David Iseminger
Series Editor

Active Directory™
Programmer's Guide

PUBLISHED BY
Microsoft Press
A Division of Microsoft Corporation
One Microsoft Way
Redmond, Washington 98052-6399

Library of Congress Cataloging-in-Publication Data
Iseminger, David, 1969-
    Microsoft Active Directory Developer's Reference Library / David Iseminger.
       p. cm.
    Includes index.
    ISBN 0-7356-0992-6
    1. Computer software--Development.   2. Directory services (Computer network technology) I. Title.
    QA76.76.D47 I84   2000
    005.7'1369--dc21   00-020462

Printed and bound in the United States of America.

1 2 3 4 5 6 7 8 9   WCWC   5 4 3 2 1 0

Distributed in Canada by Penguin Books Canada Limited.

A CIP catalogue record for this book is available from the British Library.

Microsoft Press books are available through booksellers and distributors worldwide. For further information about international editions, contact your local Microsoft Corporation office or contact Microsoft Press International directly at fax (425) 936-7329. Visit our Web site at mspress.microsoft.com.

Intel is a registered trademark of Intel Corporation. Active Directory, BackOffice, FrontPage, Microsoft, Microsoft Press, MSDN, MS-DOS, Visual Basic, Visual C++, Visual FoxPro, Visual InterDev, Visual J++, Visual SourceSafe, Visual Studio, Win32, Windows, and Windows NT are either registered trademarks or trademarks of Microsoft Corporation in the United States and/or other countries. Other product and company names mentioned herein may be the trademarks of their respective owners.

The example companies, organizations, products, people, and events depicted herein are fictitious. No association with any real company, organization, product, person, or event is intended or should be inferred.

Acquisitions Editor: Ben Ryan
Project Editor: Wendy Zucker

Part No. 097-0002778

Acknowledgements

First, thanks to **Ben Ryan** at Microsoft Press for continuing to share my enthusiasm about the series. Many thanks to Ben and **Steve Guty** for also managing the business details associated with publishing this series. We're just getting started!

Wendy Zucker again kept step with the difficult and tight schedule at Microsoft Press and orchestrated things in the way only project editors can endure. **John Pierce** was also instrumental in seeing the publishing process through completion, many thanks to both of them. The cool cover art that will continue through the series is directed by **Greg Hickman**—thanks for the excellent work. I'm a firm believer that artwork and packaging are integral to the success of a project.

Thanks also to the marketing team at Microsoft Press that handles this series: **Cora McLaughlin** and **Cheri Chapman** on the front lines and **Jocelyn Paul** each deserve recognition for their coordination efforts with MSDN, openness to my ideas and suggestions, creative marketing efforts, and other feats of marketing ingenuity.

On the Windows SDK side of things, thanks again to **Morgan Seeley** for introducing me to the editor at Microsoft Press, and thereby routing this series to the right place.

Thanks also to **Margot (Maley) Hutchison** for doing all those agent-ish things so well.

Author's Note   In Part 2 you'll see some code blocks that have unusual margin settings, or code that wraps to a subsequent line. This is a result of physical page constraints of printed material; the original code in these places was indented too much to keep its printed form on one line. I've reviewed every line of code in this library in an effort to ensure it reads as well as possible (for example, modifying comments to keep them on one line, and to keep line-delimited comment integrity). In some places, however, the word wrap effect couldn't be avoided. As such, please ensure that you check closely if you use and compile these examples.

Contents

C H A P T E R   1

Using the Active Directory Library

A fundamental change in the way Microsoft Windows operates has occurred. With Microsoft Active Directory and Windows 2000, a comprehensive directory service has been developed that enables users, administrators, and application programmers to get more out of the operating system than ever before. My prediction? (I'm an author—I'm supposed to make such predictions.) The advent of Active Directory services in Windows 2000 is going to blur the lines between networks, and will result in a basic but extraordinary change in the way users and applications operate. Just as global e-mail was a basic but extraordinary change only a few years ago (try working without e-mail today), we will reflect on Active Directory in a few years and wonder how we (or our applications) functioned effectively without it.

As a Windows programmer—whether you're writing complex applications in C/C++ or using Microsoft Visual Basic to automate administrative tasks—you need to be familiar with Active Directory and its various programming features. That familiarity (and that multiple programming language coverage) is exactly what the *Active Directory Developer's Reference Library* is geared to provide.

The Active Directory Library is *the* comprehensive reference guide to Active Directory development. This library, like all libraries in the Windows Programming Reference Series (WPRS), is designed to deliver the most complete, authoritative, and accessible reference information available on a given subject of Windows programming—without sacrificing focus. Each book in the library is dedicated to a logical group of technologies or development concerns; I've taken this approach specifically to enable you to find the information you need quickly, efficiently, and intuitively.

In addition to its Active Directory development information, the Active Directory Library contains tips designed to make your programming life easier. For example, a thorough explanation and detailed tour of MSDN Online are included, as is a section that helps you get the most out of your MSDN subscription. Just in case you don't have an MSDN subscription or don't know why you should, I've provided information about that too, including the differences between the three levels of MSDN subscription, what each level offers, and why you'd want a subscription when MSDN Online is available over the Internet.

To ensure you don't get lost in all the information provided in the Active Directory Library, each volume's appendixes provide an all-encompassing programming directory to help you easily find the particular programming element you're looking for. This directory suite, which covers all the functions, structures, enumerations, and other programming elements found in Active Directory and Active Directory Service Interface (ADSI) development, gets you quickly to the volume and page you need, saving you hours of time and bucketsful of frustration.

How the Active Directory Library Is Structured

The Active Directory Library consists of five volumes, each of which focuses on a particular aspect of Active Directory programming. These guides and programming reference volumes have been divided into the following:

- Volume 1: Active Directory Programmer's Guide
- Volume 2: Active Directory Reference
- Volume 3: ADSI Programmer's Guide
- Volume 4: ADSI Reference
- Volume 5: Active Directory Schema

Dividing the Active Directory Library into these categories enables you, the reader, to quickly identify the Active Directory volume you need based on your task, and facilitates your maintenance of focus for that task. This approach enables you to keep one reference book open and handy, or tucked under your arm while researching that aspect of Windows programming on sandy beaches, without risking back problems (from toting around all 3,200+ pages of the Active Directory Library) and without having to shuffle among multiple, less-focused books.

Within the Active Directory Library—and, in fact, in all WPRS Libraries—each volume has a deliberate structure. This per-volume structure has been created to further focus the reference material in a developer-friendly manner, to maintain consistency within each volume and each Library throughout the series, and to enable you (the developer) to easily gather the information you need. To that end, each volume in the Active Directory Library contains the following parts:

- Part 1: Introduction and Overview
- Part 2: Guides, Examples, and Programmatic Reference
- Part 3: Indexes and Active Directory Glossary

Part 1 provides an introduction to the Active Directory Library and to the Windows Programming Reference Series (what you're reading now), and a handful of chapters designed to help you get the most out of Active Directory, MSDN, and MSDN Online. MSDN and WPRS Libraries are your tools in the development process; knowing how to use them to their fullest will enable you to be more efficient and effective (both of which are generally desirable traits). In certain volumes (where appropriate), I've also provided additional information that you'll need in your Active Directory development efforts and included such information as concluding chapters in Part 1. For example, this volume includes a chapter that introduces crucial concepts about Active Directory—concepts you need to know before you dive into Active Directory programming. Some of the other volumes in the Active Directory Library conclude their Part 1 with chapters that include information crucial to their volume's contents.

Part 2 contains the Active Directory programming guides or reference material particular to its volume. You'll notice that the programmatic reference volumes contain much more than simple collections of function and structure definitions. Because a comprehensive reference resource should include information about how to use a particular technology as well as its definitions of programming elements, the information in Part 2 combines complete programming element definitions as well as instructional and explanatory material for each programming area.

Part 3 is a collection of indexes. One of the biggest challenges of the IT professional is finding information in the sea of available resources, and Active Directory programming is certainly no exception. In order to help you get a handle on Active Directory programming references (and Microsoft technologies in general), Part 3 puts all such information into an understandable, manageable directory (in the form of indexes) that enables you to quickly find the information you need. To enhance your understanding of the content in each volume, I've also included a glossary of Active Directory terms in each volume. This enables you to refresh your knowledge of a given Active Directory term regardless of which volume you're using, without the need to refer to another book (if the glossary were in only one volume).

How the Active Directory Library Is Designed

The Active Directory Library, like all libraries in the Windows Programming Reference Series, is designed to deliver the most pertinent information in the most accessible way possible. The Active Directory Library is also designed to integrate seamlessly with MSDN and MSDN Online by providing a look and feel consistent with their electronic means of disseminating Microsoft reference information. In other words, the way that a given function reference appears on the pages of this book has been designed specifically to emulate the way that MSDN and MSDN Online present their function reference pages.

The reason for maintaining such integration is simple: to make it easy for you—the developer of Windows applications—to use the tools and get the ongoing information you need to create quality programs. By providing a "common interface" among reference resources, your familiarity with the Active Directory Library reference material can be immediately applied to MSDN or MSDN Online, and vice-versa. In a word, it means *consistency*.

You'll find this philosophy applied throughout Windows Programming Reference Series publications. I've designed the series to go hand-in-hand with MSDN and MSDN Online resources. Such consistency lets you leverage your familiarity with electronic reference material, then apply that familiarity to enable you to get away from your computer if you'd like, take a book with you, and—in the absence of keyboards and e-mail and upright chairs—get your programming reading and research done. Of course, each of the Active Directory Library volumes fits nicely right next to your mouse pad as well, even when opened to a particular reference page.

With any job, the simpler and more consistent your tools are, the more time you can spend doing work rather than figuring out how to use your tools. The structure and design of the Active Directory Library provide you with a comprehensive, presharpened toolset to build compelling Windows applications.

C H A P T E R   2

What's In This Volume?

Volume 1 of the *Active Directory Developer's Reference Library* is a great place to start your directory-enabled development effort. Of course, that's why it's the first volume in this library—getting you acquainted with Microsoft Active Directory development and arming you with the knowledge you need to make great directory-enabled applications (or tools) is the primary objective of this volume. This first volume of the Active Directory Library provides guidance for the questions you're likely to have when developing applications or tools that can leverage the capabilities of Active Directory services.

So let's drill down into what exactly you'll find in this volume. First and foremost, in Chapter 5, you get the lowdown on information you need to become acquainted and familiar with terms and concepts that are particular to Active Directory services. This information is crucial, and I highly recommend that you take the time to read through Chapter 5 before diving into the rest of this library (let alone the rest of this book). The time it takes you to read through Chapter 5 will be saved repeatedly throughout your development process.

You'll also find a glossary of Active Directory terms in the back of this volume and in each volume in the Active Directory Library. If you've read through the first chapter in any of the WPRS libraries (including this one), you know that my primary objective is to ensure that these volumes provide you with the information you need in as convenient and useful a way as possible. To that end, you might run into unfamiliar Active Directory terms in any of these volumes; by having a glossary in the back of each volume, you know that the definition for unfamiliar terms is a few page flips away, rather than a book, or (if you're not near the rest of the volumes) a long walk away.

Part 2 of this volume is the Active Directory Programmer's Guide. The following list provides a synopsis of what you'll find in each chapter in the guide, beginning with Chapter 6 and continuing through the last chapter in the volume.

Chapter 6: Searching Active Directory
Searching is a primary and key feature of Active Directory. A search operation enables you to find objects in Active Directory based on selection criteria (query) and to retrieve specified properties for the objects found.

Searching Active Directory is simply a matter of finding a Microsoft Windows 2000 domain controller, binding to the object in the directory where you want to begin your search, submitting a query, and processing the results. This chapter explains, in a step-by-step fashion, how to search Active Directory.

Chapter 7: Binding

Accessing Active Directory requires finding a Windows 2000 domain controller and then binding to an object in the directory. This chapter explains how to perform binding operations.

Chapter 8: Reading and Writing Properties of Active Directory Objects

All objects have properties, and all ADSI COM objects have one or more interfaces with methods for retrieving the properties of the directory object that the COM object represents. This chapter guides you through the process involved in these operations.

Chapter 9: Controlling Access to Active Directory Objects

Every object in Active Directory is protected by Windows 2000 security. This security protection controls the operations that each security principal can perform in the directory. This chapter includes sections that explain how a directory-enabled application can cope with and take advantage of the access-control features of Active Directory.

Chapter 10: Extending the User Interface

This chapter provides a wealth of information about how to tailor the user interface (UI) to meet your needs or the needs of your customers. This chapter explains how to extend the UI for viewing and managing Active Directory objects in the Windows shell and Active Directory administrative snap-ins. This chapter also covers what you need to do to make it easy for your customers to deploy the UI extensions to the users' desktops.

Chapter 11: Object Picker Dialog Box

This chapter explains how to use the Object Picker Dialog Box. The Object Picker Dialog Box provides applications with a standard user interface for selecting computer, user, group, and contact objects. The dialog box can be used to select objects stored in Active Directory on a Windows 2000 system or in the security databases used by earlier versions of Windows NT.

Chapter 12: Replication and Data Integrity

Active Directory provides *multi-master update*. Multi-master update means that all full replicas of a given partition are writeable (partial replicas on global catalog servers are not writeable), and also means that updates are not blocked even when some replicas are down. Active Directory propagates changes from the updated replica to all other replicas. Replication is automatic and transparent.

This chapter covers the concepts of replication and data integrity in terms that are relevant to application programmers.

Chapter 13: Managing Users

This chapter addresses user accounts. User accounts are created and stored as objects in Active Directory, and represent users and computers. This chapter defines what users are and how they are used, and explains how to programmatically manage users in Active Directory.

Chapter 14: Managing Groups

This chapter addresses what you need to know to use groups in Active Directory, including issues such as creating groups, adding members, deleting groups, moving groups, and all other functions that are group-related.

Chapter 15: Tracking Changes

Many applications need to maintain consistency between specific data stored in Active Directory and other data (such as in a Microsoft SQL Server table, a file, or the registry). When data stored in Active Directory changes, the other data might need to change in order to remain consistent. This chapter explains how to address such change-tracking issues.

Chapter 16: Service Publication

Services advertise themselves using objects stored in Active Directory, a concept that is known as *service publication*. Clients query the directory to locate services of interest, a concept called *client-service rendezvous.* This chapter discusses the types of directory objects used for service publication, and explains how they are used for client-service rendezvous.

Chapter 17: Service Logon Accounts

A service, like any process, has a primary security identity that determines its access rights and privileges to local and network resources. This security identity (or security context) also determines the service's potential for damaging resources on the local computer and the network. This chapter addresses programming issues and best practices associated with the service logon account used by Microsoft Win32 services, and focuses on directory-enabled services.

Chapter 18: Mutual Authentication Using Kerberos

Mutual authentication is a security feature in which a client process must prove its identity to a service, and the service must prove its identity to the client, before any application traffic is sent over the client/service connection. This chapter explains the process of mutual authentication, and then details the information you need to know to work with mutual authentication and Kerberos.

Chapter 19: Backing Up and Restoring Active Directory

Active Directory provides functions for backing up and restoring data in the directory database. This chapter describes how to back up and restore Active Directory programmatically.

CHAPTER 3

Using Microsoft Reference Resources

Keeping current with all the latest information on the latest networking technology is like trying to count the packets going through routers at the MAE-WEST Internet service exchange by watching their blinking activity lights: It's impossible. Often times, application developers feel like those routers might feel at a given day's peak activity; too much information is passing through them, none of which is being absorbed or passed along fast enough for their boss' liking.

For developers, sifting through all the *available* information to get to the *required* information is often a major undertaking, and can impose a significant amount of overhead upon a given project. What's needed is either a collection of information that has been sifted for you, shaking out the information you need the most and putting that pertinent information into a format that's useful and efficient, or direction on how to sift the information yourself. The *Active Directory Developer's Reference Library* does the former, and this chapter and the next provide you with the latter.

This veritable white noise of information hasn't always been a problem for network programmers. Not long ago, getting the information you needed was a challenge because there wasn't enough of it; you had to find out where such information might be located and then actually get access to that location, because it wasn't at your fingertips or on some globally available backbone, and such searching took time. In short, the availability of information was limited.

Today, the volume of information that surrounds us sometimes numbs us; we're overloaded with too much information, and if we don't take measures to filter out what we don't need to meet our goals, soon we become inundated and unable to discern what's "white noise" and what's information that we need to stay on top of our respective fields. In short, the overload of available information makes it more difficult for us to find what we *really* need, and wading through the deluge slows us down.

This fact applies equally to Microsoft's reference material, because there is so much information that finding what *you* need can be as challenging as figuring out what to do with it once you have it. Developers need a way to cut through what isn't pertinent to them and to get what they're looking for. One way to ensure you can get to the information you need is to understand the tools you use; carpenters know how to use nail-guns, and it makes them more efficient. Bankers know how to use ten-keys, and it makes them more adept. If you're a developer of Windows applications, two tools you should know are MSDN and MSDN Online. The third tool for developers—reference books from the WPRS—can help you get the most out of the first two.

Books in the WPRS, such as those found in the *Active Directory Developer's Reference Library*, provide reference material that focuses on a given area of Windows programming. MSDN and MSDN Online, in comparison, contain all of the reference material that all Microsoft programming technologies have amassed over the past few years, and create one large repository of information. Regardless of how well such information is organized, there's a lot of it, and if you don't know your way around, finding what you need (even though it's in there, somewhere) can be frustrating, time-consuming, and just an overall bad experience.

This chapter will give you the insight and tips you need to navigate MSDN and MSDN Online and enable you to use each of them to the fullest of their capabilities. Also, other Microsoft reference resources are investigated, and by the end of the chapter, you'll know where to go for the Microsoft reference information you need (and how to quickly and efficiently get there).

The Microsoft Developer Network

MSDN stands for Microsoft Developer Network, and its intent is to provide developers with a network of information to enable the development of Windows applications. Many people have either worked with MSDN or have heard of it, and quite a few have one of the three available subscription levels to MSDN, but there are many, many more who don't have subscriptions and could use some concise direction on what MSDN can do for a developer or development group. If you fall into any of these categories, this section is for you.

There is some clarification to be done with MSDN and its offerings; if you've heard of MSDN, or have had experience with MSDN Online, you may have asked yourself one of these questions during the process of getting up to speed with either resource:

- Why do I need a subscription to MSDN if resources such as MSDN Online are accessible for free over the Internet?
- What is the difference between the three levels of MSDN subscriptions?
- Is there a difference between MSDN and MSDN Online, other than the fact that one is on the Internet and the other is on a CD? Do their features overlap, separate, coincide, or what?

If you have asked any of these questions, then lurking somewhere in the back of your thoughts has probably been a sneaking suspicion that maybe you aren't getting the most out of MSDN. Maybe you're wondering whether you're paying too much for too little, or not enough to get the resources you need. Regardless, you want to be in the know and not in the dark. By the end of this chapter, you'll know the answers to all these questions and more, along with some effective tips and hints on how to make the most effective use of MSDN and MSDN Online.

Comparing MSDN with MSDN Online

Part of the challenge of differentiating between MSDN and MSDN Online comes with determining which has the features you need. Confounding this differentiation is the fact that both have some content in common, yet each offers content unavailable with the other. But can their difference be boiled down? Yes, if broad strokes and some generalities are used:

- MSDN provides reference content *and* the latest Microsoft product software, all shipped to its subscribers on CD or DVD.
- MSDN Online provides reference content *and* a development community forum, and is available only over the Internet.

Each delivery mechanism for the content that Microsoft is making available to Windows developers is appropriate for the medium, and each plays on the strength of the medium to provide its "customers" with the best possible presentation of material. These strengths and medium considerations enable MSDN and MSDN Online to provide developers with different feature sets, each of which has its advantages.

MSDN is perhaps less "immediate" than MSDN Online because it gets to its subscribers in the form of CDs or DVDs that come in the mail. However, MSDN can sit in your CD/DVD drive (or on your hard drive), and isn't subject to Internet speeds or failures. Also, MSDN has a software download feature that enables subscribers to automatically update their local MSDN content over the Internet, as soon as it becomes available, without having to wait for the update CD/DVD to come in the mail. The interface with which MSDN displays its material—which looks a whole lot like a specialized browser window—is also linked to the Internet as a browser-like window. To further coordinate MSDN with the immediacy of the Internet, MSDN Online has a section of the site dedicated to MSDN subscribers that enable subscription material to be updated (on their local machines) as soon as it's available.

MSDN Online has lots of editorial and technical columns that are published directly to the site, and are tailored (not surprisingly) to the issues and challenges faced by developers of Windows applications or Windows-based Web sites. MSDN Online also has a customizable interface (somewhat similar to *MSN.com*) that enables visitors to tailor the information that's presented upon visiting the site to the areas of Windows development in which they are most interested. However, MSDN Online, while full of up-to-date reference material and extensive online developer community content, doesn't come with Microsoft product software, and doesn't reside on your local machine.

Because it's easy to confuse the differences and similarities between MSDN and MSDN Online, it makes sense to figure out a way to quickly identify how and where they depart. Figure 3-1 puts the differences—and similarities—between MSDN and MSDN Online into a quickly identifiable format.

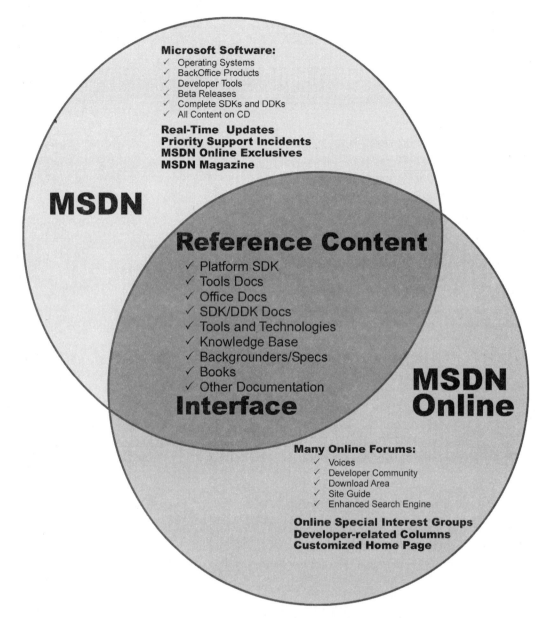

Figure 3-1:   The similarities and differences in coverage between MSDN and MSDN Online.

One feature you'll notice is shared between MSDN and MSDN Online is the interface—they are very similar. That's almost certainly a result of attempting to ensure that developers' user experience with MSDN is easily associated with the experience had on MSDN Online, and vice-versa.

Remember, too, that if you are an MSDN subscriber, you can still use MSDN Online and its features. So it isn't an "either/or" question with regard to whether you need an MSDN subscription or whether you should use MSDN Online; if you have an MSDN subscription, you will probably continue to use MSDN Online and the additional features provided with your MSDN subscription.

MSDN Subscriptions

If you're wondering whether you might benefit from a subscription to MSDN, but you aren't quite sure what the differences between its subscription levels are, you aren't alone. This section aims to provide a quick guide to the differences in subscription levels, and even provides an estimate for what each subscription level costs.

The three subscription levels for MSDN are: Library, Professional, and Universal. Each has a different set of features. Each progressive level encompasses the lower level's features, and includes additional features. In other words, with the Professional subscription, you get everything provided in the Library subscription plus additional features; with the Universal subscription, you get everything provided in the Professional subscription plus even more features.

MSDN Library Subscription

The MSDN Library subscription is the basic MSDN subscription. While the Library subscription doesn't come with the Microsoft product software that the Professional and Universal subscriptions provide, it does come with other features that developers may find necessary in their development effort. With the Library subscription, you get the following:

- The Microsoft reference library, including SDK and DDK documentation, updated quarterly
- Lots of sample code, which you can cut-and-paste into your projects, royalty free
- The complete Microsoft Knowledge Base—*the* collection of bugs and workarounds
- Technology specifications for Microsoft technologies
- The complete set of product documentation, such as Microsoft Visual Studio, Microsoft Office, and others
- Complete (and in some cases, partial) electronic copies of selected books and magazines
- Conference and seminar papers—if you weren't there, you can use MSDN's notes

In addition to these items, you also get:

- Archives of MSDN Online columns
- Periodic e-mails from Microsoft chock full of development-related information
- A subscription to MSDN News, a bi-monthly newspaper from the MSDN folks
- Access to subscriber-exclusive areas and material on MSDN Online

MSDN Professional Subscription

The MSDN Professional subscription is a superset of the Library subscription. In addition to the features outlined in the previous section, MSDN Professional subscribers get the following:

- Complete set of Windows operating systems, including release versions of Windows 95, Windows 98, and Windows NT 4 Server and Workstation.
- Windows SDKs and DDKs in their entirety
- International versions of Windows operating systems (as chosen)
- Priority technical support for two incidents in a development and test environment

MSDN Universal Subscription

The MSDN Universal subscription is the all-encompassing version of the MSDN subscription. In addition to everything provided in the Professional subscription, Universal subscribers get the following:

- The latest version of Visual Studio, Enterprise Edition
- The Microsoft BackOffice test platform, which includes all sorts of Microsoft product software incorporated in the BackOffice family, each with a special 10-connection license for use in the development of your software products
- Additional development tools, such as Office Developer, Microsoft FrontPage, and Microsoft Project
- Priority technical support for two additional incidents in a development and test environment (for a total of four incidents)

Purchasing an MSDN Subscription

Of course, all the features that you get with MSDN subscriptions aren't free. MSDN subscriptions are one-year subscriptions, which are current as of this writing. Just as each MSDN subscription escalates in functionality of incorporation of features, so does each escalate in price. Please note that prices are subject to change.

The MSDN Library subscription has a retail price of $199, but if you're renewing an existing subscription you get a $100 rebate in the box. There are other perks for existing Microsoft customers, but those vary. Check out the Web site for more details.

The MSDN Professional subscription is a bit more expensive than the Library, with a retail price of $699. If you're an existing customer renewing your subscription, you again get a break in the box, this time in the amount of a $200 rebate. You also get that break if you're an existing Library subscriber who's upgrading to a Professional subscription.

The MSDN Universal subscription takes a big jump in price, sitting at $2,499. If you're upgrading from the Professional subscription, the price drops to $1,999, and if you're upgrading from the Library subscription level, there's an in-the-box rebate for $200.

As is often the case, there are academic and volume discounts available from various resellers, including Microsoft, so those who are in school or in the corporate environment can use their status (as learner or learned) to get a better deal—and in most cases, the deal is in fact much better. Also, if your organization is using lots of Microsoft products, whether or not MSDN is a part of that group, ask your purchasing department to look into the Microsoft Open License program; the Open License program gives purchasing breaks for customers who buy lots of products. Check out *www.microsoft.com/licensing* for more details. Who knows, if your organization qualifies you could end up getting an engraved pen from your purchasing department, or if you're really lucky maybe even a plaque of some sort for saving your company thousands of dollars on Microsoft products.

You can get MSDN subscriptions from a number of sources, including online sites specializing in computer-related information, such as *www.iseminger.com* (shameless self-promotion, I know), or from your favorite online software site. Note that not all software resellers carry MSDN subscriptions; you might have to hunt around to find one. Of course, if you have a local software reseller that you frequent, you can check out whether they carry MSDN subscriptions.

As an added bonus for owners of this *Active Directory Developer's Reference Library*, in the back of Volume 1, you'll find a $200 rebate good toward the purchase of an MSDN Universal subscription. For those of you doing the math, that means you actually *make* money when you purchase the *Active Directory Developer's Reference Library* and an MSDN Universal subscription. With this rebate, every developer in your organization can have the *Active Directory Developer's Refence Library* on their desk and the MSDN Universal subscription on thier desktop, and still come out $50 ahead. That's the kind of math even accountants can like.

Using MSDN

MSDN subscriptions come with an installable interface, and the Professional and Universal subscriptions also come with a bunch of Microsoft product software such as Windows platform versions and BackOffice applications. There's no need to tell you how to use Microsoft product software, but there's a lot to be said for providing some quick but useful guidance on getting the most out of the interface to present and navigate through the seemingly endless supply of reference material provided with any MSDN subscription.

To those who have used MSDN, the interface shown in Figure 3-2 is likely familiar; it's the navigational front-end to MSDN reference material.

The interface is familiar and straightforward enough, but if you don't have a grasp on its features and navigation tools, you can be left a little lost in its sea of information. With a few sentences of explanation and some tips for effective navigation, however, you can increase its effectiveness dramatically.

Navigating MSDN

One of the primary features of MSDN—and to many, its primary drawback—is the sheer volume of information it contains, over 1.1GB and growing. The creators of MSDN likely realized this, though, and have taken steps to assuage the problem. Most of those steps relate to enabling developers to selectively navigate through MSDN's content.

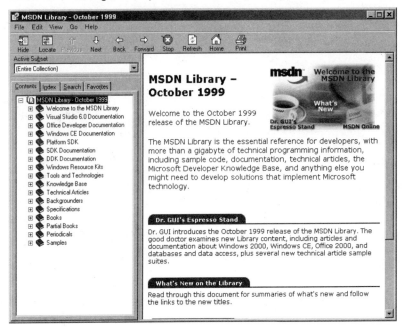

Figure 3-2:   The MSDN interface.

Basic navigation through MSDN is simple and is a lot like navigating through Microsoft Windows Explorer and its folder structure. Instead of folders, MSDN has books into which it organizes its topics; expand a book by clicking the + box to its left, and its contents are displayed with its nested books or reference pages, as shown in Figure 3-3. If you don't see the left pane in your MSDN viewer, go to the View menu and select Navigation Tabs and they'll appear.

The four tabs in the left pane of MSDN—increasingly referred to as property sheets these days—are the primary means of navigating through MSDN content. These four tabs, in coordination with the Active Subset drop-down box above the four tabs, are the tools you use to search through MSDN content. When used to their full extent, these coordinated navigation tools greatly improve your MSDN experience.

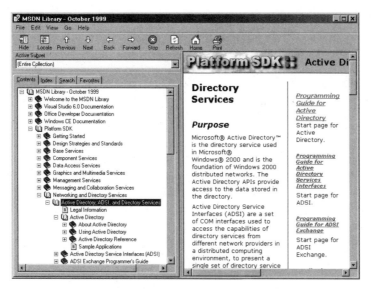

Figure 3-3:   Basic navigation through MSDN.

The Active Subset drop-down box is a filter mechanism; choose the subset of MSDN information you're interested in working with from the drop-down box, and the information in each of the four Navigation Tabs (including the Contents tab) limits the information it displays to the information contained in the selected subset. This means that any searches you do in the Search tab, and in the index presented in the Index tab, are filtered by their results and/or matches to the subset you define, greatly narrowing the number of potential results for a given inquiry. This enables you to better find the information you're *really* looking for. In the Index tab, results that might match your inquiry but *aren't* in the subset you have chosen are grayed out (but still selectable). In the Search tab, they simply aren't displayed.

MSDN comes with the following predefined subsets (these subsets are subject to change, based on documentation updates and TOC reorganizations):

Entire Collection
MSDN, Books and Periodicals
MSDN, Content on Disk 2 only
  (CD only – not in DVD version)
MSDN, Content on Disk 3 only
  (CD only – not in DVD version)
MSDN, Knowledge Base
MSDN, Technical Articles and
  Backgrounders
Office Developer Documentation
Platform SDK, BackOffice
Platform SDK, Base Services
Platform SDK, Component Services

Platform SDK, Networking Services
Platform SDK, Security
Platform SDK, Tools and Languages
Platform SDK, User Interface Services
Platform SDK, Web Services
Platform SDK, Win32 API
Repository 2.0 Documentation
Visual Basic Documentation
Visual C++ Documentation
Visual C++, Platform SDK and
  WinCE Docs
Visual C++, Platform SDK, and
  Enterprise Docs

Platform SDK, Data Access Services
Platform SDK, Getting Started
Platform SDK, Graphics and
  Multimedia Services
Platform SDK, Management Services
Platform SDK, Messaging and
  Collaboration Services

Visual FoxPro Documentation
Visual InterDev Documentation
Visual J++ Documentation
Visual SourceSafe Documentation
Visual Studio Product Documentation
Windows CE Documentation

As you can see, these filtering options essentially mirror the structure of information delivery used by MSDN. But what if you are interested in viewing the information in a handful of these subsets? For example, what if you want to search on a certain keyword through the Platform SDK's ADSI, Networking Services, and Management Services subsets, as well as a little section that's nested way into the Base Services subset? Simple—you define your own subset by choosing the View menu, and then selecting the Define Subsets menu item. You're presented with the window shown in Figure 3-4.

Defining a subset is easy; just take the following steps:

1. Choose the information you want in the new subset; you can choose entire subsets or selected books/content within available subsets.

2. Add your selected information to the subset you're creating by clicking the Add button.

3. Name the newly created subset by typing in a name in the Save New Subset As box. Note that defined subsets (including any you create) are arranged in alphabetical order.

You can also delete entire subsets from the MSDN installation. Simply select the subset you want to delete from the Select Subset To Display drop-down box, and then click the nearby Delete button.

Once you have defined a subset, it becomes available in MSDN just like the predefined subsets, and filters the information available in the four Navigation Tabs, just like the predefined subsets do.

Quick Tips

Now that you know how to navigate MSDN, there are a handful of tips and tricks that you can use to make MSDN as effective as it can be.

Use the Locate button to get your bearings. Perhaps it's human nature to need to know where you are in the grand scheme of things, but regardless, it can be bothersome to have a reference page displayed in the right pane (perhaps jumped to from a search), without the Contents tab in the left pane being synchronized in terms of the reference page's location in the information tree. Even if you know the general technology in which your reference page resides, it's nice to find out where it is in the content structure.

This is easy to fix. Simply click the Locate button in the navigation toolbar and all will be synchronized.

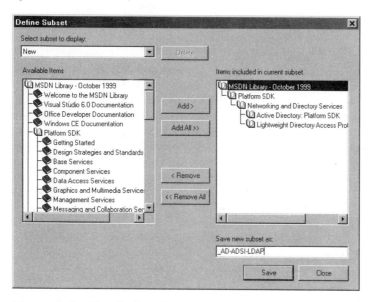

Figure 3-4:   The Define Subsets window.

Use the Back button just like a browser. The Back button in the navigation toolbar functions just like a browser's Back button; if you need information on a reference page you viewed previously, you can use the Back button to get there, rather than going through the process of doing another search.

Define your own subsets, and use them. Like I said at the beginning of this chapter, the volume of information available these days can sometimes make it difficult to get our work done. By defining subsets of MSDN that are tailored to the work you do, you can become more efficient.

Use an underscore at the beginning of your named subsets. Subsets in the Active Subset drop-down box are arranged in alphabetical order, and the drop-down box shows only a few subsets at a time (making it difficult to get a grip on available subsets, I think). Underscores come before letters in alphabetical order, so if you use an underscore on all of your defined subsets, you get them placed at the front of the Active Subset listing of available subsets. Also, by using an underscore, you can immediately see which subsets you've defined, and which ones come with MSDN—it saves a few seconds at most, but those seconds can add up.

Using MSDN Online

MSDN underwent a redesign in December of 1999, aimed at streamlining the information provided, jazzing things up with more color, highlighting hot new technologies, and various other improvements. Despite its visual overhaul, MSDN Online still shares a lot of content and information delivery similarities with MSDN, and those similarities are by design; when you can go from one developer resource to another and immediately work with its content, your job is made easier. However, MSDN Online is different enough that it merits explaining in its own right—it's a different delivery medium, and can take advantage of the Internet in ways that MSDN simply cannot.

If you've used MSN's home page before (*www.msn.com*), you're familiar with the fact that you can customize the page to your liking; choose from an assortment of available national news, computer news, local news, local weather, stock quotes, and other collections of information or news that suit your tastes or interests. You can even insert a few Web links and have them readily accessible when you visit the site. The MSDN Online home page can be customized in a similar way, but its collection of headlines, information, and news sources are all about development. The information you choose specifies the information you see when you go to the MSDN Online home page, just like the MSN home page.

There are a couple of ways to get to the customization page; you can go to the MSDN Online home page (*msdn.microsoft.com*) and click the Personalize This Site button near the top of the page, or you can go there directly by pointing your browser to *msdn.microsoft.com/msdn-online/start/custom*. However you get there, the page you'll see is shown in Figure 3-5.

As you can see from Figure 3-5, there are lots of technologies to choose from (many more options can be found when you scroll down through available technologies). If you're interested in Web development, you can select the checkbox at the left of the page next to Standard Web Development, and a predefined subset of Web-centered technologies is selected. For technologies centered more on Active Directory, you can go through and choose the appropriate technologies. If you want to choose all the technologies in a given technology group more quickly, click the Select All button in the technology's shaded title area.

You can also choose which tab is selected by default in the home page that MSDN Online presents to you, which is convenient for dropping you into the category of MSDN Online information that interests you most. All five of the tabs available on MSDN Online's home page are available for selection; those tabs are the following:

- Features
- News
- Columns
- Technical Articles
- Training & Events

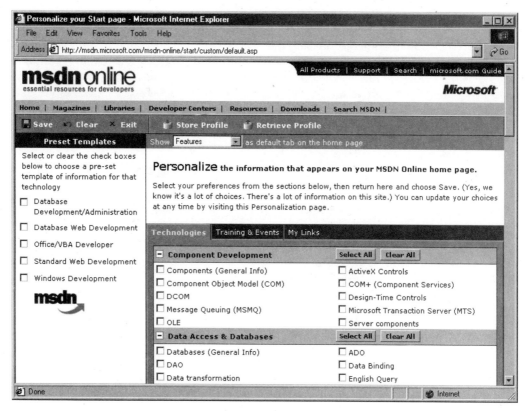

Figure 3-5:   The MSDN Online Personalize Page.

Once you've defined your profile—that is, customized the MSDN Online content you want to see—MSDN Online shows you the most recent information pertinent to your profile when you go to MSDN Online's home page, with the default tab you've chosen displayed upon loading of the MSDN Online home page.

Finally, if you want your profile to be available to you regardless of which computer you're using, you can direct MSDN Online to store your profile. Storing a profile for MSDN Online results in your profile being stored on MSDN Online's server, much like roaming profiles in Windows 2000, and thereby makes your profile available to you regardless of the computer you're using. The option of storing your profile is available when you customize your MSDN Online home page (and can be done any time thereafter). The storing of a profile, however, requires that you become a registered member of MSDN Online. More information about becoming a registered MSDN Online user is provided in the section titled *MSDN Online Registered Users*.

Navigating MSDN Online

Once you're done customizing the MSDN Online home page to get the information you're most interested in, navigating through MSDN Online is easy. A banner that sits just below the MSDN Online logo functions as a navigation bar, with drop-down menus that can take you to the available areas on MSDN Online, as Figure 3-6 illustrates.

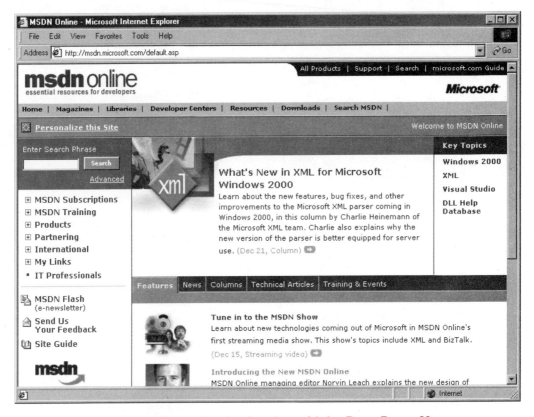

Figure 3-6:   The MSDN Online Navigation Bar with Its Drop-Down Menus.

Following is a list of available menu categories, which groups the available sites and features within MSDN Online:

Home

Magazines

Libraries

Developer Centers

Resources

Downloads

Search MSDN

The navigation bar is available regardless of where you are in MSDN Online, so the capability to navigate the site from this familiar menu is always available, leaving you a click away from any area on MSDN Online. These menu categories create a functional and logical grouping of MSDN Online's feature offerings.

MSDN Online Features

Each of MSDN Online's seven feature categories contains various sites that comprise the features available to developers visiting MSDN Online.

Home is already familiar; clicking on Home in the navigation bar takes you to the MSDN Online home page that you've (perhaps) customized, showing you all the latest information about technologies that you've indicated you're interested in reading about.

Magazines is a collection of columns and articles that comprise MSDN Online's magazine section, as well as online versions of Microsoft's magazines such as MSJ, MIND, and the MSDN Show (a Webcast feature introduced with the December 1999 remodeling of MSDN Online). The Magazines feature of MSDN Online can be linked to directly at *msdn.microsoft.com/resources/magazines.asp*. The Magazines home page is shown in Figure 3-7.

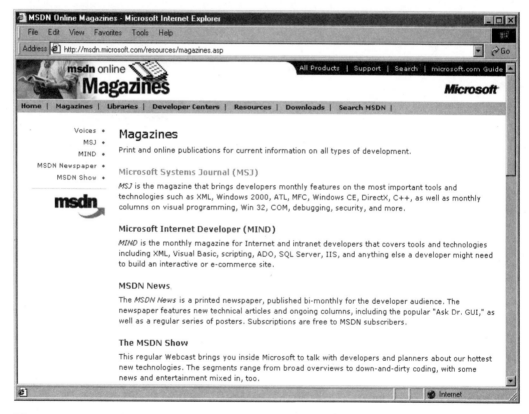

Figure 3-7:   The Magazines Home Page.

For those of you familiar with the **Voices** feature section that formerly found its home on the MSDN Online navigation banner, don't worry; all content formerly in the Voices section is included the Magazines section as a subsite (or menu item, if you prefer) of the Magazines site. For those of you who aren't familiar with the Voices subsite, you'll find a bunch of different articles or "voices" there, each of which adds its own particular twist on the issues that face developers. Both application and Web developers can get their fill of magazine-like articles from the sizable list of different articles available (and frequently refreshed) in the Voices subsite. With the combination of columns and online developer magazines offered in the Magazines section, you're sure to find plenty of interesting insights.

Libraries is where the reference material available on MSDN Online lives. The Libraries site is divided into two sections: Library and Web Workshop. This distinction divides the reference material between Windows application development and Web development. Choosing Library from the Libraries menu takes you to a page through which you can navigate in traditional MSDN fashion, and gain access to traditional MSDN reference material. The Library home page can be linked to directly at *msdn.microsoft.com/library*. Choosing Web Workshop takes you to a site that enables you to navigate the Web Workshop in a slightly different way, starting with a bulleted list of start points, as shown in Figure 3-8. The Web Workshop home page can be linked to directly at *msdn.microsoft.com/workshop*.

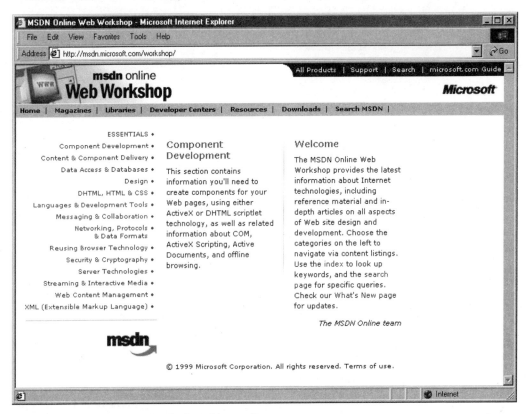

Figure 3-8:   The Web Workshop Home Page.

Developer Centers is a hub from which developers who are interested in a particular area of development—such as Windows 2000, SQL Server, or XML—can go to find focused Web site centers within MSDN Online. Each developer center is dedicated to providing all sorts of information associated with its area of focus. For example, the Windows 2000 developer center has information about what's new with Windows 2000, including newsgroups, specifications, chats, knowledge base articles, and news, among others. At publication time, MSDN Online had the following developer centers:

- Microsoft Windows 2000
- Microsoft Exchange
- Microsoft SQL Server
- Microsoft Windows Media
- XML

In addition to these developer centers is a promise that new centers would be added to the site in the future. To get to the Developer Centers home page directly, link to *msdn.microsoft.com/resources/devcenters.asp*. Figure 3-9 shows the Developer Centers home page.

Figure 3-9:   The Developer Centers Home Page.

Resources is a place where developers can go to take advantage of the online forum of Windows and Web developers, in which ideas or techniques can be shared, advice can be found or given (through MHM, or Members Helping Members), and the MSDN User Group Program can be joined or perused to find a forum to voice their opinions or chat with other developers. The Resources site is full of all sorts of useful stuff, including featured books, a DLL help database, online chats, case studies, and more. The Resources home page can be linked to directly at *msdn.microsoft.com/resources*. Figure 3-10 provides a look at the Resources home page.

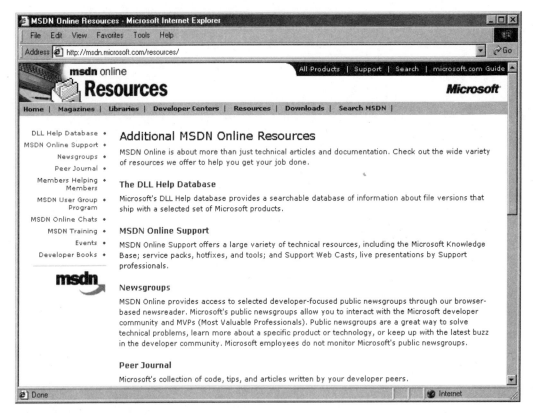

Figure 3-10:   The Resources Home Page.

The **Downloads** site is where developers can find all sorts of useable items fit to be downloaded, such as tools, samples, images, and sounds. The Downloads site is also where MSDN subscribers go to get their subscription content updated over the Internet to the latest and greatest releases, as described previously in this chapter in the *Using MSDN* section. The Downloads home page can be linked to directly at *msdn.microsoft.com/downloads*. The Downloads home page is shown in Figure 3-11.

Figure 3-11:   The Downloads Home Page.

The **Search MSDN** site on MSDN Online has been improved over previous versions, and includes the capability to restrict searches to either library (Library or Web Workshop), as well as other fine-tune search capabilities. The Search MSDN home page can be linked to directly at *msdn.microsoft.com/search*. The Search MSDN home page is shown in Figure 3-12.

There are two other destinations within MSDN Online of specific interest, neither of which is immediately reachable through the MSDN navigation bar. The first is the **MSDN Online Member Community** home page, and the other is the **Site Guide**.

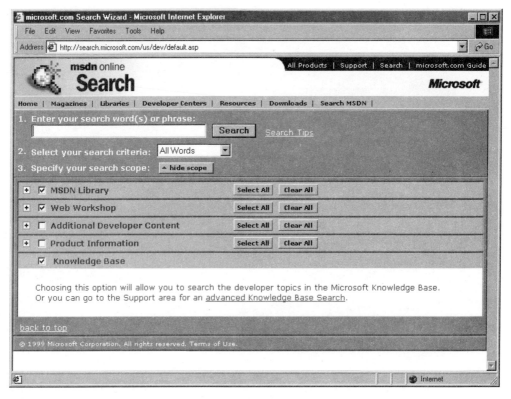

Figure 3-12:   The Search MSDN Home Page.

The MSDN Online Member Community home page can be directly reached at *msdn.microsoft.com/community*. Many of the features found in the **Resources** navigation menu are actually subsites of the Community page. Of course, becoming a member of the MSDN Online member community requires that you register (see the next section for more details on joining), but doing so enables you to get access to Online Special Interest Groups (OSIGs) and other features reserved for registered members. The Community page is shown in Figure 3-13.

Another destination of interest on MSDN Online that isn't displayed on the navigation banner is the **Site Guide**. The Site Guide is just what its name suggests—a guide to the MSDN Online site that aims at helping developers find items of interest, and includes links to other pages on MSDN Online such as a recently posted files listing, site maps, glossaries, and other useful links. The Site Guide home page can be linked to directly at *msdn.microsoft.com/siteguide*.

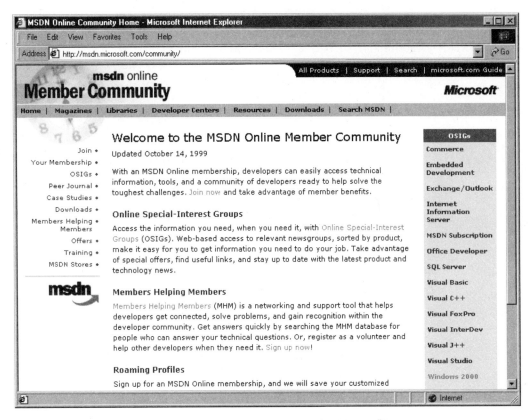

Figure 3-13: The MSDN Online Member Community Home Page.

MSDN Online Registered Users

You may have noticed that some features of MSDN Online—such as the capability to create a store profile of the entry ticket to some community features—require you to become a registered user. Unlike MSDN subscriptions, becoming a registered user of MSDN Online won't cost you anything more but a few minutes of registration time.

Some features of MSDN Online require registration before you can take advantage of their offerings. For example, becoming a member of an OSIG requires registration. That feature alone is enough to register; rather than attempting to call your developer buddy for an answer to a question (only to find out that she's on vacation for two days, and your deadline is in a few hours), you can go to MSDN Online's Community site and ferret through your OSIG to find the answer in a handful of clicks. Who knows; maybe your developer buddy will begin calling you with questions—you don't have to tell her where you're getting all your answers.

There are a number of advantages to being a registered user, such as the choice to receive newsletters right in your inbox if you want to. You can also get all sorts of other timely information, such as chat reminders that let you know when experts on a given subject will be chatting in the MSDN Online Community site. You can also sign up to get newsletters based on your membership in various OSIGs—again, only if you want to. It's easy for me to suggest that you become a registered user for MSDN Online—I'm a registered user, and it's a great resource.

The Windows Programming Reference Series

The WPRS provides developers with timely, concise, and focused material on a given topic, enabling developers to get their work done as efficiently as possible. In addition to providing reference material for Microsoft technologies, each Library in the WPRS also includes material that helps developers get the most out of its technologies, and provides insights that might otherwise be difficult to find.

The WPRS currently includes the following libraries:

- *Microsoft Win32 Developer's Reference Library*
- *Active Directory Developer's Reference Library*
- *Network Services Developer's Reference Library*

In the near future (subject, of course, to technology release schedules, demand, and other forces that can impact publication decisions), you can look for these prospective WPRS Libraries that cover the following material:

- Web Technologies Library
- Web Reference Library
- MFC Developer's Reference Library
- Com Developer's Reference Library

What else might you find in the future? Planned topics such as a Security Library, Programming Languages Reference Library, BackOffice Developer's Reference Library, or other pertinent topics that developers using Microsoft products need in order to get the most out of their development efforts, are prime subjects for future membership in the WPRS. If you have feedback you want to provide on such libraries, or on the WPRS in general, you can send email to *winprs@microsoft.com*.

If you're sending mail about a particular library, make sure you put the name of the library in the subject line. For example, e-mail about the *Active Directory Developer's Reference Library* would have a subject line that reads "*Active Directory Developer's Reference Library*." There aren't any guarantees that you'll get a reply, but I'll read all of the mail and do what I can to ensure your comments, concerns, or (especially) compliments get to the right place.

C H A P T E R   4

Finding the Developer Resources You Need

Despite Microsoft Active Directory's relatively recent arrival onto the Microsoft Windows development scene, several developer resources are available to those interested in developing Active Directory applications. Right out the (Windows 2000 release) door, Microsoft has ensured that ample developer support and resources are in place. Microsoft wants you to make good use of Active Directory and therefore provides you with as much help as possible. It's in Microsoft's best interest to do so, because in a very real sense the success of your Active Directory-enabled application results in success of the Windows 2000 (and Active Directory) effort to make life easier and better for users. As such, there are resources at your disposal—you just have to know where to look for them. That's where this chapter steps in.

Despite all of the resources available for developers of Active Directory applications and the answers they can provide to questions or problems that developers face every day, finding such resources is sometimes harder than solving the original problem. This chapter is your one-stop resource for finding as many developer resources as are available, again making your job of actually developing the application just a little easier.

While Microsoft provides lots of resource material through MSDN and MSDN Online, and although the WPRS provides lots of focused reference material and development tips and tricks, there is *much* more information to be had. Some of it is from Microsoft, some is from the general development community, and some is from companies that specialize in such development services. Regardless of which resource you choose, this chapter helps you become more informed about the resources that are available to you.

Microsoft provides developer resources through a number of different media, channels, and approaches. The extensiveness of Microsoft's resource offerings mirrors the fact that many are appropriate under various circumstances. For example, you wouldn't go to a conference to find the answer to a specific development problem in your programming project; instead, you might use one of the other Microsoft resources.

Developer Support

Microsoft's support sites cover a wide variety of support issues and approaches, including all of Microsoft's products, but most of those sites are not pertinent to developers. Some sites, however, *are* designed for developer support; the Product Services Support page for developers is a good central place to find the support information you need. Figure 4-1 shows the Product Services Support page for developers, which can be reached at *www.microsoft.com/support/customer/develop.htm*.

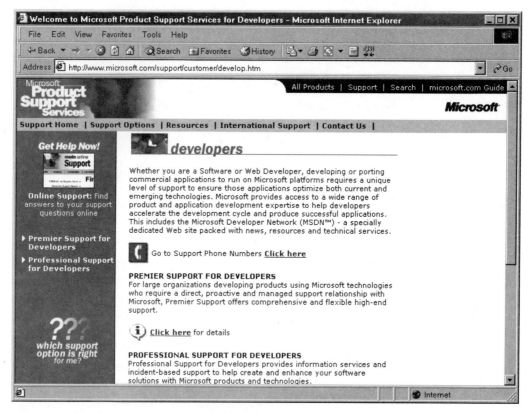

Figure 4-1:   The Product Services Support page for developers.

Note that there are a number of options for support from Microsoft, including everything from simple online searches of known bugs in the Knowledge Base to hands-on consulting support from Microsoft Consulting Services, and everything in between. The Web page displayed in Figure 4-1 is a good starting point from which you can find out more information about Microsoft's support services.

Premier Support from Microsoft provides extensive support for developers and includes different packages geared toward specific Microsoft customer needs. The packages of Premier Support that Microsoft provides are:

- Premier Support for Enterprises
- Premier Support for Developers
- Premier Support for Microsoft Certified Solution Providers
- Premier Support for OEMs

If you're a developer, you could fall into any of these categories. To find out more information about Microsoft's Premier Support, contact them at (800) 936-2000.

Priority Annual Support from Microsoft is geared toward developers or organizations that have more than an occasional need to call Microsoft with support questions and need priority handling of their support questions or issues. There are three packages of Priority Annual Support offered by Microsoft:

- Priority Comprehensive Support
- Priority Developer Support
- Priority Desktop Support

The best support option for you as a developer is the Priority Developer Support. To obtain more information about Priority Developer Support, call Microsoft at (800) 936-3500.

Microsoft also offers a **Pay-Per-Incident Support** option, so you can get help if there's just one question that you must have answered. With Pay-Per-Incident Support, you call a toll-free number and provide your Visa, MasterCard, or American Express account number, after which you receive support for your incident. In loose terms, an incident is a problem or issue that can't be broken down into subissues or subproblems (that is, it can't be broken down into smaller pieces). The number to call for Pay-Per-Incident Support is (800) 936-5800.

Note that Microsoft provides two priority technical support incidents as part of the MSDN Professional subscription and provides four priority technical support incidents as part of the MSDN Universal subscription.

You can also **submit questions** to Microsoft engineers through Microsoft's support Web site, but if you're on a time line you might want to rethink this approach and consider going to MSDN Online and looking into the Community site for help with your development question. To submit a question to Microsoft engineers online, go to *support.microsoft.com/support/webresponse.asp*.

Online Resources

Microsoft also provides extensive developer support through its community of developers found on MSDN Online. At MSDN Online's Community site, you will find OSIGs that cover all sorts of issues in an online, ongoing fashion. To get to MSDN Online's Community site, simply go to *msdn.microsoft.com/community*.

Microsoft's MSDN Online also provides its **Knowledge Base** online, which is part of the Personal Support Center on Microsoft's corporate site. You can search the Knowledge Base online at *support.microsoft.com/support/search*.

Microsoft provides a number of **newsgroups** that developers can use to view information on newsgroup-specific topics, providing yet another developer resource for information about creating Windows applications. To find out which newsgroups are available and how to get to them, go to *support.microsoft.com/support/news*.

The following handful of newsgroups will probably be of particular interest to readers of the *Active Directory Developer's Reference Library*:

- *microsoft.public.win2000.**
- *microsoft.public.msdn.general*
- *microsoft.public.platformsdk.active.directory*
- *microsoft.public.platformsdk.adsi*
- *microsoft.public.platformsdk.dist_svcs*
- *microsoft.public.vb.**
- *microsoft.public.vc.**
- *microsoft.public.vstudio.*microsoft.public.cert.**
- *microsoft.public.certification.**

Of course, Microsoft isn't the only newsgroup provider on which newsgroups pertaining to developing on Windows are hosted. Usenet has all sorts of newsgroups—too many to list—that host ongoing discussions pertaining to developing applications on the Windows platform. You can access newsgroups on Windows development just as you access any other newsgroup; generally, you'll need to contact your ISP to find out the name of the mail server and then use a newsreader application to visit, read, or post to the Usenet groups.

Learning Products

Microsoft provides a number of products that enable developers to get versed in the particular tasks or tools that they need to achieve their goals (or to finish their tasks). One product line geared toward developers is called the Mastering Series. Its products provide comprehensive, well-structured interactive teaching tools for a wide variety of development topics.

The Mastering Series from Microsoft contains interactive tools that group books and CDs together so that you can master the topic in question. The Mastering Series has an entire section devoted to Windows 2000 (which includes Active Directory), so your Active Directory development effort can get specific help from this Microsoft Press series. To get more information about the Mastering series of products or to find out what kind of offerings the Mastering series has, check out *msdn.microsoft.com/mastering*.

Other learning products are available from other vendors as well, such as other publishers, other application providers that create tutorial-type content and applications, and companies that issue videos (both taped and broadcast over the Internet) on specific technologies. For one example of a company that issues technology-based instructional or overview videos, take a look at *www.compchannel.com*.

Another way of learning about development in a particular language (such as C++, FoxPro, or Microsoft Visual Basic), for a particular operating system, or for a particular product (such as Microsoft SQL Server or Microsoft Commerce Server) is to read the preparation materials available to get certified as a Microsoft Certified Solutions Developer (MCSD). Before you get defensive about not having enough time to get certified or not having any interest in getting your certification (maybe you do—there *are* benefits, you know), let me just state that the point of the journey is not necessarily to arrive. In other words, you don't have to get your certification for the preparation materials to be useful; in fact, the materials might teach you things that you thought you knew well, but actually didn't know as well as you thought you did. The fact of the matter is that the coursework and the requirements to get through the certification process are rigorous, difficult, and quite detail-oriented. If you have what it takes to get your certification, you have an extremely strong grasp of the fundamentals (and then some) of application programming and the developer-centric information about Windows platforms.

You are required to pass a set of core exams to get an MCSD certification, and then you must choose one topic from many available electives exams to complete your certification requirements. Core exams are chosen from among a group of available exams; you must pass a total of three exams to complete the core requirements. There are "tracks" that candidates generally choose which point their certification in a given direction, such as C++ development or Visual Basic development. The core exams and their exam numbers (at the time of publication) are as follows:

Desktop Applications Development (one required):

- Designing and Implementing Desktop Applications with Visual C++ 6.0 (70-016)
- Designing and Implementing Desktop Applications with Visual FoxPro 6.0 (70-156)
- Designing and Implementing Desktop Applications with Visual Basic 6.0 (70-176)

Distributed Applications Development (one required):

- Designing and Implementing Distributed Applications with Visual C++ 6.0 (70-015)
- Designing and Implementing Distributed Applications with Visual FoxPro 6.0 (70-155)
- Designing and Implementing Distributed Applications with Visual Basic 6.0 (70-175)

Solutions Architecture:

- Analyzing Requirements and Defining Solution Architectures (70-100)

Elective exams enable candidates to choose from a number of additional exams to complete their MCSD exam requirements. The following MCSD elective exams are available:

- Any Desktop or Distributed exam not used as a core requirement
- Designing and Implementing Data Warehouses with Microsoft SQL Server 7.0 (70-019)
- Developing Applications with C++ Using the Microsoft Foundation Class Library (70-024)
- Implementing OLE in Microsoft Foundation Class Applications (70-025)
- Implementing a Database Design on Microsoft SQL Server 6.5 (70-027)
- Designing and Implementing Databases with Microsoft SQL Server 7.0 (70-029)
- Designing and Implementing Web Sites with Microsoft FrontPage 98 (70-055)
- Designing and Implementing Commerce Solutions with Microsoft Site Server 3.0, Commerce Edition (70-057)
- Application Development with Microsoft Access for Windows 95 and the Microsoft Access Developer's Toolkit (70-069)
- Designing and Implementing Solutions with Microsoft Office 2000 and Microsoft Visual Basic for Applications (70-091)
- Designing and Implementing Database Applications with Microsoft Access 2000 (70-097)
- Designing and Implementing Collaborative Solutions with Microsoft Outlook 2000 and Microsoft Exchange Server 5.5 (70-105)
- Designing and Implementing Web Solutions with Microsoft Visual InterDev 6.0 (70-152)
- Developing Applications with Microsoft Visual Basic 5.0 (70-165)

The good news is that because you must pass exams to become certified, there are books and other material out there to teach you how to meet the knowledge level necessary to pass the exams. That means those resources are available to you—regardless of whether you care one whit about becoming an MCSD.

The way to leverage this information is to get study materials for one or more of these exams and go through the exam preparation material. (Don't be fooled by believing that if the book is bigger it must be better, because that certainly isn't always the case.) Exam preparation material is available from such publishers as Microsoft Press, IDG, Sybex, and others. Most exam preparation texts also contain practice exams that let you assess your grasp of the material. You might be surprised how much you learn, even though you may have been in the field working on complex projects for some time.

Exam requirements, and the exams themselves, can change over time; more electives become available, exams based on previous versions of software are retired, and so on. You should check the status of individual exams (such as whether one of the exams listed has been retired) before moving forward with your certification plans. For more information about the certification process or for more information about the exams, check out Microsoft's certification Web site at *www.microsoft.com/train_cert/dev*.

Conferences

Like any industry, Microsoft and the development industry as a whole sponsor conferences on various topics throughout the year and around the world. There are probably more conferences available than any one human could possibly attend and still maintain his or her sanity. However, often a given conference is geared toward a focused topic, so choosing to focus on a particular development topic enables developers to winnow the number of conferences relevant to their efforts and interests.

MSDN itself hosts or sponsors almost one hundred conferences a year (some of them are regional and duplicated in different locations, so these could be considered one conference that happens multiple times). Other conferences are held in one central location, such as the big one—the Professional Developers Conference (PDC). Regardless of which conference you're looking for, Microsoft has provided a central site for event information, enabling users to search the site for conferences based on many different criteria. To find out what conferences or other events are going on in your area of interest of development, go to *events.microsoft.com*.

Other Resources

Other resources are available for developers of Windows applications, some of which might be mainstays for one developer and unheard of for another. The listing of developer resources in this chapter has been geared toward getting you more than started with finding the developer resources you need; it's geared toward getting you 100 percent of the way, but there are always exceptions.

Perhaps you're just getting started and you want more hands-on instruction than MSDN Online or MCSD preparation materials provide. Where can you go? One option is to check out your local college for instructor-led courses. Most community colleges offer night classes, and increasingly, community colleges are outfitted with pretty nice computer labs that enable you to get hands-on development instruction and experience without having to work on a 386/20.

There are undoubtedly other resources that some people know about that have been useful, or maybe invaluable. If you know of a resource that should be shared with others, send me an e-mail at *winprs@microsoft.com*, and who knows—maybe someone else will benefit from your knowledge.

If you're sending mail about a particularly useful resource, simply put "Resources" in the subject line. There aren't any guarantees that you'll get a reply, but I'll read all of the mail and do what I can to ensure that your resource idea gets considered.

CHAPTER 5

What You Need to Know First About Active Directory

This chapter provides overview information and explains specific concepts that you, the application developer or tool-developing administrator, need to understand in order to get the most out of your development effort.

If you're developing a distributed application for Microsoft Windows 2000, there are many compelling reasons to integrate Microsoft Active Directory. The intent of this first volume in the *Active Directory Developer's Reference Library* is to give you the knowledge you need to best write to Active Directory.

A directory service is a fundamental service for distributed applications. A directory service, at a minimum, must provide the following:

Location transparency
 The ability to find information about a user, group, networked service, or resource, without knowing addressing information.

Information on people and services
 The ability to store user, group, organization, and service information in a structured, hierarchical tree.

Rich query
 The ability to locate objects of interest by querying for properties of the object.

High availability
 The ability to locate a replica of the directory at a location that is maximally efficient for the read/write operations.

Active Directory provides these capabilities and much more, including the following advanced features:

Support for Internet standards
 Active Directory global namespace roots in the domain name service (DNS), and then uses LDAP to access objects within the directory service data store.

Tightly integrated and flexible security
 Advantages include:

 - Choice of authentication packages depending on your application needs. Kerberos, secure sockets layer (SSL), or a combination can be used. For example, establish an SSL channel for encryption and then use Kerberos for authentication.

 - Central management of service and resource access by using Active Directory users and groups.

- Delegation of administration so that central administrators can delegate administrative tasks such as password changing or specific object creation and deletion.

- The same access control mechanisms that are used on the Windows NT and Windows 2000 file system are used for Active Directory. Thus, the same tools that manage access control on a file system work for Active Directory.

- Comprehensive Public Key infrastructure. The Microsoft Certificate Server and Smart Card support are integrated with Active Directory to provide Smart Card logon and Certificate management.

Scriptable interfaces for easy access

The primary and recommended application programming interface (API) for Active Directory is Active Directory Service Interfaces (ADSI). ADSI enables access to Active Directory by exposing objects stored in the directory as COM objects. A directory object is manipulated using the methods on one or more COM interfaces. You can already get ADSI providers from Microsoft for Novell NetWare Directory Services (NDS) and NetWare 3, Windows NT, the Lightweight Directory Access Protocol (LDAP), Microsoft Exchange 5.5, and the Microsoft Internet Information Server (IIS) metabase. ADSI can be used from any tools from Microsoft Office applications to C/C++. ADSI supports extensibility so that additional functionality can be added to a provider to support new properties and methods. ADSI has a very simple programming model. ADSI abstracts the data management overhead that is characteristic of non-COM interfaces such as the LDAP C APIs . Because ADSI is fully scriptable, it easy to develop rich Web applications. ADO and OLE DB are supported for querying. Several tools make it easy to create an ADO or OLE DB connection and get results. By supporting ADO and OLE DB, Active Directory is just another OLE DB data provider.

Directory enabled system services

The ZAW technologies are written to take advantage of Active Directory. By creating an MSI package and using the application deployment feature of Windows 2000, your client application can be easily deployed to many desktops.

Key application integration

Key distributed applications such as Exchange will be tightly integrated with Active Directory. By doing so, companies can reduce the number of directory services that need to be managed.

Rich and extensible schema

The schema defines what objects and properties can be written and read from a directory service. Active Directory's schema is very rich. Most of the objects and properties a service needs are probably already there. If not, a distributed application can extend the schema to support the application's additional requirements.

Active Directory Basics

Too many times, we gloss over basic definitions and explanations that really need to be explained. Such omissions can make (development) life more difficult down the road, because the absence of our grasp on these basic definitions result in a half-understanding of them, which leaves us on shaky development ground. This section intends to firm up that ground, and start your directory-enabled development effort on firm footing.

What Is a Directory Service?

A directory is a source used to store information about interesting objects. A telephone directory stores information about telephone subscribers. In a file system, the directory stores information about files.

In a distributed computing system or a public computer network like the Internet, there are many interesting objects such as printers, fax servers, applications, databases, and other users. Users want to find and use these objects. Administrators want to manage how these objects are used.

In this document the terms *directory* and *directory service* refer to the directories found in public and private networks. A directory service differs from a directory in that it is both the directory information source *and* the services making the information available and usable to the users.

Why Have a Directory Service?

A directory service is one of the most important components of an extended computer system. Users and administrators frequently do not know the exact name of the objects they are interested in. They might know one of more *attributes* of the objects and can *query* the directory to get a list of objects that match the attributes (for example, "Find all duplex printers in Building 26."). A directory service allows a user to find any object, given one of its attributes.

A directory service can:

- Enforce security that is defined by administrators in order to keep information safe from intruders.
- Distribute a directory across many computers in a network.
- Replicate a directory to make it available to more users and resistant to failure.
- Partition a directory into multiple stores to allow the storage of a very large numbers of objects.

A directory service is both a management tool and an end user tool. As the number of objects in a network grows, the directory service becomes essential. The directory service is the hub around which a large distributed system turns.

What Is Active Directory?

Active Directory is the directory service included with Windows 2000. It extends the features of previous Windows-based directory services and adds entirely new features. Active Directory is *secure, distributed, partitioned*, and *replicated*. It is designed to work well in any size installation, from a single server with a few hundred objects to thousands of servers and millions of objects. Active Directory adds many new features that make it easy to navigate and manage large amounts of information, generating savings for both administrators and end users.

Active Directory Core Concepts

Some concepts and terms that are used to describe Active Directory are new and some aren't. Unfortunately, some of the terms that have been around for a while are used to mean more than one particular thing. Before continuing, it is important that you understand what the following concepts and terms mean in the context of Active Directory.

Scope

The *scope* of Active Directory is large. It can include every single object (printer, file, or user), every server, and every domain in a single wide area network. It can also include several wide area networks combined. Some of the following terms apply to more than a single network, so it is important to keep in mind that Active Directory can scale from a single computer, to a single computer network, to many computer networks combined.

Namespace

Active Directory is primarily a *namespace*, as is any directory service. A telephone directory is a namespace. A namespace is any bounded area in which a given name can be resolved. Name resolution is the process of translating a name into some object or information that the name represents. A telephone book forms a namespace in which the names of telephone subscribers can be resolved to telephone numbers. The NTFS file system forms a namespace in which the name of a file can be resolved to the file itself. Active Directory forms a namespace in which the name of an object in the directory can be resolved to the object itself.

Object

An *object* is a distinct, named set of attributes that represents something concrete, such as a user, a printer, or an application. The attributes hold data describing the thing that is identified by the directory object. Attributes of a user might include the user's given name, surname, and e-mail address.

Containers and Leaves

Active Directory is a hierarchy of objects in which every object instance (except the root of the directory hierarchy) is contained by some other object. But the structure of this hierarchy is more flexible than a file system where you just have directories and files. Instead, there are rules (in the Active Directory Schema) that determine which object classes can contain instances of which other object classes. For example, the default schema definition of the **User** object class includes the **Organizational-Unit** and **Container** object classes as possible superiors (that is, possible parents or containers) of a **User** object instance. This means that an **Organizational-Unit** object can contain a **User** object, but a **User** object cannot contain another **User** object (unless the schema definition of the **User** class is changed).

Except for schema objects (that is, the **classSchema** or **attributeSchema** objects that define the classes and attributes that can exist in an Active Directory forest), any object in Active Directory may be a container. Specifically, any object class that appears in the **possSuperiors** or **systemPossSuperiors** attribute of an object class definition is potentially a container. To find out the possible superiors of a predefined object class, see the reference page for the class in the Active Directory Schema Reference of the *Active Directory Reference*. Programmatically, you can bind to the abstract schema and use the **IADsClass::get_Containment** or **IADsClass::get_PossibleSuperiors** methods to get the classes that a given class can contain or be contained by (see *Reading the Abstract Schema*). You can also read the **possibleInferiors** attribute of any object instance to determine the object classes that the object can contain. Note that **possibleInferiors** is a constructed attribute, which means it's calculated from the **possSuperior/systemPossSuperiors** values of the other class definitions and is not actually stored in the directory.

Notice that the Active Directory Schema defines a **Container** class. As you can see from the discussion above, an object does not have to be an instance of the **Container** class to be a container. There's also a **Leaf** class, and although subclasses of this class are typically not containers, there's no reason why they couldn't be.

Finally, you can set a flag on the display specifier associated with an object class to indicate that user interfaces should always display instances of the class as leaves rather than containers. This helps prevent the user interface from being cluttered by too many containers. For more information, see *Viewing Containers as Leaf Nodes*.

Object Names and Identities

In Active Directory, an object has several identities:

- The distinguished name (DN) is the current name of the object. This is the **distinguishedName** property of the object. The distinguished name is a string, formed by concatenating the *relative distinguished names* of the object and each of its ancestors all the way to *Root*. For example, the DN of the Users container in the ArcadiaBay.Com domain would be CN=Users, DC=ArcadiaBay, DC=Com. DNs are unique within a forest. An object's distinguished name changes when the object is moved or renamed.

- The relative distinguished name (RDN) is the name defined by an object's naming attribute. The **rDnAttID** attribute of a **classSchema** object identifies the naming attribute for instances of the class. Most object classes use **cn** (Common-Name) as the naming attribute. An object's RDN must be unique in the container where the object resides. There can be many object instances with the same RDN, but no two can be in same container. For more information about the **rDnAttID** attribute and **classSchema** objects, see *Characteristics of Object Classes*.

- The object GUID (objectGUID) is a globally unique identifier (GUID) assigned by Active Directory when the object instance is created. A GUID is a 128-bit number guaranteed to be unique in space and time. Object GUIDs never change—if an object is renamed or moved anywhere in the enterprise forest, the **objectGUID** remains the same. Applications that save references to Active Directory objects must use the **objectGUID** to be rename-safe. The distinguished name for an object might change, but the **objectGUID** will not.

Object instances can have many other attributes, and the attributes can be used for identification by applications. For example, security principal objects (instances of the **user**, **computer**, and **group** object classes) have **userPrincipalName**, **sAMAccountName**, and **objectSid** attributes. These attributes are very important "names" for Windows 2000 security, but these are not part of the object's identity from the directory's perspective.

Naming Contexts and Partitions

For replication purposes, an Active Directory forest has a number of directory partitions (also called naming contexts). A directory partition is a contiguous Active Directory subtree that is replicated on one or more Windows 2000 domain controllers (DCs) in a forest.

Each DC has a replica of three directory partitions:

- The schema partition, which contains the **classSchema** and **attributeSchema** objects that define the types of objects that can exist in the Active Directory forest. Every DC in the forest has a replica of the same schema partition.

- The configuration partition, which contains replication topology and other configuration information that must be replicated throughout the forest. Every DC in the forest has a replica of the same configuration partition.

- A domain partition, which contains the objects, such as users and computers, associated with the local domain. A domain can have multiple DCs; a forest can have multiple domains. Each DC stores a full replica of the domain partition for its local domain, but does not store replicas of the domain partitions for other domains.

Note that a Global Catalog contains *partial* replicas of the all the objects from every partition in a forest.

For more information about how Active Directory maintains consistency between the various replicas of a directory partition, see *Replication and Data Integrity*.

Domains

A *domain* is a single security boundary of a Windows NT computer network. For more information on Windows NT domains, see your Windows NT documentation. Active Directory is made up of one or more domains. On a standalone workstation, the domain is the computer itself. A domain can span more than one physical location. Every domain has its own security policies and security relationships with other domains. When multiple domains are connected by trust relationships and share a common schema, configuration, and global catalog, you have a *domain tree*. Multiple domain trees can be connected together into a *forest*. All the domains in a forest also share a common schema, configuration, and global catalog.

Domain Trees

A domain tree (tree) is comprised of several domains that share a common schema and configuration, forming a contiguous namespace. Domains in a tree are also linked together by trust relationships. Active Directory is a set of one or more trees.

Trees can be viewed two ways. One view is the trust relationships between domains. The other view is the namespace of the domain tree.

Viewing Trust Relationships

You can draw a picture of a domain tree based on the individual domains and how they trust each other.

Windows NT establishes trust relationships between domains based on the Kerberos security protocol. Kerberos trust is transitive and hierarchical—if domain A trusts domain B and domain B trusts domain C, domain A trusts domain C as well. (See Figure 5-1.)

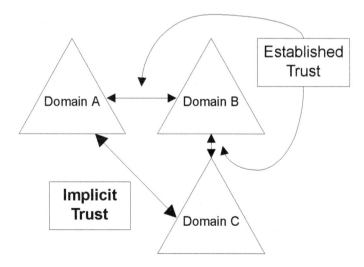

Figure 5-1:   Trust between individual domains.

Viewing the Namespace

You can also draw a picture of a domain tree based on the namespace. You can determine an object's distinguished name by following the path up the domain tree's namespace. This view is useful for grouping objects together into a logical hierarchy. The chief advantage of a contiguous namespace is that a deep search from the root of the namespace will search the entire hierarchy. (See Figure 5-2.)

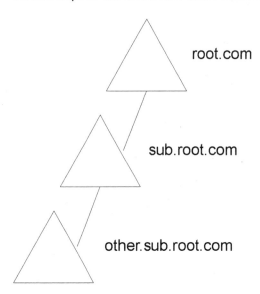

Figure 5-2:   Domain tree based on the namespace.

Forests

A forest is a set of one or more trees that *do not* form a contiguous namespace. All trees in a forest share a common schema, configuration, and global catalog. All trees in a given forest trust each other according to transitive hierarchical Kerberos trust relationships. Unlike trees, a forest does not need a distinct name. A forest exists as a set of cross-reference objects and Kerberos trust relationships known to the member trees. Trees in a forest form a hierarchy for the purposes of Kerberos trust; the tree name of at the root of the trust tree can be used to refer to a given forest. (See Figure 5-3.)

Active Directory Servers and Dynamic DNS

Active Directory servers publish their addresses such that clients can find them knowing only the domain name. Active Directory servers are published using the Service Resource Records (SRV RRs) in DNS. The SRV RR is a DNS record used to map the name of a service to the address of a server offering that service. The name of a SRV RR is in this format:

<service>.<protocol>.<domain>

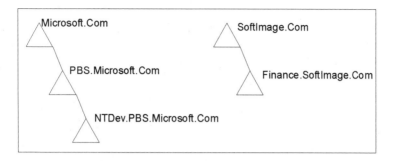

Figure 5-3:   View of a forest.

Active Directory servers offer the LDAP service over the TCP protocol so that published names are "ldap.tcp.<domain>". Thus, the SRV RR for Microsoft.com is "ldap.tcp.microsoft.com". Additional information on the SRV RR indicates the priority and weight for the server, allowing clients to choose the best server for their needs.

When an Active Directory server is installed, it uses *Dynamic DNS* to publish itself. Since TCP/IP addresses are subject to change over time, servers periodically check their registrations to make sure they are correct, updating them if necessary.

Dynamic DNS is a recent addition to the DNS standard. Dynamic DNS defines a protocol for updating a DNS server with new or changed values dynamically. Prior to Dynamic DNS, administrators needed to manually configure the records stored by DNS servers.

Sites

A *site* is a location in a network holding Active Directory servers. A site is defined as one or more well-connected TCP/IP subnets. "Well-connected" means that network connectivity is highly reliable and fast. Defining a site as a set of subnets allows administrators to quickly and easily configure Active Directory access and replication topology to take advantage of the physical network. When users log in, Active Directory clients find Active Directory servers in the same site as the user. Since machines in the same site are close to each other in network terms, communication among machines in the site is reliable, fast, and efficient. Determining the local site at login time is easy because the user's workstation already knows what TCP/IP subnet it is on, and subnets translate directly to Active Directory sites.

Active Directory Architecture

This short section introduces some of the primary architectural components of Active Directory.

Directory System Agent

The *directory system agent* (DSA) is the process that provides access to the *store*. The store is the physical store of directory information located on a hard disk. In Active Directory, the DSA is part of the local system authority (LSA) subsystem in Windows NT. Clients access the directory using one of the following mechanisms supported by the DSA:

- LDAP clients connect to the DSA using the LDAP protocol. LDAP is an acronym for Lightweight Directory Access Protocol. Active Directory supports LDAP 3.0, defined by RFC 2251, and LDAP 2.0, defined by RFC 1777. Windows 2000 clients (and Windows 95 and Windows 98 clients) with Active Directory client components installed use LDAP 3.0 to connect to the DSA.

- MAPI clients such as Microsoft Exchange connect to the DSA using the MAPI remote procedure call interface.

- Windows clients that use a previous version of Windows NT connect to the DSA using the Security Account Manager (SAM) interface.

- Active Directory DSAs connect to each other to perform replication using a proprietary remote procedure call interface.

Data Model

Active Directory data model is derived from the X.500 data model. The directory holds objects that represent things of various sorts, described by attributes. The universe of objects that can be stored in the directory is defined in the schema. For each object class, the schema defines what attributes an instance of the class must have, what additional attributes it may have, and what object class can be a parent of the current object class.

Schema

Active Directory schema is implemented as a set of object class instances stored in the directory. This is very different than many directories that have a schema but store it as a text file read at startup. Storing the schema in the directory has many advantages. For example, user applications can read it to discover what objects and properties are available.

Active Directory schema can be updated dynamically. That is, an application can extend the schema with new attributes and classes and use the extensions immediately. Schema updates are accomplished by creating or modifying the schema objects stored in the directory. Like every object in Active Directory, access-control lists (ACLs) protect schema objects, so only authorized users may alter the schema.

For more information, see Volume 5 of this library, *The Active Directory Schema*.

Administration Model

Authorized users perform administration in Active Directory. A user is authorized by a higher authority to perform a specified set of actions on a specified set of objects and object classes in some identified subtree of the directory. This is called *delegated administration.* Delegated administration allows fine-grained control over who can do what and enables delegation of authority without granting elevated privileges.

Global Catalog

Active Directory can consist of many partitions or naming contexts. The distinguished name (DN) of an object includes enough information to locate a replica of the partition that holds the object. Many times however, the user or application does not know the DN of the target object or which partition might contain the object. The *global catalog* (GC) allows users and applications to find objects in an Active Directory domain tree, given one or more attributes of the target object.

The global catalog contains a partial replica of every naming context in the directory. It contains the schema and configuration naming contexts as well. This means the GC holds a replica of every object in Active Directory but with only a small number of their attributes. The attributes in the GC are those most frequently used in search operations (such as a user's first and last names or login names) and those required to locate a full replica of the object. The GC allows users to quickly find objects of interest without knowing what domain holds them and without requiring a contiguous extended namespace in the enterprise.

The global catalog is built automatically by Active Directory replication system. The replication topology for the global catalog is generated automatically. The properties replicated into the global catalog include a base set defined by Microsoft. Administrators can specify additional properties to meet the needs of their installation.

Active Directory Security

Active Directory is part of the Windows 2000 trusted computing base and is a full participant in the Windows 2000 security infrastructure. Every object in Active Directory is protected by its own security descriptor. The system validates any attempt to access an object or attribute in Active Directory by checking the access permissions allowed by the object's security descriptor.

The following topics describe the highlights of Active Directory security. For more information and code samples, see *Controlling Access to Active Directory Objects.*

Object and Attribute Protection

An access-control list (ACL) protects all objects in Active Directory. ACLs determine who can see the object, what attributes they can see, and what actions each user can perform on the object. The existence of an object or an attribute is never revealed to a user who is not allowed to see it.

An ACL is a list of access-control entries (ACEs) stored with the object it protects. In Windows NT/Windows 2000, an ACL is stored as a binary value, called a security descriptor. Each ACE contains a security identifier (SID), which identifies the *principal* (user or group) to whom the ACE applies, and information on what type of access the ACE grants or denies.

ACLs on directory objects contain ACEs that apply to the object as a whole and ACEs that apply to the individual attributes of the object. This allows an administrator to control not just which users can see an object, but what properties those users can see. For example, all users might be granted read access to the e-mail and telephone number attributes for all other users, but security properties of users might be denied to all but members of a special security administrators group. Individual users might be granted write access to personal attributes such as the telephone and mailing addresses on their own user objects.

Delegation

Delegation is one of the most important security features of Active Directory. Delegation allows a higher administrative authority to grant specific administrative rights for containers and subtrees to individuals and groups. This eliminates the need for domain administrators with sweeping authority over large segments of the user population.

ACEs can grant specific administrative rights on the objects in a container to a user or group. Rights are granted for specific operations on specific object classes using ACEs in the container's ACL. For example, to allow a user named "user 1" to be an administrator of the "Corporate Accounting" organizational unit, you would add ACEs to the ACL on "Corporate Accounting" as follows:

```
"user 1";Grant ;Create, Modify, Delete;Object-Class User
"user 1";Grant ;Create, Modify, Delete;Object-Class Group
"user 1";Grant ;Write;Object-Class User; Attribute Password
```

Now user 1 can create new users and groups in Corporate Accounting and set the passwords on existing users, but he cannot create any other object classes and he cannot affect users in any other containers (unless, of course, ACEs grant him access on the other containers.

Inheritance

Inheritance allows a given ACE to be propagated from the container where it was applied to all children of the container. Inheritance can be combined with delegation to grant administrative rights to a whole subtree of the directory in a single operation.

C H A P T E R   6

Searching Active Directory

Searching is one of the key features of Microsoft® Active Directory™. A search operation enables you to find objects in Active Directory based on selection criteria (query) and to retrieve specified properties for the objects found.

Searching Active Directory is simply a matter of finding a Microsoft® Windows® 2000 domain controller, binding to the object where you want to begin your search in the directory, submitting a query, and processing the results.

The process for searching Active Directory includes the following steps:

1. Decide what you want to find.
2. Decide where to search.
3. Choose the data access technology to use.
4. Create a query filter (search criteria).
5. List the properties to return.
6. Bind to the object where you want to start the search.
7. Specify the scope of the search.
8. Specify other search options.
9. Execute the search and process the results.

Deciding What to Find

Before you search the directory, you need to consider what you want to find. It sounds trivial, but what you want to find and what properties you want to return affects where you bind to start your search, the depth of your search, your query filter, and search performance.

For example, if you are searching for all user objects with surname Smith, you need to first decide where you want to search: a specific container or OU within a domain, a specific domain, a specific domain tree, or the entire forest. If you are looking for objects within a specific container or domain, you will get better performance by binding directly to that container or domain—instead of performing a subtree search on a domain tree.

Next, if you are checking for the existence of, or retrieving the properties of a particular object that has a distinguished name (DN) you already know, you should do a base search, which searches only the object you have bound to. If you know an object is a direct descendant of a particular container, bind to that container and do a one-level search (**attributeSchema** and **classSchema** objects in the schema container and extended-right objects in the extended-rights container are good examples). If you don't know exactly where the object is, or if you want to search the object you've bound to and all the child objects below it in the directory hierarchy, do a subtree search.

Finally, if you are looking for a specific class of object, the query filter should have expressions that evaluate properties that are defined for that class. In addition, you should specify the **objectCategory** of the class of object you want to find as one of the expressions. You should use **objectCategory** instead of **objectClass** because **objectCategory** is indexed. Indexed attributes can increase the performance of the search. For example, to search for group objects, include the expression (objectCategory=group) in the filter. To search for user objects, you need to specify (&(objectClass=user)(objectCategory=person)) because the computer class derives from the user class, so (objectClass=user) would return both users and computers and also because both contact and user objects have an **objectCategory** of person, so (objectCategory=person) would return both users and contacts. For more information, see *Object Class and Object Category* and *Indexed Attributes*.

Example Code for Searching for Users

The following programs search for users in the domain of the user account under which the calling process is running.

C++

The following program searches the current domain for all users (or a specific user based on a specified filter).

```
#include <objbase.h>
#include <wchar.h>
#include <activeds.h>
//Make sure you define UNICODE
//Need to define version 5 for Windows 2000
#define _WIN32_WINNT 0x0500
#include <sddl.h>

HRESULT FindUsers(IDirectorySearch *pContainerToSearch,  //IDirectorySearch
pointer to the container to search.
        LPOLESTR szFilter, //Filter for finding specific users.
                    //NULL returns all user objects.
        LPOLESTR *pszPropertiesToReturn, //Properties to return for
                                // user objects found
                                //NULL returns all set
```

```
                                              // properties.
          BOOL bIsVerbose            //TRUE means display all
                                     // properties for the found objects.
                                     //FALSE means only the RDN
                          );


void wmain( int argc, wchar_t *argv[ ])
{


//Handle the command line arguments.
LPOLESTR pszBuffer = new OLECHAR[MAX_PATH*2];
wcscpy(pszBuffer, L"");
BOOL bReturnVerbose = FALSE;


for (int i = 1;i<argc;i++)
{
    if (_wcsicmp(argv[i],L"/V") == 0)
    {
    bReturnVerbose = TRUE;
    }
  else if ((_wcsicmp(argv[i],L"/?") == 0)||
      (_wcsicmp(argv[i],L"-?") == 0))
    {
    wprintf(L"This program queries for users in the current user's domain.\n");
    wprintf(L"Syntax: queryusers [/V][querystring]\n");
    wprintf(L"where /V specifies that all properties for the found users should
be returned.\n");
    wprintf(L"querystring is the query criteria in ldap query format.\n");
    wprintf(L"Defaults: If no /V is specified, the query returns only the RDN and
DN of the items found.\n");
    wprintf(L"If no querystring is specified, the query returns all users.\n");
    wprintf(L"Example: queryusers (sn=Smith)\n");
    wprintf(L"Returns all users with surname Smith.\n");
    return;
    }
    else
    {
    wcscpy(pszBuffer,argv[i]);
    }
}
if (_wcsicmp(pszBuffer,L"") == 0)
  wprintf(L"\nFinding all user objects...\n\n");
else
    wprintf(L"\nFinding user objects based on query: %s...\n\n", pszBuffer);
```

(continued)

(continued)

```
//Initialize COM
CoInitialize(NULL);
HRESULT hr = S_OK;
//Get rootDSE and the current user's domain container
// distinguished name.
IADs *pObject = NULL;
IDirectorySearch *pContainerToSearch = NULL;
LPOLESTR szPath = new OLECHAR[MAX_PATH];
VARIANT var;
hr = ADsOpenObject(L"LDAP://rootDSE",
        NULL,
        NULL,
        ADS_SECURE_AUTHENTICATION, //Use Secure Authentication
        IID_IADs,
        (void**)&pObject);
if (FAILED(hr))
{
    wprintf(L"Could not execute query. Could not bind to LDAP://rootDSE.\n");
    if (pObject)
    pObject->Release();
    return;
}
if (SUCCEEDED(hr))
{
    hr = pObject->Get(L"defaultNamingContext",&var);
    if (SUCCEEDED(hr))
    {
    //Build path to the domain container.
    wcscpy(szPath,L"LDAP://");
    wcscat(szPath,var.bstrVal);
    hr = ADsOpenObject(szPath,
            NULL,
            NULL,
            ADS_SECURE_AUTHENTICATION, //Use Secure Authentication
            IID_IDirectorySearch,
            (void**)&pContainerToSearch);

    if (SUCCEEDED(hr))
    {
      hr = FindUsers(pContainerToSearch, //IDirectorySearch pointer
                                        //to domainDNS container.
          pszBuffer,
          NULL, //Return all properties
          bReturnVerbose
          );
      if (SUCCEEDED(hr))
```

```
      {
        if (S_FALSE==hr)
          wprintf(L"No user object could be found.\n");
      }
      else if (0x8007203e==hr)
        wprintf(L"Could not execute query. An invalid filter was specified.\n");
      else
        wprintf(L"Query failed to run. HRESULT: %x\n",hr);
    }
    else
    {
      wprintf(L"Could not execute query. Could not bind to the container.\n");
    }
    if (pContainerToSearch)
      pContainerToSearch->Release();
    }
    VariantClear(&var);
}
if (pObject)
    pObject->Release();


// Uninitialize COM
CoUninitialize();
return;
}

HRESULT FindUsers(IDirectorySearch *pContainerToSearch,
                        //IDirectorySearch pointer to the
                        // container to search.
    LPOLESTR szFilter,  //Filter for finding specific users.
                        // NULL returns all user objects.
    LPOLESTR *pszPropertiesToReturn,
                        //Properties to return for user objects found
                        // NULL returns all set properties.
    BOOL bIsVerbose     //TRUE means all properties for
                        // the found objects are displayed.
                        // FALSE means only the RDN
            )
{
    if (!pContainerToSearch)
    return E_POINTER;
    //Create search filter
    LPOLESTR pszSearchFilter = new OLECHAR[MAX_PATH*2];
    //Add the filter.
```

(continued)

(continued)

```
    wsprintf(pszSearchFilter,
L"(&(objectClass=user)(objectCategory=person)%s)",szFilter);

    //Specify subtree search
    ADS_SEARCHPREF_INFO SearchPrefs;
    SearchPrefs.dwSearchPref = ADS_SEARCHPREF_SEARCH_SCOPE;
    SearchPrefs.vValue.dwType = ADSTYPE_INTEGER;
    SearchPrefs.vValue.Integer = ADS_SCOPE_SUBTREE;
    DWORD dwNumPrefs = 1;

    // COL for iterations
    LPOLESTR pszColumn = NULL;
    ADS_SEARCH_COLUMN col;
    HRESULT hr;

    // Interface Pointers
    IADs  *pObj = NULL;
    IADs  * pIADs = NULL;

    // Handle used for searching.
    ADS_SEARCH_HANDLE hSearch = NULL;

    // Set the search preference.
    hr = pContainerToSearch->SetSearchPreference( &SearchPrefs, dwNumPrefs);
    if (FAILED(hr))
    return hr;

    LPOLESTR pszBool = NULL;
    DWORD dwBool;
    PSID pObjectSID = NULL;
    LPOLESTR szSID = NULL;
    LPOLESTR szDSGUID = new WCHAR [39];
    LPGUID pObjectGUID = NULL;
    FILETIME filetime;
    SYSTEMTIME systemtime;
    DATE date;
    VARIANT varDate;
    LARGE_INTEGER liValue;
    LPOLESTR *pszPropertyList = NULL;
    LPOLESTR pszNonVerboseList[] = {L"name",L"distinguishedName"};

    LPOLESTR szName = new OLECHAR[MAX_PATH];
    LPOLESTR szDN = new OLECHAR[MAX_PATH];

    int iCount = 0;
    DWORD x = 0L;
```

```
if (!bIsVerbose)
  {
   //Return non-verbose list properties only.
   hr = pContainerToSearch->ExecuteSearch(pszSearchFilter,
              pszNonVerboseList,
              sizeof(pszNonVerboseList)/sizeof(LPOLESTR),
              &hSearch
              );
  }
  else
  {
  if (!pszPropertiesToReturn)
  {
    //Return all properties.
    hr = pContainerToSearch->ExecuteSearch(pszSearchFilter,
              NULL,
              0L,
              &hSearch
              );
  }
  else
  {
    //Specified subset.
    pszPropertyList = pszPropertiesToReturn;
     //Return specified properties.
     hr = pContainerToSearch->ExecuteSearch(pszSearchFilter,
              pszPropertyList,
              sizeof(pszPropertyList)/sizeof(LPOLESTR),
              &hSearch
              );
  }
  }
  if ( SUCCEEDED(hr) )
  {
  // Call IDirectorySearch::GetNextRow() to retrieve the next row
  //of data.
  hr = pContainerToSearch->GetFirstRow( hSearch);
  if (SUCCEEDED(hr))
  {
  while( hr != S_ADS_NOMORE_ROWS )
  {
    //Keep track of count.
    iCount++;
    if (bIsVerbose)
```

(continued)

(continued)

```
      wprintf(L"----------------------------------\n");
  // Loop through the array of passed column names,
  // print the data for each column.

  while( pContainerToSearch->GetNextColumnName( hSearch, &pszColumn ) !=
S_ADS_NOMORE_COLUMNS )
    {
    hr = pContainerToSearch->GetColumn( hSearch, pszColumn, &col );
    if ( SUCCEEDED(hr) )
    {
      // Print the data for the column and free the column.
      if(bIsVerbose)
      {
      // Get the data for this column.
      wprintf(L"%s\n",col.pszAttrName);
      switch (col.dwADsType)
      {
        case ADSTYPE_DN_STRING:
          for (x = 0; x< col.dwNumValues; x++)
          {
            wprintf(L"  %s\r\n",col.pADsValues[x].DNString);
          }
          break;
        case ADSTYPE_CASE_EXACT_STRING:
        case ADSTYPE_CASE_IGNORE_STRING:
        case ADSTYPE_PRINTABLE_STRING:
        case ADSTYPE_NUMERIC_STRING:
        case ADSTYPE_TYPEDNAME:
        case ADSTYPE_FAXNUMBER:
        case ADSTYPE_PATH:
        case ADSTYPE_OBJECT_CLASS:
          for (x = 0; x< col.dwNumValues; x++)
          {
            wprintf(L"  %s\r\n",col.pADsValues[x].CaseIgnoreString);
          }
          break;
        case ADSTYPE_BOOLEAN:
          for (x = 0; x< col.dwNumValues; x++)
          {
            dwBool = col.pADsValues[x].Boolean;
            pszBool = dwBool ? L"TRUE" : L"FALSE";
            wprintf(L"  %s\r\n",pszBool);
          }
          break;
        case ADSTYPE_INTEGER:
          for (x = 0; x< col.dwNumValues; x++)
```

```
      {
        wprintf(L"   %d\r\n",col.pADsValues[x].Integer);
      }
      break;
  case ADSTYPE_OCTET_STRING:
    if ( _wcsicmp(col.pszAttrName,L"objectSID") == 0 )
    {
      for (x = 0; x< col.dwNumValues; x++)
      {
        pObjectSID = (PSID)(col.pADsValues[x].OctetString.lpValue);
        //Convert SID to string.
        ConvertSidToStringSid(pObjectSID, &szSID);
        wprintf(L"   %s\r\n",szSID);
        LocalFree(szSID);
      }
    }
    else if ( (_wcsicmp(col.pszAttrName,L"objectGUID") == 0) )
    {
      for (x = 0; x< col.dwNumValues; x++)
      {
      //Cast to LPGUID
      pObjectGUID = (LPGUID)(col.pADsValues[x].OctetString.lpValue);
      //Convert GUID to string.
      ::StringFromGUID2(*pObjectGUID, szDSGUID, 39);
      //Print the GUID
      wprintf(L"   %s\r\n",szDSGUID);
      }
    }
    else
      wprintf(L"   Value of type Octet String. No Conversion.");
    break;
  case ADSTYPE_UTC_TIME:
    for (x = 0; x< col.dwNumValues; x++)
    {
    systemtime = col.pADsValues[x].UTCTime;
    if (SystemTimeToVariantTime(&systemtime,
                  &date) != 0)
    {
      //Pack in variant.vt.
      varDate.vt = VT_DATE;
      varDate.date = date;
      VariantChangeType(&varDate,&varDate,VARIANT_NOVALUEPROP,VT_BSTR);
      wprintf(L"   %s\r\n",varDate.bstrVal);
      VariantClear(&varDate);
    }
    else
```

(continued)

(continued)

```
          wprintf(L"  Could not convert UTC-Time.\n",pszColumn);
        }
        break;
  case ADSTYPE_LARGE_INTEGER:
    for (x = 0; x< col.dwNumValues; x++)
    {
    liValue = col.pADsValues[x].LargeInteger;
    filetime.dwLowDateTime = liValue.LowPart;
    filetime.dwHighDateTime = liValue.HighPart;
    if((filetime.dwHighDateTime==0) && (filetime.dwLowDateTime==0))
      {
      wprintf(L"  No value set.\n");
      }
    else
    {
      //Check for properties of type LargeInteger
      //  that represent time.
      //If TRUE, then convert to variant time.
      if ((0==wcscmp(L"accountExpires", col.pszAttrName))|
        (0==wcscmp(L"badPasswordTime", col.pszAttrName))||
        (0==wcscmp(L"lastLogon", col.pszAttrName))||
        (0==wcscmp(L"lastLogoff", col.pszAttrName))||
        (0==wcscmp(L"lockoutTime", col.pszAttrName))||
        (0==wcscmp(L"pwdLastSet", col.pszAttrName))
          )
      {
        //Handle special case for Never Expires
        //  where low part is -1
        if (filetime.dwLowDateTime==-1)
        {
          wprintf(L"  Never Expires.\n");
        }
        else
          {
          if (FileTimeToLocalFileTime(&filetime, &filetime) != 0)
            {
            if (FileTimeToSystemTime(&filetime,
                    &systemtime) != 0)
              {
              if (SystemTimeToVariantTime(&systemtime,
                      &date) != 0)
                {
                //Pack in variant.vt.
                varDate.vt = VT_DATE;
                varDate.date = date;
```

```
VariantChangeType(&varDate,&varDate,VARIANT_NOVALUEPROP,VT_BSTR);
                        wprintf(L"  %s\r\n",varDate.bstrVal);
                        VariantClear(&varDate);
                        }
                    else
                        {
                        wprintf(L"  FileTimeToVariantTime failed\n");
                        }
                    }
                else
                    {
                    wprintf(L"  FileTimeToSystemTime failed\n");
                    }

                    }
                else
                    {
                    wprintf(L"  FileTimeToLocalFileTime failed\n");
                    }
                }
            }
        }
        else
            {
            //Print the LargeInteger.
            wprintf(L"  high: %d low: %d\r\n",filetime.dwHighDateTime,
filetime.dwLowDateTime);
            }
          }
        }
        break;
      case ADSTYPE_NT_SECURITY_DESCRIPTOR:
        for (x = 0; x< col.dwNumValues; x++)
          {
          wprintf(L"  Security descriptor.\n");
          }
        break;
      default:
        wprintf(L"Unknown type %d.\n",col.dwADsType);
      }
      else
      {
      //Verbose handles only the two single-valued
      //  attributes: cn and ldapdisplayname
      //  so this is a special case.
```

(continued)

(continued)

```
        if (0==wcscmp(L"name", pszColumn))
        {
          wcscpy(szName,col.pADsValues->CaseIgnoreString);
        }
        if (0==wcscmp(L"distinguishedName", pszColumn))
         {
          wcscpy(szDN,col.pADsValues->CaseIgnoreString);
         }
      }
      pContainerToSearch->FreeColumn( &col );
    }
    FreeADsMem( pszColumn );
  }
  if (!bIsVerbose)
    wprintf(L"%s\n  DN: %s\n\n",szName,szDN);
  //Get the next row
  hr = pContainerToSearch->GetNextRow( hSearch);
}

}
// Close the search handle to clean up
pContainerToSearch->CloseSearchHandle(hSearch);
}
if (SUCCEEDED(hr) && 0==iCount)
hr = S_FALSE;

return hr;
}
```

Visual Basic

The following routine searches the current domain for users with the specified surname and returns the name and **distinguishedName** attributes for the objects that are found.

This routine uses ADO to perform the search.

```
Dim Con As ADODB.Connection
Dim ocommand As ADODB.Command
Dim gc As IADs

On Error Resume Next
'Maximum number of items to list on a msgbox.
MAX_DISPLAY = 5

'Prompt for surname to search for.
strName = InputBox("This routine searches in the current domain for users with the
specified surname." & vbCrLf & vbCrLf &"Specify the surname:")
```

```
If strName = "" Then
    msgbox "No surname was specified. The routine will search for all users."
End If


'Create ADO connection object for Active Directory
Set Con = CreateObject("ADODB.Connection")
    If (Err.Number <> 0) Then
      BailOnFailure Err.Number, "on CreateObject"
    End If
Con.Provider = "ADsDSOObject"
    If (Err.Number <> 0) Then
      BailOnFailure Err.Number, "on Provider"
    End If
Con.Open "Active Directory Provider"
    If (Err.Number <> 0) Then
      BailOnFailure Err.Number, "on Open"
    End If

'Create ADO command object for the connection.
Set ocommand = CreateObject("ADODB.Command")
    If (Err.Number <> 0) Then
      BailOnFailure Err.Number, "on CreateObject"
    End If
ocommand.ActiveConnection = Con
    If (Err.Number <> 0) Then
      BailOnFailure Err.Number, "on Active Connection"
    End If

'Get the ADsPath for the domain to search.
Set root = GetObject("LDAP://rootDSE")
    If (Err.Number <> 0) Then
      BailOnFailure Err.Number, "on GetObject for rootDSE"
    End If
sDomain = root.Get("defaultNamingContext")
    If (Err.Number <> 0) Then
      BailOnFailure Err.Number, "on Get on defaultNamingContext"
    End If
Set domain = GetObject("LDAP://" & sDomain)
    If (Err.Number <> 0) Then
      BailOnFailure Err.Number, "on GetObject for domain"
    End If

'Build the ADsPath element of the commandtext
sADsPath = "<" & domain.ADsPath & ">"
```

(continued)

(continued)

```
'Build the filter element of the commandtext
If (strName = "") Then
    sFilter = "(&(objectCategory=person)(objectClass=user))"
Else
    sFilter = "(&(objectCategory=person)(objectClass=user)(sn=" & strName & "))"
End If

'Build the returned attributes element of the commandtext.
sAttribsToReturn = "name,distinguishedName"

'Build the depth element of the commandtext.
sDepth = "subTree"

'Assemble the commandtext.
ocommand.CommandText = sADsPath & ";" & sFilter & ";" & sAttribsToReturn & ";" & sDepth
    If (Err.Number <> 0) Then
      BailOnFailure Err.Number, "on CommandText"
    End If
'Display
show_items "CommandText: " & ocommand.CommandText, ""

'Execute the query.
Set rs = ocommand.Execute
    If (Err.Number <> 0) Then
      BailOnFailure Err.Number, "on Execute"
    End If

strText = "Found " & rs.RecordCount & " Users in the domain:"
intNumDisplay = 0
intCount = 0

' Navigate the record set
rs.MoveFirst
While Not rs.EOF
    intCount = intCount + 1
    strText = strText & vbCrLf & intCount & ") "
    For i = 0 To rs.Fields.Count - 1
        If rs.Fields(i).Type = adVariant And Not (IsNull(rs.Fields(i).Value)) Then
          strText = strText & rs.Fields(i).Name & " = "
          For j = LBound(rs.Fields(i).Value) To UBound(rs.Fields(i).Value)
              strText = strText & rs.Fields(i).Value(j) & " "
          Next
        Else
          strText = strText & rs.Fields(i).Name & " = " & rs.Fields(i).Value & vbCrLf
        End If
```

```
      Next
      intNumDisplay = intNumDisplay + 1
      'Display in msgbox if there are MAX_DISPLAY items to display
      If intNumDisplay = MAX_DISPLAY Then
            Call show_items(strText, "Users in domain")
            strText = ""
            intNumDisplay = 0
      End If
      rs.MoveNext
Wend

show_items strText, "Users in domain"
'''''''''''''''''''''''''''''''''''''
'Display subroutines
'''''''''''''''''''''''''''''''''''''
Sub show_items(strText, strName)
      MsgBox strText, vbInformation, "Search domain for users with Surname " & strName
End Sub

Sub BailOnFailure(ErrNum, ErrText)      strText = "Error 0x" & Hex(ErrNum) & " " & ErrText
      MsgBox strText, vbInformation, "ADSI Error"
      WScript.Quit
End Sub
```

Where to Search

An object can be in one of the following naming contexts:

- *Domain.* This contains most of the highly used objects such as users, contacts, groups, organizational units, computers, and so on. Most queries will search a domain.

- *Schema container.* This contains the **attributeSchema** and **classSchema** objects that define the types of objects and properties that can exist in the directory.

- *Configuration container.* This contains configuration information that is relevant to the entire forest, such as sites, display specifiers, extended rights, partitions, and so on.

- *Global catalog.* This contains a partial replica of all objects in the directory. It includes partial replicas of all domains in the forest as well as partial replicas of the schema and configuration containers.

Searching Domain Contents

Before discussing where to bind to begin a search for objects in domains, you need to know a little about how information is stored in Active Directory.

If you have a forest with more than one domain, Active Directory does not store all information about all objects (that is, all properties for every object) on a single domain controller—for performance, scalability, and reliability reasons. A domain controller holds all information about the domain that it is a member of (it has a full replica of the domain). But a domain controller does not hold complete information about any other domain.

So, if you bind to the domain object (with referral chasing turned off—see *Referrals*), you can search for any object in that domain (and only that domain). The search can retrieve any property and can use a query filter containing any property.

In a forest, domains are arranged hierarchically as domain trees. A domain tree can be just a single domain or a domain with one or more child domains. These child domains, in turn, can have child domains beneath them and so on. A domain tree is also a contiguous namespace. A contiguous namespace means that the child domains are a continuation of the naming hierarchy. For example, a domain Microsoft.com (or DC=Microsoft,DC=COM) could have a child domain mydivision (mydivision.AcadiaBay.com or DC=mydivision,DC=Microsoft,DC=COM), which in turn could have a child mydev (mydev.mydivision.AcadiaBay.com or DC=mydev,DC=mydivision,DC=Microsoft,DC=COM).

So, if you bind to a domain object (with referral chasing turned on) for a domain within a domain tree, you will search that domain and the entire hierarchy below it. The search can retrieve any property and can use a query filter containing any property.

If a domain controller contains a full replica of only its own domain, how can you perform a subtree search on a domain tree? A domain holds references to its child domains. When a domain controller processes a subtree search request against its own domain, the domain controller searches that domain and then returns referrals to each of its child domains to the client. A referral is the way that a directory server communicates that it does not contain the information required to complete a request (such as a query) but has a reference to a server that may contain the required information. In the case of a subtree search of a domain tree, a referral is returned for each direct child domain so that the search can be continued at a domain controller in each child domain. If referral chasing is turned on, the LDAP client library (Wldap32.dll) uses those referrals to bind to a domain controller in each child domain and continue the search. If referral chasing is turned off, the LDAP client does not resolve the referrals and the search is complete. For information, see *Referral Chasing*.

A subtree search on a domain tree with referral chasing turned on can be time-consuming if there is a slow connection to the domain controllers for the child domains. If you want to search only a single domain, you should turn referral chasing off to avoid having to search the child domains unnecessarily.

Searching the Schema

To search for **attributeSchema** or **classSchema** objects, bind to an IDirectorySearch pointer on the schema container on any domain controller. The schema container is a full replica of the schema and is available on all domain controllers. Note that the schema container's distinguished name should be retrieved from the **schemaNamingContext** property from rootDSE. For sample code that retrieves the DN of the schema container, see *Example Code for Getting the Distinguished Name for the Naming Context* in the Binding chapter.

For additional information on reading from the schema container or from the abstract schema, see *Guidelines for Binding to the Schema*.

Searching the Configuration Container

To search for objects in the configuration container, bind to the configuration container on any domain controller. The configuration container is a full replica and is available on all domain controllers. Note that the configuration container's distinguished name should be retrieved from the **configurationNamingContext** property from rootDSE. For sample code that retrieves the DN of the configuration container, see Example Code for Getting the Distinguished Name for the Naming Context in the Binding chapter.

Searching Global Catalog Contents

Active Directory also has a global catalog (GC), which contains a partial replica of all objects in the directory. It also contains partial replicas of the schema and configuration containers. One or more domain controllers in a domain can hold a copy of the global catalog. For information about binding to a global catalog, see Binding to the Global Catalog.

The global catalog holds a replica of every object in Active Directory but with only a small number of their attributes. The attributes in the global catalog are those most frequently used in search operations (such as a user's first and last names, login names, and so on). The global catalog attributes also include those required to locate a full replica of the object. The global catalog allows users to quickly find objects of interest without knowing what domain holds them and without requiring a contiguous extended namespace in the enterprise; that is, you can search the entire forest.

So, if you bind to an object in the global catalog, you will search that object and the entire hierarchy below it—without having to go to any other server. However, the search can only use a query filter containing properties in the global catalog and can retrieve only properties in the global catalog.

Searching the global catalog has the following benefits:

- Global catalog enables you to search the entire forest or any part of the forest as well as the schema and configuration containers.

- Global catalog enables you to perform a complete search on a single server. No referrals or referral chasing is required.

Searching the global catalog has the following disadvantages:

- Global catalog contains a small subset of the properties on each object. If your query filter includes properties that are not in the global catalog, the query will evaluate the expressions containing those properties as false. If you specify non-global catalog properties in the list of properties to return, those properties are not retrieved.
- To search the global catalog, a domain controller containing a global catalog must be available. If one is not available, you will not be able to perform a global catalog search.
- The global catalog is read-only. This means you cannot bind to an object in the global catalog to create, modify, or delete objects.

Choosing the Data Access Technology

You can use the following technologies to search Active Directory:

IDirectorySearch
ADSI provides the **IDirectorySearch** interface to query Active Directory (as well as other directory services such as NDS) using LDAP. **IDirectorySearch** is a COM interface that returns richly typed data, such as Integer, Octet String, String, Security Descriptor, UTC-Time, Large Integer, or Boolean. For more information about how to use **IDirectorySearch**, see Searching with IDirectorySearch.

OLE DB
OLE DB is a set of COM interfaces that provide applications with uniform access to data stored in diverse information sources, regardless of location or type. ADSI also provides an OLE DB provider for ADSI that enables applications to use OLE DB to access Active Directory. The ADSI OLE DB provider uses the **IDirectorySearch** interfaces to submit queries to Active Directory and to collect the results.

ADO and other OLE DB-based data access technologies
The ADSI OLE DB provider enables any data-access technology based on OLE DB (such as ADO) to search Active Directory.

LDAP API
Microsoft® Windows® 2000 domain controllers are directory servers that are compliant with LDAP version 3. The LDAP API is a C-style function library. Applications can use the LDAP API to search Active Directory.

Which one do you choose?

For Microsoft® Visual Basic® and Visual Basic Scripting Edition (VBScript), ADO is recommended.

For C/C++, you can choose any of the technologies.

If your application extensively uses ADSI, it may be simpler to use **IDirectorySearch**. If you use **IDirectoryObject** to manage objects in Active Directory, use **IDirectorySearch** to make handling the properties returned from the search easier. **IDirectorySearch** uses the same **ADSVALUE** structures as **IDirectoryObject** to represent properties. In addition, **IDirectorySearch** is exposed on almost all ADSI COM objects. If you have a pointer to an ADSI COM object, you can simply call **QueryInterface** to get an **IDirectorySearch** pointer that you can use to perform a search starting at the directory object represented by the ADSI COM object.

If your application already uses OLE DB, ADO or LDAP API, you can continue to use those technologies to search Active Directory as well.

If your application needs to join data from Active Directory and a SQL Server 7 database, use OLE DB. By using OLE DB, your application can perform distributed queries that reference Active Directory and tables and rowsets from one or more Microsoft SQL Server 7 databases.

Creating a Query Filter

A query filter is simply the act of telling Active Directory what you want to find—in LDAP query syntax. All the specified data access technologies listed in the Choosing the Data Access Technology topic support the LDAP query syntax.

The LDAP query syntax is the following:

<expression><expression>...

A filter can contain one or more expressions. An expression has the following form:

(<logicaloperator><comparison><comparison...>)

where <logicaloperator> is the following:

Logical operator	Meaning
|	OR
&	AND
!	NOT

and <comparison> is the following:

(<attribute><operator><value>)

where <attribute> is the **IDAPDisplayName** of the attribute to evaluate, <value> is the value to compare against, and <operator> is one of the following comparison operators:

Logical operator	Meaning
=	Equals
~=	Approximately equals
<=	Less than or equal to
>=	Greater than or equal to

In addition, depending on the attribute syntax, the <value> may contain the * wildcard. Note that a <value> containing only * checks for the existence of the <attribute>.

Finding Objects by Class

Usually, you will want to find a specific class of objects. For example, you may want to find computers with location equal to Building 26.

```
(&(objectCategory=computer)(location=Building 26))
```

Why wasn't **objectClass** used? You should not use **objectClass** without another comparison containing an indexed attribute. Index attributes help increase the efficiency of a query. The **objectClass** attribute is multi-valued and not indexed. To specify the type or class of an object, you should use **objectCategory** instead.

```
//Inefficient
(objectClass=computer)

//More Efficient
(objectCategory=computer)
```

Note that there are some cases where a combination of **objectClass** and **objectCategory** must be used. The user class and contact class should be specified in the following manner:

```
(&(objectClass=user)(objectCategory=person))

(&(objectClass=contact)(objectCategory=person))
```

Note that you could search for both users and contacts with the following:

```
(objectCategory=person)
```

Finding Objects by Name

Most objects have **cn** (Common-Name) as their naming attribute. However, a few have naming attributes that are not **cn** (such as **domainDNS**, which is DC, and **organizationalUnit**, which is OU). To avoid having to remember what the naming attribute is, use the **name** (RDN) attribute.

Example Code for Filtering Objects by Name

The following filter finds all objects:

```
(objectClass=*)
```

The following filter finds all computers:

```
(objectCategory=computer)
```

The following filter finds all users and groups (note how an expression can be contained by another expression):

```
(|(&(objectClass=user)(objectCategory=person))(objectCategory=group))
```

The following filter finds all computers with names that begin with leased or corp:

```
(&(objectCategory=computer)(|(name=leased*)(name=corp*)))
```

Finding a List of Attributes to Query

If you are searching for objects of a particular class, the comparisons in your search filter should specify attributes that actually exist on the objects of that class. To get the list attributes on an object of a particular class, bind to that class in the abstract schema and call both **IADsClass::get_MandatoryProperties** and **IADsClass::get_OptionalProperties** to get the list of all properties for that object. For more information, see *Reading the Abstract Schema*.

In addition, all objects inherit from the top abstract class. Therefore, any attribute in **top** can exist (although it may not be set) on any object.

If you are searching the global catalog, you should make sure you specify only attributes that are in the global catalog. Attributes that are included in the global catalog have the **isMemberOfPartialAttributeSet** set to TRUE on their **attributeSchema** objects. Note that this information is not available in the abstract schema, so you need to read it directly from the **attributeSchema** object in the schema container.

In the global catalog, a back link attribute can be queried only if both of the following conditions are met: First, the attribute is marked for inclusion in the global catalog and second, the corresponding forward link is also marked for inclusion in the global catalog. This applies to query filters as well as query results. See *Linked Attributes*.

In addition, some attributes (mostly on the user object) are constructed. Query filters cannot contain constructed attributes. Constructed attributes cannot be evaluated in query filters; however, they can be returned in query results. This applies to all the naming contexts and the global catalog. Attributes that are constructed have ADS_SYSTEMFLAG_ATTR_IS_CONSTRUCTED (0x00000004) in the **systemFlags** property on their **attributeSchema** objects.

Note   You can get information about the predefined classes and attributes that ship with the system from the reference pages in the Active Directory Schema Reference in the *Active Directory Reference*. These pages list the mandatory and optional attributes of each object class. For attributes, the reference page indicates whether the attribute is indexed, constructed, linked, or in the global catalog.

Checking the Query Filter Syntax

The LDAP API provides a simple syntax-checking function. Note that it only checks the syntax and not the existence of the properties specified in the filter.

The following function checks the syntax of the query filter and returns S_OK if the filter is valid or S_FALSE if it is not.

```
HRESULT CheckFilterSyntax(
    LPOLESTR szServer, // NULL binds to a DC in the current domain.
    LPOLESTR szFilter) // Filter to check.
{
HRESULT hr = S_OK;
DWORD dwReturn;
LDAP *hConnect = NULL;   //Connection handle

if (!szFilter)
  return E_POINTER;

// LDAP_PORT is the default port, 389

hConnect = ldap_open(szServer,  LDAP_PORT);

// Bind using the preferred authentication method on Windows 2000
// and the calling thread's security context.

dwReturn = ldap_bind_s( hConnect, NULL, NULL, LDAP_AUTH_NEGOTIATE );
if (dwReturn==LDAP_SUCCESS) {
    dwReturn = ldap_check_filter(hConnect, szFilter);
    if (dwReturn==LDAP_SUCCESS)
        hr = S_OK;
    else
        hr = S_FALSE;
}

// Unbind to free the connection.
```

```
ldap_unbind( hConnect );

return hr;
}
```

Specifying Comparison Values

Each attribute type has a syntax that determines the type of comparison values that you can specify in a search filter for that attribute.

The following sections describe what is required for each attribute syntax. For more information on attribute syntaxes, see *Syntaxes for Active Directory Attributes*.

Boolean

The value specified in a filter must be one of the following string values:

TRUE

FALSE

Examples of Boolean

Filter specifying showInAdvancedViewOnly set to TRUE:

```
(showInAdvancedViewOnly=TRUE)
```

Filter specifying showInAdvancedViewOnly set to FALSE:

```
(showInAdvancedViewOnly=FALSE)
```

Integer and Enumeration

The value specified in a filter must be a decimal Integer. Hexadecimal values must be converted to decimal.

Note that the LDAP matching rule controls can be used to perform bit-wise comparisons.

Matching rules have the following syntax:

attributename:*ruleOID*:=*value*

where *attributename* is the IDAPDisplayName of the attribute, *ruleOID* is the OID for the matching rule control, and *value* is the value you want to use for comparison.

Active Directory supports the following matching rules.

Matching rule OID	Description
1.2.840.113556.1.4.803	LDAP_MATCHING_RULE_BIT_AND
	The matching rule is true only if all bits from the property match the value. This rule is like the bit-wise AND operator.
1.2.840.113556.1.4.804	LDAP_MATCHING_RULE_BIT_OR
	The matching rule is true if any bits from the property match the value. This rule is like the bit-wise OR operator.

Examples of Integer and Enumeration

Filter specifying groupType of Universal group
(ADS_GROUP_TYPE_UNIVERSAL_GROUP is 0x00000008).

```
(groupType=8)
```

Filter specifying groupType of security-enabled Universal group
(ADS_GROUP_TYPE_SECURITY_ENABLED is 0x80000000), since
ADS_GROUP_TYPE_SECURITY_ENABLED |
ADS_GROUP_TYPE_UNIVERSAL_GROUP is 0x80000008 and converted to
decimal value is 2147483650.

```
(groupType=2147483650)
```

Bit-wise comparisons

Filter specifying groupType with the ADS_GROUP_TYPE_SECURITY_ENABLED
bit set:

```
(groupType:1.2.840.113556.1.4.804:=2147483648) )
```

The following query string searches for Universal distribution groups (that is, Universal
groups without ADS_GROUP_TYPE_SECURITY_ENABLED flag):

```
(&(objectCategory=group)((&(groupType:1.2.840.113556.1.4.804:=8)(!(groupType:
1.2.840.113556.1.4.803:=2147483650)))))
```

OctetString

The value specified in a filter is the data to be found. The data must be represented
as an encoded byte string where each byte is preceded by a \ character.

Use the **ADsEncodeBinaryData** function to create an encoded string representation
of binary data.

Note that wildcards are allowed.

Example of OctetString

Filter containing encoded string for schemaIDGUID with GUID value (in
StringFromGUID2 format) of {BF967ABA-0DE6-11D0-A285-00AA003049E2}:

```
(schemaidguid=\BAz\96\BF\E6\0D\D0\11\A2\85\00\AA\000I\E2)
```

Filter containing encoded string for objectGUID with GUID value (in
StringFromGUID2 format) of {FB4B7B35-E0AF-11D2-868C-00C04F8607E2}:

```
(objectguid=5\7BK\FB\AF\E0\D2\11\86\8C\00\C00\86\07\E2)
```

The following code fragment prints the encoded string for the GUID
guidmyTestAttributeDNString:

```
static const GUID guidmyTestAttributeDNString =
    {
    /* 9cb304e4-d60d-11d2-81a7-00c04fb98c1a */
    0x9cb304e4,
    0xd60d,
    0x11d2,
    {0x81, 0xa7, 0x00, 0xc0, 0x4f, 0xb9, 0x8c, 0x1a}
```

```
    };

LPOLESTR szTestBuffer = NULL;
HRESULT hrTemp = E_FAIL;

hrTemp = ADsEncodeBinaryData((LPBYTE)&guidmyTestAttributeDNString,
                            sizeof(GUID), &szTestBuffer);
if (SUCCEEDED(hrTemp))
    wprintf(L"%s\n",szTestBuffer);


if(szTestBuffer)
    FreeADsMem(szTestBuffer);
```

Sid

The value specified in a filter is the encoded byte string representation of the SID. See the discussion of encoded byte strings in the preceding discussion of the OctetString syntax.

Example of SID

Filter containing encoded string for objectSid with SID string value of S-1-5-21-1935655697-308236825-1417001333:

```
(ObjectSid=\01\04\00\00\00\00\00\05\15\00\00\00\11\C3\5Fs\19R\5F\12u\B9uT)
```

DN

The entire distinguished name that you want to match must be supplied.

Wildcards are not allowed.

Note that the **objectCategory** property also allows you to specify the **lDAPDisplayName** of the class set on the property. See the example that follows.

Examples of DN

Filter specifying a member containing CN=TestUser,DC=Microsoft,DC=COM:

```
(member=CN=TestUser,DC=Microsoft,DC=COM)
```

Two equivalent filters specifying an **objectCategory** set to CN=Attribute-Schema,CN=Schema,CN=Configuration,DC=Microsoft,DC=COM:

```
(objectCategory=CN=Attribute-
Schema,CN=Schema,CN=Configuration,DC=Microsoft,DC=COM)
```

```
(objectCategory=attributeSchema)
```

INTEGER8

The value specified in a filter must be a decimal Integer. Hexadecimal values must be converted to decimal.

Examples of Integers

Filter specifying a creationTime set to a FILETIME of 3/10/99 3:31:32 PM:

```
(creationTime=125655822921406250)
```

The following functions create an exact match (=) filter for a large integer attribute and verify the existence of the attribute in the schema and its syntax:

```
HRESULT CreateExactMatchFilterLargeInteger(
              LPOLESTR szAttribute,
              INT64 liValue,
              LPOLESTR *pszFilter
              )
{
HRESULT hr = E_FAIL;

if ((!szAttribute)||(!pszFilter))
    return E_POINTER;

// Check that attribute exists and has
// Integer8 (Large Integer) syntax.

hr = CheckAttribute(szAttribute, L"Integer8");
if (S_OK==hr) {
    LPOLESTR szTempFilter = new OLECHAR[MAX_PATH];
    swprintf(szTempFilter, L"%s=%I64d", szAttribute, liValue);

    // Allocate buffer for the filter string.
    // Caller must free the buffer using CoTaskMemFree.
    *pszFilter = (OLECHAR *)CoTaskMemAlloc (
                     sizeof(OLECHAR)*(wcslen(szTempFilter)+1));
    if (*pszFilter) {
        wcscpy(*pszFilter, szTempFilter);
        hr = S_OK;
    }
    else
        hr=E_FAIL;
}
return hr;
}


HRESULT CheckAttribute(
              LPOLESTR szAttribute,
              LPOLESTR szSyntax
              )
{
HRESULT hr = E_FAIL;
BSTR bstr;
IADsProperty *pObject = NULL;
LPOLESTR szPath = new OLECHAR[MAX_PATH];
```

```
if ((!szAttribute)||(!szSyntax))
    return E_POINTER;

swprintf(szPath,L"LDAP://schema/%s",szAttribute);
hr = ADsOpenObject(szPath,
           NULL,
           NULL,
           ADS_SECURE_AUTHENTICATION, //Use Secure Authentication
           IID_IADsProperty,
           (void**)&pObject);
if (SUCCEEDED(hr)) {
    hr = pObject->get_Syntax(&bstr);
    if (SUCCEEDED(hr)) {
        if (0==_wcsicmp(bstr, szSyntax))
            hr = S_OK;
        else
            hr = S_FALSE;
    }
    SysFreeString(bstr);
}
if (pObject)
    pObject->Release();
return hr;
}
```

PrintableString

Attributes that have these syntaxes are supposed to adhere to specific character sets (see *Syntaxes for Active Directory Attributes*). Currently, Active Directory does not enforce those character sets but it may enforce them in the future.

The value specified in a filter is a string. The comparison is case-sensitive.

```
(myAttribute=TheValue)
```

GeneralizedTime

The value specified in a filter is a string that represents the date in the following form:

```
YYYYMMDDHHMMSS.0Z
```

Z means no time differential. Note that Active Directory stores date/time as Greenwich mean time (GMT) time. If you specify a time with no time differential, you are specifying the time in GMT time.

If you are not in the GMT time zone, you can use a differential value (instead of specifying Z) to specify a time according to your time zone and then add the differential between your zone and GMT. The differential is based on the following: GMT=Local+differential.

To specify a differential, use the following format:

```
YYYYMMDDHHMMSS.0[+/-]HHMM
```

Examples of GeneralizedTime

Filter specifying a whenCreated time set to 3/23/99 8:52:58 PM:

```
(whenCreated=19990323205258.0Z)
```

Filter specifying a whenCreated time set to 3/23/99 8:52:58 PM New Zealand Standard Time (differential is 12 hours):

```
(whenCreated=19990323205258.0+1200)
```

Calculating Time Zone Differential

The following function returns the differential between the current local time zone and GMT. The value returned is a string in the following format:

```
[+/-]HHMM
```

For example, Pacific Standard Time would be –0800.

```
HRESULT GetLocalTimeZoneDifferential (
                    LPOLESTR *pszDifferential
                )
{
HRESULT hr = E_FAIL;
DWORD dwReturn = 0L;
TIME_ZONE_INFORMATION timezoneinfo;
LONG lTimeDifferential = 0;
LONG lHours = 0;
LONG lMinutes = 0;
LPOLESTR szString = new OLECHAR[MAX_PATH];
dwReturn = GetTimeZoneInformation(&timezoneinfo);
switch (dwReturn)
{
    case TIME_ZONE_ID_STANDARD:
    lTimeDifferential = timezoneinfo.Bias + timezoneinfo.StandardBias;
    //Bias is in minutes--calculate the hours for HHMM format.
    lHours = -(lTimeDifferential/60);
    //Bias is in minutes--calculate the minutes for HHMM format.
    lMinutes = lTimeDifferential%60L;
      swprintf(szString, L"%+03d%02d",lHours,lMinutes);
    hr = S_OK;
    break;
    case TIME_ZONE_ID_DAYLIGHT:
    lTimeDifferential = timezoneinfo.Bias + timezoneinfo.DaylightBias;
    //Bias is in minutes--calculate the hours for HHMM format.
    //Need to take the additive inverse.
    //Bias is based on GMT=Local+Bias.
    //We need a differential based on GMT=Local-Bias.
    lHours = -(lTimeDifferential/60);
    //Bias is in minutes--calculate the minutes for HHMM format.
    lMinutes = lTimeDifferential%60L;
```

```
        swprintf(szString, L"%+03d%02d",lHours,lMinutes);
    hr = S_OK;
    break;
    case TIME_ZONE_ID_INVALID:
    default:
    hr = E_FAIL;
    break;
}

if (SUCCEEDED(hr))
{
  *pszDifferential = (OLECHAR *)CoTaskMemAlloc
(sizeof(OLECHAR)*(wcslen(szString)+1));
    if (*pszDifferential)
    {
    wcscpy(*pszDifferential, szString);
    //Call must free using CoTaskMemFree
    hr = S_OK;
    }
    else
    hr=E_FAIL;
}

return hr;
}
```

UTCTime

The value specified in a filter is a string that represents the date in the following form:

```
YYMMDDHHMMSSZ
```

Z means no time differential. Note that Active Directory stores date/time as GMT time. If you specify a time with no time differential, you are specifying the time in GMT time.

Note that the seconds (SS) value is optional.

If you are not in the GMT time zone, you can use a differential value (instead of specifying Z) to specify a time according to your time zone and then add the differential between your zone and GMT. The differential is based on the following: GMT=Local+differential.

To specify a differential, use the following format:

```
YYMMDDHHMMSS[+/-]HHMM
```

Examples of UTCTime

Filter specifying a myTimeAttrib time set to 3/23/99 8:52:58 PM:

```
(myTimeAttrib=990323205258Z)
```

Filter specifying a myTimeAttrib time set to 3/23/99 8:52:58 PM without seconds specified:

```
(myTimeAttrib=9903232052Z)
```

Filter specifying a myTimeAttrib time set to 3/23/99 8:52:58 PM New Zealand Standard Time (differential is 12 hours). This is equivalent to 3/23/99 8:52:58 AM GMT.

```
(myTimeAttrib=990323205258+1200)
```

DirectoryString

The value specified in a filter is a string. DirectoryString can contain Unicode characters. The comparison is case-insensitive.

```
(myAttribute2=THEVALUE)
```

OID

The entire OID that you want to match must be supplied.

Wildcards are not allowed.

Note that the **objectCategory** property also allows you to specify the **IDAPDisplayName** of the class set on the property. See the example below.

Examples of OID

Filter specifying **governsID** for volume class:

```
(governsID=1.2.840.113556.1.5.36)
```

Two equivalent filters specifying **systemMustContain** property containing uNCName, which has an OID of 1.2.840.113556.1.4.137:

```
(SystemMustContain=uNCName)
```

```
(SystemMustContain=1.2.840.113556.1.4.137)
```

Other Syntaxes

The following syntaxes are evaluated in a filter in the same manner as an octet string. See the discussion of the OctetString syntax earlier in this topic.

- ObjectSecurityDescriptor
- AccessPointDN
- PresentationAddresses
- ReplicaLink
- DNWithString
- DNWithOctetString
- ORName

Listing Properties to Retrieve for Each Object Found

If you are searching for objects of a particular class, it only makes sense if you retrieve attributes that actually exist on the objects of that class. Follow the same rules discussed in *Finding a List of Attributes To Query*. Note that constructed attributes *can* be retrieved in query—but constructed attributes cannot be used in filters.

Retrieving the objectClass Property

The **objectClass** property contains the class of which the object is an instance, as well as all classes from which that class is derived. For example, the **user** class inherits from **top**, **person**, and **organizationalPerson**; therefore, the **objectClass** property contains the names of those classes, as well as user. So, how do you find out what class the object is an instance of? The **objectClass** property is the only property with multiple values that has ordered values—the first value is the top of the class inheritance tree, which is the top class, and the last value is the most derived class, which is the class that the object is an instance of.

The following function takes a pointer to a column containing an **objectClass** property and returns the instantiated **objectClass** of the object:

```
HRESULT GetClass(ADS_SEARCH_COLUMN *pcol, LPOLESTR *ppClass)
{
    if (!pcol)
    return E_POINTER;

    HRESULT hr = E_FAIL;
    if (ppClass)
    {
    LPOLESTR szClass = new OLECHAR[MAX_PATH];
    wcscpy(szClass, L"");
    if ( _wcsicmp(pcol->pszAttrName,L"objectClass") == 0 )
    {
      for (DWORD x = 0; x< pcol->dwNumValues; x++)
      {
        wcscpy(szClass, pcol->pADsValues[x].CaseIgnoreString);
      }
    }
    if (0==wcscmp(L"", szClass))
    {
      hr = E_FAIL;
    }
    else
    {
      //Allocate memory for string.
      //Caller must free using CoTaskMemFree.
```

(continued)

(continued)

```
    *ppClass = (OLECHAR *)CoTaskMemAlloc (
                         sizeof(OLECHAR)*(wcslen(szClass)+1));
    if (*ppClass)
    {
      wcscpy(*ppClass, szClass);
      hr = S_OK;
    }
    else
    hr=E_FAIL;
  }
  }
  return hr;
}
```

Binding to a Search Start Point

You can bind to any object in any of the following areas:

- Domain
- Schema
- Configuration

In addition, you can bind to the global catalog, which contains a partial replica of all domains, as well as partial replicas of the schema and configuration containers. For more information on when to search in the domain, schema, configuration, and global catalog, see *Where to Search*.

For information on binding to an object, domain, the root of domain tree, and the root of the global catalog, see *Binding*.

Specifying Other Search Options

Active Directory™ enables you to control how the search is performed:

- Search Scope
- Synchronous vs. Asynchronous
- Paging
- Result Caching
- Sorting the Search Results
- Referral Chasing
- Size Limit
- Server Time Limit
- Client Time-Out
- Returning Only Attribute Names

To set these options, call **IDirectorySearch::SetSearchPreference** and specify the options as an array of **ADS_SEARCHPREF_INFO** structures.

Search Scope

You can specify the scope of a search as either a base, one-level, or subtree search. Use the ADS_SEARCHPREF_SEARCH_SCOPE flag with the values of the **ADS_SCOPEENUM** enumeration to specify the search scope.

- *Base.* A base search limits the search to only the base object. The maximum number of objects returned is always one. This search is useful to verify the existence of an object for retrieving group membership. For example, if you have an object's distinguished name, and you need to verify the object's existence based on the path, you can use a one-level search. If the search fails, you can assume that the object may have been renamed or moved to a different location, or you were given the wrong information about the object. (Note that you should store the globally unique identifier (GUID) of the object instead of the distinguished name, if you wish to revisit an object. The GUID will always reference the same object, regardless of where the object is moved within the directory hierarchy.)

- *One-level.* A one-level search is restricted to the immediate children of a base object, but excludes the base object itself. This setting can perform a targeted search for immediate child objects of a parent object. For example, consider a parent object P1 and its immediate children: C1, C2, and C3. A one-level search evaluates C1, C2, and C3 against the search criteria, but does not evaluate P1. You can use a one-level search to enumerate all children of an object. In fact, an **IADsContainer** enumeration translates to a one-level search.

- *Subtree.* A subtree search (or a deep search) includes all child objects as well as the base object. You can request the LDAP provider to chase referrals to other LDAP directory services, including other Active Directory domains or forests.

Synchronous vs. Asynchronous

When you perform a search using **IDirectorySearch**, the **IDirectorySearch::ExecuteSearch** method does not send the search request to the server—this method only saves the search parameters. The search request is sent when you call **IDirectorySearch::GetFirstRow** or **IDirectorySearch::GetNextRow**.

For Active Directory searches, the primary difference between synchronous and asynchronous is when the first row of the result is returned (that is, when the first **GetFirstRow** or **GetNextRow** call returns):

- *Synchronous.* If paging is not enabled, the first row is returned when the server has constructed and returned the entire result set to the client.

  If paging is enabled, the first row is returned when the first page of the result set is returned.

- *Asynchronous.* The first row is returned when the server has constructed the first row of the result set.

  If paging is enabled, the first row is returned when the first page of the result set is returned.

To specify the asynchronous option, include a **ADS_SEARCHPREF_INFO** structure with ADS_SEARCHPREF_ASYNCHRONOUS set to TRUE in the array passed in the **IDirectorySearch::SetSearchPreference** call.

If the ADS_SEARCHPREF_ASYNCHRONOUS search preference is not set, the default is synchronous.

Paging

Paging specifies how many rows at a time the server returns to the client. A page can be defined by the number of rows or a time limit. The ADSI COM object takes care of retrieving each page of results based on the following settings. The caller simply calls **IDirectorySearch::GetNextRow** when the caller has reached the end of a page, and the ADSI COM object takes care of retrieving the next page.

ADS_SEARCHPREF_PAGESIZE
: Specifies the number of rows to return in a page.

ADS_SEARCHPREF_PAGED_TIME_LIMIT
: Specifies the maximum time (in seconds) that the server should spend collecting a page of results before returning the page to the client. If the limit is reached, the server stops searching and returns the rows retrieved for the page up to that point.

If neither of these search preferences is set, the default is no paging.

A search operation may result in a return of a large number of objects. If the server returns the result in one big chunk, it could downgrade the performance of the client and server as well as the network load. Paged search can be used to prevent this from happening. In a paged search, the client may elect to accept results in smaller chunks. The size of a chunk is known as the search page size.

Paged search offers benefits to both the client and the server. The client can be more responsive in presenting the results to end users. This is especially relevant to graphical user interface tools that can begin the window display process while the other thread concurrently receives the data.

On the server side, paged search makes the operation scalable. Suppose that one hundred clients issue search requests simultaneously and, on the average, each client gets back two hundred objects. If no page size is specified, the server must have sufficient memory to hold 20,000 objects in the worst case scenario. On the other hand, if each client specifies a page size to be, say, ten (10) objects, the memory requirement on the server is thus reduced by a factor of 20.

In addition, using a paged search, a client can abandon the operation in progress. In contrast, in a non-paged search, the client receives a result set in one big chunk. This may potentially put a heavy burden on the network.

On behalf of the client, ADSI handles the page size transparently. The client does not have to count the number of objects in progress. ADSI encapsulates the server interaction for the client. From the client's perspective, the search comes back with a complete result set.

It is recommended that you turn on paging.

Result Caching

The ADS_SEARCHPREF_CACHE_RESULTS preference caches the result set on the client. Result caching enables an application to retain a retrieved result set and go through the retrieved rows again. It also enables cursor support (the **IDirectorySearch::GetNextRow** and **IDirectorySearch::GetPreviousRow** methods can be used to go up and down the result set).

Recommendations:

- Turn on caching if your application needs to go through the result set more than once without performing the search again on the server. If your application needs the result set and performing the search is expensive on the server (slow connection, large result set, or complex query), consider turning on caching.
- Turn on caching if you need cursor support.
- Turn off caching if your application needs to reduce memory requirements for caching a large result set at the client.

The default is for caching to be **on**.

Sorting the Search Results

The ADS_SEARCHPREF_SORT_ON preference tells the server to sort the result set. Use the **ADS_SORTKEY** structure to specify the attribute on which to sort.

It is recommended that you specify an indexed attribute. Otherwise, the server must retrieve the complete result set and sort it before sending any results to the client. This also applies to paged searches. Note that you will increase performance of a sorted search if the filter includes an indexed attribute and that attribute is specified as the sort key (in this case, Active Directory can satisfy the sort while processing the filter). For example, an efficient sort query for a set of users could have a filter that included (sn>smith) and a sort key of sn.

You should use sorting only if you really need it.

The default is for sorting to be **off**.

Referral Chasing

A referral is the mechanism that a directory server uses to direct a client to another server when it does not contain sufficient information about the object(s) requested by a query.

In a one-level or subtree search (see *Search Scope*), referrals are returned for known, immediately subordinate domain, schema or configuration containers only (that is, child domains that are direct descendants).

In a directory, not all information is available on a single server, rather, it is distributed over several different servers across the network. If the servers share the knowledge of the information that other servers can provide, they can provide referrals to a client when a requested query cannot be resolved on the originating server. For example, when a client asks Server A to query a user object (U), then A can suggest that the client continue the search on Server B if U does not reside on A, but is known to be on B. The client has the choice to pursue the referral or not. Search referrals free the client from possessing previous knowledge of the capability of each server. But the client must specify the type of referrals a server should make.

To enable referral chasing, use the ADS_SEARCHPREF_CHASE_REFERRALS preference with values from the **ADS_CHASE_REFERRALS_ENUM** enumeration. A client can choose any of the following four types of referral chasing:

- *Never.* The server should not generate a referral to a client even though it knows that another server holds the requested information. This is the default setting.
- *External.* The server should generate referrals if the request can be resolved on another server of a different directory tree. For example, a client queries OU=Sales, DC=Microsoft, DC=COM on the *msft01* server on the Microsoft.com domain. However, the object does not belong to *msft01*, but is known to be on the *arc01* server on the Microsoft.com domain. Thus, *msft01* will refer *arc01* to the client.
- *Subordinate.* The server should generate referrals if the request can be resolved on a server whose name forms a contiguous path from the originating server. The search scope must be at the subtree level. For example, Server A contains objects in DC=Sales, DC=Microsoft, DC=Com. Server B contains objects in DC=Seattle, DC=Sales, DC=Microsoft, DC=Com. Notice that the name of Server B forms a contiguous path from Server A. When a client contacts Server A, requests a sub-tree search on DC=Sales, DC=Microsoft, DC=Com, and specifies the referral to be the Subordinate type, the following event occurs:
  - Server A returns all objects that it knows within its scope.
  - Server A informs the client that objects in DC=Seattle, DC=Sales, DC=Microsoft, DC=COM can be found on Server B.

  The client can choose to contact Server B. If so, the following event occurs:
  - Server B responds with the requested objects.
  - If Server B detects other servers on the contiguous naming path, the process continues.

- *Always.* The server generates referrals if the search can be resolved based on either the external type or the subordinate type.

For more information, see *Referrals*.

Size Limit

To reduce the memory requirement or for other purposes, the client can focus on a small number of objects returned from the server and ignore the rest of the result set that are of no interest. To accomplish this, the client specifies the search size limit and other appropriate search criteria. For example, if the directory stores the SAT scores of a school district, you can query the top ten students with the highest SAT scores by specifying a size limit of 10 (ten) and a descending sort order.

The default for size limit is **no limit**.

Use the ADS_SEARCHPREF_SIZE_LIMIT preference to specify a size limit.

Server Time Limit

When you request a search on a server under a heavy workload, you may want to tell the server to restrict the search to a specified time limit. For example, you want to run an application to generate a weekly report on a server that is running near its capacity. To avoid using up all the CPU time and preventing other operations from running at all, you can specify the search time limit to a small value and then re-run the application later if it fails to generate the report.

Some servers might impose their own administrative time limit. In these cases, if you specify a search time limit value greater than the administrative time limit, the server will ignore your specification and use its internal time limit value instead.

The default time limit is **no limit**.

Use the ADS_SEARCHPREF_TIME_LIMIT preference to specify a server time limit.

Client Time-Out

A client can also impose a time limit that it is willing to wait for a server to return the result set. The value of the search **time-out** property specifies this client-side time limit. When the server fails to respond to a query within the specified time period, the client can abandon the search and try it again later.

The **time-out** property is useful when a client requests an asynchronous search. In an asynchronous search, the client makes a request and then proceeds with other tasks while waiting for the server to return the results. It is possible that the server can go offline without notifying the client. In this case, the client will have no way of knowing whether the server is still processing the query, or if it has ceased to be live. The **time-out** property gives the client some control of situations like this.

The default time-out is **no limit**.

Use the ADS_SEARCHPREF_TIMEOUT preference to specify a client time-out.

Returning Only Attribute Names

Sometimes you do a search to determine what type of information is available for a particular object. In this case, you are only interested in the attributes, not the values, of the object. To accomplish this, set the ADS_SEARCHPREF_ATTRIBTYPES_ONLY option. Specifying this option will return the attribute names without their values. However, the result set includes only those attributes that have values assigned. For example, consider an object with the following attributes:

```
name = James
sn = Smith
department = Empty
phone = (206) 555-0111
```

When the Search Attributes Only option is set, the result set includes:

```
name
sn
department
phone
```

The default is for both values and names to be returned.

Example Code for Searching for Attributes

The following function creates an array of **ADS_SEARCHPREF_INFO** structures and sets the specified search preferences. An application can use the returned array to call **IDirectorySearch**.

```
HRESULT SetSearchPreferences(
    DWORD dwScope,              //-1 means use default: subtree
    DWORD dwOverallTimeOut,     // 0 means use default: no time-out
    DWORD dwOverallSizeLimit,   // 0 means use default: no size limit
    DWORD dwOverallTimeLimit,   // 0 means use default: no time limit
    BOOL bCacheResult,          // True means use default.
    BOOL bIsAsynchronous,       // False means use default
    DWORD dwPageSize,           // 0 means use default
    DWORD dwPageTimeLimit,      // 0 means use default
    DWORD dwChaseReferral,      // 0 means use default
    LPOLESTR szSortKey,         // NULL means don't sort.
    BOOL bIsDescending,
    BOOL bReturnAttributeNamesOnly, //False means use default.
    ADS_SEARCHPREF_INFO **ppSearchPref,   // Returns array of
                                //   search preferences.
    DWORD *pdwSearchPrefCount
```

```
        )
{
HRESULT hr = S_OK;
DWORD dwCountPref = 0L;

//Determine size of preferences array.
DWORD dwTotal = 11L;

if(dwScope==-1)
    dwTotal--;
if(dwOverallTimeOut<=0)
    dwTotal--;
if(dwOverallSizeLimit<=0)
    dwTotal--;
if(dwOverallTimeLimit<=0)
    dwTotal--;
if(bCacheResult)
    dwTotal--;
if(!bIsAsynchronous)
    dwTotal--;
if(dwPageSize<=0)
    dwTotal--;
if(dwPageTimeLimit<=0)
    dwTotal--;
if(dwChaseReferral<=0)
    dwTotal--;
if(!bReturnAttributeNamesOnly)
    dwTotal--;
if (!szSortKey)
    dwTotal--;

ADS_SEARCHPREF_INFO *prefInfo = new ADS_SEARCHPREF_INFO[ dwTotal ];
ADS_SORTKEY SortKey;

    ////////////////////
    // Search Scope
    ////////////////////
    if(dwScope>=0)
    {
    prefInfo[dwCountPref].dwSearchPref =
                ADS_SEARCHPREF_SEARCH_SCOPE;
    prefInfo[dwCountPref].vValue.dwType = ADSTYPE_INTEGER;
    prefInfo[dwCountPref].vValue.Integer = dwScope;
    dwCountPref++;
    }
```

(continued)

(continued)

```
///////////////////
// Time-out
///////////////////
if(dwOverallTimeOut>0)
  {
  prefInfo[dwCountPref].dwSearchPref = ADS_SEARCHPREF_TIMEOUT;
  prefInfo[dwCountPref].vValue.dwType = ADSTYPE_INTEGER;
  prefInfo[dwCountPref].vValue.Integer = dwOverallTimeOut;
  dwCountPref++;
  }

///////////////
// Size Limit
///////////////
if(dwOverallSizeLimit>0)
  {
  prefInfo[dwCountPref].dwSearchPref = ADS_SEARCHPREF_SIZE_LIMIT;
  prefInfo[dwCountPref].vValue.dwType = ADSTYPE_INTEGER;
  prefInfo[dwCountPref].vValue.Integer = dwOverallSizeLimit;
  dwCountPref++;
  }

///////////////
// Time Limit
///////////////
if(dwOverallTimeLimit>0)
  {
  prefInfo[dwCountPref].dwSearchPref = ADS_SEARCHPREF_TIME_LIMIT;
  prefInfo[dwCountPref].vValue.dwType = ADSTYPE_INTEGER;
  prefInfo[dwCountPref].vValue.Integer = dwOverallTimeLimit;
  dwCountPref++;
  }

///////////////////
// Cache Result
///////////////////

if (!bCacheResult)
{
  prefInfo[dwCountPref].dwSearchPref =
             ADS_SEARCHPREF_CACHE_RESULTS;
  prefInfo[dwCountPref].vValue.dwType = ADSTYPE_BOOLEAN;
  prefInfo[dwCountPref].vValue.Boolean = bCacheResult;
  dwCountPref++;
}
```

```
///////////////
// Page Size
///////////////
if(dwPageSize>0)
{
  prefInfo[dwCountPref].dwSearchPref = ADS_SEARCHPREF_PAGESIZE;
  prefInfo[dwCountPref].vValue.dwType = ADSTYPE_INTEGER;;
  prefInfo[dwCountPref].vValue.Integer = dwPageSize;
  dwCountPref++;
}


///////////////
// Page Time Limit
///////////////
if(dwPageTimeLimit>0)
{
  prefInfo[dwCountPref].dwSearchPref = ADS_SEARCHPREF_PAGED_TIME_LIMIT;
  prefInfo[dwCountPref].vValue.dwType = ADSTYPE_INTEGER;;
  prefInfo[dwCountPref].vValue.Integer = dwPageTimeLimit;
  dwCountPref++;
}


///////////////////
// Chase Referrals
///////////////////
if(dwChaseReferral>0)
{
  prefInfo[dwCountPref].dwSearchPref =
            ADS_SEARCHPREF_CHASE_REFERRALS;
  prefInfo[dwCountPref].vValue.dwType = ADSTYPE_INTEGER;
  prefInfo[dwCountPref].vValue.Integer = dwChaseReferral;
  dwCountPref++;
}


///////////////
// Sort
///////////////
  if (szSortKey)
  {
      prefInfo[dwCountPref].dwSearchPref = ADS_SEARCHPREF_SORT_ON;
      prefInfo[dwCountPref].vValue.dwType = ADSTYPE_PROV_SPECIFIC;
      SortKey.pszAttrType = (LPWSTR)LocalAlloc(
                      LPTR,
                      wcslen(szSortKey)*sizeof(WCHAR) +sizeof(WCHAR)
                      );
  wcscpy(SortKey.pszAttrType,szSortKey);
```

(continued)

(continued)

```
        SortKey.pszReserved = NULL;
        SortKey.fReverseorder = 0;
        prefInfo[dwCountPref].vValue.ProviderSpecific.dwLength =
sizeof(ADS_SORTKEY);
        prefInfo[dwCountPref].vValue.ProviderSpecific.lpValue = (LPBYTE)
&SortKey;
        dwCountPref++;
    }

    /////////////////////
    // Asynchronous
    /////////////////////
  if(bIsAsynchronous)
  {
    prefInfo[dwCountPref].dwSearchPref =
                ADS_SEARCHPREF_ASYNCHRONOUS;
    prefInfo[dwCountPref].vValue.dwType = ADSTYPE_BOOLEAN;
    prefInfo[dwCountPref].vValue.Integer = bIsAsynchronous;
    dwCountPref++;
  }


    ////////////////////////////
    // Attribute Type Only
    ////////////////////////////
  if(bReturnAttributeNamesOnly)
  {
    prefInfo[dwCountPref].dwSearchPref =
                ADS_SEARCHPREF_ATTRIBTYPES_ONLY;
    prefInfo[dwCountPref].vValue.dwType = ADSTYPE_BOOLEAN;
    prefInfo[dwCountPref].vValue.Integer = bReturnAttributeNamesOnly;
    dwCountPref++;
  }

if (SUCCEEDED(hr))
{
  *pdwSearchPrefCount = dwCountPref;
  *ppSearchPref  = prefInfo;
}
else
{
  *pdwSearchPrefCount = 0L;
  *ppSearchPref  = NULL;
}


return hr;
}
```

Checking Search Preferences

The **IDirectorySearch::SetSearchPreference** method writes a status value to the *dwStatus* member of each **ADS_SEARCHPREF_INFO** structure specified in the method call to indicate whether the search preference was set. The **ADS_STATUSENUM** enumeration defines the possible status values.

Example Code for Checking the Status of ADS_SEARCHPREF_INFO

The following function checks the status of an array of **ADS_SEARCHPREF_INFO** structures and displays the status in a message box:

```
HRESULT CheckPreferences(
    ADS_SEARCHPREF_INFO *pSearchPref, // Array of search preferences.
    DWORD dwSearchPrefCount
    )
{
 if ((!pSearchPref)||(dwSearchPrefCount<1))
   return E_INVALIDARG;
 HRESULT hr = S_OK;
 LPOLESTR szString = new OLECHAR[MAX_PATH*5];
 LPOLESTR szTemp = new OLECHAR[MAX_PATH];
 LPOLESTR szStatus = new OLECHAR[MAX_PATH];
 LPOLESTR szPref = new OLECHAR[MAX_PATH];
  wcscpy(szString,L"Check preferences:\r\n");
 for (DWORD i=0; i<dwSearchPrefCount; i++)
 {
      switch (pSearchPref[i].dwStatus)
    {
    case ADS_STATUS_S_OK:
         wcscpy(szStatus, L"ADS_STATUS_S_OK");
     break;
    case ADS_STATUS_INVALID_SEARCHPREF:
     wcscpy(szStatus, L"ADS_STATUS_INVALID_SEARCHPREF");
     break;
    case ADS_STATUS_INVALID_SEARCHPREFVALUE:
     wcscpy(szStatus, L"ADS_STATUS_INVALID_SEARCHPREFVALUE");
     break;
    default:
     swprintf(szStatus, L"Unknown status: %d",
                     pSearchPref[i].dwStatus);
     break;
    }
     switch (pSearchPref[i].dwSearchPref)
    {
```

(continued)

(continued)

```
    case ADS_SEARCHPREF_ASYNCHRONOUS:
            wcscpy(szPref, L"ADS_SEARCHPREF_ASYNCHRONOUS");
       break;
    case ADS_SEARCHPREF_SIZE_LIMIT:
       wcscpy(szPref, L"ADS_SEARCHPREF_SIZE_LIMIT");
       break;
    case ADS_SEARCHPREF_TIME_LIMIT:
       wcscpy(szPref, L"ADS_SEARCHPREF_TIME_LIMIT");
       break;
    case ADS_SEARCHPREF_ATTRIBTYPES_ONLY:
       wcscpy(szPref, L"ADS_SEARCHPREF_ATTRIBTYPES_ONLY");
       break;
    case ADS_SEARCHPREF_SEARCH_SCOPE:
       wcscpy(szPref, L"ADS_SEARCHPREF_SEARCH_SCOPE");
       break;
    case ADS_SEARCHPREF_TIMEOUT:
       wcscpy(szPref, L"ADS_SEARCHPREF_TIMEOUT");
       break;
    case ADS_SEARCHPREF_PAGESIZE:
       wcscpy(szPref, L"ADS_SEARCHPREF_PAGESIZE");
       break;
    case ADS_SEARCHPREF_PAGED_TIME_LIMIT:
       wcscpy(szPref, L"ADS_SEARCHPREF_PAGED_TIME_LIMIT");
       break;
    case ADS_SEARCHPREF_CHASE_REFERRALS:
       wcscpy(szPref, L"ADS_SEARCHPREF_CHASE_REFERRALS");
       break;
    case ADS_SEARCHPREF_SORT_ON:
       wcscpy(szPref, L"ADS_SEARCHPREF_SORT_ON");
       break;
    case ADS_SEARCHPREF_CACHE_RESULTS:
       wcscpy(szPref, L"ADS_SEARCHPREF_CACHE_RESULTS");
       break;
    default:
       swprintf(szPref, L"Unknown preference: %d",
                        pSearchPref[i].dwSearchPref);
       break;
    }
    swprintf(szTemp, L"%d. %s = %s\r\n",
                     i, szPref, szStatus );
    wcscat(szString,szTemp);
    }
MessageBox(NULL,szString,L"Check Preference Status",MB_OK);

return hr;
}
```

Effects of Security on Queries

Security is an implicit filter when performing searches, enumerating containers, or reading properties.

ADSI can return NO_SUCH_PROPERTY or NO_SUCH_OBJECT errors even when the object exists if you do not have access to read attributes on the object.

For example, a caller may be able to enumerate the child objects in a container because the caller has LIST_CONTENTS rights on the container. But the same caller may not be able to access the enumerated objects if the caller does not have read access to the child objects. In this case, a query for a child object may return NO_SUCH_OBJECT even though the caller successfully enumerated the object.

If the caller does not have sufficient rights, the following return codes may be returned:

E_ADS_INVALID_DOMAIN_OBJECT

E_ADS_PROPERTY_NOT_SUPPORTED

E_ADS_PROPERTY_NOT_FOUND

Processing Query Results

After the first call to **IDirectorySearch::GetFirstRow** or **IDirectorySearch::GetNextRow**, either S_OK, S_ADS_NOMORE_ROWS, or an error result is returned.

If the return value is S_ADS_NOMORE_ROWS, no object matching the filter was found. If an error result is returned, the query failed. In both cases, you don't need to process the rows in the result because nothing was returned.

If the return is S_OK, a row has been retrieved. You can iterate through the columns by name using **IDirectorySearch::GetColumn**. The name is the IDAPDisplayName of the attribute in the column. The set of all columns was defined by the pAttributeNames parameter of the **IDirectorySearch::ExecuteSearch** method. If NULL was specified, the set of all columns is the union of all properties found for all the objects returned. To read the entire set of columns returned for an object, use the **IDirectorySearch::GetNextColumnName** to iterate each column, and use the column name returned to call **IDirectorySearch::GetColumn**.

The **IDirectorySearch::GetColumn** method returns an **ADS_SEARCH_COLUMN** structure that contains the attribute name, the type of the attribute, count of values, and a pointer to an array of **ADSVALUE** structures that contain the values. You can loop through the **ADSVALUE** structures to read the values for the property returned by the column. You must read the appropriate member of the **ADSVALUE** structure based on the ADSTYPE specified by the **dwADsType** member of the **ADS_SEARCH_COLUMN** structure (or the **dwType** member of the **ADSVALUE** structure). For example, if **dwADsType** was ADSTYPE_INTEGER, you would read the **Integer** member of each ADSVALUE structure.

For sample code, see *Example Code for Searching for Users*.

Creating Efficient Queries

There are several concepts you should consider when executing a query. The following list identifies the most important ones.

- Make sure the query filter contains at least one indexed attribute. See *Indexed Attributes*.

- Search on **objectCategory** instead of **objectClass**, because **objectClass** is not an indexed property. The statement (objectClass=foo) refers to directory objects in which foo represents any class in the object's class hierarchy, whereas (*objectCategory=foo*), refers to those directory objects in which *foo* identifies a specific class in the object's class hierarchy. The **objectClass** property can take multiple values, whereas **objectCategory** takes a single value and is, thus, better suited for type matching of objects in a directory search. ADSI uses this as the default matching criterion. Searches using one **objectClass** are not scalable to large databases. ADSI supports (*objectCategory=SomeDN*) and (*objectCategory*=Ldap_Display_Name_of_Class), for example, (*objectCategory=user*). The exception to this is that the LDAP search filter (objectClass=*) does not specify a search on object class, but merely tests for the presence of the objects. See *Object Class and Object Category*.

- Avoid searching for text in the middle and on the end of a string. For example, "cn=*hille*" or "cn=*larouse". Using more specific matching criteria tends to boost search performance. This is because Active Directory™ evaluates all predicates, identifies the indices, and then picks one index that it considers most likely to yield the smallest set of returned values.

- Chasing referrals is expensive. Try to take advantage of the global catalog if you are considering subtree searches. See *Referral Chasing*.

- Assume a subtree search will return a large result set. Use paging when performing subtree searches. The server will then be able to stream a large result set in chunks reducing the server side memory resources. This effectively flattens out network usage and reduces the need for sending extremely large chunks of data over a network. See *Paging*.

- Restrict queries to retrieve only what is necessary.

- One search of an object that reads two attributes is cheaper than two searches of the same object, each returning one attribute.

- Bind to an object once and hang onto the binding handle for the rest of your session. Do not bind and unbind for each call. If you are using ADO or OLE DB, do not create many connection objects.

- Read the rootDSE once and remember its contents for the rest of your session. See *Serverless Binding and RootDSE* in the Binding chapter.

- Persist references to objects as GUIDs, not distinguished names, in order to be rename and delete safe. For more information, see *Using objectGUID to Bind to an Object*.

Referrals

Active Directory maintains referral information in **crossRef** objects stored in the partitions container (**crossRefContainer**) in the configuration container. Earlier in this chapter (the *Where to Search* section), referrals were discussed in the context of a domain within a domain tree and the generation of referrals to subordinate domains on a subtree search.

Active Directory automatically creates and maintains **crossref** objects for all domains in the forest. In addition, there are **crossRef** objects for the configuration and schema containers. These **crossRef** objects are used to generate referrals in queries that request information about objects that are in the forest, but not contained on the directory server handling the request. These are called *internal cross references*, because they refer to domains, schema, and configuration containers within the forest itself. In the case of a subtree search, the directory server returns referrals to the subordinate domains that are direct descendants of the directory server's domain. It is up to the client to resolve the referrals by binding to the path specified by the referral and submitting a query. If referral chasing is turned on, the WLDAP32.DLL library takes care of chasing the referral. If referral chasing is turned off, the calling application receives the referral information and then it can decide whether to chase the referral.

In addition to the dnsRoot (DNS name of the domain) and **nCName** (distinguished name for the domain) properties, the **crossRef** object also contains the **nETBIOSName** (NetBIOS name of the domain) and **trustParent** (distinguished name for the **crossRef** object representing the domain's direct parent domain) properties.

Active Directory can also have *external cross references* that refer to objects outside of the forest. External cross references must be added explicitly by an administrator. Note that the target server of the external cross reference must have a DNS root, that is, it must adhere to RFC 2247.

External cross references are used for the following purposes:

- To refer to a name that is totally disjointed from any name in the forest. The "name" can refer to another LDAP server on your network or on the Internet. For example, LDAP client applications used by your company may submit operations to your directory servers for Microsoft.com. You create a **crossRef** object for Microsoft.com. Now, instead of returning an object not found error, your directory servers can return a referral to Microsoft.com and the clients can chase the referral.
- To refer to an immediate child of an object in the forest.

  For example, suppose you have an object with the following distinguished name:

  ```
  CN=SomeObject,OU=SomeOU,DC=Microsoft,DC=Com
  ```

  You can add an external cross reference for an object with the name **ChildOfSomeObject**:

  ```
  CN=ChildOfSomeObject,CN=SomeObject,OU=SomeOU,DC=Microsoft,DC=Com
  ```

A subtree search that contains **SomeObject** will also return a referral to **ChildOfSomeObject**. Note that there really exists an LDAP server at the address specified by the referral (one of the properties on the **crossRef** object) and that this LDAP server serves the namespace identified by **ChildOfSomeObject**.

If referral chasing is turned on, the WLDAP32.DLL library will chase the referral by binding to the server specified by the **dNSRoot** property of the **crossRef** object and continue the search on the distinguished name specified by the **nCName** property or a specific object within the naming context specified by **nCName**. The credentials used to read the **crossRef** object are used to bind to the server specified by **dNSRoot**. Note that the search results from the referral will be returned as part of the results for the original search. This means the client application will see all the rows for both the original search and any referred searches as a single result set.

If referral chasing is turned off, the calling application receives the referral information and then it can decide whether to chase the referral. To chase the referral, the client application must submit another search request to the server, distinguished name, and query filter specified by the referral. Referrals resolved in this way will return separate result sets from the original search request.

Because **crossRef** objects are stored in the configuration container, every domain controller (DC) has a copy of all **crossRef** objects. Therefore, every DC contains information about every domain in the forest (as well as their superior/subordinate relationships). This gives every DC the ability to generate referrals to any domain in the forest *and* referrals for unexplored subordinate domain, schema, or configuration containers on a subtree search.

Example Code for Binding to a Partitions Container

The following examples bind to the partitions container and enumerate all **crossRef** objects.

C++

```
// This application enumerates crossrefs in the partitions container.
//
#include <objbase.h>
#include <wchar.h>
#include <activeds.h>

//Make sure you define UNICODE
//Need to define version 5 for Windows 2000
#define _WIN32_WINNT 0x0500

#include <sddl.h>

HRESULT FindCrossRefs(IDirectorySearch *pConfigNC,
```

```
                    //IDirectorySearch pointer to Partitions container.
                       LPOLESTR szFilter,
            //Filter for finding specific crossrefs.
            //NULL returns all attributeSchema objects.
                       LPOLESTR *pszPropertiesToReturn,
            //Properties to return for crossRef objects found
            //NULL returns all set properties.
                       BOOL bIsVerbose
            //TRUE means all properties for the found objects
            //  are displayed.  FALSE means only the RDN
                       );


void wmain( int argc, wchar_t *argv[ ])
{
    //Handle the command line arguments.
    LPOLESTR pszBuffer = new OLECHAR[MAX_PATH*2];
    wcscpy(pszBuffer, L"");

    BOOL bReturnVerbose = FALSE;
    wprintf(L"\nFinding all crossRef objects in the Partitions container\n");

    //Intialize COM
    CoInitialize(NULL);
    HRESULT hr = S_OK;

    //Get rootDSE and the config container's DN.
    IADs *pObject = NULL;
    IDirectorySearch *pConfigNC = NULL;
    LPOLESTR szPath = new OLECHAR[MAX_PATH];
    VARIANT var;
    hr = ADsOpenObject(L"LDAP://rootDSE",
                    NULL,
                    NULL,
                    ADS_SECURE_AUTHENTICATION,
                                //Use Secure Authentication
                    IID_IADs,
                    (void**)&pObject);

    if (FAILED(hr))
    {
    wprintf(L"Could not execute query. Could not bind to LDAP://rootDSE. HR: %x\n",hr);

    if (pObject)
      pObject->Release();
```

(continued)

(continued)

```
return;
}

if (SUCCEEDED(hr))
{
hr = pObject->Get(L"configurationNamingContext",&var);

if (SUCCEEDED(hr))
{
  //Build path to the partitions container.
      wcscpy(szPath,L"LDAP://cn=Partitions,");
      wcscat(szPath,var.bstrVal);
      hr = ADsOpenObject(szPath,
                         NULL,
                         NULL,
                         ADS_SECURE_AUTHENTICATION,
                                    //Use Secure Authentication
                         IID_IDirectorySearch,
                         (void**)&pConfigNC);

  if (SUCCEEDED(hr))
  {
    hr = FindCrossRefs(pConfigNC,
          //IDirectorySearch pointer to Partitions container.
                     NULL,      //Find all
                     NULL,      //Return all properties
                     TRUE       //Display all properties
                     );

    if (SUCCEEDED(hr))
    {
      if (S_FALSE==hr)
        wprintf(L"No crossRef object could be found.\n");
    }
    else if (0x8007203e==hr)
      wprintf(L"Could not execute query. An invalid filter was specified.\n");
    else
      wprintf(L"Query failed to run. HRESULT: %x\n",hr);
  }
  else
  {
    wprintf(L"Could not execute query. Could not bind to the schema container.\n");
  }

  if (pConfigNC)
    pConfigNC->Release();
```

```
    }

    VariantClear(&var);

}

    if (pObject)
    pObject->Release();

    // Uninitialize COM
    CoUninitialize();
    return;
}
HRESULT FindCrossRefs(IDirectorySearch *pConfigNC,
        //IDirectorySearch pointer to Partitions container.
                      LPOLESTR szFilter,
        //Filter for finding specific crossrefs.
        //NULL returns all attributeSchema objects.
                      LPOLESTR *pszPropertiesToReturn,
        //Properties to return for crossRef objects found
        //NULL returns all set properties.
                      BOOL bIsVerbose
        //TRUE means all properties for the found objects are displayed.
        //FALSE means only the RDN
                      )
{
    if (!pConfigNC)
    return E_POINTER;

  //Create search filter
    LPOLESTR pszSearchFilter = new OLECHAR[MAX_PATH*2];
    LPOLESTR szCategory = NULL;

    wsprintf(pszSearchFilter, L"(&(objectCategory=crossRef)%s)",szFilter);

    //Attributes are one-level deep in the schema
    // container so only need to search one level.
    ADS_SEARCHPREF_INFO SearchPrefs;
    SearchPrefs.dwSearchPref = ADS_SEARCHPREF_SEARCH_SCOPE;
    SearchPrefs.vValue.dwType = ADSTYPE_INTEGER;
    SearchPrefs.vValue.Integer = ADS_SCOPE_ONELEVEL;
    DWORD dwNumPrefs = 1;

    // COL for iterations
```

(continued)

(continued)

```
LPOLESTR pszColumn = NULL;
ADS_SEARCH_COLUMN col;
HRESULT hr;

// Interface Pointers
IADs    *pObj = NULL;
IADs  * pIADs = NULL;

// Handle used for searching
ADS_SEARCH_HANDLE hSearch = NULL;

// Set the search preference
hr = pConfigNC->SetSearchPreference( &SearchPrefs, dwNumPrefs);

if (FAILED(hr))
return hr;

LPOLESTR pszBool = NULL;
DWORD dwBool;
PSID pObjectSID = NULL;
LPOLESTR szSID = NULL;
LPOLESTR szDSGUID = new WCHAR [39];
LPGUID pObjectGUID = NULL;
FILETIME filetime;
SYSTEMTIME systemtime;
DATE date;
VARIANT varDate;
LARGE_INTEGER liValue;
LPOLESTR *pszPropertyList = NULL;
LPOLESTR pszNonVerboseList[] = {L"lDAPDisplayName",L"cn"};

LPOLESTR szCNValue = new OLECHAR[MAX_PATH];
LPOLESTR szLDAPDispleyNameValue = new OLECHAR[MAX_PATH];

int iCount = 0;
DWORD x = 0L;

if (!bIsVerbose)
{
//Return non-verbose list properties only
hr = pConfigNC->ExecuteSearch(pszSearchFilter,
                          pszNonVerboseList,
                          sizeof(pszNonVerboseList)/sizeof(LPOLESTR),
                          &hSearch
                          );
}
```

```
    else
    {
    if (!pszPropertiesToReturn)
    {
      //Return all properties.
      hr = pConfigNC->ExecuteSearch(pszSearchFilter,
                                    NULL,
                                    0L,
                                    &hSearch
                                    );
    }
    else
    {
      //specified subset.
      pszPropertyList = pszPropertiesToReturn;
      //Return specified properties
      hr = pConfigNC->ExecuteSearch(pszSearchFilter,
                                    pszPropertyList,
                                    sizeof(pszPropertyList)/sizeof(LPOLESTR),
                                    &hSearch
                                    );
    }
}

    if ( SUCCEEDED(hr) )
    {
    // Call IDirectorySearch::GetNextRow() to retrieve the next row
    //of data
    hr = pConfigNC->GetFirstRow( hSearch);

    if (SUCCEEDED(hr))
    {
      while( hr != S_ADS_NOMORE_ROWS )
      {
        //Keep track of count.
        iCount++;

        if (bIsVerbose)
          wprintf(L"----------------------------------\n");

        // loop through the array of passed column names,
        // print the data for each column
        while( pConfigNC->GetNextColumnName( hSearch, &pszColumn ) != S_ADS_NOMORE_COLUMNS
)
        {
          hr = pConfigNC->GetColumn( hSearch, pszColumn, &col );
```

(continued)

(continued)

```
if ( SUCCEEDED(hr) )
{
  // Print the data for the column and free the column
  if(bIsVerbose)
  {
    // Get the data for this column
    wprintf(L"%s\n",col.pszAttrName);

    switch (col.dwADsType)
    {
      case ADSTYPE_DN_STRING:
        for (x = 0; x< col.dwNumValues; x++)
        {
          wprintf(L"  %s\r\n",col.pADsValues[x].DNString);
        }
        break;

      case ADSTYPE_CASE_EXACT_STRING:
      case ADSTYPE_CASE_IGNORE_STRING:
      case ADSTYPE_PRINTABLE_STRING:
      case ADSTYPE_NUMERIC_STRING:
      case ADSTYPE_TYPEDNAME:
      case ADSTYPE_FAXNUMBER:
      case ADSTYPE_PATH:
      case ADSTYPE_OBJECT_CLASS:
        for (x = 0; x< col.dwNumValues; x++)
        {
          wprintf(L"  %s\r\n",col.pADsValues[x].CaseIgnoreString);
        }
        break;

      case ADSTYPE_BOOLEAN:
        for (x = 0; x< col.dwNumValues; x++)
        {
          dwBool = col.pADsValues[x].Boolean;
          pszBool = dwBool ? L"TRUE" : L"FALSE";
          wprintf(L"  %s\r\n",pszBool);
        }
        break;

      case ADSTYPE_INTEGER:
        for (x = 0; x< col.dwNumValues; x++)
        {
          wprintf(L"  %d\r\n",col.pADsValues[x].Integer);
        }
```

```
      break;

case ADSTYPE_OCTET_STRING:
   if ( _wcsicmp(col.pszAttrName,L"objectSID") == 0 )
   {
      for (x = 0; x< col.dwNumValues; x++)
      {
         pObjectSID = (PSID)(col.pADsValues[x].OctetString.lpValue);

         //Convert SID to string.
         ConvertSidToStringSid(pObjectSID, &szSID);
         wprintf(L"   %s\r\n",szSID);

         LocalFree(szSID);
      }
   }
   else if ( (_wcsicmp(col.pszAttrName,L"objectGUID") == 0)
      || (_wcsicmp(col.pszAttrName,L"schemaIDGUID") == 0)
      || (_wcsicmp(col.pszAttrName,L"attributeSecurityGUID") == 0) )
   {
      for (x = 0; x< col.dwNumValues; x++)
      {
         //Cast to LPGUID
         pObjectGUID = (LPGUID)(col.pADsValues[x].OctetString.lpValue);

         //Convert GUID to string.
         ::StringFromGUID2(*pObjectGUID, szDSGUID, 39);

         //Print the GUID
         wprintf(L"   %s\r\n",szDSGUID);
      }
   }
   else if ( _wcsicmp(col.pszAttrName,L"oMObjectClass") == 0 )
   {
      //TODO:
      wprintf(L"   TODO:No conversion for this.");
   }
   else
      wprintf(L"   Value of type Octet String. No Conversion.");

   break;

case ADSTYPE_UTC_TIME:
   for (x = 0; x< col.dwNumValues; x++)
   {
      systemtime = col.pADsValues[x].UTCTime;
```

(continued)

(continued)

```c
      if (SystemTimeToVariantTime(&systemtime, &date) != 0)
      {
        //Pack in variant.vt
        varDate.vt = VT_DATE;
        varDate.date = date;
        VariantChangeType(&varDate,&varDate,VARIANT_NOVALUEPROP,VT_BSTR);
        wprintf(L"  %s\r\n",varDate.bstrVal);
        VariantClear(&varDate);
      }
      else
        wprintf(L"  Could not convert UTC-Time.\n",pszColumn);
    }

    break;

  case ADSTYPE_LARGE_INTEGER:
    for (x = 0; x< col.dwNumValues; x++)
    {
      liValue = col.pADsValues[x].LargeInteger;
      filetime.dwLowDateTime = liValue.LowPart;
      filetime.dwHighDateTime = liValue.HighPart;

      if((filetime.dwHighDateTime==0) && (filetime.dwLowDateTime==0))
      {
        wprintf(L"  No value set.\n");
      }
      else
      {
        //Check for properties of type LargeInteger
        // that represent time
        //if TRUE, then convert to variant time.
        if ((0==wcscmp(L"accountExpires", col.pszAttrName))|
            (0==wcscmp(L"badPasswordTime", col.pszAttrName))||
            (0==wcscmp(L"lastLogon", col.pszAttrName))||
            (0==wcscmp(L"lastLogoff", col.pszAttrName))||
            (0==wcscmp(L"lockoutTime", col.pszAttrName))||
            (0==wcscmp(L"pwdLastSet", col.pszAttrName))
           )
        {
          //Handle special case for Never Expires
          //where low part is -1
          if (filetime.dwLowDateTime==-1)
          {
            wprintf(L"  Never Expires.\n");
          }
```

```
                        else
                        {
                          if (FileTimeToLocalFileTime(&filetime, &filetime) != 0)
                          {
                            if (FileTimeToSystemTime(&filetime,
                                                      &systemtime) != 0)
                            {
                              if (SystemTimeToVariantTime(&systemtime,
                                                           &date) != 0)
                              {
                                //Pack in variant.vt
                                varDate.vt = VT_DATE;
                                varDate.date = date;

VariantChangeType(&varDate,&varDate,VARIANT_NOVALUEPROP,VT_BSTR);
                                wprintf(L"  %s\r\n",varDate.bstrVal);
                                VariantClear(&varDate);
                              }
                              else
                              {
                                wprintf(L"  FileTimeToVariantTime failed\n");
                              }

                            }
                            else
                            {
                              wprintf(L"  FileTimeToSystemTime failed\n");
                            }

                          }
                          else
                          {
                            wprintf(L"  FileTimeToLocalFileTime failed\n");
                          }
                        }
                      }
                      else
                      {
                        //Print the LargeInteger.
                        wprintf(L"   high: %d low: %d\r\n",filetime.dwHighDateTime,
filetime.dwLowDateTime);
                      }
                    }
                  }
                break;
```

(continued)

(continued)

```
                case ADSTYPE_NT_SECURITY_DESCRIPTOR:
                  for (x = 0; x< col.dwNumValues; x++)
                  {
                    wprintf(L"  Security descriptor.\n");
                  }
                  break;

                default:
                  wprintf(L"Unknown type %d.\n",col.dwADsType);
              }
            }
          else
          {
            //Verbose handles only the two single-valued
            //  attributes: cn and ldapdisplayname
            //so this is a special case.
            if (0==wcscmp(L"cn", pszColumn))
            {
              wcscpy(szCNValue,col.pADsValues->CaseIgnoreString);
            }

            if (0==wcscmp(L"lDAPDisplayName", pszColumn))
            {
              wcscpy(szLDAPDispleyNameValue,col.pADsValues->CaseIgnoreString);
            }
          }

          pConfigNC->FreeColumn( &col );
        }

      FreeADsMem( pszColumn );
      }

      if (!bIsVerbose)
      wprintf(L"%s (%s)\n",szLDAPDispleyNameValue,szCNValue);
      //Get the next row
      hr = pConfigNC->GetNextRow( hSearch );
    }
  }


  // Close the search handle to clean up
  pConfigNC->CloseSearchHandle(hSearch);


}
```

```
if (SUCCEEDED(hr) && 0==iCount)
    hr = S_FALSE;


return hr;


}
```

Visual Basic

```
'.................................
'Parse the arguments
'.................................
On Error Resume Next

msgbox "This script enumerates crossRef objects in the partitions container."


sPrefix = "LDAP://"


'Get distinguished name for config container and
'build ADsPath to partitions container.
    Set root= GetObject(sPrefix & "rootDSE")
    If (Err.Number <> 0) Then
        BailOnFailure Err.Number, "on GetObject method for rootDSE"
    End If
    sConfigDN = root.Get("configurationNamingContext")
    If (Err.Number <> 0) Then
        BailOnFailure Err.Number, "on Get method"
    End If
    sContainerDN = "cn=Partitions," & sConfigDN


'.................................
'Bind to the container
'.................................
Set cont= GetObject(sPrefix & sContainerDN)
If (Err.Number <> 0) Then
    BailOnFailure Err.Number, "on GetObject method for partitions container"
End If
'.................................
'Enumerate the container.
'.................................
For Each obj In cont
    strText = strText & "Name: " & obj.Get("name") & vbCrLf
    values = obj.GetEx("objectClass")
    For Each value In values
    sValue = value
```

(continued)

(continued)

```
    Next
    strText = strText & "  objectClass: " & sValue & vbCrLf
    strText = strText & "  DnsRoot: " & obj.Get("dnsRoot") & vbCrLf
    strText = strText & "  NCName: " & obj.Get("NCName") & vbCrLf
    sTrustParent = obj.Get("trustParent")
    If (Err.Number = 0) Then
    strText = strText & "  TrustParent: " & sTrustParent & vbCrLf
    Else
    Err.Clear
    End If
    sNetBIOSName = obj.Get("nETBIOSName")
    If (Err.Number = 0) Then
   strText = strText & "  NETBIOSName: " & sNetBIOSName & vbCrLf
    Else
    Err.Clear
    End If

Next
 show_items strText, "Display crossRef"
.......................................
'Display subroutines
.......................................
Sub show_items(strText, strName)
    MsgBox strText, vbInformation, "Create CrossRef"
End Sub

Sub BailOnFailure(ErrNum, ErrText)     strText = "Error 0x" & Hex(ErrNum) & " " &
ErrText
    MsgBox strText, vbInformation, "ADSI Error"
    WScript.Quit
End Sub
```

When Referrals are Generated

A referral is the way that a directory server communicates that it does not contain the information required to complete a request (such as a query), but has a reference to a server that may contain the required information. Note that referrals are not just generated by query requests.

The following operations can result in one or more referrals.

- *Binding to a server that does not contain the object specified by the requested distinguished name but has information about a server or domain that may contain that object.* For ADSI, this can occur if the application calls **ADsGetObject** or **ADsOpenObject** to bind to an object that exists in another domain in the forest (internal referral) or a naming context that is completely separate from the forest (external referral). For the LDAP API, this can occur when performing add, modify, delete, or search operations that specify an object that exists in another domain in the forest (internal referral) or a naming context that is completely separate from the forest (external referral).

  What about other forests? A Windows 2000 domain controller will automatically generate an external referral based on the domain controller components of the distinguished name. If name resolution fails to find an object locally and there are no **crossRef** objects for that portion of namespace, the domain controller will attempt the following: 1) Check if the distinguished name specified has DC= naming attributes for its upper components 2) If it does, it constructs an external referral based on the upper components of the distinguished name. For example, if your search was based at "cn=a,cn=b,dc=c,dc=d,dc=e", the domain controller will construct a referral to the LDAP server at DNS address "c.d.e".

  This means that all Windows 2000 domain controllers (which support only DC= naming for the upper components) automatically have knowledge of each other, and no external crossrefs are ever required for a client to bind from one forest to another. If other non-Windows 2000 directory servers (such as a Netscape server) is using DC= naming and has an appropriate SRV RR registered in DNS, it will get the advantage of the automatic referrals as well. If not, an external **crossRef** object must be added manually.

- *Performing a subtree search on a domain that contains subordinate domains in the forest or subordinate external domains, schema, or configuration containers.*

Creating an External Referral

If you create an external **crossRef** and a domain controller uses it to generate a referral (see the previous section for situations where this can occur), the **crossRef** provides the two key pieces of information in the following properties:

dnsRoot
  Specifies the server or domain that can serve information from the naming context specified in **nCName**.

nCName
  Specifies the distinguished name for the domain, schema, or configuration container rooted at the server or domain specified by **dnsRoot**.

For example, if the server with DNS address of serv1.northwest.Microsoft.com serves the naming context rooted at CN=MyContainer,OU=MyDOM,O=Microsoft, you would set the **dnsRoot** to that server's DNS address and the **nCName** to the distinguished name of the domain, schema, or configuration container.

Example Code for Creating an External crossRef Object

The following VBScript examples create an external **crossRef** object.

```
''''''''''''''''''''''''''''''''''''''''
'Parse the arguments
''''''''''''''''''''''''''''''''''''''''
On Error Resume Next
Set oArgs = WScript.Arguments

If oArgs.Count = 3 Then
    sCrossRefCN = oArgs.item(0)
    sCrossRefDNSRoot = oArgs.item(1)
    sCrossRefNCName = oArgs.item(2)
Else
    sCrossRefCN = InputBox("This script creates a cross reference object." &
vbCrLf & vbCrLf &"Specify the name (cn) of the new crossRef object:")
    sCrossRefDNSRoot = InputBox("Specify the DNS root of the server or domain
containing the external naming context:")
    sCrossRefNCName = InputBox("Specify the distinguished name (DN) of the
external naming context:")
End If

If sCrossRefCN = "" Then
    WScript.Echo "No CN was specified. You must specify a CN."
    WScript.Quit(1)
End If

If sCrossRefNCName = "" Then
    WScript.Echo "No DN was specified. You must specify a DN."
    WScript.Quit(1)
End If

If sCrossRefDNSRoot = "" Then
    WScript.Echo "No DNS root was specified. You must specify a DNS root."
    WScript.Quit(1)
End If

sPrefix = "LDAP://"

'Get distinguished name for config container and
' build ADsPath to partitions container.
    Set root= GetObject(sPrefix & "rootDSE")
    If (Err.Number <> 0) Then
        BailOnFailure Err.Number, "on GetObject method"
    End If
```

```
    sConfigDN = root.Get("configurationNamingContext")
    If (Err.Number <> 0) Then
        BailOnFailure Err.Number, "on Get method"
    End If
    sContainerDN = "cn=Partitions," & sConfigDN

'''''''''''''''''''''''''''''''''''''''''''''
'Bind to the container
'''''''''''''''''''''''''''''''''''''''''''''
Set cont= GetObject(sPrefix & sContainerDN)
If (Err.Number <> 0) Then
    BailOnFailure Err.Number, "on GetObject method for partitions container"
End If
'''''''''''''''''''''''''''''''''''''''''''''
'Add the user
'''''''''''''''''''''''''''''''''''''''''''''
Set newCrossRef  = cont.Create("crossRef", "cn=" & sCrossRefCN)
'If (Err.Number <> 0) Then
    BailOnFailure Err.Number, "on Create method"
End If
newCrossRef.put "dnsRoot", sCrossRefDNSRoot
If (Err.Number <> 0) Then
    BailOnFailure Err.Number, "on Put method call for dnsRoot"
End If
newCrossRef.put "nCName", sCrossRefNCName
If (Err.Number <> 0) Then
    BailOnFailure Err.Number, "on Put method call for nCName"
End If
newCrossRef.SetInfo
If (Err.Number <> 0) Then
    BailOnFailure Err.Number, "on SetInfo method"
End If
strText = "The crossRef " & sCrossRefCM & " was successfully added."
strText = strText & vbCrLf & "The crossRef has the following properties:"
'Refresh the property cache
newCrossRef.GetInfo
count = newCrossRef.PropertyCount
If (Err.Number <> 0) Then
    BailOnFailure Err.Number, "on PropertyCount method"
End If
strText = strText & "Number of properties: " & count

'Set v = user.Next()
'cprop = 1
'If (Err.Number <> 0) Then
'  BailOnFailure Err.Number, "on Next method"
```

(continued)

(continued)

```
'End If

'While (Not (IsNull(v)) And Err.Number = 0)
'   cprop = cprop+1
'   Set v = user.Next()
'If (Err.Number <> 0) Then
'   BailOnFailure Err.Number, "on Next method"
'End If
'Wend
For cprop=1 to count
    Set v = newCrossRef.Next()
    If IsNull(v) Then
    Exit For
    End If
    strText = strText & vbCrLf & cprop & ") " & v.Name & " "
    cattr = 0
    attr = v.Values
    For Each attrval In attr
    cattr = cattr+1
    if (v.adstype=3) then
        strText = strText & vbCrLf & "        " & attrval.caseignorestring
    end if
    if (v.adstype=1) then
        strText = strText & vbCrLf & "        " & attrval.DNstring
    end if
    if (v.adstype=7) then
        strText = strText & vbCrLf & "        " & attrval.Integer
    end if
    if (v.adstype=6) then
        strText = strText & vbCrLf & "        " & attrval.Boolean
    end if
    if (v.adstype=9) then
        strText = strText & vbCrLf & "        " & attrval.UTCTime
    end if
    if (v.adstype=10) then
        strText = strText & vbCrLf & "        " & "Type: LargeInteger"
    end if
    if (v.adstype=8) then
        strText = strText & vbCrLf & "        " & "Type: OctetString"
    end if
    if (v.adstype=25) then
        strText = strText & vbCrLf & "        " & "Type: NTSecurityDescriptor"
    end if
    Next
```

```
Next
show_items strText, "Create crossRef"

'''''''''''''''''''''''''''''''''''''''''''''
'Display subroutines
'''''''''''''''''''''''''''''''''''''''''''''
Sub show_items(strText, strName)
    MsgBox strText, vbInformation, "Create CrossRef"
End Sub

Sub BailOnFailure(ErrNum, ErrText)    strText = "Error 0x" & Hex(ErrNum) & " " &
ErrText
    MsgBox strText, vbInformation, "ADSI Error"
    WScript.Quit
End Sub
```

C H A P T E R   7

Binding

Accessing Active Directory™ is simply a matter of finding a Microsoft® Windows® 2000 domain controller and binding to an object in the directory. Use the ADSI LDAP provider to access Active Directory in a Windows 2000 environment.

For Microsoft® Windows NT® 4.0, Microsoft Corporation provides the WinNT provider for access to directory information such as users, user groups, computers, services, and other network objects in the Windows NT 4.0 environment.

Do not use the WinNT provider to access Active Directory in Windows 2000—unless you want to use the limited functionality of the WinNT provider.

When you bind to a directory object using ADSI, the directory object is represented as a COM object. This way, the binding operations require you to specify the COM interface that you want to use to access the directory object. All ADSI COM objects that represent directory objects have an **IADs** interface. A COM object representing a directory object also has other interfaces available, depending on the type of directory object. For example, a user object has an **IADsUser** interface in addition to an **IADs** interface. As with all COM objects, you can call the **QueryInterface** method to get pointers to the other interfaces supported on an object.

To bind to an object on a directory server, use one of the following functions or methods:

- **ADsGetObject** function (C/C++ only)
- **ADsOpenObject** function (C/C++ only)
- **GetObject** method (Visual Basic and VBScript only)
- **IADsOpenDSObject::OpenDSObject** method (VB and VBScript)

In general, the Get operations use the security context of the calling thread, which is either the security context of the current user or of a client that the thread is impersonating. In contrast; the Open operations enable you to supply specific user credentials. Similarly, the Get operations use default binding options and the Open operations use explicit binding options.

You would use the Open operations in the following cases:

- If your application needs to bind using a user context that is different from the primary or impersonation context of the calling thread
- If your application needs to enforce secure authentication (your application requires binding with the specified account, or as the user that is logged on)

- If your application needs encryption to protect the data exchange over the network between your application and the directory server
- If your application needs to explicitly bypass authentication and bind as Everyone or Guest

If your application is written in C/C++, use **ADsGetObject** or **ADsOpenObject**.

If your application is written in Visual Basic, use the **GetObject** function provided by COM or the **OpenDSObject** method of the **IADsOpenDSObject**.

All these operations require the ADsPath binding string. The binding string has the following form:

LDAP://hostname/ObjectName

or

GC://hostname/ObjectName

In this example, **LDAP:** specifies the LDAP provider, which is the provider for Active Directory. **GC:** uses the LDAP provider to bind to the global catalog service in order to execute fast queries.

The *hostname* is optional. Avoid specifying a specific machine to bind to.

The *ObjectName* represents a specific Active Directory object. The *ObjectName* can be a distinguished name or an object GUID.

You can use an ADsPath of LDAP or GC to bind to the root of the namespace. When you bind to the root of the namespace, you get a pointer to a namespace object which contains no properties and contains the domain object for LDAP and a container object containing a partial replica of all domains in the forest for GC.

Remember the following key points when binding:

- Active Directory uses the ADSI LDAP provider.
- Use serverless binding and rootDSE to eliminate dependencies on hardcoded server and domain names. The rootDSE is the root of the directory information tree on a directory server. The rootDSE has properties that contain information about the directory server itself.
- Bind to the global catalog service for fast search. The global catalog service contains selected properties for all objects within Active Directory tree or forest.
- If you want to access objects within the directory in a manner that is protected from renaming or movement of an object, you need to access the object using the object's **objectGUID**.
- When possible, bind using the security context of the calling thread, that is, do not specify explicit user credentials.
- Use the encryption option to use an SSL encrypted channel to communicate between your application and Active Directory.

Serverless Binding and RootDSE

You should never hardcode a server name. Additionally, you should avoid unnecessarily tying your binding to a single server under most circumstances. Active Directory supports serverless binding, which means you can bind to Active Directory on the default domain without specifying the name of a domain controller. When processing your serverless binding call, ADSI finds the "best" Windows 2000 domain controller in the default domain, which is the domain associated with the current security context of the thread that's doing the binding. For ordinary applications, this is typically the domain of the logged-on user. For service applications, this is either the domain of the service's logon account or that of the client the service is impersonating.

In LDAP 3.0, rootDSE is defined as the root of the directory information tree on a directory server. The rootDSE is not part of any namespace. The purpose of the rootDSE is to provide information about the directory server.

ADsPath string for rootDSE:

```
LDAP://rootDSE
```

or

```
LDAP://servername/rootDSE
```

In this example, *servername* is the name of the server. If the servername is not specified, ADSI uses a domain controller in the domain associated with the current security context of the calling thread. ADSI attempts to find a domain controller within the client computer's site (a site is usually defined as an IP subnet) and connect to that domain controller. If a domain controller cannot be accessed within the site, ADSI uses the first domain controller that can be found.

For an Active Directory server (a Windows NT domain controller), the rootDSE contains the following properties:

Property	Description
currentTime	Current time set on this directory server.
subschemaSubentry	Distinguished name for the **subSchema** object. The **subSchema** object contains properties that expose the supported attributes (in the **attributeTypes** property) and classes (in the **objectClasses** property).
	The **subschemaSubentry** property and subschema are defined in LDAP 3.0 (see RFC 2251).
dsServiceName	The distinguished name of the NTDS settings object for this directory server.

(continued)

(continued)

Property	Description
namingContexts	Multi-valued. DISTINGUISHED NAMEs for all naming contexts stored on this directory server. By default, a Windows 2000 domain controller contains at least three namespaces: Schema, Configuration, and one for the domain of which the server is a member.
defaultNamingContext	By default, the distinguished name for the domain of which this directory server is a member.
schemaNamingContext	Distinguished name for the schema container.
configurationNamingContext	Distinguished name for the configuration container.
RootDomainNamingContext	Distinguished name for the first domain in the forest that contains the domain of which this directory server is a member.
SupportedControl	Multi-valued. OIDs for extension controls supported by this directory server.
SupportedLDAPVersion	Multi-valued. LDAP versions (specified by major version number) supported by this directory server.
HighestCommittedUSN	Highest USN used on this directory server. Used by directory replication.
SupportedSASLMechanisms	Security mechanisms supported for SASL negotiation (see LDAP RFCs). By default, GSSAPI is supported.
DnsHostName	DNS address for this directory server.
LdapServiceName	Service Principal Name (SPN) for the LDAP server. Used for mutual authentication.
ServerName	Distinguished name for the server object for this directory server in the configuration container.

The rootDSE is a well-known and reliable location on every directory server to get distinguished names to the domain container, schema container, configuration container, and other information about the server and the contents of its directory information tree. These properties rarely change on a particular server. Your application can read these properties at startup and use them throughout the session.

In summary, your application should use serverless binding to bind to the directory on the current domain, use rootDSE to get the distinguished name for a namespace, and use that distinguished name to bind to objects in the namespace.

Example Code for Getting the Distinguished Name of the Domain

The following code fragments use serverless binding to get a binding string for the default naming context on the domain associated with the current security context of the calling thread.

Visual Basic

```
Dim rootDSE as IADs
Dim sADsPath as String

On Error GoTo NonAD

Set rootDSE = GetObject("LDAP://rootDSE")
SADsPath = "LDAP://" & rootDSE.Get("defaultNamingContext")
'Clean up
Set rootDSE = Nothing
NonAD:
    'Notify couldn't bind to rootDSE
```

C++

```
IADs *pRootDSE;
IADs *pObject;
HRESULT hr;
VARIANT var;
LPOLESTR szDSPath = new OLECHAR[MAX_PATH];

hr = ADsGetObject(L"LDAP://rootDSE",
                  IID_IADs,
                  (void**)&pRootDSE);
if (SUCCEEDED(hr))
{
    hr = pRootDSE->Get(L"defaultNamingContext",&var);
    wcscpy(szDSPath,L"LDAP://");
    wcscat(szDSPath,var.bstrVal);
    hr = ADsGetObject(szDSPath, IID_IADs, (void**) &pObject);
}
    // Clean up
    pRootDSE->Release();
    pObject->Release();
    VariantClear(&var);
```

Example Code for Getting the Distinguished Name for the Naming Context

The following code fragments contain a function that returns the distinguished name of the specified naming context (defined in the enumerated type NAMING_CONTEXT) using serverless binding and rootDSE.

Visual Basic

```vb
Function GetNamingContext(ByVal sPropertyName As String) As String
    Dim IADsRootDSE As IADs
    GetNamingContext = ""
    Set IADsRootDSE = GetObject("LDAP://rootDSE")
    GetNamingContext = IADsRootDSE.Get(sPropertyName)
    Set IADsRootDSE = Nothing
End Function
```

C++

```cpp
typedef enum
{
    NC_CURRENT_DOMAIN = 0x0,
    NC_ROOT_OF_DOMAIN_TREE,
    NC_SCHEMA,
    NC_CONFIG
} NAMING_CONTEXT;

HRESULT GetNamingContextDN(
        NAMING_CONTEXT namingcontext,
        LPOLESTR *ppDNString
        )
{
    LPOLESTR pszDSPath = L"LDAP://rootDSE";
    LPOLESTR pszProperty = NULL;
    HRESULT hr = S_OK;
    VARIANT var;
    IADs *pObj = NULL;

    //Get the rootDSE.
    hr = ADsGetObject(pszDSPath,
                    IID_IADs,
                    (void**)&pObj);
    if (SUCCEEDED(hr))
    {
        //String to specify property to get based on namingcontext.
        switch (namingcontext)
        {
            //Ask for DN of root of domain tree that contains
            //the current domain.
            case NC_ROOT_OF_DOMAIN_TREE:
                pszProperty = L"rootDomainNamingContext";
                break;
```

```
                //Ask for DN of schema container in the current domain.
                case NC_SCHEMA:
                    pszProperty = L"schemaNamingContext";
                    break;
                //Ask for DN of config container in the current domain.
                case NC_CONFIG:
                    pszProperty = L"configurationNamingContext";
                    break;
                //Ask for DN for current domain.
                case NC_CURRENT_DOMAIN:
                default:
                    pszProperty = L"defaultNamingContext";
                    break;
            }
            //Get the DN from the specified property of rootDSE.
            if (pszProperty)
            {
                hr = pObj->Get(pszProperty,&var);
                if (SUCCEEDED(hr))
                {
                    *ppDNString = (OLECHAR *)CoTaskMemAlloc
(sizeof(OLECHAR)*(wcslen(var.bstrVal)+1));
                    if (*ppDNString)
                        wcscpy(*ppDNString, var.bstrVal);
                }
            }
        }
        // Clean up
        if (pObj)
            pObj->Release();
        VariantClear(&var);
        return hr;
        //The caller needs to call CoTaskMemFree on ppDNString.
}
```

Binding to the Global Catalog

The global catalog is a namespace that contains directory information from all domains in a forest. The global catalog contains a partial replica of every domain directory. It contains an entry for every object in the enterprise forest, but does not contain all the properties of each object. Instead, it contains only the properties that are specified for inclusion in the global catalog.

The global catalog is kept on specific servers throughout the enterprise. Only domain controllers can serve as global catalog servers. Administrators indicate whether a given domain controller will hold a global catalog by using the Active Directory Sites and Services Manager.

When you bind to the global catalog with ADSI, use the **GC:** moniker.

There are two ways to bind to the global catalog:

- Bind to the enterprise root object to search across all domains in the forest.
- Bind to a specific object to search that object and its children. For example, if you bind to a domain that has two domains beneath it in a domain tree in the forest, you can search across those three domains. Note that the distinguished name for the object you want to bind to is exactly the same as the distinguished name used to bind to the **LDAP:** namespace. Recall that **LDAP:** is a full replica of a single domain and that **GC:** is a partial replica of all domains in the forest.

As with the **LDAP:** moniker, you can use serverless binding (recommended) or bind to a specific global catalog server.

▶ To search the entire forest

1. Bind to the root of the GC namespace (**GC:**).
2. Enumerate the GC container. The GC container contains a single object that you can use to search the entire forest.
3. Use the object in the container to perform the search. In C/C++, call **QueryInterface** to get an **IDirectorySearch** pointer on the object so that you can use the **IDirectorySearch** interface to perform the search. In Visual Basic, use the object returned from the enumeration in your ADO query.

Example Code for Searching a Forest

Visual Basic

The following code fragment binds to the root of the global catalog (**GC:**) and enumerates the single object (which is the root of the forest) so that it can be used to search the entire forest.

```
Set gc = GetObject("GC:")
For each child in gc
    Set entpr = child
Next
' Now entpr is an object that can used
' to search the entire forest.
```

C++

The following code fragment contains a function that returns an **IDirectorySearch** pointer that can be used to search the entire forest.

The function does a serverless bind to the root of **GC:**, enumerates the single item (which is the root of the forest and can be used to search the entire forest), calls **QueryInterface** to get an **IDirectorySearch** pointer to the object, and returns that pointer for use by the caller to search the forest.

```
HRESULT GetGC(IDirectorySearch **ppDS)
{
HRESULT hr;
IEnumVARIANT *pEnum = NULL;
IADsContainer *pCont = NULL;
VARIANT var;
IDispatch *pDisp = NULL;
ULONG lFetch;

// Set IDirectorySearch pointer to NULL.
*ppDS = NULL;

// First, bind to the GC: namespace container object.
hr = ADsOpenObject(TEXT("GC:"),
              NULL,
              NULL,
              ADS_SECURE_AUTHENTICATION, //Use Secure Authentication
              IID_IADsContainer,
              (void**)&pCont);
if (FAILED(hr)) {
    _tprintf(TEXT("ADsOpenObject failed: 0x%x\n"), hr);
    goto cleanup;
}

// Get an enumeration interface for the GC container to enumerate the
// contents. The "real" GC is the only child of the GC container.
hr = ADsBuildEnumerator(pCont, &pEnum);
if (FAILED(hr)) {
    _tprintf(TEXT("ADsBuildEnumerator failed: 0x%x\n"), hr);
    goto cleanup;
}

// Now enumerate. There's only one child of the GC: object.
hr = pEnum->Next(1, &var, &lFetch);
if (FAILED(hr)) {
    _tprintf(TEXT("ADsEnumerateNext failed: 0x%x\n"), hr);
    goto cleanup;
}

// Get the IDirectorySearch pointer.
if (( hr == S_OK ) && ( lFetch == 1 ) )
```

(continued)

(continued)

```
{
    pDisp = V_DISPATCH(&var);
    hr = pDisp->QueryInterface( IID_IDirectorySearch, (void**)ppDS);
}

cleanup:

if (pEnum)
    ADsFreeEnumerator(pEnum);
if (pCont)
    pCont->Release();
if (pDisp)
    (pDisp)->Release();
return hr;
}
```

Using objectGUID to Bind to an Object

Since an object's distinguished name changes if the object is renamed or moved, the distinguished name is not a reliable identifier for an object. In Active Directory, an object's **objectGUID** property is never changed, even if the object is renamed or moved to different places. For more information on **objectGUID** and identifiers, see *Object Names and Identities*.

You can bind to an object directly using an object's GUID. Binding with the object's GUID is only supported in Active Directory (that is, the LDAP provider). The binding string format is the following:

LDAP://*servername*/<GUID=*XXXXX*>

In this example, *servername* is the name of the directory server and *XXXXX* is the string representation of hexidecimal value of the GUID. The *servername* is optional. Note that this is *not* the string produced by **StringFromGUID2** function in the COM library. Use the **IADs::get_GUID** method to retrieve the bindable string form of the **objectGUID**.

There are some **IADs** and **IADsContainer** methods that are not supported if you bind using an objectGUID. For the **IADs** interface, the **Name**, **Parent**, and **ADsPath** methods (**get_Name**, **get_Parent**, and **get_ADsPath** for C++ programmers) are not supported for GUID bindings. For the **IADsContainer** interface, the **GetObject**, **Create**, **Delete**, **CopyHere**, and **MoveHere** methods are not supported for GUID bindings. To use these methods after binding to an object using the objectGUID, use the **IADs::Get** method to retrieve the object's distinguished name (DN), and then use the DN to bind again to the object. For more information and sample code that illustrates these limitations, see *IADs Property Methods* and **IADsContainer**.

Example Code for Using ObjectGUID to Bind to an Object

If your application stores or caches identifiers or references to objects stored in the directory, the **objectGUID** is the best identifier to keep because 1) it stays the same even if the object is renamed or moved and 2) you can bind easily to the object using its GUID. In addition, if the object is renamed or moved, the **objectGUID** provides a single identifier that you can use to easily find and identify the object—rather than forcing you to compose a query that has conditions for all properties that would identify that object.

Visual Basic

```
Dim myObject as IADs

Set myObject = GetObject("LDAP://<GUID=63560110f7e1d111a6bfaaaf842b9cfa>")
```

C++

```
IADs *pADs;
LPWSTR pszFilter = L"LDAP://dc08/<GUID=63560110f7e1d111a6bfaaaf842b9cfa>";
hr = ADsGetObject( pszFilter, IID_IADs, (void**)&pADs);
```

Reading an objectGUID and Creating a String Representation of the GUID

The **objectGUID** property of each Active Directory object is stored in the directory as an octet string (an array of one-byte characters). Use the **IADs::get_GUID** method to retrieve the bindable string form of a directory object's **objectGUID**.

The following code fragments show a function that reads the **objectGUID** attribute and returns a string representation of the GUID that can be used to bind to the object.

Visual Basic

```
Dim sADsPathObject As String
Dim sObjectGUID As String
Dim sBindByGuidStr As String

Dim IADsObject As IADs
On Error Resume Next

' Ask the user for an ADsPath to start
sADsPathObject = InputBox("This code binds to a directory object by ADsPath,
retrieves the GUID, then rebinds by GUID." & vbCrLf & vbCrLf & "Specify the
ADsPath of the object to bind to :")

If sADsPathObject = "" Then
    Exit Sub
End If
```

(continued)

(continued)

```
MsgBox "Binding to " & sADsPathObject


' Bind to initial object
Set IADsObject = GetObject(sADsPathObject)

If (Err.Number <> 0) Then
   MsgBox Err.Number, "on GetObject method"
   Exit Sub
End If


' Save the GUID of the object
sObjectGUID = IADsObject.Guid

MsgBox "The GUID for " & vbCrLf & vbCrLf & sADsPathObject & vbCrLf & vbCrLf & "
is " & vbCrLf & vbCrLf & sObjectGUID

' Release the initial object
Set IADsObject = Nothing

' Build a string for Binding to the object by GUID
sBindByGuidStr = "LDAP://<GUID=" & sObjectGUID & ">"

' Bind BACK to the Same object using the GUID
Set IADsObject = GetObject("LDAP://<GUID=" & sObjectGUID & ">")

If (Err.Number <> 0) Then
   MsgBox Err.Number, "on GetObject method"
   Exit Sub
End If

MsgBox "Successfully RE bound to " & sADsPathObject & vbCrLf & vbCrLf & " using
the path:" & vbCrLf & vbCrLf & sBindByGuidStr

' Release bind by GUID Object
Set IADsObject = Nothing
```

C++

```cpp
#define INC_OLE2
#define UNICODE 1
#define _WIN32_DCOM

#include <windows.h>
#include <winuser.h>
```

```c
#include <stdio.h>
#include <stdlib.h>
#include <string.h>
#include <malloc.h>

#include <winldap.h>
#include <activeds.h>
#include "ADSIhelpers.h"
#include <assert.h>


void main()
{
// Initialize COM
CoInitialize(0);

WCHAR pwszADsPathObject[1024];
WCHAR pwszObjectGUID[1024];
WCHAR pwszBindByGuidStr[1024];
HRESULT hr;

IADs * pIADsObject = NULL;
IADs * pIADsObjectByGuid = NULL;

// Ask the user for a ADsPath to start
_putws(L"This code binds to a directory object by ADsPath, retrieves the GUID,\n"
       L" then rebinds by GUID. \n\nSpecify the ADsPath of the object to bind to
:\n");
_getws(pwszADsPathObject);


if (pwszADsPathObject[0] == NULL)
    return;

wprintf(L"\nBinding to %s\n",pwszADsPathObject);

// Bind to initial object
hr = ADsGetObject( pwszADsPathObject,IID_IADs, (void **)& pIADsObject);
if (SUCCEEDED(hr))
{
    BSTR bsGuid = NULL;
    hr = pIADsObject->get_GUID(&bsGuid);

    if (SUCCEEDED(hr))
    {
        wprintf(L"\n The GUID for\n\n%s\n\nis\n\n%s\n",pwszADsPathObject,bsGuid);
```

(continued)

(continued)

```
        // Build a string for Binding to the object by GUID
        wsprintf(pwszBindByGuidStr,L"LDAP://<GUID=%s>",bsGuid);

        // Bind BACK to the Same object using the GUID
        hr = ADsGetObject( pwszBindByGuidStr,IID_IADs, (void **)&
pIADsObjectByGuid);

        if (SUCCEEDED(hr))
        {
            wprintf(L"\nSuccessfully RE bound to\n\n%s\n\nUsing the
path:\n\n%s\n", pwszADsPathObject,pwszBindByGuidStr);

            // Release bind by GUID Object
            pIADsObjectByGuid->Release();
            pIADsObjectByGuid = NULL;
        }

        SysFreeString(bsGuid);
    }

    pIADsObject->Release();
    pIADsObject = NULL;
}

if (FAILED(hr))
    _putws(L"Failed");

}
```

Binding to Well-Known Objects Using WKGUID

The containers can have one or more sub-objects that are important but can be renamed or moved. It can be cumbersome to keep track of these sub-objects and build correct binding strings for them, especially if they are renamed or moved.

To support rename-safe binding to these objects within these containers, the Active Directory has two properties: **wellKnownObjects** and **otherWellKnownObjects**. These properties have an attribute syntax of **SYNTAX_DISTNAME_BINARY**. They allow multiple values and contain the GUID/DN tuples of well-known objects within the containers on which they are set. The Active Directory maintains the distinguished name portion of each **wellKnownObjects** and **otherWellKnownObjects** entry so that it contains the current distinguished name of the object originally specified when the entry was created.

The **otherWellKnownObjects** property can be set and used on any object.

The **wellKnownObjects** property is used on the domainDNS and configuration containers. The **wellKnownObjects** property is a system-only property and can only be modified by the operating system.

The domainDNS container has the following well-known objects:

- Users
- Computers
- System
- Domain Controllers
- Infrastructure
- Deleted Objects
- Lost and Found

The configuration container has the following well-known object:

- Deleted Objects

These objects are always in every domainDNS and configuration container in the Active Directory.

You can bind to a well-known object using the WKGUID binding format. Binding with WKGUID is only supported in Active Directory (that is, the LDAP provider).

Important   Always use the WKGUID binding format to bind to the well-known objects (listed above) in the domain and configuration containers. This ensures that you are able to bind to those containers even if they are moved or renamed.

The WKGUID binding string format is the following:

```
LDAP://servername/<WKGUID=XXXXX,ContainerDN>
```

In this example, *servername* is the name of the directory server. The *servername* is optional.

XXXXX is the string representation of the hexadecimal value of the GUID that represents the well-known object. Note that 1) *XXXXX* is *not* the string produced by the **StringFromGUID2**function in the COM library and 2) *XXXXX* is *not* the object's **objectGUID**.

To bind to an object specified in **otherWellKnownObjects** in an object, specify *XXXXX* as the bindable string form of the well-known object GUID of the object. See *Reading an Object's objectGUID* and *Creating a String Representation of the GUID*. For more information on setting the **otherWellKnownObjects** property on objects, see *Enabling Rename-Safe Binding with the otherWellKnownObjects Property*.

To bind to an object specified in **wellKnownObjects** in **domainDNS** or configuration containers, specify *XXXXX* as one of the constants defined in ntdsapi.h:

> GUID_USERS_CONTAINER_W
>
> GUID_COMPUTRS_CONTAINER_W
>
> GUID_SYSTEMS_CONTAINER_W
>
> GUID_DOMAIN_CONTROLLERS_CONTAINER_W
>
> GUID_INFRASTRUCTURE_CONTAINER_W
>
> GUID_DELETED_OBJECTS_CONTAINER_W
>
> GUID_LOSTANDFOUND_CONTAINER_W

For example, if you wanted to bind to the users container in a domain, you would specify GUID_USERS_CONTAINER_W as *XXXXX*.

ContainerDN is the distinguished name of the container object that has this object represented as a value in its **wellKnownObjects** property. For example, if you wanted to bind to the users container in a domain, you would specify the domain's distinguished name as the *ContainerDN*.

For example, you would use the following binding to bind to the users container of the domain Microsoft.com:

```
LDAP://<WKGUID=a9d1ca15768811d1aded00c04fd8d5cd,dc=Microsoft,dc=com>
```

Example Code for Binding to the Users Container and Displaying the ADsPath

The following C++ program binds to the users container of the current user's domain and displays the users container's ADsPath (showing a live example of a WKGUID binding string). It also contains a function that binds to the specified well-known object (WKO) based on its WKO GUID in the current user's domain.

You can use similar code to bind to other wellknown containers. To bind to the Deleted Objects container using the **ADsOpenObject** function, you must specify the ADS_FAST_BIND option.

```
#include <wchar.h>
#include <objbase.h>

//For ADSI
#include <activeds.h>

//Make sure you define UNICODE
//Need to define version 5 for Windows 2000
#define _WIN32_WINNT 0x0500
#include <ntdsapi.h>

HRESULT GetWKDomainObject(LPOLESTR szBindableWKGUID,
        //IN. Bindable string GUID of well-known object.
            IADs **ppObject
```

```
                           //OUT. Return a pointer to the specified well-known object.
                              );


void wmain( int argc, wchar_t *argv[ ])
{
wprintf(L"This program finds the user's container in the current Window 2000
domain\n");
//Intialize COM
CoInitialize(NULL);
HRESULT hr = S_OK;
//Get rootDSE and the domain container's DN.
IADs *pObject = NULL;
hr = GetWKDomainObject(GUID_USERS_CONTAINER_W,
              //IN. Bindable string GUID of well-known object.
                       &pObject
              //OUT. Return a pointer to the specified well-known object.
                       );
if (FAILED(hr))
{
   wprintf(L"Not Found. Could not bind to the user container.\n");
   if (pObject)
     pObject->Release();
   return;
}

BSTR bstr;
pObject->get_ADsPath(&bstr);
wprintf (L"ADsPath of users Container: %s\n", bstr);
FreeADsStr(bstr);
if (pObject)
    pObject->Release();

//uninitialize COM
CoUninitialize();
return;

}


// This function gets the specified well-known object
// for the current user's domain.

HRESULT GetWKDomainObject(LPOLESTR szBindableWKGUID,
              //IN. Bindable string GUID of well-known object.
                    IADs **ppObject
              //OUT. Return a pointer to the specified well-known object.
```

(continued)

(continued)

```
                                    )
{
HRESULT hr = E_FAIL;
//Get rootDSE and the domain container's DN.
IADs *pObject = NULL;
LPOLESTR szPath = new OLECHAR[MAX_PATH];
VARIANT var;
hr = ADsOpenObject(L"LDAP://rootDSE",
                NULL,
                NULL,
                ADS_SECURE_AUTHENTICATION, //Use Secure Authentication
                IID_IADs,
                (void**)&pObject);

//Get current domain DN.
if (SUCCEEDED(hr))
{
    hr = pObject->Get(L"defaultNamingContext",&var);
    if (SUCCEEDED(hr))
    {
        //Build the WKGUID binding string.
        wcscpy(szPath,L"LDAP://");
        wcscat(szPath,L"<WKGUID=");
        wcscat(szPath,szBindableWKGUID);
        wcscat(szPath,L",");
        wcscat(szPath,var.bstrVal);
        wcscat(szPath,L">");
        //Print the binding string.
        //wprintf(L"WKGUID binding string: %s\n",szPath);
        VariantClear(&var);
        //Bind to the well-known object.
        hr = ADsOpenObject(szPath,
                        NULL,
                        NULL,
                        ADS_SECURE_AUTHENTICATION,
                                //Use Secure Authentication
                        IID_IADs,
                        (void**)ppObject);
        if (FAILED(hr))
        {
            if (*ppObject)
            {
                (*ppObject)->Release();
                (*ppObject) = NULL;
            }
```

```
        }
    }
}
if (pObject)
  pObject->Release();

return hr;
}
```

Example Code for Creating a Bindable String Representation of a GUID

The following C++ code fragment shows a function that returns a string representation of a GUID that can be used to bind to the object:

```
HRESULT GUIDtoBindableString (LPGUID pGUID, LPOLESTR *ppGUIDString)
{
HRESULT hr = E_FAIL;
if (!pGUID)
  return E_INVALIDARG;
//Build bindable GUID string
LPOLESTR szDSGUID = new WCHAR [128];
DWORD dwLen = sizeof(*pGUID);
LPBYTE lpByte = (LPBYTE) pGUID;
//Copy a blank string to make it a zero length string.
wcscpy( szDSGUID, L"" );
//Loop through to add each byte to the string.
for( DWORD dwItem = 0L; dwItem < dwLen ; dwItem++ )
{
  //Append to szDSGUID, double-byte, byte at dwItem index.
  swprintf(szDSGUID + wcslen(szDSGUID), L"%02x", lpByte[dwItem]);
  if( wcslen( szDSGUID ) > 128 )
    break;
}
//Allocate memory for string
*ppGUIDString = (OLECHAR *)CoTaskMemAlloc
(sizeof(OLECHAR)*(wcslen(szDSGUID)+1));
if (*ppGUIDString)
  wcscpy(*ppGUIDString, szDSGUID);
else
  hr=E_FAIL;
//Caller must free ppGUIDString using CoTaskMemFree.
return hr;
}
```

Enabling Rename-Safe Binding with the otherWellKnownObjects Property

Objects of the Container class have an **otherWellKnownObjects** attribute that you can use to associate a GUID with the distinguished name (DN) of a child object in the container. If the child object is moved or renamed, Active Directory automatically updates the DN in the **otherWellKnownObjects** value for that child object. This enables you to use the WKGUID binding feature to bind to the child object using the GUID and the DN of the container rather than the child object's DN.

The **otherWellKnownObjects** attribute is equivalent to the **wellKnownObjects** attribute except that applications and services can write an **otherwellKnownObjects** value but only the system can write **wellKnownObjects**.

Using **otherWellKnownObjects** property and WKGUID binding is beneficial in the following situation where rename-safe binding is required in relation to a specific container object:

- You have a container object and it contains other important objects.
- The important objects can be renamed or moved.
- The important objects always exist for each instance of the container object. For example, the system uses the **wellKnownObjects** attribute of each **domainDNS** object to store a value for the Users container, which exists in every instance of a **domainDNS** object. This enables applications to bind to the Users container in a rename-safe way by specifying the well-known GUID and the DN of the **domainDNS** container. Applications can use a container's **otherWellKnownObjects** attribute in the same way.
- You need rename-safe binding and/or search capability on the important objects.

▶ **To add rename-safe binding and search capabilities**

1. Add a value to the **otherWellKnownObjects** property of the container object when the important object is created within that container. The value contains the GUID that represents the well-known object (note that this is *not* the **objectGUID**) and the distinguished name for that object.
2. Use the WKGUID binding feature to bind to or search the important object.

The **otherWellKnownObjects** attribute can have multiple values and contains the GUID/DN tuples of well-known objects within the containers on which they are set. The **otherWellKnownObjects** attribute has the DNWithBinary syntax in which values have the following form:

```
B:CharCount:WKOGUID:ObjectDN
```

In this example, *CharCount* is the count of hexadecimal digits in *WKOGUID*, which is 32 (number of hex digits in a GUID) for both **otherWellKnownObjects** and **wellKnownObjects**. *WKOGUID* is the hexadecimal digit representation of the well-known GUID. *ObjectDN* is the distinguished name of the object represented by this WKO value. Active Directory maintains the ObjectDN portion of each **wellKnownObjects** and **otherWellKnownObjects** value so that it contains the current distinguished name of the object originally specified when the value was created.

For example, if {df447b5e-aa5b-11d2-8d53-00c04f79ab81} is the well-known GUID of the MyObject object in the MyContainer container in the Microsoft.com domain, the **otherWellKnownObjects** value would specify the well-known GUID and the DN of MyObject:

```
B:32:df447b5eaa5b11d28d5300c04f79ab81:cn=MyObject,cn=MyContainer,dc=Microsoft,dc=
com
```

To bind to this object, you would use the following WKGUID binding string that specifies the well-known GUID of the object and the DN of the container:

```
LDAP://<WKGUID=df447b5eaa5b11d28d5300c04f79ab81,cn=MyContainer,dc=Microsoft,dc=co
m>
```

After binding to this object, you can use the ADSI COM interfaces to search, read, modify, or delete the object.

Example Code for Creating a Container Object

The following program creates two objects: a container object and a sub-container object within it. A value for the sub-container object is added to the **otherWellKnownObjects** property of the container object. The program binds to the sub-container object using the WKGUID binding and displays its ADsPath. It then renames the sub-container object and binds again using the same WKGUID binding.

```
#include <wchar.h>
#include <objbase.h>
#include <activeds.h>

//Make sure you define UNICODE
//Need to define version 5 for Windows 2000
#define _WIN32_WINNT 0x0500
//FOR LDAP API...Required for Beta 3 only.
#include <winldap.h>
//Need to link against the following LIBs:
//wldap32.lib


static GUID MyWKOTestObjectGUID = { /* df447b5e-aa5b-11d2-8d53-00c04f79ab81 */
    0xdf447b5e,
    0xaa5b,
```

(continued)

(continued)

```
    0x11d2,
    {0x8d, 0x53, 0x00, 0xc0, 0x4f, 0x79, 0xab, 0x81}
  };


HRESULT GUIDtoBindableString (LPGUID pGUID, LPOLESTR *ppGUIDString);

HRESULT AddValueToOtherWKOProperty(LPOLESTR szContainerDN,
                        //DN for container whose otherWellKnownObjects
                        // property to modify
                                LPGUID pWKOGUID,
                        //WKO GUID for the well-known object.
                                LPOLESTR szWKOObjectDN
                        //DN of the well-known object.
                                );




void wmain( int argc, wchar_t *argv[ ])
{

LPOLESTR pszBuffer = new OLECHAR[MAX_PATH*2];
    wprintf(L"This program does the following:\n");
    wprintf(L"1. Creates a container (MyWKOTestContainer) in the current Window 2000
domain.\n");
    wprintf(L"2. Creates a container object (MyWKOTestObject) within the container.\n");
    wprintf(L"3. Adds a value for the container object on the otherWellKnownObject
property of the container.\n");
    wprintf(L"4. Binds to the container object using WKGUID binding string.\n");
    wprintf(L"5. Renames the container object using WKGUID binding string.\n");
    wprintf(L"6. Binds to the container object using WKGUID binding string.\n");
    wprintf(L"7. Optionally, cleans up by removing the container and container
object.\n\n");


//Intialize COM
CoInitialize(NULL);

HRESULT hr = S_OK;
IADs *pObject = NULL;
IADsContainer *pDomain = NULL;
IDispatch *pDisp = NULL;
IDispatch *pDispNewObject = NULL;
IADsContainer *pNewContainer = NULL;
```

```
IADs *pIADsObject = NULL;
IADs *pNewObject = NULL;
IADs *pTestWKO1 = NULL;
IADs *pTestWKO2 = NULL;
VARIANT vartest;
BSTR bstr;

LPOLESTR szNewContainerDN = new OLECHAR[MAX_PATH];
LPOLESTR szPath = new OLECHAR[MAX_PATH];
LPOLESTR szRelPath = new OLECHAR[MAX_PATH];
LPOLESTR szGUIDString = NULL;

//Names of the container and child object.
LPOLESTR szContainer = L"MyWKOTestContainer";
LPOLESTR szNewObject = L"MyWKOTestObject";

LPOLESTR szNewObjectRenameRDN = L"cn=ObjectwithNEWNAME";

//Get rootDSE and the domain container's DN.
VARIANT var;
hr = ADsOpenObject(L"LDAP://rootDSE",
                   NULL,
                   NULL,
                   ADS_SECURE_AUTHENTICATION, //Use Secure Authentication
                   IID_IADs,
                   (void**)&pObject);
if (FAILED(hr))
{
   wprintf(L"Not Found. Could not bind to the domain.\n");
   if (pObject)
     pObject->Release();
   return;
}

hr = pObject->Get(L"defaultNamingContext",&var);
if (SUCCEEDED(hr))
{
    //Build the ADsPath to the domain
    wcscpy(szPath,L"LDAP://");
    wcscat(szPath,var.bstrVal);
    VariantClear(&var);
    //Bind to the current domain.
    hr = ADsOpenObject(szPath,
                       NULL,
                       NULL,
                       ADS_SECURE_AUTHENTICATION,
```

(continued)

(continued)

```
                            //Use Secure Authentication
                IID_IADsContainer,
                (void**)&pDomain);
if (SUCCEEDED(hr))
{
  //Create the container.
  wcscpy(szRelPath,L"cn=");
  wcscat(szRelPath,szContainer);
  hr = pDomain->Create(L"container",
          //ldapDisplayName of the class of the object to create.
                      szRelPath,
          //relative path in RDN=value format
                      &pDisp);
          //return an IDispatch pointer to the new object.
  if (SUCCEEDED(hr))
  {
    //QI for an IADs interface.
    hr = pDisp->QueryInterface(IID_IADs, (void **)&pIADsObject);
    //Commit the new object to the directory.
    hr = pIADsObject->SetInfo();
    //QI for an IADsContainer interface.
    hr = pDisp->QueryInterface(IID_IADsContainer, (void **)&pNewContainer);
    if (SUCCEEDED(hr))
    {
      //Create the new container object in the container.
      wcscpy(szRelPath,L"cn=");
      wcscat(szRelPath,szNewObject);
      hr = pNewContainer->Create(L"container",
                    //ldapDisplayName of the class of
                    // the object to create.
                szRelPath,
                    //relative path in RDN=value format
                &pDispNewObject);
                    //return an IDispatch pointer to the new object.
      if (SUCCEEDED(hr))
      {
        //Get the DN of the new container object
        hr = pIADsObject->Get(L"distinguishedName", &var);
        if (SUCCEEDED(hr))
        {
          wcscpy(szNewContainerDN, var.bstrVal);
          VariantClear(&var);
          wprintf(L"Created new container with DN: %s\n",szNewContainerDN);
          hr = pDispNewObject->QueryInterface(IID_IADs, (void **)&pNewObject);
          if (SUCCEEDED(hr))
          {
```

```
                    //Commit the new object to the directory.
                    hr = pNewObject->SetInfo();
                    //Get the DN for the new object
                    hr = pNewObject->Get(L"distinguishedName", &var);
                    if (SUCCEEDED(hr))
                    {
                        wprintf(L"Created new child object with DN: %s\n",var.bstrVal);
                      //FOR BETA 3 only. Need to use LDAP API
                      //  to set the otherWellKnownObjects property.
                      wprintf(L"Call AddValueToOtherWKOProperty with:\n");
                      wprintf(L"szContainer DN: %s\n",szNewContainerDN);
                      GUIDtoBindableString (&MyWKOTestObjectGUID, &szGUIDString);
                      wprintf(L"pWKOGUID (bindable string format): %s\n",szGUIDString);
                      wprintf(L"szWKOObjectDN: %s\n",var.bstrVal);
                      hr = AddValueToOtherWKOProperty(szNewContainerDN,
                              //DN for container whose otherWellKnownObjects
                              //  property to modify
                                      &MyWKOTestObjectGUID,
                              //WKO GUID for the well-known object.
                                      var.bstrVal
                              //DN of the well-known object.
                                      );
                      wprintf(L"AddValueToOtherWKOProperty returned: %x\n",hr);
                      if (SUCCEEDED(hr))
                      {
                          //Now bind using WKGUID binding
                          //Build the ADsPath to the well-known object
                          wcscpy(szPath,L"LDAP://<WKGUID=");
                          wcscat(szPath,szGUIDString);
                          wcscat(szPath,L",");
                          wcscat(szPath,szNewContainerDN);
                            wcscat(szPath,L">");
                          wprintf(L"Bind with the following WKGUID binding string:
%s\n",szPath);

                          hr = ADsOpenObject(szPath,
                              NULL,
                              NULL,
                              ADS_SECURE_AUTHENTICATION,
                                          //Use Secure Authentication
                              IID_IADs,
                              (void**)&pTestWKO1);
                          if (SUCCEEDED(hr))
                          {
                              hr = pTestWKO1->Get(L"distinguishedName",&vartest);
                                if (SUCCEEDED(hr))
```

(continued)

(continued)

```
                        {
                                wprintf(L"Successfully bound to object. DN:
%s\n",vartest.bstrVal);

                                VariantClear(&vartest);
                        }
                }
                else
                        wprintf(L"Binding failed with hr: %x\n",hr);

                if (pTestWKO1)
                        pTestWKO1->Release();
                                        //Bind again using the DN to get
                                        //  a regular ADsPath.
                wcscpy(szPath,L"LDAP://");
                wcscat(szPath,var.bstrVal);
                hr = ADsOpenObject(szPath,
                        NULL,
                        NULL,
                        ADS_SECURE_AUTHENTICATION,
                                        //Use Secure Authentication
                        IID_IADs,
                        (void**)&pTestWKO1);
                hr = pTestWKO1->get_ADsPath(&bstr);
                //Rename the WKO object
                hr = pNewContainer->MoveHere(bstr,szNewObjectRenameRDN,NULL);
                FreeADsStr(bstr);
                if (pTestWKO1)
                        pTestWKO1->Release();
                //Now AGAIN bind using WKGUID binding
                //Build the ADsPath to the well-known object
                wcscpy(szPath,L"LDAP://<WKGUID=");
                wcscat(szPath,szGUIDString);
                wcscat(szPath,L",");
                wcscat(szPath,szNewContainerDN);
                  wcscat(szPath,L">");
                wprintf(L"Bind AGAIN with the following WKGUID binding string:
%s\n",szPath);

                hr = ADsOpenObject(szPath,
                        NULL,
                        NULL,
                        ADS_SECURE_AUTHENTICATION,
                                        //Use Secure Authentication
                        IID_IADs,
                        (void**)&pTestWKO2);
                if (SUCCEEDED(hr))
```

```
                        {
                            hr = pTestWKO2->Get(L"distinguishedName",&vartest);
                             if (SUCCEEDED(hr))
                            {
                                wprintf(L"Successfully bound to object (Note the DN reflects
the rename). DN: %s\n",vartest.bstrVal);
                                VariantClear(&vartest);
                            }
                        }
                        else
                            wprintf(L"Binding failed with hr: %x\n",hr);
                    }
                    CoTaskMemFree(szGUIDString);
                }
            }
            if (pNewObject)
                pNewObject->Release();
        }
        VariantClear(&var);
    }
    if (pIADsObject)
        pIADsObject->Release();
    if (pDispNewObject)
        pDispNewObject->Release();
}

//Ask user if they want us to delete the test containers.
wprintf(L"Do you want to delete the test container and object (Y/N):");
_getws(pszBuffer);
if (0==wcsnicmp(L"Y", pszBuffer,1))
{
    //Delete the object
    //Delete the container
    hr = pNewContainer->Delete(L"container",szNewObjectRenameRDN);
    if (SUCCEEDED(hr))
    {
        wprintf(L"Successfully deleted test object.\n");
        wcscpy(szRelPath,L"cn=");
        wcscat(szRelPath,szContainer);
        //Delete the container
        hr = pDomain->Delete(L"container",szRelPath);
        if (SUCCEEDED(hr))
            wprintf(L"Successfully deleted test container and its contents.\n");
```

(continued)

(continued)

```
            else
               wprintf(L"Failed to delete test container and its contents. hr: %x\n",hr);
         }
         else
            wprintf(L"Failed to delete test container and its contents. hr: %x\n",hr);
      }

      if (pNewContainer)
        pNewContainer->Release();
    }
    if (pDisp)
        pDisp->Release();
   }
   if (pDomain)
   pDomain->Release();
}
if (pObject)
   pObject->Release();

//Uninitialize COM
CoUninitialize();

   return;
}

HRESULT AddValueToOtherWKOProperty(LPOLESTR szContainerDN,
                   //DN for container whose otherWellKnownObjects
                   //  property to modify
                              LPGUID pWKOGUID,
                   //WKO GUID for the well-known object.
                              LPOLESTR szWKOObjectDN
                   //DN of the well-known object.
                              )
{
HRESULT hr = E_FAIL;
LPOLESTR szGUIDString = new OLECHAR[MAX_PATH];
LPOLESTR szDNwithOctetString = new OLECHAR[MAX_PATH*2];
DWORD dwReturn;
//Connection handle
LDAP *hConnect = NULL;
//Specify NULL to bind to a DC in the current computer's domain.
//LDAP_PORT is the default port, 389
hConnect = ldap_open(NULL, LDAP_PORT);
//Bind using the preferred authentication method on Windows 2000
//and the caller's security context.
```

```
dwReturn = ldap_bind_s( hConnect, NULL, NULL, LDAP_AUTH_NEGOTIATE );
if (dwReturn==LDAP_SUCCESS)
{

  //Create the WKO value to add.
  GUIDtoBindableString (pWKOGUID, &szGUIDString);
  DWORD dwGUIDSize = (wcslen(szGUIDString));
  //Build the DNwithoctetstring
  swprintf(szDNwithOctetString, L"B:%d:%s:%s", dwGUIDSize, szGUIDString,szWKOObjectDN);
//   ULONG ulBerSize = (wcslen(szDNwithOctetString));
  //Build the BerVal
//   PCHAR pByteVal = (PCHAR)szDNwithOctetString;
//   berval berWKO;
//   berWKO.bv_len = ulBerSize;
//   berWKO.bv_val = pByteVal;
  //Build the mod structure to add the value.
  LDAPMod ldWKO;
  //mod_values takes a NULL terminated array of WCHARs.
  //We're adding a single value.
  WCHAR *StrValues[] = {szDNwithOctetString , NULL };
  //Operation
  ldWKO.mod_op = LDAP_MOD_ADD;
  //Attribute
  ldWKO.mod_type = L"otherWellKnownObjects";
  //Value to set.
  ldWKO.mod_vals.modv_strvals = StrValues;
  //mods is a NULL terminated array of LDAPMod structures.
  //We're adding a single value.
  LDAPMod *pMod[] = {&ldWKO,NULL};

  //Modify the object specified by szContainerDN.
  dwReturn = ldap_modify_s(  hConnect,
                             szContainerDN,
                             pMod);
  CoTaskMemFree(szGUIDString);

  if (dwReturn==LDAP_SUCCESS)
      hr = S_OK;
}
return hr;
}
```

(continued)

(continued)

```
HRESULT GUIDtoBindableString (LPGUID pGUID, LPOLESTR *ppGUIDString)
{
HRESULT hr = E_FAIL;
if (!pGUID)
  return E_INVALIDARG;
//Build bindable GUID string
LPOLESTR szDSGUID = new WCHAR [128];
DWORD dwLen =  sizeof(*pGUID);
LPBYTE lpByte = (LPBYTE) pGUID;
//Copy a blank string to make it a zero length string.
wcscpy( szDSGUID, L"" );
//Loop through to add each byte to the string.
for( DWORD dwItem = 0L; dwItem < dwLen ; dwItem++ )
{
  //Append to szDSGUID, double-byte, byte at dwItem index.
  swprintf(szDSGUID + wcslen(szDSGUID), L"%02x", lpByte[dwItem]);
  if( wcslen( szDSGUID ) > 128 )
    break;
}
//Allocate memory for string
*ppGUIDString = (OLECHAR *)CoTaskMemAlloc (sizeof(OLECHAR)*(wcslen(szDSGUID)+1));
if (*ppGUIDString)
  wcscpy(*ppGUIDString, szDSGUID);
else
  hr=E_FAIL;
//Caller must free ppGUIDString using CoTaskMemFree.
return hr;
}


// This function gets the specified well-known object for the current user's domain.

HRESULT GetWKOObject(LPOLESTR szBindableWKGUID,
            //IN. Bindable string GUID of well-known object.
                    IADs **ppObject
            //OUT. Return a pointer to the specified well-known object.
                    )
{
HRESULT hr = E_FAIL;
//Get rootDSE and the domain container's DN.
IADs *pObject = NULL;
LPOLESTR szPath = new OLECHAR[MAX_PATH];
VARIANT var;
hr = ADsOpenObject(L"LDAP://rootDSE",
                NULL,
```

```
                NULL,
                ADS_SECURE_AUTHENTICATION, //Use Secure Authentication
                IID_IADs,
                (void**)&pObject);

//Get current domain DN.
if (SUCCEEDED(hr))
{
    hr = pObject->Get(L"defaultNamingContext",&var);
    if (SUCCEEDED(hr))
    {
        //Build the WKGUID binding string.
        wcscpy(szPath,L"LDAP://");
        wcscat(szPath,L"<WKGUID=");
        wcscat(szPath,szBindableWKGUID);
        wcscat(szPath,L",");
        wcscat(szPath,var.bstrVal);
        wcscat(szPath,L">");
        //Print the binding string.
        //wprintf(L"WKGUID binding string: %s\n",szPath);
        VariantClear(&var);
        //Bind to the well-known object.
        hr = ADsOpenObject(szPath,
                    NULL,
                    NULL,
                    ADS_SECURE_AUTHENTICATION,
                            //Use Secure Authentication
                    IID_IADs,
                    (void**)ppObject);
        if (FAILED(hr))
        {
            if (*ppObject)
            {
              (*ppObject)->Release();
              (*ppObject) = NULL;
            }
        }
    }
}
if (pObject)
  pObject->Release();

return hr;
}
```

Authentication

Every object in Active Directory has a unique security descriptor that defines access permissions required to read or update the object or its individual properties. Access permissions are determined by rights granted to users' accounts or by group memberships.

When an application binds to an object in the directory, the access permissions that the application has to that object are based on the user context specified during the bind operation. For the binding functions and methods (**ADsGetObject**, **ADsOpenObject**, **GetObject**, **IADsOpenDSObject::OpenDSObject**), an application can implicitly use the credentials of the caller, explicitly specify the credentials of a user account, or use an unauthenticated user context (*Guest*).

GetObject and ADsGetObject

GetObject or **ADsGetObject** provides Single Sign On with no encryption. The application need not provide any credential information when accessing Active Directory information. ADSI uses the security context of the calling thread. However, if secure authentication fails, ADSI attempts a simple bind with a NULL username and NULL password. If the simple bind succeeds, the user context for the binding is Guest. A simple bind is clear-text authentication. Because no username or password is sent, this is not a security issue.

For a service running under the LocalSystem account, the security context used by **GetObject** and **ADsGetObject** depends on the computer on which the service is running. If the service is running as LocalSystem on a domain controller, the service has full system-level access to Active Directory. If the service is not running on a DC, the service has the access rights and privileges allowed to the computer account for the computer on which the service is running (which is significantly less powerful than system-level access).

Example Code for Binding to an Object Using ADsGetObject

The following code fragment binds to an object with the name Bob in the Microsoft.com domain using **ADsGetObject**, which uses the caller's security context.

Visual Basic

```
Dim myUser as IADs
Set myUser = GetObject("LDAP://CN=Bob,DC=Microsoft,DC=com")
```

C++

```
IADs *pObject;
HRESULT hr;
hr = ADsGetObject(L"LDAP://CN=Bob,DC=Microsoft,DC=com",
        IID_IADs,
        (void**) &pObject);
```

ADsOpenObject and IADsOpenDSObject::OpenDSObject

The major advantages of using **ADsOpenObject** and **IADsOpenDSObject::OpenDSObject** are the following:

- The ability to specify an alternate user name and password to authenticate to the directory.
- The ability to use encryption to protect the data exchange over the network between your application and the directory server.

It is recommended that you implicitly use the caller's credentials whenever possible. However, if you need to supply alternate credentials, you can use these Open methods. If you choose to bind using alternate credentials, do not cache the password. You can use the same alternate credentials in multiple bind operations by specifying the user name and password for the first bind operation and then specifying only the user name to make subsequent binds. The system sets up a session on the first call and uses the same session on subsequent bind calls as long as the following conditions are met:

- You specify the same user name in each bind operation.
- You use serverless binding or bind to the same server in each bind operation.
- You keep the session open by holding on to an object reference from one of the bind operations. The session is closed when the last object reference is released.

ADsOpenObject and **IADsOpenDSObject::OpenDSObject** take advantage of the Windows NT *Security Support Provider Interfaces (SSPI)* to allow flexibility in authentication options. The major advantage of using these interfaces is to provide different types of authentication to Active Directory clients and to encrypt the session. Currently, ADSI does not allow certificates to be passed in. Therefore, you can use SSL for encryption and then Kerberos, NTLM, or simple authentication, depending on how the flags are set on the *dwReserved* parameter.

You cannot ask for a specific SSPI provider in ADSI, although you will always get the highest preference protocol. In the case of a Windows 2000 client binding to a Windows 2000 server, the protocol is Kerberos. For a Windows NT 4.0 client binding to a Windows 2000 server, the protocol is NTLM. Not allowing a certificate for authentication is fine in the case of a Web page because authentication occurs prior to running the Web page.

Although Open operations allow you to specify a user and password, you should not do so. Instead, don't specify any credentials and implicitly use the credentials of the caller's security context. To bind to a directory object using the caller's credentials with **ADsOpenObject** or **IADsOpenDSObject::OpenDSObject**, specify NULL for both username and password.

Finally, if you want to bind with no authentication, you can use the ADS_NO_AUTHENTICATION flag. No authentication means that ADSI attempts to bind as an anonymous user to the target object and performs no authentication. This is equivalent to requesting anonymous binding in LDAP and means "Everyone" is the security context.

Example Code for Binding to an Object Using ADsOpenObject

The following code fragment binds to an object with the name Bob in the Microsoft.com. The example uses secure authentication, but it does not specify any credentials, so it binds using the default credentials of the caller's security context.

Visual Basic

```
Dim np as IADsOpenDSObject
Dim myUser as IADs

Set np = GetObject("LDAP:")
Set myUser =
np.OpenDSObject("LDAP://CN=Bob,DC=Microsoft,DC=com",vbNullString,vbNullString,
ADS_SECURE_AUTHENTICATION)
```

C++

```
IADs *pObject;
HRESULT hr;
hr = ADsOpenObject(L"LDAP://CN=Bob,DC=Microsoft,DC=com",
       NULL,
       NULL,
       ADS_SECURE_AUTHENTICATION,
       IID_IADs,
       (void**) &pObject);
```

If you set the fourth parameter to zero rather than specifying an authentication flag, ADSI performs a simple bind, which is sent as clear text. If you specify a user account and password without specifying authentication flags, they go over the network as clear text, which is a breach of security. Do not specify a user and password without also specifying authentication flags.

Binding with Encryption

If you want to use encryption to protect the data exchange over the network between your application and the directory server, you must bind using **ADsOpenObject** or **IADsOpenDSObject::OpenDSObject**. You have two options for starting a session that uses encryption.

Kerberos

Specify the ADS_USE_SEALING flag to encrypt the data using Kerberos. You can also add the ADS_USE_SIGNING flag to verify data integrity (that is, to check to ensure the data received is the same as the data sent). If you just specify ADS_USE_SEALING, you get ADS_USE_SIGNING as well. Both flags require Kerberos authentication, which works only under the following conditions:

- The client must be on a Windows 2000 system, or on a Windows 9x or Windows NT 4.0 system with the DS Client installed.

- The client computer must be a member of a Windows 2000 mixed mode or native mode domain.

- The client must be logged on to the Windows 2000 domain, or to a domain trusted by a Windows 2000 domain.

- You must use **ADsOpenObject** or **IADsOpenDSObject::OpenDSObject** with NULL credentials, that is, you cannot specify alternate credentials.

SSL

Specify the ADS_USE_SSL flag to encrypt the channel with SSL. If you specify both ADS_SECURE_AUTHENTICATION and ADS_USE_SSL, ADSI first opens an SSL channel and performs a simple bind using the specified user name and password or the current user context if both user name and password are set to NULL. If you specify only the ADS_USE_SSL flag, ADSI opens SSL port 636 and then does a simple binding over that SSL channel.

To use SSL-based encryption while communicating with Active Directory, Active Directory must have enabled Public Key Infrastructure (PKI). PKI can be enabled by setting up an enterprise certificate authority on one of the servers in Active Directory (including one of the Active Directory servers itself). Setting up an enterprise certificate authority causes an Active Directory server to get a server certificate that can then be used to do SSL-based encryption.

GetObject or **ADsGetObject** does not use encryption, so the LDAP requests used by ADSI and the data returned from the directory server go across the network as clear text. For debugging purposes, you may want to turn encryption off so you can use Network Monitor to see the LDAP requests and returns going between the client and the directory server.

Fast Binding Option for Batch Write/Modify Operations

When you call **GetObject**, **ADsGetObject**, **ADsOpenObject**, or **IADsOpenDSObject::OpenDSObject**, ADSI creates a COM object that represents the specified directory object. Normally, ADSI first retrieves the **objectClass** property so that ADSI can expose the COM interfaces that are appropriate for that class of object. For example, a user object would expose the **IADsUser** interface in addition to the base ADSI interfaces supported for all objects (such as **IADs**, **IDirectorySearch**, **IDirectoryObject**, and so on).

For a single operation, this should have no effect on performance. However, if you are doing batch operations that require hundreds or thousands of bindings over a slow connection *and* those operations are write methods in the base ADSI interfaces (such as **IADs::Put** and **IDirectoryObject::SetObjectAttributes**), you may want to trade off full object support (that is, the object-specific interfaces such as **IADsUser** on user objects) for faster binding. To do this, use the ADS_FAST_BIND flag for **ADsOpenObject** and **IADsOpenDSObject::OpenDSObject**.

The ADS_FAST_BIND flag has the following effects:

- The bind operation uses **ADsOpenObject** or **IADsOpenDSObject::OpenDSObject** and goes to the directory server once instead of twice. ADSI does not read objectClass and, therefore, exposes only the base ADSI interfaces for the object.

- Only the following ADSI interfaces are supported on the ADSI COM object:

  IADs
  IADsContainer
  IDirectoryObject
  IDirectorySearch
  IADsPropertyList
  IADsObjectOptions
  ISupportErrorInfo
  IADsDeleteOps

- If you use **IADsContainer::GetObject** to bind to child objects, the object returned will also have ADS_FAST_BIND characteristics.

- No existence check for the object specified by the binding string. This means that subsequent method calls will fail if the object does not exist. Therefore, you should use the ADS_FAST_BIND option when you know the object already exists (for example, directly after performing a query that returned the distinguished names of the objects you want to bind to).

- ADSI extensions are exposed for objects of class **top**. Therefore, only the extensions for the base ADSI interfaces listed above are exposed.

Binding to an Object's Parent Container

In ADSI, a directory object is represented by an ADSI COM object and every ADSI COM object exposes an **IADs** interface. The **IADs** interface has the **IADs::get_Parent** method so that you can get the ADsPath for the parent of the directory object. You can use that ADsPath to bind to the parent object.

Example Code for Binding to the Parent of an Object

The following C++ code fragment contains a function that binds to the parent of an object:

```
HRESULT GetParentObject(IADs *pObject,
                //Pointer the object whose parent to bind to.
                        IADs **ppParent
                //Return a pointer to the parent object.
                    )
{
    if ((!pObject)||(!ppParent))
        return E_INVALIDARG;

    HRESULT hr = E_FAIL;
```

```
    BSTR bstr;
    hr = pObject->get_Parent(&bstr);
    if (SUCCEEDED(hr))
    {
        //Bind to the parent container.
        *ppParent = NULL;
        hr = ADsOpenObject(bstr,
            NULL,
            NULL,
            ADS_SECURE_AUTHENTICATION, //Use Secure Authentication
            IID_IADs,
            (void**)ppParent);
        if(FAILED(hr))
        {
            if (!(*ppParent))
            {
               (*ppParent)->Release();
               (*ppParent) = NULL;
            }
        }
    }
    FreeADsStr(bstr);
    return hr;
}
```

Binding to Child Objects

In ADSI, a container object exposes an **IADsContainer** interface. The **IADsContainer** interface has the **IADsContainer::GetObject** method so that you can get bind directly to a child object. The object returned by **IADsContainer::GetObject** has the same security context as the object on which the method was called. This means if you have pointer to a container object and you know the relative path to a child object, you can avoid having to pass credentials again when binding to the child object. This may be useful when your application is binding using alternate credentials (that is, explicitly specified credentials rather than those of the calling thread).

The **IADsContainer::GetObject** method enables you to specify the relative RDN path (that is, relative to the current object) and class name (optional) and get back an **IDispatch** pointer to the specified child object.

For example, if you had an **IADsContainer** pointer (pCont) to a **domainDNS** object (DC=Microsoft,DC=com), you could call **IADsContainer::GetObject** to bind to the Administrator user in the Users container (cn=Administrator,cn=Users,DC=Microsoft,DC=com):

```
hr = pCont->GetObject(L"user",L"cn=Administrator,cn=Users",&pDisp);
```

Note The relative path in RDN=value format, and the path is relative to object represented by **IADsContainer**.

Example Code for Binding to the Users Container

The following C++ code fragment contains a function that binds to the users container and then uses **IADsContainer::GetObject** to bind to the Administrator user object within the users container:

```
LPOLESTR szPath = new OLECHAR[MAX_PATH];
VARIANT var;
hr = ADsOpenObject(L"LDAP://rootDSE",
                NULL,
                NULL,
                ADS_SECURE_AUTHENTICATION, //Use Secure Authentication
                IID_IADs,
                (void**)&pObject);

//Get current domain DN.
if (SUCCEEDED(hr))
{
    hr = pObject->Get(L"defaultNamingContext",&var);
    if (SUCCEEDED(hr))
    {
        //Build the WKGUID binding string.
        wcscpy(szPath,L"LDAP://cn=Users,");
        wcscat(szPath,var.bstrVal);
        if (pObject)
          pObject->Release();
        hr = ADsOpenObject(szPath,
                NULL,
                NULL,
                ADS_SECURE_AUTHENTICATION, //Use Secure Authentication
                IID_IADs,
                (void**)&pObject);
        if (SUCCEEDED(hr))
        {
            hr = pObject->QueryInterface(IID_IADsContainer,(void**)&pContainer);
            if (SUCCEEDED(hr))
            {
                hr = pContainer->GetObject(L"user",L"cn=Administrator",&pDisp);
                if (SUCCEEDED(hr))
                {
                    hr = pDisp->QueryInterface(IID_IADs,(void**)&pChild);
                    if (SUCCEEDED(hr))
                    {
```

```
                        hr = pChild->get_ADsPath(&bstr);
                        if (SUCCEEDED(hr))
                        {
                          wprintf (L"ADsPath of child object: %s\n", bstr);
                          FreeADsStr(bstr);
                        }
                    }
                    if (pChild)
                        pChild->Release();
                }
                else
                  wprintf(L"GetObject failed with hr: %x\n",hr);
                if (pDisp)
                    pDisp->Release();
            }
            if (pContainer)
                pContainer->Release();
        }
    if (pObject)
        pObject->Release();
    }
    VariantClear(&var);
}
```

Choosing an Interface

When you bind to an object, you can specify the ADSI COM interface whose pointer will be returned. An ADSI object can have a number of interfaces, depending on the class of object. However, every ADSI COM object has an **IADs** interface.

For Automation clients, use the **IADs*** interfaces. These interfaces are dual-interfaced, provide a greater level of abstraction, and provide data using **VARIANT**s and VARIANT arrays.

For C/C++ clients, you can use the **IDirectorySearch** interface for search operations and the **IDirectoryObject** interface to manipulate objects. These interfaces are not dual-interfaced. However, they do allow you to control exactly which attributes to retrieve (rather than returning the whole set) and allow access to the raw data stored in a property.

For example, security descriptors are stored as an octet string in an **ntSecurityDescriptor** property. When you use the **Get** method on an **IADs** interface to retrieve the **ntSecurityDescriptor** property, you get an **IDispatch** pointer to an **IADsSecurityDescriptor** object that wraps the security descriptor. At that point, you can use the **QueryInterface** method to query for the **IADsSecurityDescriptor** interface and use its methods to manipulate the security descriptor. When you use the **GetObjectAttributes** method of an **IDirectoryObject** interface, you get a pointer to an array of bytes (LPBYTE), you can cast that pointer to PSECURITY_DESCRIPTOR flag and use the Win32 security APIs to manipulate the security descriptor.

C H A P T E R   8

Reading and Writing Properties of Active Directory Objects

All objects have properties. All Active Directory™ Service Interface (ADSI) COM objects have one or more interfaces with methods that retrieve the properties of the directory object that the COM object represents. There are a number of ways you can read properties from an object:

- *Get a specific property by name.* The **IADs** interface has two methods **IADs::Get** and **IADs::GetEx** to read a specific property. Every ADSI COM object has an **IADs** interface.

- *Get a specified list of properties.* The **IDirectoryObject** interface has the method **IDirectoryObject::GetObjectAttributes** that allows you to specify a list containing the names of the properties to read and returns an array of structures containing the requested property values.

- *Enumerate all properties on the object.* The **IADsPropertyList** interface allows you to enumerate all the properties on an object.

- *Get special properties.* The Automation interfaces (**IADs***) have property methods that allow you to get special properties that are not stored in an object. Or the property methods may allow you to get an object property in a data format that differs from the actual data type stored. For example, the **IADs** interface has property methods such as **IADs::get_Name** which is an object's relative path (of the form RDNAttributeName=RDN, for example, CN=James Smith), **IADs::get_Class** which is an object's class, **IADs::get_Parent** which is the ADsPath to the object's parent.

ADSI allows you to cache properties locally after they have been read from the directory server. So, you also have a choice of reading the properties from the local property cache or retrieving the properties directly from the directory server. ADSI also has methods to update the cache as well as specifying whether all properties for an object are cached or just those you've specified.

After you have retrieved a property, you read its value. The data type of a property depends on the definition of the property (also known as an attribute) in the Active Directory schema. For each type of property that can exist in Active Directory, there is an **attributeSchema** object in the Active Directory schema. An **attributeSchema** object defines the characteristics of the attribute. One of these characteristics is the attribute's syntax, which determines the data type of the attribute's values. For more information, see *Characteristics of Attributes* and *Syntaxes for Active Directory Attributes*.

The Automation interfaces (**IADs***) return a property value as a **VARIANT** or a pointer to an Automation interface on a COM object that represents the property. The **IDirectoryObject** and **IDirectorySearch** interfaces return a property as a pointer to a structure containing a typed property value or a pointer to a string of bytes. In addition, **IDirectoryObject** and **IDirectorySearch** retrieve properties directly from the directory server instead of using a local property cache.

Property Cache

The ADSI object model provides a client-side property cache for each ADSI object. Think of the cache as a table in memory that contains the names and values of all an object's properties. When an object is created, its property cache is empty. Calling **IADs::GetInfo** loads the object's properties from the underlying directory service. If the cache is empty, calling **get** or **get_*propertymethod*** from a client written in C or C++, or calling **object.propertymethod** from an Automation client, forces an implicit **GetInfo**. Once the cache is filled, all **Get** calls work on the contents of the cache only.

Getting Properties

This section discusses the following:

- Get Method
- GetEx Method
- GetInfo Method
- Optimization Using GetInfoEx
- Getting Properties with the IDirectoryObject Interface

Get Method

Individual properties can be retrieved from the directory using the **IADs::Get** method.

The following example retrieves a property by name from an object using **IADs::Get**.

```
Dim MyUser as IADs
Dim MyCommonName as String

' Bind to a specific user object.
set MyUser = GetObject("LDAP://CN=JamesSmith,OU=MyOrgUnit")

' Get property
MyCommonName = MyUser.Get("CN")
```

From Automation languages, you can use the property name directly using the dot notation. For example, you can write **MyObject.Name** or **MyObject.Class** to access the **Name** and **Class** properties defined on **IADs**.

The following example retrieves a property directly from an Active Directory™ object using the standard **IADs** interface and the **Name** property it supports.

```
Dim MyUser as IADs
Dim MyName as String

' Bind to a specific user object.
Set MyUser = GetObject("LDAP://MyMachine/CN=JamesSmith,DC=ArcadiaBay,DC=COM")

' Get property
MyName = MyUser.Name
```

You can also use the name of the schema object that describes the property. Pass the name of the property as it is defined in the schema as the first parameter.

```
Dim MyUser as IADs
Dim MyName as String

' Bind to a specific user object.
set MyUser = GetObject("LDAP://CN=JamesSmith,OU=MyOrgUnit")

' Get property
MyName = MyUser.Get("distinguishedName")
```

From languages that do not use Automation, you can also use the **IADs::Get** method and its related methods as described previously. In addition, you can use the **get_*propertyname*** methods supported on all ADSI interfaces.

```
IADs        *pUser;
BSTR        bstrName;
HRESULT     hr;

// Bind to user object
hr = ADsGetObject(L"WinNT://MyDomain/Users/James", IID_IADs, (void**)&pUser);

// Get property
if (SUCCEEDED(hr)) {
    hr = pUser->get_Name(&bstrName);

    if (SUCCEEDED(hr)) {
        printf("%S\n", bstrName);
    }

    SysFreeString(bstrName)
}
```

GetEx Method

Some properties are returned as multi-valued. They can contain one or more values. For instance, a list of descriptions on a domain is a multi-valued property. You can retrieve a multi-valued property as an array using the **IADs::GetEx** method.

IADs::GetEx gets properties that support single or multiple values in **VARIANT** structures from the property cache. Finding no value in the cache invokes an implicit **IADs::GetInfoEx**. **IADs::Get** can also be used to retrieve properties with a single value.

Example Code for Using GetEx

Visual Basic

```
Dim obj As IADs
Dim objList As Variant

Set obj =
GetObject("LDAP://MyMachine/CN=Administrator,CN=Users,DC=ArcadiaBay,DC=com")

objList = obj.GetEx("description")

For Each Desc In objList
    ' Print the descriptions
    Debug.Print (Desc)
Next
```

GetInfo Method

Call the **IADs::GetInfo** method to refresh all of an ADSI object's cached properties from the underlying directory service. To refresh specific properties, use the **IADs::GetInfoEx** method.

ADSI invokes an implicit **GetInfo** if a **Get** is performed on a specific property in the property cache and no value is found. Once **GetInfo** has been called, an implicit call will not be repeated. If a value already exists in the property cache, however, calling **Get** without first calling **GetInfo** will retrieve the cached value rather than the most current value from the underlying directory. To obtain the most recent values for an object, always call **GetInfo**. Any changes you have made in the property cache will be replaced with the current values from the server. If you need to preserve your changes on the server you call the **IADs::SetInfo** method to save your changes before you call **GetInfo**.

Example Code for Using GetInfo

Visual Basic

```
Dim MyUser as IADsUser
'MyUser will be used to demonstrate implicit GetInfo
Dim MyUser2 as IADsUser
```

```
'Myuser2 will show the explicit GetInfo

' Bind to a specific user object.
set MyUser = GetObject("LDAP://MyMachine/CN=JamesSmith,DC=ArcadiaBay,DC=COM")
set MyUser2 = GetObject("LDAP//MyMachine/CN=JamesSmith2,DC=ArcadiaBay,DC=COM");

'Perform some time consuming operations.

'Code assumes that the property description has a
' single value in the directory
' Note that this will IMPLICITLY call GetInfo as at the point
' this call is made GetInfo has not yet been called (implicitly or
' explicitly) on the MyUser object.
Debug.print "MyUser's description value is "; MyUser.Get("Description")

'Since the GetInfo has already been called implicitly this
' call is satisfied from the value in the cache.
Debug.print "MyUser's sAMAccountName is "; MyUser.Get("sAMAccountName")

' Refresh the cache explicitly so the most current value is available
MyUser2.GetInfo

'Perform time consuming operations

'Note that this call is satisfied from the cache has GetInfo has already been
called
'explicitly for this object.
Debug.print "MyUser2 has the description set to "; MyUser.Get("Description")
```

Optimization Using GetInfoEx

The **IADs::GetInfoEx** method is called explicitly to refresh some of an ADSI object's cached properties from the underlying namespace. To refresh all the properties, use **GetInfo**.

GetInfoEx gets specific current values for the properties of an Active Directory object from the underlying directory store, refreshing the cached values.

Example Code for Using GetInfoEx

The following Microsoft® Visual Basic® code sample shows how to use **IADs::GetInfoEx**.

Calling **GetInfoEx** after changing property values but before calling **IADs::SetInfo** results in losing those changed values. After this call, the cache reflects the property values in the underlying namespace directory store. However, the cache is only updated with the values specifically requested in the **GetInfoEx** call. Some servers will not return all properties of an object in response to an **IADs::GetInfo** call; you must do an explicit **GetInfoEx** call naming these "non-default" properties in order to get them into the cache.

```
Dim PropArray As Variant
Dim Prop As Variant
Dim DescList As Variant
Dim obj As IADs

Set obj = GetObject("LDAP://MyMachine")

' Initialize the array of properties to pass to GetInfoEx
PropArray = Array("description", "distinguishedName")

' Make the array a single variant for passing to GetInfoEx
Prop = PropArray

' Get just the description and DN properties
obj.GetInfoEx Prop, 0

DescList = obj.Get("description")

' Enumerate the descriptions
For Each Desc In DescList
    ' Print the descriptions
    Deubg.Print (Desc)
Next
```

Getting Properties with the IDirectoryObject Interface

The **IDirectoryObject** interface provides clients written in C and C++ with direct access to directory service objects. The interface uses a direct on-the-wire protocol to provide access, rather than using the ADSI property cache. In place of the properties supported by the **IADs** interface, **IDirectoryObject** provides methods that support a critical subset of an object's housekeeping methods and provides access to its attributes. With **IDirectoryObject**, a client can get or set any number of object attributes with one method call. Unlike the corresponding Automation methods, which are batched, those of **IDirectoryObject** are executed as soon as they are called. Since methods on this interface do not require creating an instance of an Automation directory object, the performance overhead is very low.

Clients written in languages such as C and C++ should call the methods of **IDirectoryObject** to optimize performance and take full advantage of native directory service interfaces. Automation clients cannot use **IDirectoryObject**. Instead, they should call the **IADs** interface.

Example Code for IDirectoryObject

```
C++
// IDirObj.cpp : Demonstrates the use of IDirectoryObject.
//

#define _WIN32_DCOM
#define UNICODE
#define _UNICODE

#include "stdafx.h"
#include "windows.h"
#include "stdio.h"
#include "activeds.h"
#include "tchar.h"

void main(void)
{
    IDirectoryObject    *pDirectoryObj;
    DWORD               dwNumAttrToGet;
    DWORD               dwNumAttrGot;
    LPWSTR              AttribNames[10];
    ADS_ATTR_INFO       *pPropEntries;
    HRESULT             hr;

    // Call to initialize COM Library
    CoInitialize(NULL);

    // Bind to a known object asking for the IDirectoryObject Interface.
    hr = ADsOpenObject(
L"LDAP://MyMachine/CN=Administrator,CN=Users,DC=MyDomain,DC=ArcadiaBay,DC=COM",
            L"Administrator",
            L"",
            ADS_SECURE_AUTHENTICATION,
            IID_IDirectoryObject,
            (void**)&pDirectoryObj);

    if(FAILED(hr)) {
        // Error code goes here.
        printf("ADsOpenObject Failed\n");
```

(continued)

(continued)

```
        exit(1);
    }

    // Create a list of attributes to get.
    AttribNames[0] = L"distinguishedName";
    dwNumAttrToGet = 1;

    // Call GetObjectAttributes with the
    // list of attributes and a pointer to
    // an array of ADS_ATTRIB_INFO structs.
    hr = pDirectoryObj->GetObjectAttributes( AttribNames,
                                             dwNumAttrToGet,
                                             &pPropEntries,
                                             &dwNumAttrGot);
    if(FAILED(hr)) {
        // Error code goes here.
        pDirectoryObj->Release();
        printf("IDirectoryObject::GetObjectAttributes Failed\n");
        exit(1);
    }

    printf("distinguishedName: %S\n",
            pPropEntries[0].pADsValues->PrintableString);

    // Cleanup.
    pDirectoryObj->Release();
    FreeADsMem(pPropEntries);

    // Call to uninitialize COM Library
    CoUninitialize();

}
```

Setting Properties

Setting properties is very similar to getting properties. However, when setting a property, the value is only written to the local property cache on the client computer until the **IADs::SetInfo** method is called. **SetInfo** is always an explicit call, it is never called implicitly.

You can change the property values in the property cache as necessary for your application using **IADs** methods or **IADsPropertyList** methods, then write the changes back out to the directory service when they are in a consistent state using **SetInfo**.

This section discusses the following:

- Put Method
- PutEx Method
- SetInfo Method

Put Method

The **IADs::Put** method saves the value for a property for an Active Directory™ object by name into the property cache. Use the **IADs::PutEx** method to save properties with multiple values to the property cache or to remove a property from an object. These values are not persisted to the underlying directory service until **IADs::SetInfo** is called.

Example Code for Using Put

Visual Basic

```
Dim Namespace As IADsOpenDSObject
Dim User As IADsUser
Dim NewName As Variant

Set Namespace = GetObject("LDAP:")

Set User =
Namespace.OpenDSObject("LDAP://MyMachine/CN=Administrator,CN=Users,DC=MyDomain,DC
=ArcadiaBay,DC=COM", "Administrator", "", ADS_SECURE_AUTHENTICATION)

NewName = "James Smith"

' Set using the IADs::Put method
User.Put "FullName", NewName
User.SetInfo
```

PutEx Method

The **IADs::PutEx** method uses the name of a property to save a single or multi-valued property into the property cache. This overwrites any value currently in the property cache. The values in the cache are not written to the underlying directory service until an **IADs::SetInfo** occurs. The first argument of **PutEx** indicates whether you want to replace or add to any existing values for the property. In the following example, any existing values of the **description** attribute would be erased in the cache when **PutEx** is called and erased on the server when **SetInfo** is called.

Example Code for Using PutEx

```
Visual Basic

Dim x As IADs
Set x = GetObject("LDAP://CN=Administrator,CN=Users,DC=ArcadiaBay,DC=com")
'--------------------------------------------------
' Assume the otherHomePhoneNumber has the following values:
' 111-1111, 222-2222
'--------------------------------------------------
x.PutEx ADS_PROPERTY_APPEND, "OtherhomePhone", Array("333-3333" )
x.SetInfo              'Now the values are 111-1111,222-222,333-3333

x.PutEx ADS_PROPERTY_DELETE, "OtherHomePhone", Array("111-1111", "222-2222")
x.SetInfo              'Now the values are 333-3333
x.PutEx ADS_PROPERTY_UPDATE, "OtherHomePhone", Array("888-8888", "999-9999")
x.SetInfo              'Now the values are 888-8888,999-9999
x.PutEx ADS_PROPERTY_CLEAR, "OtherHomePhone",  vbNull
x.SetInfo              'Now the property has no value
```

SetInfo Method

The **IADs::SetInfo** method saves the current values for the properties for this Active Directory object from the property cache to the underlying directory store. This is analogous to flushing a buffer out to disk.

SetInfo will update objects that already exist in the directory or create a new directory entry for newly created objects.

At the time of the **SetInfo** call, if any property cache values have been written with a **IADs::PutEx** control code such as ADS_PROPERTY_UPDATE or ADS_PROPERTY_CLEAR, then the appropriate requests are passed on to the underlying directory service.

Enumerating Properties

The **IADsPropertyList** interface allows you to enumerate all the properties on an object.

Providing Direct Access to the Property Cache

In addition to the **IADs** methods that get and set individual properties in the cache, ADSI provides the **IADsPropertyList**, **IADsPropertyEntry**, and **IADsPropertyValue** interfaces that allow client software to access the property cache directly. These interfaces allow you to work with the properties without having to use the individual property names.

Interface	Purpose
IADsPropertyList	Manage the entire list of properties defined on an object.
IADsPropertyEntry	Manage individual property attributes and values.
IADsPropertyValue	Read and write values for each property entry in the property cache.

The ADSI property-cache interfaces represent each property entry. **IADsPropertyEntry** allows access to a single property in the cache and includes a pointer to the list of **IADsPropertyValue** pointers needed to represent each value.

The **IADsPropertyList** interface manages a property list node in a namespace. With this interface, you can enumerate the properties in the list, add and remove properties, or purge the entire list in one step.

```
Dim propList As IADsPropertyList
Dim propEntry As IADsPropertyEntry
Dim propValue As IADsPropertyValue
Dim rootDSE As IADs

'Get the rootDSE entry that contains configuration information
Set rootDSE = GetObject("LDAP://RootDSE")

'Bind to the domain
Set propList = GetObject("LDAP://" & rootDSE.Get("defaultNamingContext"))

'Get the Property Entries

Set propEntry = propList.GetPropertyItem("allowedChildClassesEffective",
ADSTYPE_CASE_IGNORE_STRING)

'Get more info about Property Entry
Debug.Print propEntry.ADsType
Debug.Print propEntry.ControlCode
Debug.Print propList.PropertyCount

'Values contain pointers to IADsPropertyValues interfaces
For Each v In propEntry.Values
    Set propValue = v
    Debug.Print propValue.CaseIgnoreString
Next
>
```

CHAPTER 9

Controlling Access to Active Directory Objects

Every object in Active Directory™ is protected by Windows® 2000 security. This security protection controls the operations that each security principal can perform in the directory. This chapter includes the following sections that discuss how a directory-enabled application can cope with and take advantage of the access control features of Active Directory.

How Access Control Works in Active Directory

Access control for Active Directory objects is based on Windows NT/Windows 2000 access-control model. For a detailed description of this model and its components such as security descriptors, access tokens, SIDs, ACLs, ACEs, see *Access Control Model*.

The basic outline of this model is as follows:

- *Security descriptor.* Each directory object has its own *security descriptor* containing security information that protects the object. Among other things, the security descriptor can contain a discretionary access-control list (DACL). A DACL contains a list of access-control entries (ACEs). Each ACE allows or denies a set of access rights to a user or group. The access rights correspond to the operations, such as reading and writing properties, that can be performed on the object.
- *Security context.* When you try to access a directory object, your application specifies the credentials of the security principal who is making the access attempt. Once authenticated, these credentials determine your application's *security context*, which includes the group memberships and privileges associated with the security principal. See *Security Contexts and Active Directory*.
- *Access check.* The system grants access to an object only if the object's security descriptor grants the necessary access rights to the security principal attempting the operation (or to groups to which the security principal belongs).

Controlling Access to Objects and Their Properties

If your application creates objects in the directory, you probably want to control who can access those objects. To do this, you need to work with the object's security descriptor, and more specifically, with the DACL and its list of ACEs.

When an object is created, it receives a security descriptor. For a description of the rules that the system uses to create the DACL for a new object, see *How Security Descriptors are Set on New Directory Objects*. These rules reveal that there are several things you can do to control the ACEs an object receives at creation time.

- You can create a new security descriptor and attach it to the object at creation time. See *Creating a Security Descriptor*.
- An object can inherit ACEs from its parent container. You can apply inheritable ACEs at any point in the directory hierarchy such that the ACEs are inherited by objects down the tree. See *Inheritance and Delegation of Administration*.
- Every object class definition in the schema includes a default security descriptor which can have a default DACL. If you have the necessary access rights, you can specify the ACEs in the default DACL in the schema. See *Default Security Descriptor*.

In addition, you can modify the DACL of an existing object.

- You can replace the DACL with a new one
- You can read the existing DACL, modify it, and apply the modified DACL. See *Setting Access Rights on an Object*.

What can you do with these ACEs? The following list enumerates the most important capabilities of ACEs in Active Directory:

- Control who can perform specified operations on an object
- Control who has access to a specific property or set of properties of an object
- Control who can create child objects in a container, including who can create a specific type of child object.
- Define private access rights (extended rights) for an object type and control who can perform the operations protected by the private rights
- Apply an ACE to a container object at the root of a directory subtree, such that the protections can be inherited automatically by all child objects down the tree.
- Apply an ACE that is inherited automatically by a specific type of child object in a subtree
- Create ACEs that grant rights to a security group, rather than to a single user
- Apply ACEs to Group Policy Objects to control the accounts and computers affected by the policy.

Access Rights for Active Directory Objects

All directory objects use the same set of predefined access rights that correspond to the common directory operations. These rights are described in the **ADS_RIGHTS_ENUM** enumeration type.

In addition, you can define private access rights (extended rights) for operations that go beyond those covered by the predefined rights. See *Extended Rights*.

Security Contexts and Active Directory

When your application binds to Active Directory, it does so in the security context of a security principal, which can be a human user or an entity such as a computer or a Win32 service. The security context is the user account information that the system uses to enforce security when a thread tries to access a securable object. This information includes such things as the user's security identifier (SID), group memberships, and privileges.

A user establishes a security context by presenting credentials for authentication. If the credentials are authenticated, the system produces an access token that identifies the group memberships and privileges associated with the user's account. The system checks your access token whenever you try to access a directory object. It compares the information in your access token to the accounts and groups allowed or denied access by the object's security descriptor.

You can use the following methods to control the security context with which you bind to Active Directory.

- Bind using the ADS_SECURE_AUTHENTICATION option with the **ADsOpenObject** function or **IADsOpenDSObject::OpenDSObject** method and explicitly specify a username and password. The system authenticates these credentials and generates an access token that it uses for access checks for the duration of that binding. For more information, see *Authentication*.

- Bind using the ADS_SECURE_AUTHENTICATION option but without specifying credentials. If you are not impersonating a user, the system uses the primary security context of your application, that is, the security context of the user who started your application. In the case of a Win32-based service, this is the security context of the service account or the LocalSystem account.

- Impersonate a user and then bind with ADS_SECURE_AUTHENTICATION but without specifying credentials. In this case, the system uses the security context of the client being impersonated. For more information, see *Client Impersonation*.

- Bind using **ADsOpenObject** or **IADsOpenDSObject::OpenDSObject** with the ADS_NO_AUTHENTICATION option. This method binds without authentication and results in "Everyone" as the security context. Only the LDAP provider supports this option.

If possible, you should bind without specifying credentials. In other words, use the security context of the logged-on user or the impersonated client. This enables you to avoid caching credentials. If you must use alternate user credentials, prompt for the credentials, bind with them, but do not cache them. To use the same security context in multiple bind operations, you can specify the user name and password for the first bind operation and then specify only the user name to make subsequent binds. For details on using this technique, see *Authentication*.

Some security contexts are more powerful than others. For example, the LocalSystem account on a domain controller has complete access to Active Directory, whereas a typical user has only limited access to a some of the objects in the directory. In general, your application should *not* run in a powerful security context, such as LocalSystem, when a less powerful security context is sufficient to perform the operations you need to perform. This means that you may want to divide your application into separate components, each of which runs in a security context appropriate to the Active Directory operations you need to perform. For example, your application's setup could be broken up as follows:

- Perform schema changes and extensions in the context of a user who is a member of the Schema Admins group.
- Perform configuration container changes in the context of a user who is a member of the Enterprise Admins group.
- Perform domain container changes in the context of a user who is a member of the Domain Admins group.

How Security Affects Active Directory Operations

Active Directory uses access control to grant or deny access to objects, properties, and operations based on the identity of the user making the access attempt. When your application binds to the directory, it binds with specific user credentials. Once authenticated, these credentials determine your application's security context. Regardless of whether the credentials are those of the logged-on user, a specified user, a service account, a computer account, or an unauthenticated user (Guest/Everyone), Active Directory checks the user's right to access an object before any operation is performed on that object. The user may or may not have access to a particular object, its children, its properties, or operations on that object, which means that your application needs to handle the potential errors caused by denied access.

The following sections discuss security contexts and the effects of access control on various operations.

Access Control and Read Operations

Security is an implicit filter when performing searches, enumerating containers, or reading properties. If you don't have the necessary access rights, attempts to list objects or read properties can fail with the following error codes even thought the object or property exists:

E_ADS_INVALID_DOMAIN_OBJECT
E_ADS_PROPERTY_NOT_SUPPORTED
E_ADS_PROPERTY_NOT_FOUND

One important case to note is that a caller with ADS_RIGHT_ACTRL_DS_LIST access to a container can enumerate the child objects in the container. But an attempt to access a child object can still fail with an error such as E_ADS_UNKNOWN_OBJECT if the caller does not have ADS_RIGHT_ACTRL_DS_LIST_OBJECT access to the child object.

The impact of security on read operations is not necessarily manifested as an error. For example, a search operation can succeed but the search results do not include objects or properties to which the caller does not have access.

Access Control and Write Operations

Property modifications fail if the caller does not have sufficient rights. For write operations that batch modifications to multiple properties, the entire operation fails if the caller does not have the necessary rights to a single one of the modified properties. For example, you can make multiple **IADs::Put** calls to set multiple properties on an object. However, when you call **IADs::SetInfo** to write the new data from the local cache to the directory, **SetInfo** will fail if the caller does not have write access to all the modified properties. Similarly, **IDirectoryObject::SetObjectAttributes** fails to set any properties if the caller does not have access to all the properties being set. So you should batch multiple modify operations only if you know that all modifications will succeed. To determine the attributes of a directory object that the caller has the ability to modify, read the object's **allowedAttributesEffective** attribute.

If the caller does not have sufficient rights to modify a property, the following return codes may be returned:

E_ADS_PROPERTY_NOT_SET
E_ADS_PROPERTY_NOT_MODIFIED

Access Control and Object Creation

Active Directory will fail to create a child object if the caller does not have the ADS_RIGHT_DS_CREATE_CHILD for that object type on the parent container. To determine the types of child objects that the caller can create in a directory object, read the object's **allowedChildClassesEffective** attribute.

When you use the **IADsContainer::Create** method to create a child object, the object is not made persistent until **IADs::SetInfo** is called on the new object. Between the **Create** and **SetInfo** calls, the creating thread can put values into any of the new object's properties. After the **SetInfo** call, the creating thread does not necessarily have the access rights to set the new object's properties. To ensure that the caller has these rights, specify an explicit security descriptor during creation. The DACL should have an ACE that gives the caller the necessary access rights on the object.

For more information on access control and object creation, see *How Security Descriptors are Set on New Directory Objects.*

Access Control and Object Deletion

Active Directory allows you to delete an object if you have either of the following access rights:

- DELETE access to the object itself
- ADS_RIGHT_DS_DELETE_CHILD access for that object type on the parent container

Note that the system checks the security descriptor on both the object and its parent before denying the deletion. This means that an ACE that explicitly denies DELETE access to a user will have no effect if the user has DELETE_CHILD access on the parent. Similarly, an ACE that denies DELETE_CHILD access on the parent can be overridden if DELETE access is allowed on the object itself.

To perform a tree-delete operation, for example using the **IADsDeleteOps::DeleteObject** method, you must have ADS_RIGHT_DS_DELETE_TREE access to the object. If you have this access right, you can delete the object and any child objects regardless of the protections on the child objects. To delete a tree if you don't have ADS_RIGHT_DS_DELETE_TREE access, you must recursively traverse the tree, deleting each object individually. In this case, you must have the necessary DELETE or DELETE_CHILD access for each object in the tree.

APIs for Working with Security Descriptors

Every directory object has an **nTSecurityDescriptor** property that contains the object's security descriptor. There are two main ways to read and manipulate a directory object's security descriptor.

- *You can use the **IADs::Get** method to retrieve the security descriptor as an ADSI COM object with an **IADsSecurityDescriptor** interface.* You can then use the **IADsSecurityDescriptor**, **IADsAccessControlList**, and **IADsAccessControlEntry** interfaces to work with the security descriptor and its components (ACLs, ACEs, and so on). For sample code that retrieves an **IADsSecurityDescriptor** interface pointer for a specified object's security descriptor, see *Using IADs to Get a Security Descriptor*.

- *You can use the **IDirectoryObject::GetObjectAttributes** method to retrieve an object's security descriptor as a pointer to a self-relative Win32 security descriptor (**PSECURITY_DESCRIPTOR**).* Then you can use this pointer with the Win32 access-control functions such as **AccessCheck** and **BuildSecurityDescriptor** that have a **PSECURITY_DESCRIPTOR** parameter. For sample code that uses **IDirectoryObject** to retrieve a security descriptor, see *Using IDirectoryObject to Get a Security Descriptor*.

The recommended technique, and the one used by most of the samples in this guide, is to use the **IADs** interfaces because they simplify handling security descriptors, ACLs, and ACEs. For Visual Basic programmers, the **IADs** interfaces are the only easy way to work with security descriptors.

The **IDirectoryObject** technique is useful primarily when you need a **PSECURITY_DESCRIPTOR** pointer. For example, the sample code in the *Checking an Extended Right in an Object's ACL* uses this method to retrieve a security descriptor to pass to the **AccessCheckByTypeResultList** function.

Using IADs to Get a Security Descriptor

The following code fragments use the **IADs::Get** method to retrieve an **IADsSecurityDescriptor** pointer to the **nTSecurityDescriptor** property of an Active Directory object.

Visual Basic

```
Dim rootDSE As IADs
Dim ADUser As IADs
Dim sd As IADsSecurityDescriptor

'Bind to the Users container in the local domain
Set rootDSE = GetObject("LDAP://rootDSE")
Set ADUser = GetObject("LDAP://cn=users," & rootDSE.Get("defaultNamingContext"))

'Get the security descriptor on the Users container
Set sd = ADUser.Get("ntSecurityDescriptor")
Debug.Print sd.Control
Debug.Print sd.Group
Debug.Print sd.Owner
Debug.Print sd.Revision
```

C++

```
HRESULT GetSDFromIADs(
              IADs *pObject,
              IADsSecurityDescriptor **pSD )
{
VARIANT var;
HRESULT hr = E_FAIL;

// Set *pSD to NULL.
if (*pSD)
    *pSD = NULL;
VariantClear(&var);
```

(continued)

(continued)

```
// Get the nTSecurityDescriptor
hr = pObject->Get(L"nTSecurityDescriptor", &var);
if (SUCCEEDED(hr))
{
    //Type should be VT_DISPATCH--an IDispatch ptr to
    // the security descriptor object.
    if (var.vt==VT_DISPATCH)
    {
        // Use V_DISPATCH macro to get the IDispatch pointer from the
        // VARIANT structure and QI for IADsSecurityDescriptor ptr.
        hr = V_DISPATCH( &var )-
>QueryInterface(IID_IADsSecurityDescriptor,(void**)pSD);
        if (FAILED(hr)) {
            if (*pSD)
                (*pSD)->Release();
        }
    }
    else
        hr = E_FAIL;
}
VariantClear(&var);
return hr;
}
```

Using IDirectoryObject to Get a Security Descriptor

The following C++ code fragment contains a function that uses the **IDirectoryObject**
interface to retrieve the security descriptor of the specified object, create a buffer, copy
the security descriptor to the buffer, and return a **PSECURITY_DESCRIPTOR** pointer to
the security descriptor in the buffer:

```
HRESULT GetSDFromIDirectoryObject(
            IDirectoryObject *pObject,
            PSECURITY_DESCRIPTOR *pSecurityDescriptor)
{
HRESULT hr = E_FAIL;
PADS_ATTR_INFO pAttrInfo;
DWORD dwReturn= 0;
LPWSTR pAttrName= L"nTSecurityDescriptor";
PSECURITY_DESCRIPTOR pSD = NULL;

// Get the nTSecurityDescriptor.
hr = pObject->GetObjectAttributes( &pAttrName,
                                    1,
                                    &pAttrInfo,
                                    &dwReturn );
if ( (FAILED(hr)) || (dwReturn != 1) ) {
```

```
      wprintf(L" failed: 0x%x\n", hr);
      return hr;
}

// Check the attribute name and type.
if ( ( _wcsicmp(pAttrInfo->pszAttrName,L"nTSecurityDescriptor") == 0 ) &&
     (pAttrInfo->dwADsType==ADSTYPE_NT_SECURITY_DESCRIPTOR) )
{
    // Get a pointer to the security descriptor.
    pSD = (PSECURITY_DESCRIPTOR)(pAttrInfo->pADsValues-
>SecurityDescriptor.lpValue);

    DWORD SDSize = pAttrInfo->pADsValues->SecurityDescriptor.dwLength;

    // Allocate memory for the buffer and copy the security
    // descriptor to the buffer.
    *pSecurityDescriptor = (PSECURITY_DESCRIPTOR)CoTaskMemAlloc(SDSize);
    if (*pSecurityDescriptor)
        CopyMemory((PVOID)*pSecurityDescriptor, (PVOID)pSD, SDSize);
    else
        hr = E_FAIL;
    // Caller must free the memory for pSecurityDescriptor.
}

// Free memory used for the attributes retrieved.
FreeADsMem( pAttrInfo );

return hr;
}
```

Security Descriptor Components

Having used the **IADs::Get** method to retrieve an **IADsSecurityDescriptor** interface pointer, you can use the property methods of the **IADsSecurityDescriptor** interface to read or write the components of a directory object's security descriptor. For example, to get or set the object's DACL, use the **DiscretionaryAcl** property (Visual Basic) or the **put_DiscretionaryAcl** and **get_DiscretionaryAcl** methods (C++).

A security descriptor can store the following information:

- *A security identifier (SID) that identifies the owner of the object.* The owner of an object has the implicit right to modify the DACL and owner information in the object's security descriptor.

- *A discretionary access-control list (DACL) that identifies the users and groups who can perform various operations on the object.* A DACL contains a list of access-control entries (ACEs). Each ACE allows or denies a specified set of access rights to a specified user account, group account, or other trustee. See *Retrieving an Object's DACL.*

- *A system access-control list (SACL) that controls how the system audits attempts to access the object.* Each ACE in a SACL specifies the types of access attempts that generate an audit log entry for a specified user account, group account, or other trustee. See *Retrieving an Object's SACL.*

- *A set of* **SECURITY_DESCRIPTOR_CONTROL** *control flags that qualify the meaning of a security descriptor or its components.* For example, the SE_DACL_PROTECTED flag protects the security descriptor's DACL from inheriting ACEs from its parent.

- *A security identifier (SID) that identifies the primary group of the object.* Active Directory does not use this component.

For sample code that reads and displays the information in an object's security descriptor and DACL, see *Reading an Object's Security Descriptor.*

Retrieving an Object's DACL

An object's security descriptor may contain a discretionary access-control list (DACL). A DACL contains zero or more access-control entries (ACEs) that identify the users and groups who can access the object. If a DACL is empty (that is, it contains zero ACEs), no access is explicitly granted, so access is implicitly denied. However, if an object's security descriptor does not have a DACL, the object is unprotected and everyone has complete access.

To retrieve an object's DACL, you must be the object's owner or have READ_CONTROL access to the object.

To get and set the DACL of a directory object, use the **IADsSecurityDescriptor** interface. Using C++, the **IADsSecurityDescriptor::get_DiscretionaryAcl** method returns an **IDispatch** pointer. Call **QueryInterface** on that **IDispatch** pointer to get an **IADsAccessControlList** interface, and use the methods on that interface to access the individual ACEs in the DACL. The procedure for modifying a DACL is described in *Setting Access Rights on an Object.*

To enumerate the ACEs, use the **IADsAccessControlList::get__NewEnum** method. The method returns an **IUnknown** pointer. Call **QueryInterface** on that **IUnknown** pointer to get an **IEnumVARIANT** interface. Use the **IEnumVARIANT::Next** method to enumerate the ACEs in the ACL. Each ACE is returned as a **VARIANT** containing an **IDispatch** pointer (the **vt** member is VT_DISPATCH). Call **QueryInterface** on that **IDispatch** pointer to get an **IADsAccessControlEntry** interface for the ACE. You can use the methods of the **IADsAccessControlEntry** interface to set or retrieve the components of an ACE.

For more information about DACLs and ACEs, see the following topics in the Platform SDK.

- *Access-Control Lists (ACLs)*
- *Access-Control Entries (ACEs)*

Retrieving an Object's SACL

The security descriptor of an Active Directory object may contain a system access-control list (SACL). A SACL contains access-control entries (ACEs) that specify the types of access attempts that generate audit records in the security event log of a domain controller. Note that a SACL generates log entries only on the domain controller where the access attempt occurred, not on every DC that contains a replica of the object.

To set or retrieve the SACL in an object's security descriptor, the SE_SECURITY_NAME privilege must be enabled in the access token of the requesting thread. The administrators group has this privilege by default, and it can be assigned to other users or groups. For more information, see *SACL Access Right*.

To get and set the SACL of a directory object, use the **IADsSecurityDescriptor** interface. Using C++, the **IADsSecurityDescriptor::get_SystemAcl** method returns an **IDispatch** pointer. Call **QueryInterface** on that **IDispatch** pointer to get an **IADsAccessControlList** interface, and use the methods on that interface to access the individual ACEs in the SACL. The procedure for modifying a SACL is similar to that for modifying a DACL, as described in *Setting Access Rights on an Object*.

To enumerate the ACEs in a SACL, use the **IADsAccessControlList::get__NewEnum** method, which returns an **IUnknown** pointer. Call **QueryInterface** on that **IUnknown** pointer to get an **IEnumVARIANT** interface. Use the **IEnumVARIANT::Next** method to enumerate the ACEs in the ACL. Each ACE is returned as a **VARIANT** containing an **IDispatch** pointer (the **vt** member is VT_DISPATCH). Call **QueryInterface** on that **IDispatch** pointer to get an **IADsAccessControlEntry** interface for the ACE. You can use the methods of the **IADsAccessControlEntry** interface to set or retrieve the components of an ACE.

For more information about SACLs, see the following topics in the Platform SDK.

- *Access-Control Lists (ACLs)*
- *Audit Generation*

Reading an Object's Security Descriptor

This example uses the **IADs** interfaces to enumerate the properties of a directory object's security descriptor, DACL, and the ACEs of the DACL.

The code uses the **IADs::Get** method to retrieve the **nTSecurityDescriptor** property of the directory object. The C++ version of this method returns a **VARIANT** containing an **IDispatch** pointer. The code calls **QueryInterface** on that **IDispatch** pointer to get an **IADsSecurityDescriptor** interface to the object's security descriptor.

Next the code uses **IADsSecurityDescriptor** methods to retrieve information from the security descriptor. Note that the information available through **IADsSecurityDescriptor** depends on the access rights of the caller. The **get_DiscretionaryAcl** and **get_Owner** methods fail if the caller does not have READ_CONTROL access to the object. Similarly, a call to the **get_SystemAcl** method would fail if the caller does not have the SE_SECURITY_NAME privilege enabled.

Visual Basic

```
Dim rootDSE As IADs
Dim dsobject As IADs
Dim sd As IADsSecurityDescriptor
Dim dacl As IADsAccessControlList
Dim ace As IADsAccessControlEntry

Private Sub Form_Load()
'Bind to the Users container in the local domain
Set rootDSE = GetObject("LDAP://rootDSE")
Set dsobject = GetObject("LDAP://cn=users," &
rootDSE.Get("defaultNamingContext"))

'Read the security descriptor on the Users container
Set sd = dsobject.Get("ntSecurityDescriptor")
Debug.Print "****SECURITY DESCRIPTOR PROPERTIES****"
Debug.Print "Revision: " & sd.Revision
SDParseControlMasks (sd.Control)
Debug.Print "Owner: " & sd.Owner
Debug.Print "Owner Defaulted: " & sd.OwnerDefaulted
Debug.Print "Group: " & sd.Group
Debug.Print "Group Defaulted: " & sd.GroupDefaulted
Debug.Print "System ACL Defaulted: " & sd.SaclDefaulted
Debug.Print "Discretionary ACL Defaulted: " & sd.DaclDefaulted
Debug.Print "****DACL PROPERTIES****"
Set dacl = sd.DiscretionaryAcl
AceCount = 0
For Each ace In dacl
AceCount = AceCount + 1
Debug.Print "**** Properties of ACE " & AceCount & " ****"
Debug.Print "Trustee: " & ace.Trustee
SDParseAccessMask (ace.AccessMask)
AceType = ace.AceType
If (AceType = &H5) Then
Debug.Print "ACE Type: ADS_ACETYPE_ACCESS_ALLOWED_OBJECT"
ElseIf (AceType = &H6) Then
Debug.Print "ACE Type: ADS_ACETYPE_ACCESS_DENIED_OBJECT"
```

```
ElseIf (AceType = &H0) Then
Debug.Print "ACE Type: ADS_ACETYPE_ACCESS_ALLOWED"
ElseIf (AceType = &H1) Then
Debug.Print "ACE Type: ADS_ACETYPE_ACCESS_DENIED"
Else
Debug.Print "ACE Type: UNKNOWN TYPE: " & Hex(AceType)
End If
AceFlags = ace.Flags
If (AceFlags And &H1) Then
Debug.Print "Flags: ADS_FLAG_OBJECT_TYPE_PRESENT"
Debug.Print "ObjectType: " & ace.ObjectType
End If
If (AceFlags And &H2) Then
Debug.Print "Flags: ADS_FLAG_INHERITED_OBJECT_TYPE_PRESENT"
Debug.Print "InheritedObjectType: " & ace.InheritedObjectType
End If
Next ace
End Sub


'SDParseControlMasks
'Print flags set in the security descriptor Control
Sub SDParseControlMasks(lCtrl As Long)
Debug.Print "Control Mask: "
If (lCtrl And &H1) Then Debug.Print "  SE_OWNER_DEFAULTED"
If (lCtrl And &H2) Then Debug.Print "  SE_GROUP_DEFAULTED"
If (lCtrl And &H4) Then Debug.Print "  SE_DACL_PRESENT"
If (lCtrl And &H8) Then Debug.Print "  SE_DACL_DEFAULTED"
If (lCtrl And &H10) Then Debug.Print "  SE_SACL_PRESENT"
If (lCtrl And &H20) Then Debug.Print "  SE_SACL_DEFAULTED"
If (lCtrl And &H400) Then Debug.Print "  SE_DACL_AUTO_INHERITED"
If (lCtrl And &H800) Then Debug.Print "  SE_SACL_AUTO_INHERITED"
If (lCtrl And &H1000) Then Debug.Print "  SE_DACL_PROTECTED"
If (lCtrl And &H2000) Then Debug.Print "  SE_SACL_PROTECTED"
If (lCtrl And &H8000) Then Debug.Print "  SE_SELF_RELATIVE"
End Sub


'SDParseControlMasks
'Print the access rights in an access mask.
Sub SDParseAccessMask(lMask As Long)
Debug.Print "AccessMask: "
If (lMask And &H10000) Then Debug.Print "  ADS_RIGHT_DELETE"
If (lMask And &H20000) Then Debug.Print "  ADS_RIGHT_READ_CONTROL"
If (lMask And &H40000) Then Debug.Print "  ADS_RIGHT_WRITE_DAC"
If (lMask And &H80000) Then Debug.Print "  ADS_RIGHT_WRITE_OWNER"
If (lMask And &H80000000) Then Debug.Print "  ADS_RIGHT_GENERIC_READ"
```

(continued)

(continued)

```
If (lMask And &H40000000) Then Debug.Print "  ADS_RIGHT_GENERIC_WRITE"
If (lMask And &H20000000) Then Debug.Print "  ADS_RIGHT_GENERIC_EXECUTE"
If (lMask And &H10000000) Then Debug.Print "  ADS_RIGHT_GENERIC_ALL"
If (lMask And &H1) Then Debug.Print "  ADS_RIGHT_DS_CREATE_CHILD"
If (lMask And &H2) Then Debug.Print "  ADS_RIGHT_DS_DELETE_CHILD"
If (lMask And &H4) Then Debug.Print "  ADS_RIGHT_ACTRL_DS_LIST"
If (lMask And &H8) Then Debug.Print "  ADS_RIGHT_DS_SELF"
If (lMask And &H10) Then Debug.Print "  ADS_RIGHT_DS_READ_PROP"
If (lMask And &H20) Then Debug.Print "  ADS_RIGHT_DS_WRITE_PROP"
If (lMask And &H40) Then Debug.Print "  ADS_RIGHT_DS_DELETE_TREE"
If (lMask And &H80) Then Debug.Print "  ADS_RIGHT_DS_LIST_OBJECT"
If (lMask And &H100) Then Debug.Print "  ADS_RIGHT_DS_CONTROL_ACCESS"
End Sub
```

C++

```cpp
HRESULT ReadSecurityDescriptor( IADs *pObject )
{
HRESULT hr = E_FAIL;
VARIANT var,varACE;
VARIANT_BOOL boolVal;
IADsSecurityDescriptor *pSD = NULL;
IADsAccessControlList *pACL = NULL;
IADsAccessControlEntry *pACE = NULL;
IEnumVARIANT *pEnum = NULL;
IDispatch *pDisp = NULL;
LPUNKNOWN pUnk = NULL;
ULONG lFetch;
BSTR szObjectType = NULL;
BSTR szTrustee = NULL;
BSTR szProp = NULL;
long lRev,lControl;
long lAceType, lAccessMask, lTypeFlag;
DWORD dwAces = 0;

if (NULL == pObject)
    return hr;

VariantClear(&var);

// Get the nTSecurityDescriptor.
// Type should be VT_DISPATCH--an IDispatch ptr to
// the security descriptor object.
hr = pObject->Get(L"nTSecurityDescriptor", &var);
if ( FAILED(hr) || var.vt != VT_DISPATCH ) {
```

```
        wprintf(L"get nTSecurityDescriptor failed: 0x%x\n", hr);
        return hr;
}


hr = V_DISPATCH( &var )->QueryInterface(IID_IADsSecurityDescriptor,(void**)&pSD);
if ( FAILED(hr) ) {
    wprintf(L"QI for IADsSecurityDescriptor failed: 0x%x\n", hr);
    return hr;
}


wprintf(L"****SECURITY DESCRIPTOR PROPERTIES****\n");

// Get properties using IADsSecurityDescriptor property methods.
hr = pSD->get_Revision(&lRev);
wprintf(L"Revision: %d\n", lRev);

// Print out the control mask bits.
hr = pSD->get_Control(&lControl);
wprintf(L"Control Mask: \n");
SDParseControlMasks(lControl);


hr = pSD->get_Owner(&szProp);
wprintf(L"Owner: %s\n", szProp);
if (szProp)
    SysFreeString(szProp);


hr = pSD->get_OwnerDefaulted(&boolVal);
wprintf(L"Owner Defaulted: %s\n", boolVal ? L"True" : L"False");


hr = pSD->get_Group(&szProp);
wprintf(L"Group: %s\n", szProp);
if (szProp)
    SysFreeString(szProp);


hr = pSD->get_GroupDefaulted(&boolVal);
wprintf(L"Group Defaulted: %s\n", boolVal ? L"True" : L"False");


hr = pSD->get_SaclDefaulted(&boolVal);
wprintf(L"System ACL Defaulted: %s\n", boolVal ? L"True" : L"False");


hr = pSD->get_DaclDefaulted(&boolVal);
wprintf(L"Discretionary ACL Defaulted: %s\n", boolVal ? L"True" : L"False");


// Get the DACL.
wprintf(L"****DACL PROPERTIES****\n");
```

(continued)

(continued)

```
hr = pSD->get_DiscretionaryAcl(&pDisp);
if (SUCCEEDED(hr))
{
    hr = pDisp->QueryInterface(IID_IADsAccessControlList, (void**)&pACL);
    if (SUCCEEDED(hr))
    {
        hr = pACL->get__NewEnum( &pUnk );
        if (SUCCEEDED(hr))
        {
            hr = pUnk->QueryInterface( IID_IEnumVARIANT, (void**) &pEnum );
        }
    }
}
if ( FAILED(hr) ) {
    wprintf(L"Could not get DACL: 0x%x\n", hr);
    return hr;
}

// Loop to read all ACEs on the object.
hr = pEnum->Next( 1, &varACE, &lFetch );
while ( (hr == S_OK) && (lFetch == 1) && (varACE.vt==VT_DISPATCH))
{
    // QI for IADsAccessControlEntry to use to read the ACE.
    hr = V_DISPATCH(&varACE)->QueryInterface(
                            IID_IADsAccessControlEntry, (void**)&pACE );
    if ( FAILED(hr) ) {
        wprintf(L"QI for IADsAccessControlEntry failed: 0x%x\n", hr);
        break;
    }

    wprintf(L"**** Properties of ACE %u ****\n", ++dwAces);

    // Get the trustee (who the ACE applies to) and print it.
    hr = pACE->get_Trustee(&szTrustee);
    if (SUCCEEDED(hr))
    {
        wprintf(L"Trustee: %s\n", szTrustee);
        if (szTrustee)
            SysFreeString(szTrustee);
    }

    // Get the AceMask
    hr = pACE->get_AccessMask(&lAccessMask);
    if (SUCCEEDED(hr))
```

```
{
    wprintf(L"AccessMask: \n");
    SDParseAccessMask(lAccessMask);
}


// Get the AceType
hr = pACE->get_AceType(&lAceType);
if (SUCCEEDED(hr))
{
    if (lAceType == ADS_ACETYPE_ACCESS_ALLOWED_OBJECT)
        wprintf(L"ACE Type: ADS_ACETYPE_ACCESS_ALLOWED_OBJECT\n");
    else if (lAceType == ADS_ACETYPE_ACCESS_DENIED_OBJECT)
        wprintf(L"ACE Type: ADS_ACETYPE_ACCESS_DENIED_OBJECT\n");
    else if (lAceType == ADS_ACETYPE_ACCESS_ALLOWED)
        wprintf(L"ACE Type: ADS_ACETYPE_ACCESS_ALLOWED\n");
    else if (lAceType == ADS_ACETYPE_ACCESS_DENIED)
        wprintf(L"ACE Type: ADS_ACETYPE_ACCESS_DENIED\n");
    else
        wprintf(L"ACE Type: UNKNOWN TYPE: %x\n", lAceType);
}


// Get the flags. Based on flags, get
// objecttype and inheritedobjecttype.
hr = pACE->get_Flags(&lTypeFlag);
if (SUCCEEDED(hr))
{
    // If the object type GUID is present, print it.
    if (lTypeFlag & ADS_FLAG_OBJECT_TYPE_PRESENT)
    {
        wprintf(L"Flags: ADS_FLAG_OBJECT_TYPE_PRESENT\n");
        hr = pACE->get_ObjectType(&szObjectType);
        if (SUCCEEDED(hr))
        {
            wprintf(L"ObjectType: %s\n", szObjectType);
            if (szObjectType)
                SysFreeString(szObjectType);
        }
    }

    // If the inherited object type GUID is present, print it.
    if (lTypeFlag & ADS_FLAG_INHERITED_OBJECT_TYPE_PRESENT)
    {
        wprintf(L"Flags: ADS_FLAG_INHERITED_OBJECT_TYPE_PRESENT\n");
        hr = pACE->get_InheritedObjectType(&szObjectType);
        if (SUCCEEDED(hr))
```

(continued)

(continued)

```
            {
                wprintf(L"InheritedObjectType: %s\n", szObjectType);
                if (szObjectType)
                    SysFreeString(szObjectType);
            }
        }
    }


    // Clean up the enumerated ACE item.
    if (pACE)
        pACE->Release();

    // Clean up the VARIANT for the ACE item.
    VariantClear(&varACE);

    // Get the next ACE
    hr = pEnum->Next( 1, &varACE, &lFetch );

} // End of While loop

// Clean up
if (pEnum)
    pEnum->Release();
if (pUnk)
    pUnk->Release();
if (pACL)
    pACL->Release();
if (pDisp)
    pDisp->Release();
if (pSD)
    pSD->Release();
VariantClear(&var);
return hr;
}


// *******************************************************************
// SDParseControlMasks
// Function to print Control flags.
// *******************************************************************
int SDParseControlMasks( long lCtrl )
{
int iReturn = TRUE;

if (lCtrl & SE_OWNER_DEFAULTED)
```

```
      wprintf(L"  SE_OWNER_DEFAULTED\n");

if (lCtrl & SE_GROUP_DEFAULTED)
   wprintf(L"  SE_GROUP_DEFAULTED\n");

if (lCtrl & SE_DACL_PRESENT)
   wprintf(L"  SE_DACL_PRESENT\n");

if (lCtrl & SE_DACL_DEFAULTED)
   wprintf(L"  SE_DACL_DEFAULTED\n");

if (lCtrl & SE_SACL_PRESENT)
   wprintf(L"  SE_SACL_PRESENT\n");

if (lCtrl & SE_SACL_DEFAULTED)
   wprintf(L"  SE_SACL_DEFAULTED\n");

if (lCtrl & SE_DACL_AUTO_INHERIT_REQ)
   wprintf(L"  SE_DACL_AUTO_INHERIT_REQ\n");

if (lCtrl & SE_SACL_AUTO_INHERIT_REQ)
   wprintf(L"  SE_SACL_AUTO_INHERIT_REQ\n");

if (lCtrl & SE_DACL_AUTO_INHERITED)
   wprintf(L"  SE_DACL_AUTO_INHERITED\n");

if (lCtrl & SE_SACL_AUTO_INHERITED)
   wprintf(L"  SE_SACL_AUTO_INHERITED\n");

if (lCtrl & SE_DACL_PROTECTED)
   wprintf(L"  SE_DACL_PROTECTED\n");

if (lCtrl & SE_SACL_PROTECTED)
   wprintf(L"  SE_SACL_PROTECTED\n");

if (lCtrl & SE_SELF_RELATIVE)
   wprintf(L"  SE_OWNER_DEFAULTED\n");

return iReturn;

}

// **********************************************************************
// SDParseAccessMask
// Function to print AccessMask flags.
// **********************************************************************
```

(continued)

(continued)

```
int SDParseAccessMask( long lCtrl )
{
    int iReturn = TRUE;

if (lCtrl & ADS_RIGHT_DELETE)
    wprintf(L"  ADS_RIGHT_DELETE\n");

if (lCtrl & ADS_RIGHT_READ_CONTROL)
    wprintf(L"  ADS_RIGHT_READ_CONTROL\n");

if (lCtrl & ADS_RIGHT_WRITE_DAC)
    wprintf(L"  ADS_RIGHT_WRITE_DAC\n");

if (lCtrl & ADS_RIGHT_WRITE_OWNER)
    wprintf(L"  ADS_RIGHT_WRITE_OWNER\n");

if (lCtrl & ADS_RIGHT_GENERIC_READ)
    wprintf(L"  ADS_RIGHT_GENERIC_READ\n");

if (lCtrl & ADS_RIGHT_GENERIC_WRITE)
    wprintf(L"  ADS_RIGHT_GENERIC_WRITE\n");

if (lCtrl & ADS_RIGHT_GENERIC_EXECUTE)
    wprintf(L"  ADS_RIGHT_GENERIC_EXECUTE\n");

if (lCtrl & ADS_RIGHT_GENERIC_ALL)
    wprintf(L"  ADS_RIGHT_GENERIC_ALL\n");

if (lCtrl & ADS_RIGHT_DS_CREATE_CHILD)
    wprintf(L"  ADS_RIGHT_DS_CREATE_CHILD\n");

if (lCtrl & ADS_RIGHT_DS_DELETE_CHILD)
    wprintf(L"  ADS_RIGHT_DS_DELETE_CHILD\n");

if (lCtrl & ADS_RIGHT_ACTRL_DS_LIST)
    wprintf(L"  ADS_RIGHT_ACTRL_DS_LIST\n");

if (lCtrl & ADS_RIGHT_DS_SELF)
    wprintf(L"  ADS_RIGHT_DS_SELF\n");

if (lCtrl & ADS_RIGHT_DS_READ_PROP)
    wprintf(L"  ADS_RIGHT_DS_READ_PROP\n");

if (lCtrl & ADS_RIGHT_DS_WRITE_PROP)
```

```
          wprintf(L" ADS_RIGHT_DS_WRITE_PROP\n");

if (1Ctrl & ADS_RIGHT_DS_DELETE_TREE)
      wprintf(L" ADS_RIGHT_DS_DELETE_TREE\n");

if (1Ctrl & ADS_RIGHT_DS_LIST_OBJECT)
      wprintf(L" ADS_RIGHT_DS_LIST_OBJECT\n");

if (1Ctrl & ADS_RIGHT_DS_CONTROL_ACCESS)
      wprintf(L" ADS_RIGHT_DS_CONTROL_ACCESS\n");

return iReturn;

}
```

Setting Access Rights on an Object

When you are using the ADSI COM objects **IADsSecurityDescriptor** (security descriptor), **IADsAccessControlList** (DACLs and SACLs), and **IADsAccessControlEntry** (ACE) to add an ACE to a ACL, you are making changes to the **nTSecurityDescriptor** property of the specified object in the property cache. This means put methods on the objects that contain the new ACE and the **IADs::SetInfo** method must be called in order to write the updated security descriptor to the directory from the property cache.

For sample C++ and Visual Basic code that sets an ACE on an Active Directory object, see *Example Code for Setting an ACE on a Directory Object*.

Use the following steps for creating an ACE for an access right and setting that ACE on the DACL of an object.

1. Get an **IADs** interface pointer to the object.

2. Use the **IADs::Get** method to get the security descriptor of the object. The name of the property containing the security descriptor is **nTSecurityDescriptor**. The property will be returned as a **VARIANT** containing an **IDispatch** pointer (the **vt** member is VT_DISPATCH). Call **QueryInterface** on that **IDispatch** pointer to get an **IADsSecurityDescriptor** interface to use the methods on that interface to access the security descriptor's ACL.

3. Use the **IADsSecurityDescriptor::get_DiscretionaryAcl** method to get the DACL. The method returns an **IDispatch** pointer. Call **QueryInterface** on that **IDispatch** pointer to get an **IADsAccessControlList** interface to use the methods on that interface to access the individual ACEs in the ACL.

4. Use **CoCreateInstance** to create the ADSI COM object for the new ACE and get an **IADsAccessControlEntry** interface pointer to that object. Note that the class ID is CLSID_AccessControlEntry.

5. Set the properties of the ACE using the **IADsAccessControlEntry** methods:

   a. Use **IADsAccessControlEntry::put_Trustee** to set the trustee to whom this ACE applies. The trustee is a user, group, or other security principal. Your application should use the value from the appropriate property from the user or group object of the trustee to which you want to apply the ACE. The trustee is specified as a BSTR and can take the following forms:

   Domain account (the logon name used in a previous version of Windows NT®) of the form *domain\useraccount* where *domain* is the name of the Windows NT domain that contains the user and *useraccount* is the **sAMAccountName** property of the specified user. For example: Microsoft\jsmith.

   Well-known security principal that represents special identities defined by the Windows NT security system, such as everyone, local system, principal self, authenticated user, creator owner, and so on. The objects representing the well-known security principals are stored in the WellKnown Security Principals container beneath the Configuration container. For example, anonymous logon.

   Built-in group that represent the built-in user groups defined by the Windows NT security system. It has the form **BUILTIN***groupname* where *groupname* is the name of the built-in user group. The objects representing the built-in groups are stored in the Builtin container beneath the domain container. For example, BUILTIN\Administrators.

   SID (string format) of the specified user, which is the **objectSID** property of the specified user. You can convert to string form using the **ConvertSidToStringSid** function in the Win32 Security API. For example: S-1-5-32-548.

   Distinguished Name of the specified user, which is the **distinguishedName** property of the specified user. For example, CN=J Smith,OU=Northwest,dc=Microsoft,DC=Com.

   b. Use **IADsAccessControlEntry::put_AccessMask** to set the mask that specifies the access right. The **ADS_RIGHTS_ENUM** enumeration specifies the access rights you can set on a directory object.

   c. Use **IADsAccessControlEntry::put_AceType** to specify whether to allow or deny the access rights set by **put_AccessMask**. For standard rights, this can be ADS_ACETYPE_ACCESS_ALLOWED or ADS_ACETYPE_ACCESS_DENIED. For object-specific rights (rights that apply to a specific part of an object or to a specific type of object), use ADS_ACETYPE_ACCESS_ALLOWED_OBJECT or ADS_ACETYPE_ACCESS_DENIED_OBJECT. The **ADS_ACETYPE_ENUM** enumeration specifies the access types you can set on an ACE.

   d. Use **IADsAccessControlEntry::put_AceFlags** to specify whether other containers or objects beneath the specified object can inherit the ACE. The **ADS_ACEFLAG_ENUM** enumeration specifies the inheritance flags you can set on an ACE.

   e. Use **IADsAccessControlEntry::put_Flags** to specify whether the right applies to a specific part of the object, an inherited object type, or both.

    f. If **Flags** is set to ADS_FLAG_OBJECT_TYPE_PRESENT, call **IADsAccessControlEntry::put_ObjectType** to specify a string containing the GUID of the object class (for ADS_RIGHT_DS_CREATE_CHILD or ADS_RIGHT_DS_DELETE_CHILD), property, property set, or extended right that the ACE applies to. The GUID must be specified as a string of the form produced by the **StringFromGUID2** function in the COM library.

    g. If **Flags** is set to ADS_FLAG_INHERITED_OBJECT_TYPE_PRESENT, use **IADsAccessControlEntry::put_InheritedObjectType** to specify a string containing the GUID of the inherited object class that the ACE applies to. The GUID must be specified as a string of the form produced by the **StringFromGUID2** function in the COM library.

6. Use the **QueryInterface** method on the **IADsAccessControlEntry** object to get an **IDispatch** pointer. The **AddAce** method requires an **IDispatch** interface pointer to the ACE.

7. Use **IADsAccessControlList::AddAce** to add the new ACE to the DACL. Note that the order of the ACEs within the ACL can affect the evaluation of access to the object. The correct access to the object may require you to create an new ACL, add the ACEs from the existing ACL in the correct order to the new ACL, and then replace the existing ACL in the security descriptor with the new ACL. For more information, see How ACE Order in an ACL Determines Access.

8. Use **IADsSecurityDescriptor::put_DiscretionaryAcl** to write the DACL containing the new ACE to the security descriptor.

9. Use the **IADs::Put** method to write the security descriptor to the object's **nTSecurityDescriptor** property to the property cache.

10. Use the **IADs::SetInfo** method to update the property on the object in the directory.

Example Code for Setting an ACE on a Directory Object

C++

The following C++ code has a *SetRight* subroutine that adds an ACE to the DACL of the security descriptor of a specified Active Directory object. The subroutine is multipurpose, allowing you to set any of the following types of ACEs.

- Allow or deny access to the entire object.
- Allow or deny access to a specific property on the object.
- Allow or deny access to a set of properties on the object.
- Allow or deny the right to create a specific type of child object.
- Set an ACE that can be inherited by all child objects or by child objects of a specified object class.

Here's the code for the *SetRight* subroutine. Following that code are several samples that show how to call *SetRight* to set different types of ACEs.

```
HRESULT SetRight(
          IADs *pObject,
          long lAccessMask,
          long lAccessType,
          long lAccessInheritFlags,
          LPOLESTR szObjectGUID,
          LPOLESTR szInheritedObjectGUID,
          LPOLESTR szTrustee)
{
VARIANT varSD;
HRESULT hr = E_FAIL;
IADsAccessControlList *pACL = NULL;
IADsSecurityDescriptor *pSD = NULL;
IDispatch *pDispDACL = NULL;
IADsAccessControlEntry *pACE = NULL;
IDispatch *pDispACE = NULL;
long lFlags = 0L;

// This sample takes the szTrustee in an expected naming format
// and assumes it is the name for the correct trustee.
// Your application should check the validity of the specified trustee.
if (!szTrustee || !pObject)
    return E_INVALIDARG;

VariantClear(&varSD);

// Get the nTSecurityDescriptor.
// Type should be VT_DISPATCH--an IDispatch ptr to the security
// descriptor object.
hr = pObject->Get(L"nTSecurityDescriptor", &varSD);
if ( FAILED(hr) || varSD.vt != VT_DISPATCH ) {
    wprintf(L"get nTSecurityDescriptor failed: 0x%x\n", hr);
    return hr;
}

hr = V_DISPATCH( &varSD )-
>QueryInterface(IID_IADsSecurityDescriptor,(void**)&pSD);
if ( FAILED(hr) ) {
    wprintf(L"QI for IADsSecurityDescriptor failed: 0x%x\n", hr);
    goto cleanup;
}

// Get the DACL.
hr = pSD->get_DiscretionaryAcl(&pDispDACL);
if (SUCCEEDED(hr))
```

```
    hr = pDispDACL->QueryInterface(IID_IADsAccessControlList,(void**)&pACL);
if ( FAILED(hr) ) {
    wprintf(L"Could not get DACL: 0x%x\n", hr);
    goto cleanup;
}


// Create the COM object for the new ACE.
hr = CoCreateInstance(
                CLSID_AccessControlEntry,
                NULL,
                CLSCTX_INPROC_SERVER,
                IID_IADsAccessControlEntry,
                (void **)&pACE
                );
if ( FAILED(hr) ) {
    wprintf(L"Could not create ACE object: 0x%x\n", hr);
    goto cleanup;
}


// Set the properties of the new ACE.

// Set the mask that specifies the access right.
hr = pACE->put_AccessMask( lAccessMask );

// Set the trustee.
hr = pACE->put_Trustee( szTrustee );

// Set AceType.
hr = pACE->put_AceType( lAccessType );

// Set AceFlags to specify whether other objects can inherit
// the ACE from the specified object.
hr = pACE->put_AceFlags( lAccessInheritFlags );

// If an szObjectGUID is specified, add ADS_FLAG_OBJECT_TYPE_PRESENT
// to the lFlags mask and set the ObjectType.
if (szObjectGUID)
{
    lFlags |= ADS_FLAG_OBJECT_TYPE_PRESENT;
    hr = pACE->put_ObjectType( szObjectGUID );
}


// If an szInheritedObjectGUID is specified, add
// ADS_FLAG_INHERITED_OBJECT_TYPE_PRESENT
// to the lFlags mask and set the InheritedObjectType.
```

(continued)

(continued)

```
if (szInheritedObjectGUID)
{
    lFlags |= ADS_FLAG_INHERITED_OBJECT_TYPE_PRESENT;
    hr = pACE->put_InheritedObjectType( szInheritedObjectGUID );
}


// Set flags if ObjectType or InheritedObjectType were set.
if (lFlags)
    hr = pACE->put_Flags(lFlags);

// Add the ACE to the ACL to the SD to the cache to the object.
// Need to QI for the IDispatch pointer to pass to the AddAce method.
hr = pACE->QueryInterface(IID_IDispatch, (void**)&pDispACE);
if (SUCCEEDED(hr))
{
    hr = pACL->AddAce(pDispACE);
    if (SUCCEEDED(hr))
    {
        // Write the DACL
        hr = pSD->put_DiscretionaryAcl(pDispDACL);
        if (SUCCEEDED(hr))
        {
            // Write the ntSecurityDescriptor property to
            // the property cache.
            hr = pObject->Put(L"nTSecurityDescriptor", varSD);
            if (SUCCEEDED(hr))
            {
                // Call SetInfo to update the property on
                // the object in the directory.
                hr = pObject->SetInfo();
            }
        }
    }
}

cleanup:
if (pDispACE)
    pDispACE->Release();
if (pACE)
    pACE->Release();
if (pACL)
    pACL->Release();
if (pDispDACL)
    pDispDACL->Release();
```

```
if (pSD)
    pSD->Release();

VariantClear(&varSD);
return hr;
}
```

Allow or deny access to the entire object

The following C++ code fragment calls the *SetRight* subroutine to set an ACE that allows the trustee to read or write any property on the object. The code fragment assumes that *pObject* and *szTrustee* are set to valid values. For a discussion of the possible formats for the trustee string, see *Setting Access Rights on an Object*.

```
HRESULT hr;
IADs *pObject;
LPWSTR szTrustee;

hr = SetRight(
        pObject,   // IADs pointer to the object
        ADS_RIGHT_READ_PROP | ADS_RIGHT_WRITE_PROP,
        ADS_ACETYPE_ACCESS_ALLOWED,
        0,         // not inheritable
        NULL,      // no object type GUID
        NULL,      // no inherited object type GUID
        szTrustee
        );
```

Allow or deny access to a specific property on the object

This C++ code fragment calls the *SetRight* subroutine to allow the trustee to read or write a specific property on the object. Note that you must specify the **schemIDGUID** of the property and you must specify ADS_ACETYPE_ACCESS_ALLOWED_OBJECT to indicate that this is an object-specific ACE. This sample also specifies the ADS_ACEFLAG_INHERIT_ACE flag which means the ACE can be inherited by child objects.

```
// Grant trustee the right to read the Telephone-Number property
// of all child objects in the Users container.
// {bf967a49-0de6-11d0-a285-00aa003049e2} is the schemaIDGUID of
// the Telephone-Number property.
hr = SetRight(
        pObject,   // IADs pointer to the object
        ADS_RIGHT_READ_PROP | ADS_RIGHT_WRITE_PROP,
        ADS_ACETYPE_ACCESS_ALLOWED_OBJECT,
        ADS_ACEFLAG_INHERIT_ACE,
        L"{bf967a49-0de6-11d0-a285-00aa003049e2}",
        NULL,      // no inherited object type GUID
        szTrustee
        );
```

Allow or deny access to a set of properties on the object

This C++ code fragment calls the *SetRight* subroutine to allow the trustee to read or write a specific set of properties on the object. You must specify ADS_ACETYPE_ACCESS_ALLOWED_OBJECT to indicate that this is an object-specific ACE.

A property set is defined by a **controlAccessRight** object in the Extended Rights container of the Configuration partition. To identify the property set in the ACE, you must specify the **rightsGUID** property of a **controlAccessRight** object. Note that this property set GUID is also set in the **attributeSecurityGUID** property of every **attributeSchema** object included in the property set. For more information, see *Extended Rights*.

This sample also specifies inheritance flags that make the ACE inheritable by child objects but ineffective on the immediate object. In addition, the sample specifies the GUID of the User class, which means that the ACE can be inherited only by objects of that class.

```
// Grant trustee the right to read or write a set of properties.
// {77B5B886-944A-11d1-AEBD-0000F80367C1} is a GUID that identifies
// a property set (rightsGUID of a controlAccessRight object).
// {bf967aba-0de6-11d0-a285-00aa003049e2} is the schemaIDGUID of the
// User class, so this ACE is inherited only by objects of that class.
hr = SetRight(
        pObject,  // IADs pointer to the object
        ADS_RIGHT_READ_PROP | ADS_RIGHT_WRITE_PROP,
        ADS_ACETYPE_ACCESS_ALLOWED_OBJECT,
        ADS_ACEFLAG_INHERIT_ACE | ADS_ACEFLAG_INHERIT_ONLY_ACE,
        L"{77B5B886-944A-11d1-AEBD-0000F80367C1}",
        L"{bf967aba-0de6-11d0-a285-00aa003049e2}",
        szTrustee
        );
```

Allow or deny the right to create a specific type of child object

This C++ code fragment calls the *SetRight* subroutine to allow a specified trustee to create and delete User objects in the subtree under the specified object. Note that the sample specifies the GUID of the User class, which means the ACE only allows the trustee to create User objects, not objects of other classes. You must specify ADS_ACETYPE_ACCESS_ALLOWED_OBJECT to indicate that this is an object-specific ACE.

```
// Grant trustee the right to create or delete User objects
// in the specified object.
// {bf967aba-0de6-11d0-a285-00aa003049e2} is the schemaIDGUID of the
// User class.
hr = SetRight(
        pObject,  // IADs pointer to the object
```

```
      ADS_RIGHT_DS_CREATE_CHILD | ADS_RIGHT_DS_DELETE_CHILD,
      ADS_ACETYPE_ACCESS_ALLOWED_OBJECT,
      0,          // not inheritable
      L"{bf967aba-0de6-11d0-a285-00aa003049e2}",
      NULL,       // no inherited object type GUID
      szTrustee
      );
```

For the **schemaIDGUID** of a predefined attribute or class, see the attribute or class reference page in the Active Directory Schema Reference in the *Active Directory Reference*. For sample code to retrieve a **schemaIDGUID** programmatically, see *Reading attributeSchema and classSchema Objects*.

Visual Basic

The following Visual Basic code has a *SetRight* subroutine that adds an ACE to the DACL of the security descriptor of a specified Active Directory object. The subroutine is multipurpose, allowing you to set any of the following types of ACEs.

- Allow or deny access to the entire object.
- Allow or deny access to a specific property on the object.
- Allow or deny access to a set of properties on the object.
- Allow or deny the right to create a specific type of child object.
- Set an ACE that can be inherited by all child objects or by child objects of a specified object class.

Here's the code for the *SetRight* subroutine. Following that code are several samples that show how to call SetRight to set different types of ACEs.

```
Sub SetRight(objectDN As String, _
            accessrights As Long, _
            accesstype As Long, _
            aceinheritflags As Long, _
            objectGUID As String, _
            inheritedObjectGUID As String, _
            trustee As String)
Dim dsobject As IADs
Dim sd As IADsSecurityDescriptor
Dim dacl As IADsAccessControlList
Dim newace As New AccessControlEntry
Dim lflags As Long

'Bind to the specified object
Set dsobject = GetObject(objectDN)

'Read the security descriptor on the object
```

(continued)

(continued)

```
Set sd = dsobject.Get("ntSecurityDescriptor")

'Get the DACL from the security descriptor.
Set dacl = sd.DiscretionaryAcl

'Set the properties of the new ACE.
newace.accessmask = accessrights
newace.AceType = accesstype
newace.aceflags = aceinheritflags
newace.trustee = trustee

'Set the GUID for the object type or inherited object type
lflags = 0
If Not objectGUID = vbNullString Then
newace.ObjectType = objectGUID
lflags = lflags Or &H1 'ADS_FLAG_OBJECT_TYPE_PRESENT
End If
If Not inheritedObjectGUID = vbNullString Then
newace.inheritedObjectType = inheritedObjectGUID
lflags = lflags Or &H2 'ADS_FLAG_INHERITED_OBJECT_TYPE_PRESENT
End If
If Not (lflags = 0) Then newace.Flags = lflags

'Now add the ACE to the DACL and to the security descriptor.
dacl.AddAce newace
sd.DiscretionaryAcl = dacl

'And apply it to the object.
dsobject.Put "ntSecurityDescriptor", sd
dsobject.setinfo
End Sub
```

Allow or deny access to the entire object

The following code fragment builds a binding string for the Users container and then calls the *SetRight* subroutine to set an ACE on the Users container. The first example simply sets an ACE that allows the trustee to read or write any property on the object.

```
Private Sub Form_Load()
Dim rootDSE As IADs
Dim objectDN As String
ADS_RIGHT_READ_PROP = &H10
ADS_RIGHT_WRITE_PROP = &H20

'Bind to the Users container in the local domain
Set rootDSE = GetObject("LDAP://rootDSE")
```

```
objectDN = "LDAP://cn=users," & rootDSE.Get("defaultNamingContext")

'Grant trustee the right to read/write any property.
SetRight objectDN, _
        ADS_RIGHT_READ_PROP Or ADS_RIGHT_WRITE_PROP, _
        ADS_ACETYPE_ACCESS_ALLOWED, _
        0, _
        vbNullString, _
        vbNullString, _
        "bfoot@Microsoft.com" 'trustee
End Sub
```

Allow or deny access to a specific property on the object

This code fragment calls the *SetRight* subroutine to allow the trustee to read or write a specific property on the object. Note that you must specify the **schemIDGUID** of the property and you must specify ADS_ACETYPE_ACCESS_ALLOWED_OBJECT to indicate that this is an object-specific ACE. This sample also specifies the ADS_ACEFLAG_INHERIT_ACE flag which means the ACE can be inherited by child objects.

```
'Grant trustee the right to read the Telephone-Number property
'of all child objects in the Users container.
'{bf967a49-0de6-11d0-a285-00aa003049e2} is the schemaIDGUID of
'the Telephone-Number property.
SetRight objectDN, _
        ADS_RIGHT_WRITE_PROP Or ADS_RIGHT_READ_PROP, _
        ADS_ACETYPE_ACCESS_ALLOWED_OBJECT, _
        ADS_ACEFLAG_INHERIT_ACE, _
        "{bf967a49-0de6-11d0-a285-00aa003049e2}", _
        vbNullString, _
        "bfoot@twokay.local" 'trustee
```

Allow or deny access to a set of properties on the object

This code fragment calls the *SetRight* subroutine to allow the trustee to read or write a specific set of properties on the object. You must specify ADS_ACETYPE_ACCESS_ALLOWED_OBJECT to indicate that this is an object-specific ACE.

A property set is defined by a **controlAccessRight** object in the Extended Rights container of the Configuration partition. To identify the property set in the ACE, you must specify the **rightsGUID** property of a **controlAccessRight** object. Note that this property set GUID is also set in the **attributeSecurityGUID** property of every **attributeSchema** object included in the property set. For more information, see *Extended Rights*.

This sample also specifies inheritance flags that make the ACE inheritable by child objects but ineffective on the immediate object. In addition, the sample specifies the GUID of the User class, which means that the ACE can be inherited only by objects of that class.

```
'Grant trustee the right to read or write a set of properties.
'{77B5B886-944A-11d1-AEBD-0000F80367C1} is a GUID that identifies
'a property set.
'{bf967aba-0de6-11d0-a285-00aa003049e2} is a GUID that identifies the
'User class, so this ACE is inherited only by objects of that class.
SetRight objectDN, _
         ADS_RIGHT_READ_PROP Or ADS_RIGHT_WRITE_PROP, _
         ADS_ACETYPE_ACCESS_ALLOWED_OBJECT, _
         ADS_ACEFLAG_INHERIT_ACE Or ADS_ACEFLAG_INHERIT_ONLY_ACE, _
         "{77B5B886-944A-11d1-AEBD-0000F80367C1}", _
         "{bf967aba-0de6-11d0-a285-00aa003049e2}", _
         "bfoot@Microsoft.com" 'trustee
End Sub
```

Allow or deny the right to create a specific type of child object

This code fragment calls the *SetRight* subroutine to allow a specified trustee to create and delete User objects in the subtree under the specified object. Note that the sample specifies the GUID of the User class, which means the ACE only allows the trustee to create User objects, not objects of other classes. You must specify ADS_ACETYPE_ACCESS_ALLOWED_OBJECT to indicate that this is an object-specific ACE.

```
'Grant trustee the right to create or delete User objects
'in the specified object.
'{bf967aba-0de6-11d0-a285-00aa003049e2} is a GUID that identifies the
'User class.
SetRight objectDN, _
         ADS_RIGHT_DS_CREATE_CHILD Or ADS_RIGHT_DS_DELETE_CHILD, _
         ADS_ACETYPE_ACCESS_ALLOWED_OBJECT, _
         0, _
         "{bf967aba-0de6-11d0-a285-00aa003049e2}", _
         vbNullString, _
         "bfoot@twokay.local" 'trustee
```

For the **schemaIDGUID** of a predefined attribute or class, see the attribute or class reference page in the Active Directory Schema Reference in the *Active Directory Reference*. For sample code to retrieve a schemaIDGUID programmatically, see *Reading attributeSchema and classSchema Objects*.

Setting Access Rights on the Entire Object

Certain permissions can only be set for the entire object, such as Delete, List Contents, and so on. Granular permissions such as the **Read** Property can also be set for entire object so that they apply to entire object.

To set permissions that apply to the entire object:

- Set **AceType** to ADS_ACETYPE_ACCESS_ALLOWED or ADS_ACETYPE_ACCESS_DENIED
- Set **ObjectType** and **InheritedObjectType** to NULL

For a discussion of the steps for creating an ACE, see *Setting Access Rights on an Object*.

For additional C++ and Visual Basic sample code for setting an ACE, see:

- *Example Code for Setting an ACE on a Directory Object*

Example Code for Setting Read Property Rights on an Object

The following code fragment contains a function that creates an ACE that assigns read access to all properties of the object to the specified trustee:

```
//Create an ACE that assigns read property rights to all
// properties on the object. This ACE is not inherited, that is,
// it applies only to the current object.
HRESULT CreateAceEffectiveReadAllProperties(
                        LPOLESTR szTrustee,
                        IDispatch **ppDispACE)

{


HRESULT hr = E_FAIL;
IADsAccessControlEntry *pACE = NULL;
//Create the COM object for the new ACE.
hr = CoCreateInstance(

                        CLSID_AccessControlEntry,
                        NULL,
                        CLSCTX_INPROC_SERVER,
                        IID_IADsAccessControlEntry,
                        (void **)&pACE
                        );
if (SUCCEEDED(hr))
{
    //Set the properties of the new ACE.
    //Set the access mask containing the rights to assign.
    //This function assigns read property rights.
    hr = pACE->put_AccessMask(ADS_RIGHT_DS_READ_PROP);
    //Set the trustee.
    hr = pACE->put_Trustee( szTrustee );
    //Set AceType
    hr = pACE->put_AceType( ADS_ACETYPE_ACCESS_ALLOWED );
    //For this function, set AceFlags so that ACE is not inherited
    // by child objects. You can set AceFlags to 0 or let it default
```

(continued)

(continued)

```
    // to 0 by not calling put_AceFlags.
  hr = pACE->put_AceFlags(0);
    //For this function, set ObjectType to NULL because the right
    // applies to all properties and set Flags to 0. You can also not
    // call these two methods and let them default to NULL.
  hr = pACE->put_ObjectType( NULL );
  hr = pACE->put_Flags(0);
    //Is not inherited, so set object type to NULL or let it
    // default to NULL by not calling the method.
  hr = pACE->put_InheritedObjectType( NULL );
    //Need to QI for IDispatch pointer to pass to the AddAce method.
  hr = pACE->QueryInterface(IID_IDispatch,(void**)ppDispACE);
}

return hr;
}
```

Setting Permissions to a Specific Property

Permissions can be set to apply to a specific property of an object.

To set permissions that apply to a specific property of an object:

- Set the **AccessMask** to ADS_RIGHT_DS_READ_PROP and/or ADS_RIGHT_DS_WRITE_PROP.

- Set **AceType** to ADS_ACETYPE_ACCESS_ALLOWED_OBJECT or ADS_ACETYPE_ACCESS_DENIED_OBJECT.

- Set **ObjectType** to the **schemaIDGUID** of the property. This is the schemaIDGUID of the **attributeSchema** object that defines the property in the schema. The GUID must be specified as a string of the form produced by the **StringFromGUID2** function in the COM library.

  For the **schemaIDGUID** of a predefined attribute, see the Active Directory Schema Reference in the Active Directory Reference. For sample code to retrieve a schemaIDGUID programmatically, see *Reading attributeSchema and classSchema Objects*.

- Set **Flags** to ADS_FLAG_OBJECT_TYPE_PRESENT.

For a discussion of the steps for creating an ACE, see *Setting Access Rights on an Object*.

For sample C++ and Visual Basic code for setting a property-specific ACE, see:

- *Example Code for Setting an ACE on a Directory Object*

Setting Permissions on a Group of Properties

Permissions can also be applied to a group of properties. A property group is identified by the GUID in the **rightsGUID** property of a **controlAccessRight** object. This GUID is set in the **attributeSecurityGUID** property of the attributeSchema object of each property in the group.

To set permissions that apply to a group of properties in an object:

- Set the **AccessMask** to ADS_RIGHT_DS_READ_PROP and/or ADS_RIGHT_DS_WRITE_PROP.

  Do not set the ADS_RIGHT_DS_CONTROL_ACCESS flag, which is used to specify an extended right only.
- Set **AceType** to ADS_ACETYPE_ACCESS_ALLOWED_OBJECT or ADS_ACETYPE_ACCESS_DENIED_OBJECT.
- Set **ObjectType** to the GUID of the property group. This is the **rightsGUID** property of the controlAccessRights object that identifies the property group. This GUID is also set as the attributeSecurityGUID in the attributeSchema object of each property in the group.
- Set **Flags** to ADS_FLAG_OBJECT_TYPE_PRESENT.

For a discussion of the steps for creating an ACE, see *Setting Access Rights on an Object*.

For additional C++ and Visual Basic sample code for setting an ACE for a property set, see:

- *Example Code for Setting an ACE on a Directory Object*

Example Code for Setting Permissions on a Group of Properties

The following code fragment contains a function that creates an ACE that assigns read/write access to the **telephoneNumber** property of user objects to the specified trustee:

```
//Create an ACE that assigns change (Read/Write) property rights
//to properties of the Personal Information property group in user
// objects. For this function, the ACE is inherited only;
//therefore, it is not an effective right on the current object.
HRESULT CreateAceChangePersonalInfoPropGroupOfUsers(
                    LPOLESTR szTrustee,
                    BOOL bAllowed,
                    IDispatch **ppDispACE
                    )
{

HRESULT hr = E_FAIL;
```

(continued)

(continued)

```
IADsAccessControlEntry *pACE = NULL;
//Create the COM object for the new ACE.
hr = CoCreateInstance(
                        CLSID_AccessControlEntry,
                        NULL,
                        CLSCTX_INPROC_SERVER,
                        IID_IADsAccessControlEntry,
                        (void **)&pACE
                     );
if (SUCCEEDED(hr))
{
    //Set the properties of the new ACE.
    //Set the access mask containing the rights to assign.
    //This function assigns
    //ADS_RIGHT_DS_READ_PROP|ADS_RIGHT_DS_WRITE_PROP to control change.
    hr = pACE->put_AccessMask(ADS_RIGHT_DS_READ_PROP|ADS_RIGHT_DS_WRITE_PROP);
    //Set the trustee.
    hr = pACE->put_Trustee( szTrustee );
    //AceType must be ADS_ACETYPE_ACCESS_ALLOWED_OBJECT or
ADS_ACETYPE_ACCESS_DENIED_OBJECT.
    if (bAllowed)
        hr = pACE->put_AceType( ADS_ACETYPE_ACCESS_ALLOWED_OBJECT );
    else
        hr = pACE->put_AceType( ADS_ACETYPE_ACCESS_DENIED_OBJECT );
  //Set Flags to
  // ADS_FLAG_OBJECT_TYPE_PRESENT|ADS_FLAG_INHERITED_OBJECT_TYPE_PRESENT
  // so that the right applies only to a specific property of the
  // specified object class.
    hr = pACE-
>put_Flags(ADS_FLAG_OBJECT_TYPE_PRESENT|ADS_FLAG_INHERITED_OBJECT_TYPE_PRESENT);
    //Set ObjectType to the rightsGUID of the
    //personalInformation controlAccessRight object.
    hr = pACE->put_ObjectType( L"{77B5B886-944A-11d1-AEBD-0000F80367C1}" );
    //For this function, set AceFlags so that ACE is inherited
    // by child objects but not effective on the current object.
    // Set AceFlags to ADS_ACEFLAG_INHERIT_ACE and
    // ADS_ACEFLAG_INHERIT_ONLY_ACE.
    hr = pACE-
>put_AceFlags(ADS_ACEFLAG_INHERIT_ACE|ADS_ACEFLAG_INHERIT_ONLY_ACE);
    //Set InheritedObjectType to schemaIDGUID of the user class.
    hr = pACE->put_InheritedObjectType( L"{bf967aba-0de6-11d0-a285-00aa003049e2}"
);
    //Need to QI for the IDispatch pointer to pass to the AddAce method.
```

```
    hr = pACE->QueryInterface(IID_IDispatch,(void**)ppDispACE);
}

return hr;
}
```

Setting Permissions on Child Object Operations

Permissions (such as Create Child and Delete Child) can also be granted or denied for operations on all subobjects or subobjects that are of a specific class.

To set permissions for a specific subobject type:

- Set **AceType** to ADS_ACETYPE_ACCESS_ALLOWED_OBJECT or ADS_ACETYPE_ACCESS_DENIED_OBJECT.
- Set **ObjectType** to the GUID for object class. This is the **schemaIDGUID** property of the classSchema object that defines the object class. If **ObjectType** is NULL, the ACE applies to subobjects of any class.
- Set **Flags** to ADS_FLAG_OBJECT_TYPE_PRESENT.

For a discussion of the steps for creating an ACE, see *Setting Access Rights on an Object*.

For additional C++ and Visual Basic sample code for setting an ACE that controls child object operations, see:

- *Example Code for Setting an ACE on a Directory Object*

Example Code for Setting Permissions on Child Object Operations

The following code fragment contains a function that creates an ACE that assigns creation rights for user objects to the specified trustee:

```
//Create an ACE that assigns the right to create User objects
//beneath the current object.
//For this function, the ACE is inherited by all subobjects
//and is an effective right on the current object.
HRESULT CreateAceCreateUsers(
                        LPOLESTR szTrustee,
                        BOOL bAllowed,
                        IDispatch **ppDispACE
                        )

{

HRESULT hr = E_FAIL;
IADsAccessControlEntry *pACE = NULL;
//Create the COM object for the new ACE.
hr  = CoCreateInstance(
                        CLSID_AccessControlEntry,
```

(continued)

(continued)

```
                             NULL,
                             CLSCTX_INPROC_SERVER,
                             IID_IADsAccessControlEntry,
                             (void **)&pACE
                         );
if (SUCCEEDED(hr))
{
    //Set the properties of the new ACE.
    //Set the access mask containing the rights to assign.
    //This function assigns rights to create objects.
    hr = pACE->put_AccessMask(ADS_RIGHT_DS_CREATE_CHILD);
    //Set the trustee.
    hr = pACE->put_Trustee( szTrustee );
    //AceType must be ADS_ACETYPE_ACCESS_ALLOWED_OBJECT or
    //ADS_ACETYPE_ACCESS_DENIED_OBJECT.
    if (bAllowed)
        hr = pACE->put_AceType( ADS_ACETYPE_ACCESS_ALLOWED_OBJECT );
    else
        hr = pACE->put_AceType( ADS_ACETYPE_ACCESS_DENIED_OBJECT );
    //Set Flags to ADS_FLAG_OBJECT_TYPE_PRESENT
    // so that the right applies to the creation of a specific
    // object class within the current object and all its subobjects.
    hr = pACE->put_Flags(ADS_FLAG_OBJECT_TYPE_PRESENT);
    //Set ObjectType to the schemaIDGUID of the user class
    // so that the right controls creation of user objects.
    hr = pACE->put_ObjectType( L"{bf967aba-0de6-11d0-a285-00aa003049e2}" );
    //For this function, set AceFlags so that ACE is inherited
    // by child objects
    hr = pACE->put_AceFlags(ADS_ACEFLAG_INHERIT_ACE);
    //Set InheritedObjectType to NULL so that it is inherited
    // by all subobjects.
    hr = pACE->put_InheritedObjectType(NULL);
    //Need to QI for the IDispatch pointer to pass to the AddAce method.
    hr = pACE->QueryInterface(IID_IDispatch,(void**)ppDispACE);
}

return hr;
}
```

How Security Descriptors are Set on New Directory Objects

When you create a new object in the Active Directory, you can explicitly create a security descriptor and then set that security descriptor as the object's **nTSecurityDescriptor** property. For a description of how to do this, see *Creating a Security Descriptor*.

Active Directory uses the following rules to set the DACL in the new object's security descriptor.

1. If you explicitly specify a security descriptor when you create the object, the system merges any inheritable ACEs from the parent object into the specified DACL unless the SE_DACL_PROTECTED bit is set in the security descriptor's control bits.

2. If you do not specify a security descriptor, the system builds the object's DACL by merging any inheritable ACEs from the parent object into the default DACL from the **classSchema** object for the object's class.

3. If the schema does not have a default DACL, the object's DACL is the default DACL from the primary or impersonation token of the creator.

4. If there is no specified, inherited, or default DACL, the system creates the object with no DACL, which allows everyone full access to the object.

The system uses a similar algorithm to build a SACL for a directory service object.

The owner and primary group in the new object's security descriptor are set to the values you specify in the **nTSecurityDescriptor** property when you create the object. If you do not set these values, Active Directory uses the following rules to set them

Owner

The owner in a default security descriptor is set to the default owner SID from the primary or impersonation token of the creating process. For most users, the default owner SID is the same as the SID that identifies the user's account. Note that for users who are members of the built-in administrators group, the system automatically sets the default owner SID in the access token to the administrators group; therefore, objects created by a member of the administrators group are typically owned by the administrators group. To get or set the default owner in an access token, call the **GetTokenInformation** or **SetTokenInformation** function with the **TOKEN_OWNER** structure.

Primary Group

The primary group in a default security descriptor is set to the default primary group from the creator's primary or impersonation token. Note that primary group is not used in the context of Active Directory.

For more information on ACE inheritance, see *Inheritance and Delegation of Administration*.

For more information on the default security descriptors in the schema, see *Default Security Descriptor*.

For more information about **classSchema** objects, see *Active Directory Schema*.

Creating a Security Descriptor

Using ADSI, you can create a security descriptor and set it as a new object's **nTSecurityDescriptor** property or use it to replace an existing object's **nTSecurityDescriptor** property.

Use the following steps for creating a security descriptor for an object (see the code fragment that follows for an example):

1. Use **CoCreateInstance** to create the ADSI COM object for the new security descriptor and get an **IADsSecurityDescriptor** interface pointer to that object. Note that the class ID is **CLSID_SecurityDescriptor**.

2. Use the **IADsSecurityDescriptor::put_Owner** method to set the owner of the object. The trustee is a user, group, or other security principal. Your application should use the value from the appropriate property from the user or group object of the trustee to whom you want to apply the ACE.

3. Use the **IADsSecurityDescriptor::put_Control** method to control whether DACLs and SACLs are inherited by the object from its parent container.

4. Use **CoCreateInstance** to create the ADSI COM object for the DACL for the new security descriptor and get an **IADsAccessControlList** interface pointer to that object. Note that the class ID is **CLSID_AccessControlList**.

5. For each ACE to add to the DACL, use **CoCreateInstance** to create the ADSI COM object for the new ACE and get an **IADsAccessControlEntry** interface pointer to that object. Note that the class ID is CLSID_AccessControlEntry.

6. For each ACE to add to the DACL, set the properties of the ACE using the property methods of the ACE's **IADsAccessControlEntry** object. For more information on the properties to set on an ACE, see Setting Access Rights on an Object.

7. For each ACE to add to the DACL, use the **QueryInterface** method on the **IADsAccessControlEntry** object to get an **IDispatch** pointer. The **AddAce** method requires an **IDispatch** interface pointer to the ACE.

8. For each ACE to add to the DACL, use **IADsAccessControlList::AddAce** to add the new ACE to the DACL. Note that the order of the ACEs within the ACL can affect the evaluation of access to the object. The correct access to the object may require you to create a new ACL, add the ACEs from the existing ACL in the correct order to the new ACL, and then replace the existing ACL in the security descriptor with the new ACL. For more information, see *Order of ACEs in a DACL* in the Platform SDK.

9. Follow steps 4-8 to create the SACL for the new security descriptor.

10. Use the **IADsSecurityDescriptor::put_DiscretionaryAcl** method to set the DACL.

11. Use the **IADsSecurityDescriptor::put_SystemAcl** method to set the DACL.

12. Get an **IADs** interface pointer to the object.

13. Use the **IADs::Put** method to write the security descriptor to the object's **nTSecurityDescriptor** property to the property cache.

14. Use the **IADs::SetInfo** method to update the property on the object in the directory.

Inheritance and Delegation of Administration

Active Directory supports inheritance of permissions down the object tree to allow administration to be done at higher levels in the tree. This allows administrators to set up inheritable permissions on objects near the root (such as domain and organizational units) and have those permissions flow down automatically to various objects in the tree.

Inheritance can be set on a per-ACE basis. You can specify the following flags in the **AceFlags** to control inheritance of the ACE:

ADS_ACEFLAG_INHERIT_ACE
   This flag causes the ACE to be inherited down in the tree.

ADS_ACEFLAG_NO_PROPAGATE_INHERIT_ACE
   This flag causes the ACE to be inherited down only one level in the tree.

ADS_ACEFLAG_INHERIT_ONLY_ACE
   This flag causes the ACE to be ignored on the object it is specified on and only be inherited down and be effective where it has been inherited.

In addition to setting inheritance, Active Directory supports object specific inheritance. This allows the inheritable ACEs to be inherited down the tree but be effective only on a specific type of object. This is extremely useful in delegating administration. For example, this can be used to set an object specific inheritable ACE at an organizational unit that allows a group to have full control on all user objects in the organizational unit but nothing else. Thereby, the management of users in that organizational unit gets delegated to the users in that group.

- *Security Groups and Delegation of Service Administration.* Use Security groups to define and delegate administrative roles associated with your application server. For example, your service may be associated with a group MyService Admins. Users who are identified as the MyService administrators will be added to MyService Admins group. The setup program for MyService can set ACLs on the directory to allow MyService Admins sufficient permissions to read/write MyService-related attributes, create MyService specific objects, and so on.

- *Security Groups and Roles for Computers Running Your Service.* Use security groups to define the set of computers that are granted access to your service's objects in the directory. For example, your service may be associated with a group MyService Servers. All computers running the MyService server are added to MyService Servers group and this group can then be given access to parts of the directory where MyService servers need to read/write information. The setup program for MyService can set ACLs on the directory to allow MyService Servers sufficient permissions to read/write MyService-related attributes, create MyService specific objects, and so on.

Access Control Inheritance

ACEs in an object's ACL can belong to one of two categories:

- *Effective ACL.* ACEs in this category apply to the object itself.
- *Inherit ACL.* ACEs in this category are inherited by objects created in the container.

Each ACE in the DACL can be in one or more categories. The categories for where an ACE belongs are determined by the inheritance control flags set in the ACE.

There are three inheritance control flags that can be set in the **AceFlags** property of an ACE:

ADS_ACEFLAG_INHERIT_ACE
   This flag indicates that the ACE is part of the inherit ACL and that child objects will inherit the inheritance control flags of this ACE.

ADS_ACEFLAG_NO_PROPAGATE_INHERIT_ACE
   This flag indicates that the ACE is part of the inherit ACL, but that no inheritance control flags are propagated to direct child objects (direct descendants) and the ACE is effective on the direct child objects.

ADS_ACEFLAG_INHERIT_ONLY_ACE
   This flag indicates that the ACE is not part of effective ACL.

   If this flag is not set, then the ACE is part of the effective ACL. This flag is useful for setting permissions inheritable by subobjects, but do not affect accessibility of the container itself. For example, if an ACE is intended to be inherited by user objects in a organizational unit, there is a good chance that it should not be enforced for access to the organizational unit itself.

The ADS_ACEFLAG_NO_PROPAGATE_INHERIT_ACE and ADS_ACEFLAG_INHERIT_ONLY_ACE flags are meaningful only if ADS_ACEFLAG_INHERIT_ACE is present. This is because the ADS_ACEFLAG_INHERIT_ACE flag adds inheritance behavior to an inheritable ACE but does not define the type of inheritance. The ADS_ACEFLAG_NO_PROPAGATE_INHERIT_ACE and ADS_ACEFLAG_INHERIT_ONLY_ACE flags define a specific type of inheritance behavior.

Note that the system also sets the following flags based on the type and state of the ACE:

ADS_ACEFLAG_INHERITED_ACE
   This flag indicates that the ACE was inherited.

ADS_ACEFLAG_VALID_INHERIT_FLAGS
   This flag indicates that the inherit flags are valid.

The following table shows the effects of the different flag combinations for the **AceFlags** property of an ACE.

AceFlags	Effect on object containing the ACE	Effect on direct child objects	Effect on objects below direct children
No flags set.	Effective ACE: ACE applies to the object.	ACE is not inherited.	ACE is not inherited.
ADS_ACEFLAG_INHERIT_ACE	Effective ACE	ACE is inherited. ACE is an effective ACE.	ACE is inherited. ACE is an effective ACE.
ADS_ACEFLAG_INHERIT_ACE | ADS_ACEFLAG_INHERIT_ONLY_ACE	Not an Effective ACE: ACE does not apply to the object.	ACE is inherited. ACE is an effective ACE.	ACE is inherited. ACE is an effective ACE.
ADS_ACEFLAG_INHERIT_ACE | ADS_ACEFLAG_NO_PROPAGATE_ INHERIT_ACE	Effective ACE	ACE is inherited but without inheritance flags. ACE is an Effective ACE	ACE is not inherited.
ADS_ACEFLAG_INHERIT_ACE | ADS_ACEFLAG_INHERIT_ONLY_ACE | ADS_ACEFLAG_NO_PROPAGATE_ INHERIT_ACE	Not an Effective ACE.	ACE is inherited but without inheritance flags. ACE is an Effective ACE.	ACE is not inherited.

Setting Rights to Specific Types of Objects

To set an ACE that can be inherited only by a specific class of objects, you must do the following.

- Set **AceType** of ADS_ACETYPE_ACCESS_ALLOWED_OBJECT or ADS_ACETYPE_ACCESS_DENIED_OBJECT.
- Set **AceFlag** to include the ADS_ACEFLAG_INHERIT_ACE flag
- Set **InheritedObjectType** to the **schemaIDGUID** of the object class that can inherit the ACE.
- Set **Flags** to ADS_FLAG_INHERITED OBJECT_TYPE_PRESENT.

Important You must set ADS_ACEFLAG_INHERIT_ACE to cause the ACE to be inherited. In addition, you must set ADS_ACEFLAG_INHERIT_ONLY_ACE if the object type this ACE applies to does not match the object type of the container where the ACE is specified. If this is not done, the ACE will also become effective on the container and can grant unexpected rights.

For C++ and Visual Basic additional sample code for setting this kind of ACE, see:

* *Example Code for Setting an ACE on a Directory Object*

Example Code for Setting Rights to Specific Types of Objects

The following code fragment contains a function that creates an ACE that assigns rights that are inherited by the specified type of object but are not effective on the current object:

```
//Create an ACE that is inherited by child objects of the specified type
//but does not apply to the current object.
//This ACE is also propagated to all descendants of the current object.
HRESULT CreateAceNoEffectiveInheritObject(LPOLESTR szTrustee,
                          long lAccessRights,
                          long lAccessType,
                          LPOLESTR szObjectGUID,
                          LPOLESTR szInheritedObjectGUID,
                          IDispatch **ppDispACE)

{

HRESULT hr = E_FAIL;
IADsAccessControlEntry *pACE = NULL;
long lFlags = 0L;
//Create the COM object for the new ACE.
hr  = CoCreateInstance(

                          CLSID_AccessControlEntry,
                          NULL,
                          CLSCTX_INPROC_SERVER,
                          IID_IADsAccessControlEntry,
                          (void **)&pACE
                      );
if (SUCCEEDED(hr))
{
    //Set the properties of the new ACE.
    //Set the access mask containing the rights to assign.
    hr = pACE->put_AccessMask(lAccessRights);
    //Set the trustee.
    hr = pACE->put_Trustee( szTrustee );
    //Set AceType
```

```
    hr = pACE->put_AceType( lAccessType );
    //For this function, set AceFlags so that ACE is inherited
    // by child objects but not effective on the current object.
    // Set AceFlags to ADS_ACEFLAG_INHERIT_ACE and ADS_ACEFLAG_INHERIT_ONLY_ACE.
    hr = pACE-
>put_AceFlags(ADS_ACEFLAG_INHERIT_ACE|ADS_ACEFLAG_INHERIT_ONLY_ACE);
    //If an szObjectGUID is specified, add ADS_FLAG_OBJECT_TYPE_PRESENT
    // flag to the lFlags mask and set the ObjectType.
    if (szObjectGUID)
    {
        lFlags |= ADS_FLAG_OBJECT_TYPE_PRESENT;
        hr = pACE->put_ObjectType( szObjectGUID );
    }
    //If an szInheritedObjectGUID is specified, add
    // ADS_FLAG_INHERITED_OBJECT_TYPE_PRESENT flag to the lFlags

mask
    //and set the InheritedObjectType.
    if (szInheritedObjectGUID)
    {
        lFlags |= ADS_FLAG_INHERITED_OBJECT_TYPE_PRESENT;
        hr = pACE->put_InheritedObjectType( szInheritedObjectGUID );
    }
    //Set flags if ObjectType or InheritedObjectType were set.
    if (lFlags)
    {
        hr = pACE->put_Flags(lFlags);
    }
    //Need to QI for IDispatch pointer to pass to the AddAce method.
    hr = pACE->QueryInterface(IID_IDispatch,(void**)ppDispACE);
}

return hr;
}
```

Setting Rights to Specific Properties of Specific Types of Objects

Property-specific permissions can be used in combination with object specific inheritance
to provide the very powerful and granular delegation of administration. You can set a
property-specific object-inheritable ACE to allow a specified user or group to read and/or
write a specific attribute on a specified class of child objects in a container. For example,
you could set an ACE on an organizational unit to allow a group to read and write the
telephone number attribute of all user objects in the organizational unit.

To set property-specific object-inheritable ACEs:

• Set **AceType** to ADS_ACETYPE_ACCESS_ALLOWED_OBJECT or
  ADS_ACETYPE_ACCESS_DENIED_OBJECT.

- Set **ObjectType** to the **schemaIDGUID** of the attribute. For example, the **schemaIDGUID** of the **telephoneNumber** attribute is {bf967a49-0de6-11d0-a285-00aa003049e2}.
- Set **AceFlag** to ADS_ACEFLAG_INHERIT_ACE.
- Set **InheritedObjectType** to the **schemaIDGUID** of the object class that can inherit the ACE. For example, the **schemaIDGUID** of the **user** class is {bf967aba-0de6-11d0-a285-00aa003049e2}.
- Set **Flags** to ADS_FLAG_OBJECT_TYPE_PRESENT and ADS_FLAG_INHERITED OBJECT_TYPE_PRESENT.

Important You must set ADS_ACEFLAG_INHERIT_ACE to cause the ACE to be inherited. In addition, you must set ADS_ACEFLAG_INHERIT_ONLY_ACE if the object type this ACE applies to does not match the object type of the container where the ACE is specified. If this is not done, the ACE will also become effective on the container and can grant unexpected rights.

For C++ and Visual Basic sample code for setting this kind of ACE, see:

- *Example Code for Setting an ACE on a Directory Object*

Protecting Objects from the Effects of Inherited Rights

As discussed in Inheritance and Delegation of Administration, ACEs can be set on a container object (such as an organizational unit, domainDNS, container, and so on) and propagated to child objects (based on the **AceFlag** property set on those ACEs).

If you have a highly secured object or an object whose ACEs you want to explicitly control (such as a private OU or a special user), you may want to prevent ACEs from being propagated to the object by its parent container (or its parent container's predecessors).

You can use the **IADsSecurityDescriptor::put_Control** method to control whether DACLs and SACLs are inherited by the object from its parent container.

The **Control** property can be used to protect an object from the effects of inherited ACEs. The following flags force access control to be set explicitly on the object and prevent a user from effectively modifying access control to the object by setting inheritable ACEs on the object's parent container (or its parent container's predecessors):

Flag	Effect
SE_DACL_PROTECTED	Prevents ACEs set on the DACL of the parent container (and any objects above the parent container in the directory hierarchy) from being applied to the object's DACL.

Flag	Effect
SE_SACL_PROTECTED	Prevents ACEs set on the SACL of the parent container (and any objects above the parent container in the directory hierarchy) from being applied to the object's SACL.

Note that the SE_DACL_PRESENT flag needs to be present to set SE_DACL_PROTECTED and SE_SACL_PRESENT needs to be present to set SE_SACL_PROTECTED.

Example Code for Setting and Removing SACL and DACL Protection in the Control Property

The following code fragment is a function that sets/removes the SE_DACL_PROTECTED and SE_SACL_PROTECTED bits in the **Control** property of an object's security descriptor.

```
// This function sets/removes the SE_DACL_PROTECTED and
// SE_SACL_PROTECTED bits in the Control property.
// Valid values for lControl:
//  0L means remove both SE_DACL_PROTECTED and SE_SACL_PROTECTED
//  if they are set. SE_DACL_PROTECTED means add SE_DACL_PROTECTED
//  and remove SE_SACL_PROTECTED.
// ...and so on.
// Note that SE_DACL_PRESENT must be present to set SE_DACL_PROTECTED
// and SE_SACL_PRESENT must be present to set SE_SACL_PROTECTED.

HRESULT SetSDInheritProtect(
                IADs *pObject,
                long lControl
                )

{
HRESULT hr = E_FAIL;

VARIANT var;
IADsSecurityDescriptor *pSD = NULL;

long lSetControl;
bool bChange = FALSE;

if (pObject = NULL)
    return hr;

VariantClear(&var);
```

(continued)

(continued)

```
// Get the nTSecurityDescriptor
LPOLESTR szAttribute = L"nTSecurityDescriptor";
hr = pObject->Get(szAttribute,&var);
if (SUCCEEDED(hr))
{
    // Type should be VT_DISPATCH--an IDispatch ptr to
    // the security descriptor object.
    if (var.vt==VT_DISPATCH)
    {
        // Use V_DISPATCH macro to get the IDispatch pointer from
        // VARIANT structure and QI for IADsSecurityDescriptor ptr.
        hr = V_DISPATCH( &var )->QueryInterface(IID_IADsSecurityDescriptor,
(void**)&pSD);
        if (SUCCEEDED(hr))
        {
            // Get the Control property
            hr = pSD->get_Control(&lSetControl);
            // Parse the lControl and check for the bits in lSetControl

            // Check if SE_DACL_PROTECTED needs to be set.
            if (lControl & SE_DACL_PROTECTED)
            {
                // Check if SE_DACL_PROTECTED is NOT set.
                if (!(lSetControl & SE_DACL_PROTECTED))
                {
                    lSetControl = lSetControl | SE_DACL_PROTECTED;
                    bChange = TRUE;
                }
            }
            // SE_DACL_PROTECTED needs to be removed
            else
            {
                if ((lSetControl &SE_DACL_PROTECTED)==SE_DACL_PROTECTED)
                {
                    lSetControl=lSetControl-SE_DACL_PROTECTED;
                    bChange = TRUE;
                }
            }

            //Check if SE_SACL_PROTECTED needs to be set.
            if (lControl & SE_SACL_PROTECTED)
            {
                //Check if SE_SACL_PROTECTED is NOT set.
                if (!(lSetControl & SE_SACL_PROTECTED))
```

```
                {
                    lSetControl = lSetControl | SE_SACL_PROTECTED;
                    bChange = TRUE;
                }
            }
            //SE_SACL_PROTECTED needs to be removed
            else
            {
                if ((lSetControl &SE_SACL_PROTECTED)==SE_SACL_PROTECTED)
                {
                    lSetControl=lSetControl-SE_SACL_PROTECTED;
                    bChange = TRUE;
                }
            }

            //If there was change to the Control property,
            //write it to the Security Descriptor,
            //write the SD to object, and then call SetInfo
            //to write the object to the directory.
            if (bChange)
            {
                hr = pSD->put_Control(lSetControl);
                if (SUCCEEDED(hr))
                {
                    hr = pObject->Put(szAttribute,var);
                    if (SUCCEEDED(hr))
                    {
                        hr = pObject->SetInfo();
                    }
                }
            }
        }
        if (pSD)
            pSD->Release();
    }
}
VariantClear(&var);
return hr;
}
```

Default Security Descriptor

Active Directory also provides the capability of specifying default security for each type of object. This is specified in the **defaultSecurityDescriptor** attribute in the **classSchema** object definition in the Active Directory schema. This security descriptor is used to provide default protection on the object if there is no security descriptor specified during the creation of the object.

Note   ACEs from a default security descriptor are treated as if they were specified as part of object creation. Therefore, the default ACEs are placed in front of inherited ACEs and override them as appropriate. See *Order of ACEs in a DACL*.

The **defaultSecurityDescriptor** is specified in a special string format using the Security Descriptor Definition Language (SDDL). There are two functions provided to convert binary form of the security descriptor to string format and vice versa. These functions are:

- **ConvertSecurityDescriptorToStringSecurityDescriptor**
- **ConvertStringSecurityDescriptorToSecurityDescriptor**

For the default security descriptors of the predefined object classes, see the class reference pages in the Active Directory Schema Reference of the *Active Directory Reference*.

For sample code that reads or modifies the **defaultSecurityDescriptor** property of an object class, see *Reading the defaultSecurityDescriptor for an Object Class* and *Modifying the defaultSecurityDescriptor for an Object Class*.

Reading the defaultSecurityDescriptor for an Object Class

Using ADSI, you can read the **defaultSecurityDescriptor** for an object class.

▶ **To read the defaultSecurityDescriptor for an Object Class in C/C++**

If you are using ADSI, use the following steps for reading **defaultSecurityDescriptor** for an object class (see the following code fragment for an example):

1. Get an **IADs** interface pointer to the **classSchema** object for the object class.
2. Use the **IADs::Get** method to get the default security descriptor of the object. The name of the property containing the security descriptor is **defaultSecurityDescriptor**. The property will be returned as a **VARIANT** containing a BSTR with the default security descriptor in SDDL string format.
3. Use the **ConvertStringSecurityDescriptorToSecurityDescriptor** function to convert the SDDL string form to a security descriptor.
4. Use the Win32 Security APIs to read the parts of the security descriptor: **GetSecurityDescriptorDacl**, **GetSecurityDescriptorSacl**, **GetSecurityDescriptorOwner**, and **GetSecurityDescriptorControl**.

Example Code for Reading defaultSecurityDescriptor

The following code is a program that reads the **defaultSecurityDescriptor** for a specified object class:

```
#include <stdio.h>
#include <wchar.h>
#include <objbase.h>
#include <activeds.h>
#include <ACCCTRL.h>
//For security descriptor control flags
#include <winnt.h>
#define _WIN32_WINNT 0x0500
#include <Sddl.h>

HRESULT ReadDefaultSecurityDescriptor( IADs *pObject );
int SDParseControlMasks( long lCtrl );
int SDParseAccessMask( long lCtrl );

int main(int argc, char *argv[])
{
LPOLESTR szPath = new OLECHAR[MAX_PATH];
LPOLESTR pszBuffer  = new WCHAR[MAX_PATH];
HRESULT hr = S_OK;
IADs *pObject = NULL;
VARIANT var;

wprintf(L"This program displays the default security descriptor of an object class\n");
wprintf(L"Specify the object class:");
_getws(pszBuffer);
if (!pszBuffer)
    return TRUE;
wcscpy(szPath, L"LDAP://cn=");
wcscat(szPath, pszBuffer);
wcscat(szPath, L",");

// Intialize COM.
CoInitialize(NULL);

// Get rootDSE and the schema container's DN.
// Bind to current user's domain using current user's security context.
hr = ADsOpenObject(L"LDAP://rootDSE",
                NULL,
                NULL,
                ADS_SECURE_AUTHENTICATION, //Use Secure Authentication
```

(continued)

(continued)

```
                IID_IADs,
                (void**)&pObject);

if (SUCCEEDED(hr))
{
    hr = pObject->Get(L"schemaNamingContext",&var);
    if (SUCCEEDED(hr))
    {
        wcscat(szPath,var.bstrVal);
        VariantClear(&var);
        if (pObject)
        {
            pObject->Release();
            pObject = NULL;
        }
        hr = ADsOpenObject(szPath,
                    NULL,
                    NULL,
                    ADS_SECURE_AUTHENTICATION, //Use Secure Authentication
                    IID_IADs,
                    (void**)&pObject);
        if (SUCCEEDED(hr))
        {
            wprintf(L"***********Read the default SD for the %s class***********\n",
pszBuffer);
            hr = ReadDefaultSecurityDescriptor(
                            pObject
                            );
        }
    }
}

if (FAILED(hr))
    wprintf(L"Failed with the following HRESULT: %x\n",hr);

if (pObject)
    pObject->Release();

// Uninitialize COM
CoUninitialize();
return TRUE;
}
```

```
HRESULT ReadDefaultSecurityDescriptor( IADs *pObject )
{
HRESULT hr = E_FAIL;
PSECURITY_DESCRIPTOR pSDCNV = NULL;
BOOL bDaclPresent = FALSE;
BOOL bDaclDefaulted = FALSE;
PACL pDacl = NULL;
LPVOID pAce = NULL;
BYTE bAceType, bAceFlags;
PSID pSID = NULL;
DWORD dAccessMask;
OLECHAR szTrusteeName[MAX_PATH];
DWORD cbName = 0L;
OLECHAR szTrusteeDomainName[MAX_PATH];
DWORD cbReferencedDomainName = 0L;
SID_NAME_USE TrusteeType;
PACCESS_ALLOWED_ACE paace = NULL;
PACCESS_ALLOWED_OBJECT_ACE poace = NULL;
DWORD dFlags = 0L;
VARIANT var;
LPOLESTR szGUID = new WCHAR [39];

    hr = pObject->Get(L"defaultSecurityDescriptor",&var);
    if (SUCCEEDED(hr))
    {
        //Type should be VT_BSTR.
        if (var.vt==VT_BSTR)
        {
            wprintf(L"Default SD: %s\n", var.bstrVal);
            if (ConvertStringSecurityDescriptorToSecurityDescriptor(var.bstrVal,
                                                        SDDL_REVISION_1,
                                                        &pSDCNV,
                                                        NULL
                                                        ))
            {
                //Read the security descriptor.
                //Get the DACL
                if (GetSecurityDescriptorDacl(
                    pSDCNV, // address of security descriptor
                    &bDaclPresent, // address of flag for presence of disc. ACL
                    &pDacl,  // address of pointer to ACL
                    &bDaclDefaulted // address of flag for default disc. ACL
                    ))
                {
                    printf("Ace count: %d\n",pDacl->AceCount);
```

(continued)

(continued)

```
for (WORD i = 0; i < pDacl->AceCount; i++ )
{
    //Get the ACE
    if (GetAce( pDacl, // pointer to access-control list
            i, // index of ACE to retrieve
            &pAce // pointer to pointer to ACE
            ))
    {
        wprintf(L"**** ACE %d of %d ****\n", i+1, pDacl->AceCount);
        bAceType = ((ACE_HEADER *)pAce)->AceType;
        bAceFlags = ((ACE_HEADER *)pAce)->AceFlags;

        switch (bAceType)
        {
        case ACCESS_ALLOWED_ACE_TYPE:
            printf("ACE Type: ACCESS_ALLOWED_ACE_TYPE\n");
            dAccessMask = ((ACCESS_ALLOWED_ACE *)pAce)->Mask;
            paace = (PACCESS_ALLOWED_ACE)pAce;
            pSID = (PSID)&(paace->SidStart);
            break;
        case ACCESS_DENIED_ACE_TYPE:
            printf("ACE Type: ACCESS_DENIED_ACE_TYPE\n");
            dAccessMask = ((ACCESS_DENIED_ACE *)pAce)->Mask;
            paace = (PACCESS_ALLOWED_ACE)pAce;
            pSID = (PSID)&(paace->SidStart);
            break;
        case ACCESS_ALLOWED_OBJECT_ACE_TYPE:
            printf("ACE Type: ACCESS_ALLOWED_OBJECT_ACE_TYPE\n");
            dAccessMask = ((ACCESS_ALLOWED_OBJECT_ACE *)pAce)->Mask;
            poace = (PACCESS_ALLOWED_OBJECT_ACE)pAce;
            //Check Flags to see
            //if object type and/or inherited object type is set.
            dFlags = poace->Flags;
            if (dFlags & ACE_OBJECT_TYPE_PRESENT)
            {
                //Convert GUID to string.
                ::StringFromGUID2(poace->ObjectType, szGUID, 39);
                //Print the GUID
                wprintf(L"ObjectType GUID: %s\n",szGUID);
            }
            //Print the inherited object type
            //If both GUIDs are present, go to the member.
            if ( (dFlags & ACE_OBJECT_TYPE_PRESENT)
                && (dFlags & ACE_INHERITED_OBJECT_TYPE_PRESENT)
```

```
            )
        {
            //Convert GUID to string.
            ::StringFromGUID2(poace->InheritedObjectType, szGUID,
39);

            //Print the GUID
            wprintf(L"Inherited ObjectType GUID: %s\n",szGUID);
        }
        //If only the inherited object type is present,
        //we need to go to the ObjectType member.
        if ( (!(dFlags & ACE_OBJECT_TYPE_PRESENT))
            && (dFlags & ACE_INHERITED_OBJECT_TYPE_PRESENT)
            )
        {

            //Convert GUID to string.
            ::StringFromGUID2(poace->ObjectType, szGUID, 39);
            //Print the GUID
            wprintf(L"Inherited ObjectType GUID: %s\n",szGUID);
        }

        //Get the SID from the ACE.
        if ( (dFlags & ACE_OBJECT_TYPE_PRESENT)
            && (dFlags & ACE_INHERITED_OBJECT_TYPE_PRESENT)
            )
        {
          pSID = (PSID)&(poace->SidStart);
        }
        else if (dFlags & ACE_OBJECT_TYPE_PRESENT)
        {
          pSID = (PSID)&(poace->InheritedObjectType);
        }
        else if (dFlags & ACE_INHERITED_OBJECT_TYPE_PRESENT)
        {
          pSID = (PSID)&(poace->InheritedObjectType);
        }
        break;
    case ACCESS_DENIED_OBJECT_ACE_TYPE:
      printf("ACCESS_DENIED_OBJECT_ACE_TYPE\n");
      dAccessMask = ((ACCESS_DENIED_OBJECT_ACE *)pAce)->Mask;
      poace = (PACCESS_ALLOWED_OBJECT_ACE)pAce;
      //Check Flags to see
      //if object type and/or inherited object type is set.
      dFlags = poace->Flags;
      if (dFlags & ACE_OBJECT_TYPE_PRESENT)
      {
```

(continued)

(continued)

```
                          //Convert GUID to string.
                          ::StringFromGUID2(poace->ObjectType, szGUID, 39);
                          //Print the GUID
                          wprintf(L"ObjectType GUID: %s\n",szGUID);
                  }
                  //Print the inherited object type
                  //If both GUIDs are present, go to the member.
                  if ( (dFlags & ACE_OBJECT_TYPE_PRESENT)
                      && (dFlags & ACE_INHERITED_OBJECT_TYPE_PRESENT)
                      )
                  {
                      //Convert GUID to string.
                      ::StringFromGUID2(poace->InheritedObjectType, szGUID,
39);

                      //Print the GUID
                      wprintf(L"Inherited ObjectType GUID: %s\n",szGUID);
                  }
                  //If only the inherited object type is present,
                  //we need to go to the ObjectType member.
                  if ( (!(dFlags & ACE_OBJECT_TYPE_PRESENT))
                      && (dFlags & ACE_INHERITED_OBJECT_TYPE_PRESENT)
                      )
                  {
                      //Convert GUID to string.
                      ::StringFromGUID2(poace->ObjectType, szGUID, 39);
                      //Print the GUID
                      wprintf(L"Inherited ObjectType GUID: %s\n",szGUID);
                  }

                  //Get the SID from the ACE.
                  if ( (dFlags & ACE_OBJECT_TYPE_PRESENT)
                      && (dFlags & ACE_INHERITED_OBJECT_TYPE_PRESENT)
                      )
                  {
                    pSID = (PSID)&(poace->SidStart);
                  }
                  else if (dFlags & ACE_OBJECT_TYPE_PRESENT)
                  {
                    pSID = (PSID)&(poace->InheritedObjectType);
                  }
                  else if (dFlags & ACE_INHERITED_OBJECT_TYPE_PRESENT)
                  {
                    pSID = (PSID)&(poace->InheritedObjectType);
                  }
```

```
                                    break;
                        default:
                            printf("Unknown ACE TYPE\n");
                            break;
                        }
                        cbName = sizeof(szTrusteeName);
                        cbReferencedDomainName = sizeof(szTrusteeDomainName);
                        ZeroMemory(szTrusteeName, cbName);
                        ZeroMemory(szTrusteeDomainName, cbReferencedDomainName);
                        //Look up the trustee name and domain.
                        if (LookupAccountSid(
                          NULL,              // address of string for system name
                          pSID,              // address of security identifier
                          szTrusteeName,     // address of string for account name
                          &cbName,           // address of size account string
                          szTrusteeDomainName,
                                             // address of string for referenced domain
                          &cbReferencedDomainName,
                                             // address of size domain string
                          &TrusteeType       // address of structure for SID type
                          ))
                        {
                          if (wcslen(szTrusteeDomainName)==0)
                            wprintf(L"Trustee: %s\n",szTrusteeName);
                          else
                            wprintf(L"Trustee: %s\\%s\n",
szTrusteeDomainName,szTrusteeName);
                        }
                        else
                        {
                            if (GetLastError() == ERROR_NONE_MAPPED)
                            {
                                printf("Last Error: ERROR_NONE_MAPPED\n");
                            }
                            else
                            {
                                printf("Last Error: %d\n",GetLastError());
                            }
                        }
                        printf("AccessMask: \n");
                        SDParseAccessMask(dAccessMask);
                        printf("Inheritance flags: %d\n",bAceFlags);
                }
            }
        }
```

(continued)

(continued)

```
            }
            if (pSDCNV)
                LocalFree(pSDCNV);
        }
    }
    VariantClear(&var);
return hr;
}

//Function to print Control flags.
int SDParseControlMasks(
                        long lCtrl
                        )
{
    int iReturn = TRUE;

if (lCtrl & SE_OWNER_DEFAULTED)
    printf("  SE_OWNER_DEFAULTED\n");

if (lCtrl & SE_GROUP_DEFAULTED)
    printf("  SE_GROUP_DEFAULTED\n");

if (lCtrl & SE_DACL_PRESENT)
    printf("  SE_DACL_PRESENT\n");

if (lCtrl & SE_DACL_DEFAULTED)
    printf("  SE_DACL_DEFAULTED\n");

if (lCtrl & SE_SACL_PRESENT)
    printf("  SE_SACL_PRESENT\n");

if (lCtrl & SE_SACL_DEFAULTED)
    printf("  SE_SACL_DEFAULTED\n");

if (lCtrl & SE_DACL_AUTO_INHERIT_REQ)
    printf("  SE_DACL_AUTO_INHERIT_REQ\n");

if (lCtrl & SE_SACL_AUTO_INHERIT_REQ)
    printf("  SE_SACL_AUTO_INHERIT_REQ\n");

if (lCtrl & SE_DACL_AUTO_INHERITED)
    printf("  SE_DACL_AUTO_INHERITED\n");
```

```
if (lCtrl & SE_SACL_AUTO_INHERITED)
    printf(" SE_SACL_AUTO_INHERITED\n");

if (lCtrl & SE_DACL_PROTECTED)
    printf(" SE_DACL_PROTECTED\n");

if (lCtrl & SE_SACL_PROTECTED)
    printf(" SE_SACL_PROTECTED\n");

if (lCtrl & SE_SELF_RELATIVE)
    printf(" SE_OWNER_DEFAULTED\n");

return iReturn;

}

//Function to print AccessMask flags.
int SDParseAccessMask(
                      long lCtrl
                      )
{
    int iReturn = TRUE;

if (lCtrl & ADS_RIGHT_DELETE)
    printf(" ADS_RIGHT_DELETE\n");

if (lCtrl & ADS_RIGHT_READ_CONTROL)
    printf(" ADS_RIGHT_READ_CONTROL\n");

if (lCtrl & ADS_RIGHT_WRITE_DAC)
    printf(" ADS_RIGHT_WRITE_DAC\n");

if (lCtrl & ADS_RIGHT_WRITE_OWNER)
    printf(" ADS_RIGHT_WRITE_OWNER\n");

if (lCtrl & ADS_RIGHT_GENERIC_READ)
    printf(" ADS_RIGHT_GENERIC_READ\n");

if (lCtrl & ADS_RIGHT_GENERIC_WRITE)
    printf(" ADS_RIGHT_GENERIC_WRITE\n");

if (lCtrl & ADS_RIGHT_GENERIC_EXECUTE)
    printf(" ADS_RIGHT_GENERIC_EXECUTE\n");

if (lCtrl & ADS_RIGHT_GENERIC_ALL)
```

(continued)

(continued)

```
         printf("  ADS_RIGHT_GENERIC_ALL\n");

if (lCtrl & ADS_RIGHT_DS_CREATE_CHILD)
    printf("  ADS_RIGHT_DS_CREATE_CHILD\n");

if (lCtrl & ADS_RIGHT_DS_DELETE_CHILD)
    printf("  ADS_RIGHT_DS_DELETE_CHILD\n");

if (lCtrl & ADS_RIGHT_ACTRL_DS_LIST)
    printf("  ADS_RIGHT_ACTRL_DS_LIST\n");

if (lCtrl & ADS_RIGHT_DS_SELF)
    printf("  ADS_RIGHT_DS_SELF\n");

if (lCtrl & ADS_RIGHT_DS_READ_PROP)
    printf("  ADS_RIGHT_DS_READ_PROP\n");

if (lCtrl & ADS_RIGHT_DS_WRITE_PROP)
    printf("  ADS_RIGHT_DS_WRITE_PROP\n");

if (lCtrl & ADS_RIGHT_DS_DELETE_TREE)
    printf("  ADS_RIGHT_DS_DELETE_TREE\n");

if (lCtrl & ADS_RIGHT_DS_LIST_OBJECT)
    printf("  ADS_RIGHT_DS_LIST_OBJECT\n");

if (lCtrl & ADS_RIGHT_DS_CONTROL_ACCESS)
    printf("  ADS_RIGHT_DS_CONTROL_ACCESS\n");

return iReturn;

}
```

Modifying the defaultSecurityDescriptor for an Object Class

The following sample code retrieves the default security descriptor for an object class, adds an ACE to the DACL, and then sets the modified security descriptor on the object class.

Note that schema modification is disabled by default on all Windows 2000 domain controllers. To enable schema modification at a particular DC, set a REG_DWORD value named "Schema Update Allowed" under the following registry key:

```
HKEY_LOCAL_MACHINE\System\CurrentControlSet\Services\NTDS\Parameters
```

Add this value if it does not already exist. Set this value to 1 to enable schema modification. If this value is zero, schema modification is disabled. The Schema Manager MMC snap-in provides a checkbox that sets or clears this registry key.

```
#include <wchar.h>
#include <objbase.h>
#include <activeds.h>
#include <ACLAPI.h>
#include <winnt.h>
#include <Sddl.h>

#define _WIN32_WINNT 0x0500

HRESULT ModifyDefaultSecurityDescriptor( IADs *pObject );

int main(int argc, char *argv[])
{
LPOLESTR szPath = new OLECHAR[MAX_PATH];
LPOLESTR pszBuffer  = new WCHAR[MAX_PATH];
HRESULT hr = S_OK;
IADs *pObject = NULL;
VARIANT var;

wprintf(L"This program modifies the default security descriptor of an object
class\n");
wprintf(L"Specify the object class:");
_getws(pszBuffer);
if (!pszBuffer)
  return TRUE;
wcscpy(szPath, L"LDAP://cn=");
wcscat(szPath, pszBuffer);
wcscat(szPath, L",");

// Intialize COM

CoInitialize(NULL);

// Get rootDSE and the schema container's DN. Bind to the
// current user's domain using current user's security context.

hr = ADsOpenObject(L"LDAP://rootDSE",
            NULL,
            NULL,
            ADS_SECURE_AUTHENTICATION, // Use Secure Authentication
            IID_IADs,
            (void**)&pObject);
```

(continued)

(continued)

```
if (SUCCEEDED(hr)) {
  hr = pObject->Get(L"schemaNamingContext",&var);
  if (SUCCEEDED(hr)) {
    wcscat(szPath,var.bstrVal);
    VariantClear(&var);
    if (pObject) {
       pObject->Release();
       pObject = NULL;
    }
    hr = ADsOpenObject(szPath,
               NULL,
               NULL,
               ADS_SECURE_AUTHENTICATION, // Use Secure Authentication
               IID_IADs,
               (void**)&pObject);
    if (SUCCEEDED(hr)) {
      wprintf(L"Modify the default SD for the %s class\n", pszBuffer);
      hr = ModifyDefaultSecurityDescriptor( pObject );
    }
  }
}

if (FAILED(hr))
  wprintf(L"Failed with the following HRESULT: 0x%x\n", hr);

if (pObject)
  pObject->Release();

// Uninitialize COM.

CoUninitialize();
return TRUE;
}


HRESULT ModifyDefaultSecurityDescriptor(
                          IADs *pObject
                          )
{
HRESULT hr = E_FAIL;
VARIANT var;
PSECURITY_DESCRIPTOR pSDCNV = NULL;
SECURITY_DESCRIPTOR SD = {0};
DWORD dwSDSize = sizeof(SECURITY_DESCRIPTOR);
PSID pOwnerSID = NULL;
```

```
DWORD dwOwnerSIDSize = 0;
PSID pGroupSID = NULL;
DWORD dwGroupSIDSize = 0;
PACL pDACL = NULL;
DWORD dwDACLSize = 0;
PACL pSACL = NULL;
DWORD dwSACLSize = 0;
BOOL bDaclPresent = FALSE;
BOOL bDaclDefaulted = FALSE;
PACL pOldDACL, pNewDACL;
ULONG ulLen;
EXPLICIT_ACCESS ea;
DWORD dwRes;

// Get the default security descriptor. Type should be VT_BSTR.

hr = pObject->Get(L"defaultSecurityDescriptor", &var);
if (FAILED(hr) || var.vt!=VT_BSTR ) {
  wprintf(L"Error getting default SD: 0x%x\n", hr );
  goto Cleanup;
}

wprintf(L"Old Default SD: %s\n", var.bstrVal);

// Convert the security descriptor string to a security descriptor.

if ( ! ConvertStringSecurityDescriptorToSecurityDescriptor (
        var.bstrVal, SDDL_REVISION_1, &pSDCNV, NULL )) {
  wprintf(L"Error converting string security descriptor: %d\n",
        GetLastError() );
  goto Cleanup;
}

// Convert self-relative security descriptor to absolute.
// First get the required buffer sizes.

if (! MakeAbsoluteSD(pSDCNV, &SD, &dwSDSize,
        pDACL, &dwDACLSize,
        pSACL, &dwSACLSize,
        pOwnerSID, &dwOwnerSIDSize,
        pGroupSID, &dwGroupSIDSize) ) {

  // Allocate the buffers.

  pDACL = (PACL) GlobalAlloc(GPTR, dwDACLSize);
  pSACL = (PACL) GlobalAlloc(GPTR, dwSACLSize);
```

(continued)

(continued)

```
  pOwnerSID = (PACL) GlobalAlloc(GPTR, dwOwnerSIDSize);
  pGroupSID = (PACL) GlobalAlloc(GPTR, dwGroupSIDSize);
  if (! (pDACL && pSACL && pOwnerSID && pGroupSID) ) {
    wprintf(L"GlobalAlloc failed: %d\n", GetLastError() );
    goto Cleanup;
  }

  // Now do the conversion.

  if (! MakeAbsoluteSD(pSDCNV, &SD, &dwSDSize, pDACL, &dwDACLSize,
           pSACL, &dwSACLSize, pOwnerSID, &dwOwnerSIDSize,
           pGroupSID, &dwGroupSIDSize) ) {
    wprintf(L"MakeAbsoluteSD: %d\n", GetLastError() );
    goto Cleanup;
  }
}

// Get the DACL from the security descriptor.

if (! GetSecurityDescriptorDacl(&SD, &bDaclPresent,
                 &pOldDACL, &bDaclDefaulted) ) {
  wprintf(L"GetSecurityDescriptorDacl failed: %d\n", GetLastError() );
  goto Cleanup;
}

// Initialize an EXPLICIT_ACCESS structure for the new ACE.
// The ACE grants Everyone the right to read properties.

ZeroMemory(&ea, sizeof(EXPLICIT_ACCESS));
ea.grfAccessPermissions = ADS_RIGHT_DS_READ_PROP;
ea.grfAccessMode = GRANT_ACCESS;
ea.grfInheritance= 0;
ea.Trustee.TrusteeForm = TRUSTEE_IS_NAME;
ea.Trustee.ptstrName = TEXT("Everyone");

// Create a new ACL that merges the new ACE into the existing DACL.

dwRes = SetEntriesInAcl(1, &ea, pOldDACL, &pNewDACL);
if (ERROR_SUCCESS != dwRes) {
    wprintf(L"SetEntriesInAcl Error %u\n", dwRes );
    goto Cleanup;
}

// Put the modified DACL into the security descriptor.

if (! SetSecurityDescriptorDacl(&SD, TRUE, pNewDACL, FALSE) ) {
```

```
   wprintf(L"SetSecurityDescriptorOwner failed: %d\n",
         GetLastError() );
  goto Cleanup;
}

// Convert the security descriptor back to string format.

VariantClear(&var);
if ( ! ConvertSecurityDescriptorToStringSecurityDescriptor (
      &SD, SDDL_REVISION_1,
      GROUP_SECURITY_INFORMATION | OWNER_SECURITY_INFORMATION |
      DACL_SECURITY_INFORMATION | SACL_SECURITY_INFORMATION,
      &var.bstrVal, &ulLen )) {
  wprintf(L"Error converting security descriptor to string: %d\n",
      GetLastError() );
  goto Cleanup;
}

wprintf(L"New default SD: %s\n", var.bstrVal);
V_VT(&var) = VT_BSTR;

// Use Put and SetInfo to set the modified security descriptor.

hr = pObject->Put(L"defaultSecurityDescriptor", var);
if (FAILED(hr)) {
    wprintf(L"Error putting default SD: 0x%x\n", hr );
    goto Cleanup;
}

hr = pObject->SetInfo();
if (FAILED(hr)) {
    wprintf(L"Error setting default SD: 0x%x\n", hr );
    goto Cleanup;
}

Cleanup:

VariantClear(&var);
if (pSDCNV)
    LocalFree(pSDCNV);
if (pDACL)
    GlobalFree(pDACL);
if (pSACL)
    GlobalFree(pSACL);
if (pOwnerSID)
    GlobalFree(pOwnerSID);
```

(continued)

(continued)

```
if (pGroupSID)
    GlobalFree(pGroupSID);
if (pNewDACL)
    LocalFree(pNewDACL);

return hr;
}
```

Extended Rights

All Active Directory™ objects support a standard set of access rights defined in the **ADS_RIGHTS_ENUM** enumeration. You can use these access rights in the ACEs of an object's security descriptor to control access to the object, that is, to control who can perform standard operations, such as creating and deleting child objects, or reading and writing the properties of an object. However, for some objects classes you may want to control access in a way not supported by the standard access rights. So Active Directory provides a way to extend the standard access control mechanism.

Extended rights are used in two ways.

- *For special operations not covered by the standard set of access rights.* For example, the user class can be granted a **Send As** right that can be used by Exchange, Outlook, or any other mail program, to determine whether a particular user can have another user send mail on their behalf.

- *For defining property sets, to enable controlling access to a subset of an object's properties.* Using the standard access rights, a single ACE can grant or deny access to all of an object's properties or to a single property. Extended rights provide a way for a single ACE to control access to a set of properties. For example, the user class supports the **Personal-Information** property set that includes properties such as street address and telephone number.

Each extended right is represented by a **controlAccessRight** object in the Extended-Rights container of the Configuration partition. Because the Configuration container is replicated across the entire forest, extended rights are propagated across all domains in a forest. There are a number of predefined extended rights, and of course, you can define your own.

For C++ and Visual Basic® sample code that sets an ACE to control read/write access to a property set, see *Example Code for Setting an ACE on a Directory Object*.

For information on using extended rights to control access to special operations, see the following topics.

- *Creating an Extended Right*
- *Setting an Extended Right ACE in an Object's ACL*
- *Checking an Extended Right in an Object's ACL*
- *Reading an Extended Right Set in an Object's ACL*

Creating an Extended Right

To add an extended right to Active Directory, you create a **controlAccessRight** object in the Extended-Rights container of the Configuration partition. Visual Basic and C++ sample code at the end of this topic show how to do it. To use the extended right, you must do a few more things depending on whether the extended right is for a special operation or a property set.

If you are defining an extended right for a property set, you must use the **rightsGUID** of the **controlAccessRight** object to identify the properties in the set. Every property is defined by an **attributeSchema** object in the Active Directory schema. The **attributeSecurityGUID** property of an **attributeSchema** object identifies the property set, if any, that the property belongs to. Note that the **attributeSecurityGUID** property is single-valued and stores the GUID in binary format (octet string syntax).

If you are defining an extended right to control access to a special operation, it is up to your application to perform the access check when a user tries to perform the operation. The following steps show how to do this:

1. Create an extended right that defines the type of access to the application or service. See sample code below.
2. Create an Active Directory object that represents the application, service, or resource that you are protecting.
3. Add object ACEs to the DACL in the object's security descriptor to allow or deny users or groups the extended right on that object. See *Setting an Extended Right ACE in an Object's ACL.*
4. When a user tries to perform the operation, check the user's rights by passing the object's security descriptor and the user's access token to the **AccessCheckByTypeResultList** function. See *Checking an Extended Right in an Object's ACL.*
5. Based on the result of the access check on the object, the application or service can allow or deny the user access to the application or service

When you create a **controlAccessRight** object, you must set the following attributes to make the object a legal extended right that is recognized by Active Directory and the Windows NT®/Windows® 2000 security system:

cn
   A single-valued property that is the object's relative distinguished name (RDN) in the Extended-Rights container. The **cn** is the name of the extended right in Active Directory.

appliesTo
   A multi-valued property that lists the object classes that the extended right applies to. For example, the **Send-As** extended right lists the **user** and **computer** object classes in its **appliesTo** property.

In the list, each object class is identified by the **schemaIDGUID** of its **classSchema** object. The GUIDs are stored as strings of the form produced by the **StringFromGUID2** function in the COM library—but without the starting and terminating curly braces ({ }). For example, the following GUID is the **schemaIDGUID** for the **computer** class:

```
bf967a86-0de6-11d0-a285-00aa003049e2
```

Note that the **schemaIDGUID** property of a **classSchema** object is stored as a binary GUID using the octet string syntax. To convert this octet string format to the string format used in the **appliesTo** property, use the **StringFromGUID2** function and remove the curly braces from the returned string.

To get the **schemaIDGUID** property of one of the predefined object classes, such as **user** or **computer**, see the class reference page in the Active Directory Schema Reference in the *Active Directory Reference*. For sample code that retrieves a **schemaIDGUID** from a classSchema object, see *Reading attributeSchema and classSchema Objects*.

displayName

The string used to display the extended right in user interfaces such as the **Security** property page and other places in the Active Directory Users and Computers.

rightsGUID

A GUID that identifies the extended right in an ACE. The GUID is stored as a string of the form produced by the **StringFromGUID2** function but without the starting and terminating curly braces. Use UUIDGEN.EXE or some other utility to generate a GUID for the extended right.

If you are defining a new property set, you use the **rightsGUID** of the **controlAccessRight** object to identify the properties in the set. Every property is defined by an **attributeSchema** object in the Active Directory schema. The **attributeSecurityGUID** property of an **attributeSchema** object identifies the property set, if any, that the property belongs to. Note that the **attributeSecurityGUID** property is single-valued and stores the GUID in binary format (octet string syntax).

objectClass

This attribute specifies **controlAccessRight** as the object class.

Example Code for Creating a controlAccessRight Object in the Extended Rights Container

Visual Basic

The following Visual Basic code fragment creates a **controlAccessRight** object in the Extended-Rights container.

```
Dim ExContainer As IADsContainer
Dim rootdse As IADs
Dim ExRight As IADs
```

```
Set rootdse = GetObject("LDAP://rootDSE")
configpath = rootdse.Get("configurationNamingContext")
Set ExContainer = GetObject("LDAP://cn=extended-rights," & configpath)

'Create the object, specifying the object class and the cn.
Set ExRight = ExContainer.Create("controlAccessRight", "cn=MyExRight")

'Set the classes the right applies to.
'Specify the schemaIDGUID of the user and computer classes.
ExRight.PutEx ADS_PROPERTY_UPDATE, "appliesTo", _
        Array("bf967aba-0de6-11d0-a285-00aa003049e2", _
            "bf967a86-0de6-11d0-a285-00aa003049e2")

'Set the display name used in Security property pages and other UI
ExRight.PutEx ADS_PROPERTY_UPDATE, "displayName", Array("My-Extended-Right")

'Set rightsGUID to a GUID generated by uuidgen.exe.
ExRight.PutEx ADS_PROPERTY_UPDATE, "rightsGUID", _
            Array("64ad33ac-ea09-4ded-b798-a0585c50fd5a")
ExRight.SetInfo
```

C++

The following C++ code fragment is a function that creates a **controlAccessRight**
object in the Extended-Rights container. When you call this function, use the following
format to specify the GUID string for the *pszRightsGUID* parameter:

```
L"b7b13123-b82e-11d0-afee-0000f80367c1"
```

The **ADSVALUE** array for the **appliesTo** property uses the same GUID format and sets
the **dwType** member to ADSTYPE_CASE_IGNORE_STRING.

```
#define _WIN32_WINNT 0x0500

#include <windows.h>
#include <stdio.h>
#include <activeds.h>

// *****************************************************************
// CreateExtendedRight
// *****************************************************************
HRESULT CreateExtendedRight(
            LPWSTR pszCommonName,        // cn property
            LPWSTR pszDisplayName,       // displayName property
            LPWSTR pszRightsGUID,        // rightsGUID property
            ADSVALUE *pAdsvAppliesTo,    // array of GUIDs for
                                         //   appliesTo property
```

(continued)

(continued)

```
                int cAppliesTo )           // number of GUIDs in array
{
HRESULT hr = E_FAIL;
VARIANT var;
LPOLESTR szADsPath = new OLECHAR[MAX_PATH];
IADs *pRootDSE = NULL;
IDirectoryObject *pExRights = NULL;

const int cAttributes = 5;
    // Count of attributes that must be set to create an extended right.
PADS_ATTR_INFO pAttributeEntries = new ADS_ATTR_INFO[cAttributes];
    // array of attributes
ADSVALUE adsvCN,
         adsvObjectClass,
         adsvDisplayName,
         adsvRightsGUID;

LPOLESTR pszRightRelPath = new WCHAR[MAX_PATH];
IDispatch *pNewObject = NULL;

hr = ADsOpenObject(L"LDAP://rootDSE",
                   NULL,
                   NULL,
                   ADS_SECURE_AUTHENTICATION,
                                  //Use Secure Authentication
                   IID_IADs,
                   (void**)&pRootDSE);
if (FAILED(hr)) {
    wprintf(L"Bind to rootDSE failed: 0x%x\n", hr);
    return hr;
}

// Get the DN to the config container.
hr = pRootDSE->Get(L"configurationNamingContext", &var);
if (SUCCEEDED(hr))
{
    // Build ADsPath string to Extended-Rights container
    wcscpy(szADsPath,L"LDAP://cn=Extended-Rights,");
    wcscat(szADsPath,var.bstrVal);

    // Get an IDirectory Object pointer to
    // the Extended Rights Container.
    hr = ADsOpenObject(szADsPath,
             NULL,
             NULL,
```

```
                    ADS_SECURE_AUTHENTICATION, //Use Secure Authentication
                    IID_IDirectoryObject,
                    (void**)&pExRights);
}
if (FAILED (hr) ) {
    wprintf(L"Bind to Extended Rights Container failed: 0x%x\n", hr);
    goto cleanup;
}

  // Set first attribute: CN
pAttributeEntries[0].pszAttrName = L"CN";
  // Attribute name: CN
pAttributeEntries[0].dwControlCode = ADS_ATTR_APPEND;
  // Add the attribute.
pAttributeEntries[0].dwADsType = ADSTYPE_CASE_IGNORE_STRING;
  // Attribute syntax is string.
  // Fill in the ADSVALUE structure for the CN property
adsvCN.CaseIgnoreString = pszCommonName;
adsvCN.dwType = ADSTYPE_CASE_IGNORE_STRING;
pAttributeEntries[0].pADsValues = &adsvCN;
pAttributeEntries[0].dwNumValues = 1;

  // Set second attribute: objectClass
pAttributeEntries[1].pszAttrName = L"objectClass";
  // Attribute name: objectClass
pAttributeEntries[1].dwControlCode = ADS_ATTR_APPEND;
  // Add the attribute.
pAttributeEntries[1].dwADsType = ADSTYPE_CASE_IGNORE_STRING;
  // Attribute syntax is string.
  // Fill in the ADSVALUE structure for the objectClass property
adsvObjectClass.CaseIgnoreString = L"controlAccessRight";
  // objectClass is controlAccessRight
adsvObjectClass.dwType = ADSTYPE_CASE_IGNORE_STRING;
pAttributeEntries[1].pADsValues = &adsvObjectClass;
pAttributeEntries[1].dwNumValues = 1;

  // Set third attribute: appliesTo
  // Each value for this property is a schemaIDGUID of
  // a class to which the right can be applied.
pAttributeEntries[2].pszAttrName = L"appliesTo";
  // Attribute name: appliesTo
pAttributeEntries[2].dwControlCode = ADS_ATTR_APPEND;
  // Add the attribute.
pAttributeEntries[2].dwADsType = ADSTYPE_CASE_IGNORE_STRING;
  // Attribute syntax is string.
  // The ADSVALUE array for this property is passed in
```

(continued)

(continued)

```
  // as a parameter to this function.
pAttributeEntries[2].pADsValues = pAdsvAppliesTo;
pAttributeEntries[2].dwNumValues = cAppliesTo;

  // Set fourth attribute: displayName
pAttributeEntries[3].pszAttrName = L"displayName";
  // Attribute name: CN
pAttributeEntries[3].dwControlCode = ADS_ATTR_APPEND;
  // Add the attribute.
pAttributeEntries[3].dwADsType = ADSTYPE_CASE_IGNORE_STRING;
  // Attribute syntax is string.
  // Fill in the ADSVALUE structure for the displayName property.
adsvDisplayName.CaseIgnoreString = pszDisplayName;
adsvDisplayName.dwType = ADSTYPE_CASE_IGNORE_STRING;
pAttributeEntries[3].pADsValues = &adsvDisplayName;
pAttributeEntries[3].dwNumValues = 1;

  // Set fifth attribute: rightsGUID
pAttributeEntries[4].pszAttrName = L"rightsGUID";
  // Attribute name: CN
pAttributeEntries[4].dwControlCode = ADS_ATTR_APPEND;
  // Add the attribute.
pAttributeEntries[4].dwADsType = ADSTYPE_CASE_IGNORE_STRING;
  // Attribute syntax is string.
  // Fill in the ADSVALUE structure for the rightsGUID property.
adsvRightsGUID.dwType = ADSTYPE_CASE_IGNORE_STRING;
adsvRightsGUID.CaseIgnoreString = pszRightsGUID;
pAttributeEntries[4].pADsValues = &adsvRightsGUID;
pAttributeEntries[4].dwNumValues = 1;

  // Set up the relative distinguished name for the new object.
wcscpy(pszRightRelPath, L"cn=");
wcscat(pszRightRelPath, pszCommonName);

  // Create the controlAccessRight
hr = pExRights->CreateDSObject(
                   pszRightRelPath,    // Relative path of new object
                   pAttributeEntries,  // Attributes to be set
                   cAttributes,        // Number of attributes
                                       //  being set
                   &pNewObject         // receives IDispatch pointer
                                       //  to the new object
                   );

cleanup:
```

```
if (pRootDSE)
    pRootDSE->Release();
if (pExRights)
    pExRights->Release();
if (pNewObject)
    pNewObject->Release();
VariantClear(&var);
return hr;
}
```

Setting an Extended Right ACE in an Object's ACL

Using ADSI, you set an extended right ACE just as you would a property-specific ACE, except that the **ObjectType** field of the ACE is the **rightsGUID** of the extended right. Note that you can also use the Win32 security APIs to set ACLs on directory objects.

For extended rights, set the properties on the ACE in the following manner:

AccessMask
> For extended rights that control access to special operations, AccessMask must contain the ADS_RIGHT_DS_CONTROL_ACCESS flag.
>
> For extended rights that define a property set, AccessMask contains ADS_RIGHT_READ_PROP and/or ADS_RIGHT_WRITE_PROP.

Flags
> This value must include the ADS_FLAG_OBJECT_TYPE_PRESENT flag.

ObjectType
> This value must be the **StringFromGUID2** format of the **rightsGUID** property of the extended right. Note that in an ACE, the GUID string must include the starting and terminating curly braces (even though the rightsGUID property of the **controlAccessRight** object does not include the curly braces).

AceType
> Either ADS_ACETYPE_ACCESS_ALLOWED_OBJECT to grant the trustee the extended right or ADS_ACETYPE_ACCESS_DENIED_OBJECT to deny the trustee the extended right.

Trustee
> The security principal (user, group, computer, and so on) to whom the ACE applies.

For a discussion of the steps for creating an ACE, see *Setting Access Rights on an Object*.

For additional C++ and Visual Basic sample code for setting an ACE, see:

- *Example Code for Setting an ACE on a Directory Object*

Example Code for Setting an Extended Right ACE

The following code fragment is a function that adds an ACE for an extended right to the ACL of the specified object.

```
HRESULT SetExtendedRight(
                         IADs *pObject,
                         LPOLESTR pszRightsGUID,
                         LONG lAccessType,
                         LONG fInheritanceFlags,
                         LONG fAppliesToObjectType,
                         LPOLESTR szTrustee
                         )


{

BOOL bExists = FALSE;
VARIANT var,varACE;
HRESULT hr = E_FAIL;
IADsSecurityDescriptor *pSD = NULL;
IADsAccessControlList *pACL = NULL;
IDispatch *pDisp = NULL;
LPUNKNOWN pUnk = NULL;
ULONG lFetch;
IEnumVARIANT *pEnum = NULL;
IADsAccessControlEntry *pACE = NULL;
IDispatch *pDispatch = NULL;
IDispatch *pDispACE = NULL;

//Check params
//This sample takes the rightsGUID in StringFromGUID2 format
// and assumes it is the GUID for the correct extended right.
// For extended rights in a DACL, lAccessType must be
//   ADS_ACETYPE_ACCESS_ALLOWED_OBJECT or
//   ADS_ACETYPE_ACCESS_DENIED_OBJECT.
if
((lAccessType!=ADS_ACETYPE_ACCESS_ALLOWED_OBJECT)&&(lAccessType!=ADS_ACETYPE_ACCESS_DENIED
_OBJECT))
    return E_INVALIDARG;
//This sample takes the szTrustee in an expected naming format and
// assumes it is the name for the correct trustee.
if (!szTrustee)
    return E_INVALIDARG;
if (!pszRightsGUID)
    return E_INVALIDARG;

if (pObject)
{

    VariantClear(&var);
    //Get the nTSecurityDescriptor
```

```
    LPOLESTR szAttribute = L"nTSecurityDescriptor";
  hr = pObject->Get(szAttribute,&var);
  if (SUCCEEDED(hr))
  {
      //Type should be VT_DISPATCH--an IDispatch ptr to the
      // security descriptor object.
      if (var.vt==VT_DISPATCH)
      {
          //Use V_DISPATCH macro to get the IDispatch pointer
          // from the VARIANT structure
          // and QI for IADsSecurityDescriptor ptr.
          hr = V_DISPATCH( &var )-
>QueryInterface(IID_IADsSecurityDescriptor,(void**)&pSD);
          if (SUCCEEDED(hr))
          {
              //Get the DACL
              hr = pSD->get_DiscretionaryAcl(&pDisp);
              if (SUCCEEDED(hr))
              {
                  //QI for IADsAccessControlList interface
                  hr = pDisp->QueryInterface(IID_IADsAccessControlList,(void**)&pACL);
                  if (SUCCEEDED(hr))
                  {
                      //Create the COM object for the new ACE.
                      hr  = CoCreateInstance(
                                              CLSID_AccessControlEntry,
                                              NULL,
                                              CLSCTX_INPROC_SERVER,
                                              IID_IADsAccessControlEntry,
                                              (void **)&pACE
                                            );
                      if (SUCCEEDED(hr))
                      {
                          //Set the properties of the new ACE.
                          // For extended right, set the mask to
                          // ADS_RIGHT_DS_CONTROL_ACCESS.
                          hr = pACE->put_AccessMask(ADS_RIGHT_DS_CONTROL_ACCESS);
                          //Set the trustee.
                          hr = pACE->put_Trustee( szTrustee );
                          //For extended rights, set AceType to
                          // ADS_ACETYPE_ACCESS_ALLOWED_OBJECT or
                          // ADS_ACETYPE_ACCESS_DENIED_OBJECT.
                          hr = pACE->put_AceType( lAccessType );
                          //For this sample, set AceFlags so that ACE
                          // is not inherited by child objects.
                          hr = pACE->put_AceFlags(fInheritanceFlags);
```

(continued)

(continued)

```
                    //Flags specifies whether the ACE applies
                    // to the current object, child objects,
                    // or both. For this sample,
                    // fAppliesToInheritedObject is set to
                    // ADS_FLAG_OBJECT_TYPE_PRESENT so that
                    // the right applies only to
                    // the current object.
                hr = pACE->put_Flags( fAppliesToObjectType );
                //For extended rights, set ObjectType to
                // the rightsGUID of the extended right.
                if (fAppliesToObjectType & ADS_FLAG_OBJECT_TYPE_PRESENT)
                {
                    hr = pACE->put_ObjectType( pszRightsGUID );
                }
                //Set the inherited object type if right
                // applies to child objects.
                if (fAppliesToObjectType &
ADS_FLAG_INHERITED_OBJECT_TYPE_PRESENT)
                {
                    hr = pACE->put_InheritedObjectType( pszRightsGUID );
                }
                //Add the ACE to the ACL.
                // Need to QI for IDispatch pointer to
                // pass to the AddAce method.
                hr = pACE->QueryInterface(IID_IDispatch,(void**)&pDispACE);
                if (SUCCEEDED(hr))
                {
                    hr = pACL->AddAce(pDispACE);
                    if (SUCCEEDED(hr))
                    {
                        //Write the DACL
                        hr = pSD->put_DiscretionaryAcl(pDisp);
                        if (SUCCEEDED(hr))
                        {
                            //Write the ntSecurityDescriptor
                            // property to the
                            // property cache.
                            hr = pObject->Put(szAttribute, var);
                            if (SUCCEEDED(hr))
                            {
                                //Call SetInfo to update the
                                // property on the object in
                                // the directory.
                                hr = pObject->SetInfo();
```

```
                                }
                              }

                          }

                        }
                      if (pDispACE)
                          pDispACE->Release();
                  }
                  if (pACE)
                      pACE->Release();
              }

          if (pACL)
              pACL->Release();
        }
        if (pDisp)
            pDisp->Release();
    }
    if (pSD)
        pSD->Release();
    }
  }
  VariantClear(&var);
}
return hr;
}
```

Checking an Extended Right in an Object's ACL

To check an extended right on an object's ACL, use the
AccessCheckByTypeResultList function. To use this function, your application needs
a pointer to the SECURITY_DESCRIPTOR for the object (instead of an
IADsSecurityDescriptor interface to an ADSI security descriptor COM object).

If you are using ADSI, use the following steps for checking access for an extended right
on an object (see the following code fragment for an example):

1. Get an **IDirectoryObject** interface pointer to the object.

2. Use the **IDirectoryObject::Get** method to get the security descriptor of the object.
   The name of the property containing the security descriptor is **nTSecurityDescriptor**.
   The property will be returned as a **VARIANT** containing an **IDispatch** pointer (the **vt**
   member is VT_DISPATCH). Call **QueryInterface** on that **IDispatch** pointer to get an
   IADsSecurityDescriptor interface to use the methods on that interface to access the
   security descriptor's ACL.

3. Use the **IADsSecurityDescriptor::get_DiscretionaryAcl** method to get the ACL. The method returns an **IDispatch** pointer. Call **QueryInterface** on that **IDispatch** pointer to get an **IADsAccessControlList** interface to use the methods on that interface to access the individual ACEs in the ACL.

4. Get the token of the client whose access you want to check.

5. Use the **AccessCheckByTypeResultList** function to check the permissions for the specified extended right for the specified client.

Example Code for Checking an Extended Right in an Object's ACL

The following code fragment is a function that checks whether the currently logged-on user has permissions for an extended right on the specified object:

```c
// Define the Generic Mapping structure.
// generic read
#define GENERIC_READ_MAPPING      ((STANDARD_RIGHTS_READ)      | \
                                   (ADS_RIGHT_ACTRL_DS_LIST)    | \
                                   (ADS_RIGHT_DS_READ_PROP)     | \
                                   (ADS_RIGHT_DS_LIST_OBJECT))
// generic execute
#define GENERIC_EXECUTE_MAPPING   ((STANDARD_RIGHTS_EXECUTE)    | \
                                   (ADS_RIGHT_ACTRL_DS_LIST))
// generic right
#define GENERIC_WRITE_MAPPING     ((STANDARD_RIGHTS_WRITE)      | \
                                   (ADS_RIGHT_DS_SELF)          | \
                  (ADS_RIGHT_DS_WRITE_PROP))
// generic all
#define GENERIC_ALL_MAPPING       ((STANDARD_RIGHTS_REQUIRED) | \
                                   (ADS_RIGHT_DS_CREATE_CHILD)   | \
                                   (ADS_RIGHT_DS_DELETE_CHILD)   | \
                                   (ADS_RIGHT_DS_DELETE_TREE)    | \
                                   (ADS_RIGHT_DS_READ_PROP)   | \
                                   (ADS_RIGHT_DS_WRITE_PROP)  | \
                                   (ADS_RIGHT_ACTRL_DS_LIST)     | \
                                   (ADS_RIGHT_DS_LIST_OBJECT)    | \
                                   (ADS_RIGHT_DS_CONTROL_ACCESS) | \
                                   (ADS_RIGHT_DS_SELF))
// Standard DS generic access rights mapping
#define DS_GENERIC_MAPPING {GENERIC_READ_MAPPING,     \
             GENERIC_WRITE_MAPPING,   \
             GENERIC_EXECUTE_MAPPING, \
             GENERIC_ALL_MAPPING}


HRESULT CheckExtendedRight(
                          HANDLE hToken,
                          IDirectoryObject *pObject,
```

```
                                   LPOLESTR pszRightsGUID,
                                   DWORD *dwAccess
                                   )


{
HRESULT hr = E_FAIL;
*dwAccess = FALSE;
BOOL bSuccess = FALSE;
PADS_ATTR_INFO pAttrInfo = NULL;
DWORD   dwReturn= 0;
LPWSTR   pAttrNames[]= {L"nTSecurityDescriptor",L"objectSid"};
PSECURITY_DESCRIPTOR pSD = NULL;
DWORD   SDSize;
VOID    *pAbsoluteSD = NULL;
DWORD   AbsoluteSDSize = 0;
VOID    *pDacl = NULL;
DWORD   DaclSize = 0;
VOID    *pSacl = NULL;
DWORD   SaclSize = 0;
VOID    *pOwner = NULL;
DWORD   OwnerSize = 0;
VOID    *pGroup = NULL;
DWORD   GroupSize = 0;
PSID pSID = NULL;
// Get attributes for security descriptor and SID
hr = pObject->GetObjectAttributes( pAttrNames,
                                   2,
                                   &pAttrInfo,
                                   &dwReturn );
if ( (SUCCEEDED(hr)) && (dwReturn>0) )
{
    for(DWORD idx=0; idx < dwReturn;idx++, pAttrInfo++ )
    {
        //Check the attribute name
        if ( _wcsicmp(pAttrInfo->pszAttrName,L"nTSecurityDescriptor") == 0 )
        {
            //Check the attribute type.
            if (pAttrInfo->dwADsType==ADSTYPE_NT_SECURITY_DESCRIPTOR)
            {
                pSD = (PSECURITY_DESCRIPTOR)(pAttrInfo->pADsValues-
>SecurityDescriptor.lpValue);
                SDSize = (pAttrInfo->pADsValues->SecurityDescriptor.dwLength);
            }
        }
        if ( _wcsicmp(pAttrInfo->pszAttrName,L"objectSID") == 0 )
```

(continued)

(continued)

```
        {
            //Check the attribute type.
            if (pAttrInfo->dwADsType==ADSTYPE_OCTET_STRING)
            {
                pSID = (PSID)(pAttrInfo->pADsValues->OctetString.lpValue);
            }
        }
    }
}
OBJECT_TYPE_LIST sObjectList;
sObjectList.Level = ACCESS_OBJECT_GUID;
sObjectList.Sbz = 0;
CLSID pclsid;
//Make the rightsGUID string the right format
//for conversion with the COM conversion functions.
LPOLESTR pszGUID = new OLECHAR[MAX_PATH];
wcscpy(pszGUID, L"{");
wcscat(pszGUID, pszRightsGUID);
wcscat(pszGUID, L"}");
hr = CLSIDFromString(
            pszGUID,  //Pointer to the string representation
                      // of the CLSID
            &pclsid   //Pointer to the CLSID
          );
if (SUCCEEDED(hr))
{
    sObjectList.ObjectType = (GUID*)&pclsid;
}
else
    return E_FAIL;


CHAR PrivilegeSetBuffer[256];
PRIVILEGE_SET *PrivilegeSet = (PRIVILEGE_SET *)PrivilegeSetBuffer;
DWORD dwPrivSetSize = sizeof( PrivilegeSetBuffer );
DWORD GrantedAccess = 0;
ZeroMemory(PrivilegeSetBuffer, 256);
DWORD DesiredAccess = ADS_RIGHT_DS_CONTROL_ACCESS;
// Use the GENERIC_MAPPING structure to convert any
// generic access rights to object-specific access rights.
GENERIC_MAPPING GenericMapping = DS_GENERIC_MAPPING;
// Before calling AccessCheck, a convert must be done
// security descriptor into Absolute form.
if( ! MakeAbsoluteSD(
                pSD,
                (PSECURITY_DESCRIPTOR)pAbsoluteSD,
```

```
                    &AbsoluteSDSize,
                    (PACL)pDacl,
                    &DaclSize,
                    (PACL)pSacl,
                    &SaclSize,
                    (PSID)pOwner,
                    &OwnerSize,
                    (PSID)pGroup,
                    &GroupSize
                    ))
{
    pAbsoluteSD = (PSECURITY_DESCRIPTOR)LocalAlloc(0,AbsoluteSDSize);
    if(!pAbsoluteSD)
    {
        // TODO: handle this.
    }
    pDacl = (PACL)LocalAlloc(0,DaclSize);
    if(!pDacl)
    {
        // TODO: handle this.
    }
    pSacl = (PACL)LocalAlloc(0,SaclSize);
    if(!pSacl)
    {
        // TODO: handle this.
    }
    pOwner = (PSID)LocalAlloc(0,OwnerSize);
    if(!pOwner)
    {
        // TODO: handle this.
    }
    pGroup = (PSID)LocalAlloc(0,GroupSize);
    if(!pGroup)
    {
        // TODO: handle this.
    }
    if( ! MakeAbsoluteSD(
                    pSD,
                    (PSECURITY_DESCRIPTOR)pAbsoluteSD,
                    &AbsoluteSDSize,
                    (PACL)pDacl,
                    &DaclSize,
                    (PACL)pSacl,
                    &SaclSize,
                    (PSID)pOwner,
```

(continued)

(continued)

```
                          &OwnerSize,
                          (PSID)pGroup,
                          &GroupSize
                  ))
        {
            //
            // TODO: handle this
            //
            //Clean up and return
            if (pAttrInfo)
              FreeADsMem( pAttrInfo );
            return E_FAIL;

        }
    }

    bSuccess = AccessCheckByTypeResultList(
            pSD,                // security descriptor
            pSID,               // SID of object being checked
            hToken,             // handle to client access token
            DesiredAccess,      // requested access rights
            &sObjectList,       // array of object types
            1,                  // number of object type elements
            &GenericMapping,    // map generic to specific rights
            PrivilegeSet,       // receives privileges used
            &dwPrivSetSize,     // size of privilege-set buffer
            &GrantedAccess,     // retrieves mask of granted rights
            dwAccess            // retrieves results of access check
            );
    //Check if access check function call succeeded.
    if(bSuccess)
    {
        hr = S_OK;
    }
    else
        hr = E_FAIL;
}
// Use FreeADsMem for all memory obtained from ADSI call
if (pAttrInfo)
     FreeADsMem( pAttrInfo );

return hr;
}
```

Reading an Extended Right Set in an Object's ACL

Using ADSI, you read an extended right ACE just as you would any other ACE in an ACL. (Note that you can also use the Win32 security APIs to read ACLs on directory objects.) However, extended rights use the properties on the ACE in a manner that is specific to granting and denying extended rights:

- **AccessMask** must contain the following flag: ADS_RIGHT_DS_CONTROL_ACCESS
- **Flags** is ADS_FLAG_OBJECT_TYPE_PRESENT
- **ObjectType** is the string form of the **rightsGUID** property of the extended right. The string format of the GUID is the same string format as the **StringFromGUID2** COM Library function
- **AceType** is either ADS_ACETYPE_ACCESS_ALLOWED_OBJECT to grant the trustee the extended right or ADS_ACETYPE_ACCESS_DENIED_OBJECT to deny the trustee the extended right
- **Trustee** is the security principal (user, group, computer, and so on) to whom the ACE applies

▶ **To read ACEs for an extended right on an object in C/C++**

If you are using ADSI, use the following steps for reading ACEs for an extended right on an object (see the following code fragment for an example):

1. Get an **IADs** interface pointer to the object.
2. Use the **IADs::Get** method to get the security descriptor of the object. The name of the property containing the security descriptor is **nTSecurityDescriptor**. The property will be returned as a **VARIANT** containing an **IDispatch** pointer (the **vt** member is VT_DISPATCH). Call **QueryInterface** on that **IDispatch** pointer to get an **IADsSecurityDescriptor** interface to use the methods on that interface to access the security descriptor's ACL.
3. Use the **IADsSecurityDescriptor::get_DiscretionaryAcl** method to get the ACL. The method returns an **IDispatch** pointer. Call **QueryInterface** on that **IDispatch** pointer to get an **IADsAccessControlList** interface to use the methods on that interface to access the individual ACEs in the ACL.
4. Use the **IADsAccessControlList::get__NewEnum** method to enumerate the ACEs. The method returns an **IUnknown** pointer. Call **QueryInterface** on that **IUnknown** pointer to get an **IEnumVARIANT** interface.
5. Use the **IEnumVARIANT::Next** method to enumerate the ACEs in the ACL. The property will be returned as a **VARIANT** containing an **IDispatch** pointer (the **vt** member is VT_DISPATCH). Call **QueryInterface** on that **IDispatch** pointer to get an **IADsAccessControlEntry** interface to read the ACE.
6. Call the **IADsAccessControlEntry::get_AccessMask** method to get the **AccessMask**.
7. Check the **AccessMask** value for the ADS_RIGHT_DS_CONTROL_ACCESS flag. If it has this flag, the ACE contains an extended right.

8. Call **IADsAccessControlEntry::get_Flags** method to get the flag for object type.

9. Check **Flags** value for ADS_FLAG_OBJECT_TYPE_PRESENT flag.

10. If **Flags** is set to ADS_FLAG_OBJECT_TYPE_PRESENT, call the **IADsAccessControlEntry::get_ObjectType** method to get a string containing the rightsGUID of the extended right that the ACE applies to.

11. Call the **IADsAccessControlEntry::get_AceType** method to get the type of ACE. The type will be ADS_ACETYPE_ACCESS_ALLOWED_OBJECT to grant the trustee the extended right or ADS_ACETYPE_ACCESS_DENIED_OBJECT to deny the extended right.

12. Call the **IADsAccessControlEntry::get_Trustee** method to get the security principal (user, group, computer, and so on) to whom the ACE applies.

13. When you are done with for the **ObjectType** and **Trustee** strings, use **SysFreeString** to free the memory for those strings.

14. When you are done with the interfaces, call **Release** to decrement or release all the interface references.

Example Code for Checking for an Extended Right in an ACE

The following code fragment is a function that checks for a specified extended right in an ACE in the ACL of the specified object:

```
//DESCRIPTION: ReadExtendedRight checks for the specified extended
// right on the specified object. If an ACE with that extended right
// exists, it displays (using printf) the trustee and ACE type for
// the extended right.

//FLOW: Get the security descriptor of an object, get the ACL,
// enumerate the ACEs, check for extended rights ACEs,
// check for the specified right, and display the trustee and ACE type.

//NOTES: The pszRightsGUID UNICODE string should be a string
// containing the rightsGUID property value of the extended right
// and the string should have the same format as the COM Library
// function StringFromGUID2.
//For example:
// LPOLESTR pszRightsGUID = L"{8186e976-4d8a-11d2-95dd-0000f875b660}";
// The pbExists parameter specifies a BOOL that will receive
// TRUE if an ACE with the specified right exists; otherwise, FALSE.

HRESULT ReadExtendedRight(
                    IADs *pObject,
                    LPOLESTR pszRightsGUID,
                    BOOL *pbExists
                    )

{

BOOL bExists = FALSE;
```

```
VARIANT var,varACE;
HRESULT hr = E_FAIL;
IADsSecurityDescriptor *pSD = NULL;
IADsAccessControlList *pACL = NULL;
IDispatch *pDisp = NULL;
LPUNKNOWN pUnk = NULL;
ULONG lFetch;
BSTR szObjectType, szTrustee;
IEnumVARIANT *pEnum = NULL;
IADsAccessControlEntry *pACE = NULL;
IDispatch *pDispatch = NULL;
long lAceType, lAccessMask, lTypeFlag;


if (pObject)
{
    VariantClear(&var);
    //Get the nTSecurityDescriptor
    LPOLESTR szAttribute = L"nTSecurityDescriptor";
    hr = pObject->Get(szAttribute,&var);
    if (SUCCEEDED(hr))
    {
        //Type should be VT_DISPATCH--an IDispatch ptr to
        //the security descriptor object.
        if (var.vt==VT_DISPATCH)
        {
            //Use V_DISPATCH macro to get the IDispatch pointer from
            // VARIANT structure and QI for IADsSecurityDescriptor ptr.
            hr = V_DISPATCH( &var )-
>QueryInterface(IID_IADsSecurityDescriptor,(void**)&pSD);
            if (SUCCEEDED(hr))
            {
                //Get the DACL
                hr = pSD->get_DiscretionaryAcl(&pDisp);
                if (SUCCEEDED(hr))
                {
                    //QI for IADsAccessControlList interface
                    hr = pDisp->QueryInterface(IID_IADsAccessControlList,(void**)&pACL);
                    if (SUCCEEDED(hr))
                    {
                        //Enumerate the ACEs in the ACL.
                        hr = pACL->get__NewEnum( &pUnk );
                        if (SUCCEEDED(hr))
                        {
```

(continued)

(continued)

```
                              hr = pUnk->QueryInterface( IID_IEnumVARIANT, (void**) &pEnum
);
                              if (SUCCEEDED(hr))
                              {
                                  hr = pEnum->Next( 1, &varACE, &lFetch );
                                  //Loop to read all ACEs on the object.
                                  while( hr == S_OK )
                                  {
                                      //Check if 1 item is returned and
                                      // returned item is an
                                      // IDispatch pointer.
                                      if ( (lFetch == 1) && (varACE.vt==VT_DISPATCH))
                                      {
                                          pDispatch = V_DISPATCH(&varACE);
                                          //QI for IADsAccessControlEntry
                                          // to use to read the ACE.
                                          hr = pDispatch->QueryInterface(
IID_IADsAccessControlEntry, (void**)&pACE );
                                          if (SUCCEEDED(hr))
                                          {
                                              hr = pACE->get_AccessMask(&lAccessMask);
                                              //Check for control access
                                              // right flag to see if this
                                              // is an ACE for an extended
                                              // right.
                                              if (lAccessMask & ADS_RIGHT_DS_CONTROL_ACCESS)
                                              {
                                                  pACE->get_Flags(&lTypeFlag);
                                                  //Check to make sure
                                                  // this ACE applies
                                                  // to an object
                                                  if (lTypeFlag &
ADS_FLAG_OBJECT_TYPE_PRESENT)
                                                  {
                //Get the object type GUID and print it.
                                                      pACE->get_ObjectType(&szObjectType);
                                                      if (
_wcsicmp(szObjectType,pszRightsGUID) == 0 )
                                                      {
                                                          if (bExists==FALSE)
                                                              bExists = TRUE;
                                                          printf("\nObjectType: %S\n",
szObjectType);
                                                          hr = pACE->get_AceType(&lAceType);
```

```
                                                        if (lAceType ==
ADS_ACETYPE_ACCESS_ALLOWED_OBJECT)
                                                            printf("ACE Type:
ADS_ACETYPE_ACCESS_ALLOWED_OBJECT\n");

                                                        if (lAceType ==
ADS_ACETYPE_ACCESS_DENIED_OBJECT)
                                                            printf("ACE Type:
ADS_ACETYPE_ACCESS_DENIED_OBJECT\n");

            //Get the trustee (who the right applies to) and print it.
                                                    pACE->get_Trustee(&szTrustee);
                                                    printf("Trustee: %S\n",
szTrustee);
            //Free the string.
                                                    if (szTrustee)
                                                        SysFreeString(szTrustee);
                                                }
            //Free the string.
                                                if (szObjectType)
                                                    SysFreeString(szObjectType);
                                            }
                                        }
                                    }
            //Clean up the enumerated ACE item.
                                    if (pACE)
                                        pACE->Release();
                                    if (pDispatch)
                                        pDispatch->Release();
                                }
                                //Clean up the VARIANT for
                                // the ACE item.
                                VariantClear(&varACE);
                                //Get the next ACE
                                hr = pEnum->Next( 1, &varACE, &lFetch );
                        };//End of While loop
                    }
                    //Clean up
                    if (pEnum)
                        pEnum->Release();
                }
                if (pUnk)
                    pUnk->Release();
            }
            if (pACL)
```

(continued)

(continued)

```
                    pACL->Release();
             }
          if (pDisp)
              pDisp->Release();
       }
    if (pSD)
       pSD->Release();
   }
 }
 VariantClear(&var);
}
*pbExists = bExists;
return hr;
}
```

CHAPTER 10

Extending the User Interface for Directory Objects

Microsoft® Windows® 2000 ships with Microsoft Management Console (MMC) snap-ins, such as the Active Directory Users and Computers snap-in, for administration of Active Directory™. In addition, the Windows 2000 client includes user interfaces (UI) for finding objects that reside in the directory and reading and writing properties. This chapter details what you need to know to extend the UI for viewing and managing Active Directory objects in the Windows shell and Active Directory administrative snap-ins. This chapter also covers what you need to do to make it easy for your customers to deploy the UI extensions to the user's desktops.

Specifically, this chapter discusses the following:

- How to extend the UI for Active Directory objects.
- How to use display specifiers, and where to store display specifiers.
- How to add property pages to property sheets for objects of a specific Active Directory object class.
- How to add menu items to the context menus for objects of a specific Active Directory object class.
- How to set the object class and attribute display names, which are the names used to identify the class or attribute in the UI.
- How to set the icon used to represent objects of a specific Active Directory class. The icon is displayed in the Windows shell and Active Directory Administrative snap-ins.
- How to specify whether objects of a specific Active Directory class are displayed as containers or leaf objects. If an object is a leaf object, it only appears in the result (right) pane of the administrative snap-ins and Explorer view of the Windows shell. If an object is a container, it can appear in either the scope (left) or result pane.
- How to extend or replace an existing creation wizard for objects of a specific Active Directory class. Creation wizards simplify what a user needs to enter in order for the object to be created. Currently, the user, computer, group, and other Active Directory classes have creation wizards.
- How to take advantage of the standard Windows 2000 query and selection UI. The Windows 2000 operating system provides COM objects that implement dialog boxes for browsing and selecting the following directory objects: domains, containers, and specific types of objects. In addition, the query (Find) dialog box can also be used or extended.
- How to provide user interfaces for new object classes.

- How to extend Active Directory Administrative snap-ins using MMC extension snap-ins.
- How to use the Microsoft Installer (MSI) and Windows 2000 application deployment to distrubute the COM objects created to perform the tasks listed above.

About Active Directory User Interfaces

Both administrators and users must be able to view Active Directory™ objects in the user interface.

Administrators will manage Active Directory using different Microsoft Management Console (MMC) snap-ins—specifically Active Directory Users and Computers, Active Directory Sites and Services, Active Directory Domains and Trusts, and Active Directory Schema Manager.

The end user, however, will see the directory through the Microsoft® Windows® shell. Users can browse for objects stored in the directory from either the directory item in My Network Places on the desktop or through the Find dialogs available in the Start menu.

Active Directory supports a user interface (UI) that adapts to meet the needs of administrators and end users. Active Directory enables you to extend the user interface that represents existing object classes as well as new classes added to the schema. You can control or extend the following UI elements for each class defined in the schema:

- Property pages
- Context menus
- Class display name
- Attribute display names
- Object creation wizard
- Class icons
- Containers viewed as leaf nodes

In addition, the Windows 2000 operating system provides COM objects that implement common dialog boxes for handling directory objects:

- Directory Object Picker (for specific types)
- Domain Browser
- Container Browser
- Query Forms

Note that your application can use these common dialog boxes to browse for, select, or query for directory objects instead of having to implement your own dialog boxes to perform these common actions.

For Active Directory administration snap-ins, context menus and property pages can also be extended using MMC extension snap-ins. You can also implement the other MMC extensions as well: taskpads, namespace items, control bars, and toolbars. For more information, see *Extending Active Directory Administrative Snap-ins using MMC Extension Snap-ins*.

Display Specifiers

In Active Directory, an object class (or class) defines a type of object that can be created in Active Directory. The definition of each object class is stored as a **classSchema** object in the Active Directory schema. In addition to the **classSchema** definition, each object class can have one or more display specifiers that specify the user interface information for objects of that class.

A display specifier is an Active Directory object of the **displaySpecifier** class. The attributes of a **displaySpecifier** object specify localized user interface information that describes the various UI elements for a particular object class. Display specifiers store information for property sheets, context menus, icons, creation wizards, and localized class and attribute names. For property pages and context menus, the Windows shell and Active Directory administrative snap-ins use this information to form different user interfaces for administrators and end users—one set of property pages and/or context menus can be associated with administrative applications while a different set of elements can be associated with end user applications.

The **displaySpecifier** objects are stored in locale-specific containers in the **DisplaySpecifiers** container in the **Configuration** container, which is replicated to every domain controller in the enterprise forest. The **DisplaySpecifiers** container has subcontainers that correspond to the various locales supported by the enterprise installation. These subcontainers are named using language identifiers (for example, the name of the locale container for US-English is 409, which corresponds to the hexadecimal language identifier, 0x0409). Thus, an object class can have multiple display specifiers: one in each locale subcontainer. For more information about locales, see *National Language Support*.

The name of a **displaySpecifier** object is formed by appending the string "-Display" to the **lDAPDisplayName** of the object class. For example, the name of a **displaySpecifier** object for the **user** class is "user-Display".

You can add, delete, or modify properties of a class's **displaySpecifier** objects to specify the UI elements (class name, attribute names, property sheets, context menus, icon, and so on) that appear for each instance of an object of that class.

The following example shows the values set on the group-Display display specifier object:

```
[group-Display]
objectClass = displaySpecifier
ObjectCategory = Display-Specifier
cn = group-Display
```

(continued)

(continued)

```
adminPropertyPages = 1,{6dfe6489-a212-11d0-bcd5-00c04fd8d5b6}
adminPropertyPages = 2,{6dfe648b-a212-11d0-bcd5-00c04fd8d5b6}
adminPropertyPages = 3,{6dfe6488-a212-11d0-bcd5-00c04fd8d5b6}
adminPropertyPages = 4,{4E40F770-369C-11d0-8922-00A024AB2DBB}
shellPropertyPages = 1,{f5d121ee-c8ac-11d0-bcdb-00c04fd8d5b6}
shellPropertyPages = 2,{dde2c5e9-c8ae-11d0-bcdb-00c04fd8d5b6}
contextMenu = 0,{62AE1F9A-126A-11D0-A14B-0800361B1103}
adminContextMenu = 1,{08eb4fa6-6ffd-11d1-b0e0-00c04fd8dca6}
classDisplayName = Group
attributeDisplayNames = cn,Name
attributeDisplayNames = c,Country Abbreviation
attributeDisplayNames = description,Description
attributeDisplayNames = distinguishedName,X500 Distinguished Name
attributeDisplayNames = l,City
attributeDisplayNames = managedBy,Managed By
attributeDisplayNames = member,Members
attributeDisplayNames = notes,Notes
attributeDisplayNames = physicalDeliveryOfficeName,Delivery Office
attributeDisplayNames = url,Web Page Address
treatAsLeaf=True
```

DisplaySpecifiers Container

Display specifiers are stored by locale in the DisplaySpecifiers container of the Configuration container. Because the Configuration container is replicated across the entire forest, display specifiers are propagated across all domains in a forest.

The Configuration container stores the DisplaySpecifiers container, which in turn stores containers that correspond to each locale. These locale containers are named using the hexadecimal representation of that locale's LCID. For example, the US/English locale's container is named **409**, the German locale's container is named **407**, and the Japanese locale's container is named **411**.

Each locale container stores objects of the **displaySpecifier** class.

To list all display specifiers for a locale, simply enumerate all the **displaySpecifier** objects in the specified locale container within the DisplaySpecifiers container.

The following code fragment contains a function that binds to the display specifier container for the specified locale:

```
// This function returns a pointer to the display specifier container
// for the specified locale. If locale is NULL, use default system
// locale and then return the locale in the locale parameter.
HRESULT BindToDisplaySpecifiersContainerByLocale(LCID *locale,
                                    IADs **ppDispSpecCont
                                    )

{
HRESULT hr = E_FAIL;
```

```
if ((!ppDispSpecCont)||(!locale))
  return E_POINTER;

// If no locale is specified, use the default system locale.
if (!(*locale))
{
    *locale = GetSystemDefaultLCID();
    if (!(*locale))
        return E_FAIL;
}

// Make sure that it's a valid locale.
if (!IsValidLocale(*locale, LCID_SUPPORTED))
    return E_INVALIDARG;

LPOLESTR szPath = new OLECHAR[MAX_PATH*2];
IADs *pObj = NULL;
VARIANT var;

hr = ADsOpenObject(L"LDAP://rootDSE",
                    NULL,
                    NULL,
                    ADS_SECURE_AUTHENTICATION,
                                //Use Secure Authentication
                    IID_IADs,
                    (void**)&pObj);

if (SUCCEEDED(hr))
{
    // Get the DN to the configuration container.
    hr = pObj->Get(L"configurationNamingContext", &var);
    if (SUCCEEDED(hr))
    {
        // Build the string to bind to the container for the
        // specified locale in the DisplaySpecifiers container.
        wsprintf(szPath, L"LDAP://cn=%x,cn=DisplaySpecifiers,%s", *locale,
var.bstrVal);
        // Bind to the container.
        *ppDispSpecCont = NULL;
        hr = ADsOpenObject(szPath,
                    NULL,
                    NULL,
                    ADS_SECURE_AUTHENTICATION,
                                //Use Secure Authentication
                    IID_IADs,
```

(continued)

(continued)

```
                    (void**)ppDispSpecCont);

    if(FAILED(hr))
    {
        if (!(*ppDispSpecCont))
        {
            (*ppDispSpecCont)->Release();
            (*ppDispSpecCont) = NULL;
        }
    }
}
}

// Clean up
VariantClear(&var);
if (pObj)
    pObj->Release();

return hr;
}
```

Property Pages for Use with Display Specifiers

A **displaySpecifier** object has two attributes that identify property pages to display in the property sheet for instances of an object class.

adminPropertyPages
Identifies administrative property pages to display in Active Directory™ administrative snap-ins.

shellPropertyPages
Identifies end-user property pages to display in the Microsoft® Windows® shell.

You can add values to these attributes in an existing **displaySpecifier** object to specify additional property pages to include in the administrative and/or end-user property sheets. For example, suppose you added a set of mayHave attributes to the schema definition of the **contact** class (see *Extending the Schema*). To display these new attributes to end users, you could specify additional property pages in the **shellPropertyPages** attribute of the **contact-Display** object for each supported locale. Then, when a user views a contact object, your property page is displayed with the rest of the property pages in the contact property sheet.

▶ **To add custom property pages to the property sheets for an object class**

1. Write the property page COM object. The property page COM object must implement **IShellExtInit** and **IShellPropSheetExt**. See *Implementing the Property Page COM Object.*

2. Install the property page COM object on the computers where you want the extension property pages to be used. To do this, create a Microsoft® Windows® Installer package for your property page COM object's DLL and deploy the package appropriately using the group policy. See *Using MSI and Windows 2000 Application Deployment to Distribute UI Additions*.

3. Register the property page COM object in the **adminPropertyPages** and/or **shellPropertyPages** attributes of the **displaySpecifier** objects for the object class. See *Registering the Property Page COM Object in a Display Specifier*.

Note that you can register the same property page COM object for more than one object class.

Note that registration is specific to one locale. If the property page COM object applies to all locales, register it in the object class's **displaySpecifier** object in all of the locale subcontainers in the **DisplaySpecifiers** container. If the property page COM object is localized for a certain locale, register it in the **displaySpecifier** object in that locale's subcontainer.

Implementing the Property Page COM Object

To extend property sheets for directory objects, a property page COM object must implement two shell interfaces: **IShellExtInit** and **IShellPropSheetExt**.

A property page COM object is instantiated when the user views the properties for an object of a class for which the property page has been registered. If the COM object was registered in the class's **adminPropertyPages** property, the property page appears when the user views properties for objects of that class in Active Directory administrative snap-ins. If it was registered in **shellPropertyPages**, the property page appears in the Windows shell.

The **IShellExtInit** interface has only one method and it must be implemented:

IShellExtInit::Initialize

After the property page COM object is instantiated, the shell calls the **IShellExtInit::Initialize** method. This is the property page COM object's only opportunity to get the **IDataObject** pointer that enables the object to get information about the selected objects. You should store the **IDataObject** pointer in a member variable so you can use the **IDataObject::GetData** method to retrieve information with the following clipboard formats:

CFSTR_DS_DISPLAY_SPEC_OPTIONS

Provides information about whether the property page was invoked by the Windows shell or by an Active Directory administrative snap-in. The data is returned as an HGLOBAL that points to a **DSDISPLAYSPECOPTIONS** structure. The structure contains additional information that tells you about the user context and server where the shell or snap-in retrieved the data about the selected objects. This additional information is useful if you need to bind to one or more objects in the selection.

CFSTR_DSOBJECTNAMES

Provides the list of objects that were selected when the property page was invoked by the Windows shell or by an Active Directory administrative snap-in. The data is returned as an HGLOBAL that points to a **DSOBJECTNAMES** structure. The structure contains the count of items in the selection and a pointer to an array of **DSOBJECT** structures that represent each selected item. The **DSOBJECT** structure contains the ADsPath, class name, and flags (indicating whether the page should be read-only and whether the object is a container). If it is necessary to read or modify properties on the object, the ADsPath can be used to bind to the object and perform the necessary operations.

You should also store the clipboard formats as member variables. The **IShellExtInit::Initialize** method is a good place to register these formats.

CFSTR_DSPROPERTYPAGEINFO

Applies only to property pages. This clipboard format provides the *optionaldata* string at the end of property page COM object's value in the **adminPropertyPages** and **shellPropertyPages** property. If optionaldata was not specified, **IDataObject::GetData** returns E_NOTIMPL.

The following code fragment contains an implementation of the **IShellExtInit::Initialize** method. This method releases the **IDataObject** pointer if **IShellExtInit::Initialize** was called before, stores the passed **IDataObject** pointer in a member variable, and registers the two clipboard formats in a member variable.

```
STDMETHODIMP CMyDsPropertyPage::Initialize(LPCITEMIDLIST pIDFolder,
                               LPDATAOBJECT pDataObj,
                               HKEY hRegKey)
{
    // Initialize can be called more than once.
    if (m_pDataObj)
        m_pDataObj->Release();

    // Keep a pointer to the IDataObject.
    if (pDataObj)
    {
        m_pDataObj = pDataObj;
        pDataObj->AddRef();
    }

    //Register the clipboard formats to use for getting info about
    //the selected DS objects.
    m_cfDsDispSpecOptions =
RegisterClipboardFormat(CFSTR_DS_DISPLAY_SPEC_OPTIONS);
    m_cfDsObjectNames = RegisterClipboardFormat(CFSTR_DSOBJECTNAMES);

    return NOERROR;
}
```

Note that the **IShellExtInit::Initialize** method is implemented the same way for context menu extensions.

After **IShellExtInit::Initialize** returns, the **IShellPropSheetExt::AddPages** method is called.

You can implement the property page(s) in the class implementing the **IShellPropSheetExt** and **IShellExtInit** interfaces. Or you can implement each property page in a class that is completely separate from the class implementing the two shell extension interfaces.

The class that implements the two shell extension interfaces only needs to be instantiated for the creation of the pages, whereas the class for each page lasts as long as the property sheet. By implementing a class for each page, the class can be tailored for manipulating the attributes displayed on its page. If the property pages are implemented as separate classes, the class implementing the property page should be initialized with the appropriate member data such as the **IDataObject** pointer and any other data about the selected objects required by the property page class.

The **IShellPropSheetExt** interface has two methods that must be implemented:

IShellPropSheetExt::AddPages
> This method is called just before the property sheet is displayed. This is the property page COM object's opportunity to create one or more property pages using the **CreatePropertySheetPage** function. In the **PROPSHEETPAGE** structure passed to **CreatePropertySheetPage**, store a **this** pointer to the class that owns the property page in the **lParam** member, so that the dialog box procedure for the property page can access the class members. When the dialog box procedure for the property page is called, the pointer to the **PROPSHEETPAGE** structure is passed as the **lParam**. This means the dialog box procedure has access to the class members.

> **Important**   The **IShellPropSheetExt::AddPages** method call runs on the caller's main thread. The dialog box procedure runs on a different thread. Therefore, do not reference the **IDataObject** pointer in the dialog box procedure unless it is first marshaled to this thread.

> If the dialog box procedure requires data from the **IDataObject**, you can avoiding having to marshal the **IDataObject** pointer by extracting the data that the dialog box procedure needs and storing that data in member variables in the class. This can be done in the **IShellExtInit::Initialize** or the **IShellPropSheetExt::AddPages** methods. Then the dialog box procedure can access the class members via the lParam. Typically, the dialog box procedure will need only the ADsPath of the selected objects so that it can then use the ADsPath information to bind and perform operations on those objects.

IShellPropSheetExt::ReplacePage
> This method is not called. It is only called for extension pages for the Control Panel. The method should just return E_FAIL.

The following code fragment contains an implementation of the **IShellPropSheetExt**
methods and the dialog box procedure for the single property page added by the
IShellPropSheetExt::AddPages method. The property page binds to the selected
object and displays some properties for it. For the full implementation of this sample, see
the following DSSamplePage sample.

```
STDMETHODIMP DSSamplePage::AddPages(LPFNADDPROPSHEETPAGE lpfnAddPage, LPARAM
lParam)
{
    HRESULT hr = S_OK;
    STGMEDIUM ObjMedium = {TYMED_NULL};
    FORMATETC fmte = {g_cfDsObjectNames, NULL, DVASPECT_CONTENT, -1,
TYMED_HGLOBAL};
    LPDSOBJECTNAMES pDsObjectNames;
    PWSTR pwzObjName;
    PWSTR pwzClass;

    // Get the path to the DS object from the data object.
    // Note: This call runs on the caller's main thread.
    // The pages' window procs run on a different thread, so don't
    // reference the data object from a winproc unless it is first
    // marshaled on this thread. For this sample, we extract the data
    // we want and store it in member variables so that the dialog proc
    // can access the data without having to marshall
    // the IDataObject pointer.
    hr = m_pDataObj->GetData(&fmte, &ObjMedium);
    if (SUCCEEDED(hr))
    {
        pDsObjectNames = (LPDSOBJECTNAMES)ObjMedium.hGlobal;

        if (pDsObjectNames->cItems < 1)
        {
            hr = E_FAIL;
        }
        pwzObjName = (PWSTR)ByteOffset(pDsObjectNames,
                                    pDsObjectNames->aObjects[0].offsetName);
        pwzClass = (PWSTR)ByteOffset(pDsObjectNames,
                                    pDsObjectNames->aObjects[0].offsetClass);
        // Save the ADsPath of object
        m_ObjPath = new WCHAR [wcslen(pwzObjName )+1];
        wcscpy(m_ObjPath,pwzObjName);
    }

    // Now release the ObjMedium:
    // If punkForRelease is NULL, the receiver of
    // the medium is responsible for releasing it; otherwise,
```

```
// punkForRelease points to the IUnknown on the appropriate
// object so its Release method can be called.

ReleaseStgMedium(&ObjMedium);

PROPSHEETPAGE psp;
HPROPSHEETPAGE hpage;
HRESULT hres = 0;

LPCSHELLEXT lpcsext = this;
//
// Create a property sheet page object from a dialog box.
//
// We store a pointer to our class in the psp.lParam, so we
// can access our class members from within the DSSamplePageDlgProc.
//
// If the page needs more instance data, you can append
// arbitrary size of data at the end of this structure,
// and pass it to the CreatePropSheetPage. In such a case,
// the size of entire data structure (including page specific
// data) must be stored in the dwSize field.   Note that in
// general you should NOT need to do this, as you can simply
// store a pointer to data in the lParam member.
//

psp.dwSize       = sizeof(psp);   // no extra data.
psp.dwFlags      =  PSP_USETITLE | PSP_USECALLBACK;
psp.hInstance    = g_hInstance;
psp.pszTemplate  = MAKEINTRESOURCE(IDD_DSSamplePage);
psp.hIcon        = 0;
psp.pszTitle     = L"Object Stats";
psp.pfnDlgProc   = DSSamplePageDlgProc;
psp.pcRefParent  = NULL;//&g_cRefThisDll;
psp.pfnCallback  = DSSamplePageCallback;
psp.lParam       = (LPARAM)lpcsext;

AddRef();
hpage = CreatePropertySheetPage(&psp);

if (hpage)
{
    if (!lpfnAddPage(hpage, lParam))
    {
        DestroyPropertySheetPage(hpage);
        Release();
    }
```

(continued)

(continued)

```
    }

    return NOERROR;

}


STDMETHODIMP DSSamplePage::ReplacePage(UINT uPageID, LPFNADDPROPSHEETPAGE
lpfnReplaceWith, LPARAM lParam)
{
    return E_FAIL;
}


BOOL CALLBACK DSSamplePageDlgProc(HWND hDlg,
                                 UINT uMessage,
                                 WPARAM wParam,
                                 LPARAM lParam)
{
    LPPROPSHEETPAGE psp=(LPPROPSHEETPAGE)GetWindowLong(hDlg, DWL_USER);
    UINT iIndex=0;
    LPCSHELLEXT lpcs;

    switch (uMessage)
    {
        //
        // When the shell or snap-in creates a dialog box for a
        // property sheet page, it passes the pointer to the
        // PROPSHEETPAGE data structure as lParam. The dialog procedures
        // of extensions typically store it in the DWL_USER of the
        // dialog box window.
        //
        case WM_INITDIALOG:
            {
                SetWindowLong(hDlg, DWL_USER, lParam);
                BSTR bsResult;

                psp = (LPPROPSHEETPAGE)lParam;

                lpcs = (LPCSHELLEXT)psp->lParam;

                HRESULT hr;
                IADs* pIADs = NULL;

                hr = ADsGetObject( lpcs->m_ObjPath, IID_IADs,(void **)&pIADs);
```

```
if (SUCCEEDED(hr))
{
    // Retrieves the GUID for this object- The guid
    // uniquely identifies this directory object. The
    // Guid is globally unique. Also the guid is
    // rename/move safe. The ADsPath below returns the
    // CURRENT location of the object- The guid remains
    // constant regardless of name or location of the
    // directory object
    pIADs->get_GUID(&bsResult);
    SetWindowText(GetDlgItem(hDlg,IDC_GUID),bsResult);
    SysFreeString(bsResult);

    // Retrieves the RDN
    pIADs->get_Name(&bsResult);
    SetWindowText(GetDlgItem(hDlg,IDC_NAME),bsResult);
    SysFreeString(bsResult);

    // Retrieves the value in the class attribute,
    // that is, group
    pIADs->get_Class(&bsResult);
    SetWindowText(GetDlgItem(hDlg,IDC_CLASS),bsResult);
    SysFreeString(bsResult);

    // Retrieves the full literal LDAP path for
    // this object.
    // This may be used to re-bind to this object-
    // though for persistent storage (and to be
    // 'move\rename' safe) it is suggested that the
    // guid be used instead of the ADsPath
    pIADs->get_ADsPath(&bsResult);
    SetWindowText(GetDlgItem(hDlg,IDC_ADSPATH),bsResult);
    SysFreeString(bsResult);

    // Retrieves the LDAP path for the
    // parent\container for this object
    pIADs->get_Parent(&bsResult);
    SetWindowText(GetDlgItem(hDlg,IDC_PARENT),bsResult);
    SysFreeString(bsResult);

    // Retrieves the LDAP path for the Schema
    // definition of the object returned from
    // the IADs::get_Schema() member
    pIADs->get_Schema(&bsResult);
    SetWindowText(GetDlgItem(hDlg,IDC_SCHEMA),bsResult);
    SysFreeString(bsResult);
```

(continued)

(continued)

```
                pIADs->Release();
                pIADs = NULL;
            }
        }
        break;

    case WM_DESTROY:
        RemoveProp(hDlg, L"ID");
        break;

    case WM_NOTIFY:
        switch (((NMHDR FAR *)lParam)->code)
        {
            case PSN_SETACTIVE:
                break;

            case PSN_APPLY:
                //TODO: Apply changes user made here.
                break;

            default:
                break;
        }
        break;

    default:
        return FALSE;
    }

    return TRUE;
}
```

Registering the Property Page COM Object in a Display Specifier

Even after you've written and installed your property page COM object, the Windows shell and Active Directory administrative snap-ins cannot recognize it yet. For the Windows shell or Active Directory administrative snap-ins to recognize your property page, you must add a value for your property page COM object in the **adminPropertyPages** and/or **shellPropertyPages** property of the display specifier for the class whose property sheet you want to extend. Note that you can register the same property page COM object for more than one class.

If the COM object was registered in the **adminPropertyPages** property of the class's display specifier, the property page appears when the user views properties for objects of that class in Active Directory administrative snap-ins. If it was registered in **shellPropertyPages**, the property page appears in the Windows shell. If you want it to appear in both the shell and administrative snap-ins, you need to register the COM object in both properties.

The **adminPropertyPages** and **shellPropertyPages** properties are multi-valued. The **adminPropertyPages** contains the list of property pages for Active Directory administrative snap-ins to display in the property sheet for the object class. The **shellPropertyPages** contains the list for the Windows shell.

Each value is a string with the following format:

ordernumber,CLSID,optionaldata

In this example, the *ordernumber* is an unsigned number that represents the page's position on the sheet. When a property sheet is displayed, the values are sorted using a comparison of each value's *ordernumber*. If more than one value has the same *ordernumber*, those property page COM objects are loaded in the order they are read from Active Directory ; however, you should use a non-existing *ordernumber* (that is, one that has not been used by other values in the property). There is no prescribed starting position, and gaps are allowed in the *ordernumber* sequence.

The *CLSID* is the CLSID of the property page COM object in the string format produced by the **StringFromGUID2** function in the COM library.

The *optionaldata* can be retrieved by the property page COM object using the **IDataObject** pointer passed to its **IShellExtInit::Initialize** method. The *optionaldata* is not required. The property page COM object calls **IDataObject::GetData** method with the clipboard format CF_DSPROPERTYPAGEINFO and gets an global memory handle (HGLOBAL) to a **DSPROPERTYPAGEINFO** structure containing the offset to the Unicode string containing *optionaldata*. A COM object can implement more than one property page. So, one possible use of the *optionaldata* is to name the pages to display. This gives you the flexibility of choosing to implement multiple COM objects (one for each page) or a single COM object to handle multiple pages.

The following string is an example value for the **adminPropertyPages** or **shellPropertyPages** properties:

```
1,{6dfe6485-a212-11d0-bcd5-00c04fd8d5b6}
```

Important For the Windows shell, display specifier information is retrieved at user logon, and cached for the user's session. For the administrative snap-ins, the display specifier information is retrieved when the snap-in is loaded, and is cached for the lifetime of the process. For the Windows shell, this means changes to display specifiers take effect after a user logs off and back on again. For the administrative snap-ins, changes take effect when the snap-in or console file is loaded.

Adding a Value to the adminPropertyPages or shellPropertyPages properties

When you add a value for your property page COM object to **adminPropertyPages** or **shellPropertyPages**, follow these rules:

1. Make sure it hasn't already been added.

2. Add a new value at the end of the property page ordering list. This means setting the *ordernumber* portion of the value to the next value after the highest existing *ordernumber*.

3. To add the value, use the **IADs::PutEx** method with the *InControlCode* parameter set to ADS_PROPERTY_APPEND so that the value will be added to the existing values (and, therefore, not overwrite the existing values). Make sure you call **IADs::SetInfo** to commit the change to the directory.

The following program adds a property page to the group class in the computer's default locale. Note how the **AddPropertyPageToDisplaySpecifier** function checks for the property page's CLSID in the existing values, gets the highest *ordernumber*, and adds the value for the property page using **IADs::PutEx** with the ADS_PROPERTY_APPEND control code.

```
#include <wchar.h>
#include <objbase.h>
#include <activeds.h>

HRESULT AddPropertyPageToDisplaySpecifier(
    LPOLESTR szClassName, //ldapDisplayName of class
    CLSID *pPropPageCLSID //CLSID of property page COM object
    );

HRESULT BindToDisplaySpecifiersContainerByLocale(LCID *locale,
                                      IADsContainer **ppDispSpecCont
                                      );

HRESULT GetDisplaySpecifier(IADsContainer *pContainer, LPOLESTR szDispSpec, IADs
**ppObject);


void wmain( int argc, wchar_t *argv[ ])
{

wprintf(L"This program adds a sample property page to the display specifier for
group class in the local computer's default locale.\n");

//Initialize COM.
CoInitialize(NULL);
HRESULT hr = S_OK;
```

```
//Class ID for the sample property page
LPOLESTR szCLSID = L"{D9FCE809-8A10-11d2-A7E7-00C04F79DC0F}";
LPOLESTR szClass = L"group";
CLSID clsid;
//Convert to GUID.
hr = CLSIDFromString(
    szCLSID,  //Pointer to the string representation of the CLSID.
    &clsid    //Pointer to the CLSID.
    );


hr = AddPropertyPageToDisplaySpecifier(
    szClass, //ldapDisplayName of class
    &clsid //CLSID of property page COM object
    );
if (S_OK == hr)
    wprintf(L"Property page registered successfully\n");
else if (S_FALSE == hr)
    wprintf(L"Property page was not added because it was already registered.\n");
else
    wprintf(L"Property page was not added. HR: %x.\n");

//Uninitialize COM.
CoUninitialize();
return;
}


//Adds a property page to Active Directory admin snap-ins.
HRESULT AddPropertyPageToDisplaySpecifier(
    LPOLESTR szClassName, //ldapDisplayName of class.
    CLSID *pPropPageCLSID //CLSID of property page COM object.
    )
{
HRESULT hr = E_FAIL;
IADsContainer *pContainer = NULL;
LPOLESTR szDispSpec = new OLECHAR[MAX_PATH];
IADs *pObject = NULL;
VARIANT var;
LPOLESTR szProperty = L"adminPropertyPages";
LCID locale = NULL;
//Get the display specifier container using default system locale.
//Note that when you are adding your property page COM object,
//you should specify the locale because the registration is
//locale specific. This means if you created a property page
//for German, you want to explicitly add it to the 407 container
```

(continued)

(continued)

```
//so that it will be used when a computer is running with locale
//set to German AND NOT whatever locale set on the
//computer where this program is running.
hr = BindToDisplaySpecifiersContainerByLocale(&locale,
                                   &pContainer
                                        );
//TODO: Need to handle fail case where dispspec object
//is not found and give option to create one.

if (SUCCEEDED(hr))
{
    //Bind to display specifier object for the specified class.
    //Build the display specifier name.
    wcscpy(szDispSpec, szClassName);
    wcscat(szDispSpec, L"-Display");
    hr = GetDisplaySpecifier(pContainer, szDispSpec, &pObject);
    if (SUCCEEDED(hr))
    {
        //Convert GUID to string.
        LPOLESTR szDSGUID = new WCHAR [39];
        ::StringFromGUID2(*pPropPageCLSID, szDSGUID, 39);

        //Get the adminPropertyPages property.
        hr = pObject->GetEx(szProperty,&var);
        if (SUCCEEDED(hr))
        {
          LONG lstart, lend;
          SAFEARRAY *sa = V_ARRAY( &var );
          VARIANT varItem;
          // Get the lower and upper bound.
           hr = SafeArrayGetLBound( sa, 1, &lstart );
          if (SUCCEEDED(hr))
          {
            hr = SafeArrayGetUBound( sa, 1, &lend );
          }
          if (SUCCEEDED(hr))
          {
            //Now iterate the values to check if the prop page's CLSID
            //is already registered.
            VariantInit(&varItem);
            BOOL bExists = FALSE;
            UINT uiLastItem = 0;
            UINT uiTemp = 0;
            INT iOffset = 0;
            LPOLESTR szMainStr = new OLECHAR[MAX_PATH];
            LPOLESTR szItem = new OLECHAR[MAX_PATH];
```

```
LPOLESTR szStr = NULL;
for ( long idx=lstart; idx <= lend; idx++ )
{
  hr = SafeArrayGetElement( sa, &idx, &varItem );
  if (SUCCEEDED(hr))
  {
    //Check if the specified CLSID is already registered.
    wcscpy(szMainStr,varItem.bstrVal);
    if (wcsstr( szMainStr,szDSGUID))
        bExists = TRUE;
    //Get the index which is the number before
    //the first comma.
    szStr = wcschr(szMainStr, '.');
    iOffset = (int)(szStr - szMainStr);
    wcsncpy( szItem, szMainStr, iOffset );
    szItem[iOffset]=0L;
    uiTemp = _wtoi(szItem);
    if (uiTemp > uiLastItem)
        uiLastItem = uiTemp;
    VariantClear(&varItem);
  }
}
//If the CLSID is not registered, add it.
if (!bExists)
{
    //Build the value to add.
    LPOLESTR szValue = new OLECHAR[MAX_PATH];
    //Next index to add at end of list.
    uiLastItem++;
    _itow( uiLastItem, szValue, 10 );
    wcscat(szValue,L",");
    //Add the class ID for the property page.
    wcscat(szValue,szDSGUID);
    //wprintf(L"Value to add: %s\n", szValue);
    VARIANT varAdd;
    //Only one value to add
    LPOLESTR pszAddStr[1];
    pszAddStr[0]=szValue;
    ADsBuildVarArrayStr(pszAddStr, 1, &varAdd);

    hr = pObject->PutEx( ADS_PROPERTY_APPEND, szProperty, varAdd );
    if (SUCCEEDED(hr))
    {
        //Commit the change.
        hr = pObject->SetInfo();
    }
```

(continued)

(continued)

```
            }
            else
                hr = S_FALSE;
            }
        }
        VariantClear(&var);
    }
    if (pObject)
    pObject->Release();
}

return hr;
}

//This function returns a pointer to the display specifier container
//for the specified locale.
//If locale is NULL, use the default system locale and then
//return the locale in the locale param.
HRESULT BindToDisplaySpecifiersContainerByLocale(LCID *locale,
                                       IADsContainer **ppDispSpecCont
                                                )

{
HRESULT hr = E_FAIL;

if ((!ppDispSpecCont)||(!locale))
    return E_POINTER;

//If no locale is specified, use the default system locale.
if (!(*locale))
{
    *locale = GetSystemDefaultLCID();
    if (!(*locale))
    return E_FAIL;
}

//Make sure that it's a valid locale.
if (!IsValidLocale(*locale, LCID_SUPPORTED))
    return E_INVALIDARG;

LPOLESTR szPath = new OLECHAR[MAX_PATH*2];
IADs *pObj = NULL;
VARIANT var;

hr = ADsOpenObject(L"LDAP://rootDSE",
                    NULL,
                    NULL,
```

```
                              ADS_SECURE_AUTHENTICATION,
                                        //Use Secure Authentication.
                        IID_IADs,
                        (void**)&pObj);

if (SUCCEEDED(hr))
{
    //Get the DN to the config container.
    hr = pObj->Get(L"configurationNamingContext",&var);
    if (SUCCEEDED(hr))
    {
        //Build the string to bind to the DisplaySpecifiers container.
        swprintf(szPath,L"LDAP://cn=%x,cn=DisplaySpecifiers,%s", *locale,
var.bstrVal);
        //Bind to the DisplaySpecifiers container.
        *ppDispSpecCont = NULL;
        hr = ADsOpenObject(szPath,
            NULL,
            NULL,
            ADS_SECURE_AUTHENTICATION, //Use Secure Authentication
            IID_IADsContainer,
            (void**)ppDispSpecCont);

        if(FAILED(hr))
        {
            if (!(*ppDispSpecCont))
            {
                (*ppDispSpecCont)->Release();
                (*ppDispSpecCont) = NULL;
            }
        }
    }
}
//Clean up
VariantClear(&var);
if (pObj)
    pObj->Release();

return hr;
}

HRESULT GetDisplaySpecifier(IADsContainer *pContainer, LPOLESTR szDispSpec, IADs
**ppObject)
{
HRESULT hr = E_FAIL;
LPOLESTR szDSPath = new OLECHAR [MAX_PATH];
```

(continued)

(continued)

```
IDispatch *pDisp = NULL;

//Build relative path to the display specifier object.
wcscpy(szDSPath, L"CN=");
wcscat(szDSPath, szDispSpec);
if (!pContainer)
{
    hr = E_POINTER;
    return hr;
}
//TODO check the other pointers.
//Initialize the output pointer.
(*ppObject) = NULL;

//Use child object binding with IADsContainer::GetObject.
hr = pContainer->GetObject(L"displaySpecifier",
                     szDSPath,
                     &pDisp);
if (SUCCEEDED(hr))
{
    hr = pDisp->QueryInterface(IID_IADs, (void**)ppObject);
    if (FAILED(hr))
    {
        //Clean up
        if (*ppObject)
        (*ppObject)->Release();
    }
}

if (pDisp)
    pDisp->Release();

return hr;

}
```

Context Menus for Use with Display Specifiers

You can add context menus to the existing context menus for a particular object class within the Microsoft® Windows® shell or Active Directory™ administrative snap-ins. Context menu items may be either COM objects, which are activated using the standard COM instance creation methods, or an application that is invoked using the standard **ShellExecute** function.

For example, you can implement a context menu COM object that adds menu items to the context menu of the contact class. When a user views a contact object, your context menu items are displayed along with other context menu items in the contact context menu.

▶ **To extend context menus with context menu items from a COM object**

1. Write the property page COM object. The property page COM object must implement **IShellExtInit** and **IContextMenu**.

2. Install the context menu COM object on the computers where you want the extension context menu items to be used. It is recommended that you create a Microsoft Installer package for your context menu COM object's DLL and deploy the package appropriately using the group policy. See *Using MSI and Windows 2000 Application Deployment to Distribute UI Additions*.

3. Register the context menu extension for a particular object class so that the context menu is added to the context menus of objects of that class.

   For the Windows shell or Active Directory administrative snap-ins to recognize your context menu, you must add a value for your context menu COM object in the **adminContextMenu** and/or **shellContextMenu** property of the display specifier for the class whose context menu you want to extend. Note that you can register the same context menu COM object for more than one class.

   Note that registration is per locale. If the context menu COM object is specific to a certain locale, it should be registered in a displaySpecifier in the locale container that it applies to. If it applies to all locales, it should be added to the appropriate displaySpecifier (that is, the one that represents the class that should get the context menu extension) in all locale containers.

▶ **To extend context menus with context menu items that launch an application**

1. Install the application where you want the extension context menu items to be used.

2. Register the context menu extension for a particular object class so that the context menu is added to the context menus of objects of that class. Note that value added for the extension takes a slightly different format.

Implementing the Context Menu COM Object

To extend context menus with custom menu items for directory objects, a context menu COM object must implement two shell interfaces: **IShellExtInit** and **IContextMenu**.

A context menu COM object is instantiated when the user opens the context menu for an object of a class for which the context menu extension has been registered. If the COM object was registered in the class's **adminContextMenu** property, the COM object's context menu items appear in the context menu for objects of that class in Active Directory administrative snap-ins. If it was registered in **shellContextMenu**, the context menu items appear in the Windows shell.

After the context menu COM object is instantiated, the **IShellExtInit::Initialize** method is called. The **IShellExtInit** interface has only one method and it must be implemented. This is the context menu COM object's only opportunity to get the **IDataObject** pointer that enables the object to get information about the selected directory objects. Follow the same rules and recommendations as the implementation for property page COM objects. See *Implementing the Property Page COM Object*.

After **IShellExtInit::Initialize** returns, the **IContextMenu::QueryContextMenu** method is called. The **IContextMenu** interface has three methods that must be implemented:

IContextMenu::QueryContextMenu
Called just before the context menu is displayed. This is the context menu COM object's opportunity to add menu items using the **InsertMenu** function.

IContextMenu::GetCommandString
Called when a context menu item is selected. This is the context menu COM object's opportunity to display status bar text. Make sure that you cast the pszName parameter to a Unicode string when specifying the text to display.

IContextMenu::InvokeCommand
Called when a context menu item is chosen. This is the context menu COM object's opportunity to perform the action represented by the menu item.

Example Code for Implementation of the Context Menu COM Object

The following code fragment contains an implementation of the **IShellExtInit** and **IContextMenu** methods and the command handler methods for each menu command added by the **IContextMenu::QueryContextMenu** method. The context menu items display message boxes with various information (such as the contents of the two supported clipboard formats). For the full implementation of this sample, see the following MyContextMenu sample.

```
STDMETHODIMP CMyDsContextMenu::QueryContextMenu(HMENU hMenu,
                                                UINT indexMenu,
                                                UINT idCmdFirst,
                                                UINT idCmdLast,
                                                UINT uFlags)
{
    UINT idCmd = idCmdFirst;
    WCHAR szMenuText1[64];
    WCHAR szMenuText2[64];
    WCHAR szMenuText3[64];
    WCHAR szMenuText4[64];
    WCHAR *szMenuGetSupportedClipboardFormats = L"Get Supported Clipboard
Formats";
    WCHAR *szMenuGetDsDisplaySpecOptions = L"Get Data Using DsDisplaySpecOptions
Clipboard Format";
```

```
    WCHAR *szMenuGetDsObjectNames = L"Get Data Using DsObjectNames Clipboard
Format";
    BOOL bAppendItems=TRUE;

    //Check the flags
    //Normal
    //Note that the administrative snap-ins will
    //use only the CMF_NORMAL state.
    //So CMF_EXPLORE will never be set for admin snap-ins.
    if ((uFlags & 0x000F) == CMF_NORMAL)
    //Check == here, since CMF_NORMAL=0
    {
        wcscpy(szMenuText1, L"Do DoMenuCmd&1 (Normal)");
        wcscpy(szMenuText2, L"Do DoMenuCmd&2 (Normal)");
        wcscpy(szMenuText3, L"Do DoMenuCmd&3 (Normal)");
        wcscpy(szMenuText4, L"Do DoMenuCmd&4 (Normal)");
    }
    //Note that if the context menu is a shell extension,
    //the Windows shell may be displaying the object in Explorer view.
    //This can be handled differently based on what you need/want.
    else if (uFlags & CMF_EXPLORE)
    {
        wcscpy(szMenuText1, L"Do DoMenuCmd&1 (Explorer)");
        wcscpy(szMenuText2, L"Do DoMenuCmd&2 (Explorer)");
        wcscpy(szMenuText3, L"Do DoMenuCmd&3 (Explorer)");
        wcscpy(szMenuText4, L"Do DoMenuCmd&4 (Explorer)");
    }
    else if (uFlags & CMF_DEFAULTONLY)
    {
        bAppendItems = FALSE;
    }
    else
    {
        bAppendItems = FALSE;
    }

    //Insert the menu items.
    if (bAppendItems)
    {
        InsertMenuW(hMenu, indexMenu++, MF_SEPARATOR|MF_BYPOSITION, 0, NULL);

        InsertMenuW(hMenu,
                    indexMenu++,
                    MF_STRING|MF_BYPOSITION,
                    idCmd++,
                    szMenuText1);
```

(continued)

(continued)

```
        InsertMenuW(hMenu, indexMenu++, MF_SEPARATOR|MF_BYPOSITION, 0, NULL);

        InsertMenuW(hMenu,
                indexMenu++,
                MF_STRING|MF_BYPOSITION,
                idCmd++,
                szMenuText2);

        InsertMenuW(hMenu, indexMenu++, MF_SEPARATOR|MF_BYPOSITION, 0, NULL);

        InsertMenuW(hMenu,
                indexMenu++,
                MF_STRING|MF_BYPOSITION,
                idCmd++,
                szMenuText3);

        InsertMenuW(hMenu,
                indexMenu++,
                MF_STRING|MF_BYPOSITION,
                idCmd++,
                szMenuText4);

        InsertMenuW(hMenu,
                indexMenu++,
                MF_STRING|MF_BYPOSITION,
                idCmd++,
                szMenuGetSupportedClipboardFormats);

        InsertMenuW(hMenu,
                indexMenu++,
                MF_STRING|MF_BYPOSITION,
                idCmd++,
                szMenuGetDsDisplaySpecOptions);

        InsertMenuW(hMenu,
                indexMenu++,
                MF_STRING|MF_BYPOSITION,
                idCmd++,
                szMenuGetDsObjectNames);


    return ResultFromShort(idCmd-idCmdFirst);
    //Must return number of menu items we added.
    }
    return NOERROR;
```

```
}

STDMETHODIMP CMyDsContextMenu::InvokeCommand(LPCMINVOKECOMMANDINFO lpcmi)
{

    HRESULT hr = E_INVALIDARG;


    if (!HIWORD(lpcmi->lpVerb))
    {
        UINT idCmd = LOWORD(lpcmi->lpVerb);

        switch (idCmd)
        {
            case 0:
                hr = DoMenuCmd1(lpcmi->hwnd,
                               lpcmi->lpDirectory,
                               lpcmi->lpVerb,
                               lpcmi->lpParameters,
                               lpcmi->nShow);
                break;

            case 1:
                hr = DoMenuCmd2(lpcmi->hwnd,
                               lpcmi->lpDirectory,
                               lpcmi->lpVerb,
                               lpcmi->lpParameters,
                               lpcmi->nShow);
                break;

            case 2:
                hr = DoMenuCmd3(lpcmi->hwnd,
                               lpcmi->lpDirectory,
                               lpcmi->lpVerb,
                               lpcmi->lpParameters,
                               lpcmi->nShow);
                break;

            case 3:
                hr = DoMenuCmd4(lpcmi->hwnd,
                               lpcmi->lpDirectory,
                               lpcmi->lpVerb,
                               lpcmi->lpParameters,
                               lpcmi->nShow);
            case 4:
                hr = GetSupportedClipboardFormats(lpcmi->hwnd,m_pDataObj);
```

(continued)

(continued)

```
                    break;

            case 5:
                hr = GetDsDisplaySpecOptions(lpcmi->hwnd,m_pDataObj);
                break;

            case 6:
                hr = GetDsObjectNames(lpcmi->hwnd,m_pDataObj);
                break;
        }
    }
/*
    else if (HIWORD(lpcmi->lpVerb))
    {
    //Handle this for returning language independent command names.

    }
*/
    return hr;
}


//
//   FUNCTION: CMyDsContextMenu::GetCommandString
//
//   Called by the shell after the user has selected a
//   menu item that was added in QueryContextMenu().
//

STDMETHODIMP CMyDsContextMenu::GetCommandString(UINT idCmd,
                                                UINT uFlags,
                                                UINT FAR *reserved,
                                                LPSTR pszName,
                                                UINT cchMax)
{
if ((uFlags & GCS_HELPTEXT) != 0)
{
    switch (idCmd)
    {
    //Need to cast pszName to a Unicode string.
    //TODO check pszName length against cchMax
        case 0:
            wcscpy((LPOLESTR)pszName, L"New menu item number 1");
            break;

        case 1:
```

```
                wcscpy((LPOLESTR)pszName, L"New menu item number 2");
                break;

            case 2:
                wcscpy((LPOLESTR)pszName, L"New menu item number 3");
                break;

            case 3:
                wcscpy((LPOLESTR)pszName, L"New menu item number 4");
                break;
            case 4:
                wcscpy((LPOLESTR)pszName, L"Get Supported Clipboard Formats");
            case 5:
                wcscpy((LPOLESTR)pszName, L"Get Data Using DsDisplaySpecOptions
Clipboard Format");
            case 6:
                wcscpy((LPOLESTR)pszName, L"Get Data Using DsObjectNames Clipboard
Format");
        }
        return S_OK;
    }
/*
    else if (uFlags == GCS_VERB)
    {
        //Handle this flag for returning language independent command names

        }
*/
    return E_FAIL;
    }

//Command Handlers

STDMETHODIMP CMyDsContextMenu::DoMenuCmd1(HWND hParent,
                                    LPCSTR pszWorkingDir,
                                    LPCSTR pszCmd,
                                    LPCSTR pszParam,
                                    int iShowCmd)

{

    MessageBoxW(hParent, L"Menu item 1!", L"Shell Extension Sample", MB_OK);

    return NOERROR;
}

STDMETHODIMP CMyDsContextMenu::DoMenuCmd2(HWND hParent,
```

(continued)

(continued)

```
                                    LPCSTR pszWorkingDir,
                                    LPCSTR pszCmd,
                                    LPCSTR pszParam,
                                    int iShowCmd)
{

    MessageBoxW(hParent, L"Menu item 2!", L"Shell Extension Sample", MB_OK);

    return NOERROR;
}

STDMETHODIMP CMyDsContextMenu::DoMenuCmd3(HWND hParent,
                                    LPCSTR pszWorkingDir,
                                    LPCSTR pszCmd,
                                    LPCSTR pszParam,
                                    int iShowCmd)
{

    MessageBoxW(hParent, L"Menu item 3!", L"Shell Extension Sample", MB_OK);

    return NOERROR;
}

STDMETHODIMP CMyDsContextMenu::DoMenuCmd4(HWND hParent,
                                    LPCSTR pszWorkingDir,
                                    LPCSTR pszCmd,
                                    LPCSTR pszParam,
                                    int iShowCmd)
{

    MessageBoxW(hParent, L"Menu item 4!", L"Shell Extension Sample", MB_OK);

    return NOERROR;
}

STDMETHODIMP CMyDsContextMenu::Initialize(LPCITEMIDLIST pIDFolder,
                                    LPDATAOBJECT pDataObj,
                                    HKEY hRegKey)
{

    // Initialize can be called more than once

    if (m_pDataObj)
      m_pDataObj->Release();

    // Keep a pointer to the IDataObject
```

```
    if (pDataObj)
    {
      m_pDataObj = pDataObj;
      pDataObj->AddRef();
    }


    //Register the clipboard formats to use for getting info about
    //the selected DS object.
    m_cfDsDispSpecOptions =
RegisterClipboardFormat(CFSTR_DS_DISPLAY_SPEC_OPTIONS);
    m_cfDsObjectNames = RegisterClipboardFormat(CFSTR_DSOBJECTNAMES);

    return NOERROR;
}

STDMETHODIMP CMyDsContextMenu::GetSupportedClipboardFormats(HWND hParent,
IDataObject *pDO)
{
#define FORMATETC_MAX 20
    LPOLESTR szText = new OLECHAR[MAX_PATH*4];
    OLECHAR szCFName[MAX_PATH];
    HRESULT hr = E_FAIL;
    LPENUMFORMATETC lpEnumFmtEtc = NULL;
    FORMATETC rgfmtetc[FORMATETC_MAX];
    int iReturn = 0;
    ULONG j;
    ULONG cFetched = 0;

    hr = pDO->EnumFormatEtc(
        DATADIR_GET,
        (LPENUMFORMATETC FAR*)&lpEnumFmtEtc
        );
    if (FAILED(hr))
    {
    //Not implemented in Users and Computers snap-in.
    if (E_NOTIMPL==hr)
        swprintf(szText,L"EnumFormatEtc method is not implemented in the Users
and Computers snap-in.");
    else
        swprintf(szText,L"EnumFormatEtc method failed with hr: %x",hr);

    MessageBoxW(hParent,szText,L"Clipboard formats",MB_OK);
        return hr;    // unable to get format enumerator
    }
    //Is implemented in the Windows shell.
```

(continued)

(continued)

```
    //Enumerate the formats offered by the source.
    // Loop over all formats offered by the source.
    memset(rgfmtetc,0,sizeof(rgfmtetc[FORMATETC_MAX]) );
    hr = lpEnumFmtEtc->Next(FORMATETC_MAX,
                    rgfmtetc,
                    &cFetched);
    if ( SUCCEEDED(hr) || (cFetched > 0 && cFetched <= FORMATETC_MAX) )
    {
    wcscpy(szText,L"Supported clipboard formats:\n");
        for (j = 0; j < cFetched; j++)
        {
            iReturn = GetClipboardFormatNameW(
                rgfmtetc[j].cfFormat, //Clipboard format to retrieve.
                szCFName,             //Address of buffer for name.
                sizeof(szCFName)      //Length of string in characters.
                );
        if (iReturn)
        {
            wcscat(szText,szCFName );
            wcscat(szText,L"\n");
        }
        else
        {
            swprintf(szCFName,L"Unknown clipboard format
%d\n",rgfmtetc[j].cfFormat);
            wcscat(szText,szCFName );
        }
    }
    MessageBoxW(hParent,szText,L"Clipboard formats",MB_OK);
}
    else
    {
    swprintf(szText,L"Next method failed with hr: %x",hr);
    MessageBoxW(hParent,szText,L"Clipboard formats",MB_OK);
    }



    //Clean up
    if (lpEnumFmtEtc)
        lpEnumFmtEtc->Release();
    return hr;
}
```

```
STDMETHODIMP CMyDsContextMenu::GetDsDisplaySpecOptions(HWND hParent,
                                       IDataObject *pDO)
{

LPOLESTR szText = new OLECHAR[MAX_PATH*4];
HRESULT hr = S_OK;
PDSDISPLAYSPECOPTIONS pDsSpecOptions = NULL;
LPOLESTR szPrefix = NULL;

//Need to get CFSTR_DS_DISPLAY_SPEC_OPTIONS as HGLOBAL.
STGMEDIUM stgmedium = {
    TYMED_HGLOBAL,
    NULL,
    NULL
};

//Initialize formatetc for CFSTR_DS_DISPLAY_SPEC_OPTIONS format.
FORMATETC formatetc = {
    m_cfDsDispSpecOptions,
    NULL,
    DVASPECT_CONTENT,
    -1,
    TYMED_HGLOBAL
};

// Get the global memory block containing the display option
// info for the selected objects.
hr = pDO->GetData(&formatetc, &stgmedium);
if (FAILED(hr))
{
    //Not implemented.
    if (E_NOTIMPL==hr)
        swprintf(szText,L"GetData method is not implemented.");
    else
        swprintf(szText,L"GetData method failed with hr: %x",hr);

    MessageBoxW(hParent,szText,L"GetData using DsDisplaySpecOptions",MB_OK);
    return hr;     //Unable to get data.
}
// Assign pointer to DSDISPLAYSPECOPTIONS structure.
pDsSpecOptions = (PDSDISPLAYSPECOPTIONS) GlobalLock(stgmedium.hGlobal);
if (pDsSpecOptions)
{
    //Use the ByteOffset macro that was defined
    //to move to the appropriate offset based on offsetAttributePrefix.
    szPrefix = (LPOLESTR)ByteOffset(pDsSpecOptions,
```

(continued)

(continued)

```
                                    pDsSpecOptions->offsetAttribPrefix);

    if (0==wcscmp(DS_PROP_SHELL_PREFIX, szPrefix))
        swprintf(szText,L"Context menu was called from the Windows shell.\nThe
offsetAttribPrefix member is %s.", szPrefix);
    else if (0==wcscmp(DS_PROP_ADMIN_PREFIX, szPrefix))
        swprintf(szText,L"Context menu was called from an Active Directory
Administrative Snap-in.\nThe offsetAttribPrefix member is %s.", szPrefix);
    else
        swprintf(szText,L"Could not determine prefix. The offsetAttribPrefix
member is %s.", szPrefix);
    MessageBoxW(hParent,szText,L"GetData using DsDisplaySpecOptions",MB_OK);
}

//Clean up
GlobalUnlock(stgmedium.hGlobal);
ReleaseStgMedium(&stgmedium);

return hr;

}
```

Registering the Context Menu COM Object in a Display Specifier

Even after you've written and installed your context menu COM object, the Windows shell and Active Directory administrative snap-ins cannot recognize it yet. For the Windows shell or Active Directory administrative snap-ins to recognize your context menu, you must add a value for your context menu COM object in the **adminContextMenu** and/or **shellContextMenu** property of the display specifier for the class whose context menu you want to extend. Note that you can register the same context menu COM object for more than one class.

If the COM object was registered in the **adminContextMenu** property of the class's display specifier, the context menu appears when the user opens the context menu for objects of that class in Active Directory administrative snap-ins. If it was registered in **shellContextMenu**, the context menu appears in the Windows shell. If you want it to appear in both the shell and administrative snap-ins, you need to register the COM object in both properties.

The **adminContextMenu** and **shellContextMenu** properties are multi-valued. The **adminContextMenu** contains the list of context menus for Active Directory administrative snap-ins to add to the context menu for the object class. The **shellContextMenu** contains the list for the Windows shell.

For a context menu COM object, the value is a string with the following format:

ordernumber,CLSID

In this example, the *ordernumber* is a signed number that represents the menu item's position on the context menu. When a context menu is first displayed, the values are sorted using a signed comparison of each value's *ordernumber*. If more than one value has the same *ordernumber*, those context menu COM objects are loaded in the order they are read from the directory; however, you should use a non-existing *ordernumber* (that is, one that has not been used by other values in the property). There is no prescribed starting position, and gaps are allowed in the *ordernumber* sequence.

The *CLSID* is the CLSID of the context menu's COM object in the string format produced by the **StringFromGUID2** function in the COM library. Note that the COM object must implement the **IContextMenu** and **IShellExtInit** interfaces.

Example:

```
1,{08eb4fa6-6ffd-11d1-b0e0-00c04fd8dca6}
```

Adding a Value to the adminContextMenu or shellContextMenu properties

When you add a value for your property page COM object to **adminContextMenu** or **shellContextMenu**, follow these rules:

1. Make sure it hasn't already been added.
2. Add a new value at the end of the context menu ordering list. This means setting the *ordernumber* portion of the value to the next value after the highest existing *ordernumber*.
3. To add the value, use the **IADs::PutEx** method with the *lnControlCode* parameter set to ADS_PROPERTY_APPEND so that the value will be added to the existing values (and, therefore, not overwrite the existing values). Make sure you call **IADs::SetInfo** to commit the change to the directory.

See the sample code for adding values for property pages.

Registering a Context Menu Item that Starts an Application in a Display Specifier

If the context menu item starts a program, the value is a string with the following format:

ordernumber,menuitemtext,command

In this example, the *ordernumber* is a signed number that represents the menu item's position on the context menu. When a context menu is first displayed, the values are sorted using a signed comparison of each value's *ordernumber*. If more than one value has the same *ordernumber*, those context menu items are loaded in the order they are read from the directory; however, you should use a non-existing *ordernumber* (that is, one that has not been used by other values in the property). There is no prescribed starting position and gaps are allowed in the *ordernumber* sequence.

The *menuitemtext* is the text used to display this context menu item on the context menu. The *menuitemtext* cannot contain commas. The *menuitemtext* can contain an ampersand (&) to set the shortcut key for the menu item. For example, the following value makes **d** the shortcut key:

```
1,&Do this,do.exe
```

The *command* is the program that will be executed by the snap-in. Either the full path must be specified or the application must be in the computer's path environment variable. The program is invoked using the **ShellExecute** function. The *command* cannot contain additional parameters (for example, Notepad myfile.txt). Since **ShellExecute** is used, documents can be specified as the command (for example the command d:\myfile.doc will open d:\myfile.doc based on the program associated with the .doc extension). Paths and application names with spaces are allowed. Note that the selected object's distinguished name and class are passed as the first and second arguments, respectively, of the program invoked by *command*.

In the Windows shell, multi-selection is supported. The *command* is invoked for each selected object. In Active Directory administrative snap-ins, multi-selection is not supported, that is, the *command* is not invoked at all. Only single selection is supported.

Important   For the Windows shell, display specifier information is retrieved at user logon and cached for the user's session. For the administrative snap-ins, the display specifier information is retrieved when the snap-in is loaded and is cached for the lifetime of the process. For the Windows shell, this means changes to display specifiers take effect after a user logs off and back on again. For the administrative snap-ins, changes take effect when the snap-in or console file is reloaded (that is, if you start a new instance of the console file or new MMC.EXE instance and add the snap-in, the latest display specifier information will be retrieved).

Example Code for Setting Up Automatic Retrieval of Display Specifiers

The following example uses two scripts. The first script (frommenu.vbs) is the *command* that is run when the menu item is selected. The second script (addmenu.vbs) installs the display specifier context menu item to execute the script frommenu.vbs. This example assumes locale 409 (US English) and extends the user object's context menu in Active Directory administrative snap-ins.

▶ **To run the example code**

1. Copy the code for frommenu.vbs below, open Notepad, paste the code into Notepad, save the file as C:\frommenu.vbs, and close Notepad.

2. Copy the code for addmenu.vbs below, open Notepad, paste the code into Notepad, save the file as C:\addmenu.vbs, and close Notepad.

3. Run addmenu.vbs.

4. Start the Active Directory Users and Computers snap-in.

FROMMENU.VBS

```
'frommenu.vbs is the script run when the menu item is chosen.

'''''''''''''''''''''''''''''''''''
'Parse the arguments
'First arg is ADsPath of the selected object. Second is Class.
'''''''''''''''''''''''''''''''''''
On Error Resume Next

Set oArgs = WScript.Arguments
sText = "This script was run from a display specifier context menu." & vbCrLf & _
"Selected Item:"
If oArgs.Count > 1 Then
    sText = sText & vbCrLf & "  ADsPath: " & oArgs.item(0)
    sText = sText & vbCrLf & "  Class: " & oArgs.item(1)
Else
    sText = sText & vbCrLf & "Arg Count: " & oArgs.Count
End If
show_items sText
Err.Number = 0
sBind = oArgs.item(0)
Set dsobj= GetObject(sBind)
If (Err.Number <> 0) Then
    BailOnFailure Err.Number, "on GetObject method"
End If
objname = dsobj.Get("name")
If (Err.Number <> 0) Then
    BailOnFailure Err.Number, "on Get method"
End If
sText = "Use ADsPath from first argument to bind and get RDN (name) property."
sText = sText & vbCrLf & "Name: " & objname
show_items sText

'''''''''''''''''''''''''''''''''''
'Display subroutines
'''''''''''''''''''''''''''''''''''
Sub show_items(strText)
    MsgBox strText, vbInformation, "Script from Context Menu"
End Sub

Sub BailOnFailure(ErrNum, ErrText)    strText = "Error 0x" & Hex(ErrNum) & " " & _
ErrText
    MsgBox strText, vbInformation, "ADSI Error"
    WScript.Quit
End Sub
```

ADDMENU.VBS

```vbs
'addmenu.vbs adds the menu item to run frommenu.vbs
'from user object's context menu in the admin snap-ins.
On Error Resume Next
Set root= GetObject("LDAP://rootDSE")
If (Err.Number <> 0) Then
    BailOnFailure Err.Number, "on GetObject method"
End If
sConfig = root.Get("configurationNamingContext")
'hardcoded for user class.
sClass = "user"
'hardcoded for US English
sLocale = "409"
sPath = "LDAP://cn=" & sClass & "-Display,cn=" & sLocale &
",cn=DisplaySpecifiers," & sConfig
show_items "Display Specifier: " & sPath
Set obj= GetObject(sPath)
If (Err.Number <> 0) Then
    BailOnFailure Err.Number, "on GetObject method"
End If
'TODO--check if this is already there.
'Add the value for the context menu
sValue = "5,Run My Test Script,c:\frommenu.vbs"
vValue = Array(sValue)
obj.PutEx 3, "adminContextMenu", vValue
If (Err.Number <> 0) Then
    BailOnFailure Err.Number, "on IADs::PutEx method"
End If
'Commit the change
obj.SetInfo
If (Err.Number <> 0) Then
    BailOnFailure Err.Number, "on IADs::SetInfo method"
End If

show_items "Success! Added value to adminContextMenu property of user-Display: "
& sValue


'''''''''''''''''''''''''''''''''''''''''''
'Display subroutines
'''''''''''''''''''''''''''''''''''''''''''
Sub show_items(strText)
    MsgBox strText, vbInformation, "Add admin context menu"
End Sub
```

```
Sub BailOnFailure(ErrNum, ErrText)      strText = "Error 0x" & Hex(ErrNum) & " " &
ErrText
    MsgBox strText, vbInformation, "ADSI Error"
    WScript.Quit
End Sub
```

Class and Attribute Display Names

A display specifier object for an object class has two attributes that you can use to specify the display names used in the UI for objects of that class.

- The **classDisplayName** attribute is a single-valued Unicode string that specifies the class display name.
- The **attributeDisplayNames** attribute is a multi-valued property that specifies the names to use in the UI for the attributes of the object class.

The **attributeDisplayNames** values are Unicode strings, with each element consisting of a comma delimited name pair:

attrName,DisplayText

In this example, *attrName* is the **IDAPDisplayName** of an attribute and *DisplayText* is the text to display as the label (name) of that attribute in the user interface.

Guidelines for Class and Attribute Display Names

Since many vendors may be extending classes with new attributes or creating entirely new classes, it is important that the class and attribute display names are unambiguous and do not result in conflicts.

Each vendor should prefix the class display name with a unique friendly identifier based on the vendor's name. For example if the Arcadia Bay company creates a new class derived from the user class, then they could uniquely have a class display name "Arcadia Bay User".

If a vendor extends an existing class with new attributes, then they should again uniquely identify the attribute display name so that there are no conflicts with other attribute display names. Again, prefixing the attribute display name with unique friendly identifier based on the vendor's name is good practice. For example, if the Arcadia Bay company extends the user class with a new HR attribute, they could uniquely display the attribute as "Arcadia Bay HR Information".

Additionally, from a localization perspective, each vendor should localize the class and attribute display names into each language supported by Microsoft® Windows® 2000.

Adding a Value to the attributeDisplayNames Property

When you add a value for an attribute display name to **attributeDisplayNames**, follow these rules.

1. Check if a mapping for the attribute already exists. If you want to replace an existing attribute value, delete it first using **IADs::PutEx** method with the *InControlCode* parameter set to ADS_PROPERTY_DELETE and the *vProp* parameter set to the value you want removed.

   Do not use ADS_PROPERTY_CLEAR or ADS_PROPERTY_UPDATE.

2. Create the string representing the attribute display name. See the format above.

3. To add the value, use the **IADs::PutEx** method with the *InControlCode* parameter set to ADS_PROPERTY_APPEND so that the value will be added to the existing values (and, therefore, not overwrite the existing values). Make sure you call **IADs::SetInfo** to commit the change to the directory.

For more information about naming new classes and attributes, see *Naming Attributes and Classes*.

Class Icons

The iconic images used to represent a class object can be read from the Display Specifier. Moreover, each class can store multiple icon states. For example, a folder class can have bitmaps for the open, closed, and disabled states. The current implementation allows up to sixteen different icon states per class.

The attribute is named **iconPath** and can be specified in one of two ways.

   state,ICOfilename

or

   state,DLLname,resourceID

In this example, the *state* is an integer with a value between 0 and 15. The value 0 is defined to be the default or "closed" state of the icon. The value 1 is defined to be the "open" state of the icon. The value 2 is the disabled state. The other values are application-defined.

The *ICOfilename* or *DLLname* must be the name of a file in the local computer's file search path.

The *resourceID* is a zero-based index into the DLL's resource fork list of icons.

Adding a Value to the iconPath Property

When you add a value for an icon to **iconPath**, follow these rules:

1. Check if an icon for the state intended for the new icon exists. If you want to replace an existing icon value, delete it first using **IADs::PutEx** method with the *InControlCode* parameter set to ADS_PROPERTY_DELETE and the *vProp* parameter set to the value you want removed.

   Do not use ADS_PROPERTY_CLEAR or ADS_PROPERTY_UPDATE.

2. Set the *state* portion of the value to the icon state for the new icon that you want to add.

3. To add the value, use the **IADs::PutEx** method with the *InControlCode* parameter set to ADS_PROPERTY_APPEND so that the value will be added to the existing values (and, therefore, not overwrite the existing values). Make sure you call **IADs::SetInfo** to commit the change to the directory.

Viewing Containers as Leaf Nodes

Potentially, any Active Directory™ object can be a container of other objects. This can clutter the user interface (UI), so it is possible to declare that a specific class be displayed as a leaf element by default. The **treatAsLeaf** attribute holds a Boolean value that, if True, indicates that the objects of the class should only be treated as leaf elements.

Object Creation Wizards

In the Active Directory™ administrative snap-ins, the user can create new objects in the directory by opening the context menu for the container where the new object will be created, choosing New, and then choosing the class of object to create. Creating new instances of an object invokes the object creation wizard. Each class of object may specify the use of a specific creation wizard, or it may use a generic creation wizard. For well known classes (for example, **user** and **organizationalUnit**), the Active Directory Users and Computers snap-in provides a standard set of creation wizards.

Note that object creation wizards can be invoked from other applications. For more information, see *Invoking Creation Wizards from Your Application*.

There are two methods for extending creation wizards:

* *Replace an existing wizard (or provide one if one does not exist for the class).* The existing wizard is replaced through the use of a *primary extension*. A primary extension provides the first set of pages and is hosted in the same way as native pages. It also supports the extensibility mechanism so that other creation wizard extensions can be invoked. For sample code, see the scpwizard sample in the Platform SDK.

* *Extend an existing wizard.* Existing wizards can be extended with creation wizard extensions, which add additional pages following those of the native or primary extension. For sample code, see the userwizard sample in the Platform SDK.

In both cases, the extension UI has to be implemented as a COM object and it must support the **IDsAdminNewObjExt** interface.

If a creation wizard is not registered for an object class, Active Directory administrative snap-ins provide a generic creation wizard. The generic creation wizard is built at run time from the list of mandatory properties for the class of object that is being created. For each mandatory property, a page is added to the UI. The generic creation wizard is not extensible. If extensibility is required, it must be replaced with a primary extension.

▶ **To replace the existing creation wizard (or the generic creation wizard if no creation wizard is registered) for an object class**

1. Write the primary extension COM object. The COM object must implement **IDsAdminNewObjExt** and provide pages .

2. Install the context menu COM object on the computers where you want the extension context menu items to be used. It is recommended that you create a Microsoft® Windows® Installer package for your context menu COM object's DLL and deploy the package appropriately using the group policy. See *Using MSI and Windows 2000 Application Deployment to Distribute UI Additions.*

3. Register the creation wizard as the primary extension for a particular object class.

   Add the value for your creation wizard COM object in the **creationWizard** property of the display specifier for the class for which your creation wizard will be the primary extension. Note that you can register the same creation wizard COM object for more than one class.

   Note that registration is specific to one locale. If the creation wizard COM object is specific to a certain locale, it should be registered in a displaySpecifier in the locale container that it applies to. If it applies to all locales, it should be added to the appropriate displaySpecifier (that is, the one that represents the class that should get the creation wizard) in all locale containers.

▶ **To extend context menus with context menu items that launch an application**

1. Write the primary extension COM object. The COM object must implement **IDsAdminNewObjExt** and provide pages.

2. Install the creation wizard COM object on the computers where you want the creation wizard to be used. It is recommended that you create a Microsoft Installer package for your creation wizard COM object's DLL and deploy the package appropriately using the group policy. See *Using MSI and Windows 2000 Application Deployment to Distribute UI Additions.*

3. Register the creation wizard as an extension for a particular object class.

   Add a value for your creation wizard COM object to the existing values in the **creationWizardExt** property of the display specifier for the class whose creation wizard you want to extend. Note that you can register the same creation wizard COM object for more than one class.

Note that registration is per locale. If the creation wizard COM object is specific to a certain locale, it should be registered in a displaySpecifier in the locale container that it applies to. If it applies to all locales, it should be added to the appropriate displaySpecifier (that is, the one that represents the class that should get the creation wizard) in all locale containers.

Invoking Creation Wizards from Your Application

Using the **IDsAdminCreateObj** COM object, an application can use the creation wizard for a specified class to create a new object of that class. For example, an application can use **IDsAdminCreateObj** to invoke the creation wizard for creating a new user.

The following function starts the user creation wizard so that the user can create a new user in the container (specified by an **IADsContainer** pointer). The function returns an **IADs** pointer to the new user object.

```
//Need to include dsadmin.h
//Need to link dsuiext.lib

HRESULT StartCreateUserWizard(HWND hWnd,
          //Handle to window that should own the wizard.
                  IADsContainer *pContainer,
          //Container in which to create the new object
                  IADs **ppNewObject
          //Return a pointer the new object
                  )
{
if ((!pContainer)||(!ppNewObject))
    return E_POINTER;
CHAR *szText = new CHAR[MAX_PATH*4];
VARIANT varname;
BSTR bstr;
HRESULT hr = E_FAIL;
//For creating a new user, set class to user.
LPOLESTR szClass = L"user";

//Create the creation handler for creation wizards
IDsAdminCreateObj* pCreateObj = NULL;
hr = ::CoCreateInstance(CLSID_DsAdminCreateObj,
                   NULL, CLSCTX_INPROC_SERVER,
                   IID_IDsAdminCreateObj,
                   (void**)&pCreateObj);
if (SUCCEEDED(hr))
{
    // Initialize handler
    hr = pCreateObj->Initialize(pContainer, szClass);
    if (SUCCEEDED(hr))
```

(continued)

(continued)

```
    {
        //Invoke the creation wizard.
        hr = pCreateObj->CreateModal(hWnd, ppNewObject);
        //S_FALSE means user clicked Cancel
        if (hr == S_FALSE)
        {
        MessageBox(hWnd,"User cancelled the wizard\nThe new object was not
created.","Start Create User Wizard",MB_OK);
        //Set *ppNewObject to NULL
        *ppNewObject = NULL;
        hr = E_FAIL;
        }
        //S_OK means user clicked OK
        else if (hr==S_OK)
        {
        //Display the new user object's name and ADsPath
        hr = (*ppNewObject)->Get(L"name",&varname);
        hr = (*ppNewObject)->get_ADsPath(&bstr);
        if (SUCCEEDED(hr))
            {
            wsprintf(szText,"The new user %ws was successfully created. \nNew
object ADsPath: %ws",varname.bstrVal,bstr);
            MessageBox(NULL,szText,"Start Create User Wizard",MB_OK);
            VariantClear(&varname);
            SysFreeString(bstr);
            }
        else
            {
            wsprintf(szText,"The new object was successfully created. But
properties could not be read from the new object.");
            MessageBox(hWnd,szText,"Start Create User Wizard",MB_OK);
            //Return S_FALSE to tell caller that the
            //property read failed.
            hr = S_FALSE;
            }
        }
        else
        {
        wsprintf(szText,"Creation Wizard could not be started. hr: %x",hr);
        MessageBox(hWnd,szText,"Start Create User Wizard",MB_OK);
        }
    }
}
if (pCreateObj)
    pCreateObj->Release();
```

```
return hr;
}
```

Using MSI and Windows 2000 Application Deployment to Distribute UI Additions

To distribute the COM objects, applications, and/or files used by the extensions you've added to a display specifier (property page, context menu, and creation wizard COM objects, ICO files for class icons, scripts or applications started by context menu extensions, and so on), you can create a Microsoft Installer package and use group policy to deploy it to users or computers.

Using Standard Dialog Boxes for Handling Active Directory Objects

Microsoft® Windows® provides a Common Dialog Box library for common operations (such as File Open, File Browse, and so on). Microsoft® Windows® 2000 provides some dialog boxes that you can use for common UI operations in Active Directory™.

Windows 2000 operating system provides COM objects that implement dialog boxes for handling directory objects:

- Directory Object Picker (for specific types)
- Domain Browser
- Container Browser

In addition, Active Directory creation wizards can also be invoked from an application. For more information, see *Invoking Creation Wizards from Your Application.*

Directory Object Picker

Using the **IDsObjectPicker** COM object, an application can display a dialog box that enables a user to select one or more objects from the directory and get back information about the selected objects. Note that the object picker supports only the selection of user, contact, group, and computer objects. Note that well-known security principals (such as Everyone, Anonymous, and so on) can also be included as selectable object in the object picker.

To display an object picker dialog box, call the **CoCreateInstance** or **CoCreateInstanceEx** function to create an instance of the system's **IDsObjectPicker** implementation. Then call the **IDsObjectPicker::Initialize** method to initialize the dialog box and the **IDsObjectPicker::InvokeDialog** method to display it.

When you initialize an object picker dialog box, you specify a set of scope types and filters.

- The specified scope types determine the locations, for example domains or computers, from which the user can select objects.

- The filters determine the types of objects the user can select from a given scope type.

The **Look in** drop-down list contains the scope locations that correspond to the specified scope types. When the user selects a scope from the list, the dialog box applies the filters for that scope type to display a list of objects.

By default, the user can select a single object. To enable multiple selections, set the DSOP_FLAG_MULTISELECT flag in the **flOptions** member of the **DSOP_INIT_INFO** structure when you initialize the dialog box.

For more information about the **IDsObjectPicker** interface and its related structures, see the *Platform SDK* documentation.

The following functions display the object picker dialog box so that the user can select computer objects. The **SelectComputersAndDo** function is the main function and calls the **InitObjectPicker** and **ProcessSelectedObjects** functions. The **InitObjectPicker** function initializes the IDsObjectPicker object to search for computers in the current domain. The **ProcessSelectedObjects** function displays the name, objectClass, and ADsPath of the selected objects in message boxes.

```
//Need to include objsel.h
UINT g_cfDsObjectPicker; //for clipboard format.


HRESULT SelectComputersAndDo(HWND hWnd)
//Handle to window that should own the object picker.
{
HRESULT hr = E_FAIL;
IDsObjectPicker *pDsObjectPicker = NULL;
IDataObject *pdo = NULL;
// Create an instance of the object picker.
hr = CoCreateInstance(CLSID_DsObjectPicker,
    NULL,
    CLSCTX_INPROC_SERVER,
    IID_IDsObjectPicker,
    (void **) &pDsObjectPicker);
if (SUCCEEDED(hr))
{
    // Initialize the object picker instance.
    hr = InitObjectPicker(pDsObjectPicker);
    // Invoke the modal dialog.
    if (SUCCEEDED(hr))
    {
    hr = pDsObjectPicker->InvokeDialog(hWnd, &pdo);
    if (hr == S_OK) //S_OK means User clicked OK
    {
```

```
            //Process the selected objects and display
            //each in a message box.
        ProcessSelectedObjects(pdo);
        if (pdo)
            pdo->Release();
        }
    else if (hr == S_FALSE) //S_FALSE means User clicked Cancel
        MessageBoxA(hWnd,"User canceled object picker dialog\n","Object Picker
dialog",MB_OK);
    else
        MessageBoxA(hWnd,"Object picker dialog failed.","Object Picker
dialog",MB_OK);
    }
}
if (pDsObjectPicker)
    pDsObjectPicker->Release();
return hr;
}
HRESULT InitObjectPicker(
    IDsObjectPicker *pDsObjectPicker) {

g_cfDsObjectPicker =    RegisterClipboardFormat(CFSTR_DSOP_DS_SELECTION_LIST);

static const int      SCOPE_INIT_COUNT = 1;
DSOP_SCOPE_INIT_INFO aScopeInit[SCOPE_INIT_COUNT];
DSOP_INIT_INFO  InitInfo;
// Initialize the DSOP_SCOPE_INIT_INFO array.

ZeroMemory(aScopeInit,
    sizeof(DSOP_SCOPE_INIT_INFO) * SCOPE_INIT_COUNT);

// Combine multiple scope types in a single array entry.

aScopeInit[0].cbSize = sizeof(DSOP_SCOPE_INIT_INFO);
aScopeInit[0].flType = DSOP_SCOPE_TYPE_UPLEVEL_JOINED_DOMAIN
                     | DSOP_SCOPE_TYPE_DOWNLEVEL_JOINED_DOMAIN;

// Set uplevel and downlevel filters to include only computer objects.
// Uplevel filters apply to both mixed and native modes.
// Notice that the uplevel and downlevel flags are different.

aScopeInit[0].FilterFlags.Uplevel.flBothModes =
        DSOP_FILTER_COMPUTERS;
aScopeInit[0].FilterFlags.flDownlevel =
        DSOP_DOWNLEVEL_FILTER_COMPUTERS;
```

(continued)

(continued)

```
// Initialize the DSOP_INIT_INFO structure.

ZeroMemory(&InitInfo, sizeof(InitInfo));

InitInfo.cbSize = sizeof(InitInfo);
InitInfo.pwzTargetComputer = NULL;  // Target is the local computer.
InitInfo.cDsScopeInfos = SCOPE_INIT_COUNT;
InitInfo.aDsScopeInfos = aScopeInit;
InitInfo.flOptions = DSOP_FLAG_MULTISELECT;

// You can call Initialize multiple times; last call wins.
// Note that object picker makes its own copy of InitInfo.

return pDsObjectPicker->Initialize(&InitInfo);
}

void ProcessSelectedObjects(
    IDataObject *pdo  // Data object containing user's selections
)
{

CHAR *szText = new CHAR[MAX_PATH*3];
HRESULT hr = S_OK;
BOOL fGotStgMedium = FALSE;
PDS_SELECTION_LIST pDsSelList = NULL;
ULONG i;
STGMEDIUM stgmedium = {
    TYMED_HGLOBAL,
    NULL,
    NULL
};
FORMATETC formatetc = {
    g_cfDsObjectPicker,
    NULL,
    DVASPECT_CONTENT,
    -1,
    TYMED_HGLOBAL
};

do {
    // Get the global memory block containing the user's selections.

    hr = pdo->GetData(&formatetc, &stgmedium);
    if (FAILED(hr)) break;
    fGotStgMedium = TRUE;
```

```
        // Retrieve pointer to DS_SELECTION_LIST structure.

        pDsSelList = (PDS_SELECTION_LIST) GlobalLock(stgmedium.hGlobal);
        if (!pDsSelList) break;

        // Loop through DS_SELECTION array of selected objects.

        for (i = 0; i < pDsSelList->cItems; i++) {
            wsprintf(szText,"Object: %u\nName: %ws\nClass: %ws\nADsPath: %ws",
                i,
                    pDsSelList->aDsSelection[i].pwzName,
                    pDsSelList->aDsSelection[i].pwzClass,
                    pDsSelList->aDsSelection[i].pwzADsPath);
        MessageBox(NULL,szText,"Selection",MB_OK);
        }

        GlobalUnlock(stgmedium.hGlobal);
} while (0);

if (fGotStgMedium)
    ReleaseStgMedium(&stgmedium);

}
```

Domain Browser

Using the **IDsBrowseDomainTree** COM object, an application can display a domain browser dialog box and get back the DNS name of the domain selected by the user. The **IDsBrowseDomainTree** interface also has other methods to enumerate and retrieve information about all domain trees and domains within a forest.

The following function displays the domain browser dialog box where the user selects a domain. The function returns the DNS name of the domain:

```
//Need to include DSCLIENT.H
//Must link dsuiext.lib

HRESULT BrowseForDomain(HWND hWnd,            //Handle to window that should
                                             // own the browse dialog.

            LPOLESTR *ppDomainDNSName //Return the DNS name of
                                      // selected domain.

                    )
{
HRESULT hr = E_FAIL;
IDsBrowseDomainTree *pDsDomains = NULL;
//CoCreate the domain tree browser.
hr = ::CoCreateInstance(CLSID_DsDomainTreeBrowser,
```

(continued)

(continued)

```
                NULL,
                CLSCTX_INPROC_SERVER,
                IID_IDsBrowseDomainTree,
                (void **)(&pDsDomains));
if (SUCCEEDED(hr))
{
hr = pDsDomains->BrowseTo(
                hWnd, //Handle to window that owns the dialog.
                ppDomainDNSName, //String to return DNS Name.
                0L //Flags
            );
//User must free string with CoTaskMemFree.
}
if (pDsDomains)
  pDsDomains->Release();
return hr;
}
```

Container Browser

Using the **DsBrowseForContainer** function, an application can display a container browser dialog box and get back the path to the container selected by the user (ADS_FORMAT_X500_NO_SERVER is the default—see the ADS_FORMAT_ENUM enumeration for the list of all formats) and optionally the ldapDisplayName of the container's object class. The function takes a pointer to a **DSBROWSEINFO** structure that contains the caption and dialog box text, ADsPath to the root of the browser tree, credentials (user and password), and flags to control the appearance of the dialog box.

The following function displays the container browser dialog box where the user selects a container. The function returns the ADsPath and class of the container:

```
//Must include DSCLIENT.H
//Must link dsuiext.lib

HRESULT BrowseForContainer(HWND hWnd,
            //Handle to window that should own the browse dialog.
                LPOLESTR szRootPath,
            //Root of the browse tree. NULL for entire forest.
                LPOLESTR *ppContainerADsPath,
            //Return the ADsPath of the selected container.
                LPOLESTR *ppContainerClass
            //Return the ldapDisplayName of the container's class.
                )
{
HRESULT hr = E_FAIL;
DSBROWSEINFO dsbi;
```

```
OLECHAR szPath[MAX_PATH*2];
OLECHAR szClass[MAX_PATH];
DWORD result;

if (!ppContainerADsPath)
  return E_POINTER;


::ZeroMemory( &dsbi, sizeof(dsbi) );
dsbi.hwndOwner = hWnd;
dsbi.cbStruct = sizeof (DSBROWSEINFO);
dsbi.pszCaption = "Browse for Container"; // The caption (titlebar text)
dsbi.pszTitle = "Select a container."; //Text for the dialog.
dsbi.pszRoot = szRootPath;
  //ADsPath for the root of the tree to display in the browser.
  // Specify NULL with DSBI_ENTIREDIRECTORY flag for entire forest.
  // NULL without DSBI_ENTIREDIRECTORY flag displays current domain
  // rooted at LDAP.
dsbi.pszPath = szPath; //Pointer to a unicode string buffer.
dsbi.cchPath = sizeof(szPath)/sizeof(OLECHAR);
  //count of characters for buffer.
dsbi.dwFlags = DSBI_INCLUDEHIDDEN |
  //Include hidden objects
            DSBI_IGNORETREATASLEAF|
  //Ignore the treat as leaf flag on the object for display purposes.
            DSBI_RETURN_FORMAT |
  //Return the path to object in format specified in dwReturnFormat
            DSBI_RETURNOBJECTCLASS;
  //Return the object class
dsbi.pfnCallback = NULL;
dsbi.lParam = 0;
dsbi.dwReturnFormat = ADS_FORMAT_X500;
  //Specify the format. This one returns an ADsPath. See
  // ADS_FORMAT_ENUM enumeration in IADS.H
dsbi.pszObjectClass = szClass;
  //Pointer to a unicode string buffer.
dsbi.cchObjectClass = sizeof(szClass)/sizeof(OLECHAR);
  //count of characters for buffer.

//if root path is NULL, make the forest the root.
if (!szRootPath)
  dsbi.dwFlags |= DSBI_ENTIREDIRECTORY;
```

(continued)

(continued)

```
//Display browse dialog box.
result = DsBrowseForContainer( &dsbi );
// returns -1, 0, IDOK or IDCANCEL
if (result == IDOK)
{
    //Allocate memory for string
    *ppContainerADsPath = (OLECHAR *)CoTaskMemAlloc
(sizeof(OLECHAR)*(wcslen(szPath)+1));
    if (*ppContainerADsPath)
    {
        wcscpy(*ppContainerADsPath, szPath);
        //Caller must free using CoTaskMemFree
        hr = S_OK;
    }
    else
        hr=E_FAIL;
    if (ppContainerClass)
    {
        //Allocate memory for string
        *ppContainerClass = (OLECHAR *)CoTaskMemAlloc
(sizeof(OLECHAR)*(wcslen(szClass)+1));
        if (*ppContainerClass)
        {
            wcscpy(*ppContainerClass, szClass);
            //Call must free using CoTaskMemFree
            hr = S_OK;
        }
        else
            hr=E_FAIL;
    }
}
else
    hr = E_FAIL;

return hr;

}
```

How Applications Should Use Display Specifiers

Most of this chapter has discussed how the Microsoft® Windows® shell and Active Directory™ administrative snap-ins take advantage of display specifiers. How should you use them in your application?

1. For labels for class and attribute names, use the **classDisplayName** and **attributeDisplayNames** properties of the display specifier objects for the appropriate locale. This enables you to take advantage of the localized display names *and* avoid doing unnecessary localization of the class and attribute names. Display specifiers also provide a single location (that is, in the directory) for localized text labels for class and attribute names.

   Do not use the **cn**, **classDisplayName**, **ldapDisplayName** properties on the classSchema or attributeSchema objects to display text labels in your applications—these properties are not localized.

2. Use creation wizards to create new objects.

3. Using localized icons.

Localization

Each locale container will hold Display-Specifier objects that have been localized for that locale. Active Directory UI applications will first look in a locale container named after the locale identifier for the current user's session. If a folder of that name is not found, the US-English locale will be used.

COM objects can be localized either by having a separate binary for each language or by having multiple language resources in a single binary.

Similarly, the class and attribute display names will be translated. Different icons can be specified for each locale.

User Interface Extension for New Object Classes

When creating a new class, you determine how objects of that class will be displayed. The classSchema object itself has properties that determine when a object is visible in the user interface. To provide class display name, attribute display names, icons, context menus, property pages, and creation wizards for the class in Active Directory™ administrative snap-ins and the Microsoft® Windows® shell, you need to create a display specifier for the class. Note that you need to create a display specifier for each locale your class supports.

When you create a new class, consider the following settings and their effects on how the Windows shell and Active Directory administrative snap-ins will display objects of that class:

defaultHidingValue

If you do not set defaultHidingValue, it defaults to TRUE. This means that instances of the object are hidden in the Administrative snap-ins and the Windows shell. It also means that a menu item for the new object class will not appear in the New context menu of the Administrative snap-ins—even if the appropriate creation wizard properties are set on the new object class's displaySpecifier object.

Set this property to FALSE if you want to be able to see instances of the class in the administrative snap-ins and the shell *and* enable a creation wizard and its menu item in the New menu of the administrative snap-ins.

showInAdvancedViewOnly

If you do not set showInAdvancedViewOnly, it defaults to TRUE.

When set to TRUE, instances of the object appear in the Users and Computers snap-in in Advanced View only and do not appear in the Windows shell.

Set this property to FALSE if you want to be able to see instances of the class in Normal view in the Users and Computers snap-in and the Windows shell.

Note that you can also set this value on an individual object to override the value set on the object's class. For example, the **container** class has this value set to TRUE but the Users container has this value set to FALSE; therefore, the Users container appears in the shell and in Normal view in the Users and Computers snap-in but other containers that do not have showInAdvancedViewOnly set to FALSE will appear only in Advanced view in the Users and Computers snap-in.

Creating Display Specifiers for New Classes

Users of Active Directory can customize it to suit their unique requirements. The user interface can also be changed to suit their needs. Active Directory permits the schema to be modified by creating new classes and attributes or modifying existing classes. Display Specifiers can be modified to reflect the new user interface elements that schema modifications require.

A Display-Specifier object is created for the new class. If multiple locales are present, new Display-Specifier objects are created for each supported locale. If the new class is derived from a parent class and the parent class already has an acceptable UI, that UI is specified and additional pages, menu items, and display names can be added for the new attributes. Otherwise, a completely new UI is created and specified. In either case, a new icon and class display name can be used.

Note that a new class that inherits from an existing class does not inherit the parent class's display specifier. If you want the new class to use some or all of the parent class's display specifier properties, you must create a new display specifier for the new class and copy the properties you want from the parent class's display specifier to the new display specifier. This must be done for all locales for which you want to use the parent class's display specifier properties.

Modifying Existing Classes

New attributes can be added to an existing class. New UI components (pages, menu items, and attribute display names) can be added or the existing UI replaced. It is also possible to design new property pages that expose fewer attributes of a class and to create context menus with fewer actions.

Extending Active Directory Administrative Snap-ins Using MMC Extension Snap-ins

MMC enables you to create extension snap-ins that extend the namespace, context menus, property pages, control bars, toolbars, and taskpads of other snap-ins. Active Directory™ administrative snap-ins are standalone snap-ins that can be extended by extension snap-ins.

The following tutorial provides all the steps required to create an MMC context menu extension.

Context Menu Extension Tutorial

Using the conventional MMC extension snap-in mechanisms, only the All Tasks and Create New context menus can be extended.

1. Register the node type for the object class whose context menu you want to extend.

   Note that the node type that you want the snap-in to extend must be registered in the MMC registry key. For more information on registering a node type for nodes (objects of a specific class) in Active Directory Manager, see *Registering Node Types for Active Directory Manager*.

2. Create a new project using the ATL COM AppWizard with the server type Dynamic Link Library (DLL).

   For this tutorial, type MyExtensionSnapin as the Project Name.

   To create a new project, choose **New** from the **File** menu, select the **Projects** tab, select **ATL COM AppWizard**, type the project name in the **Project Name** box, and click **OK**. The ATL COM AppWizard page appears. Select **Dynamic Link Library (DLL)** and click **Finish**. For this tutorial, do not select the other options in wizard page. **The New Project Information** dialog box appears. Click **OK**.

3. Add an MMC Snapin object by choosing **New ATL Object** from the **Insert** menu.

4. In the **ATL Object Wizard** dialog box, select **Objects** from the **Category** list and **MMC SnapIn** from the **Objects** list. Click **Next**.

5. In the **ATL Object Wizard Properties** dialog box, select the **Names** tab and type the control name in the **Short Name** box. The other boxes are filled in based on this name. For this tutorial, type **MyContextMenu** in the **Short Name** box.

6. Select the MMC Snapin tab and make the following settings:

   a. Check the **Extension** box, click on the browse (...) button **for Extends Node**, and select the node type from the **Snap-In Nodes** dialog box. For this tutorial, select BF967ABA-0DE6-11D0-A285-00AA003049E2 in the **Snap-In Nodes** dialog box so that this snap-in extends the user class.

Note that the node type that you want the snap-in to extend must be registered in the MMC registry key. For more information on registering a node type for nodes (objects of a specific class) in Active Directory Manager, see *Registering Node Types for Active Directory Manager.*

b. Make sure that the IComponentData, IComponent, ISnapInAbout, and IExtendContextMenu are checked. If you want to add a property sheet or control bar, check those options as well. For this tutorial, just select the specified four items: IComponentData, IComponent, ISnapInAbout, and IExtendContextMenu.

c. Clear the **Supports Persistence** box. If you want to save the state of your snap-in, you can use the persistence interfaces. For this tutorial, clear the **Supports Persistence** box.

7. Click **OK**. The **CMyContextMenuExtData** class is created. This class implements the extension snap-in. A menu resource is also created.

Note that the following classes are also created: **CMyContextMenuData** (implements IComponentData, which interacts with scope pane), **CMyContextMenuComponent** (implements IComponentData, which interacts with result pane), and **CMyContextMenuAbout** (implements ISnapinAbout, which controls **About** box information and some information in the **Add/Remove Snap-ins** dialog box).

8. Open the menu resource by clicking on the **Resource** tab, expanding the MyExtensionSnapin resources folder, expanding the Menu folder, and double-clicking the menu resource IDR_MYCONTEXTMENU_MENU. The menu has four menu items: TOP, NEW, TASK, and VIEW.

Note that an extension snap-in can only add menu items to the NEW and TASK menus.

9. Add a menu item to the **TASK** menu by clicking on **TASK** and double-clicking on the empty menu item that appears beneath **TASK**. The **Menu Item Properties** box appears.

10. In the **Caption** box, type the text for the menu item.

For this tutorial, type the following: Do Some Extension Thing.

11. In the **Prompt** box, type the description for the menu item that you want to display in the status bar when the menu item is selected.

For this tutorial, type the following: Does some extension thing.

12. In the **ID** box, type the command ID for the menu item. You can leave this blank if you want an ID to be automatically generated.

For this tutorial, type the following: ID_DO_SOMETHING.

13. Close the **Menu Item Properties** dialog box.

14. Open the header file containing the class definition of CMyExtensionSnapinExtData. Click the **ClassView** tab and then double-click CMyExtensionSnapinExtData.

15. Find the following two lines:

```
BEGIN_SNAPINCOMMAND_MAP(CMyExtensionSnapinExtData ExtData, FALSE)
END_SNAPINCOMMAND_MAP()
```

16. Change the FALSE parameter to TRUE to indicate that the snap-in is an extension. The line should look like this:

```
BEGIN_SNAPINCOMMAND_MAP(CMyExtensionSnapinExtData, TRUE)
```

17. Add the SNAPINCOMMAND_ENTRY macro between the two lines and specify the command ID for the menu item as the first parameter and the name of the method that serves as the command handler for the command ID as the second. The snap-in command map should now look like this:

```
BEGIN_SNAPINCOMMAND_MAP(CMyExtensionSnapinExtData, TRUE)
    SNAPINCOMMAND_ENTRY(ID_DO_SOMETHING, OnDoSomeThing)
END_SNAPINCOMMAND_MAP()
```

18. Add the command handler as a method in the class. The command handler must take the following form:

```
HRESULT MethodName (bool& bHandled,
        CSnapInObjectRootBase* pObj)
```

For this tutorial, add the following method to the class:

```
HRESULT OnDoSomeThing (bool& bHandled,
    CSnapInObjectRootBase* pObj)
{
    ::MessageBoxW( NULL, L" OnDoSomeThing ", L" CMyExtensionSnapinExtData ",
MB_OK);
    return S_OK;
}
```

19. Build the project.
20. Load the Active Directory Manager snap-in into MMC or open the DSA.MSC console file. Open the Active Directory Manager, then the domain node, then the Users container, right-click on a user such as Administrator, select All Tasks. The menu item Do Some Extension Thing should appear. Choose the menu item. The OnDoSomeThing method is called and the message box appears.

Registering Node Types for Active Directory Manager

A critical part of extending Active Directory Manager is registering the node type that you want to extend. Note that Active Directory Manager does not register all the possible node types that it can display. Because the schema is extensible (new types of objects can be added as classes to the schema and those objects can be represented in the Active Directory Manager), the Active Directory Manager does not attempt to add every single class defined in the schema as a node type. For Active Directory Manager, the GUID for the node type is the GUID stored in the **schemaIDGUID** property of the classSchema object that represents the type of object that you want to extend. For example, if you wanted to add a context menu item to the Tasks menu of user objects in Active Directory Manager, you would use the COM string representation of GUID stored in the **schemaIDGUID** property of the user classSchema object as the node type GUID.

If the node type you want to extend is not registered, you must add the appropriate node type keys to the registry. The following keys must exist for the node type:

HKEY_LOCAL_MACHINE\Software\Microsoft\MMC\NodeTypes\{*nodetype*}

HKEY_LOCAL_MACHINE\Software\Microsoft\MMC\SnapIns\{*snapinCLSID*}\ NodeTypes\{*nodetype*}

For Active Directory Manager, the {*nodetype*} key is the schemaIDGUID of the object class whose node you want to extend. The {*snapinCLSID*} key is the class ID of the Active Directory Manager snap-in, which is {E355E538-1C2E-11D0-8C37-00C04FD8FE93}.

For example, the following registry entries must exist for a taskpad extension snap-in (with CLSID of {897C0FB4-8850-11D2-9523-00C04F8607E2}) to extend the user objects:

```
HKEY_LOCAL_MACHINE\Software\Microsoft\MMC\NodeTypes\{BF967ABA-0DE6-11D0-A285-
00AA003049E2}

HKEY_LOCAL_MACHINE\Software\Microsoft\MMC\NodeTypes\{BF967ABA-0DE6-11D0-A285-
00AA003049E2}\extensions\Task\{897C0FB4-8850-11D2-9523-00C04F8607E2}

HKEY_LOCAL_MACHINE\Software\Microsoft\MMC\SnapIns\{E355E538-1C2E-11D0-8C37-
00C04FD8FE93}\NodeTypes\{BF967ABA-0DE6-11D0-A285-00AA003049E2}
```

For information about reading the schemaIDGUID of classes and registering them as MMC node types for Active Directory Manager, see the sample code below. For more detail on MMC node types, see MMC node types.

The following program registers a class as a node type and adds an extension snap-in as a context menu extension to that node type:

1. Finds the user classSchema object and gets its **schemaIDGUID** property, which will be used to register the node type for the user object class. This GUID is converted using the GetCOMGUIDStr function.
2. Uses RegisterNodeType to register the user object class as a node type.
3. Uses AddExtensionToNodeType to add an extension snap-in as a context menu extension with the CLSID of {275C0FB4-8850-11D2-9523-00C04F8607E2} to the user class object node type (which was previously created by RegisterNodeType).

```c
#include <wchar.h>
#include <activeds.h>


#define MMC_REG_NODETYPES L"software\\microsoft\\mmc\\nodetypes"
#define MMC_REG_SNAPINS L"software\\microsoft\\mmc\\snapins"
#define MMC_REG_SNAPINS L"software\\microsoft\\mmc\\snapins"
```

```
//MMC Extension subkeys

#define MMC_REG_EXTENSIONS L"Extensions"
#define MMC_REG_NAMESPACE L"NameSpace"
#define MMC_REG_CONTEXTMENU L"ContextMenu"
#define MMC_REG_TOOLBAR L"ToolBar"
#define MMC_REG_PROPERTYSHEET L"PropertySheet"
#define MMC_REG_TASKPAD L"Task"

//DSADMIN key
#define MMC_DSADMIN_CLSID L"{E355E538-1C2E-11D0-8C37-00C04FD8FE93}"


WCHAR * GetDirectoryObjectAttrib(IDirectoryObject *pDirObject,LPWSTR pAttrName);

HRESULT GetCOMGUIDStr(LPOLESTR *ppAttributeName,IDirectoryObject *pDO, LPOLESTR
*ppGUIDString);

HRESULT   RegisterNodeType( LPOLESTR pszSchemaIDGUID );

HRESULT   AddExtensionToNodeType(LPOLESTR pszSchemaIDGUID,
                  LPOLESTR pszExtensionType,
                  LPOLESTR pszExtensionSnapinCLSID,
                  LPOLESTR pszRegValue
                  );


int main(int argc, char* argv[])
{
LPOLESTR szPath = new OLECHAR[MAX_PATH];
HRESULT hr = S_OK;
IADs *pObject = NULL;
VARIANT var;
IDirectoryObject *pDO = NULL;
LPOLESTR pAttributeName = L"schemaIDGUID";
LPOLESTR pGUIDString = NULL;


wcscpy(szPath, L"LDAP://");
CoInitialize(NULL);
//Get rootDSE and the schema container's DN.
//Bind to current user's domain using current user's security context.
hr = ADsOpenObject(L"LDAP://rootDSE",
          NULL,
          NULL,
```

(continued)

(continued)

```
            ADS_SECURE_AUTHENTICATION, //Use Secure Authentication
            IID_IADs,
            (void**)&pObject);

if (SUCCEEDED(hr))
{
    hr = pObject->Get(L"schemaNamingContext",&var);
    if (SUCCEEDED(hr))
    {
        wcscat(szPath, L"cn=user,");
        wcscat(szPath,var.bstrVal);
        if (pObject)
        {
            pObject->Release();
            pObject = NULL;
        }
        hr = ADsOpenObject(szPath,
                NULL,
                NULL,
                ADS_SECURE_AUTHENTICATION, //Use Secure Authentication
                IID_IDirectoryObject,
                (void**)&pDO);
        if (SUCCEEDED(hr))
        {
            hr = GetCOMGUIDStr(&pAttributeName,
                        pDO,
                        &pGUIDString);
        if (SUCCEEDED(hr))
        {
            wprintf(L"schemaIDGUID: %s\n", pGUIDString);
            hr = RegisterNodeType( pGUIDString);
            wprintf(L"hr %x\n", hr);
            hr = AddExtensionToNodeType(pGUIDString,
                        MMC_REG_CONTEXTMENU,
                        L"{275C0FB4-8850-11D2-9523-00C04F8607E2}",
                        L"MySnapin"
                        );

        }
        }
    }
}
if (pDO)
    pDO->Release();
```

```
VariantClear(&var);

// Uninitialize COM
CoUninitialize();
return 0;
}


/////////////////////////////////////////////////////////////////////////
/*
    GetDirectoryObjectAttrib()      - Returns the value of the attribute
                                      named in pAttrName from the
                                      IDirectoryObject passed

    Parameters

    IDirectoryObject *pDirObject  - Object from which to retrieve an
                                    attribute value
    LPWSTR pAttrName              - Name of attribute to retrieve
*/
WCHAR * GetDirectoryObjectAttrib(IDirectoryObject *pDirObject,LPWSTR pAttrName)
{
    HRESULT    hr;
    ADS_ATTR_INFO    *pAttrInfo=NULL;
    DWORD    dwReturn;
    static WCHAR pwReturn[1024];

    pwReturn[0] = 01;

    hr = pDirObject->GetObjectAttributes( &pAttrName,
                                          1,
                                          &pAttrInfo,
                                          &dwReturn );
    if ( SUCCEEDED(hr) )
    {
        for(DWORD idx=0; idx < dwReturn;idx++, pAttrInfo++ )
        {
            if ( _wcsicmp(pAttrInfo->pszAttrName,pAttrName) == 0 )
            {
                wcscpy(pwReturn,pAttrInfo->pADsValues->CaseIgnoreString);
                break;
            }
        }
        FreeADsMem( pAttrInfo );
    }
    return pwReturn;
```

(continued)

(continued)

```
}


HRESULT GetCOMGUIDStr(LPOLESTR *ppAttributeName,IDirectoryObject *pDO, LPOLESTR
*ppGUIDString)
{
    HRESULT hr = S_OK;
    PADS_ATTR_INFO  pAttributeEntries;
    VARIANT varX;
    DWORD dwAttributesReturned = 0;
    hr = pDO->GetObjectAttributes(  ppAttributeName, //objectGUID
                                    1, //Only objectGUID
                                    &pAttributeEntries, // Returned attributes
                                    &dwAttributesReturned //Number of attributes
returned
                                 );
    if (SUCCEEDED(hr) && dwAttributesReturned>0)
    {
        //Make sure that we got the right type--GUID is
        //ADSTYPE_OCTET_STRING
        if (pAttributeEntries->dwADsType == ADSTYPE_OCTET_STRING)
        {
            LPGUID pObjectGUID = (GUID*)(pAttributeEntries-
>pADsValues[0].OctetString.lpValue);
            //OLE str to fit a GUID
            LPOLESTR szDSGUID = new WCHAR [39];
            //Convert GUID to string.
            ::StringFromGUID2(*pObjectGUID, szDSGUID, 39);
        *ppGUIDString = (OLECHAR *)CoTaskMemAlloc
(sizeof(OLECHAR)*(wcslen(szDSGUID)+1));
        if (*ppGUIDString)
            wcscpy(*ppGUIDString, szDSGUID);
        else
            hr=E_FAIL;
    }
    else
        hr = E_FAIL;
    //Free the memory for the attributes.
    FreeADsMem(pAttributeEntries);
    VariantClear(&varX);
    }
    return hr;
}
```

```
HRESULT   RegisterNodeType(LPOLESTR pszSchemaIDGUID)
{
    LONG      lResult;
    HKEY      hKey;
    HKEY      hSubKey, hNewKey;
    DWORD     dwDisposition;
    LPOLESTR szRegSubKey = new OLECHAR[MAX_PATH];

        // first, open the HKEY_LOCAL_MACHINE
        lResult = RegConnectRegistry( NULL, HKEY_LOCAL_MACHINE, &hKey );
        if ( ERROR_SUCCESS == lResult )
    {
        //go to the MMC_REG_NODETYPES subkey
            lResult = RegOpenKey( hKey, MMC_REG_NODETYPES, &hSubKey );
            if ( ERROR_SUCCESS == lResult )
            {
            // Create a key for the node type of the
            // class represented by pszSchemaIDGUID
            lResult = RegCreateKeyEx( hSubKey,

                                                    // handle of an open key
                        pszSchemaIDGUID,        // address of subkey name
                        0L ,                    // reserved
                        NULL,
                        REG_OPTION_NON_VOLATILE, // special options flag
                        KEY_ALL_ACCESS,
                        NULL,
                        &hNewKey,
                        &dwDisposition );
            RegCloseKey( hSubKey );
        if ( ERROR_SUCCESS == lResult )
        {
            hSubKey = hNewKey;
                // Create an extensions key
            lResult = RegCreateKeyEx( hSubKey,
                    MMC_REG_EXTENSIONS,
                            0L ,
                            NULL,
                            REG_OPTION_NON_VOLATILE,
                            KEY_ALL_ACCESS,
                            NULL,
                            &hNewKey,
                            &dwDisposition );
            //go to the MMC_REG_SNAPINS subkey
            RegCloseKey( hSubKey );
            //Build the subkey path to the NodeTypes key of dsadmin
```

(continued)

(continued)

```
            wcscpy(szRegSubKey, MMC_REG_SNAPINS); //Snapins key
            wcscat(szRegSubKey, L"\\");
            wcscat(szRegSubKey, MMC_DSADMIN_CLSID); //CLSID for DSADMIN
            wcscat(szRegSubKey, L"\\NodeTypes");
            lResult = RegOpenKey( hKey, szRegSubKey, &hSubKey );
            if ( ERROR_SUCCESS == lResult )
            {
                // Create a key for the node type of the class
                // represented by pszSchemaIDGUID
                lResult = RegCreateKeyEx( hSubKey,
                    // handle of an open key
                                pszSchemaIDGUID,
                    // address of subkey name
                                0L ,                      // reserved
                                NULL,
                                REG_OPTION_NON_VOLATILE,
                    // special options flag
                                KEY_ALL_ACCESS,
                                NULL,
                                &hNewKey,
                                &dwDisposition );
                    RegCloseKey( hSubKey );
                }

            }
        }
    }
    RegCloseKey( hSubKey );
    RegCloseKey( hNewKey );
    RegCloseKey( hKey );
        return lResult;
}

HRESULT  AddExtensionToNodeType(LPOLESTR pszSchemaIDGUID,
                    LPOLESTR pszExtensionType,
                    LPOLESTR pszExtensionSnapinCLSID,
                    LPOLESTR pszRegValue
                    )
{
    LONG      lResult;
    HKEY      hKey;
    HKEY      hSubKey, hNewKey;
    DWORD     dwDisposition;
    LPOLESTR szRegSubKey = new OLECHAR[MAX_PATH];
    HRESULT hr = S_OK;
```

```
    // first, open the HKEY_LOCAL_MACHINE
    lResult = RegConnectRegistry( NULL, HKEY_LOCAL_MACHINE, &hKey );
    if ( ERROR_SUCCESS == lResult )
{
    //Build the subkey path to the NodeType specified
    //by pszSchemaIDGUID
wcscpy(szRegSubKey, MMC_REG_NODETYPES);
wcscat(szRegSubKey, L"\\");
wcscat(szRegSubKey, pszSchemaIDGUID);
//go to the subkey
    lResult = RegOpenKey( hKey, szRegSubKey, &hSubKey );
    if ( ERROR_SUCCESS != lResult )
{
    // Create the key for the nodetype if it doesn't already exist.
    hr = RegisterNodeType(pszSchemaIDGUID);
        if ( ERROR_SUCCESS != lResult )
        return E_FAIL;
        lResult = RegOpenKey( hKey, szRegSubKey, &hSubKey );
}
// Create an extensions key if one doesn't already exist
lResult = RegCreateKeyEx( hSubKey,
                MMC_REG_EXTENSIONS,
                        0L ,
                        NULL,
                        REG_OPTION_NON_VOLATILE,
                        KEY_ALL_ACCESS,
                        NULL,
                        &hNewKey,
                        &dwDisposition );
RegCloseKey( hSubKey );
if ( ERROR_SUCCESS == lResult )
{
    hSubKey = hNewKey;
    // Create an extension type subkey if one doesn't already exist
    lResult = RegCreateKeyEx( hSubKey,
                pszExtensionType,
                        0L ,
                        NULL,
                        REG_OPTION_NON_VOLATILE,
                        KEY_ALL_ACCESS,
                        NULL,
                        &hNewKey,
                        &dwDisposition );
    RegCloseKey( hSubKey );
```

(continued)

(continued)

```
    if ( ERROR_SUCCESS == lResult )
    {
    hSubKey = hNewKey;
    // Add your snap-in to the
    //extension type key if it hasn't been already.
    lResult  = RegSetValueEx( hSubKey,
            pszExtensionSnapinCLSID,
                    0L ,
                    REG_SZ,
                    (const BYTE*)pszRegValue,
                    (wcslen(pszRegValue)+1)*sizeof(OLECHAR)
            );
    }


    }
    }
    RegCloseKey( hSubKey );
    RegCloseKey( hNewKey );
    RegCloseKey( hKey );
    return lResult;
}
```

MMC Node Types

All node types that can be extended have their own subkey in the
HKEY_LOCAL_MACHINE\Software\Microsoft\MMC\NodeTypes key. A node type key
contains an Extensions subkey. The Extensions key contains subkeys that represent the
types of extensions (such as NameSpace for namespace extensions, and so on). Each
extension type subkey contains values that represent the CLSIDs of the snap-ins that
extend that node type with that type of extension. For example, you would add the
CLSID of a snap-in that extended the namespace of the node type in the
MMC\NodeTypes\{*nodeguid*}\Extensions\NameSpace subkey.

MMC uses the NodeTypes key to determine the extension snap-ins that can extend the
node types for each snap-in. An extension snap-in must register itself for each node type
that it extends as well as register what type of extensions it provides.

A snap-in with node types that can be extended must add those node types as node
type keys in the HKEY_LOCAL_MACHINE\Software\Microsoft\MMC\NodeTypes key.
A node type key is represented as a key whose name is the GUID of the node type.
The node type must also be added as a value in the snap-in's
HKEY_LOCAL_MACHINE\Software\Microsoft\MMC\SnapIns\{*snapinCLSID*}\NodeTypes
key.

An extension snap-in must add its CLSID as a value to the extension type key for each
type of extension it provides for a particular node type.

The NodeTypes key has the following form:

```
HKEY_LOCAL_MACHINE\Software\Microsoft\MMC\NodeTypes\
    {nodetypeGUID}
        Extensions
            NameSpace
                {extensionsnapinCLSID}
            ContextMenu
                {extensionsnapinCLSID}
            ToolBar
                {extensionsnapinCLSID}
            PropertySheet
                {extensionsnapinCLSID}
            Task
                {extensionsnapinCLSID}
        Dynamic Extensions
            {extensionsnapinCLSID}
```

C H A P T E R   1 1

Object Picker Dialog Box

The object picker dialog box provides applications with a standard user interface for selecting computer, user, group, and contact objects. The dialog box can be used to select objects stored in Active Directory™ on a Windows® 2000 system or in the security databases used by earlier versions of Windows NT®.

About the Object Picker Dialog Box

The object picker dialog box enables a user to select one or more objects from the Active Directory global catalog, a Microsoft Windows 2000 domain or computer, a Microsoft Windows NT 4.0 domain or computer, or a workgroup. The object types from which the user can select include user, contact, group, and computer objects. For more information about Active Directory, see the *Active Directory Programmer's Guide*.

To display an object picker dialog box, call the **CoCreateInstance** or **CoCreateInstanceEx** function to create an instance of the system's **IDsObjectPicker** implementation. Then call the **IDsObjectPicker::Initialize** method to initialize the dialog box and the **IDsObjectPicker::InvokeDialog** method to display it.

The following illustration shows a typical object picker dialog box.

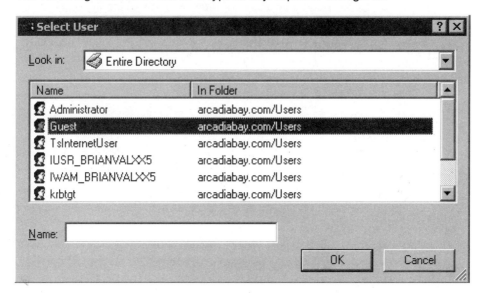

When you initialize an object picker dialog box, you specify a set of scope types and filters.

- The specified scope types determine the locations, for example domains or computers, from which the user can select objects.
- The filters determine the types of objects the user can select from a given scope type.

The **Look in** drop-down list contains the scope locations that correspond to the specified scope types. When the user selects a scope from the list, the dialog box applies the filters for that scope type to display a list of objects.

By default the user can select a single object. To enable multiple selections, set the DSOP_FLAG_MULTISELECT flag in the **flOptions** member of the **DSOP_INIT_INFO** structure when you initialize the dialog box.

Object Picker Scopes and Filters

The **Look in** drop-down list contains the scopes from which the user can select objects. A scope is a domain, computer, workgroup, or global catalog that stores information about and provides access to a set of available objects. The entries in the scope list depend on the scope types and the target computer specified when you last called the **IDsObjectPicker::Initialize** method to initialize the dialog box.

A scope type is a generic category of scopes, such as all domains in the enterprise to which the target computer belongs, or the global catalog for the target computer's enterprise, or the target computer itself. For each specified scope type, the dialog box uses the context of the target computer to determine the scope list entries.

When you call the **Initialize** method, you must specify a **DSOP_INIT_INFO** structure containing an array of **DSOP_SCOPE_INIT_INFO** structures. Each entry in the array specifies one or more scope types as well as applicable filters and other attributes. The filters determine the types of objects—such as users, groups, contacts, and computers— the user can select from a given scope type. When the user selects a scope from the list, the dialog box applies the filters for that scope type to display a list of objects from which the user can select.

Each **DSOP_SCOPE_INIT_INFO** structure contains a **DSOP_FILTER_FLAGS** structure that specifies the filters for that scope type. The **DSOP_FILTER_FLAGS** structure distinguishes between *uplevel* and *downlevel* scopes.

- An uplevel scope is a global catalog or a Windows 2000 domain that supports the ADSI LDAP provider.
- Downlevel scopes include Windows NT 4.0 domains, workgroups, and all individual computers, whether running Windows 2000 or Windows NT 4.0. The dialog box uses the ADSI WinNT provider to access downlevel scopes.

Objsel.h defines two sets of filter flags: one for uplevel scopes and one for downlevel scopes.

- You must use the DSOP_FILTER_* flags in the **DSOP_UPLEVEL_FILTER_FLAGS** structure to specify filters for uplevel scopes.
- You must use the DSOP_DOWNLEVEL_FILTER_* flags in the **flDownlevel** member of the **DSOP_FILTER_FLAGS** structure to specify filters for downlevel scopes.

Using the Object Picker Dialog Box

The topics in this section provide sample code for using the object picker dialog box.

Displaying the Object Picker Dialog Box

The sample code in this topic shows the main function of a process that uses the object picker dialog box. The main function performs the following steps:

- Calls the **CoInitializeEx** function to initialize COM and specify the apartment-threaded model.
- Calls the **CoCreateInstance** function to create an instance of the system's **IDsObjectPicker** interface.
- Calls a subroutine to initialize the interface instance. For a description and sample code, see Initializing the Object Picker Dialog Box.
- Calls the **IDsObjectPicker::InvokeDialog** method to display the dialog box.
- Calls a subroutine to process the user's selections. For a description and sample code, see Processing the Selected Objects.

Note   **RegisterClipboardFormat** call that registers the CFSTR_DSOP_DS_SELECTION_LIST clipboard format. **RegisterClipboardFormat** returns an identifier used in the **IDataObject::GetData** call made by the subroutine that processes the user's selections.

```
#include <objsel.h>

UINT g_cfDsObjectPicker =
    RegisterClipboardFormat(CFSTR_DSOP_DS_SELECTION_LIST);


void _cdecl
main(int argc, char * argv[]) {

HRESULT hr = S_OK;
IDsObjectPicker *pDsObjectPicker = NULL;
```

(continued)

(continued)

```
IDataObject *pdo = NULL;
HWND hwndParent = NULL; // Supply a window handle to your application.

hr = CoInitializeEx(NULL, COINIT_APARTMENTTHREADED);
if (FAILED(hr)) return;

do {

    // Create an instance of the object picker.

    hr = CoCreateInstance(CLSID_DsObjectPicker,
                NULL,
                CLSCTX_INPROC_SERVER,
                IID_IDsObjectPicker,
                (void **) &pDsObjectPicker);
    if (FAILED(hr)) break;

    // Initialize the object picker instance.

    hr = InitObjectPicker(pDsObjectPicker);
    if (FAILED(hr)) break;

    // Invoke the modal dialog.

    hr = pDsObjectPicker->InvokeDialog(hwndParent, &pdo); if (FAILED(hr)) break;

    if (hr == S_OK) {
        ProcessSelectedObjects(pdo);
        pdo->Release();
    }
    else if (hr == S_FALSE)
        printf("User canceled object picker dialog\n");

} while (0);

pDsObjectPicker->Release();
CoUninitialize();
}
```

Initializing the Object Picker Dialog Box

This topic describes a subroutine that initializes the **IDsObjectPicker** interface instance.
The sample code initializes a **DSOP_INIT_INFO** structure and passes it to the
IDsObjectPicker::Initialize method.

The sample code first initializes a **DSOP_SCOPE_INIT_INFO** structure to specify that the user can select computer objects from the domain to which the target computer is joined. This example uses a single **DSOP_SCOPE_INIT_INFO** structure because all specified scope types use the same filters and attributes. To specify additional scope types with different filters and attributes, modify the example to use an array of multiple **DSOP_SCOPE_INIT_INFO** structures.

The example enables multiple selections by setting the DSOP_FLAG_MULTISELECT flag in the **flOptions** member of the **DSOP_INIT_INFO** structure. To allow only a single selection, do not set this flag.

```
HRESULT InitObjectPicker(
    IDsObjectPicker *pDsObjectPicker) {

static const int      SCOPE_INIT_COUNT = 1;
DSOP_SCOPE_INIT_INFO aScopeInit[SCOPE_INIT_COUNT];
DSOP_INIT_INFO  InitInfo;

// Initialize the DSOP_SCOPE_INIT_INFO array.

ZeroMemory(aScopeInit,
    sizeof(DSOP_SCOPE_INIT_INFO) * SCOPE_INIT_COUNT);

// Combine multiple scope types in a single array entry.

aScopeInit[0].cbSize = sizeof(DSOP_SCOPE_INIT_INFO);
aScopeInit[0].flType = DSOP_SCOPE_TYPE_UPLEVEL_JOINED_DOMAIN
                 | DSOP_SCOPE_TYPE_DOWNLEVEL_JOINED_DOMAIN;

// Set uplevel and downlevel filters to include only computer objects.
// Uplevel filters apply to both mixed and native modes.
// Notice that the uplevel and downlevel flags are different.

aScopeInit[0].FilterFlags.Uplevel.flBothModes =
        DSOP_FILTER_COMPUTERS;
aScopeInit[0].FilterFlags.flDownlevel =
        DSOP_DOWNLEVEL_FILTER_COMPUTERS;

// Initialize the DSOP_INIT_INFO structure.

ZeroMemory(&InitInfo, sizeof(InitInfo));

InitInfo.cbSize = sizeof(InitInfo);
InitInfo.pwzTargetComputer = NULL;  // Target is the local computer.
InitInfo.cDsScopeInfos = SCOPE_INIT_COUNT;
```

(continued)

(continued)

```
InitInfo.aDsScopeInfos = aScopeInit;
InitInfo.flOptions = DSOP_FLAG_MULTISELECT;

// You can call Initialize multiple times; last call wins.
// Note that object picker makes its own copy of InitInfo.

return pDsObjectPicker->Initialize(&InitInfo);
}
```

Processing the Selected Objects

This topic describes a subroutine that retrieves and processes information about the objects the user selected from the object picker dialog box.

The *ProcessSelectedObjects* subroutine calls the **GetData** method of the **IDataObject** instance returned by the object picker dialog box. **GetData** retrieves a **STGMEDIUM** structure containing a handle to the global memory block. Calling the **GlobalLock** function on this handle returns a pointer to a **DS_SELECTION_LIST** structure containing data describing the user's selections.

```
void ProcessSelectedObjects(
    IDataObject *pdo  // Data object containing user's selections
) {

HRESULT hr = S_OK;
BOOL fGotStgMedium = FALSE;
PDS_SELECTION_LIST pDsSelList = NULL;
ULONG i;
STGMEDIUM stgmedium = {
    TYMED_HGLOBAL,
    NULL,
    NULL
};
FORMATETC formatetc = {
    g_cfDsObjectPicker,
    NULL,
    DVASPECT_CONTENT,
    -1,
    TYMED_HGLOBAL
};

do {
    // Get the global memory block containing the user's selections.

    hr = pdo->GetData(&formatetc, &stgmedium);
```

```
    if (FAILED(hr)) break;
    fGotStgMedium = TRUE;

    // Retrieve pointer to DS_SELECTION_LIST structure.

    pDsSelList = (PDS_SELECTION_LIST) GlobalLock(stgmedium.hGlobal); if
(!pDsSelList) break;

    // Loop through DS_SELECTION array of selected objects.

    for (i = 0; i < pDsSelList->cItems; i++) {
        printf("Object %u'\n", i);
        printf("  Name '%ws'\n",
                pDsSelList->aDsSelection[i].pwzName);
        printf("  Class '%ws'\n",
                pDsSelList->aDsSelection[i].pwzClass);
        printf("  Path '%ws'\n",
                pDsSelList->aDsSelection[i].pwzADsPath);
        printf("  UPN '%ws'\n",
                pDsSelList->aDsSelection[i].pwzUPN);
    }


    GlobalUnlock(stgmedium.hGlobal);
} while (0);

if (fGotStgMedium)
    ReleaseStgMedium(&stgmedium);

}
```

C H A P T E R   1 2

Replication and Data Integrity

Microsoft® Active Directory™ provides *multi-master update*. Multi-master update means that all full replicas of a given partition are writeable (the partial replicas on global catalog servers are not writeable.) Multi-master update means that updates are not blocked even when some replicas are down. Active Directory propagates the changes from the updated replica to all other replicas. Replication is automatic and transparent.

Active Directory Replication Model

This section discusses the following:

- What is the Active Directory Replication Model?
- Why Active Directory uses This Replication Model
- A Programmer's Model of Active Directory Replication

What is the Active Directory Replication Model?

The replication model used in Microsoft® Active Directory™ is called *multi-master loose consistency with convergence*. In this model, the directory can have many replicas; a replication system propagates changes made at any given replica to all other replicas. The replicas are **not** guaranteed to be consistent with each other at any particular point in time ("loose consistency"), since changes can be applied to any replica at any time ("multi-master"). If the system is allowed to reach a steady state, in which no new updates are occurring and all previous updates have been completely replicated, all replicas are **guaranteed** to converge on the same set of values ("convergence").

Why Active Directory Uses This Replication Model

Active Directory is a loosely coupled system for the following reasons:

- Customers require a highly distributed solution in which parts of the directory can be spread across their networks and administered locally.
- Large customers need to grow to many millions of objects, hundreds or thousands of replicas, or both.
- Many customer networks provide only intermittent connectivity to some locations; for example, remote oil drilling platforms and ships at sea, so the system must be tolerant of partly connected or disconnected operations.

There is no way to guarantee complete knowledge of the current or future state of a distributed system because knowledge of state changes must be propagated and propagation takes time, during which more state changes may occur. This is an axiom of distributed computing.

Tightly coupled systems deal with uncertainty by attempting to eliminate it. This is done through constraints on updates, requiring all nodes or some majority of nodes to be available before updates can be performed, using distributed locking schemes or single-mastering for critical resources, constraining all nodes to be well connected, or some combination of these techniques. The more tightly coupled the computing nodes in a distributed system are, the lower the scaling limit.

Loosely coupled systems deal with uncertainty by tolerating it. A loosely coupled system allows the nodes to have differing views of the overall system state and provides algorithms for resolving conflicts.

Tightly coupled solutions were rejected as unsuitable for Active Directory because of the requirements for local administration, disconnected operation, and scalability to very large numbers of nodes. The loosely coupled model chosen, **multi-master loose consistency with convergence**, satisfies all of these requirements.

A Programmer's Model of Active Directory Replication

The following does not describe how Active Directory replication works—instead it gives a much simpler *model*, which is equivalent from an application programmer's perspective.

All updates to Active Directory are performed using LDAP requests that create, modify, or delete one object for each request. A single request can set or modify any number of attributes on an object.

An update request is processed as an atomic transaction at some domain controller (DC). Either the entire update happens or none of it does. If the requester receives a successful response to an update request, that entire request has succeeded (committed). That's called an *originating write*. You can't group multiple LDAP requests into a single larger transaction.

As part of performing an originating write, a DC computes a "stamp" for each new or modified attribute value, and attaches this stamp to the value so when the value is replicated, the stamp is replicated too. The new stamp is guaranteed to be different from all other stamps, and in case of an update the new stamp is always *larger* than the stamp on the old value at that DC.

Occasionally, a DC selects the set of objects that have changed since the last time the DC performed replication. Then, for each object, it sends a single message to all other DCs containing all the current values of attributes changed since the last time the object was replicated. Replication messages are reliable and are delivered in order but may take a long time to be delivered.

When one DC receives a replication message from another DC, it processes it as follows: For each modified attribute, if the stamp on the value in the replication message is larger than the stamp on the current value, the DC applies the update; otherwise the DC discards the update. Each replication message is applied as an atomic transaction, just like an originating write.

That's the complete model of how Active Directory replication works. Key properties of this model:

- An originating write to a single object is atomic.
- When replicating changes, either all the changes made by an originating write are sent, or none of them are.
- A replicated write to a single object is atomic, but conflicts are resolved attribute-by-attribute.

The model does *not* guarantee the replication ordering of changes made to different objects.Don't write applications that assume changes will be replicated in originating-write order. The model does *not* guarantee that if an attribute of an object is changed twice, both values will be replicated: Replication sends only the current value at the time of replication.

The model differs from reality in several ways that only affect performance.For instance, Active Directory actually sends replication messages containing the changes to multiple objects, but it processes the contents of such a multi-object message as if it were a series of single-object messages.And Active Directory does not perform point-to-point replication as described in the model, but instead performs a more complex and more efficient transitive replication that is functionally equivalent to the model.

Active Directory Replication Behavior

Replication behavior is consistent and predictable; given a set of changes to a given replica, the outcome can be predicted—the changes will be propagated to all other replicas. Devising a reliable general model for predicting *when* the changes will be applied at all other replicas, or at a particular replica, is impossible, because the future state of the distributed system as a whole cannot be known. This is called *nondeterministic latency*, and applications that use the directory **must** understand and allow for it.

The situation is not as complex at it might appear. There are only threestates that an application must accommodate:

- *Version Skew*. This is when none of the changes applied to a given source replica have propagated to a given destination replica. An application reading the source replica sees the new version of the information, while an application reading the destination sees the old version (or nothing, if the new information was added for the first time). Version skew applies to all directory service consumers.

- *Partial Update*. This is when some of the changes applied to a given source replica have propagated to a given destination replica. An application reading the source replica sees the new information, while an application reading the destination sees a mix of old and new (or only some of the new, if the new information was added for the first time). Partial update applies to directory service consumers that use two or more related objects to store their information.
- *Fully Replicated State*. All of the changes applied to a given source replica have propagated to a given destination replica. Applications at the source and destination replicas see the same information.

Impact on Directory-Enabled Applications

Version Skew

Version skew occurs when applications read the **same** objects from **different** replicas before a change has replicated. Applications reading the remote replica see the unchanged object. Version skew is an issue when a given application or set of applications use the information in the directory to interoperate.

For example, an RPC Service can publish its endpoints in the directory using standard RPC APIs (such as RpcNsBindingExport). Clients connect to the service by looking up the desired endpoint in the directory (RpcNsBindingLookupBegin, RpcNsBindingLookupNext, and so on) and binding to it.

Assume that an RPC Service S_1 publishes endpoint E_{s1} and subsequently moves to a different computer. The original endpoint E_{s1} is changed to E_{s2}, reflecting the new computer's address. Clients reading remote replicas of the directory service are unable to connect to the service until the updated endpoint is replicated. However, moving a service from one computer to another is a rare occurrence; therefore, this interruption/delay should rarely be encountered, especially if the movement of the service is well planned.

Partial Updates

In general, partial update occurs when one application is reading a set of data while another application is writing to that same set of data. This is a situation that can occur with any application in a multi-mastered system. There are many ways this can occur. You could have *n* applications writing to the same data set at once. If you look at it this way, the directory replication service is just another application that could potentially be writing to the same data set that another application may be reading. This could be a potential problem for an application. However, the window of time in which a partial update can affect your application is relatively small. This should rarely if ever be an issue for applications that are not dependent on the synchronization of multiple objects. If your application is highly dependent on the synchronization of a related set of objects, you should consider the effects of a partial update in your application design.

In terms of the directory replication, partial update occurs when applications read the **same set** of objects from **different** replicas while replication is in progress. Applications at the remote replica see some of the changes but not all.

Note that the window in which partial update can affect an application is small: the application must start reading objects while inbound replication is in progress, after one or more of the related, changed objects have been received but before all have been received. The time between the updates at the source replica directly affects the size of this window—updates that occur close together in time will be replicated close together in time. Partial update can be an issue when an application uses a related set of objects.

For example, a remote access service can use the directory to store policy and profile information. The policy information is stored in one set of objects, and the profile in another set. When a user connects to the remote access service, the remote access service reads the policy to determine whether the user is allowed to connect, and if so what profile to apply to the user's session. Partial update can affect the remote access service in several ways:

- If the policy is complex and consists of multiple objects, the remote access service might read a partially updated policy resulting in incorrect denial or granting of service to the user, inability to process the policy due to internal inconsistency, and so on.

- If both the policy and profiles have been updated, the service might correctly process the policy but apply a stale profile, because the policy objects have replicated but the profile objects have not.

- If the profile is complex and consists of multiple objects, the service might correctly process the policy but apply a partially updated profile because the policy objects have replicated but only some of the profile objects have done so.

Collisions

Collisions occur when the same attributes of two or more replicas of a given object are changed during the same replication interval. The replication process reconciles the collision; because of reconciliation a user or application may "see" a value other than the one they wrote.

A simple example is user address information: A user changes a mailing address at replica R1 and an administrator changes the same mailing address at replica R2. A written value propagates until another value is selected over that value by the collision reconciliation mechanism. As long as a value continues to "win" against other values in the collision resolution process, the value continues to propagate. Ultimately, this "winning" value will be propagated to R1,R2, and all other replicas if no other changes are made.

Collision resolution is an issue for applications that make assumptions about the internal consistency of objects or sets of objects. For example, a network bandwidth allocation management service stores network bandwidth information for a given network segment in the directory in an object O1. The object contains the bandwidth available in bits-per-second and the maximum bandwidth any single user can reserve. The service expects that the user reservable bandwidth will always be less than or equal to the bandwidth available.

- The object in the initial fully replicated state gives the available bandwidth as 56 kilobits-per-second, and the user reservable bandwidth as 9,600 bits-per-second.
- An administrator at replica R_1 changes the values to 64k and 19,200 respectively.
- An administrator at replica R_2 changes the values to 10 million and 1 million respectively before the update from R_1 arrives.

Assuming the attributes in question have equal version numbers when the updates occur, there is a small but real possibility that the object will end up with a maximum bandwidth of 64k and a user reservable maximum of 1 million—if the application performs the updates as separate write operations. The application should always update both properties in a single operation.

Detecting and Avoiding Replication Latency

Replication latency is a fact of life in a loosely coupled distributed system. Applications must accommodate this. The best way to accommodate replication latency is to design applications to minimize the effects. The ideal directory-enabled application:

- Is insensitive to version skew.
- Does not depend on relationships among multiple objects.
- Has no intra- or inter-object consistency requirements.

Applications and services that fit this profile need not be concerned with replication latency. Other applications must be designed with replication latency in mind. The key to success in designing such an application is awareness of the replication process. Steps taken at design time to reduce inter-object dependencies and minimize partial update windows will pay large dividends at run time. Approaches to dealing with replication latency are divided into two classes—**avoidance strategies** that reduce the impact of latency and **detection strategies** that allow an application to detect latency-induced states.

What Can You Know, and When Can You Know It?

Applications that are sensitive to latency-induced states must recognize problem states and take appropriate action. There are two problem states: version skew and partial update. Version skew is not detectable by examining the Directory Service (remember the axiom of distributed computing stated in Why Active Directory Uses This Replication Model). Partial update can be detected by adding metadata to the objects that compose the related set. Suggestions for such metadata appear in subsequent sections of this document. There are avoidance strategies applications can take to reduce the possibility of both version skew and partial update. These strategies are also discussed in subsequent sections of this document.

Temporal Locality

Temporal locality is an avoidance strategy that reduces the window for partial updates. Replication of changes from a given source replica proceeds in ascending USN order. Writes that occur close together in time will have USNs that are "near" each other, and will be propagated close together in time. Applications that create or update multiple, related objects should write the objects as close together in time as possible. For example, the application could gather all necessary input from the user and apply it to the directory when the user clicks an "Apply" button.

Temporal Locality also reduces the odds of collision resolution introducing intra-object inconsistencies.

Out-of-Band Signaling

Cooperating applications that share common data using the directory can use out-of-band signaling to avoid both version skew and partial updates. Put simply, the cooperating applications use a mechanism separate from directory replication to inform each other of changes in the shared common data. Out-of-band signaling is most effective when used in combination with a versioning mechanism—this allows the partner detecting the change to notify remote partners what version of the shared data to wait for.

Returning to the RPC example given in "Version Skew," the RPC server could call back into connected clients to inform them of the move to a new server: "I am going to move. Please stand by, replication will bring you the new address shortly" so that the client can handle the transition period.

Applications that require identical policies to be in force in order to communicate with each other can use out-of-band signaling to ensure that a new policy is not employed until all involved parties have received it. For example, if the IP Security policy between two machines is changed, an agent on the source machine could contact an agent on the destination machine to negotiate the application of the changed policy, with the source machine delaying application until the destination machine has received the new policy as well.

Effective Date and Time

Effective date and time is an avoidance strategy that prevents version skew and partial updates by deferring the effective data of information to some point in the future when the change has a very high probability of being fully replicated. To implement effective dates, the application objects must include an effective date timestamp, which is filled in when the object is created or changed. Consumers of the objects check the timestamp and defer use of the objects until that date and time are reached.

Some important considerations:

- Applications that choose this approach must ensure that there is a set of applicable data to use until the updated objects become effective.

- Distributed time service in Microsoft® Windows NT® 4.0 keeps the clocks of the connected Microsoft® Windows® 2000 systems synchronized. No time service is perfect, however, so there is a small window for version skew.

- Setting a good effective date presumes knowledge of the overall replication latency for the distributed system in question. In a stable network a good rule of thumb for effective dates is the time of the update plus 2*(average overall latency). So, for a system whose overall latency averages 4 hours, a delay of 8 hours is reasonable.

- In an unstable network, determining a "good" value for effective dates is much more difficult, since the latency may be highly variable. Effective date is most "effective" in an unstable network when combined with other avoidance or detection strategies such as checksums or consistency GUIDs (see the next section for more information).

Checksums and Object Counts

Checksums and object counts are detection strategies that allow an application to detect a partial update state. Checksums can also be used to detect inconsistencies introduced by collision resolution. Both checksums and object counts require a place to store the value used for verifying a checksum or object count. This can be on a "master" object chosen from among those involved in the application-specific relationship or on a parent object under which the related objects are stored.

For checksums, applications reading the related objects verify the checksum by calculating a local result and comparing it with the stored value. If the values do not match, the replica is in a partial update state and the objects cannot be used.

For object counts, applications count the related objects (typically children of a single parent) and compare the count with the stored value. If the counts do not match, the replica is in a partial update state and the objects cannot be used.

Some important considerations:

- For the checksum approach to work, the one or more attributes used in computing the checksum must be updated. The algorithm used to compute the checksum must reliably reflect differences in input. If many different inputs product the same checksum, the algorithm will not reliably detect partial updates. "Salting" the input with values like the **objectGUID** of the source computer and the date and time of the update is also helpful.

- Object counts work best when used with new sets of objects, or in combination with consistency GUIDs (see the next section for more information). The application performing the update must either know *a priori* the number of objects that will be in the container when the update is completed. or use some other means of marking the container invalid while the update proceeds (for example, setting the count to zero). After completing the update the source application marks the container with the count of objects contained.

Consistency GUIDs

Consistency GUIDs are a detection strategy that allows an application to detect partial updates. A consistency GUID (Globally Unique Identifier) is applied to each object in a related set. In implementation, a source application generates a new GUID and applies it to each object it updates in the set of related objects. It then applies the new GUID to the rest of the objects in the set, and finishes by applying the new GUID to the "master" object. Typically, the "master" object will be a container that is the parent of the other objects in the set.

Some important considerations:

- Consistency GUIDs combined with object counts or checksums are more effective than consistency GUIDs alone, because the application reading the objects may not know how many objects with the GUID should be present.

- Applications must generate their own GUIDs (a Microsoft® Win32® API, UuidCreate, provides this function), and not use the system-generated GUIDs found in an object's **objectGUID** attribute. This is because a consistency GUID needs to change each time the set of objects is updated. Object identity GUIDs found in **objectGUID** never change after the object has been created.

- Consistency GUIDs assume that no object is shared among sets, so each set can have a unique consistency GUID.

Versioning and Fallback Strategies

When an application detects a partial update using one of the preceding techniques or reads a set of objects whose effective date has not yet been reached, the application must deal with the situation gracefully. For some applications, the graceful response is to "fall back" to a previous version of the objects in question. Active Directory does not provide a versioning facility—applications that want this capability must provide it themselves. Approaches to versioning include keeping the "last known good" values cached locally and storing multiple sets of objects in the directory, for example, in "old," "current," and "new" containers. Many other schemes are possible.

Implementations must take care to avoid unintended consequences. An earlier version of objects should be used only when a partial update is detected or the new objects are not yet "effective." Falling back because something in the application "doesn't work" might circumvent an administrator's intent. For example, two computers that formerly could communicate might find themselves unable to do so because of a change in IP Security policy. If this is intentional on the part of the administrator, the affected systems should not fall back to the policy that allowed them to communicate, as this would be a security breach.

CHAPTER 13

Managing Users

User accounts are created and stored as objects in Active Directory™. These user objects represent users and computers. This chapter defines what users are and how they are used, and explains how to programmatically manage users in Active Directory. This chapter discusses the following topics:

- Users in Active Directory
- Security Principals
- What is a User?
- Reading a user object
- Creating a user
- Deleting a user
- Enumerating users
- Querying for users
- Moving users
- Managing users on member servers and Windows 2000 Professional

Users in Active Directory

In Windows® 2000, Active Directory™ is a generalized directory service that includes storage of domain, user, user group, and security information.

In Windows NT® 4.0 and earlier, you used the Net functions (such as **NetUserAdd**, **NetUserEnum**, **NetUserDel**, and so on) to manage users, user groups, and other network items. With Windows 2000, ADSI provides uniform and secure access to these items and their properties. Note that ADSI provides a Windows NT 4.0 provider that enables you to use ADSI to manage user, user groups, and computers on Windows NT 4.0 systems. There are also providers for Microsoft® Exchange 5.5, Microsoft Internet Information Server, Novell NetWare® Directory Services (NDS) and Novell NetWare® 3. This means a single set of standardized methods for managing users and user groups for Windows NT, NDS, and NetWare 3.

In addition, Windows 2000 is a multi-master directory. This means that changes to users, user groups, and other information stored in the directory can be made at *any* domain controller. On Windows 2000, you no longer need to locate the primary domain controller (PDC) and make user and user group changes on the PDC.

Windows 2000 also introduces a new hierarchical namespace within a domain called an organizational unit (OU). An OU can contain computers, users, user groups, and other network objects. Usually, an OU is used for the purpose of grouping things for administrative purposes, such as delegating administrative rights and assigning policies to the group as a single unit.

Domains, OUs, users, user groups, computers, and other network items are stored as objects in Active Directory. In Windows 2000, you still add users, user groups, and computers to a domain. However, you now have the option of adding these objects to an OU container or any other type of container that the object you want to add defines in its **classSchema** object's **Poss-Superiors** attribute (this is a property on an object's **classSchema** object and this property restricts what types of objects can contain that object).

Security Principals

In Windows® 2000, a security principal is a user, group, or computer—an entity that the security system recognizes. This includes human users as well as autonomous processes. Strictly speaking, the security system cannot tell the difference between users who are logged in and processes running on the computer. It sees both as security principals with security principal names.

Users, groups, and computers are created and stored as objects in Active Directory™. There are also well-known security principals that represent special identities defined by the Windows 2000 security system, such as Everyone, Local System, Principal Self, Authenticated User, Creator Owner, and so on. Objects representing the well-known security principals, such as Anonymous Logon, are stored in the WellKnown Security Principals container beneath the Configuration container.

What Is a User?

User accounts are created and stored as objects in Active Directory™. User accounts can be used by human users or programs such as Win32 services use to log on to a computer. When a user logs on, the system verifies the user's password by comparing it with information stored in the user's user object in Active Directory. If the password is authenticated (that is, the password presented matches the password stored in the user object), the system produces an access token. An access token is an object that describes the security context of a process or thread. The information in a token includes the security identity and group memberships of the user account associated with the process or thread. Every process executed on behalf of this user has a copy of this access token.

Each user or application that accesses resources in a Windows® 2000 domain must have an account in Active Directory. Windows 2000 uses this user account to verify that the user or application has permission to use a resource.

A user account can be used to do the following:

- Enable human users to log on to a computer and to access resources based on that user account's identity.
- Enable programs and services to run under a specific security context.
- Manage user access to shared resources such as Active Directory objects and their properties, network shares, files, directories, printer queues, and so on.

Groups can contain members, which are references to users and other groups. Groups can also be used to control access to shared resources. When assigning permissions for resources (file shares, printers, and so on), administrators should assign those permissions to a group rather than to the individual users. The permissions are assigned once to the group, instead of several times to each individual user. This helps simplify the maintenance and administration of a network.

Users vs. Contacts

Both users and contacts can be used to represent human users. However, a user is a security principal; a contact is not.

A user can be used to enable a human user to log on and access shared resources.

A contact is used only for distribution list and e-mail purposes. However, a contact can contain most of the information stored in a user object such as address, phone numbers, and so on—since both user and contact are derived from the person **classSchema** object. A contact has no security context; therefore, a contact cannot be used to control access to shared resources and cannot be used to log on to a computer.

Users vs. Computers

The computer object class inherits from the user object class. A computer object represents a computer; however, the computer and the computer's local services often require access to the network and shared resources. When the computer accesses shared resources (not the user logged on to the computer), it needs an access token just as a human user logged on as a user does. When a computer accesses the network, it uses an access token containing the security identifier for the computer's computer account and the groups that account is a member of.

A service can run in the context of LocalSystem or a specific service account. On computers running Windows 2000, a service that runs in the context of the LocalSystem account uses the credentials of the computer.

Reading a User Object

To read the properties of a user object, bind to the user object and use the methods provided by the **IADs**, **IADsPropertyList**, or **IADsUser** interfaces. In C/C++, you can also use **IDirectoryObject** to retrieve specific properties. For information on reading properties of an object, see *Accessing and Manipulating Data with ADSI*.

Binding to a User Object

To bind to a user object, specify the user object's distinguished name or its **objectGUID** as you would with any other object.

For information about binding, see *Chapter 7: Binding.*

User Object Properties

A user object has a number of properties. This section documents the key properties that are used by the Windows® 2000 operating system, administrative tools, and the Windows Address Book (WAB). It does not describe *all* properties (many are not used) on the user object.

Some properties are stored in the directory (such as **cn**, **nTSecurityDescriptor**, **objectGUID**, and so on) and replicated to all domain controllers within a domain. A subset of these properties is also replicated to the global catalog.

Non-replicated properties are stored on each domain controller but are not replicated elsewhere (such as **badPwdCount**, **lastLogon**, **lastLogoff**, and so on). The non-replicated properties are properties that pertain to a particular domain controller. For example, **lastLogon** is the last date and time that the user's network logon was validated by the particular domain controller that is returning the property.

A user object also has constructed properties that are not stored in the directory but are calculated by the domain controller (such as **canonicalName**, **distinguishedName**, **allowedAttributes**, **ADsPath**, and so on). Note that **distinguishedName** and **ADsPath** are not defined in the schema.

Properties for user objects fall into the following categories:

- *Base object.* This category covers properties required on all directory objects, such as **objectClass**, **nTSecurityDescriptor**, and so on.
- *Naming/Identity.* This category covers properties that are referring to or identifying the object, such as **distinguishedName**, **objectGUID**, **objectSid**, and so on.
- *Security.* This category covers properties for logon and access control purposes.
- *Address book.* This category covers properties for e-mail and general information about the user.
- *Application-specific information.* This category covers user-specific configuration information for specific applications such as dial-up networking.

Naming Properties

As with other directory objects, a user object has names in the form of **cn**, **name**, **distinguishedName**, and **objectGUID** properties. Note that a user's relative distinguished name (RDN) is the value of the **cn** property. These properties can be viewed and managed by the Active Directory™ User and Computers snap-in.

Since a user object is a security principal, it has the following additional naming properties:

userPrincipalName (User-Principal-Name)

The **userPrincipalName** is a single-valued and indexed property that is a string that specifies the user principal name (UPN) of the user. The UPN is an Internet-style login name for the user based on the Internet standard RFC 822. The UPN is shorter than the distinguished name and easier to remember. By convention, this should map to the user's e-mail name. The point of the UPN is to consolidate the e-mail and logon namespaces so that the user need only remember a single name.

The UPN is the preferred logon name for Windows 2000 users. Users should be using their UPNs to log on to the domain. At logon time, a UPN is validated first by searching the local domain, then the global catalog. Failure to find the UPN in the local domain or the GC results in rejection of the UPN.

The UPN can be assigned, but is not required, when the user account is created. Once assigned, the UPN is unaffected by changes to other properties of the user object (for example, if the user is renamed or moved) or changes to the domains in the tree (for example, if a parent domain was renamed or a domain was moved). Thus, a user can keep the same login name, although the directory may be radically restructured. Note that the UPN can be changed administratively at any time.

The UPN is a string property that can contain any string value. However, the following scheme is recommended:

The user principal name has two parts: the UPN prefix (the user account name) and the UPN suffix (a DNS domain name). The parts are joined together by the @ (at sign) symbol to make the complete UPN. For example, the user Someone who has an account in the Microsoft domain would have a UPN of someone@Microsoft.com.

The UPN must be unique among all security principal objects within the directory forest. By default (that is, for the built-in user accounts and user accounts created using the Active Directory Users and Computers snap-in), the UPN can consist of any name for the user (such as the **sAMAccountName** property of the user) and the domain tree name to which the user belongs in the following form:

Name@treeName

The *treeName* is the domain name system (DNS) name of a domain, but is not required to be the name of the domain containing the user. However, the *treeName* portion of the UPN must be the name of a domain in the current forest or an alternate name listed in the **upnSuffixes** property of the Partitions container within the Configuration container. You can add or remove UPN suffixes by modifying the **upnSuffixes** property (or by choosing Properties for the root node of the Active Directory Domains and Trusts and modifying the UPN suffixes on the UPN Suffixes tab). Usually, the *treeName* is the name of the first domain in the first tree of the forest. In most cases, this domain name is the domain name registered as the enterprise domain on the Internet. The tree name is stored in a property ("treeName") stored on the **domainDNS** object.

When creating a new user object, you should check the local domain and the global catalog for the proposed name to ensure it does not already exist.

objectGUID (Object-GUID)

The **objectGUID** property is a single-valued property that is the unique identifier for the object. This property is a Globally Unique Identifier (GUID). When an object is created in the directory, Active Directory generates a GUID and assigns it to the object's **objectGUID** property. The GUID is unique across the enterprise and anywhere else.

The **objectGUID** is a 128-bit GUID structure stored as an OctetString.

Because an object's distinguished name changes if the object is renamed or moved, the domain name is not a reliable identifier for an object. In Active Directory, an object's **objectGUID** property is never changed, even if the object is renamed or moved to different places. Note that you can retrieve the string form of the **objectGUID** using the **IADs::get_GUID** method.

sAMAccountName (SAM-Account-Name)

The **sAMAccountName** property is a single-valued property that is the logon name used to support clients and servers from a previous version of Windows (such as Windows NT® 4.0 and earlier, Windows 95, Windows 98, and LAN Manager). The **sAMAccountName** should be less than 20 characters to support these clients and servers.

The **sAMAccountName** must be unique among all security principal objects within the domain.

You should query for the new name against the domain to verify that the **sAMAccountName** is unique in the domain.

The **sAMAccountName** must be unique among all security principal objects within a domain container.

objectSid (Object-Sid)

The **objectSid** property is a single-valued property that specifies the security identifier (SID) of the user. The SID is a unique value used to identify the user as a security principal. It is a binary value that is set by the system when the user is created.

Each user has a unique SID issued by a Windows 2000 domain and stored in **objectSid** property of the user object in the directory. Each time a user logs on, the system retrieves the user's SID from the directory and places it in the user's access token. The user's SID is also used to retrieve the SIDs for the groups of which the user is a member and places them in the user's access token. The system uses the SIDs in the user's access token to identify the user and his/her group memberships in all subsequent interactions with Windows NT security.

When a SID has been used as the unique identifier for a user or group, it cannot ever be used again to identify another user or group.

sIDHistory (SIDHistory)

The **sIDHistory** property is a multi-valued property that contains previous SIDs used for the user object if the user was moved from another domain. Whenever a user is moved from one domain to another, a new SID is created and that new SID becomes the **objectSID**. The previous SID is added to the **sIDHistory** property, which contains the SIDs from the user's previous domain moves.

Security Properties

In addition to naming properties for user objects (**objectGUID**, **objectSid**, **cn**, **distinguishedName**, and so on), there are other security properties that are used for logon, network access, and access control. These properties are used by the Windows 2000 security system. These properties can be viewed and managed by the Active Directory User and Computers snap-in.

accountExpires

The **accountExpires** property specifies when the account will expire. This value is stored as a large integer that represents the number of seconds elapsed since 00:00:00, January 1, 1970. A value of TIMEQ_FOREVER indicates that the account never expires.

This value is defined in LMACCESS.H.

altSecurityIdentities

The **altSecurityIdentities** property is a multi-valued property that contains mappings for X.509 certificates or external Kerberos user accounts to this user for the purpose of authentication. Various security packages (including Public Key authentication package and Kerberos) use this information to authenticate users when they present the alternative form of identification (such as certificate, Unix Kerberos ticket, and so on.) and build a Windows 2000 token based on the corresponding user account such that they can access system resources.

For X.509 certificates, the values should be the Issuer and Subject names in 509v3 certificates (issued by an external public Certificate Authority) that map to the user account used to find an account for authentication. The SSL (schannel) package uses the following syntax: X509:*<somecertinfotype>somecertinfo*. For example, the following value specifies the issuer DN "<I>" with the DN C=US,O=InternetCA,CN=APublicCertificateAuthority and the subject DN "<S>" with the DN C=US,O=Microsoft,OU=FOO,CN=John Smith:

```
X509:<I>C=US,O=InternetCA,CN=APublicCertificateAuthority<S>C=US,O=Microsoft,O
U=FOO,CN=John Smith
```

Note that <I> or <I> and <S> are supported. Having only <S> is not supported. Applications should not modify the values within <I> or <S> because partial DN matching is not supported.

For external Kerberos accounts, the values should be the Kerberos account name. The Kerberos package uses the following syntax: Kerberos:MITaccountname. For example, the following is the value for an account at Microsoft.com:

```
Kerberos:John.Doe@Microsoft.com
```

badPasswordTime (Non-replicated)

The **badPasswordTime** property specifies the last time the user tried to log onto the account using an incorrect password. This value is stored as a large integer that represents the number of seconds elapsed since 00:00:00, January 1, 1970. This property is maintained separately on each domain controller in the domain. A value of zero means that the last bad password time is unknown. To get an accurate value for the user's last bad password time in the domain, each domain controller in the domain must be queried and the largest value should be used.

badPwdCount (Non-replicated)

The **badPwdCount** property specifies the number of times the user tried to log on to the account using an incorrect password. This property is maintained separately on each domain controller in the domain. A value of 0 indicates that the value is unknown. To get an accurate value for the user's total bad password attempts in the domain, each domain controller in the domain must be queried and the sum of the values should be used.

codePage

The **codePage** property specifies the code page for the user's language of choice. This value is not used by Windows 2000.

countryCode

The **countryCode** property specifies the country code for the user's language of choice. This value is not used by Windows 2000.

homeDirectory

The **homeDirectory** property specifies the path of the home directory for the user. The string can be null.

If **homeDrive** is set and specifies a drive letter, **homeDirectory** should be a UNC path. The path must be a network UNC path of the form *server**share**directory*. This value can be a null string.

If **homeDrive** is not set, **homeDirectory** should be a local path (such as C:\mylocaldir).

homeDrive

The **homeDrive** property specifies the drive letter to which to map the UNC path specified by **homeDirectory**. The drive letter must be specified in the following form:

driveletter**:**

where driveletter is the letter of the drive to map. For example:

Z:

If this property is not set, the **homeDirectory** should be a local path (such as C:\mylocaldir).

lastLogoff (Non-replicated)

The **lastLogoff** property specifies when the last logoff occurred. This value is stored as a large integer that represents the number of seconds elapsed since 00:00:00, January 1, 1970. This property is maintained separately on each domain controller in the domain. A value of zero means that the last logoff time is unknown. To get an accurate value for the user's last logoff in the domain, each domain controller in the domain must be queried and the largest value should be used.

lastLogon (Non-replicated)

The **lastLogon** property specifies when the last logon occurred. This value is stored as a large integer that represents the number of seconds elapsed since 00:00:00, January 1, 1970. This property is maintained separately on each domain controller in the domain. A value of zero means that the last logon time is unknown. To get an accurate value for the user's last logon in the domain, each domain controller in the domain must be queried and the largest value should be used.

lmPwdHistory

The **lmPwdHistory** property is the password history of the user in LAN Manager (LM) one-way format (OWF). The LM OWF is used for compatibility with LAN Manager 2.x clients, Windows 95, and Windows 98. This property is used only by the operating system. Note that you cannot derive the clear password back from the OWF form of the password.

logonCount (Non-replicated)

The **logonCount** property counts the number of successful times the user tried to log on to this account. This property is maintained separately on each domain controller in the domain. A value of 0 indicates that the value is unknown. To get an accurate value for the user's total number of successful logon attempts in the domain, each domain controller in the domain must be queried and the sum of the values should be used.

mail (E-mail-Addresses)

The **mail** property is a single-valued property that contains the SMTP address for the user (such as john@Microsoft.com).

memberOf

The **memberOf** property is a multi-valued property that contains groups of which the user is a direct member, depending on the domain controller (DC) from which this property is retrieved:

- At a DC for the domain containing the user, **memberOf** for the user is complete with respect to membership for groups in that domain; however, **memberOf** does not contain the user's membership in domain local and global groups in other domains.

- At a GC server, **memberOf** for the user is complete with respect to all universal group memberships.

If both conditions are true about the DC, both sets of information are contained in **memberOf**.

Note that this property lists the groups that contain the user in their member property—it does not contain the recursive list of nested predecessors. For example, if user O is a member of group C and group B and group B were nested in group A, the **membersOf** property of user O would list group C and group B but not group A.

This property is not stored—it is a computed back-link attribute.

ntPwdHistory

The **ntPwdHistory** property is the password history of the user in Windows NT (NT) one-way format (OWF). Windows® 2000 uses the NT OWF. This property is used only by the operating system. Note that you cannot derive the clear password back from the OWF form of the password.

otherMailbox

The **otherMailbox** property is a multi-valued property containing other additional mail addresses in a form such as CCMAIL: JohnDoe.

PasswordExpirationDate

The password expiration date is not a property on the user object. It is a calculated value based on the sum of **pwdLastSet** for the user and **maxPwdAge** of the user's domain. To get the password expiration date, call the **IADsUser::get_PasswordExpirationDate** method. You cannot modify this property for a user; instead, call **IADsDomain::put_MaxPasswordAge** method to change the setting for the domain.

primaryGroupID

The **primaryGroupID** property is a single-valued property containing the relative identifier (RID) for the primary group of the user. By default, this is the RID for the Domain Users group. This property is not used in the context of the Active Directory.

profilePath

The **profilePath** property specifies a path to the user's profile. This value can be a null string, a local absolute path, or a UNC path.

pwdLastSet

The **pwdLastSet** property specifies when the user last set the password. This value is stored as a large integer that represents the number of seconds elapsed since 00:00:00, January 1, 1970.

The system uses the value of this property and the **maxPwdAge** property of the domain containing the user object to calculate the password expiration date (sum of **pwdLastSet** for the user and **maxPwdAge** of the user's domain).

This property controls whether the user must change the password the next time the user logs on. If **pwdLastSet** is zero (the default), the user must change the password at next logon. The value -1 means the user does not need to change the password at next logon. The system sets this value to -1 after user has set the password.

sAMAccountType

The **sAMAccountType** property specifies an integer that represents the account type. This is set by the operating system when the object is created.

scriptPath

The **scriptPath** property specifies the path of the user's logon script, .CMD, .EXE, or .BAT file. The string can be null.

unicodePwd

The **unicodePwd** property is the password for the user.

For setting the password of the user, you should use the **IADsUser::ChangePassword** method (if your script or application is allowing the user to change his/her own password) or **IADsUser::SetPassword** method (if your script or application is allowing an administrator to reset a password).

The password of the user in Windows NT (NT) one-way format (OWF). Windows® 2000 uses the NT OWF. This property is used only by operating system. Note that you cannot derive the clear password back from the OWF form of the password.

userAccountControl

The **userAccountControl** property specifies flags that control password, lockout, disable/enable, script, and home directory behavior for the user. This property also contains a flag that indicates the account type of the object. The user object usually has the UF_NORMAL_ACCOUNT set.

The flags are defined in LMACCESS.H.

Value	Meaning
UF_SCRIPT	The logon script executed. This value must be set for LAN Manager 2.0 or Windows NT.
UF_ACCOUNTDISABLE	The user's account is disabled.
UF_HOMEDIR_REQUIRED	The home directory is required. This value is ignored in Windows NT and Windows 2000.
UF_PASSWD_NOTREQD	No password is required.
UF_PASSWD_CANT_CHANGE	The user cannot change the password.
UF_LOCKOUT	The account is currently locked out. This value can be cleared to unlock a previously locked account. This value cannot be used to lock a previously locked account.
UF_DONT_EXPIRE_PASSWD	Represents the password, which should never expire on the account.

The following values describe the account type. Only one value can be set. You cannot change the account type.

Value	Meaning
UF_NORMAL_ACCOUNT	This is a default account type that represents a typical user.
UF_TEMP_DUPLICATE_ACCOUNT	This is an account for users whose primary account is in another domain. This account provides user access to this domain, but not to any domain that trusts this domain. The User Manager refers to this account type as a *local* user account.
UF_WORKSTATION_TRUST_ACCOUNT	This is a computer account for a Windows NT Workstation/Windows 2000 Professional or Windows NT Server/Windows 2000 Server that is a member of this domain.
UF_SERVER_TRUST_ACCOUNT	This is a computer account for a Windows NT Backup Domain Controller that is a member of this domain.
UF_INTERDOMAIN_TRUST_ACCOUNT	This is a *permit to trust* account for a Windows NT domain that *trusts* other domains.

userCertificate (X509-Cert)

The **userCertificate** property is a multi-valued property that contains the DER-encoded X509v3 certificates issued to the user. Note that this property contains the public key certificates issued to this user by Microsoft® Certificate Service.

userSharedFolder

The **userSharedFolder** property specifies a UNC path to the user's shared documents folder. The path must be a network UNC path of the form *server**share**directory*. This value can be a null string.

userWorkstations

The **userWorkstations** property is a single-valued property containing the NetBIOS names of the computers running Windows NT Workstation/Windows 2000 Professional from which the user can log on. Each NetBIOS name is separated by a comma. The NetBIOS name of a computer is the **sAMAccountName** property of a computer object.

If there are no values set, it indicates that there is no restriction. To disable logons from all computers running Windows NT Workstation/Windows 2000 Professional to this account, set the UF_ACCOUNTDISABLE value in **userAccountControl** property.

This value is defined in LMACCESS.H.

maxStorage

The **maxStorage** property specifies the maximum amount of disk space the user can use. Use the value specified in USER_MAXSTORAGE_UNLIMITED to use all available disk space.

This value is defined in LMACCESS.H.

Address Book Properties

The address book properties are used to provide supplementary identification and information for a user. Their content is defined by the user and the user's organization. These properties can be viewed and managed by the Active Directory User and Computers snap-in or the Windows Address Book (WAB).

c (Country-Name)

The **Country-Name** property is the country in the user's address.

The country is represented as the two-character country code based on ISO-3166. For the country codes, see Values for countryCode.

co (Text-Country)

The **co** property is the country in which the user is located.

notes (Comment)

The **notes** property is a comment. This string can be a null string.

department (Department)

The **department** property is a single-valued property that contains the name for the department in which the user works.

description (Description)

The **description** property is a single-valued property that contains the description to display for the user.

displayName (Display-Name)

The **displayName** property is the name displayed in the address book for a particular user. This is usually the combination of the user's first name, middle initial, and last name.

directReports (Reports)

The **directReports** property is a multi-valued property that contains the list of users that directly report to the user. The users listed as reports are those that have the property manager property set to this user. Each item in the list is a linked reference to the object that represents the user; therefore, Active Directory automatically updates the **directReports** property when a user's manager property adds or removes this user as a manager. The items are represented as distinguished names.

facsimileTelephoneNumber (Facsimile-Telephone-Number)

The **facsimileTelephoneNumber** property is a single-valued property that contains the telephone number of the user's business fax machine.

givenName (Given-Name)

The **givenName** property is a single-valued property that contains the given name (first name) of the user.

homePhone (Phone-Home-Primary)

The **homePhone** property is a single-valued property containing the primary home telephone number for the user.

initials (Initials)

The **initials** property is single-valued property containing the initials for parts of the user's full name. This may be used as the middle initial in the Windows Address Book.

ipPhone (Phone-Ip-Primary)
The **ipPhone** property is used by Telephony.

l (Locality-Name)
The **l** property is a single-valued property containing the locality, such as the town or city, in the user's address.

managedObjects (Managed-Objects)
The **managedObjects** property is a multi-valued property that contains the list of objects that are managed by the user. The objects listed are those that have the **managedBy** property set to this user. Each item in the list is a linked reference to the managed object; therefore, Active Directory automatically updates the **managedObjects** property when an object's **managedBy** property adds or removes this user as its manager. The items are represented as distinguished names.

manager (Manager)
The **manager** property is a single-valued property that contains the user who is the user's manager. The manager's user object contains a **directReports** property that contains references to all user objects that have their manager properties set to the manager's user object. See **directReports**.

mobile (Phone-Mobile-Primary)
The **mobile** property is a single-valued property containing the primary cellular telephone number for the user.

otherFacsimileTelephoneNumber (Phone-Fax-Other)
The **otherFacsimileTelephoneNumber** property is a multi-valued property that contains telephone numbers of alternate fax machines for the user.

otherIpPhone (Phone-Ip-Other)
The **otherIpPhone** property is used by Telephony.

otherMobile (Phone-Mobile-Other)
The **otherMobile** property is a multi-valued property that contains alternate cellular telephone numbers for the user.

otherPager (Phone-Pager-Other)
The **otherPager** property is a multi-valued property that contains alternate pager telephone numbers for the user.

otherTelephone (Phone-Office-Other)
The **otherTelephone** property is a multi-valued property that contains alternate business telephone numbers for the user.

pager (Phone-Pager-Primary)
The **pager** property is a single-valued property containing the primary pager telephone number for the user.

physicalDeliveryOfficeName (Physical-Delivery-Office-Name)
The **physicalDeliveryOfficeName** property is a single-valued property that contains the office location in the user's place of business.

postalAddress (Postal-Address)
The **postalAddress** property is a single-valued property containing the user's postal address.

postalCode (Postal-Code)
> The **postalCode** property is a single-valued property containing postal code for the user's postal address. The postal code is specific to the user's country. In the United States of America, this property contains the ZIP code.

postOfficeBox (Post-Office-Box)
> The **postOfficeBox** property is a single-valued property containing the number or identifier of the user's post office box.

sn (Surname)
> The **sn** property is a single-valued property that specifies the user's surname (family name or last name).

st (State-Or-Province-Name)
> The **st** property is the state or province in the user's address.

street (Street-Address)
> The **street** property is a single-valued property that contains the street address of the user's place of business.

telephoneNumber (Telephone-Number)
> The **telephoneNumber** property is a single-valued property that contains the primary telephone number of the user's place of business.

title (Title)
> The **title** property is a single-valued property that contains the user's job title. This property is commonly used to indicate the formal job title, such as Senior Programmer, rather than occupational class, such as programmer. It is not typically used for "suffix" titles such as Esq. or DDS.
>
> Examples: Managing Director, Programmer II, Associate Professor, and Development Lead.

url (WWW-Page-Other)
> The **url** property is a multi-valued property that contains the URLs for the user's alternate web pages.

wWWHomePage (WWW-Home-Page)
> The **wWWHomePage** property is a single-valued property that contains the URL for the user's primary web page.

Reading User Object Properties

For general information about reading properties, see *Accessing and Manipulating Data with ADSI*.

All objects have properties; however, the user object has three types of properties that are stored differently.

Domain-replicated, stored properties

Some properties are stored in the directory (such as **cn**, **nTSecurityDescriptor**, **objectGUID**, and so on) and replicated to all domain controllers within a domain. A subset of these properties is also replicated to the global catalog. If you enumerate properties on user object from the global catalog, only the properties that are replicated to the global catalog are returned. Some properties are also indexed—including an indexed property in a query improves the performance of a query.

These properties can be retrieved using the **IADs::Get** method, **IADsProperty*** methods, **IDirectoryObject::GetObjectAttributes** method, and **IDirectorySearch** methods.

Non-replicated, locally stored properties

Non-replicated properties are stored on each domain controller but are not replicated elsewhere (such as **badPwdCount**, **lastLogon**, **lastLogoff**, and so on). The non-replicated properties are properties that pertain to a particular domain controller. For example, **lastLogon** is the last date/time that the user's network logon was validated by the particular domain controller that is returning the property. These properties can be retrieved in the same way as the domain-wide properties described previously. However, for these properties, each domain controller stores only values that pertain to that particular domain controller. For example, if you want to get the last time a user logged on to the domain, you would have to read the **lastLogon** property for the user at every domain controller in the domain and find latest time.

Non-stored, constructed properties

A user object also has constructed properties that are not stored in the directory but are calculated by the domain controller (such as **canonicalName**, **distinguishedName**, **allowedAttributes**, **ADsPath**, and so on). Note that **distinguishedName** and **ADsPath** are not defined in the schema. All the constructed properties can be retrieved by **IDirectoryObject** and **IDirectorySearch** methods. Most are automatically retrieved and cached with a **IADs::GetInfo** call on the user object (Note **IADs::Get** does an implicit **IADs::GetInfo** call if the cache is empty). However, some constructed properties are not automatically retrieved and cached and, therefore, require an **IADs::GetInfoEx** call to explicitly retrieve them. For example, **canonicalName** is not retrieved with a **IADs::GetInfo** call and therefore **IADs::Get** will return a E_ADS_PROPERTY_NOT_FOUND error. Enumeration of all properties using **IADsPropertyList** will not include the **canonicalName** property.

Determining Which Properties Are Non-Replicated, Constructed, Global Catalog, and Indexed

The **systemFlags** property of an **attributeSchema** object contains flags that indicate various qualities of the attribute object, such as whether the attribute is constructed or nonreplicated. The **ADS_SYSTEMFLAG_ENUM** enumeration contains values for various **systemFlags** bits, including the following bits for constructed and nonreplicated properties.

```
ADS_SYSTEMFLAG_ATTR_NOT_REPLICATED = 0x00000001
ADS_SYSTEMFLAG_ATTR_IS_CONSTRUCTED = 0x00000004
```

You can use these bits to query for attributes that are constructed or nonreplicated. For example, the following query string finds all **attributeSchema** objects that are not replicated. Note that the query string uses the decimal equivalent of the value, not a hexadecimal number or the ADS_SYSTEMFLAG_ATTR_NOT_REPLICATED constant name. For more information about the matching rule OID used by this query string, see *How to Specify Comparison Values*.

```
(&(objectCategory=attributeSchema)(systemFlags:1.2.840.113556.1.4.804:=1))
```

The **searchFlags** property of each property's **attributeSchema** object defines whether a property is indexed (indexed has a value of 1, non-indexed is 0). For example, the following query string finds the **attributeSchema** objects representing indexed properties:

```
(&(objectCategory=attributeSchema)(searchFlags=1))
```

The **isMemberOfPartialAttributeSet** property of each property's **attributeSchema** object defines whether a property is replicated to the global catalog (in the global catalog that has a value of TRUE, not in the global catalog that is FALSE). For example, the following query string finds the **attributeSchema** objects representing global catalog properties:

```
(&(objectCategory=attributeSchema)(isMemberOfPartialAttributeSet=TRUE))
```

Example Code for Reading Properties

The following code fragments enumerate the properties of the specified user in the current domain, by searching for the user and then using **IADsPropertyList** to enumerate its properties (note how time/date values as large integers are handled and how octet strings for **objectSID** and **objectGUID** are handled.).

C++

```cpp
//For the pow function to calculate powers of 2
#include <math.h>
#include <wchar.h>
#include <objbase.h>
#include <activeds.h>


//Make sure you define UNICODE
//Need to define version 5 for Windows 2000
#define _WIN32_WINNT 0x0500
//For SID conversion API.
#include <sddl.h>


HRESULT GetUserProperties(IADs * pObj);
```

(continued)

(continued)

```
HRESULT EnumeratePropertyValue(
        IADsPropertyEntry *pEntry
        );

HRESULT FindUserByName(IDirectorySearch *pSearchBase, //Container to search
                LPOLESTR szFindUser, //Name of user to find.
                IADs **ppUser); //Return a pointer to the user


void wmain( int argc, wchar_t *argv[ ])
{

//Handle the command line arguments.
LPOLESTR pszBuffer = new OLECHAR[MAX_PATH*2];
if (argv[1] == NULL)
{
    wprintf(L"This program finds a user in the current Window 2000 domain\n");
    wprintf(L"and displays its properties.\n");
    wprintf(L"Enter Common Name of the user to find:");
    _getws(pszBuffer);
}
else
    wcscpy(pszBuffer, argv[1]);
//if empty string, exit.
if (0==wcscmp(L"", pszBuffer))
    return;

wprintf(L"\nFinding user: %s...\n",pszBuffer);

//Intialize COM
CoInitialize(NULL);
HRESULT hr = S_OK;
//Get rootDSE and the domain container's DN.
IADs *pObject = NULL;
IDirectorySearch *pDS = NULL;
LPOLESTR szPath = new OLECHAR[MAX_PATH];
VARIANT var;
hr = ADsOpenObject(L"LDAP://rootDSE",
            NULL,
            NULL,
            ADS_SECURE_AUTHENTICATION, //Use Secure Authentication
            IID_IADs,
            (void**)&pObject);
if (FAILED(hr))
```

```
{
    wprintf(L"Not Found. Could not bind to the domain.\n");
    if (pObject)
        pObject->Release();
    return;
}

hr = pObject->Get(L"defaultNamingContext",&var);
if (SUCCEEDED(hr))
{
    wcscpy(szPath,L"LDAP://");
    wcscat(szPath,var.bstrVal);
    VariantClear(&var);
    if (pObject)
    {
        pObject->Release();
        pObject = NULL;
    }
    //Bind to the root of the current domain.
    hr = ADsOpenObject(szPath,
                NULL,
                NULL,
                ADS_SECURE_AUTHENTICATION, //Use Secure Authentication
                IID_IDirectorySearch,
                (void**)&pDS);
    if (SUCCEEDED(hr))
    {
        hr =  FindUserByName(pDS, //Container to search
                    pszBuffer, //Name of user to find.
                    &pObject); //Return a pointer to the user
        if (SUCCEEDED(hr))
        {
            wprintf (L"------------------------------------------------\n");
            wprintf (L"--------Call GetUserProperties----------\n");
            hr = GetUserProperties(pObject);
            wprintf (L"GetUserProperties HR: %x\n", hr);
        }
        else
        {
            wprintf(L"User \"%s\" not Found.\n",pszBuffer);
            wprintf (L"FindUserByName failed with the following HR: %x\n", hr);
        }
        if (pObject)
            pObject->Release();
```

(continued)

(continued)

```
        }

    if (pDS)
        pDS->Release();
}


//uninitialize COM
CoUninitialize();

    return;
}

HRESULT GetUserProperties(IADs * pObj)
{
    HRESULT hr = E_FAIL;
    LPOLESTR szDSPath = new OLECHAR [MAX_PATH];
    IADsPropertyList *pObjProps = NULL;
    IADsPropertyEntry *pEntry = NULL;
    VARIANT var;
    BSTR szString;
    long lCount = 0L;
    long lCountTotal = 0L;
    long lPType = 0L;
    if (!pObj)
        return E_INVALIDARG;
    //Call GetInfo to load all properties for the object into the cache.
    //Must do this because IADsPropertyList methods read from the cache.
    hr = pObj->GetInfo();
    if (SUCCEEDED(hr))
    {
        //QI for an IADsPropertyList pointer.
        hr = pObj->QueryInterface(IID_IADsPropertyList, (void**)&pObjProps);
        if (SUCCEEDED(hr))
        {
            //Enumerate the properties of the object
            hr = pObjProps->get_PropertyCount(&lCountTotal);
            wprintf(L"Property Count: %d\n",lCountTotal);
            hr = pObjProps->Next(&var);
            if (SUCCEEDED(hr))
            {
                lCount = 1L;
                while (hr==S_OK)
                {
                    if (var.vt==VT_DISPATCH)
```

```
                {
                    hr = V_DISPATCH(&var)->QueryInterface(IID_IADsPropertyEntry,
(void**)&pEntry);

                    if (SUCCEEDED(hr))
                    {
                        hr = pEntry->get_Name(&szString);
                        wprintf(L"%s: ",szString);
                        SysFreeString(szString);
                        hr = pEntry->get_ADsType(&lPType);
                        if (lPType != ADSTYPE_INVALID)
                        {
                            hr = EnumeratePropertyValue(pEntry);
                            if(FAILED(hr))
                                printf("EnumeratePropertyValue failed. hr:
%x\n",hr);

                        }
                        else
                        {
                        wprintf(L"Invalid type\n");
                        }
                    }
                    else
                    {
                    printf("IADsPropertyEntry QueryInterface call failed. hr:
%x\n",hr);

                    }
                    //Clean up
                    if (pEntry)
                        pEntry->Release();
                }
                else
                {
                    printf("Unexpected returned type for VARIANT: %d",var.vt);
                }
                VariantClear(&var);
                hr = pObjProps->Next(&var);
                if (SUCCEEDED(hr))
                {
                    lCount++;
                }
            }
```

(continued)

(continued)

```
                }
            }
        wprintf(L"Total properties retrieved: %d\n",lCount);
        //Clean up
        if (pObjProps)
            pObjProps->Release();
    }
    //Return success if all properties were retrieved.
    if (lCountTotal==lCount)
        hr=S_OK;
    return hr;
}


HRESULT EnumeratePropertyValue(
            IADsPropertyEntry *pEntry
            )
{
HRESULT hr = E_FAIL;
IADsPropertyValue *pValue = NULL;
IADsLargeInteger *pLargeInt = NULL;
long lType, lValue;
BSTR bstr,szString;
VARIANT var,varOS,varDate;
VARIANT *pVar;
CHAR *pszBOOL = NULL;

FILETIME filetime;
SYSTEMTIME systemtime;
IDispatch *pDisp = NULL;
DATE date;

//For Octet Strings
void HUGEP *pArray;
ULONG dwSLBound;
ULONG dwSUBound;


hr = pEntry->get_Values(&var);
if (SUCCEEDED(hr))
{
    //Should be safe array containing variants
    if (var.vt==(VT_VARIANT|VT_ARRAY))
    {
```

```
hr = SafeArrayAccessData((SAFEARRAY*)(var.pparray), (void HUGEP* FAR*)&pVar);
long lLBound, lUBound;
//One dimensional array. Get the bounds for the array.
hr = SafeArrayGetLBound((SAFEARRAY*)(var.pparray), 1, &lLBound);
hr = SafeArrayGetUBound((SAFEARRAY*)(var.pparray), 1, &lUBound);
//Get the count of elements
long cElements = lUBound-lLBound + 1;
//Get the elements of the array
if (SUCCEEDED(hr))
{
    for (int i = 0; i < cElements; i++ )
    {
        switch (pVar[i].vt)
        {
        case VT_BSTR:
            wprintf(L"%s ",pVar[i].bstrVal);
            break;
        case VT_DISPATCH:
            hr = V_DISPATCH(&pVar[i])->QueryInterface(IID_IADsPropertyValue,
(void**)&pValue);
            if (SUCCEEDED(hr))
            {
            hr = pValue->get_ADsType(&lType);
            switch (lType)
            {
            case ADSTYPE_DN_STRING:
                hr = pValue->get_DNString(&bstr);
                wprintf(L"%s ",bstr);
                SysFreeString(bstr);
                break;
            case ADSTYPE_CASE_IGNORE_STRING:
                hr = pValue->get_CaseIgnoreString(&bstr);
                wprintf(L"%s ",bstr);
                SysFreeString(bstr);
                break;
            case ADSTYPE_BOOLEAN:
                hr = pValue->get_Boolean(&lValue);
                pszBOOL = lValue ? "TRUE" : "FALSE";
                wprintf(L"%s ",pszBOOL);
                break;
            case ADSTYPE_INTEGER:
                hr = pValue->get_Integer(&lValue);
                wprintf(L"%d ",lValue);
                break;
```

(continued)

(continued)

```
                 case ADSTYPE_OCTET_STRING:
                     //Get the name of the property to handle
                     //the properties we're interested in.
                     pEntry->get_Name(&szString);
                     hr = pValue->get_OctetString(&varOS);
                     //Get a pointer to the bytes
                     //in the octet string.
                     if (SUCCEEDED(hr))
                     {
                         hr = SafeArrayGetLBound( V_ARRAY(&varOS),
                                                  1,
                                                  (long FAR

*) &dwSLBound );

                         hr = SafeArrayGetUBound( V_ARRAY(&varOS),
                                                  1,
                                                  (long FAR

*) &dwSUBound );

                         if (SUCCEEDED(hr))
                         {
                             hr = SafeArrayAccessData( V_ARRAY(&varOS),

&pArray );

                         }
                         if (0==wcscmp(L"objectGUID", szString))
                         {
                             LPOLESTR szDSGUID = new WCHAR [39];
                             //Cast to LPGUID
                             LPGUID pObjectGUID = (LPGUID)pArray;
                             //Convert GUID to string.
                             ::StringFromGUID2(*pObjectGUID, szDSGUID, 39);
                             //Print the GUID
                             wprintf(L"%s ",szDSGUID);
                         }
                         else if (0==wcscmp(L"objectSid", szString))
                         {
                             PSID pObjectSID = (PSID)pArray;
                             //Convert SID to string.
                             LPOLESTR szSID = NULL;
                             ConvertSidToStringSid(pObjectSID, &szSID);
                             wprintf(L"%s ",szSID);
                             LocalFree(szSID);
```

```
                            }
                            else
                            {
                                wprintf(L"Value of type Octet String. No
Conversion.");

                            }
                                SafeArrayUnaccessData( V_ARRAY(&varOS) );
                                VariantClear(&varOS);
                        }

                    SysFreeString(szString);

                    break;
                case ADSTYPE_UTC_TIME:
                    //wprintf(L"Value of type UTC_TIME\n");
                    hr = pValue->get_UTCTime(&date);
                    if (SUCCEEDED(hr))
                    {
                        //Pack in variant.vt
                        varDate.vt = VT_DATE;
                        varDate.date = date;

VariantChangeType(&varDate,&varDate,VARIANT_NOVALUEPROP,VT_BSTR);
                        wprintf(L"%s ",varDate.bstrVal);
                        VariantClear(&varDate);
                    }
                    break;
                case ADSTYPE_LARGE_INTEGER:
                    //wprintf(L"Value of type Large Integer\n");
                    //Get the name of the property to handle
                    //the properties we're interested in.
                    pEntry->get_Name(&szString);
                    hr = pValue->get_LargeInteger(&pDisp);
                    if (SUCCEEDED(hr))
                    {
                        hr = pDisp->QueryInterface(IID_IADsLargeInteger,
(void**)&pLargeInt);

                        if (SUCCEEDED(hr))
                        {
                            hr =
```

(continued)

(continued)

```
pLargeInt->get_HighPart((long*)&filetime.dwHighDateTime);
                            hr =

pLargeInt->get_LowPart((long*)&filetime.dwLowDateTime);
                            if((filetime.dwHighDateTime==0) &&

(filetime.dwLowDateTime==0))

                                {
                                    wprintf(L"No Value ");
                                }
                                else
                                {
    //Check for properties of type LargeInteger
    // that represent time if TRUE, then convert to variant time.
                                    if ((0==wcscmp(L"accountExpires", szString))|
                                        (0==wcscmp(L"badPasswordTime",

szString))||

                                        (0==wcscmp(L"lastLogon", szString))||
                                        (0==wcscmp(L"lastLogoff",

szString))||

                                        (0==wcscmp(L"lockoutTime",

szString))||

                                        (0==wcscmp(L"pwdLastSet", szString))
                                        )
                                    {
    //Handle special case for Never Expires where low part is -1
                                        if (filetime.dwLowDateTime==-1)
                                        {
                                            wprintf(L"Never Expires ");
                                        }
                                        else
                                        {
                                            if

(FileTimeToLocalFileTime(&filetime, &filetime) != 0)
                                            {
                                                if

(FileTimeToSystemTime(&filetime,
```

```
       &systemtime) != 0)
                                                  {
                                                   if
(SystemTimeToVariantTime(&systemtime,

               &date) != 0)
                                                   {

//Pack in variant.vt

varDate.vt = VT_DATE;

varDate.date = date;

VariantChangeType(&varDate,&varDate,VARIANT_NOVALUEPROP,VT_BSTR);

wprintf(L"%s ",varDate.bstrVal);

VariantClear(&varDate);
                                               }
                                               else
                                               {

wprintf(L"FileTimeToVariantTime failed ");
                                               }
                                             }
                                             else
                                             {

wprintf(L"FileTimeToSystemTime failed ");
                                             }
```

(continued)

(continued)

```
                                            }
                                            else
                                            {

wprintf(L"FileTimeToLocalFileTime failed ");
                                            }
                                        }
                                    }
                                    //Print the LargeInteger.
                                    else
                                    {
                                        wprintf(L"Large Integer: high: %d

low: %d ",filetime.dwHighDateTime, filetime.dwLowDateTime);
                                    }
                                }
                            }
                        if (pLargeInt)
                            pLargeInt->Release();
                    }
                    else
                    {
                        wprintf(L"Could not get Large Integer");
                    }

                    if (pDisp)
                        pDisp->Release();

                    break;
                case ADSTYPE_NT_SECURITY_DESCRIPTOR:
                    wprintf(L"Value of type NT Security Descriptor ");
                    break;
                case ADSTYPE_PROV_SPECIFIC:
                    wprintf(L"Value of type Provider Specific ");
                    break;
                default:
                    wprintf(L"Unhandled ADSTYPE for property value: %d ",lType);
                    break;
                }
            }
            else
            {
```

```
                              wprintf(L"QueryInterface failed for IADsPropertyValue. HR: %x\n",
hr);
                    }
                    if (pValue)
                        pValue->Release();
                    break;
                default:
                    wprintf(L"Unhandled Variant type for property value array:
%d\n",pVar[i].vt);
                    break;
                }
            }
        wprintf(L"\n");
    }
    //Decrement the access count for the array.
    SafeArrayUnaccessData((SAFEARRAY*)(var.pparray));

    }
}



    return hr;
}



HRESULT FindUserByName(IDirectorySearch *pSearchBase,
                                            //Container to search
                    LPOLESTR szFindUser, //Name of user to find.
                    IADs **ppUser)       //Return a pointer to
                                         // the user
{
    HRESULT hrObj = E_FAIL;
    HRESULT hr = E_FAIL;
    if ((!pSearchBase)||(!szFindUser))
        return E_INVALIDARG;
    //Create search filter
    LPOLESTR pszSearchFilter = new OLECHAR[MAX_PATH];
    LPOLESTR szADsPath = new OLECHAR[MAX_PATH];
    wcscpy(pszSearchFilter, L"(&(objectCategory=person)(objectClass=user)(cn=");
    wcscat(pszSearchFilter, szFindUser);
    wcscat(pszSearchFilter,    L"))");
        //Search entire subtree from root.
    ADS_SEARCHPREF_INFO SearchPrefs;
    SearchPrefs.dwSearchPref = ADS_SEARCHPREF_SEARCH_SCOPE;
```

(continued)

(continued)

```
SearchPrefs.vValue.dwType = ADSTYPE_INTEGER;
SearchPrefs.vValue.Integer = ADS_SCOPE_SUBTREE;
    DWORD dwNumPrefs = 1;
// COL for iterations
    ADS_SEARCH_COLUMN col;
    // Handle used for searching
    ADS_SEARCH_HANDLE hSearch;
// Set the search preference
    hr = pSearchBase->SetSearchPreference( &SearchPrefs, dwNumPrefs);
    if (FAILED(hr))
        return hr;
// Set attributes to return
CONST DWORD dwAttrNameSize = 1;
    LPOLESTR pszAttribute[dwAttrNameSize] = {L"ADsPath"};


    // Execute the search
    hr = pSearchBase->ExecuteSearch(pszSearchFilter,
                            pszAttribute,
                                dwAttrNameSize,
                                &hSearch
                            );
if (SUCCEEDED(hr))
{

// Call IDirectorySearch::GetNextRow() to retrieve the next row
//of data
    while( pSearchBase->GetNextRow( hSearch) != S_ADS_NOMORE_ROWS )
    {
        // loop through the array of passed column names,
        // print the data for each column
        for (DWORD x = 0; x < dwAttrNameSize; x++)
        {
            // Get the data for this column
            hr = pSearchBase->GetColumn( hSearch, pszAttribute[x], &col );
            if ( SUCCEEDED(hr) )
            {
                // Print the data for the column and free the column
                // Note the requested attribute is
                //  type CaseIgnoreString.
                wcscpy(szADsPath, col.pADsValues->CaseIgnoreString);
                hr = ADsOpenObject(szADsPath,
                            NULL,
                            NULL,
                            ADS_SECURE_AUTHENTICATION,
```

```
                                              //Use Secure Authentication
                                IID_IADs,
                                (void**)ppUser);
                    if (SUCCEEDED(hr))
                    {
                        wprintf(L"Found User.\n",szFindUser);
                        wprintf(L"%s: %s\r\n",pszAttribute[x],col.pADsValues-
>CaseIgnoreString);

                        hrObj = S_OK;
                    }
                    pSearchBase->FreeColumn( &col );
                }
                else
                    hr = E_FAIL;
            }
        }
        // Close the search handle to clean up
        pSearchBase->CloseSearchHandle(hSearch);
    }
    if (FAILED(hrObj))
        hr = hrObj;
    return hr;
}
```

Visual Basic

```
Dim sUserName As String
    Dim sSearchFilter As String
    Dim lScope As Integer
    Dim iIndex As Integer
    iIndex = 0
    Dim v, j, i
    Dim ds As IADs
    Dim con As New Connection, rs As New Recordset
    Dim Com As New Command
    Dim oIADs As IADs
    Dim sLdap As String
    Dim sUserADsPath As String

    sUserName = InputBox("This script Enumerates the properties of a user on a domain." &
vbCrLf & vbCrLf & "Specify the name of the user:")

    If sUserName = "" Then
        Exit Sub
```

(continued)

(continued)

```
End If

' Bind to the rootDSE
Set ds = GetObject("LDAP://RootDSE")
sLdap = "LDAP://" & ds.Get("defaultNamingContext")
Set ds = Nothing

Set oIADs = GetObject(sLdap)

sSearchFilter = "CN='" & sUserName & "'"

'Open a Connection object
con.Provider = "ADsDSOObject"

'-----------------------------------------------------------------
' To be authenticated using alternate credentials
' use connection properties of User ID and Password
'-----------------------------------------------------------------
' con.Properties("User ID") = "Administrator"
' con.Properties("Password") = ""

' Open the connection
con.Open "Active Directory Provider"

' Create a command object on this connection
Set Com.ActiveConnection = con

' set the query string using SQL Dialect
Com.CommandText = "select name,AdsPath from '" & oIADs.ADsPath & "' where " &
sSearchFilter & " ORDER BY NAME"

' Tell the user what the search filter is
'MsgBox "Search Filter = " & Com.CommandText

'----------------------------------------------------
' Or you can use LDAP Dialect, for example,
'----------------------------------------------------
' Ex Com.CommandText =
'"<LDAP://ntdsdc1/dc=NTDEV,DC=microsof,DC=com>;(objectClass=*);name"
' For LDAP Dialect, the valid search scope are base,
' oneLevel and subtree
' Com.CommandText = "<" & adDomainPath &
' ">;(objectClass=*);name;subtree"
' For LDAP Dialect (<LDAP:...>), there is no way to
```

```
' specify sort order in the string,
' However, you can use this SORT ON property to specify sort order.
' for SQL Dialect you can use ORDER BY in the SQL Statement
' Ex. Com.Properties("Sort On") = "Name"

'Set the preferences for Search
Com.Properties("Page Size") = 1000
Com.Properties("Timeout") = 30 'seconds
Com.Properties("searchscope") = ADS_SCOPE_SUBTREE
Com.Properties("Chase referrals") = ADS_CHASE_REFERRALS_EXTERNAL
Com.Properties("Cache Results") = False
  ' do not cache the result, it results in less memory requirements
Com.Properties("Size Limit") = 1 ' Limit to 1 Result

'Execute the query
Set rs = Com.Execute

' Navigate the record set
 If Not rs.EOF Then
    rs.MoveFirst
End If

On Error Resume Next
If Not rs.EOF Then
    ' Display the LDAP path for the row
    MsgBox "Found the user " & sUserName & " at " & rs.Fields("AdsPath")
    sUserADsPath = rs.Fields("AdsPath")
    rs.MoveNext
Else
    MsgBox "Did not find the username " & sUserName & " in the directory"
    Exit Sub
End If

Set ds = Nothing
Set con = Nothing
Set rs = Nothing
Set Com = Nothing
Set oIADs = Nothing

' Now enumerate the properties
Dim propList As IADsPropertyList
Dim propEnty As IADsPropertyEntry
Dim propVal As IADsPropertyValue
Dim count As Long
```

(continued)

(continued)

```
Dim sOutput As String
Dim currentcount As Long

Const NumToDisplayAtAtime As Integer = 10

' Bind to the user
Set propList = GetObject(sUserADsPath)

' Bring the properties into the cache
propList.GetInfo

count = propList.PropertyCount
sOutput = "No of Property Found: " & Str(count) & vbCrLf & vbCrLf

For i = 0 To count - 1
    currentcount = currentcount + 1
    'Each item in property list has a property entry
    Set propEntry = propList.Item(i)

    ' Append to outputstring
    sOutput = sOutput & "PROPERTYENTRY NAME:" & propEntry.Name & vbCrLf & " ------" &
vbCrLf

    'Each value in property entry has property values
    For Each v In propEntry.Values
        Set propVal = v
        ' Append to outputstring
        sOutput = sOutput & propVal.CaseIgnoreString vbCrLf
    Next
    If currentcount = NumToDisplayAtAtime Then
        MsgBox sOutput
        sOutput = ""
        currentcount = 0
    End If
Next
Set propList = Nothing
Set propEnty = Nothing
Set propVal = Nothing
```

Example Code for List Non-Replicated, Global Catalog, and Constructed Properties

The following C/C++ program queries for four types of properties that are 1) non-replicated, 2) indexed, 3) global catalog, and 4) constructed.

```
// Displays attributes of different types.
//
#include "stdafx.h"
#include <wchar.h>
#include <activeds.h>

HRESULT FindAttributesByType(IDirectorySearch *pSchemaNC,
  //IDirectorySearch pointer to schema naming context.
        DWORD dwAttributeType,
  //Bit flags to search for in systemFlags
        LPOLESTR pszAttributerNameType,
  //ldapDisplayName of the naming attribute you want
  // to display for each returned attribute.
  // NULL returns common name.
        BOOL bIsExactMatch
  //TRUE to find attributes that have systemFlags
  // exactly matching dwAttributeType
  //FALSE to find attributes that have the
  // dwAttributeType bit set (and possibly others).
        );

HRESULT FindIndexedAttributes(IDirectorySearch *pSchemaNC,
  //IDirectorySearch pointer to schema naming context.
        LPOLESTR pszAttributeNameType,
  //ldapDisplayName of the naming attribute you want to
  // display for each returned attribute.
  // NULL returns common name.
        BOOL bIsIndexed
  //TRUE to find indexed attributes.
  //FALSE to find non-indexed attributes.
        );

HRESULT FindGCAttributes(IDirectorySearch *pSchemaNC,
  //IDirectorySearch pointer to schema naming context.
        LPOLESTR pszAttributeNameType,
  //ldapDisplayName of the naming attribute you want to display
  // for each returned attribute.
  // NULL returns common name.
        BOOL bInGC
  //TRUE to find indexed attributes.
  //FALSE to find non-indexed attributes.
        );

int main(int argc, char* argv[])
```

(continued)

(continued)

```
{
HRESULT hr = E_FAIL;
LPOLESTR szPath = new OLECHAR[MAX_PATH];
IDirectorySearch *pSchemaNC = NULL;
IADs *pObject = NULL;
VARIANT var;

//Intialize COM
CoInitialize(NULL);

//Get rootDSE and the schema container's distinguished name.
//Bind to current user's domain using current user's security context.
hr = ADsOpenObject(L"LDAP://rootDSE",
                NULL,
                NULL,
                ADS_SECURE_AUTHENTICATION, //Use Secure Authentication
                IID_IADs,
                (void**)&pObject);
if (SUCCEEDED(hr))
{
    hr = pObject->Get(L"schemaNamingContext",&var);
    if (SUCCEEDED(hr))
    {
    wcscpy(szPath,L"LDAP://");
    wcscat(szPath,var.bstrVal);
    hr = ADsOpenObject(szPath,
                    NULL,
                    NULL,
                    ADS_SECURE_AUTHENTICATION,
                                //Use Secure Authentication
                    IID_IDirectorySearch,
                    (void**)&pSchemaNC);
    if (SUCCEEDED(hr))
    {
    //Find non-replicated attributes
    wprintf(L"Find non-replicated attributes\n");
    hr = FindAttributesByType(pSchemaNC,
            //IDirectorySearch pointer to schema naming context.
        ADS_SYSTEMFLAG_ATTR_NOT_REPLICATED,
            //Bit flags to search for in systemFlags
        NULL,
        TRUE
        );
```

```
    //Find attributes included in the global catalog
    wprintf(L"Find attributes included in the global catalog\n");
    hr = FindGCAttributes(pSchemaNC,
        NULL,
        TRUE
        );

    //Find constructed attributes
    wprintf(L"Find constructed attributes\n");
    hr = FindAttributesByType(pSchemaNC,
            //IDirectorySearch pointer to schema naming context.
        ADS_SYSTEMFLAG_ATTR_IS_CONSTRUCTED,
            //Bit flags to search for in systemFlags
        NULL,
        FALSE
        );

    //Find indexed attributes
    wprintf(L"Find indexed attributes\n");
    hr = FindIndexedAttributes(pSchemaNC,
            //IDirectorySearch pointer to schema naming context.
        NULL,
        TRUE
        );
    }
    if (pSchemaNC)
        pSchemaNC->Release();
    }
}
if (pObject)
    pObject->Release();
VariantClear(&var);

// Uninitialize COM
CoUninitialize();
return 0;
}


HRESULT FindAttributesByType(IDirectorySearch *pSchemaNC,
            //IDirectorySearch pointer to schema naming context.
        DWORD dwAttributeType,
            //Bit flags to search for in systemFlags
        LPOLESTR pszAttributeNameType,
            //ldapDisplayName of the naming attribute you want
```

(continued)

(continued)

```
                 // to display for each returned attribute.
                 //NULL returns common name.
        BOOL bIsExactMatch
                 //TRUE to find attributes that have systemFlags exactly
                 // matching dwAttributeType
                 //FALSE to find attributes that have the dwAttributeType
                 // bit set (and possibly others).
        )
{
    //Create search filter
    LPOLESTR pszSearchFilter = new OLECHAR[MAX_PATH*2];
    if (bIsExactMatch)
        //Find attributes with systemFlags that exactly match dwAttributeType
        wsprintf(pszSearchFilter,
L"(&(objectCategory=attributeSchema)(systemFlags=%d))",dwAttributeType);
    else
        //Find attributes with systemFlags that contain dwAttributeType
        wsprintf(pszSearchFilter,
L"(&(objectCategory=attributeSchema)(systemFlags:1.2.840.113556.1.4.804:=%d))",dwAttribute
Type);

    //Attributes are one-level deep in the Schema container
    // so only need to search one level.
    ADS_SEARCHPREF_INFO SearchPrefs;
    SearchPrefs.dwSearchPref = ADS_SEARCHPREF_SEARCH_SCOPE;
    SearchPrefs.vValue.dwType = ADSTYPE_INTEGER;
    SearchPrefs.vValue.Integer = ADS_SCOPE_ONELEVEL;
    DWORD dwNumPrefs = 1;

    // COL for iterations
        ADS_SEARCH_COLUMN col;
        HRESULT hr;

        // Interface Pointers
        IADs    *pObj = NULL;
        IADs    * pIADs = NULL;

    // Handle used for searching
    ADS_SEARCH_HANDLE hSearch;

    // Set the search preference
        hr = pSchemaNC->SetSearchPreference( &SearchPrefs, dwNumPrefs);
        if (FAILED(hr))
            return hr;
```

```
        CONST DWORD dwAttrNameSize = 1;
            LPOLESTR pszAttribute[dwAttrNameSize];
            if (!pszAttributeNameType)
                pszAttribute[0] = L"cn";
            else
                pszAttribute[0] = pszAttributeNameType;
        // Execute the search
        hr = pSchemaNC->ExecuteSearch(pszSearchFilter,
                                      pszAttribute,
                                       dwAttrNameSize,
                                       &hSearch
                                       );
        if ( SUCCEEDED(hr) )
        {
        // Call IDirectorySearch::GetNextRow() to retrieve the next row
        //of data
            while( pSchemaNC->GetNextRow( hSearch) != S_ADS_NOMORE_ROWS )
            {
                // loop through the array of passed column names,
                // print the data for each column
                for (DWORD x = 0; x < dwAttrNameSize; x++)
                {
                    // Get the data for this column
                    hr = pSchemaNC->GetColumn( hSearch, pszAttribute[x], &col );
                    if ( SUCCEEDED(hr) )
                    {
                        // Print the data for the column and free the column
                        wprintf(L"%s: %s\r\n",pszAttribute[x],col.pADsValues-
>CaseIgnoreString);

                        pSchemaNC->FreeColumn( &col );
                    }
                    else
                        wprintf(L"<%s property is not a string>",pszAttribute[x]);
                }
            }
            // Close the search handle to clean up
            pSchemaNC->CloseSearchHandle(hSearch);
        }
        return hr;
}

HRESULT FindIndexedAttributes(IDirectorySearch *pSchemaNC,
            //IDirectorySearch pointer to schema naming context.
```

(continued)

(continued)

```
        LPOLESTR pszAttributeNameType,
              //ldapDisplayName of the naming attribute you want to
              // display for each returned attribute.
              //NULL returns common name.
        BOOL bIsIndexed
              //TRUE to find indexed attributes.
              //FALSE to find non-indexed attributes.
        )
{
    //Create search filter
    LPOLESTR pszSearchFilter = new OLECHAR[MAX_PATH*2];
    DWORD dwIndexed;
    if (bIsIndexed)
        dwIndexed = 1;
    else
        dwIndexed = 0;

    wsprintf(pszSearchFilter,
L"(&(objectCategory=attributeSchema)(searchFlags=%d))",dwIndexed);

    //Attributes are one-level deep in the Schema container so
    // only need to search one level.
    ADS_SEARCHPREF_INFO SearchPrefs;
    SearchPrefs.dwSearchPref = ADS_SEARCHPREF_SEARCH_SCOPE;
    SearchPrefs.vValue.dwType = ADSTYPE_INTEGER;
    SearchPrefs.vValue.Integer = ADS_SCOPE_ONELEVEL;
    DWORD dwNumPrefs = 1;

    // COL for iterations
    ADS_SEARCH_COLUMN col;
    HRESULT hr;

    // Interface Pointers
    IADs    *pObj = NULL;
    IADs    * pIADs = NULL;

    // Handle used for searching
    ADS_SEARCH_HANDLE hSearch;

    // Set the search preference
    hr = pSchemaNC->SetSearchPreference( &SearchPrefs, dwNumPrefs);
    if (FAILED(hr))
        return hr;
```

```
    CONST DWORD dwAttrNameSize = 1;
    LPOLESTR pszAttribute[dwAttrNameSize];

    if (!pszAttributeNameType)
        pszAttribute[0] = L"cn";
    else
        pszAttribute[0] = pszAttributeNameType;

    // Execute the search
    hr = pSchemaNC->ExecuteSearch(pszSearchFilter,
                                  pszAttribute,
                                   dwAttrNameSize,
                                   &hSearch
                                   );
    if ( SUCCEEDED(hr) )
    {
    // Call IDirectorySearch::GetNextRow() to retrieve the next row
    //of data
        while( pSchemaNC->GetNextRow( hSearch) != S_ADS_NOMORE_ROWS )
        {
            // loop through the array of passed column names,
            // print the data for each column
            for (DWORD x = 0; x < dwAttrNameSize; x++)
            {
                // Get the data for this column
                hr = pSchemaNC->GetColumn( hSearch, pszAttribute[x], &col );
                if ( SUCCEEDED(hr) )
                {
                    // Print the data for the column and free the column
                    wprintf(L"%s: %s\r\n",pszAttribute[x],col.pADsValues-
>CaseIgnoreString);

                    pSchemaNC->FreeColumn( &col );
                }
                else
                    wprintf(L"<%s property is not a string>",pszAttribute[x]);
            }
        }
        // Close the search handle to clean up
        pSchemaNC->CloseSearchHandle(hSearch);
    }
    return hr;
}

HRESULT FindGCAttributes(IDirectorySearch *pSchemaNC,
```

(continued)

(continued)

```
               //IDirectorySearch pointer to schema naming context.
       LPOLESTR pszAttributeNameType,
               //ldapDisplayName of the naming attribute you want to
               // display for each returned attribute.
               // NULL returns common name.
       BOOL bInGC
               //TRUE to find GC attributes.
               //FALSE to find non-GC attributes.
       )
{
    //Create search filter
    LPOLESTR pszSearchFilter = new OLECHAR[MAX_PATH*2];
    LPOLESTR szBool = NULL;
    if (bInGC)
        szBool = L"TRUE";
    else
        szBool = L"FALSE";

    wsprintf(pszSearchFilter,
L"(&(objectCategory=attributeSchema)(isMemberOfPartialAttributeSet=%s))",szBool);
    //Attributes are one-level deep in the Schema container so
    // only need to search one level.
    ADS_SEARCHPREF_INFO SearchPrefs;
    SearchPrefs.dwSearchPref = ADS_SEARCHPREF_SEARCH_SCOPE;
    SearchPrefs.vValue.dwType = ADSTYPE_INTEGER;
    SearchPrefs.vValue.Integer = ADS_SCOPE_ONELEVEL;
    DWORD dwNumPrefs = 1;
    // COL for iterations
    ADS_SEARCH_COLUMN col;
    HRESULT hr;
    // Interface Pointers
    IADs    *pObj = NULL;
    IADs    * pIADs = NULL;
    // Handle used for searching
    ADS_SEARCH_HANDLE hSearch;
    // Set the search preference
    hr = pSchemaNC->SetSearchPreference( &SearchPrefs, dwNumPrefs);
    if (FAILED(hr))
        return hr;

    CONST DWORD dwAttrNameSize = 1;
    LPOLESTR pszAttribute[dwAttrNameSize];

    if (!pszAttributeNameType)
```

```
            pszAttribute[0] = L"cn";
    else
            pszAttribute[0] = pszAttributeNameType;


    // Execute the search
    hr = pSchemaNC->ExecuteSearch(pszSearchFilter,
                                    pszAttribute,
                                    dwAttrNameSize,
                                    &hSearch
                                    );
    if ( SUCCEEDED(hr) )
    {
    // Call IDirectorySearch::GetNextRow() to retrieve the next row
    //of data
            while( pSchemaNC->GetNextRow( hSearch) != S_ADS_NOMORE_ROWS )
            {
                // loop through the array of passed column names,
                // print the data for each column
                for (DWORD x = 0; x < dwAttrNameSize; x++)
                {
                    // Get the data for this column
                    hr = pSchemaNC->GetColumn( hSearch, pszAttribute[x], &col );
                    if ( SUCCEEDED(hr) )
                    {
                        // Print the data for the column and free the column
                        wprintf(L"%s: %s\r\n",pszAttribute[x],col.pADsValues-
>CaseIgnoreString);
                        pSchemaNC->FreeColumn( &col );
                    }
                    else
                        wprintf(L"<%s property is not a string>",pszAttribute[x]);
                }
            }

            // Close the search handle to clean up
            pSchemaNC->CloseSearchHandle(hSearch);
    }
    return hr;
}
```

Example Code for Reading a Constructed Property

The code fragments on the next page read the **canonicalName** property of the
Administrator.

C++

```cpp
//Read the canonicalName of Administrator
#include <wchar.h>
#include <objbase.h>
#include <activeds.h>

void wmain( int argc, wchar_t *argv[ ])
{

//Intialize COM
CoInitialize(NULL);
HRESULT hr = S_OK;
//Get rootDSE and the domain container's DN.
IADs *pObject = NULL;
LPOLESTR szPath = new OLECHAR[MAX_PATH];
VARIANT var;
hr = ADsOpenObject(L"LDAP://rootDSE",
            NULL,
            NULL,
            ADS_SECURE_AUTHENTICATION, //Use Secure Authentication
            IID_IADs,
            (void**)&pObject);
if (FAILED(hr))
{
   wprintf(L"Not Found. Could not bind to the domain.\n");
   if (pObject)
     pObject->Release();
   return;
}

hr = pObject->Get(L"defaultNamingContext",&var);
if (SUCCEEDED(hr))
{
   wcscpy(szPath,L"LDAP://");
   wcscat(szPath,L"cn=Administrator,cn=Users,");
   wcscat(szPath,var.bstrVal);
   VariantClear(&var);
   if (pObject)
   {
      pObject->Release();
      pObject = NULL;
   }
   //Bind to the Administrator user object.
```

```c
    hr = ADsOpenObject(szPath,
                NULL,
                NULL,
                ADS_SECURE_AUTHENTICATION, //Use Secure Authentication
                IID_IADs,
                (void**)&pObject);
  if (SUCCEEDED(hr))
  {
    //
       LPOLESTR pwszArray[] = {L"canonicalName"};
    DWORD dwArrayItems = sizeof(pwszArray)/sizeof(LPOLESTR);
       VARIANT vArray;
       VariantInit(&vArray);
       // Build a Variant of array type, using the
       // specified string array.
       hr = ADsBuildVarArrayStr(pwszArray, dwArrayItems, &vArray);
       if (SUCCEEDED(hr))
       {
        hr = pObject->GetInfoEx(vArray,0L);
        hr = pObject->Get(L"canonicalName", &var);
        if (SUCCEEDED(hr))
           wprintf(L"canonicalName: %s\n",var.bstrVal);
        else
           wprintf(L"Get failed with hr: %x\n",hr);
       VariantClear(&var);
    }
  }
  if (pObject)
     pObject->Release();
}

//Uninitialize COM
CoUninitialize();

  return;
}
```

Visual Basic

```vb
'Read the canonicalName of Administrator
Dim rootDSE As IADs
Dim user As IADs

sPrefix = "LDAP://"
```

(continued)

(continued)

```
Set rootDSE = GetObject(sPrefix & "rootDSE")
If (Err.Number <> 0) Then
   BailOnFailure Err.Number, "on GetObject method"
End If
sDomain = rootDSE.Get("defaultNamingContext")
If (Err.Number <> 0) Then
   BailOnFailure Err.Number, "on Get method"
End If
sUserDN = "cn=Administrator,cn=users," + sDomain
'''''''''''''''''''''''''''''''''''''''''''''
'Bind to the Administrator user
'''''''''''''''''''''''''''''''''''''''''''''
Set user = GetObject(sPrefix & sUserDN)
user.GetInfoEx Array("canonicalName"), 0
strText = "Canonical Name: " & user.Get("canonicalName")
If (Err.Number <> 0) Then
  BailOnFailure Err.Number, "on Get method"
End If
show_items strText, sComputer


'''''''''''''''''''''''''''''''''''''''''''''
'Display subroutines
'''''''''''''''''''''''''''''''''''''''''''''
Sub show_items(strText, strName)
   MsgBox strText, vbInformation, "Get canonicalName for Administrator"
End Sub

Sub BailOnFailure(ErrNum, ErrText)     strText = "Error 0x" & Hex(ErrNum) & " " &
ErrText
   MsgBox strText, vbInformation, "ADSI Error"
   WScript.Quit
End Sub
```

Setting Properties on a User Object

There are two ways to set properties on a user object (or any object):

- *IDirectoryObject::SetObjectAttributes method*. You can set properties at the server directly (no local caching).

- *Property cache methods (IADs and IADsPropertyList)*. You can set the property values in the property cache as necessary for your application using **IADs** methods or **IADsPropertyList** methods, then write the changes back out to the directory service when they are in a consistent state using **SetInfo**.

Regardless of the way you set properties, you need to know at least two pieces of information about the property: 1) What is the property's syntax (data type)? and 2) Does the property allow multiple values?

For more information about the User class, see User in the Active Directory Schema reference.

For a sample application that sets properties, see the CreateUser sample, which creates a user from properties specified in an initialization file.

Setting Passwords

For the password of the user, you should use the **IADsUser::ChangePassword** method (if your script or application is allowing the user to change his/her own password) or **IADsUser::SetPassword** method (if your script or application is allowing an administrator to reset a password).

Example Code for Setting User Passwords

The following Visual Basic® code snippet shows how to set the user password, assuming the caller has the permission to set the password.

```
Set usr = GetObject("LDAP://cn=foobar,cn=Users,dc=Microsoft,dc=com")
usr.SetPassword "topsecret98"
```

Creating a User

To add a user to Active Directory™, you create a user object in the domain container of the domain where you want to place the user. Users can be created at the root of the domain, within an organizational unit, or within a container.

When you create a user object, you must also set the following attributes to make the object a legal user that is recognized by Active Directory and the Windows® Security system:

cn

Required. Specify the name of the user object in the directory. This will be the object's relative distinguished name (RDN) within the container where you create the user.

sAMAccountName

Required. Specify a string that is the name used to support clients and servers from a previous version of Windows®. The **sAMAccountName** should be less than 20 characters to support clients from a previous version of Windows.

The **sAMAccountName** must be unique among all security principal objects within the domain. You should perform a query against the domain to verify that the **sAMAccountName** is unique within the domain.

Optionally, you can also set other properties. The following user properties are set with default values if you do not explicitly set them at creation time.

Property	Value
accountExpires	Default is Never.
cn	Specified in **IADsContainer::Create**.
nTSecurityDescriptor	A security descriptor is created based on the rules specified in *How Security Descriptors are Set on New Directory Objects*.
objectCategory	Person
name	RDN is the **cn**.
pwdLastSet	Controls whether user must change password at next logon. Default is 0. Zero (0) means the user must change the password at next logon.
UserAccountControl	Contains values that determine several logon and account features for the user. By default, the following flags are set: UF_ACCOUNTDISABLE UF_PASSWD_NOTREQD UF_NORMAL_ACCOUNT UF_ACCOUNTDISABLE means the user's account is disabled. UF_PASSWD_NOTREQD means no password is required for the user to log on. UF_NORMAL_ACCOUNT is a default account type that represents a typical user.
memberOf	Domain Users

Example Code for Creating a User

C++

The following code snippet contains a function that creates a user with only the essential properties explicitly set (**cn**, **sAMAccountType**) and returns an **IDirectoryObject** pointer to the new user object:

```
/////////////////////////////////////////////////////////////////////////////
/*  CreateUser()   - Function for creating a basic User

    Parameters

        IDirectoryObject *pDirObject     -   Parent Directory Object for
                                             the new User
        LPWSTR pwCommonName              -   Common Name for the new User
        IDirectoryObject ** ppDirObjRet -   Pointer to the Pointer which
```

```
                                         will receive the new User
*/
HRESULT CreateUser(IDirectoryObject *pDirObject, LPWSTR pwCommonName,LPWSTR
pwSamAcctName,IDirectoryObject ** ppDirObjRet)
{
    assert(pDirObject);
    if (wcslen(pwSamAcctName) >20)
    {
        MessageBox(NULL,L"SamAccountName CANNOT be bigger than 20
characters",L"Error: CreateSimpleUser()",MB_ICONSTOP);
        assert(0);
        return E_FAIL;
    }

    HRESULT    hr;
    ADSVALUE   sAMValue;
    ADSVALUE   classValue;
    LPDISPATCH pDisp;
    WCHAR          pwCommonNameFull[1024];

    ADS_ATTR_INFO  attrInfo[] =
    {
        { L"objectClass", ADS_ATTR_UPDATE,
                            ADSTYPE_CASE_IGNORE_STRING, &classValue, 1 },
        {L"sAMAccountName", ADS_ATTR_UPDATE,
                            ADSTYPE_CASE_IGNORE_STRING, &sAMValue, 1},
    };

    DWORD dwAttrs = sizeof(attrInfo)/sizeof(ADS_ATTR_INFO);
    classValue.dwType = ADSTYPE_CASE_IGNORE_STRING;
    classValue.CaseIgnoreString = L"User";

    sAMValue.dwType=ADSTYPE_CASE_IGNORE_STRING;
    sAMValue.CaseIgnoreString = pwSamAcctName;

    wsprintfW(pwCommonNameFull,L"CN=%s",pwCommonName);

    hr = pDirObject->CreateDSObject( pwCommonNameFull,  attrInfo,
                                dwAttrs, &pDisp );
    if (SUCCEEDED(hr))
    {
        hr = pDisp->QueryInterface(IID_IDirectoryObject,(void**) ppDirObjRet);

        pDisp->Release();
```

(continued)

(continued)

```
        pDisp = NULL;
    }
    return hr;
}
```

Visual Basic

The following code snippet creates a user with only the essential properties explicitly set (**cn**, **sAMAccountType**) and displays the properties of the new user:

```
Dim IADsRootDSE As IADs

sComputer = InputBox("This creates a user in a Windows 2000 domain." & vbCrLf &
vbCrLf & "Specify the domain name or the name of a domain controller in the
domain. (for example, MyDomain.development.microsoft.com ):")
sContainer = InputBox("Specify the name of the container where you want to create
the user : (for example,
CN=Users,DC=MyDomain,DC=Development,DC=microsoft,DC=com")
sUser = InputBox("Specify the name of the user to create: (for example, Bob )")

If sUser = "" Then
  MsgBox "No user name was specified. You must specify a user name."
  Exit Sub
End If

If sComputer = "" Then
  On Error GoTo 0
  MsgBox "No computer or domain was specified. Script will use the current user's
domain " & WshNetwork.UserDomain & "."
  Exit Sub
Else
  sPrefix = "LDAP://" & sComputer & "/"
End If

If sContainer = "" Then
  WScript.Echo "No container was specified. Script will use the Users container
in the specified domain."
  Set IADsRootDSE = GetObject(sPrefix & "rootDSE")
  If (Err.Number <> 0) Then
    BailOnFailure Err.Number, "on GetObject method"
  End If
  sDomain = IADsRootDSE.Get("defaultNamingContext")
  If (Err.Number <> 0) Then
    BailOnFailure Err.Number, "on Get method"
```

```
    End If
      sContainerDN = "cn=Users," + sDomain
Else
      sContainerDN = sContainer
End If


''''''''''''''''''''''''''''''''''''''''''
'Bind to the container
''''''''''''''''''''''''''''''''''''''''''
Set cont = GetObject(sPrefix & sContainerDN)
If (Err.Number <> 0) Then
    BailOnFailure Err.Number, "on GetObject method"
End If
''''''''''''''''''''''''''''''''''''''''''
'Add the user
''''''''''''''''''''''''''''''''''''''''''
Set user = cont.Create("user", "cn=" & sUser)
If (Err.Number <> 0) Then
    BailOnFailure Err.Number, "on Create method"
End If
user.put "samAccountName", sUser
If (Err.Number <> 0) Then
    BailOnFailure Err.Number, "on Put samAccountName method"
End If
user.SetInfo
If (Err.Number <> 0) Then
    BailOnFailure Err.Number, "on SetInfo method"
End If
strText = "The user " & sUser & " was successfully added."
strText = strText & vbCrLf & "The user has the following properties:"
'Refresh the property cache
user.GetInfo
'zz Count = user.PropertyCount
If (Err.Number <> 0) Then
    BailOnFailure Err.Number, "on PropertyCount method"
End If
strText = strText & "Number of properties: " & Count

For cprop = 1 To Count
  Set v = user.Next()
  If IsNull(v) Then
      Exit For
  End If
  strText = strText & vbCrLf & cprop & ") " & v.Name & " (" & v.ADsType & ") "
```

(continued)

(continued)

```
Next
show_items strText, sComputer
strText = "User operational attributes"
user.GetInfoEx Array("canonicalName", "allowedAttributes",
"allowedAttributesEffective"), 0
  strText = strText & vbCrLf & "Canonical Name:" & user.Get("canonicalName")
If (Err.Number <> 0) Then
  BailOnFailure Err.Number, "on Get method"
End If
show_items strText, sComputer

cattr = 0
strText = "Attributes Allowed"
attr = user.GetEx("allowedAttributes")
For Each attrval In attr
  cattr = cattr + 1
Next
strText = strText & vbCrLf & cattr
show_items strText, sComputer

cattr = 0
strText = "Attributes Effective"
attr = user.GetEx("allowedAttributesEffective")
For Each attrval In attr
  cattr = cattr + 1
Next
strText = strText & vbCrLf & cattr
show_items strText, sComputer
'''''''''''''''''''''''''''''''''''''''''''
'Display subroutines
'''''''''''''''''''''''''''''''''''''''''''
Sub show_items(strText, strName)
    MsgBox strText, vbInformation, "Create User on " & strName
End Sub

Sub BailOnFailure(ErrNum, ErrText)     strText = "Error 0x" & Hex(ErrNum) & " " &
ErrText
    MsgBox strText, vbInformation, "ADSI Error"
    WScript.Quit
End Sub
```

Deleting a User

To delete a user from a domain, you need to bind to the container containing the user and specify "user" as the class using **IADsContainer::Delete**. You do not need to call **IADs::SetInfo** to commit the change to the container. The **IADsContainer::Delete** call commits the deletion of the user directly to the directory.

Using C/C++, you can also bind to the container and use the **IDirectoryObject::DeleteDSObject** method.

Example Code for Deleting a User

```
C++
```

The following code fragment deletes a user in a domain:

```
//////////////////////////////////////////////////////////////////////////
/*  DeleteADObject()    - Deletes the passed object by AdsPath

    Parameters

        LPOLESTR pwszAdsPath        - AdsPath of object to delete

    Optional Parameters:

        LPOLESTR pwszUser           - User Name and Password, if the
                                      parameters are NOT passed,
        LPOLESTER pwszPassWord      - Binding will use ADsGetObject, if
                                      the parameters
                                    - Are specified, will use
                                      ADsOpenObject, passing user
                                      name and password

*/
HRESULT DeleteADObject(LPOLESTR pwszAdsPath, LPOLESTR  pwszUser,LPOLESTR  pwszPassWord)
{
    HRESULT             hr;
    BSTR                bsParentPath;
    IADs *              pIADsToDelete = NULL;
    IDirectoryObject *  pIDirObjectParent= NULL;
    VARIANT             vCNToDelete;
    WCHAR               pwszTemp[512];

    VariantInit(&vCNToDelete);
    // Bind to the object being deleted
```

(continued)

(continued)

```
assert((pwszUser==NULL && pwszPassWord == NULL) || (pwszUser && pwszPassWord));

// If a username and password are passed in, use ADsOpenObject()
// otherwise use ADsGetObject()
if (!pwszUser) // No user password passed, use ADsOpenObject
{
    hr = ADsGetObject( pwszAdsPath, IID_IADs,(void **)& pIADsToDelete);
}
else
{
    hr = ADsOpenObject(pwszAdsPath, pwszUser, pwszPassWord,
                    ADS_SECURE_AUTHENTICATION,IID_IADs, (void**) & pIADsToDelete);
}

if (SUCCEEDED(hr))
{
    // Get the parent path
    hr = pIADsToDelete->get_Parent(&bsParentPath);

    // Get the CN property for the object to delete
    hr = pIADsToDelete->Get(L"cn",&vCNToDelete);

    if (SUCCEEDED(hr))
    {
        // ***********************************************************
        // Now bind to the parent
        // If a username and password are passed in,
        // use ADsOpenObject()
        // otherwise use ADsGetObject()
        if (!pwszUser) // No user password passed, use ADsOpenObject
        {
            hr = ADsGetObject( bsParentPath, IID_IDirectoryObject,(void **)&
pIDirObjectParent);
        }
        else
        {
            hr = ADsOpenObject(bsParentPath, pwszUser, pwszPassWord,
                            ADS_SECURE_AUTHENTICATION,IID_IDirectoryObject,
(void**) & pIDirObjectParent);
        }
        if (SUCCEEDED(hr))
        {
            // Release the object to delete
```

```
                    pIADsToDelete->Release();
                    pIADsToDelete =NULL;

                    // Put the CN property into a string beginning with CN=
                    swprintf(pwszTemp,L"cn=%s\n",vCNToDelete.bstrVal);

                    // Ask the parent to delete the child
                    hr =pIDirObjectParent->DeleteDSObject(pwszTemp);
                    // Release the Parent Object
                    pIDirObjectParent->Release();
                    pIDirObjectParent = NULL;
                }
            }
        SysFreeString(bsParentPath);
    }
    // If there is an IADs Object, release it
    if ( pIADsToDelete)
    {
        // Release the object to delete
        pIADsToDelete->Release();
        pIADsToDelete =NULL;
    }

    VariantClear(&vCNToDelete);
 return hr;
}
```

Visual Basic

The following code deletes a user in a domain:

```
Set x = GetObject("LDAP://OU=myou,DC=Microsoft,DC=com")
x.Delete("user", "cn=userguy")
```

Enumerating Users

Unlike Windows NT® 4.0 domains, Windows® 2000 users can be placed in any container or organizational unit in a domain as well as the root of the domain. This means that users can be in numerous locations in the directory hierarchy. Therefore, you have two choices for enumerating users:

1. *Enumerate the users directly contained in a container, OU, or at the root of the domain.*

   Explicitly bind to the container object containing the users you are interested in enumerating, set a filter containing "user" as the class using the **IADsContainer::put_Filter** method, and use the **IADsContainer::get__NewEnum** method to enumerate the user objects.

This technique is useful if you want to enumerate users that are directly contained in a container or OU object. If the container contains other containers that can potentially contain other users, you need to bind to those containers and recursively enumerate the users on those containers. If you do not need to manipulate the user objects and only need to read specific properties, you should use the deep search described in option 2.

Because enumeration returns pointers to ADSI COM objects representing each user object, you can call **QueryInterface** to get **IADs**, **IADsUser**, and **IADsPropertyList** interface pointers to the user object. This means you can get interface pointers to each enumerated user object in a container without having to explicitly bind to each user object. If you wanted to perform operations on all the users directly within a container, enumeration saves you from having to bind to each user in order to call **IADs** or **IADsUser** methods. If you only want to retrieve specific properties from users, use **IDirectorySearch** as described in option 2.

2. *Perform a deep search for (&(objectClass=user)(objectCategory=person)) to find all users in a tree.*

First, bind to the container object where you want to begin the search. For example, if you wanted to find all users in a domain, you would bind to root of the domain; if you wanted to find all users in the forest, you would bind to the global catalog and search from the root of the GC.

Then use **IDirectorySearch** to query using a search filter containing (&(objectClass=user)(objectCategory=person)) and search preference of ADS_SCOPE_SUBTREE.

You can perform a search with a search preference of ADS_SCOPE_ONELEVEL to limit the search to the direct contents of the container object that you bound to.

IDirectorySearch retrieves only the values of specific properties from users. If you only want to retrieve values, use **IDirectorySearch**. If you want to manipulate the user objects returned from a search (that is, you want to use **IADs** or **IADsUser** methods), you must explicitly bind to them (to do this, specify **distinguishedName** as one of the properties to return from the search and use the returned distinguished names to bind to each user returned in the search).

Only specific properties are retrieved. You cannot retrieve all attributes without explicitly specifying every possible attribute of the user class.

Querying for Users

To query for a user, the query must contain the following search expression:

```
(&(objectClass=user)(objectCategory=person))
```

Why? Because the computer class is a subclass of user, a query containing only (objectClass=user) would return user objects *and* computer objects. Also, the object category of the user object is person (not user); therefore, the expression (objectCategory=user) does not return any users. If you use the expression (objectCategory=user), the query returns user objects *and* contact objects.

Users can be placed in any container or organizational unit in a domain as well as the root of the domain. This means that users can be in numerous locations in the directory hierarchy. You can perform a deep search for (objectCategory=user) to find all users in a container, organizational unit, domain, domain tree, or forest—depending on the object that the **IDirectorySearch** pointer you're using is bound to.

Example Code for Using the Global Catalog to Find Users in a Forest

Visual Basic

The following code finds all users in the forest by querying the global catalog using ADO:

```
Dim Con As ADODB.Connection
Dim ocommand As ADODB.Command
Dim gc As IADs

On Error Resume Next
'Maximum number of items to list on a msgbox.
MAX_DISPLAY = 5

'ADO Connection object
Set Con = CreateObject("ADODB.Connection")
  If (Err.Number <> 0) Then
    BailOnFailure Err.Number, "on CreateObject"
  End If
Con.Provider = "ADsDSOObject"
  If (Err.Number <> 0) Then
    BailOnFailure Err.Number, "on Provider"
  End If
Con.Open "Active Directory Provider"
  If (Err.Number <> 0) Then
    BailOnFailure Err.Number, "on Open"
  End If
'ADO Command object
Set ocommand = CreateObject("ADODB.Command")
  If (Err.Number <> 0) Then
    BailOnFailure Err.Number, "on CreateObject"
  End If
ocommand.ActiveConnection = Con
```

(continued)

(continued)

```
  If (Err.Number <> 0) Then
     BailOnFailure Err.Number, "on Active Connection"
  End If
Set gc = GetObject("GC:")
For Each child In gc
    Set entpr = child
Next
  If (Err.Number <> 0) Then
     BailOnFailure Err.Number, "on GetObject for GC"
  End If
show_items entpr.ADsPath, "foo"

ocommand.CommandText = "<" & entpr.ADsPath &
">;(&(objectCategory=person)(objectClass=user));distinguishedName,name;subTree"
  If (Err.Number <> 0) Then
     BailOnFailure Err.Number, "on CommandText"
  End If
Set rs = ocommand.Execute
  If (Err.Number <> 0) Then
     BailOnFailure Err.Number, "on Execute"
  End If
strText = "Found " & rs.RecordCount & " Users in Forest:"
intNumDisplay = 0
intCount = 0
' Navigate the record set
rs.MoveFirst
While Not rs.EOF
    intCount = intCount + 1
    strText = strText & vbCrLf & intCount & ") "
    For i = 0 To rs.Fields.Count - 1
        If rs.Fields(i).Type = adVariant And Not (IsNull(rs.Fields(i).Value)) Then
           strText = strText & rs.Fields(i).Name & " = "
           For j = LBound(rs.Fields(i).Value) To UBound(rs.Fields(i).Value)
              strText = strText & rs.Fields(i).Value(j) & " "
           Next
        Else
           strText = strText & rs.Fields(i).Name & " = " & rs.Fields(i).Value & vbCrLf
        End If
    Next
    intNumDisplay = intNumDisplay + 1
    'Display in msgbox if there are MAX_DISPLAY items to display
    If intNumDisplay = MAX_DISPLAY Then
        Call show_items(strText, "Users in forest")
        strText = ""
```

```
         intNumDisplay = 0
      End If
      rs.MoveNext
Wend
show_items strText, "foo"
''''''''''''''''''''''''''''''''''''''''''
'Display subroutines
''''''''''''''''''''''''''''''''''''''''''
Sub show_items(strText, strName)
    MsgBox strText, vbInformation, "Search GC for users" & strName
End Sub

Sub BailOnFailure(ErrNum, ErrText)    strText = "Error 0x" & Hex(ErrNum) & " " & ErrText
    MsgBox strText, vbInformation, "ADSI Error"
    WScript.Quit
End Sub
```

C++

The following code fragment contains a function that finds all users in the forest by querying the global catalog:

```
HRESULT FindAllUsersInGC()
{
    HRESULT hr = E_FAIL;
    HRESULT hrGC = S_OK;

    VARIANT var;
    ULONG lFetch;

    // Interface Pointers
    IDirectorySearch *pGCSearch = NULL;
    IADsContainer *pContainer = NULL;
    IUnknown *pUnk = NULL;
    IEnumVARIANT *pEnum = NULL;
    IDispatch *pDisp = NULL;
    IADs *pADs = NULL;




    //Bind to global catalog
    hr = ADsOpenObject(L"GC:",
                NULL,
                NULL,
                ADS_SECURE_AUTHENTICATION, //Use Secure Authentication
```

(continued)

(continued)

```
                IID_IADsContainer,
                (void**)&pContainer);

    if (SUCCEEDED(hr))
    {
        hr = pContainer->get__NewEnum( &pUnk );
        if (SUCCEEDED(hr))
        {
            hr = pUnk->QueryInterface( IID_IEnumVARIANT, (void**) &pEnum );
            if (SUCCEEDED(hr))
            {
            // Now Enumerate--there should be only one item.
            hr = pEnum->Next( 1, &var, &lFetch );
            if (SUCCEEDED(hr))
            {
                while( hr == S_OK )
                {
                    if ( lFetch == 1 )
                    {
                        pDisp = V_DISPATCH(&var);
                        hr = pDisp->QueryInterface( IID_IDirectorySearch,
(void**)&pGCSearch);
                        hrGC = hr;
                    }
                    VariantClear(&var);
                    hr = pEnum->Next( 1, &var, &lFetch );
                };
            }
            }
            if (pEnum)
                pEnum->Release();
            }
            if (pUnk)
            pUnk->Release();
    }
    if (pContainer)
        pContainer->Release();


    if (FAILED(hrGC))
    {
        if (pGCSearch)
            pGCSearch->Release();
        return hrGC;
```

```
}

//Create search filter
LPOLESTR pszSearchFilter = L"(&(objectCategory=person)(objectClass=user))";
//Search entire subtree from root.
ADS_SEARCHPREF_INFO SearchPrefs;
SearchPrefs.dwSearchPref = ADS_SEARCHPREF_SEARCH_SCOPE;
SearchPrefs.vValue.dwType = ADSTYPE_INTEGER;
SearchPrefs.vValue.Integer = ADS_SCOPE_SUBTREE;
DWORD dwNumPrefs = 1;

// COL for iterations
ADS_SEARCH_COLUMN col;

// Handle used for searching
ADS_SEARCH_HANDLE hSearch;

// Set the search preference
hr = pGCSearch->SetSearchPreference( &SearchPrefs, dwNumPrefs);
if (FAILED(hr))
    return hr;
// Set attributes to return
CONST DWORD dwAttrNameSize = 2;
LPOLESTR pszAttribute[dwAttrNameSize] = {L"cn",L"distinguishedName"};

// Execute the search
hr = pGCSearch->ExecuteSearch(pszSearchFilter,
                              pszAttribute,
                                dwAttrNameSize,
                                &hSearch
                                );

if ( SUCCEEDED(hr) )
{

// Call IDirectorySearch::GetNextRow() to retrieve the next row
//of data
    while( pGCSearch->GetNextRow( hSearch) != S_ADS_NOMORE_ROWS )
    {

        // loop through the array of passed column names,
        // print the data for each column
        for (DWORD x = 0; x < dwAttrNameSize; x++)
        {
```

(continued)

(continued)

```
                // Get the data for this column
                hr = pGCSearch->GetColumn( hSearch, pszAttribute[x], &col );

                if ( SUCCEEDED(hr) )
                {
                    // Print the data for the column and free the column
                    // Note the requested attributes are type CaseIgnoreString.
                    wprintf(L"%s: %s\r\n",pszAttribute[x],col.pADsValues-
>CaseIgnoreString);

                    pGCSearch->FreeColumn( &col );
                }
                else
                    wprintf(L"<%s property is not a string>",pszAttribute[x]);
            }
            wprintf(L"-----------------------------\n");
        }

        // Close the search handle to clean up
        pGCSearch->CloseSearchHandle(hSearch);
    }
    if (pGCSearch)
        pGCSearch->Release();
    return hr;
}
```

Moving Users

Users can be moved within a domain.

However, you can only move objects between domains using the movetree.exe utility. When a user is moved to a different domain, the **objectSID** is changed to reflect the new domain and the old **objectSID** is added as a value to the **sIDHistory** property. The **objectGUID** remains the same.

▶ **To move a user**

1. Bind to the user to move and get an **IADs** pointer.
2. Get the **ADsPath** using the **IADs::get_ADsPath** method. The **ADsPath** will be used to specify the user to move.
3. Bind to the container object where you want to move the user to and get an **IADsContainer** pointer.
4. Move the user using the **IADsContainer::MoveHere** method.

   If you have a pointer to the user object before it was moved, the pointer to the object is still valid, but the object's methods are no longer valid since the directory object it represents is no longer valid.

For sample code for moving objects, see *Moving Groups*.

Managing Users on Member Servers and Windows 2000 Professional

On member servers and Windows® 2000 Professional, there is a local security database. That local security database can contain its own local users whose scope is only the particular computer where they are created. When managing these types of users on member servers and workstations, you use the WinNT provider.

When managing users on a Windows 2000 domain using ADSI, you use the LDAP provider. When managing users on member servers and workstations, you use the WinNT provider.

Enumerating Users on Member Servers and Windows 2000 Professional

On member servers and computers running Windows 2000 Professional, you can easily enumerate all the users in local security database.

▶ **To enumerate the users on a member server or computer running Windows 2000 Professional**

1. Bind to the computer using the following rules:

   a. Use an account that has sufficient rights to access that computer.

   b. Use the following binding string format using the WinNT provider, computer name, and an extra parameter to tell ADSI that it is binding to a computer:

   WinNT://*sComputerName*, computer

   where *sComputerName* is the name of the computer whose groups you want to access.

   In the binding string, the ",computer" parameter tells ADSI that it is binding to a computer and allows the WinNT: provider's parser to skip some ambiguity-resolution queries to determine what type of object you are binding to.

   c. Bind to the **IADsContainer** interface.

2. Set a filter containing "user" using the **IADsContainer::put_Filter** method. This enables you to enumerate the container and retrieve only users.

3. Enumerate the user objects, using the **IADsContainer::get__NewEnum** method.

4. For each user object, use the **IADs** or **IADsUser** methods to read the properties of the user.

Example Code for Enumerating Users on a Member Server or Windows 2000 Professional

The following script enumerates all users on a member server or Windows 2000 Professional:

```
Dim cont As IADsContainer

'Example: Enumerating all local users on member server or workstation
''''''''''''''''''''''''''''''''''''''''''
'Parse the arguments
''''''''''''''''''''''''''''''''''''''''''
sComputer = InputBox("This script lists the users on a member server or workstation." &
vbCrLf & vbCrLf & "Specify the computer name:")

If sComputer = "" Then
  Exit Sub
End If


''''''''''''''''''''''''''''''''''''''''''
'Bind to the computer
''''''''''''''''''''''''''''''''''''''''''
'Note that this sample uses the logged-on user's context
'To specify a user account other than the user account under
'which your application is running, use IADsOpenDSObject.
Set cont = GetObject("WinNT://" & sComputer & ",computer")
If (Err.Number <> 0) Then
   BailOnFailure Err.Number, "on GetObject method"
End If


''''''''''''''''''''''''''''''''''''''''''
'Filter to view only user objects
''''''''''''''''''''''''''''''''''''''''''
cont.Filter = Array("User")
If (Err.Number <> 0) Then
   BailOnFailure Err.Number, "on IADsContainer::Filter method"
End If

strText = ""
intIndex = 0
intNumDisplay = 0
```

```
cmember = 0
'Maximum number of users to list on a msgbox.
MAX_DISPLAY = 20


''''''''''''''''''''''''''''''''''''''''''
'Get each user
''''''''''''''''''''''''''''''''''''''''''
For Each user In cont
    intIndex = intIndex + 1
    'Get the name
    strText = strText & vbCrLf & Right("   " & intIndex, 4) & " " & user.Name
    intNumDisplay = intNumDisplay + 1
    'Display in msgbox if there are MAX_DISPLAY users to display
    If intNumDisplay >= MAX_DISPLAY Then
        Call show_users(strText, sComputer)
        strText = ""
        intNumDisplay = 0
    End If
    'Reset the count of members within the current group
    cmember = 0
Next
Call show_users(strText, sComputer)
''''''''''''''''''''''''''''''''''''''''''
'Display subroutines
''''''''''''''''''''''''''''''''''''''''''
Sub show_users(strText, strName)
    MsgBox strText, vbInformation, "Users on " & strName
End Sub

Sub BailOnFailure(ErrNum, ErrText)     strText = "Error 0x" & Hex(ErrNum) & " " & ErrText
    MsgBox strText, vbInformation, "ADSI Error"
    WScript.Quit
End Sub
```

C++

The following code fragment contains a function that enumerates all objects of a specified class (such as user) and displays the members contained in each object on a member server or Windows 2000 Professional:

```
/////////////////////////////////////////////////////////////////////////
/*  ListObjectsWithWinNtProvider()     - Uses the WinNT provider to list
                                         children based on a filter
                                         Returns S_OK on success
```

(continued)

(continued)

```
Parameters

LPWSTR pwszComputer      - Computer to list
LPWSTR pwszClass         - Filter for listing
LPWSTR pwszUSER = NULL   - User Name for ADsOpenObject() binding-
                           If NOT passed - Bind Though ADsGetObject()
LPWSTR pwszPASS = NULL   - Password for ADsOpenObject() binding-
                           If NOT passed - Bind Though ADsGetObject()

*/
HRESULT ListObjectsWithWinNtProvider(LPWSTR pwszComputer,LPWSTR pwszClass, LPWSTR pwszUSER
= NULL, LPWSTR pwszPASS = NULL)
{
    HRESULT hr;
    LPWSTR   pwszBindingString = NULL;

    IADsContainer * pIADsCont = NULL;

    // Allocate a String for Binding..
    // This should definitely be big enough..
    pwszBindingString = new WCHAR[(wcslen(gbsComputer) *2) + 20];

    swprintf(pwszBindingString,L"WinNT://%s,computer",pwszComputer);

    // Make sure either NO user is passed - or BOTH
    // user and password are passed
    assert(!pwszUSER || (pwszUSER && pwszPASS));

    // Bind to the container passed
    // If USER and PASS passed in, use ADsOpenObject()
    if (pwszUSER)
        hr = ADsOpenObject( pwszBindingString,
                            pwszUSER,
                            pwszPASS,
                            ADS_SECURE_AUTHENTICATION,
                            IID_IADsContainer,
                            (void**) &pIADsCont);
    else
        hr = ADsGetObject( pwszBindingString, IID_IADsContainer,(void **)&pIADsCont);

    if (SUCCEEDED(hr))
    {
        VARIANT vFilter;
        VariantInit(&vFilter);
```

```
LPWSTR pwszFilter = pwszClass;

// Build a Variant of array type, using the filter passed
hr = ADsBuildVarArrayStr(&pwszFilter, 1, &vFilter);
if (SUCCEEDED(hr))
{
    // Set the filter for the results of the Enum
    hr = pIADsCont->put_Filter(vFilter);
    if (SUCCEEDED(hr))
    {
        IEnumVARIANT * pEnumVariant = NULL;
                // Ptr to the IEnumVariant Interface
        VARIANT Variant;
                // Variant for retrieving data
        ULONG   ulElementsFetched;
                // Number of elements fetched

        // Builds an enumerator interface- this will be
        // used to enumerate the objects contained in
        // the IADsContainer
        hr = ADsBuildEnumerator(pIADsCont,&pEnumVariant);
        // While no errors- Loop through and print the data
        while (SUCCEEDED(hr) && hr != S_FALSE)
        {
            // Object comes back as a VARIANT holding
            // an IDispatch *
            hr = ADsEnumerateNext(pEnumVariant,1,&Variant,&ulElementsFetched);
            if (hr != S_FALSE)
            {
                assert(HAS_BIT_STYLE(Variant.vt,VT_DISPATCH));
                IDispatch *pDispatch = NULL;
                IADs *pIADs= NULL;
                pDispatch = Variant.pdispVal;
                // QI the Variant's IDispatch * for
                // the IADs interface
                hr = pDispatch->QueryInterface(IID_IADs,(VOID **) &pIADs) ;

                if (SUCCEEDED(hr))
                {
                    // Print some information about the object
                    BSTR bsResult;
                    pIADs->get_Name(&bsResult);
                    wprintf(L" NAME: %s\n",(LPOLESTR) bsResult);
                    SysFreeString(bsResult);
```

(continued)

(continued)

```
                        pIADs->get_ADsPath(&bsResult);
                        wprintf(L" ADSPATH: %s\n",(LPOLESTR) bsResult);
                        SysFreeString(bsResult);

                        puts("---------------------------------------------------------
");
                        pIADs->Release();
                        pIADs = NULL;
                    }
                }
            }

            // Since the hr from iteration was lost, free
            // the interface if the ptr is != NULL
            if (pEnumVariant)
            {
                pEnumVariant->Release();
                pEnumVariant = NULL;
            }
            VariantClear(&Variant);
        }
    }
    VariantClear(&vFilter);
}

delete [] pwszBindingString;
pwszBindingString = NULL;

return hr;
}
```

Creating Users on Member Servers and Windows 2000 Professional

▶ **To create a user on a member server or computer running Windows 2000 Professional**

1. Bind to the computer using the following rules:

    a. Use an account that has sufficient rights to access that computer.

    b. Use the binding string format on the next page using the WinNT provider, computer name, and an extra parameter to tell ADSI that it is binding to a computer.

WinNT://*sComputerName*, computer

where *sComputerName* is the name of the computer whose groups you want to access.

In the binding string, the ",computer" parameter tells ADSI that it is binding to a computer and allows the WinNT: provider's parser to skip some ambiguity resolution queries to determine what type of object you are binding to.

   c. Bind to the **IADsContainer** interface.

2. Specify "user" as the class using **IADsContainer::Create** to add the user.

3. Write the user to the computer's security database using **IADs::SetInfo**.

Example Code for Creating Users on a Member Server or Windows 2000 Professional

The following Visual Basic code creates a user on a member server or Windows 2000 Professional:

```
'Example: Creating a user on a member server or workstation

Dim cont As IADsContainer
Dim oUser As IADsUser
Dim v As Variant

'''''''''''''''''''''''''''''''''''''''''''''''''
'Parse the arguments
'''''''''''''''''''''''''''''''''''''''''''''''''
On Error Resume Next

sComputer = InputBox("This script creates a user on a member server or
workstation." & vbCrLf & vbCrLf & "Specify the computer name:")
sUser = InputBox("Specify the user name:")

If sComputer = "" Then
    Exit Sub
End If
If sUser = "" Then
    Exit Sub
End If

'''''''''''''''''''''''''''''''''''''''''''''''''
'Bind to the computer
'''''''''''''''''''''''''''''''''''''''''''''''''
Set cont = GetObject("WinNT://" & sComputer & ",computer")
If (Err.Number <> 0) Then
```

(continued)

(continued)

```
    BailOnFailure Err.Number, "on GetObject method"
End If

'''''''''''''''''''''''''''''''''''''''''
'Create the user
'''''''''''''''''''''''''''''''''''''''''
Set oUser = cont.Create("user", sUser)
If (Err.Number <> 0) Then
    BailOnFailure Err.Number, "on IADsContainer::Create method"
End If

'''''''''''''''''''''''''''''''''''''''''
'Write the user to the computer's security database.
'''''''''''''''''''''''''''''''''''''''''
oUser.SetInfo
If (Err.Number <> 0) Then
    BailOnFailure Err.Number, "on IADs::SetInfo method"
End If
'''''''''''''''''''''''''''''''''''''''''
'Read the user that was just created
'and display its name and its properties.
'''''''''''''''''''''''''''''''''''''''''
If (Err.Number <> 0) Then
    BailOnFailure Err.Number, "on SetInfo method"
End If
strText = "The user " & sUser & " was successfully added."
strText = strText & vbCrLf & "The user has the following properties:"
'Refresh the property cache
oUser.GetInfo

strText = strText & "Number of properties: " & Count
For cprop = 1 To Count
  Set v = oUser.Next()
  If IsNull(v) Then
    Exit For
  End If
  strText = strText & vbCrLf & cprop & ") " & v.Name & " (" & v.ADsType & ") "
Next
show_items strText, sComputer
'''''''''''''''''''''''''''''''''''''''''
'Display subroutines
'''''''''''''''''''''''''''''''''''''''''
Sub show_items(strText, strName)
    MsgBox strText, vbInformation, "Create user on ", & strName
End Sub
```

Deleting Users on Member Servers and Windows 2000 Professional

▶ **To delete a user from a member server or computer running Windows® 2000 Professional**

1. Bind to the computer using the following rules:

   a. Use an account that has sufficient rights to access that computer.

   b. Use the following binding string format using the WinNT provider, computer name, and an extra parameter to tell ADSI that it is binding to a computer:

   WinNT://*sComputerName*, computer

   In this example, *sComputerName* is the name of the computer whose groups you want to access.

   In the binding string, the ",computer" parameter tells ADSI that it is binding to a computer and allows the WinNT: provider's parser to skip some ambiguity resolution queries to determine what type of object you are binding to.

   c. Bind to the **IADsContainer** interface.

2. Specify "user" as the class using **IADsContainer::Delete** to delete the user.

   Note that you do not need to call **IADs::SetInfo** to commit the change to the container. The **IADsContainer::Delete** call commits the deletion of the user directly to the directory.

Example Code for Deleting Users on a Member Server or Windows 2000 Professional

The following Visual Basic code deletes a user on a member server or workstation:

```
Dim cont As IADsContainer
Dim oGroup As IADsGroup


'Example: Deleting a user on a member server or workstation


''''''''''''''''''''''''''''''''''''''''''
'Parse the arguments
''''''''''''''''''''''''''''''''''''''''''
On Error Resume Next
sComputer = InputBox("This script deletes a user from a member server or
workstation." & vbCrLf & vbCrLf & "Specify the computer name:")
If sComputer = "" Then
    Exit Sub
End If

sUser = InputBox("Specify the user name:")
```

(continued)

(continued)

```
If sUser = "" Then
    Exit Sub
End If


''''''''''''''''''''''''''''''''''''''''''
'Bind to the computer
''''''''''''''''''''''''''''''''''''''''''
Set cont = GetObject("WinNT://" & sComputer & ".computer")
If (Err.Number <> 0) Then
    BailOnFailure Err.Number, "on GetObject method"
End If


''''''''''''''''''''''''''''''''''''''''''
'Delete the user
''''''''''''''''''''''''''''''''''''''''''
cont.Delete "user", sUser

If (Err.Number <> 0) Then
    BailOnFailure Err.Number, "on IADsContainer::Delete method"
End If

strText = "The user " & sUser & " was deleted on computer " & sComputer & "."

Call show_users(strText, sComputer)
''''''''''''''''''''''''''''''''''''''''''
'Display subroutines
''''''''''''''''''''''''''''''''''''''''''
Sub show_users(strText, strName)
    MsgBox strText, vbInformation, "Delete user on " & strName
End Sub
```

Values for countryCode

The following table lists the countries and regions that can be displayed in the Active Directory™ Users and Computers interface, and the corresponding value that is set in the **countryCode** property.

Name displayed on the Users and Computers interface	Values for countryCode
AFGHANISTAN	AF
ALBANIA	AL
ALGERIA	DZ
AMERICAN SAMOA	AS
ANDORRA	AD

Name displayed on the Users and Computers interface	Values for countryCode
ANGOLA	AO
ANGUILLA	AI
ANTARCTICA	AQ
ANTIGUA AND BARBUDA	AG
ARGENTINA	AR
ARMENIA	AM
ARUBA	AW
AUSTRALIA	AU
AUSTRIA	AT
AZERBAIJAN	AZ
BAHAMAS	BS
BAHRAIN	BH
BANGLADESH	BD
BARBADOS	BB
BELARUS	BY
BELGIUM	BE
BELIZE	BZ
BENIN	BJ
BERMUDA	BM
BHUTAN	BT
BOLIVIA	BO
BOSNIA AND HERZEGOWINA	BA
BOTSWANA	BW
BOUVET ISLAND	BV
BRAZIL	BR
BRITISH INDIAN OCEAN TERRITORY	IO
BRUNEI DARUSSALAM	BN
BULGARIA	BG
BURKINA FASO	BF
BURUNDI	BI
CAMBODIA	KH
CAMEROON	CM
CANADA	CA
CAPE VERDE	CV

(continued)

(continued)

Name displayed on the Users and Computers interface	Values for countryCode
CAYMAN ISLANDS	KY
CENTRAL AFRICAN REPUBLIC	CF
CHAD	TD
CHILE	CL
CHINA	CN
CHRISTMAS ISLAND	CX
COCOS (KEELING) ISLANDS	CC
COLOMBIA	CO
COMOROS	KM
CONGO	CG
CONGO, THE DEMOCRATIC REPUBLIC OF THE	CD
COOK ISLANDS	CK
COSTA RICA	CR
COTE D'IVOIRE	CI
CROATIA (local name: Hrvatska)	HR
CUBA	CU
CYPRUS	CY
CZECH REPUBLIC	CZ
DENMARK	DK
DJIBOUTI	DJ
DOMINICA	DM
DOMINICAN REPUBLIC	DO
EAST TIMOR	TP
ECUADOR	EC
EGYPT	EG
EL SALVADOR	SV
EQUATORIAL GUINEA	GQ
ERITREA	ER
ESTONIA	EE
ETHIOPIA	ET
FALKLAND ISLANDS (MALVINAS)	FK
FAROE ISLANDS	FO
FIJI	FJ
FINLAND	FI

Name displayed on the Users and Computers interface	Values for countryCode
FRANCE	FR
FRANCE, METROPOLITAN	FX
FRENCH GUIANA	GF
FRENCH POLYNESIA	PF
FRENCH SOUTHERN TERRITORIES	TF
GABON	GA
GAMBIA	GM
GEORGIA	GE
GERMANY	DE
GHANA	GH
GIBRALTAR	GI
GREECE	GR
GREENLAND	GL
GRENADA	GD
GUADELOUPE	GP
GUAM	GU
GUATEMALA	GT
GUINEA	GN
GUINEA-BISSAU	GW
GUYANA	GY
HAITI	HT
HEARD AND MC DONALD ISLANDS	HM
HOLY SEE (VATICAN CITY STATE)	VA
HONDURAS	HN
HONG KONG S. A. R.	HK
HUNGARY	HU
ICELAND	IS
INDIA	IN
INDONESIA	ID
IRAN (ISLAMIC REPUBLIC OF)	IR
IRAQ	IQ
IRELAND	IE
ISRAEL	IL
ITALY	IT

(continued)

(continued)

Name displayed on the Users and Computers interface	Values for countryCode
JAMAICA	JM
JAPAN	JP
JORDAN	JO
KAZAKHSTAN	KZ
KENYA	KE
KIRIBATI	KI
KOREA, DEMOCRATIC PEOPLE'S REPUBLIC OF	KP
KOREA, REPUBLIC OF	KR
KUWAIT	KW
KYRGYZSTAN	KG
LAO PEOPLE'S DEMOCRATIC REPUBLIC	LA
LATVIA	LV
LEBANON	LB
LESOTHO	LS
LIBERIA	LR
LIBYAN ARAB JAMAHIRIYA	LY
LIECHTENSTEIN	LI
LITHUANIA	LT
LUXEMBOURG	LU
MACAU S. A. R.	MO
MACEDONIA, THE FORMER YUGOSLAV REPUBLIC OF	MK
MADAGASCAR	MG
MALAWI	MW
MALAYSIA	MY
MALDIVES	MV
MALI	ML
MALTA	MT
MARSHALL ISLANDS	MH
MARTINIQUE	MQ
MAURITANIA	MR
MAURITIUS	MU
MAYOTTE	YT
MEXICO	MX
MICRONESIA, FEDERATED STATES OF	FM

Name displayed on the Users and Computers interface	Values for countryCode
MOLDOVA, REPUBLIC OF	MD
MONACO	MC
MONGOLIA	MN
MONTSERRAT	MS
MOROCCO	MA
MOZAMBIQUE	MZ
MYANMAR	MM
NAMIBIA	NA
NAURU	NR
NEPAL	NP
NETHERLANDS	NL
NETHERLANDS ANTILLES	AN
NEW CALEDONIA	NC
NEW ZEALAND	NZ
NICARAGUA	NI
NIGER	NE
NIGERIA	NG
NIUE	NU
NORFOLK ISLAND	NF
NORTHERN MARIANA ISLANDS	MP
NORWAY	NO
OMAN	OM
PAKISTAN	PK
PALAU	PW
PANAMA	PA
PAPUA NEW GUINEA	PG
PARAGUAY	PY
PERU	PE
PHILIPPINES	PH
PITCAIRN	PN
POLAND	PL
PORTUGAL	PT
PUERTO RICO	PR
QATAR	QA

(continued)

(continued)

Name displayed on the Users and Computers interface	Values for countryCode
REUNION	RE
ROMANIA	RO
RUSSIAN FEDERATION	RU
RWANDA	RW
SAINT KITTS AND NEVIS	KN
SAINT LUCIA	LC
SAINT VINCENT AND THE GRENADINES	VC
SAMOA	WS
SAN MARINO	SM
SAO TOME AND PRINCIPE	ST
SAUDI ARABIA	SA
SENEGAL	SN
SEYCHELLES	SC
SIERRA LEONE	SL
SINGAPORE	SG
SLOVAKIA (Slovak Republic)	SK
SLOVENIA	SI
SOLOMON ISLANDS	SB
SOMALIA	SO
SOUTH AFRICA	ZA
SOUTH GEORGIA AND THE SOUTH SANDWICH ISLANDS	GS
SPAIN	ES
SRI LANKA	LK
ST. HELENA	SH
ST. PIERRE AND MIQUELON	PM
SUDAN	SD
SURINAME	SR
SVALBARD AND JAN MAYEN ISLANDS	SJ
SWAZILAND	SZ
SWEDEN	SE
SWITZERLAND	CH
SYRIAN ARAB REPUBLIC	SY
TAIWAN	TW

Name displayed on the Users and Computers interface	Values for countryCode
TAJIKISTAN	TJ
TANZANIA, UNITED REPUBLIC OF	TZ
THAILAND	TH
TOGO	TG
TOKELAU	TK
TONGA	TO
TRINIDAD AND TOBAGO	TT
TUNISIA	TN
TURKEY	TR
TURKMENISTAN	TM
TURKS AND CAICOS ISLANDS	TC
TUVALU	TV
UGANDA	UG
UKRAINE	UA
UNITED ARAB EMIRATES	AE
UNITED KINGDOM	GB
UNITED STATES	US
UNITED STATES MINOR OUTLYING ISLANDS	UM
URUGUAY	UY
UZBEKISTAN	UZ
VANUATU	VU
VENEZUELA	VE
VIET NAM	VN
VIRGIN ISLANDS (BRITISH)	VG
VIRGIN ISLANDS (U.S.)	VI
WALLIS AND FUTUNA ISLANDS	WF
WESTERN SAHARA	EH
YEMEN	YE
YUGOSLAVIA	YU
ZAMBIA	ZM
ZIMBABWE	ZW

C H A P T E R   1 4

Managing Groups

This chapter details what you need to know to use groups in Active Directory™, and therefore discusses the following topics:

- What are groups and how are they used
- Group objects
- Groups on mixed- and native-mode domains
- Creating groups
- Adding members to groups
- Removing members from groups in a domain
- Nesting groups
- Determining a user's or group's membership in a group
- Enumerating groups
- Querying for groups in a domain
- Changing a group's scope or type
- Deleting groups
- Moving groups
- Getting the domain account-style name of a group
- Managing groups on member servers and a computer running Windows NT Workstation/Windows 2000 Professional
- What application and service developers need to know about groups

Groups in Active Directory

Groups are Active Directory™ or local computer objects that can contain users, contacts, computers, and other groups. Groups can be used to do the following:

- Manage user and computer access to shared resources such as Active Directory objects and their properties, network shares, files, directories, printer queues, and so on.
- Create e-mail distribution lists.
- Filter group policy.

Groups can be used for security purposes (such as access control and policy) or they can be used for grouping purposes (such as distribution lists). Specify whether a group is used for security purposes when you create the group.

When assigning permissions for resources (file shares, printers, and so on), administrators should assign those permissions to a group rather than to the individual users. The permissions are assigned once to the group, instead of several times to each individual user. This helps simplify the maintenance and administration of a network.

To control access to a frequently used resource, create a group that will contain users that require that type of access, add one or more ACEs to set the access for that group on the security descriptor for the resource, and then add any users who require that type of access to the resource as members of the group. For more information about setting access on directory objects, see *Controlling Access to Active Directory Objects*.

When a user is made a member of a group, that user is given all the rights and permissions granted to the group. However, if the user is already logged on, the rights of the newly assigned group will not take effect until he/she logs off and logs on again.

Contacts in a group can be sent e-mail, but cannot be assigned rights and permissions. Although a contact can be added to a security group as well as to a distribution group, contacts cannot be used to assign rights and permissions.

Groups vs. Organizational Units

Groups are distinct from organizational units (OUs). OUs are useful for creating a hierarchy for administrative delegation or setting group policy. Groups are used for granting access and creating distribution lists.

Groups and organizational units also differ in regard to the domain boundaries to which they are applied. You can create groups to contain users, computers, or shared resources on a local server, a single domain, or multiple domains in a forest. Organizational units represent a collection of objects (including group objects) only within the context of a single domain.

Native vs. Mixed Mode

In Windows® 2000, domains can operate in two different modes:

- *Mixed Mode*. Windows NT® 4.0 domain controllers may be present in this environment. This is the default mode when a domain is created. Clients and member servers may be still running previous versions of Windows NT, Windows 98, or Windows 95.

- *Native Mode*. All domain controllers must be running a Windows 2000 Server. Clients and member servers may still be running Windows NT 4.0. Clients and member servers may still be running previous versions of Windows NT, Windows 98, or Windows 95.

A domain must be in native mode to use the following Windows 2000 group features:

- Universal security groups. Universal groups are a new type of group that can be created and used in any domain in the forest.
- Nesting security groups.
- Conversion of groups.

Mixed mode supports all types of distribution groups (including Universal) and nesting of distribution groups. Mixed mode should only be used to support Windows NT 4.0 domain controllers during the migration process. A domain tree or forest can contain both mixed-mode and native-mode domains.

Before creating or converting groups that require native mode, your application should check the operation mode of the domain.

Nesting

In Windows 2000, groups can contain other groups. This is called nesting. Nesting is supported only for distribution groups in domains running in mixed mode. A domain must be in native mode to nest security groups (as well as distribution groups).

Nesting can be an efficient way to handle large memberships as well as delegate management of group membership. For example, the top group could be a universal group that contains only global groups. The domain administrators of the domains containing those global groups can manage the membership within their own domains. The enterprise administrator can simply manage the global group membership of the universal group (that is, adding and removing global groups) and let the domain administrators handle the membership requests from users in their own domain.

Types of Groups

A group can be a security group or a distribution group.

Security groups are listed in access-control lists (ACLs), which define permissions on resources and objects. Security groups can also be used as an e-mail entity. Sending an e-mail message to the group sends the message to all the members of the group.

Distribution groups are not security enabled. Distribution groups provide a subset of the functionality of security groups. Distribution groups cannot be listed in ACLs. Distribution groups can be used only for grouping purposes. For example, distribution lists can be used with e-mail applications (such as Exchange) to send e-mail to collections of users.

If you do not need a group for security purposes, create a distribution group instead. Using a distribution group improves performance because distribution groups are ignored when Windows 2000 builds the user security token during the logon process. This also reduces the size of the token, improving performance as the token is sent to various computers the user accesses.

How Security Groups are Used in Access Control

The security identifier (SID) is the object identifier of the user or security group when the user or group is used for security purposes. The name of the user or group is not used as the unique identifier within the system. The SID is stored in the **objectSid** property of user objects and security group objects. Active Directory generates the **objectSid** when the user or group is created. The system ensures that the SIDs are unique across a forest. Note that the **objectGuid** is the unique identifier of a user, group, or any other directory object. The SID changes if a user or group is moved to another domain; the **objectGuid** always remains the same.

When a user or group is given permission to access a resource (such as a printer or a file share), the SID of the user or group is added to the access control entry (ACE) defining the granted permission in the resource's discretionary access control list (DACL). In Active Directory, each object has an **nTSecurityDescriptor** property that stores a DACL defining the access to that particular object or properties on that object. For more information about setting access control on objects in Active Directory, see *Controlling Access to Active Directory Objects*.

When a user logs on to a Windows 2000 domain, the operating system generates an access token. This access token is used when determining which resources the user may access. Among other information, the user's access token includes the following:

- User's SID
- SIDs of the global and universal security groups of which the user is a member

Every process executed on behalf of this user has a copy of this access token.

When the user attempts to access resources on a computer, the service through which the user accesses the resource impersonates the user by creating a new access token based on the access token created at user logon time. This new access token additionally contains SIDs for all domain local groups that 1) are in the target resource's domain *and* 2) include the user. The service uses this new access token to evaluate access to the resource. If a SID in the access token appears in any ACEs in the DACL, the service gives the user the permissions specified in those ACEs.

Where Groups Can Be Created

In Active Directory, groups are created in domains. Groups can be created at the root of the domain (domainDNS), in an organizational unit (OU), or in a container (container) object.

The domain where you create a group can make a difference based on the scope of the group. The scope of a group determines 1) domains where members can be added from and 2) domains where the group can be used to grant permissions.

You should choose the particular container (domain, OU, or container) where you create a group based on the administration required for the group. For example, if your directory has multiple OUs, each of which has a different user to administer it, you may want to create global groups within those OUs so that those administrators can manage group membership for users in those OUs. If groups are required for access control outside the OU, the groups within the OUs can be nested in universal groups (or other global groups) that can be used elsewhere in the domain and forest.

Note   Groups can be moved within a domain; however, only universal groups can be moved from one domain to another.

Scope of Groups

Each security and distribution group has a scope:

- Domains from which members can be added to the group
- Domains where the group can be used to grant permissions
- Domains where the group can be nested in other groups

There are three scopes for groups, as shown in the following table.

Scope	Members	Grant Permissions	Member of Other Groups
Universal	From any Windows NT/Windows 2000 domain in the forest: Universal Groups, Global Groups and users (including contacts) from any domain in the forest.	On any domain in the forest	Can be a member of the following groups in the forest: Local Groups and Universal Groups.
Global	Only from the domain containing the group: Global Groups and users (including contacts) from the domain containing the group.	On any domain in the forest	Can be a member of any group in the forest: Global Groups, Local Groups, and Universal Groups.
Domain Local	From any domain in the forest: Global Groups, Universal Groups, and users (including contacts) from any domain in the forest. Domain local groups from the domain containing the group.	Only on the domain containing the group	Only can be a member of Local Groups in the domain containing the group.

If you have multiple forests, users from one forest cannot be placed in groups in another, and groups from one forest cannot be given permissions in another.

In short, a universal group can contain users and groups from any domain and can be used for access control in any domain. A global group can contain only users and groups from a single domain and can be used for access control on any domain. A domain local group can contain users and groups from any domain and can only be used for access control on a single domain.

Group Scope and the Global Catalog

Universal groups and their members are listed in the global catalog.

Global and domain local groups are also listed in the global catalog, but their members are not. This reduces the size of the global catalog and dramatically reduces the replication traffic needed to keep the global catalog up-to-date.

Changes in membership in global and domain local groups have no effect on the global catalog.

Effects of Universal Groups on the Global Catalog

For customers using universal groups in larger systems with slow connections, the following issues should be addressed to avoid performance and availability problems:

- *Authentication of a user requires global knowledge of the user's group memberships in order to compute all the groups that user (directly or indirectly) belongs to.* With universal groups, the global catalog service (GC) is used to perform this membership computation. If a GC is not available at logon time, the user is not able to log on to a native-mode domain. On a mixed-mode domain, the user may not have the appropriate access to resources according to universal group memberships in other domains.

  Solution: To avoid GC availability problems when using Universal groups, configure one or more GC servers per site.

- *Because authentication requires the GC to compute a user's universal group memberships, the GC must contain all universal group memberships.* If only universal groups are used, a high level of GC replication traffic may be generated if the universal group memberships are changed frequently. A medium-sized branch office might not be able to afford the network bandwidth required to keep a GC up-to-date.

  Solution: To avoid unnecessary GC replication traffic with frequently changing group memberships, nest global groups within universal groups and make membership changes in the global groups. This leaves the universal group membership static (this avoids the need to replicate membership changes in the GC) and enables administrators to make changes frequently to global groups (global group membership is replicated only within the domain).

What Type of Group to Use

Which type of group should you create? When you create a group, you specify the type and scope. However, how you intend to use the group for access control also affects the type and scope.

Type

Groups use following types:

- *Security*. Use security groups to control access to resources. Security groups can also be used as e-mail distribution lists.

- *Distribution*. Use distribution groups if the group is *only* used for e-mail distribution lists or for grouping purposes. The primary purpose of this type of group is to group related objects together. Distribution groups cannot be used for access control. You can explicitly disable security on these groups to avoid unnecessary evaluation of these groups during a user's logon process. This avoids the expense of examining them when the logon process creates the user's security token (this makes logon more efficient) and reduces the size of the security token (this makes evaluation of access rights more efficient).

If the domain containing the group is running in native mode, you can convert the type of a group after it has been created. The type cannot be converted in mixed mode.

Scope

Groups use the following scopes:

- *Universal.* Use universal groups to define functional groups that span domains. To do this, nest global groups within universal groups and make membership changes in the global groups. The universal group should change infrequently (add/remove global groups) while its membership might change much more frequently (add/remove members from the global groups). For example, define the group system administrators from Microsoft.com as a universal group that contains the global groups sys-admins from northamericadom.Microsoft.com, sys-admins from europedom.Microsoft.com, and so on. Each of these account groups would contain the individual system administrators from a single domain.

Note   Universal groups require access to a global catalog server. For more information about the impact of universal groups on the global catalog, see *Group Scope and the Global Catalog.*

  Enterprises with a single domain should not use universal groups. Instead, use global groups and domain local groups as appropriate. Avoiding universal groups in the single domain scenario makes the transition easier if the enterprise subsequently expands to multiple domains.

- *Global.* Use global groups for membership maintenance (adding and removing users) should occur within the global groups.

  If a domain contains a hierarchy of organizational units and administration is delegated to administrators at each OU, it may be simpler and more efficient to nest global groups. For example, if OU 1 contained OU 2 and OU 3, a global group in OU 1 could contain global groups in OU 2 and OU 3. In OU 1, the administrator would add/remove users from OU 1 and the administrators of OU 2 and 3 would add/remove members for users from their own OUs.

- *Domain Local.* Use domain local groups to define access policies on resources within a domain. Depending upon the situation, domain local groups contain global groups, universal groups, individual accounts, other domain local groups, or a mixture of these.

Usage

If you intend a group to be used to set access rights on directory objects, you must create a group with Global scope. Why? All objects and their security descriptors (which control access to the object) are replicated to every global catalog server. The Configuration container (which contains objects that also have security descriptors) is also replicated to all DCs in the forest. If you use a domain local group to assign rights in a security descriptor, there are circumstances when the group is not in the user's access token and, therefore, the right assigned is not enforced. When the directory object is replicated to the Configuration container or global catalog in another domain and a user requests access to the object in that other domain, the DC handling the access request is not able to add the domain local group to the access token. Effectively, the access that the assigned right containing the domain local group defines is not enforced in these domains. The assigned right is enforced only on the domain containing the domain local group.

Domain Local groups should only be used to manage resources that 1) are not stored in the directory (such as file shares, printer queues, and so on) and 2) are on computers in the domain containing the Domain Local group.

Group Objects

A group is represented as a group object in Active Directory. The group object has seven important properties:

cn

The **cn** (or Common-Name) is a single-valued property that is the object's relative distinguished name. The **cn** is the name of the group in Active Directory. As with all other objects, the **cn** of a group must be unique among the sibling objects in the container containing the group.

member

The **member** property is a multi-valued property that contains the list of distinguished names for the user, group, and contact objects that are members of the group. Each item in the list is a linked reference to the object that represents the member; therefore, Active Directory automatically updates the distinguished names in the member property when a member object is moved or renamed.

groupType

The **groupType** property is a single-valued property that is an integer that specifies the group type and scope using the following bit flags:

ADS_GROUP_TYPE_DOMAIN_LOCAL_GROUP

ADS_GROUP_TYPE_GLOBAL_GROUP

ADS_GROUP_TYPE_SECURITY_ENABLED

ADS_GROUP_TYPE_UNIVERSAL_GROUP

The first three flags specify the group scope.

The ADS_GROUP_TYPE_SECURITY_ENABLED flag indicates the type of the group. If this flag is set, the group is a security group. If this flag is not set, the group is a distribution group.

memberOf

The **memberOf** property is a multi-valued property that contains the list of distinguished names for groups that contain the group as a member. This property lists the groups beneath which the group is directly nested—it does not contain the recursive list of nested predecessors. For example, if group D were nested in group C and group B and group B were nested in group A, the **membersOf** property of group D would list group C and group B but not group A.

objectGUID

The **objectGUID** property is a single-valued property that is the unique identifier for the object. This property is a GUID (Globally Unique Identifier). When an object is created in the directory, Active Directory generates a GUID and assigns it to the object's **objectGUID** property. The GUID is unique across the enterprise and anywhere else.

The **objectGUID** is a 128-bit GUID structure stored as an OctetString.

objectSid (Object-Sid)

The objectSid property is a single-valued property that specifies the security identifier (SID) of the group. The SID is a unique value used to identify the group as a security principal. It is a binary value that the system sets when the group is created.

Each group has a unique SID that the Windows NT®/Windows® 2000 Server domain issues that is stored in the **objectSid** property of the group object in the directory. Each time a user logs on, the system retrieves the SID for the groups of which the user is a member and places it in the user's access token. The system uses the SIDs in the user's access token to identify the user and his/her group memberships in all subsequent interactions with Windows NT/Windows 2000 security.

When a SID has been used as the unique identifier for a user or group, it cannot ever be used again to identify another user or group.

sAMAccountName

The **sAMAccountName** property is a single-valued property that is the logon name used to support clients and servers from a previous version (Windows® 95, Windows® 98, and LAN Manager). The **sAMAccountName** should be less than 20 characters to support clients and servers from a previous version.

The **sAMAccountName** must be unique among all security principal objects within a domain.

Groups on Mixed- and Native-Mode Domains

In Windows® 2000, domains can operate in two different modes: mixed or native. Groups behave differently depending on the domain mode.

A mixed-mode domain supports only the following:

- Global security groups can contain only user accounts.
- Domain local security groups can contain other global groups and user accounts.
- Universal security groups cannot be created.
- Universal distribution groups can be created.
- Only distribution groups can be nested.
- No conversion of scope or type is allowed.

A native-mode domain provides all the group features for Windows 2000:

- Universal groups are available as security groups and distribution groups.
- Full group nesting is allowed.
- Groups can be converted freely between security groups and distribution groups. Global groups and domain local groups can be converted to universal groups.

Before creating or converting groups that require native mode, your application should check the operation mode of the domain.

Detecting the Operation Mode of a Domain

In Windows® 2000, a domain can run in two operation modes: mixed and native. Mixed mode should be used to include domain controllers running Windows NT® 4.0 in a Windows 2000 domain. Mixed mode does not support universal groups or nested groups. If all domain controllers in the domain are running Windows 2000, you can use native mode.

To programmatically detect the operation mode of a Windows 2000 domain, you can read the **ntMixedDomain** property of the **domainDNS** object for that domain. A zero value (0) means the domain is in native mode. A value of one (1) means the domain is in mixed mode. You can also use the **DsRoleGetPrimaryDomainInformation** function to get the operation mode as well as other information about the domain and its state.

To bind to the **domainDNS** object of the domain of the user account under which your application is running, use serverless binding and rootDSE to get the distinguished name for the domain and then use that distinguished name to bind to the **domainDNS** object that represents that domain. For more information on serverless binding and rootDSE, see *Serverless Binding and RootDSE*.

Example Code for Determining the Operation Mode

```
C++
```

The code fragment on the next page contains a function that reads the **ntMixedDomain** property of a domain and determines the operation mode.

```
HRESULT GetDomainMode(IADs *pDomain, BOOL *bIsMixed)
{
HRESULT hr = E_FAIL;
VARIANT var;
if (pDomain)
{

    VariantClear(&var);

    //Get the ntMixedDomain attribute
    LPOLESTR szAttribute = L"ntMixedDomain";
    hr = pDomain->Get(szAttribute,&var);
    if (SUCCEEDED(hr))
    {

        //Type should be VT_I4.
        if (var.vt==VT_I4)
        {

            //Zero means native mode.
            if (var.lVal == 0)
                *bIsMixed = FALSE;

            //One means mixed mode.
            else if (var.lVal == 1)
                *bIsMixed = TRUE;
            else
                hr=E_FAIL;
        }
    }
    VariantClear(&var);
}
return hr;

}
```

Visual Basic

The script reads the **ntMixedDomain** property of a domain and determines the operation mode:

```
'Example: Detects if a domain is in mixed mode or native mode

Dim IADsRootDSE As IADs
Dim IADsDomain As IADs
```

(continued)

(continued)

```
On Error Resume Next
sComputer = InputBox("This script detects if a Windows 2000 domain is running in
mixed or native mode." & vbCrLf & vbCrLf & "Specify the domain name or the name
of a domain controller in the domain :")

sPrefix = "LDAP://" & sComputer & "/"

'''''''''''''''''''''''''''''''''''''''
'Bind to a ds server
'''''''''''''''''''''''''''''''''''''''
Set IADsRootDSE = GetObject(sPrefix & "rootDSE")
If (Err.Number <> 0) Then
    BailOnFailure Err.Number, "on GetObject method"
    Exit Sub
End If
sDomain = IADsRootDSE.Get("defaultNamingContext")
If (Err.Number <> 0) Then
    BailOnFailure Err.Number, "on Get method"
    Exit Sub
End If
Set IADsDomain = GetObject(sPrefix & sDomain)
If (Err.Number <> 0) Then
    BailOnFailure Err.Number, "on GetObject method"
    Exit Sub
End If


'''''''''''''''''''''''''''''''''''''''
'Get ntMixedDomain property
'''''''''''''''''''''''''''''''''''''''
sMode = IADsDomain.Get("ntMixedDomain")
If (Err.Number <> 0) Then
    BailOnFailure Err.Number, "on Get ntMixedDomain property"
    Exit Sub
End If
'''''''''''''''''''''''''''''''''''''''
'Get name property
'''''''''''''''''''''''''''''''''''''''
sName = IADsDomain.Get("name")
If (Err.Number <> 0) Then
    BailOnFailure Err.Number, "on Get name property"
    Exit Sub
End If
```

```
If (sMode = 0) Then
    sModeString = "Native"
ElseIf (sMode = 1) Then
    sModeString = "Mixed"
Else
    BailOnFailure sMode, "Invalid ntMixedDomain value: " & sMode
    Exit Sub
End If

 strText = "The domain " & sName & " is in " & sModeString & " mode."

MsgBox strText
''''''''''''''''''''''''''''''''''''''''
'Display subroutines
''''''''''''''''''''''''''''''''''''''''
Sub show_groups(strText, strName)
    MsgBox strText, vbInformation, "Groups on " & strName
End Sub

Sub BailOnFailure(ErrNum, ErrText)     strText = "Error 0x" & Hex(ErrNum) & " " &
ErrText
    MsgBox strText, vbInformation, "ADSI Error"
    WScript.Quit
End Sub
```

Creating Groups in a Domain

To add a group to Active Directory, you create a group object in the domain container of the domain where you want to place the group. Groups can be created at the root of the domain, within an organizational unit, or within a container.

When you create a group object, you must also set the following attributes to make the object a legal group that Active Directory and the Windows® security system can recognize.

cn
　　Required. Specify the name of the group object in the directory. This will be the object's relative distinguished name within the container where you create the group.

groupType
　　Required. Specify an integer that contains the flags that specify the group type and scope using the following combinations.

Group	Flags
Domain Local Distribution	ADS_GROUP_TYPE_DOMAIN_LOCAL_GROUP

(continued)

(continued)

Group	Flags
Domain Local Security	ADS_GROUP_TYPE_DOMAIN_LOCAL_GROUP | ADS_GROUP_TYPE_SECURITY_ENABLED
Global Distribution	ADS_GROUP_TYPE_GLOBAL_GROUP
Global Security	ADS_GROUP_TYPE_GLOBAL_GROUP | ADS_GROUP_TYPE_SECURITY_ENABLED
Universal Distribution	ADS_GROUP_TYPE_UNIVERSAL_GROUP
Universal Security	ADS_GROUP_TYPE_UNIVERSAL_GROUP | ADS_GROUP_TYPE_SECURITY_ENABLED

If the group is intended for setting access control on directory objects, you should create Global Security or Universal Security groups.

Note Universal Security groups can only be created on Windows® 2000 domains running in native mode. For more information about detecting mixed and native mode, see *Detecting the Operation Mode of a Domain*.

sAMAccountName

Required. Specify a string that is the name used to support clients and servers from a previous version. The **sAMAccountName** should be less than 20 characters to support clients of a previous version of Windows NT®.

The **sAMAccountName** must be unique among all security principal objects within the domain. You should perform a query against the domain to verify that the **sAMAccountName** is unique within the domain.

Optionally, you can set the member property when creating the group object (using **IDirectoryObject::CreateDSObject**) to add members (users, groups, or contacts). Or if you use **IADsContainer::Create** to create the group, you can use **IADsGroup::Add** to set the member property directly after creation. For more information about adding members to a group, see *Adding Members to Groups in a Domain*.

Example Code for Creating a Group

```
C++
```

The following code fragment contains a function that creates a group with only the essential properties explicitly set (**cn**, **sAMAccountType**, **groupType**) and containing no members:

```
/////////////////////////////////////////////////////////////////////////
/*  CreateSimpleGroup()   - Function for creating a basic group
```

```
    Parameters

        IDirectoryObject *pDirObject     -    Parent Directory Object for
                                              the new group
        LPWSTR pwCommonName              -    Common Name for the new
                                              group
        IADs ** ppObjRet                -    Pointer to the Pointer which
                                              will receive the new Group
        int iGroupType                  -    Bitflags for new group:
                                         ADS_GROUP_TYPE_GLOBAL_GROUP,
                                         ADS_GROUP_TYPE_DOMAIN_LOCAL_GROUP,
                                         ADS_GROUP_TYPE_UNIVERSAL_GROUP,
                                         ADS_GROUP_TYPE_SECURITY_ENABLED
*/
HRESULT CreateSimpleGroup(IDirectoryObject *pDirObject, LPWSTR
pwCommonName,LPWSTR pwSamAcctName,IADs *ppObjRet,int iGroupType)
{
    if(!pDirObject)
        return E_INVALIDARG;

//Check if the group type is Universal Security
//if true, make sure domain is in native mode.
    if(((iGroupType &
ADS_GROUP_TYPE_UNIVERSAL_GROUP)==ADS_GROUP_TYPE_UNIVERSAL_GROUP)&&((iGroupType &
ADS_GROUP_TYPE_SECURITY_ENABLED)==ADS_GROUP_TYPE_SECURITY_ENABLED))
    {
        //Check whether the domain containing the container is in mixed mode
        hr = CheckDomainModeOfObject(pDirObject, &bIsMixed);

        if (SUCCEEDED(hr))
        {
            if (bIsMixed)
                return E_INVALIDARG;
        }
        else
        {
            return hr;
        }
    }

    //SamAccountName CANNOT be bigger than 20 characters.
    if (wcslen(pwSamAcctName) >20)
    {
        return E_FAIL;
```

(continued)

(continued)

```
}

HRESULT    hr;

/*
    ADSVALUE is used to specify attribute information for calling
    IDirectoryObject::CreateDSObject()
    When Creating a new group, the required attributes are :
      objectClass,sAMAccountName and groupType.

    In this function the "objectClass" is set to "group".
    The  "sAMAccountName" is the Windows NT 4.0 name.
    In Windows 2000/Windows NT 4 mixed-mode environment,
    this attribute will be exposed to the Windows NT 4 computers.
    Therefore, this name must be globally unique throughout the
    network and cannot exceed 20 characters in length.
*/
ADSVALUE    sAMValue;
ADSVALUE    classValue;
ADSVALUE    groupType;

LPDISPATCH pDisp;
WCHAR      pwCommonNameFull[1024];

// Build an Array of ADS_ATTR_INFO structures
// Note that the sAMAccountName and groupType entries contain
// a pointer to the respective ADSVALUE structures
// defined previously
ADS_ATTR_INFO  attrInfo[] =
{
    { L"objectClass", ADS_ATTR_UPDATE,
                      ADSTYPE_CASE_IGNORE_STRING, &classValue, 1 },
    {L"sAMAccountName", ADS_ATTR_UPDATE,
                      ADSTYPE_CASE_IGNORE_STRING, &sAMValue, 1},
    {L"groupType", ADS_ATTR_UPDATE,
                      ADSTYPE_CASE_IGNORE_STRING, &groupType, 1}
};

// Get the size of the array
DWORD dwAttrs = sizeof(attrInfo)/sizeof(ADS_ATTR_INFO);

/*
    For ADSVALUES, the dwType member and
    the data value member (in this case "CaseIgnoreString")
```

```
        must be set.
    */

    // To create a group, this parameter must be set to "group".
    classValue.dwType = ADSTYPE_CASE_IGNORE_STRING;
    classValue.CaseIgnoreString = L"group";

    // Set sAMAccountName to the name passed to this function
    sAMValue.dwType=ADSTYPE_CASE_IGNORE_STRING;
    sAMValue.CaseIgnoreString = pwSamAcctName;

    // Set the groupType to the group type passed to this function
    groupType.dwType=ADSTYPE_INTEGER;
    groupType.Integer =  iGroupType;

    //Note that CN is limited to 64 characters.
    // Take the passed commonname and prefix a 'CN=' to conform
    // to the format that  IDirectoryObject::CreateDSObject() requires
    wsprintfW(pwCommonNameFull,L"CN=%s",pwCommonName);

    // Create the new group
    hr = pDirObject->CreateDSObject( pwCommonNameFull,  attrInfo,
                                dwAttrs, &pDisp );
    if (SUCCEEDED(hr))
    {
        // Query the new group for an IADs to be returned
        // from this function
        hr = pDisp->QueryInterface(IID_IADs,(void**) ppObjRet);

        pDisp->Release();
        pDisp = NULL;
    }
    return hr;
}


HRESULT GetDomainMode(IADs *pDomain, BOOL *bIsMixed)
{
HRESULT hr = E_FAIL;
VARIANT var;
if (pDomain)
{
    VariantClear(&var);
    //Get the ntMixedDomain attribute
```

(continued)

(continued)

```
    LPOLESTR szAttribute = L"ntMixedDomain";
    hr = pDomain->Get(szAttribute,&var);
    if (SUCCEEDED(hr))
    {
        //Type should be VT_I4.
        if (var.vt==VT_I4)
        {
            //Zero means native mode.
            if (var.lVal == 0)
                *bIsMixed = FALSE;
            //One means mixed mode.
            else if (var.lVal == 1)
                *bIsMixed = TRUE;
            else
                hr=E_FAIL;
        }
    }
    VariantClear(&var);
}
return hr;

}

HRESULT CheckDomainModeOfObject(IDirectoryObject *pDirObject, BOOL *bIsMixed)
{
    HRESULT hr = E_FAIL;
    IADs *pDomain = NULL;
    VARIANT VarTest;
    WCHAR *pFound = NULL;
    int iLen;
    WCHAR *pDomainPath = new WCHAR[MAX_PATH*2];

    //Check whether the domain containing the container is in mixed mode
    WCHAR *pVal = NULL;
    pVal = GetDirectoryObjectAttrib(pDirObject,L"canonicalName");

    if (pVal)
    {
        //Parse the canonical name for the DNS name of the domain
        pFound = wcschr(pVal,'/');
        //Bind to the domain using the dns name,
        //get defaultnamingcontext,
        if (pFound)
        {
```

```
    iLen = pFound - pVal;
    wcscpy(pDomainPath, L"LDAP://");
    wcsncat(pDomainPath, pVal,iLen);
    wcscat(pDomainPath, L"/rootDSE");
    wprintf(L"DNS Name: %s\n", pDomainPath);
    VariantClear(&VarTest);
    hr = ADsOpenObject(pDomainPath,
                   NULL,
                   NULL,
                   ADS_SECURE_AUTHENTICATION,
                              //Use Secure Authentication
                   IID_IADs,
                   (void**)&pDomain);
if (SUCCEEDED(hr))
{
    hr = pDomain->Get(L"defaultNamingContext",&VarTest);
    if (SUCCEEDED(hr))
    {
        wcscpy(pDomainPath, L"LDAP://");
         wcsncat(pDomainPath, pVal,iLen);
        wcscat(pDomainPath, L"/");
        wcscat(pDomainPath, VarTest.bstrVal);
        VariantClear(&VarTest);
        if (pDomain)
            pDomain->Release();
        if (SUCCEEDED(hr))
        {
            hr = ADsOpenObject(pDomainPath,
                           NULL,
                           NULL,
                           ADS_SECURE_AUTHENTICATION,
                                      //Use Secure Authentication
                           IID_IADs,
                           (void**)&pDomain);
            if (SUCCEEDED(hr))
            {
                hr = GetDomainMode(pDomain, bIsMixed);
            }
        }
    }
}
if (pDomain)
    pDomain->Release();
}
```

(continued)

(continued)

```
    }
    return hr;
}


////////////////////////////////////////////////////////////////////////////
/*

    GetDirectoryObjectAttrib()      -   Returns the value of the
                                        attribute named in pAttrName
                                        from the IDirectoryObject passed

      Parameters

        IDirectoryObject *pDirObject    - Object from which to retrieve
                                          an attribute value

        LPWSTR pAttrName                - Name of attribute to retrieve
*/
WCHAR * GetDirectoryObjectAttrib(IDirectoryObject *pDirObject,LPWSTR pAttrName)
{
    HRESULT    hr;
    ADS_ATTR_INFO   *pAttrInfo=NULL;
    DWORD   dwReturn;
    static WCHAR pwReturn[1024];

    pwReturn[0] = 01;

    hr = pDirObject->GetObjectAttributes( &pAttrName,
                                          1,
                                          &pAttrInfo,
                                          &dwReturn );
    if ( SUCCEEDED(hr) )
    {
        for(DWORD idx=0; idx < dwReturn;idx++, pAttrInfo++ )
        {
            if ( _wcsicmp(pAttrInfo->pszAttrName,pAttrName) == 0 )
            {
                wcscpy(pwReturn,pAttrInfo->pADsValues->CaseIgnoreString);
                break;
            }
        }
        FreeADsMem( pAttrInfo );
    }
    return pwReturn;
}
```

Visual Basic

The following subroutine creates a group with only the essential properties explicitly set (**cn**, **sAMAccountType**, **groupType**) and containing no members:

```
'///////////////////////////////////////////////////////////////////////
'     CreateSimpleGroup()   - Function for creating a basic group
'
'     Parameters
'
'         oDirObject As IDirectoryObject    -   Parent Directory Object
'                                               for the new group
'         ByVal sCommonName As String       -   Common Name for the new
'                                               group
'         ByVal sSAMAcctName As String      -   Pointer to the Pointer
'                                               which will receive the
'                                               new Group
'         oDirObject As IDirectoryObject    -   Parent Directory Object
'                                               for the new group
'         ByVal sCommonName As String       -   Common Name for the new
'                                               group
'         ByVal sSAMAcctName As String      -   Sam Account Name for the
'                                               new group
'         oDirObjectRet As IDirectoryObject -   New object returned
'         ByVal iGroupType As Long          -   Bitflags for new group:
'
'                                   ADS_GROUP_TYPE_GLOBAL_GROUP,
'                                   ADS_GROUP_TYPE_DOMAIN_LOCAL_GROUP,
'                                   ADS_GROUP_TYPE_UNIVERSAL_GROUP,
'                                   ADS_GROUP_TYPE_SECURITY_ENABLE
Sub CreateSimpleGroup(oDirObject As IDirectoryObject, ByVal sCommonName As
String, ByVal sSAMAcctName As String, oDirObjectRet As IDirectoryObject, ByVal
iGroupType As Long)

    If Len(sSAMAcctName) > 20 Then
        MsgBox "SamAccountName CANNOT be bigger than 20 characters"
        Exit Sub
    End If

    Dim sGroupType As String
    Dim oNewObject As IADs
    Dim oIadsContDirObj As IADsContainer
    Set oIadsContDirObj = oDirObject
```

(continued)

(continued)

```
    ' Get the string value for the group type
    sGroupType = Str(iGroupType)

    ' Get a New group object
    Set oNewObject = oIadsContDirObj.Create("group", "CN=" & sCommonName)

    ' Put the required attributes
    oNewObject.Put "sAMAccountName", sSAMAcctName
    oNewObject.Put "GroupType", iGroupType

    ' Commit the new group
    oNewObject.SetInfo

    ' Print group vitals
    DisplayMessage ">>> Created new GROUP with a groupeType of " &
Str(iGroupType)
    PrintIADSObject oNewObject

    Set oDirObjectRet = oNewObject
    Set oNewObject = Nothing
    Set oIadsContDirObj = Nothing


End Sub
```

Adding Members to Groups in a Domain

You can add users, groups, or contacts to groups. The member property of the group object contains all direct members of the group.

The simplest way to control group membership is to use the **IADsGroup::Add** and **IADsGroup::Remove** methods on the **IADsGroup** object representing the group you want to add or remove members from.

The following properties of the group object control group membership:

member

Use the **member** property to specify the list of distinguished names for the user, group, and contact objects that are members of the group.

After creating the group object, use the **IADsGroup::Add** method to add members to the group. Note that **IADsGroup::Add** uses the ADsPath instead of the distinguished name. To get the ADsPath, use the **IADs::get_ADsPath** method on the object representing the user, group, or contact you want to add.

memberOf

Optionally, use the **memberOf** property to specify the list of distinguished names of groups that contain the group as a member.

Active Directory™ maintains this property. When this group's distinguished name is added to the **member** property of another group, that other group's distinguished name is automatically added to this group's **memberOf** property.

The **IADsGroup** methods are simplest for adding and removing members. However, you can also use **IDirectoryObject** methods to add and remove members. The **IDirectoryObject** methods may be more efficient if you are adding multiple members at creation time where you can specify the members in the *pAttributeEntries* parameter of the **IDirectoryObject::CreateDSObject** method. If you use the **IDirectoryObject** methods to add members, you must specify distinguished names for the users, groups, or contacts to add.

When using **IDirectoryObject**, be careful when adding members. The member property is also multi-valued. Therefore, if members already exist in the **member** property, you must retrieve the array of members using **IDirectoryObject::GetObjectAttributes**, add the new members to the array, and write the updated array to the **member** property again using **IDirectoryObject::SetObjectAttributes**.

Example Code for Adding a Member to a Group

C++

The following code fragment contains a function that adds a member to a group:

```
////////////////////////////////////////////////////////////////////////
/*  AddMemberToGroup()    -        Adds the passed directory object as a
                                   member of passed group

    Parameters

        IADsGroup * pGroup          - Group to hold the new
                                      IDirectoryObject
        IADs* pIADsNewMember        - Object which will become a member of
                                      the group.
                                      Object can be a user, contact,
                                      or group.
*/
HRESULT AddMemberToGroup(IADsGroup * pGroup, IADs* pIADsNewMember)
{
    HRESULT hr = E_INVALIDARG;
    if ((!pGroup)||(!pIADsNewMember))
        return hr;
```

(continued)

(continued)

```
    // Use the IADs::get_ADsPath() member to get the ADsPath
    // Once the ADsPath string is returned, all that is needed
    // to add the new member to the group, is to call the
    // IADsGroup::Add() member, passing in the ADsPath string.
    // Ask the new member for it's AdsPath
    // This is a fully qualified LDAP path to the object to add.
    BSTR bsNewMemberPath;
    hr = pIADsNewMember->get_ADsPath(&bsNewMemberPath);
    if (SUCCEEDED(hr))
    {

        // Use the IADsGroup interface to add the new member.
        // Pass the LDAP path to the
        // new member to the IADsGroup::Add() member
        hr = pGroup->Add(bsNewMemberPath);

        // Free the string returned from IADs::get_ADsPath()
        SysFreeString(bsNewMemberPath);
    }
    return hr;
}
```

Visual Basic

The following subroutine adds a member to a group:

```
'//////////////////////////////////////////////////////////////////////
' AddUsersToGroup ()    - Function for adding users to a group
'
'     Parameters
'
'         IDirectoryObject    oDirObject     -    Parent Directory Object for
'                                                 the new group
String array   UsersList             - List of Users to add.

Sub AddUsersToGroup(oDirObject As IDirectoryObject, sUsersList() As String, ByVal
iNumUsers As Integer)
    Dim x As Integer


    ' Add the passed Users
    ' go through the list and pull out the ADsPath properties
    ' contained therein
    ' use this path to call IADsGroup::Add(), thereby adding the object
```

```
         ' to the group
     For x = 0 To iNumUsers
         Dim oIADsGroup_NewGroup As IADsGroup
         Set oIADsGroup_NewGroup = oDirObjectRet
         oIADsGroup_NewGroup.Add sUsersList(x)
Set oIADsGroup_NewGroup = Nothing
     Next x

End Sub
```

Removing Members from Groups in a Domain

You can remove users, groups, or contacts from groups. The **member** property of the group object contains all direct members of the group.

The simplest way to remove a member from a group is to use the **IADsGroup::Remove** methods on the **IADsGroup** object representing the group you want to remove members from.

Example Code for Removing a Member from a Group

The following code fragment contains a function that removes a member from a group:

```
///////////////////////////////////////////////////////////////////////
/*  RemoveMemberFromGroup()    -        Removes the passed directory object from
the membership of passed group


     Parameters

         IADsGroup * pGroup       - Group to remove the member from
         IADs* pIADsNewMember     - Object to remove.
                                    Object can be a user, contact,
                                    or group.
*/
HRESULT RemoveMemberFromGroup(IADsGroup * pGroup, IADs* pIADsNewMember)
{
    HRESULT hr = E_INVALIDARG;
    if ((!pGroup)||(!pIADsNewMember))
        return hr;

    // Use the IADs::get_ADsPath() member to get the ADsPath
    // Once the ADsPath string is returned, all that is needed to
    // remove the member from the group, is to call the
    // IADsGroup::Remove() method, passing in the ADsPath string.
    // Ask the member for it's AdsPath
```

(continued)

(continued)

```
    // This is a fully qualified LDAP path to the object to remove.
    BSTR bsNewMemberPath;
    hr = pIADsNewMember->get_ADsPath(&bsNewMemberPath);
    if (SUCCEEDED(hr))
    {

        // Use the IADsGroup interface to remove the member.
        // Pass the LDAP path to the
        // member to the IADsGroup::Remove() method
        hr = pGroup->Remove(bsNewMemberPath);

        // Free the string returned from IADs::get_ADsPath()
        SysFreeString(bsNewMemberPath);
    }
    return hr;
}
```

Nesting a Group in Another Group

Adding a group as a member of a group is called *nesting*. For distribution groups, nesting is supported in both mixed mode and native mode. For security groups, nesting is supported only on domains running in native mode.

To nest a group in another group, you use the same techniques described in Adding members to groups in a domain.

Note that depending of the scope of the group, the group can contain only specific types of groups from certain domains. For more information about the effect of group scope on members, see *Scope of groups*.

Your nesting options depend on whether the domain is in mixed mode or native mode.

Nesting in Native Mode

The following list describes what can be contained in a group that exists in a native-mode domain. This same list also applies to distribution groups in mixed-mode domains. The scope of the group determines these containment rules. Universal groups can contain user accounts, universal groups, and global groups from any domain.

Global groups can contain user accounts from the same domain, and global groups from the same domain.

Domain local groups can contain user accounts, universal groups, and global groups, all from any domain. They can also contain other domain local groups from within the same domain.

Nesting in Mixed Mode

Security groups in a mixed-mode domain can contain only the following:

- Global groups can contain only user accounts.
- Domain local groups can contain other global groups and user accounts.
- Universal groups cannot be created in mixed-mode domains because the universal scope is supported only in Windows® 2000 native-mode domains.

Note that distribution groups can be nested according to the nesting rules for native mode.

Common Errors

The following table contains a list of common errors that can occur based on the scope of the group being nested.

HRESULT	Meaning
0x8007001F	General failure. This error occurs if you attempt to add 1) a Domain Local group to a Global or Universal group, 2) a Universal group to a Global group, or 3) a Domain Local.
	Domain Local groups can only be added as members to other Domain Local groups in the same domain.
	Universal groups can be added to Universal and Domain Local groups but not Global groups.
0x8007202F	ERROR_DS_CONSTRAINT_VIOLATION. This error occurs if you attempt to nest a security group (that is, add a group as a member of another group) in another group in a domain running in mixed mode. Security groups cannot be nested in mixed mode; security groups can only be nested in native mode.

Determining a User's or Group's Membership in a Group

The **IADsGroup** interface has an **IADsGroup::IsMember** method. This method returns TRUE if the specified object is a direct member of the group, that is, the group's member property contains the specified object.

Note   A group can contain other groups (nesting). The **IADsGroup::IsMember** method does not recursively check the member properties of groups in its member property, groups within those groups, and so on. To recursively check if an object is a member of a group, you must enumerate the groups in the member property, check the members of those groups to see if the object is a member, and if those groups contain other groups, check their members, and so on.

Example Code for Checking for Membership in a Group

The following code fragment contains a function that checks for absolute membership of an object by recursively checking whether an object is a member of a group or any groups nested within that group:

```
///////////////////////////////////////////////////////////////////////////
/*  RecursiveIsMember()                             - Recursively scans the
                                                      members of passed
                                                      IADsGroup ptr
                                                      and any groups belonging
                                                      to the passed ptr- for
                                                      membership
                                                      of Passed group
                                                      Will return a TRUE if
                                                      the member is found in
                                                      the passed group,
                                                      Or if the passed member
                                                      is a member of any group
                                                      which is a member
                                                      of the passed group

    Parameters

        IADsGroup  *     pADsGroup         - Group from which to check
                                             members
        LPWSTR           pwszMember        - LDAP path for object to check
                                             membership
        BOOL             bVerbose          - IF TRUE, will output verbose
                                             information on the scanning

    OPTIONAL Parameters

        LPOLESTR  pwszUser                 - User Name and Password, if the
                                             parameters are NOT passed,
        LPOLESTER pwszPassword             - Binding will use ADsGetObject, if
                                             the parameters
                                           - Are specified, will use
```

```
                                        ADsOpenObject, passing user name
                                        and password
*/


BOOL RecursiveIsMember(IADsGroup * pADsGroup,LPWSTR pwszMemberGUID,LPWSTR
pwszMemberPath,

                                        BOOL bVerbose, LPOLESTR  pwszUser,
LPOLESTR pwszPassword)
{
    HRESULT          hr                = S_OK;       // COM Result Code
    IADsMembers *    pADsMembers       = NULL;       // Ptr to Members of
                                                     // the IADsGroup

    BOOL             fContinue         = TRUE;       // Looping Variable
    IEnumVARIANT *   pEnumVariant      = NULL;       // Ptr to the Enum
                                                     // variant

    IUnknown *       pUnknown          = NULL;       // IUnknown for
                                                     // getting the ENUM
                                                     // initially

    VARIANT          VariantArray[FETCH_NUM];        // Variant array for
                                                     // temp holding
                                                     // returned data

    ULONG            ulElementsFetched = NULL;       // Number of elements
                                                     // fetched

    BSTR             bsGroupPath       = NULL;
    BOOL             bRet              = FALSE;

    // Get the path of the object passed in
    hr = pADsGroup->get_ADsPath(&bsGroupPath);

    if (!SUCCEEDED(hr))
        return hr;

    if (bVerbose)
    {
        WCHAR pwszOutput[2048];
        wsprintf(pwszOutput,L"Checking the Group:\n\n%s\n\n for the
member:\n\n%s\n\n",bsGroupPath,pwszMemberPath);
        PrintBanner(pwszOutput);
    }

    // Get an interface pointer to the IADsCollection of members
    hr = pADsGroup->Members(&pADsMembers);

    if (SUCCEEDED(hr))
```

(continued)

(continued)

```
{
    // Ask the IADsCollection of members for a new ENUM Interface
    // Note the enum comes back as an IUnknown *
    hr = pADsMembers->get__NewEnum(&pUnknown);

    if (SUCCEEDED(hr))
    {
        // QI the IUnknown * for an IEnumVARIANT interface
        hr = pUnknown->QueryInterface(IID_IEnumVARIANT, (void
**)&pEnumVariant);

        if (SUCCEEDED(hr))
        {
            // While have not hit errors or end of data....
            while (fContinue)
            {
                ulElementsFetched = 0;
                // Get a "batch" number of group members- number
                // of rows specified by FETCH_NUM
                hr = ADsEnumerateNext(pEnumVariant, FETCH_NUM, VariantArray,
&ulElementsFetched);

                if (ulElementsFetched )
                {
                    // Loop through the current batch- printing
                    // the path for each member
                    for (ULONG i = 0; i < ulElementsFetched; i++ )
                    {
                        IDispatch * pDispatch       = NULL;
                            // ptr for holding dispath of element
                        BSTR        bstrCurrentPath  = NULL;
                            // Holds path of object
                        BSTR        bstrGuidCurrent  = NULL;
                            // Holds path of object
                        IDirectoryObject * pIDOCurrent = NULL;
                            // Holds the current object

                        // Get the dispatch ptr for the variant
                        pDispatch = VariantArray[i].pdispVal;

assert(HAS_BIT_STYLE(VariantArray[i].vt,VT_DISPATCH));

                        // Get the IADs interface for the "member"
```

```
                                    // of this group
                                    hr = pDispatch->QueryInterface(IID_IDirectoryObject,
                                                        (VOID **) &pIDOCurrent
);

                                    if (SUCCEEDED(hr))
                                    {
                                        // Retrieve the GUID for the
                                        // current object
                                        hr = GetObjectGuid(pIDOCurrent,bstrGuidCurrent);

                                        if (FAILED(hr))
                                            return hr;

                                        IADs * pIADsCurrent = NULL;

                                        // Retrieve the IADs Interface
                                        // for the current object
                                        hr = pIDOCurrent-
>QueryInterface(IID_IADs,(void**)&pIADsCurrent);
                                        if (FAILED(hr))
                                            return hr;

                                        // Get the ADsPath property for
                                        // this member
                                        hr = pIADsCurrent->get_ADsPath(&bstrCurrentPath);

                                        if (SUCCEEDED(hr))
                                        {
                                            if (bVerbose)

wprintf(L"Comparing:\n\n%s\nWITH:\n%s\n\n",bstrGuidCurrent,pwszMemberGUID);

                                            // Is the "member of this group
                                            // Equal to passed?
                                            if
(_wcsicmp(bstrGuidCurrent,pwszMemberGUID)==0)
                                            {
                                                if (bVerbose)
                                                    wprintf(L"!!!!!Object:\n\n%s\n\nIs a
member of\n\n%s\n\n",pwszMemberPath,bstrGuidCurrent);

                                                bRet = TRUE;
                                                break;
```

(continued)

(continued)

```
                                                       }
                                                    else //Otherwise, we should bind to
                                                        //this and see if it is a group
                                                    {    // If is it a group then the QI
                                                         // to IADsGroup will succeed

                                                        IADsGroup * pIADsGroupAsMember = NULL;

                                                        if (pwszUser)
                                                            hr = ADsOpenObject( bstrCurrentPath,
                                                                                pwszUser,
                                                                                pwszPassword,
ADS_SECURE_AUTHENTICATION,

                                                                                IID_IADsGroup,
                                                                                (void**)
&pIADsGroupAsMember);
                                                    else
                                                        hr = ADsGetObject( bstrCurrentPath,
IID_IADsGroup,(void **)&pIADsGroupAsMember);

                                                        // If we DID bind, then this IS
                                                        // a group
                                                        if (SUCCEEDED(hr))
                                                        {
                                                            // Recursively call
                                                            // ourselves to check THIS
                                                            // group
                                                            BOOL bRetRecurse;
                                                            bRetRecurse =
RecursiveIsMember(pIADsGroupAsMember,pwszMemberGUID,pwszMemberPath,bVerbose,pwszU
ser ,pwszPassword );

                                                            if (bRetRecurse)
                                                            {
                                                                bRet = TRUE;
                                                                break;
                                                            }
                                                            pIADsGroupAsMember->Release();
                                                            pIADsGroupAsMember = NULL;
                                                        }
                                                    }
                                                    SysFreeString(bstrCurrentPath);
                                                    bstrCurrentPath = NULL;
```

```
                                    SysFreeString(bstrGuidCurrent);
                                    bstrGuidCurrent = NULL;
                                }
                                // Release
                                pIDOCurrent->Release();
                                pIDOCurrent = NULL;
                                if (pIADsCurrent)
                                {
                                    pIADsCurrent->Release();
                                    pIADsCurrent = NULL;
                                }
                            }
                        }
                        // Clear the variant array
                        memset(VariantArray, 0, sizeof(VARIANT)*FETCH_NUM);
                    }
                    else
                        fContinue = FALSE;
                }
                pEnumVariant->Release();
                pEnumVariant = NULL;
            }
            pUnknown->Release();
            pUnknown = NULL;
        }
        pADsMembers ->Release();
        pADsMembers  = NULL;
    }

    // Free the group path if it was retrieved.
    if (bsGroupPath)
    {
        SysFreeString(bsGroupPath);
        bsGroupPath = NULL;
    }
    return bRet;
}
//////////////////////////////////////////////////////////////////////////
/*  GetObjectGuid()     - Retrieves the GUID in String form from the
                          passed Directory Object
                          Returns S_OK on success

    Parameters
```

(continued)

(continued)

```
        IDirectoryObject *  pDO    -  Directory Object from where GUID
                                      will be retrieved.
        BSTR               &  bsGuid -  Returned GUID
*/

HRESULT GetObjectGuid(IDirectoryObject * pDO,BSTR &bsGuid)
{

    GUID *pObjectGUID    = NULL;
    PADS_ATTR_INFO       pAttributeEntries;
    LPWSTR               pAttributeName = L"objectGUID";
                                    //Get the GUID for the object
    DWORD                dwAttributesReturned = 0;
    HRESULT              hr;
    hr = pDO->GetObjectAttributes(  &pAttributeName, //objectGUID
                                    1, //Only objectGUID
                                    &pAttributeEntries,
                                        // Returned attributes
                                    &dwAttributesReturned
                                        //Number of attributes returned
                                    );


    if (SUCCEEDED(hr) && dwAttributesReturned>0)
    {
        //Make sure that we got the right type--objectGUID is
ADSTYPE_OCTET_STRING
        if (pAttributeEntries->dwADsType == ADSTYPE_OCTET_STRING)
        {
            //Get COM converted string version of the GUID
            // lpvalue should be LPBYTE. Should be able to
            // cast it to ptr to GUID.
            pObjectGUID = (GUID*)(pAttributeEntries-
>pADsValues[0].OctetString.lpValue);


            //OLE str to fit a GUID

            LPOLESTR szGUID = new WCHAR [64];
            szGUID[0]=NULL;
            //Convert GUID to string.
            ::StringFromGUID2(*pObjectGUID, szGUID, 39);
            bsGuid = SysAllocString(szGUID);

            delete [] szGUID;
```

```
        }
    }

    return hr;

}
////////////////////////////////////////////////////////////////////////////
/*  PrintBanner()    -        Prints a banner on the screen

    Parameters

            LPOLESTR pwszBanner   - String to print
*/
void PrintBanner(LPOLESTR pwszBanner)
{
    _putws(L"");
    _putws(L"///////////////////////////////////////////////////////");
    wprintf(L"\t");
    _putws(pwszBanner);
    _putws(L"///////////////////////////////////////////////////////\n");
}
```

Enumerating Groups

This section contains the following information:

- Enumerating Groups in a Domain
- Enumerating Groups by Scope or Type in a Domain
- Enumerating Members in a Group
- Enumerating Groups That Contain Many Members

Enumerating Groups in a Domain

Unlike Windows NT® 4.0 domains, Windows® 2000 groups can be placed in any container or organizational unit in a domain as well as the root of the domain. This means that groups can be in numerous locations in the directory hierarchy. Therefore, you have two choices for enumerating groups:

1. Enumerate the groups directly contained in a container, OU, or at the root of the domain.

   Explicitly bind to the container object containing the groups you are interested in enumerating, set a filter containing "groups" as the class using the **IADsContainer::put_Filter** property method, and use the **IADsContainer::get__NewEnum** method to enumerate the group objects.

This technique is useful if you want to enumerate groups that are directly contained in a container or OU object. If the container contains other containers that can potentially contain other groups, you need to bind to those containers and recursively enumerate the groups on those containers. If you do not need to manipulate the group objects and only need to read specific properties, you should use the deep search described in option 2.

2. Because enumeration returns pointers to ADSI COM objects representing each group object, you can call **QueryInterface** to get **IADs**, **IADsGroup**, and **IADsPropertyList** interface pointers to the group object. This means you can get interface pointers to each enumerated group object in a container without having to explicitly bind to each group object. If you wanted to perform operations on all the groups directly within a container, enumeration saves you from having to bind to each group in order to call **IADs** or **IADsGroup** methods. If you only want to retrieve specific properties from groups, you should use **IDirectorySearch** as described in option 3.

3. Perform a deep search for objectCategory=group to find all groups in a tree.

   First, bind to the container object where you want to begin the search. For example, if you wanted to find all groups in a domain, you would bind to root of the domain; if you wanted to find all groups in the forest, you would bind to global catalog and search from the root of the GC.

   Then use **IDirectorySearch** to query using a search filter containing (objectCategory=group) and search preference of ADS_SCOPE_SUBTREE.

   Note   You can perform a search with a search preference of ADS_SCOPE_ONELEVEL to limit the search to the direct contents of the container object that you bound to.

   IDirectorySearch retrieves only the values of specific properties from groups. If you only want to retrieve values, you should use **IDirectorySearch**. If you want to manipulate the group objects returned from a search (that is, you want to use **IADs** or **IADsGroup** methods), you must explicitly bind to them (to do this, specify **distinguishedName** as one of the properties to return from the search and use the returned distinguished names to bind to each group returned in the search).

   Only specific properties are retrieved. You cannot retrieve all attributes without explicitly specifying every possible attribute of the group class.

Enumerating Groups by Scope or Type in a Domain

In Windows® 2000 domains, there is single class called group for all group scopes (Domain Local, Global, Universal) and types (security, distribution). The **groupType** property of the group object specifies the group type and scope.

To use type or scope to enumerate or search for groups on Windows 2000 domains, you must use a filter that contains a matching rule for the **groupType** property.

Matching rules have the following syntax:

attributename:*ruleOID*:=*value*

where *attributename* is the ldapDisplayName of the attribute, *ruleOID* is the OID for the matching rule, and *value* is the value you want to use for comparison. Spaces are not allowed in this string. Also, *value* must be a decimal number; it cannot be a hexadecimal number or a constant name such as ADS_GROUP_TYPE_SECURITY_ENABLED.

Active Directory supports the two matching rules shown in the following table.

Matching Rule OID	Description
1.2.840.113556.1.4.803	LDAP_MATCHING_RULE_BIT_AND
	The matching rule is true only if all bits from the property match the value. This rule is like the bit-wise AND operator.
1.2.840.113556.1.4.804	LDAP_MATCHING_RULE_BIT_OR
	The matching rule is true if any bits from the property match the value. This rule is like the bit-wise OR operator.

Example Query Strings

The following query string searches for security groups. It uses the decimal equivalent of the ADS_GROUP_TYPE_SECURITY_ENABLED flag:

```
(&(objectCategory=group)(groupType:1.2.840.113556.1.4.804:=2147483648) )
```

The following query string searches for Universal distribution groups (that is, Universal groups without ADS_GROUP_TYPE_SECURITY_ENABLED flag). The filter uses 8 as the decimal equivalent of ADS_GROUP_TYPE_UNIVERSAL_GROUP, and 2147483656 as the decimal equivalent of ADS_GROUP_TYPE_UNIVERSAL_GROUP + ADS_GROUP_TYPE_SECURITY_ENABLED.

```
(&(objectCategory=group)((&(groupType:1.2.840.113556.1.4.804:=8)(!(groupType:1.2.
840.113556.1.4.803:=2147483656)))) )
```

The following query string searches for all Universal groups—this includes Universal groups that are of type security as well as distribution:

```
(&(objectCategory=group)(groupType:1.2.840.113556.1.4.804:=8) )
```

The following query string searches for Universal security groups:

```
(&(objectCategory=group)(groupType:1.2.840.113556.1.4.803:=2147483656) )
```

Example Code for Building a Query String to Search for Groups by Type/Scope

```
C++
```

The following code fragment contains a function that creates a query string that uses type or scope for enumerating or searching for groups.

```
////////////////////
// Enum Definitions
//This first enum should be defined for Beta 3 and later.
enum
    {    ADS_GROUP_TYPE_GLOBAL_GROUP     = 0x2,
    ADS_GROUP_TYPE_DOMAIN_LOCAL_GROUP    = 0x4,
    ADS_GROUP_TYPE_UNIVERSAL_GROUP     = 0x8,
    ADS_GROUP_TYPE_SECURITY_ENABLED    = 0x80000000
    };

// (used for telling BuildGroupTypeQueryString() how
// to build the string)
enum ELDAPMatchingRule
{
    lmrAND,
    lmrOR
};
///////////////////////////////////////////////////////////////////////
/*  BuildGroupTypeQueryString()   - Builds a Query String for searching
                                   on groupType

    Parameters

        ELDAPMatchingRule elmrRule      - Specifies whether the passed
                                          bitmask is ANDed or ORed
        DWORD dwGroupTypeBits           - Bitflags for groupType

*/
WCHAR * BuildGroupTypeQueryString(ELDAPMatchingRule elmrRule, DWORD
dwGroupTypeBits)
{
    static WCHAR wszRet [255];
    wszRet[0] = 01;
    /*
        The LDAP_MATCHING RULE is defined as follows:

        LDAP_MATCHING_RULE_BIT_OR 1.2.840.113556.1.4.804
        LDAP_MATCHING_RULE_BIT_AND 1.2.840.113556.1.4.803

        These strings are used to describe the bits in dwGroupTypeBits.
        Specifying an "and" (using LDAP_MATCHING_RULE_BIT_AND) causes
        the query to mean a bit-wise "and" for the bits in
        dwGroupTypeBits. Alternatively, specifying
        LDAP_MATCHING_RULE_BIT_OR denotes a bit-wise "or" of the flags
```

```
            present in dwGroupTypeBits
    */
    switch (elmrRule)
    {
        case lmrAND:

wsprintf(wszRet,L"(groupType:1.2.840.113556.1.4.803:=%d)",dwGroupTypeBits);
        break;
        case lmrOR:

wsprintf(wszRet,L"(groupType:1.2.840.113556.1.4.804:=%d)",dwGroupTypeBits);
        break;
    }
    OutputDebugStringW(wszRet);
    OutputDebugStringW(L"\r\n");
    return wszRet;
}
```

Visual Basic

When using Visual Basic®, use the ADO SQL syntax for specifying Group Type.

Definitions for bit values:

```
Public Const ADS_GROUP_TYPE_GLOBAL_GROUP = &H2
Public Const ADS_GROUP_TYPE_DOMAIN_LOCAL_GROUP = &H4
Public Const ADS_GROUP_TYPE_UNIVERSAL_GROUP = &H8
Public Const ADS_GROUP_TYPE_SECURITY_ENABLED = &H80000000
```

Query Strings:

ALL GLOBAL GROUPS

```
"GroupType=" & Str(ADS_GROUP_TYPE_GLOBAL_GROUP) & " or " & "GroupType=" &
Str(ADS_GROUP_TYPE_GLOBAL_GROUP Or ADS_GROUP_TYPE_SECURITY_ENABLED)
```

ALL DOMAIN LOCAL GROUPS (With and without Security)

```
"GroupType=" & Str(ADS_GROUP_TYPE_DOMAIN_LOCAL_GROUP) & " or " & "GroupType=" &
Str(ADS_GROUP_TYPE_DOMAIN_LOCAL_GROUP Or ADS_GROUP_TYPE_SECURITY_ENABLED)
```

ALL SECURITY ENABLED GROUPS

```
"GroupType=" & Str(ADS_GROUP_TYPE_SECURITY_ENABLED)
```

The code fragment on the next page searches for groups based on type using the BuildGroupTypeQueryString subroutine.

```
'**********************************
'  QueryAndOutputGroups()  -  Performs several sample searches using ADO
'
'
'    Parameters
'
'        oDirObjectRoot As IDirectoryObject - The root from where
'                                             searches will be performed
'
Sub QueryAndOutputGroups(oDirObjectRoot As IDirectoryObject)

    '*****************************
    ' Search for all the groups
    DisplayMessage " "
    DisplayMessage "<<<<<<<<<<<<<<<<<<<<<<<ALL GROUPS>>>>>>>>>>>>>>>>>>" 'cn = 'UG*'
objectCategory
    SimpleDirectorySearch oDirObjectRoot, "objectCategory = 'group'", ADS_SCOPE_SUBTREE

    '*****************************************
    ' Search for all the GLOBAL groups
    DisplayMessage " "
    DisplayMsgWaitForInput "Hit OK to perform a subtree search of all the GLOBAL groups"
    DisplayMessage " "
    DisplayMessage "<<<<<<<<<<<<<<<<<<<<<<<ALL GLOBAL Groups>>>>>>>>>>>>>>>>>>"
    SimpleDirectorySearch oDirObjectRoot, "GroupType=" & Str(ADS_GROUP_TYPE_GLOBAL_GROUP)
& " or " & _
                          "GroupType=" & Str(ADS_GROUP_TYPE_GLOBAL_GROUP Or
ADS_GROUP_TYPE_SECURITY_ENABLED), _
                          ADS_SCOPE_SUBTREE

    '*****************************************
    ' Search for all the DOMAIN LOCAL  groups
    DisplayMessage " "
    DisplayMsgWaitForInput "Hit OK to perform a subtree search of all the DOMAIN LOCAL
groups"
    DisplayMessage " "
    DisplayMessage "<<<<<<<<<<<<<<<<<<<<<<<ALL Domain Local Groups>>>>>>>>>>>>>>>>>>"
    SimpleDirectorySearch oDirObjectRoot, "GroupType=" &
Str(ADS_GROUP_TYPE_DOMAIN_LOCAL_GROUP) & " or " & _
                          "GroupType=" & Str(ADS_GROUP_TYPE_DOMAIN_LOCAL_GROUP Or
ADS_GROUP_TYPE_SECURITY_ENABLED), _
                          ADS_SCOPE_SUBTREE

    '        #ifdef USE_UNIVERSAL_GROUPS
```

```
'*******************************************
' Search for all the UNIVERSAL  groups
DisplayMessage " "
DisplayMsgWaitForInput "Hit OK to perform a subtree search of all the UNIVERSAL
groups"
DisplayMessage " "
DisplayMessage "<<<<<<<<<<<<<<<<<<<<<<ALL Universal Groups>>>>>>>>>>>>>>>>>"
SimpleDirectorySearch oDirObjectRoot, "GroupType=" &
Str(ADS_GROUP_TYPE_UNIVERSAL_GROUP) & " or " & _
                         "GroupType=" & Str(ADS_GROUP_TYPE_UNIVERSAL_GROUP Or
ADS_GROUP_TYPE_SECURITY_ENABLED), _
                         ADS_SCOPE_SUBTREE
'         #End If


'*******************************************
' Search for all the Security Enabled  groups
DisplayMessage " "
DisplayMsgWaitForInput "Hit OK to perform a subtree search of all Security Enabled
groups"
DisplayMessage " "
DisplayMessage "<<<<<<<<<<<<<<<<<<<<<<<ALL Security Enabled Groups>>>>>>>>>>>>>>>>>"
SimpleDirectorySearch oDirObjectRoot, "GroupType=" &
Str(ADS_GROUP_TYPE_SECURITY_ENABLED) & " or " & _
                         "GroupType=" & Str(ADS_GROUP_TYPE_SECURITY_ENABLED Or
ADS_GROUP_TYPE_SECURITY_ENABLED), _
                         ADS_SCOPE_SUBTREE


'*******************************************
' Search for all the Security Enabled LOCAL groups
DisplayMessage " "
DisplayMsgWaitForInput "Hit OK to perform a subtree search of all Security Enabled
LOCAL groups"
DisplayMessage " "
DisplayMessage "<<<<<<<<<<<<<<<<<<<<<<<<ALL Security Enabled Domain Local
Groups>>>>>>>>>>>>>>>>>"
SimpleDirectorySearch oDirObjectRoot, "GroupType=" &
Str(ADS_GROUP_TYPE_DOMAIN_LOCAL_GROUP Or _
                         ADS_GROUP_TYPE_SECURITY_ENABLED), _
                         ADS_SCOPE_SUBTREE


'*******************************************
' Search for all the DOMAIN LOCAL groups whose
```

(continued)

(continued)

```
    ' name begins with 'UGExercise'
    DisplayMessage " "
    DisplayMsgWaitForInput "Hit OK to perform a subtree search of all DOMAIN LOCAL  groups
that begin with the text 'UGExercise'"
    DisplayMessage " "
    DisplayMessage "<<<<<<<<<<<<<<<<<<<<<<<ALL Domain Local Groups Beginnig with
'UGExercise' >>>>>>>>>>>>>>>>"

    SimpleDirectorySearch oDirObjectRoot, "cn='UGExercise*' and (GroupType=" & _
                         Str(ADS_GROUP_TYPE_DOMAIN_LOCAL_GROUP) & " or GroupType=" & _
                         Str(ADS_GROUP_TYPE_DOMAIN_LOCAL_GROUP Or
ADS_GROUP_TYPE_SECURITY_ENABLED) & _
                         ")", ADS_SCOPE_SUBTREE


    '****************************************
    ' Search for ALL the groups whose
    ' name begins with 'UGExercise'
    DisplayMessage " "
    DisplayMsgWaitForInput "Hit OK to perform a subtree search of ALL groups that begin
with the text 'UGExercise '"
    DisplayMessage " "
    DisplayMessage "<<<<<<<<<<<<<<<<<<<<<<<ALL Groups Beginning with 'UGExercise'
>>>>>>>>>>>>>>>>"

    SimpleDirectorySearch oDirObjectRoot, " cn='UGExercise*' and objectCategory='group'",
ADS_SCOPE_SUBTREE

End Sub

'///////////////////////////////////////////////////////////////////////
'    SimpleDirectorySearch()    - Uses ADO to search the directory
'                                 Results are displayed in the list box
'    Parameters
'
'        oDirObjectRoot As IDirectoryObject    - Root of the search
'        ByVal sSearchFilter As String         - LDAP Search filter
'        ByVal lScope As Integer               - Scope for Searching
'                                                possible values are:
'                                                ADS_SCOPE_BASE
'                                                ADS_SCOPE_ONELEVEL
'                                                ADS_SCOPE_SUBTREE
'
'        (See IDirectorySearch and ADS_SCOPEENUM in the
```

```
'       docs for more info)
'
Sub SimpleDirectorySearch(oDirObjectRoot As IDirectoryObject, ByVal sSearchFilter As
String, ByVal lScope As Integer)

    Dim iIndex As Integer
    iIndex = 0
    Dim v, j, i

    Dim con As New Connection, rs As New Recordset
    Dim Com As New Command
    Dim oIADs As IADs
    Dim sAdsPathRoot As String

    ' Get the LDAP path to the passed in object
    sAdsPathRoot = GetAdsPath(oDirObjectRoot)

    'Open a Connection object
    con.Provider = "ADsDSOObject"

    '------------------------------------------------------------------------
    ' To be authenticated using alternate credentials
    ' use connection properties of User ID and Password
    '------------------------------------------------------------------------
    ' con.Properties("User ID") = "Administrator"
    ' con.Properties("Password") = ""

    '. Open the connection
    con.Open "Active Directory Provider"

    ' Create a command object on this connection
    Set Com.ActiveConnection = con

    ' set the query string using SQL Dialect
    Com.CommandText = "select name,AdsPath from '" & sAdsPathRoot & "' where " &
sSearchFilter & " ORDER BY NAME"

    ' Tell the user what the search filter is
    DisplayMessage "Search Filter = " & Com.CommandText

    '---------------------------------------------------------
    ' Or you can use LDAP Dialect, for example,
    '---------------------------------------------------------
    ' Ex Com.CommandText =
```

(continued)

(continued)

```
' "<LDAP://Microsoftsvr1/dc=Microsoft,DC=com>;(objectClass=*);name"
' For LDAP Dialect, the valid search scope are base,
' oneLevel and subtree
' Com.CommandText = "<" & adDomainPath &
' ">;(objectClass=*);name;subtree"
' For LDAP Dialect (<LDAP:...>), there is no way to specify
' sort order in the string,
' However, you can use this SORT ON property to specify sort order.
' for SQL Dialect you can use ORDER BY in the SQL Statement
' Ex. Com.Properties("Sort On") = "Name"

'Set the preferences for Search
Com.Properties("Page Size") = 1000
Com.Properties("Timeout") = 30 'seconds
Com.Properties("searchscope") = lScope
Com.Properties("Chase referrals") = ADS_CHASE_REFERRALS_EXTERNAL
Com.Properties("Cache Results") = False ' do not cache the result, it results in less
memory requirements

'Execute the query
Set rs = Com.Execute

' Tell the user how many rows
DisplayMessage "Returned " & Str(rs.RecordCount) & " rows"

' Navigate the record set
If Not rs.EOF Then
    rs.MoveFirst
End If

On Error Resume Next
While Not rs.EOF
    ' Display the LDAP path for the row
    DisplayMessage rs.Fields("AdsPath")
    rs.MoveNext
Wend

End Sub
```

Enumerating Members in a Group

The members of a group are stored in a multi-valued property called **member**. For groups with a small to medium-sized membership, you can use the **IADsGroup::Members** method to get a pointer to an **IADsMembers** object containing the list of all members and then use the **IADsMembers::get__NewEnum** to get an enumerator object that you can use to enumerate the members.

For the group membership is potentially large, you should use ranging to retrieve users one range at a time. For information on using ranging to enumerate members, see *Enumerating Groups That Contain Many Members*.

Example Code for Displaying Members of a Group

C++

The following code fragment contains a function that displays the members of a group using **IADsGroup** and **IADsMembers**:

```
/////////////////////////////////
/*  PrintGroupObjectMembers()
- Prints the members of the group that the pADsGroup passes.
    Parameters
        IADsGroup * pADsGroup      - Group from which to list members
*/
HRESULT PrintGroupObjectMembers(IADsGroup * pADsGroup)
{
    HRESULT          hr                = S_OK;      // COM Result Code
    IADsMembers *    pADsMembers       = NULL;      // Ptr to Members of
                                                    // the IADsGroup
    BOOL             fContinue         = TRUE;      // Looping Variable
    IEnumVARIANT *   pEnumVariant      = NULL;      // Ptr to the Enum
                                                    // variant
    IUnknown *       pUnknown          = NULL;      // IUnknown for
                                                    // getting the ENUM
                                                    // initially
    VARIANT          VariantArray[FETCH_NUM];       // Variant array for
                                                    // temp holding
                                                    // returned data
    ULONG            ulElementsFetched = NULL;      // Number of elements
                                                    // fetched

    // Get an interface pointer to the IADsCollection of members
    hr = pADsGroup->Members(&pADsMembers);

    if (SUCCEEDED(hr))
    {

        // Ask the IADsCollection of members for a new ENUM Interface
        // Note the enum comes back as an IUnknown *
        hr = pADsMembers->get__NewEnum(&pUnknown);

        if (SUCCEEDED(hr))
```

(continued)

(continued)

```
        {

                // QI the IUnknown * for a IEnumVARIANT interface
                hr = pUnknown->QueryInterface(IID_IEnumVARIANT, (void
**)&pEnumVariant);

                if (SUCCEEDED(hr))
                {

                        // While have not hit errors or end of data....
                        while (fContinue)
                        {
                            ulElementsFetched = 0;

                                // Get a "batch" number of group members- number
                                // of rows that FETCH_NUM specifies
                                hr = ADsEnumerateNext(pEnumVariant, FETCH_NUM, VariantArray,
&ulElementsFetched);

                                if (ulElementsFetched )//SUCCEEDED(hr) && hr != S_FALSE)
                                {

                                        // Loop through the current batch, printing
                                        // the path for each member
                                        for (ULONG i = 0; i < ulElementsFetched; i++ )
                                        {
                                            IDispatch * pDispatch        = NULL;
                                            // ptr for holding dispath of element
                                            IADs       * pIADsGroupMember = NULL;
                                            // IADs ptr to group member
                                            BSTR         bstrPath         = NULL;
                                            // Holds path of object

                                            // Get the dispatch ptr for the variant
                                            pDispatch = VariantArray[i].pdispVal;
assert(HAS_BIT_STYLE(VariantArray[i].vt,VT_DISPATCH));

                                            // Get the IADs interface for the "member"
                                            // of this group
                                            hr = pDispatch->QueryInterface(IID_IADs,
                                                                    (VOID **)
&pIADsGroupMember) ;
```

```
                              if (SUCCEEDED(hr))
                              {

                              // Get the ADsPath property for
                              //this member
                                  hr = pIADsGroupMember->get_ADsPath(&bstrPath) ;

                                  if (SUCCEEDED(hr))
                                  {

                                      // Print the ADsPath of the
                                      //group member
                                      wprintf(L"\tMember Object: %ws\n", bstrPath);
                                      SysFreeString(bstrPath);
                                  }
                                  pIADsGroupMember->Release();
                                  pIADsGroupMember   = NULL;

                              }
                          }

                      // Clear the variant array
                      memset(VariantArray, 0, sizeof(VARIANT)*FETCH_NUM);
                  }
                  else
                      fContinue = FALSE;
              }
          pEnumVariant->Release();
          pEnumVariant = NULL;
          }
      pUnknown->Release();
      pUnknown = NULL;
      }
    pADsMembers ->Release();
    pADsMembers  = NULL;
    }

// If everything WENT ok, all the data
// was printed,  and an S_FALSE (indicating
// no more data) was received. If that is the case,
// you REALLY want to return an S_OK
if (hr == S_FALSE)
    hr = S_OK;


return hr;
}
```

Visual Basic

The following code fragment contains a function that displays the members of a group:

```
'////////////////////////////////////////////////////////////////////////////
'    PrintGroupObjectMembers()     - Prints the members of passed
'                                    IADsGroup ptr
'
'    Parameters
'
'        oADsGroup As IADsGroup    - Group from which to list members
'
'HRESULT PrintGroupObjectMembers(IADsGroup * pADsGroup)
Sub PrintGroupObjectMembers(oADsGroup As IADsGroup)

    Dim child As IADs
    For Each child In oADsGroup.Members
        PrintIADSObject child
    Next child

End Sub
```

Enumerating Groups That Contain Many Members

The members of a group are stored in a multi-valued property called **member**. The group membership may potentially contain a large number of values. This can be inconvenient or even impossible when the number of values in a multi-valued attribute becomes very large.

Active Directory supports incremental retrievals for this purpose. You may specify the range specifiers for multi-valued properties.

Range specifiers for a property take the following form:

attributename;Range=*range*

where *attributename* is the ldapDisplayName of the attribute and *range* is the range of values that you want to retrieve from the property. The * wildcard can be used to specify "to the end of the list" and 0 is used to specify the first entry in the list.

The following table contains examples of range specifiers.

Example	Meaning
Member;Range=0-500	Retrieve entries from 0 to 500 inclusively. The maximum potential entries are 501 values.
Member;Range=2-3	Retrieve the 3rd and 4th entries.
Member;Range=501-*	Retrieve the 502nd entry and beyond.

IDirectorySearch, **IDirectoryObject**, and ADO support range retrievals.

ADO SQL Dialect

In ADO using SQL dialect, you must use single quotes around the attribute and range specifier.

For example:

```
Command.Text = "select Name, 'member;Range=0-50' from
'LDAP://CN=Group1,DC=Microsoft,DC=Com'  where objectCategory='group'"
```

ADO LDAP Dialect

In ADO using LDAP dialect, the attribute and its range specifier do not use quotes.

For example:

```
Command.Text = <LDAP://CN=NewGroup,DC=Microsoft,DC=Com>;(objectCategory=group);
name,member;Range=51-*;base"
```

IDirectorySearch and IDirectoryObject

When you use **IDirectorySearch** or **IDirectoryObject**, the attribute and range specifier replace the name of the attribute in the **pAttributesName** array that specifies the names of the attributes to return from the **IDirectorySearch::ExecuteSearch** and **IDirectoryObject::GetObjectAttributes** methods.

For example:

```
LPWSTR pszAttrs[2];

pszAttrs[0] = L"Name";
pszAttrs[1] = L"member;Range=0-100";
```

Example Code for Using Ranging to Retrieve Members of a Group

```
C++
```

The following code fragment contains a function that uses ranging to retrieve the members of a group using **IDirectoryObject**:

```
//////////////////////////////////////////////////////////////////////////
/*  PrintAttributeWithRanging()    - Uses IDirectoryObject to read an
                                      attribute with ADSI ranging


    Parameters

        IDirectoryObject * pDirObject    - Object from which the
                                           attribute will be read

        LPOLESTR pwszAttribute           - Name of the attribute
        int iNumToDisplayAtATime         - Number of Attributes to
                                           retrieve at a time
```

(continued)

(continued)

```
*/
HRESULT PrintAttributeWithRanging(IDirectoryObject * pDirObject,LPOLESTR
pwszAttribute, int iNumToDisplayAtATime)
{
    HRESULT hr = S_OK;

    ADS_ATTR_INFO    *pAttrInfo=NULL;
    // Returned Data
    DWORD            dwReturn;
    // number of returned elements
    WCHAR            pwszRangeAttrib[512];
    // String for building Range
    LPWSTR           pAttrNames[]={pwszRangeAttrib};
    // Array for passing attribute array
    DWORD            dwNumAttr =sizeof(pAttrNames)/sizeof(LPWSTR);
    // Number of attributes requested

    // Do a series of range searches, grabbing
    // iNumToDisplayAtATime at a time.
    int iRange = 0;
    DWORD dAttribsGotten = 0;

    while (SUCCEEDED(hr))
    {
        int     iAttribsGottenLastSrch =0;

        // Build the Range String : ex: L"Member;Range=0-5"
        swprintf(pwszRangeAttrib,L"%s;Range=%d-
%d",pwszAttribute,iRange,iRange+iNumToDisplayAtATime-1);

        // Get the object Attributes
        hr = pDirObject->GetObjectAttributes(pAttrNames,
                                             dwNumAttr,
                                             &pAttrInfo,
                                             &dwReturn );

        if(SUCCEEDED(hr))
        {

            // Loop through all the rows returned
            for (DWORD x = 0; x< dwReturn; x++)
            {

                // Switch on TYPE returned
```

```
            switch ((pAttrInfo+x)->dwADsType)
            {
                case ADSTYPE_DN_STRING:
                case ADSTYPE_CASE_EXACT_STRING:
                case ADSTYPE_CASE_IGNORE_STRING:
                case ADSTYPE_PRINTABLE_STRING:
                {

                    // If the returned value is multi-valued
                    //(which it is when using ranging),
                    // then loop through all the values in
                    //the multi-value
                    for (DWORD dwVal = 0 ; dwVal < (pAttrInfo+x)-
>dwNumValues; dwVal++)
                    {

                        // Print the values in the multi-valued
                        //return data
                        wprintf(L"%d: %s =
%s\n",dAttribsGotten,(pAttrInfo+x)->pszAttrName,((pAttrInfo+x)-
>pADsValues+dwVal)->CaseIgnoreString);

                        // Increment some counters for checking
                        // whether LESS data was
                        // returned than was asked for (which
                        // means you are done)
                        dAttribsGotten++;
                        iAttribsGottenLastSrch++;
                    }
                    break;
                }
                default:
                    wprintf(L"%d: %s = !!UnHandled
Type!!\n",dAttribsGotten,(pAttrInfo+x)->pszAttrName);

                FreeADsMem( pAttrInfo );
                pAttrInfo = NULL;
            }
        }
    }

    if (FAILED(hr) || hr ==S_ADS_NOMORE_ROWS || iAttribsGottenLastSrch== 0 ||
                                        iAttribsGottenLastSrch<
iNumToDisplayAtATime  )
```

(continued)

(continued)

```
        break;

    // Increment the range counter, so the next string that is
    // built will get the next range
    iRange += iNumToDisplayAtATime;
    }


    // Use FreeADsMem for all memory obtained from ADSI call
    return S_OK;
}
```

Visual Basic

The following code fragment contains a subroutine that uses ranging to retrieve the
members of a group:

```
'///////////////////////////////////////////////////////////////////////
'    PrintAttributeWithRanging()     - Uses ADO to read an attribute with
'                                      ADSI Ranging
'
'    Parameters
'
'        oDirObject  pDirObject As IDirectoryObject - Object from which
'                                                      the attribute will
'                                                      be read
'        ByVal sAttribute As String                 - Name of the
'                                                      attribute
'        ByVal iNumToDisplayAtATime As Integer       - Number of
'                                                      Attributes to
'                                                      retrieve at a time
'
'
Sub PrintAttributeWithRanging(oDirObject As IDirectoryObject, ByVal sAttribute As
String, ByVal iNumToDisplayAtATime As Integer)
    Dim iIndex As Integer
    iIndex = 0
    Dim j, i

    Dim con As New Connection, rs As New Recordset
    Dim Com As New Command
    Dim oIADs As IADs
    Dim sAdsPathRoot As String

    ' Get the LDAP path to the passed in object
    sAdsPathRoot = GetAdsPath(oDirObject)
```

```
'Open a Connection object
con.Provider = "ADsDSOObject"

'-------------------------------------------------------------
' To be authenticated using alternate credentials
' use connection properties of User ID and Password
'-------------------------------------------------------------
' con.Properties("User ID") = "Administrator"
' con.Properties("Password") = ""

' Open the connection
con.Open "Active Directory Provider"

' Create a command object on this connection
Set Com.ActiveConnection = con

Dim iNumLastReturned As Integer
Dim iTotalAttribs As Integer          .
Dim iRange As Integer

iTotalAttribs = 0
iRange = 0

Do
     ' set the query string using SQL Dialect
     Com.CommandText = "SELECT  '" & sAttribute & "';Range=" &
Trim(Str(iRange)) & "-" & Trim(Str(iRange + iNumToDisplayAtATime)) & "' FROM '" &
sAdsPathRoot & "' WHERE CN='*'"
     ' Tell the user what the search filter is
     DisplayMessage "Search Filter = " & Com.CommandText


     '-----------------------------------------------------
     ' Or you can use LDAP Dialect, for example,
     '-----------------------------------------------------
     ' Ex Com.CommandText =
     ' "<LDAP://Microsoft1/dc=Microsoft,DC=com>;(objectClass=*);name"
     ' For LDAP Dialect, the valid search scope are base, oneLevel
     ' and subtree
     ' Com.CommandText = "<" & adDomainPath &
     ' ">;(objectClass=*);name;subtree"
     ' For LDAP Dialect (<LDAP:...>), there is no way to specify sort
     ' order in the string,
     ' However, you can use this SORT ON property to specify sort
```

(continued)

(continued)

```
' order.
' for SQL Dialect you can use ORDER BY in the SQL Statement
' Ex. Com.Properties("Sort On") = "Name"

'Set the preferences for Search
Com.Properties("Page Size") = 1000
Com.Properties("Timeout") = 30 'seconds
Com.Properties("searchscope") = ADS_SCOPE_BASE
Com.Properties("Chase referrals") = ADS_CHASE_REFERRALS_EXTERNAL
Com.Properties("Cache Results") = False ' do not cache the
                                        ' result, it results in
                                        ' less memory
                                        ' requirements


'Execute the query
Set rs = Com.Execute


' Tell the user how many rows
DisplayMessage "Returned " & Str(rs.RecordCount) & " rows"
iNumLastReturned = 0
' Navigate the record set
If Not rs.EOF Then
    rs.MoveFirst
End If
Dim f As Field
Dim iCount As Integer
iCount = 0

On Error Resume Next
While Not rs.EOF
    For Each f In rs.Fields
        ' Is the value a Variant Array?
        If TypeName(f.Value) = "Variant()" Then
            Dim v As Variant
            For Each v In f.Value
                DisplayMessage f.Name & " (" & iTotalAttribs & ")" & "-"
& v
                iCount = iCount + 1
                iNumLastReturned = iNumLastReturned + 1
                iTotalAttribs = iTotalAttribs + 1
            Next v
        Else
            ' Otherwise display a single valued attribute
            DisplayMessage f.Name & f.Value 'rs.Fields("AdsPath")
```

```
              End If
          Next f
          rs.MoveNext
      Wend
      Set rs = Nothing
      Set f = Nothing
      iRange = iRange + iNumToDisplayAtATime
  Loop While iNumLastReturned > 0

End Sub
```

Example Code for Ranging with IDirectorySearch

The following C++ code fragment contains a function that uses ranging to retrieve the members of a group using **IDirectorySearch**:

```
//////////////////////////////////////////////////////////////////////////
/*   PrintAttributeWithRanging()     - Uses IDirectorySearch to read an
                                       attribute with ADSI ranging


     Parameters

         IDirectoryObject * pDirObject   - Object from which the
                                           attribute will be read
         LPOLESTR pwszAttribute          - Name of the attribute
         int iScope                      - Scope of the search
         int iNumToDisplayAtATime        - Number of Attributes to
                                           retrieve at a time

*/
HRESULT PrintAttributeWithRanging(IDirectoryObject * pDirObject,LPOLESTR
pwszAttribute, int iScope,int iNumToDisplayAtATime)
{
    HRESULT hr;
    ADS_SEARCH_COLUMN col;

    // Interface Pointers
    IDirectorySearch *pDSSearch=NULL;

    // Get an IDirectorySearch * from the passed IDirectoryObject
    hr = pDirObject->QueryInterface(IID_IDirectorySearch,(void**)&pDSSearch);
    if (FAILED(hr))
        return hr;

    // The attribute which will come back from the search
```

(continued)

(continued)

```
    WCHAR pszAttr[512];
    DWORD dwAttrNameSize = 1;//sizeof(pszAttr)/sizeof(LPWSTR);

    // Preferences on Search
    ADS_SEARCHPREF_INFO arSearchPrefs[1];
    DWORD dwNumPrefs;

    // Set the scope to the passed value
    arSearchPrefs [0].dwSearchPref = ADS_SEARCHPREF_SEARCH_SCOPE ;
    arSearchPrefs [0].vValue.dwType = ADSTYPE_INTEGER;
    arSearchPrefs [0].vValue.Integer = ADS_SCOPE_BASE;

    // Number of elements in arSearchPrefs
    dwNumPrefs = 1;

    ADS_SEARCH_HANDLE hSearch;  // Handle for searching. ADSI uses this
                                // to keep its place

    // Set the preferences for search
    hr = pDSSearch->SetSearchPreference( arSearchPrefs, dwNumPrefs);
    if (FAILED(hr))
        return hr;

    // Do a series of Range searches, grabbing 10 at a time.
    int iRange = 0;
    DWORD dAttribsGotten = 0;
    while (SUCCEEDED(hr))
    {

        LPWSTR  pSrchFilter = (LPWSTR)&pszAttr;
        int     iAttribsGottenLastSrch =0;

        // Build the Range String : ex: L"Member;Range=0-5"
        swprintf(pSrchFilter ,L"%s;Range=%d-
%d",pwszAttribute,iRange,iRange+iNumToDisplayAtATime-1);

        // Display info to the user
        wprintf(L"\nPerforming a Range IDirectorySearch for the attribute '%s'\n"
                L"The search filter is %s\n\nEntries %d through %d:\n\n"
                ,pwszAttribute,pSrchFilter,iRange,iRange+iNumToDisplayAtATime-1);

        // Executing a BASE level search
        hr = pDSSearch->ExecuteSearch(L"(CN=*)",&pSrchFilter,dwAttrNameSize,
&hSearch );
```

```
        // Execute the Search

        if ( SUCCEEDED(hr) )
        {

            while( pDSSearch->GetNextRow( hSearch) != S_ADS_NOMORE_ROWS )
             {
                LPWSTR pszColumn;
                while(pDSSearch->GetNextColumnName( hSearch, &pszColumn )!=
S_ADS_NOMORE_COLUMNS )
                {        //printf("%S ", pszColumn );

                    // Get the ADsPath and save it in the list
                    hr = pDSSearch->GetColumn( hSearch, pszColumn, &col );
                    if ( SUCCEEDED(hr) )
                    {
                        for (DWORD x = 0; x< col.dwNumValues; x++)
                        {
                            wprintf(L"%d:
%s\n",dAttribsGotten,(col.pADsValues+x)->CaseIgnoreString);
                            dAttribsGotten++;
                            iAttribsGottenLastSrch++;
                        }

                        // Copy the BSTR
                        // Free the column that GetColumn returns
                        pDSSearch->FreeColumn( &col );
                    }

                    FreeADsMem( pszColumn );
                }
             }

            // Close the search handle and release the IDirectorySearch interface
            pDSSearch->CloseSearchHandle(hSearch);
        }

        if (FAILED(hr) || hr ==S_ADS_NOMORE_ROWS || iAttribsGottenLastSrch== 0 ||
iAttribsGottenLastSrch< iNumToDisplayAtATime  )
            break;
        iRange += iNumToDisplayAtATime;
    }
    pDSSearch->Release();
    pDSSearch= NULL;
    return hr;

}
```

Querying for Groups in a Domain

Groups can be placed in any container or organizational unit in a domain as well as the root of the domain. This means that groups can be in numerous locations in the directory hierarchy.

You can perform a deep search for (objectClass=group) to find all groups in a tree. You can also use a query string of the form, which uses the matching rule OID to search for the ADS_GROUP_TYPE_SECURITY_ENABLED bit in the **groupType** attribute. For more information on using matching rules, see *How to Specify Comparison Values*.

```
(&(objectClass=group)(groupType:1.2.840.113556.1.4.804:=2147483648) )
```

Example Code for Performing a Query in a Domain

C++

The following code fragment contains two functions that perform a query against a specified root object and displays all groups and groups by type:

```
///////////////////////////////////////////////////////////////////////////
/*  QueryAndOutputGroups()    -           Gets an IDirectorySearch
                                          Interface on the passed root
                                          Performs several sample searches
                                          using IDirectorySearch


    Parameters

        IDirectoryObject * pDirObjectRoot - The root from where searches
                                            will be performed
*/
void QueryAndOutputGroups(IDirectoryObject * pDirObjectRoot)
{
    HRESULT hr;
    DisplayConsoleMsgWaitForEnter(L"To look at the new Active Directory structure, use\n"
                                  L"IDirectorySearch, to perform several querys on the
directory\n"
                                  L" NOTE: All of the samples object that this program\n
creates"
                                  L" begin with the text 'UGExercise'.\n\n"
                                  L"Hit ENTER to perform a subtree search of ALL the
groups.\n" );

        /////////////////////////////////////////////////
        // Search for  groups

        // Interface Pointers
        IDirectorySearch *pDSSearch=NULL;
```

```
// The attributes that are needed
LPWSTR pszAttr[] ={  L"Name", L"ADsPath" };
DWORD dwAttrNameSize = sizeof(pszAttr)/sizeof(LPWSTR);

// Preferences on Search
// Do a DEEP SUBTREE search for all accounts
ADS_SEARCHPREF_INFO arSearchPrefs[1];
DWORD dwNumPrefs;

arSearchPrefs [0].dwSearchPref = ADS_SEARCHPREF_SEARCH_SCOPE ;
arSearchPrefs [0].vValue.dwType = ADSTYPE_INTEGER;
arSearchPrefs [0].vValue.Integer = ADS_SCOPE_SUBTREE;

dwNumPrefs = 1;

hr = pDirObjectRoot->QueryInterface(IID_IDirectorySearch,(void**)&pDSSearch);

if (SUCCEEDED(hr))
{

    //////////////////////////////////////////////////
    // Search for all the groups
    puts("<<<<<<<<<<<<<<<<<<<<<<ALL GROUPS>>>>>>>>>>>>>>>>>>");
    hr = SimpleDirectorySearch(pDSSearch,
                               L"(objectCategory=group)",
                               pszAttr,dwAttrNameSize,
                               arSearchPrefs,
                               dwNumPrefs);

    //////////////////////////////////////////////////
    // Search for all the GLOBAL groups

    DisplayConsoleMsgWaitForEnter(
        L"Hit ENTER to perform a subtree search of all the GLOBAL groups\n");
    puts("<<<<<<<<<<<<<<<<<<<<<<ALL GLOBAL Groups>>>>>>>>>>>>>>>>>>");
    hr = SimpleDirectorySearch(pDSSearch,

BuildGroupTypeQueryString(lmrOR,ADS_GROUP_TYPE_GLOBAL_GROUP),
                               pszAttr,dwAttrNameSize,arSearchPrefs,
                               dwNumPrefs);

    //////////////////////////////////////////////////
    // Search for all the DOMAIN LOCAL  groups
```

(continued)

(continued)

```
    DisplayConsoleMsgWaitForEnter(
        L"Hit ENTER to perform a subtree search of all the DOMAIN LOCAL groups\n");
    puts("<<<<<<<<<<<<<<<<<<<<<ALL Domain Local Groups>>>>>>>>>>>>>>>>>");
    hr = SimpleDirectorySearch(pDSSearch,

BuildGroupTypeQueryString(lmrOR,ADS_GROUP_TYPE_DOMAIN_LOCAL_GROUP),
                                pszAttr,dwAttrNameSize,
                                arSearchPrefs,
                                dwNumPrefs);


    if (bUseUniversalGroups)
    {
        /////////////////////////////////////////////////
        // Search for all the UNIVERSAL  groups
        DisplayConsoleMsgWaitForEnter(
            L"Hit ENTER to perform a subtree search of all the UNIVERSAL groups\n");
        puts("<<<<<<<<<<<<<<<<<<<<<ALL Universal Groups>>>>>>>>>>>>>>>>>");
        hr = SimpleDirectorySearch(pDSSearch,
                                BuildGroupTypeQueryString(lmrOR,
                                ADS_GROUP_TYPE_UNIVERSAL_GROUP),
                                pszAttr,dwAttrNameSize,
                                arSearchPrefs,
                                dwNumPrefs);
    }


    /////////////////////////////////////////////////
    // Search for all the Security Enabled  groups

    DisplayConsoleMsgWaitForEnter(
        L"Hit ENTER to perform a subtree search of all Security Enabled groups\n");
    puts("<<<<<<<<<<<<<<<<<<<<<ALL Security Enabled Groups>>>>>>>>>>>>>>>>>");
    hr = SimpleDirectorySearch(pDSSearch,

BuildGroupTypeQueryString(lmrOR,ADS_GROUP_TYPE_SECURITY_ENABLED),
                                pszAttr,dwAttrNameSize,
                                arSearchPrefs,
                                dwNumPrefs);


    /////////////////////////////////////////////////
    // Search for all the Security Enabled LOCAL groups

    DisplayConsoleMsgWaitForEnter(
        L"Hit ENTER to perform a subtree search of all Security Enabled LOCAL
groups\n");
```

```
            puts("<<<<<<<<<<<<<<<<<<<<<<<<<ALL Security Enabled Domain Local
Groups>>>>>>>>>>>>>>>>>");
        hr = SimpleDirectorySearch(pDSSearch,

BuildGroupTypeQueryString(lmrAND,ADS_GROUP_TYPE_DOMAIN_LOCAL_GROUP |
ADS_GROUP_TYPE_SECURITY_ENABLED),
                                pszAttr,dwAttrNameSize,
                                arSearchPrefs,
                                dwNumPrefs);

        /////////////////////////////////////////////////
        // Search for all the DOMAIN LOCAL groups whose
        // name begins with 'UGExercise'

        DisplayConsoleMsgWaitForEnter(
            L"Hit ENTER to perform a subtree search of all DOMAIN LOCAL  groups that begin
with the text \'UGExercise\'\n");
        puts("<<<<<<<<<<<<<<<<<<<<<<<<<ALL Domain Local Groups Beginnig with \'UGExercise\'
>>>>>>>>>>>>>>>>>");

        // Build a string for the Query - this helper
        // aids in taking the BITMASK passed to it and
        // converting it into a string
        WCHAR * szwGTQuery =
BuildGroupTypeQueryString(lmrOR,ADS_GROUP_TYPE_DOMAIN_LOCAL_GROUP );
        WCHAR   szwQuery[512];

        // Add the bit value to the LDAP query string
        // Look for all objects which have
        // DOMAIN LOCAL and a groupType == the domain local bitmask
        // built previously with BuildGroupTypeQueryString()
        wsprintf(szwQuery,L"(&(cn=UGExercise*)%s)",szwGTQuery);
        OutputDebugString(szwQuery);
        OutputDebugString(L"\r\n");

        // Perform the search using the query string
        // built previously (szwQuery)
        hr =
SimpleDirectorySearch(pDSSearch,szwQuery,pszAttr,dwAttrNameSize,arSearchPrefs,dwNumPrefs);

        /////////////////////////////////////////////////
        // Search for ALL the groups whose
        // name begins with 'UGExercise'
```

(continued)

(continued)

```
        DisplayConsoleMsgWaitForEnter(
            L"Hit ENTER to perform a subtree search of ALL groups that begin with the text
\'UGExercise \'\n");

        puts("<<<<<<<<<<<<<<<<<<<<<<<<ALL Groups Beginning with \'UGExercise \'
>>>>>>>>>>>>>>>>");
        hr = SimpleDirectorySearch(pDSSearch,
                                    L"(&(cn=UGExercise*)(objectCategory=group))",
                                    pszAttr,dwAttrNameSize,
                                    arSearchPrefs,
                                    dwNumPrefs);

        // Release the Search interface
        pDSSearch->Release();
        pDSSearch= NULL;
    }
    else
        puts("ERROR: pDirObjectRoot-
>QueryInterface(IID_IDirectorySearch,(void**)&pDSSearch); FAILED!");


}
//////////////////////////////////////////////////////////////////////
/*  SimpleDirectorySearch()    - Uses IDirectorySearch to search
                                 the directory. Results are printed to
                                 the console window

    Parameters

        IDirectorySearch *pDSSearch         - IDirectorySearch interface
                                              from the object
                                              which will serve as the
                                              root of the search
        LPWSTR pszSearchFilter              - LDAP Search filter
        LPWSTR pszAttr[]                    - Array of Attribute names
                                              to retrieve
        DWORD dwAttrNameSize                - Number of elements in
                                              pszAttr
        PADS_SEARCHPREF_INFO pSearchPrefs   - ADSI Array of preferences
        DWORD dwNumPrefs                    - Number of elements in
                                              pSearchPrefs
*/
HRESULT SimpleDirectorySearch(IDirectorySearch *pDSSearch,LPWSTR pszSearchFilter, LPWSTR
pszAttr[],DWORD dwAttrNameSize,
                        PADS_SEARCHPREF_INFO pSearchPrefs,DWORD dwNumPrefs  )
```

```
{
    wprintf(L"\nSearch Filter =%s\n",pszSearchFilter);
    // COL for iterations
    ADS_SEARCH_COLUMN col;
    HRESULT hr;

    // Interface Pointers
    IADs     *pObj = NULL;
    IADs     * pIADs = NULL;

    // Handle used for searching
    ADS_SEARCH_HANDLE hSearch;

    // if the preferences were passed in, call
    // IDirectorySearch::SetSearchPreference()
    if (dwNumPrefs &&  pSearchPrefs)
    {
        hr = pDSSearch->SetSearchPreference( pSearchPrefs, dwNumPrefs);
        if (FAILED(hr))
            return hr;
    }
    // Execute the search using the passed search filter, the
    // attributes and the address of the search handle
    hr = pDSSearch->ExecuteSearch(pszSearchFilter,pszAttr ,dwAttrNameSize, &hSearch );

    if ( SUCCEEDED(hr) )
    {

    // Call IDirectorySearch::GetNextRow() to retrieve the next row
    //of data
        while( pDSSearch->GetNextRow( hSearch) != S_ADS_NOMORE_ROWS )
        {

            // loop through the array of passed column names,
            // print the data for each column
            for (DWORD x = 0; x < dwAttrNameSize; x++)
            {

                // Get the data for this column
                hr = pDSSearch->GetColumn( hSearch, pszAttr[x], &col );

                if ( SUCCEEDED(hr) )
                {
```

(continued)

(continued)

```
                // Print the data for the column and free the column
                wprintf(L"%s: %s\r\n",pszAttr[x],col.pADsValues->CaseIgnoreString);
                pDSSearch->FreeColumn( &col );
            }
            else
                wprintf(L"<%s property NOT available>",pszAttr[x]);
        }
        puts("------------------------------------------------");
    }

    // Close the search handle to clean up
    pDSSearch->CloseSearchHandle(hSearch);
    }
    return hr;
}
```

Visual Basic

The following subroutine performs a query against a specified root object and display all groups and groups by type:

```
'***********************************
'   QueryAndOutputGroups()  - Performs several sample searches using ADO
'
'
'   Parameters
'
'       oDirObjectRoot As IDirectoryObject - The root from where
'                                            searches will be performed
'
Sub QueryAndOutputGroups(oDirObjectRoot As IDirectoryObject)

    '*******************************
    ' Search for all the groups
    DisplayMessage " "
    DisplayMessage "<<<<<<<<<<<<<<<<<<<<<<<ALL GROUPS>>>>>>>>>>>>>>>>>>" 'cn = 'UG*'
objectCategory
    SimpleDirectorySearch oDirObjectRoot, "objectCategory = 'group'", ADS_SCOPE_SUBTREE

    '***************************************
    ' Search for all the GLOBAL groups
    DisplayMessage " "
    DisplayMsgWaitForInput "Hit OK to perform a subtree search of all the GLOBAL groups"
    DisplayMessage " "
    DisplayMessage "<<<<<<<<<<<<<<<<<<<<<<<ALL GLOBAL Groups>>>>>>>>>>>>>>>>>>"
```

```
    SimpleDirectorySearch oDirObjectRoot, "GroupType=" & Str(ADS_GROUP_TYPE_GLOBAL_GROUP)
& " or " & _
                            "GroupType=" & Str(ADS_GROUP_TYPE_GLOBAL_GROUP Or
ADS_GROUP_TYPE_SECURITY_ENABLED), _
                            ADS_SCOPE_SUBTREE


    '******************************************
    ' Search for all the DOMAIN LOCAL  groups
    DisplayMessage " "
    DisplayMsgWaitForInput "Hit OK to perform a subtree search of all the DOMAIN LOCAL
groups"
    DisplayMessage " "
    DisplayMessage "<<<<<<<<<<<<<<<<<<<<<<ALL Domain Local Groups>>>>>>>>>>>>>>>>>>"
    SimpleDirectorySearch oDirObjectRoot, "GroupType=" &
Str(ADS_GROUP_TYPE_DOMAIN_LOCAL_GROUP) & " or " & _
                            "GroupType=" & Str(ADS_GROUP_TYPE_DOMAIN_LOCAL_GROUP Or
ADS_GROUP_TYPE_SECURITY_ENABLED), _
                            ADS_SCOPE_SUBTREE


    '       #ifdef USE_UNIVERSAL_GROUPS


    '******************************************
    ' Search for all the UNIVERSAL  groups
    DisplayMessage " "
    DisplayMsgWaitForInput "Hit OK to perform a subtree search of all the UNIVERSAL
groups"
    DisplayMessage " "
    DisplayMessage "<<<<<<<<<<<<<<<<<<<<<<ALL Universal Groups>>>>>>>>>>>>>>>>>>"
    SimpleDirectorySearch oDirObjectRoot, "GroupType=" &
Str(ADS_GROUP_TYPE_UNIVERSAL_GROUP) & " or " & _
                            "GroupType=" & Str(ADS_GROUP_TYPE_UNIVERSAL_GROUP Or
ADS_GROUP_TYPE_SECURITY_ENABLED), _
                            ADS_SCOPE_SUBTREE
    '       #End If


    '******************************************
    ' Search for all the Security Enabled  groups
    DisplayMessage " "
    DisplayMsgWaitForInput "Hit OK to perform a subtree search of all Security Enabled
groups"
    DisplayMessage " "
    DisplayMessage "<<<<<<<<<<<<<<<<<<<<<<ALL Security Enabled Groups>>>>>>>>>>>>>>>>>>"
    SimpleDirectorySearch oDirObjectRoot, "GroupType=" &
Str(ADS_GROUP_TYPE_SECURITY_ENABLED) & " or " & _
```

(continued)

(continued)

```
                              "GroupType=" & Str(ADS_GROUP_TYPE_SECURITY_ENABLED Or
ADS_GROUP_TYPE_SECURITY_ENABLED), _
                              ADS_SCOPE_SUBTREE


    '*****************************************
    ' Search for all the Security Enabled LOCAL groups
    DisplayMessage " "
    DisplayMsgWaitForInput "Hit OK to perform a subtree search of all Security Enabled
LOCAL groups"
    DisplayMessage " "
    DisplayMessage "<<<<<<<<<<<<<<<<<<<<<<ALL Security Enabled Domain Local
Groups>>>>>>>>>>>>>>>>>"
    SimpleDirectorySearch oDirObjectRoot, "GroupType=" &
Str(ADS_GROUP_TYPE_DOMAIN_LOCAL_GROUP Or _
                              ADS_GROUP_TYPE_SECURITY_ENABLED), _
                              ADS_SCOPE_SUBTREE


    '*****************************************
    ' Search for all the DOMAIN LOCAL groups whose
    ' name begins with 'UGExercise'
    DisplayMessage " "
    DisplayMsgWaitForInput "Hit OK to perform a subtree search of all DOMAIN LOCAL  groups
that begin with the text 'UGExercise'"
    DisplayMessage " "
    DisplayMessage "<<<<<<<<<<<<<<<<<<<<<<ALL Domain Local Groups Beginnig with
'UGExercise' >>>>>>>>>>>>>>>>>"

    SimpleDirectorySearch oDirObjectRoot, "cn='UGExercise*' and (GroupType=" & _
                              Str(ADS_GROUP_TYPE_DOMAIN_LOCAL_GROUP) & " or GroupType=" & _
                              Str(ADS_GROUP_TYPE_DOMAIN_LOCAL_GROUP Or
ADS_GROUP_TYPE_SECURITY_ENABLED) & _
                              ")", ADS_SCOPE_SUBTREE


    '*****************************************
    ' Search for ALL the groups whose
    ' name begins with 'UGExercise'
    DisplayMessage " "
    DisplayMsgWaitForInput "Hit OK to perform a subtree search of ALL groups that begin
with the text 'UGExercise '"
    DisplayMessage " "
    DisplayMessage "<<<<<<<<<<<<<<<<<<<<<<<ALL Groups Beginning with 'UGExercise'
>>>>>>>>>>>>>>>>>"
```

```
    SimpleDirectorySearch oDirObjectRoot, " cn='UGExercise*' and objectCategory='group'",
ADS_SCOPE_SUBTREE

End Sub
                                           -
'/////////////////////////////////////////////////////////////////////////
'    SimpleDirectorySearch()    - Uses ADO to search the directory
'                                 Results are displayed in the list box
'    Parameters
'
'        oDirObjectRoot As IDirectoryObject  - Root of the search
'        ByVal sSearchFilter As String       - LDAP Search filter
'        ByVal lScope As Integer             - Scope for Searching
'                                              possible values are:
'                                                 ADS_SCOPE_BASE
'                                                 ADS_SCOPE_ONELEVEL
'                                                 ADS_SCOPE_SUBTREE
'
'    (See IDirectorySearch and ADS_SCOPEENUM in the docs for more info)
'
Sub SimpleDirectorySearch(oDirObjectRoot As IDirectoryObject, ByVal sSearchFilter As
String, ByVal lScope As Integer)

    Dim iIndex As Integer
    iIndex = 0
    Dim v, j, i

    Dim con As New Connection, rs As New Recordset
    Dim Com As New Command
    Dim oIADs As IADs
    Dim sAdsPathRoot As String

    ' Get the LDAP path to the passed in object
    sAdsPathRoot = GetAdsPath(oDirObjectRoot)

    'Open a Connection object
    con.Provider = "ADsDSOObject"

    '-----------------------------------------------------------------
    ' To be authenticated using alternate credentials
    ' use connection properties of User ID and Password
    '-----------------------------------------------------------------
    ' con.Properties("User ID") = "Administrator"
    ' con.Properties("Password") = ""
```

(continued)

(continued)

```
' Open the connection
con.Open "Active Directory Provider"

' Create a command object on this connection
Set Com.ActiveConnection = con

' set the query string using SQL Dialect
Com.CommandText = "select name,AdsPath from '" & sAdsPathRoot & "' where " &
sSearchFilter & " ORDER BY NAME"

' Tell the user what the search filter is
DisplayMessage "Search Filter = " & Com.CommandText

'-----------------------------------------------------
' Or you can use LDAP Dialect, for example,
'-----------------------------------------------------
' Ex Com.CommandText =
' "<LDAP://Microsoft1/dc=Microsoft,DC=com>;(objectClass=*);name"
' For LDAP Dialect, the valid search scope are base, oneLevel and
' subtree
' Com.CommandText = "<" & adDomainPath &
' ">;(objectClass=*);name;subtree"
' For LDAP Dialect (<LDAP:...>), there is no way to specify sort
' order in the string,
' However, you can use this SORT ON property to specify sort order.
' for SQL Dialect you can use ORDER BY in the SQL Statement
' Ex. Com.Properties("Sort On") = "Name"

'Set the preferences for Search
Com.Properties("Page Size") = 1000
Com.Properties("Timeout") = 30 'seconds
Com.Properties("searchscope") = lScope
Com.Properties("Chase referrals") = ADS_CHASE_REFERRALS_EXTERNAL
Com.Properties("Cache Results") = False ' do not cache the result,
                                        ' it results in less memory
                                        ' requirements

'Execute the query
Set rs = Com.Execute

' Tell the user how many rows
DisplayMessage "Returned " & Str(rs.RecordCount) & " rows"
```

```
' Navigate the record set
If Not rs.EOF Then
    rs.MoveFirst
End If

On Error Resume Next
While Not rs.EOF
    ' Display the LDAP path for the row
    DisplayMessage rs.Fields("AdsPath")
    rs.MoveNext
Wend

End Sub
```

Changing a Group's Scope or Type

Changing a group's scope or type is not allowed in mixed-mode domains. However, the following conversions are allowed in native-mode domains:

Global group to universal group. However, this is only allowed if the global group is not a member of another global group.

Domain local group to universal group. However, the domain local group being converted cannot contain another domain local group.

Universal group to global or domain local group. For conversion to global group, the universal group being converted cannot contain users or global groups from another domain. For conversion to domain local group, the universal group being converted cannot be a member of any universal group or a domain local group from another domain.

In native mode, a group's type can be converted freely between security groups and distribution groups.

Note that if a group is used to set access control, changing the scope or type can affect the access control entries (ACEs) that contain that group. The security system will ignore ACEs that contain groups that are not security groups.

Example Code for Changing the Scope of a Group

C++

The following code fragment changes the scope of a group:

```
WCHAR pwszLDAPPath[MAX_PATH*2];

    HRESULT hr;
```

(continued)

(continued)

```cpp
    IADsGroup * pGroup = NULL;

    // Initialize COM
    CoInitialize(0);

    // Bind to the container passed
hr = ADsGetObject( pwszLDAPPath, IID_IADsGroup,(void **)&pGroup);

    if (SUCCEEDED(hr))
    {
        VARIANT vValue;
        BSTR     bsValue = SysAllocString(L"groupType");
        VariantInit(&vValue);
    // Set a new GroupType Value
        vValue.vt = VT_I4;
        vValue.lVal = ADS_GROUP_TYPE_GLOBAL_GROUP ;

        hr = pGroup->Put(bsValue,vValue);
        hr = pGroup->SetInfo();
        pGroup->Release();
        pGroup= NULL;
    }

    CoUninitialize();
```

Visual Basic

The following code fragment changes the scope of a group:

```vb
Dim x as IADs
Set x = GetObject("LDAP://CN=mygroup,OU=myou,DC=Microsoft,DC=com")
x.Put "groupType", ADS_GROUP_TYPE_UNIVERSAL_GROUP|ADS_GROUP_TYPE_SECURITY_ENABLED
```

Deleting Groups

To delete a group from a domain, bind to the container containing the group and specify "group" as the class using **IADsContainer::Delete** to delete the group. You do not need to call **IADs::SetInfo** method to commit the change to the container. The **IADsContainer::Delete** call commits the deletion of the group directly to the directory.

Example Code for Deleting a Group in a Domain

C++

The code fragment on the next page contains a function that deletes a group in a domain.

```
///////////////////////////////////////////////////////////////////////////
/*  DeleteADObject()   - Deletes the passed object by AdsPath

    Parameters

        LPOLESTR pwszAdsPath         -         AdsPath of object to delete

    Optional Parameters:

        LPOLESTR pwszUser            - User Name and Password, if the
                                       parameters are NOT passed,
        LPOLESTER pwszPassWord       - Binding will use ADsGetObject, if
                                       the parameters
                                     - Are specified, will use
                                       ADsOpenObject, passing user
                                       name and password

*/
HRESULT DeleteADObject(LPOLESTR pwszAdsPath, LPOLESTR  pwszUser,LPOLESTR
pwszPassWord)
{
    HRESULT             hr;
    BSTR                bsParentPath;
    IADs *              pIADsToDelete = NULL;
    IDirectoryObject *  pIDirObjectParent= NULL;
    VARIANT             vCNToDelete;
    WCHAR               pwszTemp[512];

    VariantInit(&vCNToDelete);
    OutputDebugString(pwszAdsPath);
    OutputDebugString(L"\r\n");

    // Bind to the object being deleted

    assert((pwszUser==NULL && pwszPassWord == NULL) || (pwszUser &&
pwszPassWord));

    // If a username and password are passed in, use ADsOpenObject()
    // otherwise use ADsGetObject()
    if (!pwszUser) // No user password passed, use ADsOpenObject
    {
        hr = ADsGetObject( pwszAdsPath, IID_IADs,(void **)& pIADsToDelete);
    }
    else
```

(continued)

(continued)

```
    {
        hr = ADsOpenObject(pwszAdsPath, pwszUser, pwszPassWord,
                        ADS_SECURE_AUTHENTICATION,IID_IADs, (void**) &
pIADsToDelete);
    }

    if (SUCCEEDED(hr))
    {
        // Get the parent path
        hr = pIADsToDelete->get_Parent(&bsParentPath);

        // Get the CN property for the object to delete
        hr = pIADsToDelete->Get(L"cn",&vCNToDelete);
        if (SUCCEEDED(hr))
        {
            // **********************************************************
            // Now bind to the parent
            // If a username and password are passed in,
            // use ADsOpenObject() otherwise use ADsGetObject()
            if (!pwszUser) // No user password passed, use ADsOpenObject
            {
                hr = ADsGetObject(  bsParentPath, IID_IDirectoryObject,(void **)&
pIDirObjectParent);
            }
            else
            {
                hr = ADsOpenObject(bsParentPath, pwszUser, pwszPassWord,

ADS_SECURE_AUTHENTICATION,IID_IDirectoryObject, (void**) & pIDirObjectParent);
            }
            if (SUCCEEDED(hr))
            {
                // Release the object to delete
                pIADsToDelete->Release();
                pIADsToDelete =NULL;

                // Put the CN property into a string beginning with CN=
                swprintf(pwszTemp,L"cn=%s\n",vCNToDelete.bstrVal);

                // Ask the parent to delete the child
                hr =pIDirObjectParent->DeleteDSObject(pwszTemp);
                // Release the Parent Object
                pIDirObjectParent->Release();
                pIDirObjectParent = NULL;
```

```
            }
        }
        SysFreeString(bsParentPath);
    }
    // If we have a IADsObject- we need to release it
    if ( pIADsToDelete)
    {
        // Release the object to delete
        pIADsToDelete->Release();
        pIADsToDelete =NULL;
    }

    VariantClear(&vCNToDelete);
return hr;
}
```

Visual Basic

The following code deletes a group in domain:

```
Dim x as IADs
Set x = GetObject("LDAP://OU=myou,DC=Microsoft,DC=com")
x.Delete("group", "cn=mygroup")
```

Moving Groups

Groups can be moved within a domain.

However, you can only move objects between domains using the movetree.exe utility and then using that utility only universal groups can be moved from one domain to another. A global or domain local group can be converted to a universal group, moved to another domain, and converted back again.

▶ **To move a group**

1. Bind to the group to move and get an **IADs** pointer.
2. Get the ADsPath using the **IADs::get_ADsPath** property method. The ADsPath will be used to specify the group to move.
3. Bind to the container object where you want to move the group to and get an **IADsContainer** pointer.
4. Move the group using the **IADsContainer::MoveHere** method.

   If you have a pointer to the group object before it was moved, the pointer to the object is still valid, but the object's methods is no longer valid because the directory object it represents is no longer valid.

Example Code for Moving a Group

C++

The following code fragment contains a function that moves a group (or any object) to another location in the domain:

```
/////////////////////////////////////////////////////////////////////
/*
    MoveObject()      -     Moves an object in the directory from the
                            IDirectoryObject passed
                            The Object at the NEW location is Queried for
                            an updated IDirectoryObject interface, and the
                            passed PTR is updated..
    Parameters

        IDirectoryObject *pIDODestination  - Place to move the object to
        IDirectoryObject **ppIDOToMove     - Object to move (note
                                               returned is a different PTR
                                               (but it points to the
                                               moved object)
*/

HRESULT MoveObject(IDirectoryObject * pIDODestination,IDirectoryObject
**ppIDOToMove)
{
    IADsContainer * pIADsContainerDestination = NULL;
    IADs          * pIADsToMove;
    HRESULT         hr;
    BSTR            bsPathToMove;

    // QI a IADs ptr from the ToMove object
    hr =(*ppIDOToMove)->QueryInterface(IID_IADs,(void**)&pIADsToMove);

    if (SUCCEEDED(hr))
    {

        //The ADS path of the object to MOVE
        hr =pIADsToMove->get_ADsPath(&bsPathToMove);
        if (SUCCEEDED(hr))
        {

            //printf("\n%s\n",QueryAllInterfaces( pIDODestination));
            // Get an IADsContainer * from the Destination
```

```
            hr =pIDODestination->QueryInterface(IID_IADsContainer
,(void**)&pIADsContainerDestination );
          if (SUCCEEDED(hr))
          {
              IDispatch * pIDispatchNewObject = NULL;

              // Actually MOVE the object
              hr = pIADsContainerDestination-
>MoveHere(bsPathToMove,NULL,&pIDispatchNewObject );
              if (SUCCEEDED(hr))
              {
                  IDirectoryObject * pIDONewOneToReturn = NULL;

                  // Now get a IDirectoryObject * from
                  // the IDispatch returned from MoveHere()
                  hr =pIDispatchNewObject->QueryInterface(IID_IDirectoryObject
,(void**)pIDONewOneToReturn );

                  if (SUCCEEDED(hr))
                  {

                      // Now take the PASSED interface. FREE it and reassign
the new ptr
                      // (note if there are ANY outstanding refs to the com
object behind the ptr- they will still be
                      // valid (from a COM point of view), but this
                      // object will return errors if you try to do
                      // anything with it)
                      (*ppIDOToMove)->Release();

                      // Copy the ptr from the QI'd one to
                      // the return for this function
                      ppIDOToMove = &pIDONewOneToReturn;
                  }
                  pIDispatchNewObject->Release();
                  pIDispatchNewObject = NULL;
              }

              pIADsContainerDestination->Release();
              pIADsContainerDestination  = NULL;
          }
          SysFreeString(bsPathToMove);
      }
      pIADsToMove->Release();
```

(continued)

(continued)

```
        pIADsToMove = NULL;
    }

    return hr;
}
```

Visual Basic

The following code fragment moves a group (or any object) to another location in the domain:

```
Dim oDirObjTo As IADsContainer
Dim oNewObj As IADs

Set oDirObjTo = GetObject(txtTo.Text)

Set oNewObj = oDirObjTo.MoveHere(txtFrom.Text, vbNullString)

MsgBox "New Object has been moved to " & oNewObj.ADsPath

Set oDirObjTo = Nothing

Set oNewObj = Nothing
```

Getting the Domain Account-Style Name of a Group

Users, groups, computers, and other security principals can also be represented in domain account form. Domain account (the logon name used in previous versions of Windows NT®) has the following form:

domain\account

where *domain* is the name of the Windows NT domain that contains the user and *account* is the **samAccountName** property of the specified user. For example: Microsoft\jsmith.

The domain account form can be used to specify the trustee in an ACE in a security descriptor. It is also used for the logon name on computers running Windows version NT 4.0 and earlier.

```
//Need to include the following headers to use DsGetDcName
//#include <LMCONS.H>
//#include <dsgetdc.h>
//#include <lmapibuf.h>
//This function returns the previous version name of the security principal
//specified by the distinguished name specified by szDN.
//The szDomain parameter should be NULL to use the current domain
```

```
//to get the name translation. Otherwise, you should specify the
//domain you want to use as just the domain name (such as northwestdom)
//or in dotted format (such as northwestdom.Microsoft.com).
HRESULT GetDownlevelName(LPOLESTR szDomainName, LPOLESTR szDN, LPOLESTR
*ppNameString)
{
HRESULT hr = E_FAIL;
IADsNameTranslate *pNameTr = NULL;
IADs *pObject = NULL;
LPOLESTR szPath = new OLECHAR[MAX_PATH];
LPOLESTR szInitDomain = new OLECHAR[MAX_PATH];
BSTR szNameTr;

if ((!szDN)||(!ppNameString))
    return hr;

//Use the current domain if none is specified.
if (!szDomainName)
{
    //Call DsGetDcName to get the name of this computer's domain.
    PDOMAIN_CONTROLLER_INFO DomainControllerInfo = NULL;
    DWORD dReturn = 0L;
    dReturn = DsGetDcName(   NULL,
                NULL,
                NULL,
                NULL,
                DS_DIRECTORY_SERVICE_REQUIRED,
                &DomainControllerInfo
    );
    if (dReturn==NO_ERROR)
    {
        wcscpy(szInitDomain, DomainControllerInfo->DomainName);
        hr = S_OK;
    }


    //Free the buffer.
    if (DomainControllerInfo)
        NetApiBufferFree(DomainControllerInfo);
}
else
{
    wcscpy(szInitDomain, szDomainName);
    hr = S_OK;
}
```

(continued)

(continued)

```
if (SUCCEEDED(hr))
{

    //Create the COM object for the IADsNameTranslate object.
    hr  = CoCreateInstance(

                            CLSID_NameTranslate,
                            NULL,
                            CLSCTX_INPROC_SERVER,
                            IID_IADsNameTranslate,
                            (void **)&pNameTr
                        );
    if (SUCCEEDED(hr))
    {

        //Initialize for the specified domain.
        hr = pNameTr->Init(ADS_NAME_INITTYPE_DOMAIN, szInitDomain);
        if (SUCCEEDED(hr))
        {
            hr = pNameTr->Set(ADS_NAME_TYPE_1779, szDN);
            hr = pNameTr->Get(ADS_NAME_TYPE_NT4, &szNameTr);
            if (SUCCEEDED(hr))
            {
                *ppNameString = (OLECHAR *)CoTaskMemAlloc
(sizeof(OLECHAR)*(wcslen(szNameTr)+1));
                if (*ppNameString)
                    wcscpy(*ppNameString, szNameTr);
                else
                    hr=E_FAIL;
            }
        }
    }
    if (pNameTr)
        pNameTr->Release();
}

//Caller must call CoTaskMemFree to free ppNameString.
return hr;
}
```

Groups on Member Servers and Windows 2000 Professional

On member servers and Windows® 2000 Professional, there is a local security database. That local security database can contain its own local user and machine local groups whose scope is only the particular computer where they are created. When managing these types of users and groups on member servers and computers running Windows NT® Workstation/Windows 2000 Professional, you use the WinNT provider.

When a member server or a computer running Windows 2000 Professional or Windows 2000 Professional is a member of a Windows 2000 domain, the groups or users in the domain can be used in the local security database to grant rights to that group on that particular computer.

When managing groups on a Windows 2000 domain using ADSI, you use the LDAP provider. When managing groups on member servers and computers running Windows NT Workstation/Windows 2000 Professional, you use the WinNT provider.

This means you need to bind at least once to each provider: 1) Bind to the LDAP provider to retrieve the ADsPath to the group or user you want to add to a group in the local database and 2) Bind to the WinNT provider to add that user or group to a machine local group.

Enumerating Groups on Member Servers and Windows 2000 Professional

On member servers and computers running Windows 2000 Professional, you can easily enumerate all the machine local groups.

Only machine local groups can be created on member servers and Windows 2000 Professional. However, those machine local groups can contain 1) Universal and Global groups from the forest containing the domain that the computer is a member of or 2) Domain local groups from that computer's domain 3) Users from any domain in the forest.

▶ **To enumerate the machine local groups on a member server or computer running Windows 2000 Professional**

1. Bind to the computer using the following rules:
   a. Use an account that has sufficient rights to access that computer.
   b. Use the following binding string format using the WinNT provider, computer name, and an extra parameter to tell ADSI that it is binding to a computer:

   WinNT://*sComputerName, computer*

   where *sComputerName* is the name of the computer who groups you want to access.

In the binding string, the "*,computer*" parameter tells ADSI that it is binding to a computer. ADSI makes this information available to the WinNT provider's parser so that it can skip some ambiguity-resolution queries to determine what type of object you are binding to.

   c. Bind to the **IADsContainer** interface.

2. Set a filter containing "groups" using the **IADsContainer::put_Filter** property method. This enables you to enumerate the container and retrieve only groups.

3. Enumerate the group objects, using the **IADsContainer::get__NewEnum** method.

4. For each the group object, using the **IADsGroup** methods to read the name and members of the group.

Example Code for Enumerating Groups

C++

The following code fragment contains a function that enumerates all objects of a specified class (such as group) and displays the members contained in each object on a member server or a computer running Windows NT Workstation/Windows 2000 Professional:

```
///////////////////////////////////////////////////////////////////////////
/*  ListMembersWithWinNtProvider()    - Uses the WinNT provider to list
                                        children based on a filter
                                        Returns S_OK on success


    Parameters

    LPWSTR pwszComputer     - Computer to list
    LPWSTR pwszClass        - Filter for listing
    LPWSTR pwszUSER = NULL   - User Name for ADsOpenObject() binding-
                              If NOT passed - Bind Though ADsGetObject()
    LPWSTR pwszPASS = NULL   - Password for ADsOpenObject() binding-
                              If NOT passed - Bind Though ADsGetObject()

*/
HRESULT ListMembersWithWinNtProvider(LPWSTR pwszComputer,LPWSTR pwszClass, LPWSTR
pwszUSER = NULL, LPWSTR pwszPASS = NULL)
{
    HRESULT hr;
    LPWSTR  pwszBindingString = NULL;

    IADsContainer * pIADsCont = NULL;

    // Allocate a String for Binding..
```

```
// This should definitely be big enough..
pwszBindingString = new WCHAR[(wcslen(gbsComputer) *2) + 20];

swprintf(pwszBindingString,L"WinNT://%s,computer",pwszComputer);

// Make sure either NO user is passed - or BOTH
// user and password are passed
assert(!pwszUSER || (pwszUSER && pwszPASS));

// Bind to the container passed
// If USER and PASS passed in, use ADsOpenObject()
if (pwszUSER)
    hr = ADsOpenObject( pwszBindingString,
                        pwszUSER,
                        pwszPASS,
                        ADS_SECURE_AUTHENTICATION,
                        IID_IADsContainer,
                        (void**) &pIADsCont);
else
    hr = ADsGetObject( pwszBindingString, IID_IADsContainer,(void
**)&pIADsCont);

if (SUCCEEDED(hr))
{
    VARIANT vFilter;
    VariantInit(&vFilter);
    LPWSTR pwszFilter = pwszClass;

    // Build a Variant of array type, using the filter passed
    hr = ADsBuildVarArrayStr(&pwszFilter, 1, &vFilter);

    if (SUCCEEDED(hr))
    {
        // Set the filter for the results of the Enum
        hr = pIADsCont->put_Filter(vFilter);

        if (SUCCEEDED(hr))
        {
            IEnumVARIANT * pEnumVariant = NULL;
                            // Ptr to the IEnumVariant Interface
            VARIANT Variant;  // Variant for retrieving data
            ULONG   ulElementsFetched; // Number of elements fetched

            // Builds an enumerator interface- this will be used
```

(continued)

(continued)

```
                // to enumerate the objects contained in
                // the IADsContainer
                hr = ADsBuildEnumerator(pIADsCont,&pEnumVariant);
                // While no errors- Loop through and print the data
                while (SUCCEEDED(hr) && hr != S_FALSE)
                {

                    // Object comes back as a VARIANT holding
                    // an IDispatch *
                    hr =
ADsEnumerateNext(pEnumVariant,1,&Variant,&ulElementsFetched);

                    if (hr != S_FALSE)
                    {
                        assert(HAS_BIT_STYLE(Variant.vt,VT_DISPATCH));

                        IDispatch *pDispatch = NULL;
                        IADs *pIADs= NULL;
                        pDispatch = Variant.pdispVal;

                        // QI the Variant's IDispatch *
                        // for the IADs interface
                        hr = pDispatch->QueryInterface(IID_IADs,(VOID **) &pIADs)
;

                        if (SUCCEEDED(hr))
                        {
                            // Print some information about the object
                            BSTR bsResult;

                            pIADs->get_Name(&bsResult);
                            wprintf(L" NAME: %s\n",(LPOLESTR) bsResult);
                            SysFreeString(bsResult);


                            pIADs->get_ADsPath(&bsResult);
                            wprintf(L" ADSPATH: %s\n",(LPOLESTR) bsResult);
                            SysFreeString(bsResult);

                            puts("-------------------------------------------------
-------");

                            pIADs->Release();
                            pIADs = NULL;
                        }
```

```
                }
            }

            // Since the hr from iteration was lost, free
            // the interface if the ptr is != NULL
            if (pEnumVariant)
            {
                pEnumVariant->Release();
                pEnumVariant = NULL;
            }
            VariantClear(&Variant);
        }
    }
    VariantClear(&vFilter);
}

delete [] pwszBindingString;
pwszBindingString = NULL;

return hr;
}
```

Visual Basic

The following code enumerates all groups and displays the members contained in each group on a member server or a computer running Windows NT Workstation/Windows 2000 Professional:

```
'Example: Enumerating all local groups on member server or
'Windows NT Workstation/Windows 2000 Professional
Dim IADsCont As IADsContainer
Dim Group As IADsGroup


sComputer = InputBox("This script lists the groups on a member server or
workstation." & vbCrLf & vbCrLf & "Specify the computer name:")

If sComputer = "" Then
  MsgBox "No computer name was specified. You must specify a computer name."
  Exit Sub
End If

'''''''''''''''''''''''''''''''''''''''''''''
'Bind to the computer
'''''''''''''''''''''''''''''''''''''''''''''
```

(continued)

(continued)

```
'Note that this sample uses the caller's security context.
'To specify a user account other than the user account under which
'which your application is running, use IADsOpenDSObject.
Set IADsCont = GetObject("WinNT://" & sComputer & ",computer")
If (Err.Number <> 0) Then
   BailOnFailure Err.Number, "on GetObject method"
End If

''''''''''''''''''''''''''''''''''''''''
'Filter to view only group objects
''''''''''''''''''''''''''''''''''''''''

IADsCont.Filter = Array("group")
If (Err.Number <> 0) Then
   BailOnFailure Err.Number, "on IADsContainer::Filter method"
End If

strText = ""
intIndex = 0
intNumDisplay = 0
cmember = 0
'Maximum number of groups to list on a msgbox.
MAX_DISPLAY = 10

''''''''''''''''''''''''''''''''''''''''
'Get each group and display its name and its members
''''''''''''''''''''''''''''''''''''''''

For Each Group In IADsCont
    intIndex = intIndex + 1
    'Get the name
    strText = strText & vbCrLf & Right("   " & intIndex, 4) & " " & Group.Name

    intNumDisplay = intNumDisplay + 1
    'Get the members object
    Set memberList = Group.members
    If (Err.Number <> 0) Then
        BailOnFailure Err.Number, "on IADsGroup::members method"
    End If

    'Get the enumerate the members of the group from the members object
    For Each member In memberList
      If cmember = 0 Then
      strText = strText & vbCrLf & "          " & "Members:"
      End If
```

```
         strText = strText & vbCrLf & "            " & member.Name & " (" & member.Class
& ")"
         cmember = cmember + 1
      Next
      If cmember = 0 Then
         strText = strText & vbCrLf & "         " & "No members"
      End If
      'Display in msgbox if there are MAX_DISPLAY groups to display
      If intNumDisplay >= MAX_DISPLAY Then
          Call show_groups(strText, sComputer)
          strText = ""
          intNumDisplay = 0
      End If
      'Reset the count of members within the current group
      cmember = 0
   Next
Call show_groups(strText, sComputer)


'''''''''''''''''''''''''''''''''''''''''''''
'Display subroutines
'''''''''''''''''''''''''''''''''''''''''''''
Sub show_groups(strText, strName)
    MsgBox strText, vbInformation, "Groups on " & strName
End Sub

Sub BailOnFailure(ErrNum, ErrText)    strText = "Error 0x" & Hex(ErrNum) & " " & ErrText
    MsgBox strText, vbInformation, "ADSI Error"
    WScript.Quit
End Sub
```

Creating Machine Local Groups on Member Servers and Windows 2000 Professional

Only machine local groups (class **localGroup**) can be created on member servers and Windows® 2000 Professional.

▶ **To create a machine local group on a member server or computer running Windows 2000 Professional**

1. Bind to the computer using the following rules:

   a. Use an account that has sufficient rights to access that computer.

   b. Use the binding string format on the next page using the WinNT provider, computer name, and an extra parameter to tell ADSI that it is binding to a computer.

WinNT://*sComputerName , computer*

where *sComputerName* is the name of the computer who groups you want to access.

In the binding string, the "*,computer*" parameter tells ADSI that it is binding to a computer. ADSI makes this information available to the WinNT provider's parser so that it can skip some ambiguity-resolution queries to determine what type of object you are binding to.

c. Bind to the **IADsContainer** interface.

2. Specify "**localGroup**" as the class using **IADsContainer::Create** to add the group.

Note   If you specify "**group**" as the class, ADSI uses "**localGroup**". Do not specify the class as "**globalGroup**". Groups of class "**globalGroup**" cannot be created on member servers or a computer running Windows NT Workstation/Windows 2000 Professional. If you specify "**globalGroup**," **IADsContainer::Create** creates the group in the property cache but **IADs::SetInfo** does not write the group to the security database and it does not return an error.

---

3. Write the group to the computer's security database using **IADs::SetInfo**.

Example Code for Creating a Group on a Member Server or Windows NT Workstation/Windows 2000 Professional

C++

The following code fragment creates a group on a member server or a computer running Windows NT Workstation/Windows 2000 Professional:

```
void wmain( int argc, wchar_t *argv[ ])
{
    HRESULT hr;
    IDirectoryObject * pDirObjectRoot            = NULL;
    IDirectoryObject * pDirObjectSampleLocal     = NULL;
    BOOL               bMixedMode;
    IADsContainer    * pIADsCont                 = NULL;

    // Initialize COM
    CoInitialize(0);
    IUnknown * pUnk;

    // Since we are using the WinNT provider,
    // bind to the specific computer name,
    // put your computer name in the string below
    #ifdef USE_OPEN_OBJECT
```

```
        hr = ADsOpenObject(L"WinNT://MyComputerName,computer", ADS_OPENOBJECT_USERNAME,
ADS_OPENOBJECT_PASSWORD ,

ADS_SECURE_AUTHENTICATION,IID_IADsContainer, (void**) &pIADsCont);
    #else
        hr = ADsGetObject(L"WinNT:// MyComputerName,computer", IID_IADsContainer, (void**)
&pIADsCont);
    #endif

    if (SUCCEEDED(hr))
    {
        IDispatch * pIDispatch = NULL;

        BSTR bsGroup = SysAllocString(L"group");
        BSTR bsName = SysAllocString(L"ThisIsAGroup");

        hr = pIADsCont->Create(bsGroup,bsName , &pIDispatch);

        if (SUCCEEDED(hr))
        {
            puts(QueryAllInterfaces(pIDispatch));

            IADsGroup   * pGroup = NULL;

            hr = pIDispatch->QueryInterface(IID_IADsGroup,(void**)&pGroup);

            if (SUCCEEDED(hr))
            {
                hr = pGroup->SetInfo();

                if(SUCCEEDED(hr))
                {
                    // NOW- add some users (fill these in with Valid Users)
                    BSTR bsUserOne = SysAllocString(L"WinNT://MyComputerName
/Administrator");
                    BSTR bsUserTwo = SysAllocString(L"WinNT://MyComputerName /jcooper");
                    hr = pGroup->Add(bsUserOne);
                    if (SUCCEEDED(hr))
                    {
                        hr = pGroup->Add(bsUserTwo);
                        if (SUCCEEDED(hr))
                        {
                            IADsMembers *   pADsMembers       = NULL;
                            // Ptr to Members of the IADsGroup
```

(continued)

(continued)

```
BOOL            fContinue        = TRUE;
  // Looping Variable
IEnumVARIANT * pEnumVariant      = NULL;
  // Ptr to the Enum variant
IUnknown *      pUnknown         = NULL;
  // IUnknown for getting the ENUM initially
VARIANT         VariantArray[FETCH_NUM];
  // Variant array for temp holding
  // returned data
ULONG           ulElementsFetched = NULL;
  // Number of elements fetched

// Get a interface pointer to the
// IADsCollection of members
hr = pGroup->Members(&pADsMembers);
if (SUCCEEDED(hr))
{
    // Ask the IADsCollection of members
    // for a new ENUM Interface
    // Note the enum comes back as an
    // IUnknown *
    hr = pADsMembers->get__NewEnum(&pUnknown);
    if (SUCCEEDED(hr))
    {
        // QI the IUnknown * for a
        // IEnumVARIANT interface
        hr = pUnknown->QueryInterface(IID_IEnumVARIANT, (void
**)&pEnumVariant);

        if (SUCCEEDED(hr))
        {
            // While have not hit errors or
            // end of data....
            while (fContinue)
            {
                ulElementsFetched = 0;
                // Get a "batch" number of
                // group members- number of
                // rows specified by
                // FETCH_NUM
                hr = ADsEnumerateNext(pEnumVariant, FETCH_NUM,
VariantArray, &ulElementsFetched);

                if (ulElementsFetched )//SUCCEEDED(hr) && hr
!= S_FALSE)
```

```
{
    // Loop through the
    // current batch-
    // printing the path
    // for each member
    for (ULONG i = 0; i < ulElementsFetched; i++ )
    {
        IDispatch * pDispatch          = NULL;
            // ptr for holding dispath of element
        IADs       * pIADsGroupMember  = NULL;
            // IADs ptr to group member
        BSTR         bstrPath          = NULL;
            // Holds path of object

        // Get the dispatch ptr for the variant
        pDispatch = VariantArray[i].pdispVal;
        assert(HAS_BIT_STYLE(VariantArray[i].vt,VT_DISPATCH));

        // Get the IADs interface for the "member" of this group
        hr = pDispatch->QueryInterface(IID_IADs,
            (VOID **) &pIADsGroupMember) ;

        if (SUCCEEDED(hr))
        {
            // Get the ADsPath property for this member
            hr = pIADsGroupMember->get_ADsPath(&bstrPath) ;

            if (SUCCEEDED(hr))
            {
                // Print the ADsPath of the group member
                printf("\tMember Object: %ws\n", bstrPath);
                SysFreeString(bstrPath);
            }
            pIADsGroupMember->Release();
            pIADsGroupMember  = NULL;
```

(continued)

(continued)

```
                                                        }
                                                      }
                                                      // Clear the variant
                                                      // array
                                                      memset(VariantArray, 0,
sizeof(VARIANT)*FETCH_NUM);

                                                }
                                                else
                                                    fContinue = FALSE;
                                          }
                                          pEnumVariant->Release();
                                          pEnumVariant = NULL;
                                    }
                                    pUnknown->Release();
                                    pUnknown = NULL;
                              }
                              pADsMembers ->Release();
                              pADsMembers  = NULL;
                        }
                      }
                    }
                  SysFreeString(bsUserOne);
                  SysFreeString(bsUserTwo);
                  bsUserOne = NULL;
                  bsUserTwo = NULL;
            }
            pGroup->Release();
            pGroup = NULL;
      }

      pIDispatch->Release();
      pIDispatch = NULL;
    }
    pIADsCont->Release();
    pIADsCont = NULL;
  }
  CoUninitialize();
}
```

Visual Basic

The code that follows creates a group on a member server or a computer running
Windows NT Workstation/Windows 2000 Professional.

```
On Error Resume Next

Dim IADsCont As IADsContainer
Dim oIADsGroup As IADsGroup
Dim ListIADsMembers As IADsMembers
Dim Member As IADs

sComputer = InputBox("This script creates a group on a member server or workstation." &
vbCrLf & vbCrLf & "Specify the computer name:")
sGroup = InputBox("Specify the group name:")

If sComputer = "" Then
  MsgBox "No computer name was specified. You must specify a computer name."
  Exit Sub
End If
If sGroup = "" Then
  MsgBox "No group name was specified. You must specify a group name."
  Exit Sub
End If

'''''''''''''''''''''''''''''''''''''''''
'Bind to the computer
'''''''''''''''''''''''''''''''''''''''''
Set IADsCont = GetObject("WinNT://" & sComputer & ",computer")
If (Err.Number <> 0) Then
   BailOnFailure Err.Number, "on GetObject method"
End If

'''''''''''''''''''''''''''''''''''''''''
'Create the group
'''''''''''''''''''''''''''''''''''''''''
'Only Local groups can be created on member servers and
'Windows NT Workstation/Windows 2000 Professional.
Set oIADsGroup = IADsCont.Create("localGroup", sGroup)
If (Err.Number <> 0) Then
   BailOnFailure Err.Number, "on IADsContainer::Create method"
End If

'''''''''''''''''''''''''''''''''''''''''
'Write the group to the computer's security database.
'''''''''''''''''''''''''''''''''''''''''
oIADsGroup.SetInfo

'''''''''''''''''''''''''''''''''''''''''
```

(continued)

(continued)

```
'Read the group that was just created
'and display its name and its members.
.......................................
strText = "The group " & oIADsGroup.Name & " was created on computer " & sComputer & "."
If (Err.Number <> 0) Then
    BailOnFailure Err.Number, "on IADsGroup::Name method"
End If
Set ListIADsMembers = oIADsGroup.members
If (Err.Number <> 0) Then
    BailOnFailure Err.Number, "on IADsGroup::members method"
End If
'Get the enumerate the members of the group from the members object
cmember = 0
For Each Member In ListIADsMembers
  If cmember = 0 Then
    strText = strText & vbCrLf & "        " & "Members:"
  End If
  strText = strText & vbCrLf & "        " & Member.Name & " (" & Member.Class & ")"
  cmember = cmember + 1
Next
If cmember = 0 Then
    strText = strText & vbCrLf & "        " & "No members"
End If

Call show_groups(strText, sComputer)


.......................................
'Display subroutines
.......................................
Sub show_groups(strText, strName)
    MsgBox strText, vbInformation, "Create group on " & strName
End Sub
```

Deleting Groups on Member Servers and Windows 2000 Professional

▶ **To delete a machine local group from a member server or computer running Windows® 2000 Professional**

1. Bind to the computer using the following rules:

   a. Use an account that has sufficient rights to access that computer.

    b. Use the following binding string format using the WinNT provider, computer name, and an extra parameter to tell ADSI that it is binding to a computer:

       WinNT://*sComputerName* , computer

       where *sComputerName* is the name of the computer that has the groups you want to access.

       In the binding string, the "*,computer*" parameter tells ADSI that it is binding to a computer and allows the WinNT provider's parser to skip some ambiguity-resolution queries to determine what type of object you are binding to.

    c. Bind to the **IADsContainer** interface.

2. Specify "group" as the class using **IADsContainer::Delete** to delete the group.

    You do not need to call **IADs::SetInfo** to commit the change to the container. The **IADsContainer::Delete** call commits the deletion of the group directly to the directory.

Example Code for Deleting a Group on a Member Server or Windows NT Workstation/Windows 2000 Professional

C++

The following function deletes a group on a member server or a computer running Windows NT Workstation/Windows 2000 Professional:

```
///////////////////////////////////////////////////////////////////////
/*  DeleteADObject()    - Deletes the passed object by AdsPath

    Parameters

        LPOLESTR pwszAdsPath          -        AdsPath of object to delete

    Optional Parameters:

        LPOLESTR pwszUser             - User Name and Password, if the
                                        parameters are NOT passed,
        LPOLESTER pwszPassWord        - Binding will use ADsGetObject,
                                        if the parameters
                                      - Are specified, will use
                                        ADsOpenObject, passing user name
                                        and password
*/
HRESULT DeleteADObject(LPOLESTR pwszAdsPath, LPOLESTR  pwszUser,LPOLESTR  pwszPassWord)
{
    HRESULT             hr;
    BSTR                bsParentPath;
    IADs *              pIADsToDelete = NULL;
    IDirectoryObject *  pIDirObjectParent= NULL;
```

(continued)

(continued)

```
VARIANT              vCNToDelete;
WCHAR                pwszTemp[512];

VariantInit(&vCNToDelete);
OutputDebugString(pwszAdsPath);
OutputDebugString(L"\r\n");

// Bind to the object being deleted

assert((pwszUser==NULL && pwszPassWord == NULL) || (pwszUser && pwszPassWord));

// If a username and password are passed in, use ADsOpenObject()
// otherwise use ADsGetObject()
if (!pwszUser) // No user password passed, use ADsOpenObject
{
    hr = ADsGetObject(  pwszAdsPath, IID_IADs,(void **)& pIADsToDelete);
}
else
{
    hr = ADsOpenObject(pwszAdsPath, pwszUser, pwszPassWord,
                   ADS_SECURE_AUTHENTICATION,IID_IADs, (void**) & pIADsToDelete);
}

if (SUCCEEDED(hr))
{
    // Get the parent path
    hr = pIADsToDelete->get_Parent(&bsParentPath);

    // Get the CN property for the object to delete
    hr = pIADsToDelete->Get(L"cn",&vCNToDelete);
    if (SUCCEEDED(hr))
    {
        // ***********************************************************
        // Now bind to the parent
        // If a username and password are passed in,
        //   use ADsOpenObject()
        // otherwise use ADsGetObject()
        if (!pwszUser) // No user password passed, use ADsOpenObject
        {
            hr = ADsGetObject(  bsParentPath, IID_IDirectoryObject,(void **)&
pIDirObjectParent);
        }
        else
```

```
            {
                hr = ADsOpenObject(bsParentPath, pwszUser, pwszPassWord,
                                ADS_SECURE_AUTHENTICATION,IID_IDirectoryObject,
(void**) & pIDirObjectParent);
            }
            if (SUCCEEDED(hr))
            {
                // Release the object to delete
                pIADsToDelete->Release();
                pIADsToDelete =NULL;

                // Put the CN property into a string beginning with CN=
                swprintf(pwszTemp,L"cn=%s\n",vCNToDelete.bstrVal);

                // Ask the parent to delete the child
                hr =pIDirObjectParent->DeleteDSObject(pwszTemp);
                // Release the Parent Object
                pIDirObjectParent->Release();
                pIDirObjectParent = NULL;
            }
        }
        SysFreeString(bsParentPath);
    }
    // If we have a IADsObject- we need to release it
    if ( pIADsToDelete)
    {
        // Release the object to delete
        pIADsToDelete->Release();
        pIADsToDelete =NULL;
    }

    VariantClear(&vCNToDelete);
 return hr;
}
```

Visual Basic

The following code deletes a group on a member server or a computer running Windows NT Workstation/Windows 2000 Professional:

```
'Example: Deleting a local group on a member server or Windows NT Workstation/Windows 2000
Professional

'''''''''''''''''''''''''''''''''''''''
'Parse the arguments
'''''''''''''''''''''''''''''''''''''''
```

(continued)

(continued)

```
On Error Resume Next

Set oArgs = WScript.Arguments
If oArgs.Count < 2 Then
    sComputer = InputBox("This script deletes a group from a member server or
workstation." & vbCrLf & vbCrLf &"Specify

the computer name:")
    sGroup = InputBox("Specify the group name:")
Else
    sComputer = oArgs.item(0)
    sGroup = oArgs.item(1)
End If


If sComputer = "" Then
    WScript.Echo "No computer name was specified. You must specify a computer name."
    WScript.Quit(1)
End If
If sGroup = "" Then
    WScript.Echo "No group name was specified. You must specify a group name."
    WScript.Quit(1)
End If

''''''''''''''''''''''''''''''''''''''''
'Bind to the computer
''''''''''''''''''''''''''''''''''''''''
Set cont= GetObject("WinNT://" & sComputer & ",computer")
If (Err.Number <> 0) Then
    BailOnFailure Err.Number, "on GetObject method"
End If


''''''''''''''''''''''''''''''''''''''''
'Delete the group
''''''''''''''''''''''''''''''''''''''''
'You do not need to specify localGroup, just group is sufficient.
Set oGroup = cont.Delete("group", sGroup)
If (Err.Number <> 0) Then
    BailOnFailure Err.Number, "on IADsContainer::Delete method"
End If

strText = "The group " & sGroup & " was deleted on computer " & sComputer & "."

Call show_groups(strText, sComputer)
```

```
' ' ' ' ' ' ' ' ' ' ' ' ' ' ' ' ' ' ' ' ' ' ' ' ' ' ' ' ' ' ' ' ' ' ' ' ' ' ' '
'Display subroutines
' ' ' ' ' ' ' ' ' ' ' ' ' ' ' ' ' ' ' ' ' ' ' ' ' ' ' ' ' ' ' ' ' ' ' ' ' ' '
Sub show_groups(strText, strName)
    MsgBox strText, vbInformation, "Create group on " & strName
End Sub
```

Adding Domain Groups to Machine Local Groups on Member Servers and Windows 2000 Professional

When a member server or a computer running Windows NT® Workstation or Windows® 2000 Professional is a member of a Windows 2000 domain, the groups or users in the domain can be used in the computer's local security database to grant rights to that group on that particular computer.

When managing groups on a Windows 2000 domain using ADSI, you use the LDAP provider. When managing groups on member servers and a computer running Windows NT Workstation/Windows 2000 Professional, you use the WinNT provider.

This means you need to bind at least once to each provider: 1) Bind to the LDAP provider to retrieve the ADsPath to the group or user you want to add to a group in the local database and 2) Bind to the WinNT provider to add that user or group to a machine local group.

Note   Only machine local groups can be created on member servers and Windows 2000 Professional. However, those machine local groups can contain 1) Universal and global groups from the forest containing the domain that the computer is a member of or 2) Domain local groups from that computer's domain 3) Users from any domain in the forest.

▶ **To enumerate the machine local groups on a member server or computer running Windows 2000 Professional**

1. Bind to the group you want to add a member to using the following rules:

   a. Use an account that has sufficient rights to access that computer.

   b. Use the following binding string format using the WinNT provider, computer name, and an extra parameter to tell ADSI that it is binding to a computer:

      WinNT://*sComputerName*, computer

      where *sComputerName* is the name of the computer group you want to add a member to.

      In the binding string, the "*,computer*" parameter tells ADSI that it is binding to a computer. ADSI makes this information available to the WinNT provider's parser so that it can skip some ambiguity-resolution queries to determine what type of object you are binding to. This can save the user a 5-20 second wait for the ambiguity to be resolved.

    c. Bind to the **IADsContainer** interface of the computer.

    d. Use **IADsContainer::GetObject** to bind to the group object and specify "**localGroup**" as the class and the group name as the name of the object.

2. Get the ADsPath of the user or group to add to the group. You should bind to the object using the WinNT provider, get an **IADs** pointer, and use the **IADs::get_ADsPath** property method to get the ADsPath of the object.

    If the user or group is in the current user's domain, use serverless binding and rootDSE to bind to the domain, get an **IADs** pointer, use the **IADs::Get** method to retrieve the dc attribute (this is the domain name), and use the dc value to bind to the domain using a binding string with the following format:

    WinNT://*sDomainName*, domain

    where *sDomainName* is the name of the domain containing the user or group you want to add to the machine local group.

    Then, use **IADsContainer::GetObject** to bind to the user or group object and use the **IADs::get_ADsPath** method to get the ADsPath of the object.

3. Add the user or group to the group, using the **IADsGroup::Add** method.

Example Code for Adding a Domain User or Group to a Matching Local Group

The following VBScript adds a domain user/group to a machine local group on a member server or a computer running Windows NT Workstation/Windows 2000 Professional:

```
'The following script adds a domain user/group to a machine local group
'on a member server or Windows NT Workstation/Windows 2000 Professional:

Dim IADsCont As IADsContainer
Dim ListIADsMembers As IADsMembers
Dim Member As IADs
Dim GroupIADsGroup As IADsGroup


sComputer = InputBox("This script adds a domain user/group to a local group on a member
server or workstation." & vbCrLf & vbCrLf & "Specify the computer name of the group where
you want to add the member:")
sGroup = InputBox("Specify the name of the group to which you want to add the member:")

If sComputer = "" Then
  MsgBox "No computer name was specified. You must specify a computer name."
  Exit Sub
End If
If sGroup = "" Then
  MsgBox "No group name was specified. You must specify a group name."
  Exit Sub
End If
```

```
''''''''''''''''''''''''''''''''''''''''
'Bind to the computer
''''''''''''''''''''''''''''''''''''''''
'
Set IADsCont = GetObject("WinNT://" & sComputer & ",computer")
Set GroupIADsGroup = IADsCont.GetObject("LocalGroup", sGroup)
If (Err.Number <> 0) Then
    BailOnFailure Err.Number, "on GetObject method"
End If

strText = ""
cmember = 0

''''''''''''''''''''''''''''''''''''''''
'Get display group name and its members
''''''''''''''''''''''''''''''''''''''''
    'Get the name
    strText = strText & vbCrLf & "The group " & GroupIADsGroup.Name & " currently has the
following members:"
    'Get the members object
    Set ListIADsMembers = GroupIADsGroup.members
    If (Err.Number <> 0) Then
        BailOnFailure Err.Number, "on IADsGroup::members method"
    End If
    'Enumerate the members of the group from the members object
    For Each Member In ListIADsMembers
        strText = strText & vbCrLf & "        " & Member.Name & " (" & Member.Class & ")"
      cmember = cmember + 1
    Next
    If cmember = 0 Then
        strText = strText & vbCrLf & "        " & "No members"
    End If
Call show_groups(strText, sComputer)

sNewMember = InputBox("Specify the ADsPath of the domain user or group to add:")
If sNewMember = "" Then
  MsgBox "No member was specified. You must specify a member to add."
  Exit Sub
End If

''''''''''''''''''''''''''''''''''''''''
'Bind to the member you want to add
''''''''''''''''''''''''''''''''''''''''
```

(continued)

(continued)

```
Set NewMember = GetObject(sNewMember)
If (Err.Number <> 0) Then
   BailOnFailure Err.Number, "Could not bind to user or group to add."
End If
'Call show_groups(member.ADsPath, sComputer)

GroupIADsGroup.Add (NewMember.ADsPath)
'group.Add("WinNT://timto1923dom/yyyy")
'group.Add("WinNT://redmond /domain users")
If (Err.Number <> 0) Then
   BailOnFailure Err.Number, "Could not add member to group."
End If

''''''''''''''''''''''''''''''''''''''''''
'Confirm success and display group name and its members
''''''''''''''''''''''''''''''''''''''''''
strText = "Member was successfully added."
strText = strText & vbCrLf & "The group " & GroupIADsGroup.Name & " now has the following
members:"
'Get the members object
Set ListIADsMembers = GroupIADsGroup.members
If (Err.Number <> 0) Then
   BailOnFailure Err.Number, "on IADsGroup::members method"
End If
'Enumerate the members of the group from the members object
For Each Member In ListIADsMembers
  strText = strText & vbCrLf & "       " & Member.Name & " (" & Member.Class & ")"
  cmember = cmember + 1
Next
If cmember = 0 Then
  strText = strText & vbCrLf & "       " & "No members"
End If
Call show_groups(strText, sComputer)

''''''''''''''''''''''''''''''''''''''''''
'Display subroutines
''''''''''''''''''''''''''''''''''''''''''
Sub show_groups(strText, strName)
    MsgBox strText, vbInformation, "Groups on " & strName
End Sub

Sub BailOnFailure(ErrNum, ErrText)    strText = "Error 0x" & Hex(ErrNum) & " " & ErrText
    MsgBox strText, vbInformation, "ADSI Error"
    WScript.Quit
End Sub
```

What Application and Service Developers Need to Know About Groups

When designing an application or service, you can use groups to delegate administration or control access to the application or service as a whole or some portion of it. For example, an application might want to control who has the right to perform various administrative operations. You can do this by creating ACEs that allow specified access rights to the appropriate groups. In general, it's better to have an ACE that allows access to a group than to have several ACEs that allow access to individual users or computers.

Applications should adhere to the following guidelines when using groups:

- Do not create dependencies on hard-coded groups, which can cause serious problems if the group, for example, is deleted or moved.
- If possible, use you the appropriate built-in group rather than creating a new group just for your application. Creating groups that have a limited use (that is, the groups only apply when running the application or accessing the service) unnecessarily adds the SIDs for the groups to the access tokens of the users who are members of those groups. This can slow logon performance for those users (access token is created at logon time) as well as access checks when accessing resources.
- If you do create your own groups:

  Protect the group by setting ACEs that control who can add or remove members.

  Use global groups if they are used for access control on Active Directory objects.

  Use universal groups only if necessary (member information is required globally using global catalog; group can contain any user/group). If you do use universal groups, place global groups in the universal group and add/remove users from the global group. Avoid excess change to universal groups for replication efficiency.

- Do not control access by checking group membership to determine whether the current user belongs to the appropriate group. Instead, use an ACE and control access by having the system perform an access check.

If you need to control access to operations that do not fit within the predefined access rights for Active Directory objects (see **ADS_RIGHTS_ENUM**), you can use the extended rights feature of access control in Windows® 2000.

▶ **To use an extended right to control the right to perform an operation**

1. Create an extended right that defines the type of access to the application or service. See *Extended Rights*.
2. Create an Active Directory object that represents the application, service, or resource.
3. Add object ACEs to the DACL in the object's security descriptor to allow or deny users or groups the extended right on that object. See *Setting Access Rights on an Object*.
4. When a user tries to perform the protected operation, your application or service uses the **AccessCheckByTypeResultList** function to determine whether the extended right is granted to the user. See *Checking an Extended Right in an Object's ACL*.

5. Based on the result of the access check on the object, your application or service can allow or deny the user access to the application or service.

A service application could also create a group whose members would be the various service instances. For instance, a service with instances installed on multiple computers throughout an enterprise might have a common log file that all service instances write to. The service installation program creates the log file and uses a DACL to allow access only to members of a group. The group members would be the user accounts under which the various service instances are running, or if the services run under the LocalSystem account, the members would be the computer accounts of the host servers.

CHAPTER 15

Tracking Changes

Many applications need to maintain consistency between specific data stored in Active Directory™ and other data. The other data might be stored in Active Directory, in a SQL Server table, in a file, in the registry—anywhere. When data stored in Active Directory changes, the other data might need to change in order to remain consistent. Applications that have this requirement include the following:

- *Directory synchronization applications.* For instance, the Active Directory Connector (ADC) is an application that maintains consistency between Active Directory and the Exchange Directory.
- *Offline address book applications.* When information about a user changes in Active Directory, the offline address book should eventually change to reflect this.
- *Service applications whose configuration information is stored in Active Directory.* When a service's configuration changes in Active Directory, the service should reconfigure itself as quickly as possible.

Active Directory contains rich support for this class of applications, which we'll call *change-tracking applications*. This support is the topic of this chapter.

This chapter discusses the following topics:

- An overview of techniques for tracking changes to Active Directory
- How to register for and process change notifications
- How to poll for changes to Active Directory using the DirSync control
- How to poll for Active Directory changes using the USNChanged attribute
- How to retrieve information about deleted objects from a Deleted Objects container

Note that this chapter does not cover mechanisms used by *monitoring applications*. These are applications that monitor directory changes not for the purpose of maintaining consistent data between separate stores, but simply as a management technique. Although monitoring applications can use the same mechanisms that support change-tracking applications, the following mechanisms (documented elsewhere) are specifically tailored for monitoring applications:

- *Security auditing.* By modifying the SACL portion of an object's security descriptor, you can cause accesses to the object on a given domain controller to generate audit records in the security event log on that DC. You can audit reads, writes, or both reads and writes; you can audit the entire object or specific attributes. For more information, see *Retrieving an Object's SACL* and *Audit Generation*.

- *Event logging.* By modifying registry settings on a given domain controller you can change the kinds of events logged to the directory service event log. Specifically, to log all modifications, set the "8 Directory Access" value under the HKEY_LOCAL_MACHINE\SYSTEM\CurrentControlSet\Services\NTDS\Diagnostics key to 4. For more information, see *Event Logging.*

- *Event tracing.* Windows® 2000 provides an Event Tracing API for tracing and logging interesting events in software or hardware. The Windows 2000 operating system, and Active Directory in particular, support the use of event tracing for capacity planning and detailed performance analysis. For more information, see *Event Tracing.*

Overview of Change Tracking Techniques

There are several dimensions on which mechanisms for tracking changes can differ:

- *Scope for tracking changes.* An application might want to track changes to a single attribute of a single object, to all objects in a domain, or something in between. If the mechanism matches an application's needs, the application will receive a minimum of irrelevant information, enhancing overall performance.

- *Timeliness.* An application might want to see every change as it happens, or might be content to see the net effect of changes that have accumulated over a period of minutes or hours.

   Processing less timely data may be more efficient, because several changes may be collapsed into one. For instance, if an attribute changes three times within a one hour interval, an application that is satisfied with changes that have accumulated over an hour will see just one attribute change, not three.

   When thinking about timeliness it is important to consider the effect of replication latency. An update that originates on one domain controller does not replicate to another domain controller instantly. Requiring change-tracking timeliness much better than the expected replication latency often gives no real benefit to the application.

- *Polling versus notification.* With polling an application periodically makes a request to a domain controller to receive change tracking information. With notification the domain controller sends changes to the application only when changes have happened.

   The overhead of polling is obvious: The application may request change tracking information when nothing of interest has changed. The overhead of notification is more subtle. The server must maintain information about notification requests and must consult this information to decide whether or not to send a notification. This can add overhead to normal update requests. In effect, normal updates pay some of the price of notifications.

- *Expressing the application's knowledge: persistent versus ephemeral.* Every change tracking mechanism must include some method for the server holding the information being tracked to understand the application's state of knowledge, so that the idea of "change" is well defined. For instance, the application's state of knowledge might be expressed as "I am fully up to date with all changes that took place on DC d before time t." A mechanism based on this way of expressing an application's state of knowledge would provide an efficient way for the application to obtain changes that have occurred later than a specified time.

  If the expression of the application's knowledge can be persisted (that is, stored recoverably, as in a file or database), application restart is less expensive and simpler than if it cannot. In the example above, the expression of the application's knowledge can be persisted by recording the DC d and the time t. Some change notification mechanisms don't allow this information to be persisted. The server and application must synchronize with some other mechanism when the application starts. This is expensive if many objects are involved, and can involve complicated programming.

You can use the following techniques to track changes in Active Directory.

- Use the change notification control to initiate a persistent asynchronous search for changes that match a specified filter. See *Change Notifications in Active Directory.*
- Use a directory synchronization (DirSync) search to retrieve changes that have occurred since the previous DirSync search. See *Polling for Changes Using the DirSync Control.*
- Use the USNChanged attribute to search for objects that have changed since the previous search. See *Polling for Changes Using USNChanged.*

The change notification control is designed for programs or services that want reasonably prompt notification of infrequent changes. An example is a service or program that stores configuration information in Active Directory™ and wants to be notified promptly when a change occurs. Note that there are limitations of the notification control.

- The promptness of notifications depends on replication latency and where the change was made. You may be notified promptly when a change replicates into the replica you are monitoring. But the change may have originated much earlier on some other replica.
- The control is restricted to monitoring a single object or the immediate children of a container. Applications that need to monitor multiple containers or unrelated objects can register up to five notification requests.
- If too many clients are listening for changes that occur frequently, it will impact the performance of the server. In general, applications should limit their use of this control for performance reasons on the server. If you don't need to know about changes immediately, it may be best to periodically poll for changes instead of using change notification.

The DirSync and USNChanged search techniques are designed for applications that maintain consistency between data in Active Directory™ and corresponding data in some other storage. These techniques are used by applications that periodically poll for changes. The DirSync technique is based on an LDAP server control that you can use through ADSI or LDAP APIs. The disadvantages of the DirSync control are that it can only be used by a highly privileged account, such as a domain administrator

- The DirSync control can only be used by a highly-privileged account, such as a domain administrator.
- The DirSync control can only monitor an entire naming context. You cannot limit the scope of a DirSync search to monitor only a specific subtree, container, or object in a naming context.

The USNChanged technique does not have these limitations, although it is somewhat more complicated to use than DirSync.

Change Notifications in Active Directory

Active Directory™ provides a mechanism for a client application to register with a domain controller to receive change notifications. To do this, the client specifies the LDAP change notification control in an asynchronous LDAP search operation. The client also specifies the following search parameters:

Base of the search
    The distinguished name of an object in the directory.

Scope
    You can specify either LDAP_SCOPE_BASE to monitor just the object itself, or LDAP_SCOPE_ONELEVEL to monitor the immediate children of the object, not including the object itself. Do not specify LDAP_SCOPE_SUBTREE. Although the subtree scope is supported if the base object is the root of a naming context, its use can severely impact server performance, because it generates an LDAP search result message every time an object in the naming context is modified. You cannot specify LDAP_SCOPE_SUBTREE for an arbitrary subtree.

Filter
    You must specify a search filter of (objectclass=*), which means you receive notifications for changes to any object in the specified scope.

Attributes
    You can specify a list of attributes to be returned when a change occurs. Note that you receive notifications when any attribute is modified, not just the specified attributes.

You can register up to five notification requests on a single LDAP connection. You must have a dedicated thread that waits for the notifications and processes them as quickly as possible. When you call the **ldap_search_ext** function to register a notification request, the function returns a message identifier that identifies that request. You then use the **ldap_result** function to wait for change notifications. When a change occurs, the server sends you an LDAP message containing the message identifier for the notification request that generated the notification. This causes the **ldap_result** function to return with search results that identify the object that changed.

It is up to the client application to determine the initial state of the object being monitored. To do this, you must first register the notification request and then read the current state.

It is also up to the client application to determine the nature of the change. For a base level search, a notification occurs when any attribute changes, or when the object is deleted or moved. For a one-level search, a notification occurs when a child object is created, deleted, moved, or modified. Note that moving or renaming an object in the hierarchy above a target object does not generate a notification even though the distinguished name of the target changed as a result. For example, suppose you are monitoring changes to the child objects in a container, you do not receive notifications if the container itself is moved or renamed.

When the client processes the search results, it can use the **ldap_get_dn** function to get the distinguished name of the object that changed. Of course, you cannot rely on distinguished names to identify the objects being tracked, because distinguished names can change. Instead, include the **objectGUID** attribute in the list of attributes to retrieve. Each object's **objectGUID** remains unchanged regardless of where the object is moved within the enterprise forest.

If an object within the search scope is deleted, the client receives a change notification and the **isDeleted** attribute of the object is set to TRUE. In this case, the search results report the new distinguished name of the object in the Deleted Objects container of its partition. It is not necessary to specify the tombstone control (LDAP_SERVER_SHOW_DELETED_OID) to get notifications of object deletions. For more information, see *Retrieving Deleted Objects*.

Once a client has registered a notification request, the client continues to receive notifications until the connection is broken or the client abandons the search by calling the **ldap_abandon** function. If the client or server disconnects, for example, if the server goes down, the notification request is terminated. When the client reconnects, it must register for notifications again, and then read the current state of the objects of interest in case there were changes while the client was disconnected.

The client can use the value of an object's **uSNChanged** attribute to determine whether the current state of the object on the server reflects the latest changes that the client has received. The system increases an object's **uSNChanged** attribute whenever the object is moved or modified. For instance, if the server goes down and the directory partition is restored from a backup, the server's replica of an object may not reflect changes previously reported to the client, in which case the **uSNChanged** value on the server will be lower than the value stored by the client.

For sample code that uses the LDAP change notification control in an asynchronous LDAP search operation, see *Example Code for Receiving Change Notifications*.

For a discussion of when to use the LDAP change notification control, see *Overview of Change Tracking Techniques*.

Example Code for Receiving Change Notifications

The following sample code demonstrates how to use the LDAP change notification control to receive notifications of changes to an object in Active Directory. The example registers for notifications, reads the initial state of the object, and then uses a loop to wait for and process changes to the object.

First, the example calls the **ldap_search_ext** function, which is an asynchronous search operation that returns after registering a notification request. After setting up the notification request, the example calls the **ldap_search_s** function, which is a synchronous search operation that reads the current state of the object. Finally, the example, uses a loop that calls **ldap_result** to wait for results of the asynchronous search operation. When **ldap_result** returns, the example processes the search results and repeats the loop.

Note that if the example read the current state and then set up the notification request, there would be a window of time during which changes could occur before the notification request was registered. By reading the object after setting up the notification request, the window works in reverse—you could receive notifications of changes that occurred before reading the initial state. To handle this possibility, the example caches the object's **uSNChanged** value when it reads the object's initial state. Then, when **ldap_result** returns with a change notification, the example compares the cached **uSNChanged** value with the value reported by **ldap_result**. If the new **uSNChanged** value is less than or equal to the cached value, the example discards the results because they indicate a change that occurred prior to the initial read operation.

This example performs a base level search that monitors a single object. You could specify the LDAP_SCOPE_ONELEVEL scope to monitor all child object's of the specified object. You could also modify the code to register up to five notification requests and then use **ldap_result** to wait for notifications from any of the requests. Remember that change notification requests impact the performance of the server, so you should limit your use as described in *Change Notifications in Active Directory*.

```
#include <windows.h>
#include <winldap.h>
#include <ntldap.h>
#include <stdio.h>
#include <rpcdce.h>

// Forward declarations.
VOID BuildGUIDString(WCHAR *szGUID, LPBYTE pGUID);
BOOL ProcessResult(LDAP *ldapConnection, LDAPMessage *message, __int64
*piUSNChanged );

//*********************************************************************
// GetChangeNotifications
// Binds to an LDAP server, registers for change notifications,
// retrieves the current state, and then goes into a loop that
// waits for and processes change notifications.
//*********************************************************************
INT GetChangeNotifications(
    LPWSTR szSearchBaseDN)  // Distinguished name of object to monitor
{
INT err, n=0;
BOOL bSuccess;
ULONG version = LDAP_VERSION3;
LDAP *ldapConnection = NULL;

LDAPControl simpleControl;
PLDAPControl controlArray[2];

ULONG ulScope = LDAP_SCOPE_BASE;
LONG msgId;
LDAPMessage *results = NULL;
LDAPMessage *message = NULL;

// attributes to retrieve
TCHAR   *szAttribs[]={
        {L"telephoneNumber"},
        {L"isDeleted"},
        {L"objectGUID"},
        {L"uSNChanged"}
    };

// stores the latest USNChanged value for the object.
__int64 iUSNChanged = 0;
```

(continued)

(continued)

```
// Connect to the default LDAP server.
ldapConnection = ldap_open( NULL, 0 );
if ( ldapConnection == NULL ) {
    wprintf( L"ldap_open failed to connect. Error: 0x%x.\n", GetLastError() );
    goto FatalExit0;
}
wprintf( L"Connected to server.\n");


// Specify LDAP version 3.
ldapConnection->ld_lberoptions = 0;
ldap_set_option( ldapConnection, LDAP_OPT_VERSION, &version );


// Bind to the server using default credentials.
err = ldap_bind_s( ldapConnection, NULL, NULL, LDAP_AUTH_NEGOTIATE );
if (LDAP_SUCCESS != err) {
    wprintf(L"Bind failed: 0x%x\n", err);
    goto FatalExit0;
}
wprintf( L"Successful bind.\n");


// Set up the change notification control.
simpleControl.ldctl_oid = LDAP_SERVER_NOTIFICATION_OID_W;
simpleControl.ldctl_iscritical = TRUE;
simpleControl.ldctl_value.bv_len = 0;
simpleControl.ldctl_value.bv_val = NULL;
controlArray[0] = &simpleControl;
controlArray[1] = NULL;


//  Start a persistent asynchronous search.
err   = ldap_search_ext( ldapConnection,
                    (PWCHAR) szSearchBaseDN,
                    ulScope,
                    L"ObjectClass=*",
                    szAttribs,      // Attributes to retrieve
                    0,              // Retrieve attributes and values
                    (PLDAPControl *) &controlArray,
                    NULL,           // Client controls
                    0,              // Timeout
                    0,              // Sizelimit
                    (PULONG)&msgId  // Receives identifier for results
                    );
if (LDAP_SUCCESS != err) {
    wprintf( L" The asynch search failed. Error: 0x%x \n", err );
    goto FatalExit0;
```

```
}
wprintf( L"Registered for change notifications on %s.\n", szSearchBaseDN);
wprintf( L"Message identifier is %d.\n", msgId);

// After starting the persistent search, perform a synchronous search
// to retrieve the current state of the object being monitored.
err = ldap_search_s( ldapConnection,
                     (PWCHAR) szSearchBaseDN,
                     ulScope,
                     L"ObjectClass=*",
                     szAttribs,      // list of attributes to retrieve
                     0,              // retrieve attributes and values
                     &results);      // receives the search results
if (LDAP_SUCCESS != err) {
    wprintf(L"ldap_search_s error: 0x%x\n", err);
    goto FatalExit0;
}
wprintf( L"\nGot current state\n");

// Process the search results.
message = ldap_first_entry( ldapConnection, results );
while (message != NULL)
{
    bSuccess = ProcessResult(ldapConnection, message, &iUSNChanged );
    message = ldap_next_entry( ldapConnection, message );
}
ldap_msgfree( results );

// Wait for a notification, process the results,
// then loop back to wait for the next notification.
wprintf( L"Waiting for change notifications...\n" );
while (n<3)
{
    // Wait for the results of the asynchronous search.
    results = NULL;
    err = ldap_result(
        ldapConnection,
        LDAP_RES_ANY,     // message identifier
        LDAP_MSG_ONE,     // retrieve one message at a time
        NULL,             // no timeout
        &results);        // receives the search results
    if ((err == (ULONG) -1) || (results) == NULL) {
        wprintf(L"ldap_result error: 0x%x\n", ldapConnection->ld_errno);
        break;
```

(continued)

(continued)

```
    }
    wprintf( L"\nGot a notification. Message ID: %d\n", results->lm_msgid);

    // Process the search results.
    message = ldap_first_entry( ldapConnection, results );
    while (message != NULL)
    {
        bSuccess = ProcessResult(ldapConnection, message, &iUSNChanged );
        message = ldap_next_entry( ldapConnection, message );
    }
    ldap_msgfree( results );
    n++;
}

FatalExit0:
if (ldapConnection)
    ldap_unbind( ldapConnection );
if (results)
    ldap_msgfree( results );
return 0;
}

//***********************************************************************
// BuildGUIDString
// Routine that makes the GUID a string in directory service bind form.
//***********************************************************************
VOID
BuildGUIDString(WCHAR *szGUID, LPBYTE pGUID)
{
    DWORD i = 0;
    DWORD dwlen = sizeof(GUID);
    WCHAR buf[4];

    wcscpy(szGUID, L"");

    for (i;i<dwlen;i++) {
        wsprintf(buf, L"%02x", pGUID[i]);
        wcscat(szGUID, buf);
    }
}

//***********************************************************************
// ProcessResult
// Routine that processes the search results.
```

```
//********************************************************************
BOOL ProcessResult(LDAP *ldapConnection,    // Connection handle
                   LDAPMessage *message,    // Result entry to process
                   __int64 *piUSNChanged ) // Latest USNChanged value
{
PWCHAR *value = NULL;
__int64 iNewUSNChanged;

PWCHAR dn = NULL, attribute = NULL;
BerElement *opaque = NULL;
berval **pbvGUID=NULL;
WCHAR szGUID[40];        // string version of the objectGUID attribute
ULONG count, total;

// First, get the uSNChanged attribute to determine whether this
// result is new information. If this uSNChanged value is less than
// the previous one, the result contains out-of-date information, so
// discard it.
value = ldap_get_values(ldapConnection, message, L"uSNChanged");
if (!value) {
    wprintf(L"ldap_get_values error\n");
    return FALSE;
}
iNewUSNChanged = _wtoi64(value[0]);      // Convert string to integer.
if (iNewUSNChanged <= *piUSNChanged)
{
    wprintf( L"Discarding outdated search results.\n");
    ldap_value_free( value );
    return TRUE;
} else
{
    *piUSNChanged = iNewUSNChanged;
    ldap_value_free( value );
}

// The search results are newer than the previous state, so process
// the results. First, print the distinguished name of the object.
dn = ldap_get_dn( ldapConnection, message );
if (!dn) {
    wprintf(L"ldap_get_dn error\n");
    return FALSE;
}
wprintf( L"    Distinguished Name is : %s\n", dn );
ldap_memfree(dn);
```

(continued)

(continued)

```
// Then loop through the attributes and display the new values.
attribute = ldap_first_attribute( ldapConnection, message, &opaque );
while (attribute != NULL)
{
    // Handle objectGUID as a binary value.
    if (_wcsicmp(L"objectGUID", attribute)==0)
    {
        wprintf(L"    %s: ", attribute);
        pbvGUID = ldap_get_values_len (ldapConnection, message, attribute);
        if (pbvGUID)
        {
            BuildGUIDString(szGUID, (LPBYTE) pbvGUID[0]->bv_val);
            wprintf(L"%s\n", szGUID);
        }
        ldap_value_free_len( pbvGUID );
    } else
    {
        // Handle other attributes as string values.
        value = ldap_get_values(ldapConnection, message, attribute);
        wprintf( L"    %s: ", attribute );
        if (total = ldap_count_values(value) > 1) {
            for (count = 0; count < total; count++ )
                wprintf( L"        %s\n", value[count] );
        } else
            wprintf( L"%s\n", value[0] );
        ldap_value_free( value );
    }
    ldap_memfree(attribute);
    attribute = ldap_next_attribute(ldapConnection, message, opaque);
}

return TRUE;
}

//*******************************************************************
// wmain
//*******************************************************************
int wmain( int   cArgs, WCHAR  *pArgs[] )
{
PWCHAR szSearchBaseDN = NULL;

wprintf( L"\n" );
```

```
if (cArgs < 2)
    wprintf(L"Usage: getchanges <distinguished name of search base>\n");

szSearchBaseDN = (PWCHAR) pArgs[1];

return GetChangeNotifications(szSearchBaseDN);

}
```

Polling for Changes Using the DirSync Control

The directory synchronization (DirSync) control is an LDAP server extension that enables an application to search an Active Directory™ partition for objects that have changed since a previous state.

Note that the DirSync caller must have the SE_SYNC_AGENT_NAME privilege, which enables the caller to read all objects and attributes in Active Directory, regardless of the access protections on the objects and attributes. By default, this privilege is assigned to the Administrator and LocalSystem accounts on domain controllers. If your application needs to run under an account that does not have this privilege, use the change-tracking technique described in *Polling for Changes Using USNChanged*. For more information about privileges, see *Privileges*.

You can use the DirSync control through ADSI by specifying the ADS_SEARCHPREF_DIRSYNC search preference when using **IDirectorySearch**. For sample code, see *Example Code Using ADS_SEARCHPREF_DIRSYNC*. You can also perform a DirSync search using the LDAP API. The following discussion describes the ADSI implementation, most of which also applies to using LDAP directly, except as noted at the end of this topic.

When you perform a DirSync search, you pass in a provider-specific blob of data (a cookie) that identifies the directory's state at the time of the previous DirSync search. For the first search, you pass in a NULL cookie, and the search returns all objects that match the filter. The search also returns a valid cookie. Store the cookie in the same storage that you are synchronizing with Active Directory. On subsequent searches, retrieve the cookie from storage and pass it with the search request. The search results now include only the objects and attributes that have changed since the previous state identified by the cookie. The search also returns a new cookie to store for the next search.

The client's search request also specifies the following search parameters:

Base of the search
   The base of a DirSync search must be the root of a directory partition, which can be a domain partition, the configuration partition, or the schema partition.

Scope

The scope of a DirSync search must be ADS_SCOPE_SUBTREE, that is, the entire subtree of the partition. Note that for a search of a domain partition, the subtree includes the heads (but not the contents) of the configuration and schema partitions. To poll for changes in a smaller scope, use the USNChanged technique instead of DirSync.

Filter

You can specify any valid search filter. For an initial search with a NULL cookie, the results include all objects that match the filter. For subsequent searches with a valid cookie, the search results include information only for objects that match the filter and have changed since the state indicated by the cookie. For information on search filters, see *Creating a Query Filter*.

Attributes

You can specify a list of attributes to be returned when a change occurs. For each object, the initial results include all the requested attributes that are set on the object. Subsequent search results include only the specified attributes that have changed. Attributes that have not changed are not included in the search results. In the ADSI implementation, the search results automatically include the ADsPath binding string and **objectGUID** of each object. Also, the specified attributes act as an additional filter; the initial search results include only objects that have at least one of the specified attributes set.

A few additional details:

- For incremental searches, the best practice is to bind to the same domain controller used in the previous search, that is, the DC that generated the cookie. If the same DC is not available, either wait until it is or bind to a new DC and perform a full synchronization. Store the DNS name of the DC in the secondary storage along with the cookie.

  You can pass a cookie generated by one DC to a different DC hosting a replica of the same directory partition. There is no chance that a client will miss out on changes by using a cookie from one DC on another DC. However, it is possible that the search results from the new DC may include changes that were already reported by the old DC; and in some cases, the new DC may return all objects and attributes, as with a full synchronization. The client should just make its database consistent with whatever search results are reported on any given DirSync call, that is, treat all incremental results as if they were the latest state. It doesn't matter whether you've seen the change before or are even going back to a previous state because repeated incremental synchronizations will converge on consistency.

- When an object is renamed or moved, its descendants (if any) are NOT included in the search results, even though the distinguished names of the descendants have changed. Similarly, when an inheritable ACE is modified in an object's security-descriptor, the descendants of the object are NOT included in the search results, even though the security-descriptors of the descendants have changed.

- Use the **objectGUID** attribute to identify the objects being tracked. Each object's **objectGUID** remains unchanged regardless of where the object is moved within the forest.

- The results of an incremental search automatically include deleted objects. If an object is deleted, the object's **isDeleted** attribute is set to TRUE. For more information, see *Retrieving Deleted Objects*.

- Note that the search results of a DirSync search indicate the state of the objects on a replica of the directory partition at the time of the search. This means that changes made on other domain controllers (DC) will not be included if they have not been replicated to the target DC. It also means that an object's attributes may have changed several times since the previous DirSync search, but the search will show only the final state, not the sequence of changes.

- In the ADSI implementation, the application must treat the cookie as opaque and not make any assumptions about its internal organization or value.

- Note that the client stores the cookie, cookie length, and DNS name of the DC in the same storage that contains the synchronized object data. This ensures that the cookie and other parameters remain in sync with the object data if the storage is ever restored from a backup.

LDAP Implementation of the DirSync Control

You can also perform a DirSync search by specifying the LDAP_SERVER_DIRSYNC_OID control with one of the LDAP search functions, such as **ldap_search_ext**. If you use the LDAP API, be sure to also specify the LDAP_SERVER_EXTENDED_DN_OID and LDAP_SERVER_SHOW_DELETED_OID controls. The EXTENDED_DN control causes an LDAP search to return an extended form of the distinguished name that includes the **objectGUID** (and **objectSID** for security principal objects such as users, groups, and computers.) The SHOW_DELETED control causes the search results to include information for deleted objects. Note that these controls are automatically included in the ADSI implementation.

Example Code Using ADS_SEARCHPREF_DIRSYNC

The following sample code uses the ADSI implementation of the directory synchronization (DirSync) control to search the local domain partition of Active Directory for user objects that have changed since the previous call.

The example uses the **IDirectorySearch** interface to search from the root of the domain partition. Before calling the **ExecuteSearch** method, the example calls the **SetSearchPreference** method to specify the ADS_SEARCHPREF_SEARCH_SCOPE, ADS_SEARCHPREF_DIRSYNC, and ADS_SEARCHPREF_TOMBSTONE search preferences. The scope must specify a subtree search. With the ADS_SEARCHPREF_DIRSYNC search preference, you must also specify an **ADS_PROV_SPECIFIC** structure containing the length of the cookie and a pointer to it.

The first time this program is called, it specifies a NULL cookie and a length of zero. This causes the search operation to perform a full read, returning all the requested attributes for all objects that match the filter. Along with the search results, the server returns a valid cookie and the cookie length. On subsequent runs, the program retrieves the cached cookie and length and uses them to retrieve changes since the previous run.

Note that this sample simply caches the cookie and cookie length in the registry. In a real synchronization application, you must store the parameters in the same storage that you are keeping consistent with Active Directory. This ensures that the parameters and object data remain in sync if your database is ever restored from a backup.

```c
#include <windows.h>
#include <stdio.h>
#include <activeds.h>

typedef struct {
    WCHAR objectGUID[40];
    WCHAR ADsPath[MAX_PATH];
    WCHAR phoneNumber[32];
    BOOL  isDeleted;
} MyUserData;

// forward declaration
VOID BuildGUIDString(WCHAR *szGUID, LPBYTE pGUID);
VOID WriteObjectDataToStorage(MyUserData *userdata, BOOL bUpdate);


//**********************************************************************
// DoDirSyncSearch
//**********************************************************************
HRESULT DoDirSyncSearch(
            LPWSTR pszSearchFilter,  // Search filter
            LPWSTR *pAttributeNames, // Attributes to retrieve
            DWORD dwAttributes,      // Number of attributes
            PUCHAR *ppCookie,        // Pointer to previous cookie
            PULONG pulCookieLength,  // Length of previous cookie
            LPWSTR szDC)             // Name of DC to bind to
{
LPOLESTR szDSPath = new OLECHAR[MAX_PATH];
LPOLESTR szServerPath = new OLECHAR[MAX_PATH];

IADs *pRootDSE = NULL;

IDirectorySearch *pSearch = NULL;
ADS_SEARCH_HANDLE hSearch = NULL;
ADS_SEARCHPREF_INFO arSearchPrefs[3];
```

```
ADS_PROV_SPECIFIC dirsync;
ADS_SEARCH_COLUMN col;

HRESULT hr;
VARIANT var;
DWORD i;
MyUserData userdata;
BOOL bUpdate = FALSE;
DWORD dwCount = 0;

// Validate input parameters.
if (!pulCookieLength || !ppCookie || !szDC) {
    wprintf(L"Invalid parameter.\n");
    return E_FAIL;
}

// If cookie is non-NULL, this is an update.
// Otherwise, it's a full read.
if (*ppCookie)
    bUpdate = TRUE;

CoInitialize(NULL);

// If we have a DC name from the previous USN sync,
// include it in the binding string.
if (szDC[0]) {
    wcscpy(szServerPath, L"LDAP://");
    wcscat(szServerPath, szDC);
    wcscat(szServerPath, L"/");
} else
    wcscpy(szServerPath, L"LDAP://");

// Bind to root DSE.
wcscpy(szDSPath, szServerPath);
wcscat(szDSPath, L"rootDSE");
wprintf(L"RootDSE binding string: %s\n", szDSPath);
hr = ADsGetObject(szDSPath,
                  IID_IADs,
                  (void**)&pRootDSE);
if (FAILED(hr)) {
    wprintf(L"failed to bind to rootDSE: 0x%x\n", hr);
    goto cleanup;
}
```

(continued)

(continued)

```
// Save the name of the DC that we connected to so we can connect to
// the same DC on the next dirsync operation.
if (! szDC[0])
{
    hr = pRootDSE->Get(L"DnsHostName",&var);
    wcscpy(szDC, var.bstrVal);
    wcscpy(szServerPath, L"LDAP://");
    wcscat(szServerPath, szDC);
    wcscat(szServerPath, L"/");
}

// Get an IDirectorySearch pointer to the root of the domain partition.
hr = pRootDSE->Get(L"defaultNamingContext",&var);
wcscpy(szDSPath, szServerPath);
wcscat(szDSPath, var.bstrVal);
hr = ADsGetObject(szDSPath, IID_IDirectorySearch, (void**) &pSearch);
if (FAILED(hr)) {
    wprintf(L"failed to get IDirectorySearch: 0x%x\n", hr);
    goto cleanup;
}

// Initialize the structure to pass in the cookie.
// On the first call, the cookie is NULL and the length is zero.
// On later calls, the cookie and length are the values returned by
// the previous call.
dirsync.dwLength = *pulCookieLength;
dirsync.lpValue = *ppCookie;

arSearchPrefs[0].dwSearchPref = ADS_SEARCHPREF_SEARCH_SCOPE;
arSearchPrefs[0].vValue.dwType = ADSTYPE_INTEGER;
arSearchPrefs[0].vValue.Integer = ADS_SCOPE_SUBTREE;

arSearchPrefs[1].dwSearchPref = ADS_SEARCHPREF_DIRSYNC;
arSearchPrefs[1].vValue.dwType = ADSTYPE_PROV_SPECIFIC;
arSearchPrefs[1].vValue.ProviderSpecific = dirsync;

hr = pSearch->SetSearchPreference(arSearchPrefs, 2);
if (FAILED(hr)) {
    wprintf(L"failed to set search prefs: 0x%x\n", hr);
    goto cleanup;
}

// Search for the objects indicated by the search filter.
hr = pSearch->ExecuteSearch(pszSearchFilter,
```

```
                       pAttributeNames, dwAttributes, &hSearch );
if (FAILED(hr)) {
    wprintf(L"failed to set execute search: 0x%x\n", hr);
    goto cleanup;
}


// Loop through the rows of the search result.
// Each row is an object that has changed since the previous call
hr = pSearch->GetNextRow( hSearch);
while ( SUCCEEDED(hr) && hr != S_ADS_NOMORE_ROWS )
{
    ZeroMemory(&userdata, sizeof(MyUserData) );

    // Get the ADsPath.
    hr = pSearch->GetColumn( hSearch, L"ADsPath", &col );
    if ( SUCCEEDED(hr) ) {
        wcscpy(userdata.ADsPath, col.pADsValues->CaseIgnoreString);
        pSearch->FreeColumn( &col );
    }

    // Get the telephone number.
    hr = pSearch->GetColumn( hSearch, L"telephoneNumber", &col );
    if ( SUCCEEDED(hr) ) {
        wcscpy(userdata.phoneNumber, col.pADsValues->CaseIgnoreString);
        pSearch->FreeColumn( &col );
    }

    // Get the objectGUID number.
    hr = pSearch->GetColumn( hSearch, L"objectGUID", &col );
    if ( SUCCEEDED(hr) ) {
        WCHAR szGUID[40]; // string version of the objectGUID attribute
        if (col.pADsValues->OctetString.lpValue) {
            BuildGUIDString(szGUID, (LPBYTE) col.pADsValues-
>OctetString.lpValue);
            wcscpy(userdata.objectGUID, szGUID);
        }
        pSearch->FreeColumn( &col );
    }

    // Get the isDeleted attribute.
    hr = pSearch->GetColumn( hSearch, L"isDeleted", &col );
    if ( SUCCEEDED(hr) ) {
        userdata.isDeleted = col.pADsValues->Boolean;
        pSearch->FreeColumn( &col );
```

(continued)

(continued)

```
        }

    WriteObjectDataToStorage(&userdata, bUpdate);
    dwCount++;
    hr = pSearch->GetNextRow( hSearch);
}
wprintf(L"dwCount: %d\n", dwCount);

// After looping through the results, get the cookie.
if (hr == S_ADS_NOMORE_ROWS )
{
    hr = pSearch->GetColumn( hSearch, ADS_DIRSYNC_COOKIE, &col );
    if ( SUCCEEDED(hr) ) {
        wprintf(L"Got cookie\n");
        *pulCookieLength = col.pADsValues->ProviderSpecific.dwLength;
        *ppCookie = (PUCHAR) AllocADsMem (*pulCookieLength);
        memcpy(*ppCookie, col.pADsValues->ProviderSpecific.lpValue,
            *pulCookieLength);
        pSearch->FreeColumn( &col );
    } else
        wprintf(L"no cookie: 0x%x\n", hr);
}

cleanup:
if (pRootDSE)
    pRootDSE->Release();
if (pSearch)
    pSearch->Release();
if (hSearch)
    pSearch->CloseSearchHandle(hSearch);
VariantClear(&var);
CoUninitialize();

return hr;
}



//**********************************************************************
// WriteObjectDataToStorage routine
//**********************************************************************
VOID WriteObjectDataToStorage(MyUserData *userdata, BOOL bUpdate)
{
if (bUpdate)
    wprintf(L"UPDATE:\n");
```

```
else
    wprintf(L"INITIAL DATA:\n");
wprintf(L"    objectGUID: %s\n", userdata->objectGUID);
wprintf(L"    ADsPath: %s\n", userdata->ADsPath);
wprintf(L"    phoneNumber: %s\n", userdata->phoneNumber);
if (userdata->isDeleted)
    wprintf(L"    DELETED OBJECT\n");
wprintf(L"----------------------------------------------\n");
return;

}


//********************************************************************
// WriteCookieAndDCtoStorage routine
// This example simply caches the cookie in the registry. In a real
// synchronization application, you must store these parameters in the
// same storage that you are keeping consistent with Active Directory.
// This ensures that the parameters and object data remain in sync if
// the storage is ever restored from a backup.
//********************************************************************
DWORD WriteCookieAndDCtoStorage(
            UCHAR *pCookie,
            ULONG ulLength,
            WCHAR *pszDCName)
{
HKEY hReg = NULL;
DWORD dwStat = NO_ERROR;

// Create a registry key under
//     HKEY_CURRENT_USER\SOFTWARE\Vendor\Product.
dwStat = RegCreateKeyExW(HKEY_CURRENT_USER,
            L"Software\\Microsoft\\Windows 2000 AD-Synchro-DirSync",
            0,
            NULL,
            REG_OPTION_NON_VOLATILE,
            KEY_ALL_ACCESS,
            NULL,
            &hReg,
            NULL);
if (dwStat != NO_ERROR) {
    wprintf(L"RegCreateKeyEx failed: 0x%x\n", dwStat);
    return dwStat;
}
```

(continued)

(continued)

```
// Cache the cookie as a value under the registry key.
dwStat = RegSetValueExW(hReg, L"Cookie", 0, REG_BINARY,
                          (const BYTE *)pCookie, ulLength);
if (dwStat != NO_ERROR)
   wprintf(L"RegSetValueEx for cookie failed: 0x%x\n", dwStat);

// Cache the cookie length as a value under the registry key.
dwStat = RegSetValueExW(hReg, L"Cookie Length", 0, REG_DWORD,
                          (const BYTE *)&ulLength, sizeof(DWORD) );
if (dwStat != NO_ERROR)
   wprintf(L"RegSetValueEx for cookie length failed: 0x%x\n", dwStat);

// Cache the DC name as a value under the registry key.
dwStat = RegSetValueExW(hReg, L"DC name", 0, REG_SZ,
                          (const BYTE *)pszDCName, 2*(wcslen(pszDCName)) );
if (dwStat != NO_ERROR)
   wprintf(L"RegSetValueEx for DC name failed: 0x%x\n", dwStat);


RegCloseKey(hReg);
return dwStat;
}


//*********************************************************************
// GetCookieAndDCfromStorage routine
//*********************************************************************
DWORD GetCookieAndDCfromStorage(
          PUCHAR *ppCookie,        // Receives pointer to cookie
          PULONG pulCookieLength,  // Receives length of cookie
          WCHAR *pszDCName)        // Receives name of DC to bind to
{
HKEY hReg = NULL;
DWORD dwStat;
DWORD dwLen;

// Open the registry key.
dwStat = RegOpenKeyExW(
          HKEY_CURRENT_USER,
          L"Software\\Microsoft\\Windows 2000 AD-Synchro-DirSync",
          0,
          KEY_QUERY_VALUE,
          &hReg);
if (dwStat != NO_ERROR) {
   wprintf(L"RegOpenKeyEx failed: 0x%x\n", dwStat);
```

```
        return dwStat;
    }


    // Get the length of the cookie from the registry.
    dwLen = sizeof(DWORD);
    dwStat = RegQueryValueExW(hReg, L"Cookie Length", NULL, NULL,
                            (LPBYTE)pulCookieLength, &dwLen );
    if (dwStat != NO_ERROR) {
        wprintf(L"RegQueryValueEx failed to get length: 0x%x\n", dwStat);
        return dwStat;
    }


    // Allocate a buffer for the cookie value.
    *ppCookie = (PUCHAR) GlobalAlloc(GPTR, *pulCookieLength);
    if (!*ppCookie) {
        wprintf(L"GlobalAlloc failed: %u\n", GetLastError() );
        return dwStat;
    }


    // Now get the cookie from the registry.
    dwStat = RegQueryValueExW(hReg, L"Cookie", NULL, NULL,
                            (LPBYTE)*ppCookie, pulCookieLength );
    if (dwStat != NO_ERROR) {
        wprintf(L"RegQueryValueEx failed to get cookie: 0x%x\n", dwStat);
        return dwStat;
    }


    // Get the DC name from the registry.
    dwLen = MAX_PATH;
    dwStat = RegQueryValueExW(hReg, L"DC name", NULL, NULL,
                            (LPBYTE)pszDCName, &dwLen );
    if (dwStat != NO_ERROR) {
        wprintf(L"RegQueryValueEx failed to get DC name: 0x%x\n", dwStat);
        return dwStat;
    }


RegCloseKey(hReg);

return NO_ERROR;
}


//*******************************************************************
// BuildGUIDString
// Routine that makes the GUID into a string in
```

(continued)

(continued)

```
// directory service bind form
//**************************************************************
VOID
BuildGUIDString(WCHAR *szGUID, LPBYTE pGUID)
{
    DWORD i = 0x0;
    DWORD dwlen = sizeof(GUID);
    WCHAR buf[4];

    wcscpy(szGUID, L"");

    for (i;i<dwlen;i++) {
        wsprintf(buf, L"%02x", pGUID[i]);
        wcscat(szGUID, buf);
    }
}


//**************************************************************
// main
//**************************************************************
int main(int argc, char* argv[])
{
DWORD dwStat;
ULONG ulLength;
UCHAR *pCookie;
WCHAR szDCName[MAX_PATH];
HRESULT hr;
LPWSTR szAttribs[] = {
    {L"telephoneNumber"}
};
LPWSTR *pszAttribs=szAttribs;
DWORD dwAttribs = sizeof(szAttribs)/sizeof(LPWSTR);

// Get all attributes.
if (argc>1)
    if (argv[1][0] == 'a') {
        pszAttribs=NULL;
        dwAttribs = -1;
    }

if (argc>2)
{
    // Perform a full synchronization.
    // Initialize the synchronization parameters to zero or NULL.
```

```
        wprintf(L"Performing a full sync.\n");
        szDCName[0] = '\0';
        ulLength = 0;
        pCookie = NULL;
    } else
    {
        // Perform an incremental synchronization.
        // Initialize synchronization parameters from storage.
        wprintf(L"Retrieving changes only.\n");
        dwStat = GetCookieAndDCfromStorage(&pCookie, &ulLength, szDCName);
        if (dwStat != NO_ERROR) {
            wprintf(L"Could not get the cookie: %u\n", dwStat);
            goto cleanup;
        }
    }

    // Perform the search and update the synchronization parameters.
    hr = DoDirSyncSearch(L"(&(objectClass=user)(objectCategory=person))",
                        pszAttribs, dwAttribs,
                        &pCookie, &ulLength,
                        szDCName);
    if (FAILED(hr)) {
        wprintf(L"DoDirSyncSearch failed: 0x%x\n", hr);
        goto cleanup;
    }

    // Cache the returned synchronization parameters in storage.
    wprintf(L"Caching the synchronization parameters.\n");
    dwStat = WriteCookieAndDCtoStorage(pCookie, ulLength, szDCName);
    if (dwStat != NO_ERROR) {
        wprintf(L"Could not cache the cookie: %u\n", dwStat);
        goto cleanup;
    }

cleanup:
    if (pCookie)
        GlobalFree (pCookie);

    return 1;
}
```

Polling for Changes Using USNChanged

The DirSync control is robust, efficient, and easy to use. But it has two significant
limitations, as mentioned on the following page.

- Only for highly-privileged programs: To use the DirSync control, a program must run under an account that has the SE_SYNC_AGENT_NAME privilege on the domain controller. Very few accounts are so highly privileged, so an application that uses the DirSync control can't be run by ordinary users.

- No subtree scoping: The DirSync control returns all changes that occur within a naming context. An application interested only in changes that occur in a small subtree of a naming context must wade through many irrelevant changes, which is inefficient both for the application and for the domain controller.

There's another way to get changes from Active Directory™ that avoids these limitations: **uSNChanged** querying. This alternative is not better than the DirSync control in all respects—it involves transmitting all attributes whenever any attribute changes, and it requires more work from the application writer to handle certain failure scenarios correctly. But it is the best way available to write certain change-tracking applications today.

Here's the technical background on the **uSNChanged** attribute:

- When a domain controller modifies an object it sets that object's **uSNChanged** to a value that's larger than the previous value of **uSNChanged** for that object, and larger than the current value of **uSNChanged** for all other objects held on that domain controller. As a consequence, an application can find the most-recently changed object on a domain controller by finding the object with the largest **uSNChanged**, the second-most-recently changed object on a domain controller by finding the object with the second-largest **uSNChanged**, and so on.

- The **uSNChanged** attribute is not replicated; therefore reading an object's **uSNChanged** attribute at two different domain controllers will typically give different values.

With that background, it is easy to see the general outline of how to use **uSNChanged** to track changes in a subtree S. First perform a "full sync" of the subtree S. Suppose the largest **uSNChanged** seen on any object in S is U. Now periodically query for all objects in subtree S whose **uSNChanged** is greater than U. The query will return all objects that have changed since the full sync. Set U to the largest **uSNChanged** among these changed objects, and you are ready to poll again when the time comes.

The subtleties of implementing a USNChanged synchronization application are as follows:

- Use the highestCommittedUSN rootDSE attribute to bound your uSNChanged filters. That is, before starting a full sync, read the highestCommittedUSN of your affiliated DC. Then, perform a full synchronization query (using paged results) to initialize the database. When this is complete, store the highestCommittedUSN value read before the full sync query; to use as the lowerBoundUSN for the next synchronization. Later, to perform an incremental synchronization, once again read the highestCommittedUSN rootDSE attribute. Then query for relevant objects (using paged results) whose uSNChanged is greater than the lowerBoundUSN value saved from the previous synchronization. Update the database using this information. When that's complete, update lowerBoundUSN from the highestCommittedUSN value read before the incremental synchronization query. Always store the lowerBoundUSN value in the same storage that the application is synchronizing with the DC's content.

Following this procedure, rather than the more obvious one based on uSNChanged values on retrieved objects, avoids making the server re-examine updated objects that fall outside the set that's interesting to the application.

- Because **uSNChanged** is a non-replicated attribute, the application must bind to the same DC every time it runs. If it cannot bind to that DC it must either wait until it can do so, or affiliate with some new DC and perform a full synchronization with that DC. When the application affiliates with a DC it records the DNS name of that DC in stable storage (the same storage it is keeping consistent with the DC's content.) Then it uses the stored DNS name to bind to the same DC for subsequent synchronizations.

- The application must detect when the DC it is currently affiliated with has been restored from backup, since this can break consistency. When the application affiliates with a DC it caches the "invocation id" of that DC in stable storage (the same storage it is keeping consistent with the DC's content.) The "invocation id" of a DC is a GUID stored in the **invocationId** property of the DC's service object. To get the distinguished name of a DC's service object, read the dsServiceName attribute of the rootDSE.

  Note that when the *application's* stable storage is restored from backup there are no consistency problems because the DC name, invocation id, and lowerBoundUSN are all stored together with the data being synchronized with the DC's content.

- Use paging when querying the server (both full and incremental synchronizations), to avoid the possibility of retrieving huge result sets all at once. See *Paging*.

- Perform index-based queries to avoid forcing the server to store large intermediate results when using paged results. See *Indexed Attributes*.

- In general, do not use server-side sorting of search results, which can force the server to store and sort large intermediate results. This applies to both full and incremental synchronizations. See *Sorting the Search Results*.

- Deal gracefully with "no parent" conditions. The application may "see" an object before it has seen its parent. Depending upon the application this may or may not be a problem. The application can always read the current state of the parent from the directory.

- To handle moved or deleted objects, you must store the objectGUID attribute of each object you are tracking. An object's objectGUID attribute remains unchanged regardless of where it is moved throughout the forest.

- To deal with moved objects, you must either perform periodic full synchronizations or increase the search scope and filter out uninteresting changes at the client end.

- To deal with deleted objects, you must either perform periodic full synchronizations or perform a separate search for deleted objects whenever you do an incremental synchronization. When you query for deleted objects, retrieve the objectGUIDs of the deleted objects to determine the objects to delete from your database. See *Retrieving Deleted Objects*.

- Remember that the search results include only the objects and attributes that the caller has permission to read (based on the security descriptors and DACLs on the various objects. See *Effects of Security on Queries*.

For sample code that demonstrates the basics of a USNChanged synchronization application, see *Example Code to Retrieve Changes Using USNChanged*.

Example Code to Retrieve Changes Using USNChanged

The following sample code uses the **uSNChanged** attribute of Active Directory objects to retrieve changes that have occurred since a previous query. The code can perform either a full synchronization or an incremental update. For a full synchronization, the sample application connects to the rootDSE of a domain controller and reads the following parameters that it stores to be used in the next incremental synchronization:

- The DNS name of the DC. Incremental synchronizations must be performed on the same DC as the previous synchronization.

- The invocationID GUID of the DC. The sample uses this value to detect that the DC has been restored from a backup, in which case, the sample must perform a full synchronization.

- The highestCommittedUSN. This value becomes the lower bound for the **uSNChanged** filter on the next incremental synchronization.

The example uses the **IDirectorySearch** interface, specifying the distinguished name of the base of the search, a search scope, and a filter. There are no restrictions on the search base or scope. In addition to specifying the objects of interest, the filter must also specify a uSNChanged comparison, such as (uSNChanged>=*lowerBoundUSN*). For a full synchronization, *lowerBoundUSN* is zero. For an incremental synchronization, it is the 1 plus the highestCommittedUSN value from the previous search.

Note that this sample program is intended only to show how to use uSNChanged to retrieve changes from Active Directory. It simple prints out the changes and does not actually synchronize the data in a secondary storage. Consequently, it does not show how to deal with issues like moved objects or "no parent" conditions. It does show how to retrieve deleted objects, but it doesn't show how an application uses the objectGUID of the deleted objects to determine the corresponding object to delete in the storage.

Also, the sample simply caches the DC name, invocation ID, and higestCommittedUSN in the registry. In a real synchronization application, you must store the parameters in the same storage that you are keeping consistent with Active Directory. This ensures that the parameters and object data remain in sync if your database is ever restored from a backup.

```c
#include <windows.h>
#include <stdio.h>
#include <activeds.h>
#include <ntdsapi.h>

typedef struct {
    WCHAR objectGUID[40];
    WCHAR distinguishedName[MAX_PATH];
    WCHAR phoneNumber[32];
} MyUserData;

// forward declaration
VOID BuildGUIDString(WCHAR *szGUID, LPBYTE pGUID);
VOID WriteObjectDataToStorage(MyUserData *userdata, BOOL bUpdate);
VOID DeleteObjectDataFromStorage(MyUserData *userdata);

//*******************************************************************
// DoUSNSyncSearch
//*******************************************************************
HRESULT DoUSNSyncSearch(
        LPWSTR szSearchBaseDN,      // Distinguished name of search base
        ULONG ulScope,              // Scope of the search
        LPWSTR *pAttributeNames,    // Attributes to retrieve
        DWORD dwAttributes,         // Number of attributes
        LPWSTR szPrevInvocationID,  // GUID string for DC's invocationID
        LPWSTR szPrevHighUSN,       // Highest USN from previous sync
        LPWSTR szDC)                // Name of DC to bind to
{
LPOLESTR szDSPath = new OLECHAR[MAX_PATH];
LPOLESTR szServerPath = new OLECHAR[MAX_PATH];

IADs *pRootDSE = NULL;
IADs *pDCService = NULL;
IADs *pDeletedObj = NULL;

IDirectorySearch *pSearch = NULL;
ADS_SEARCH_HANDLE hSearch = NULL;
ADS_SEARCHPREF_INFO arSearchPrefs[3];
WCHAR szSearchFilter[256];       // Search filter
ADS_SEARCH_COLUMN col;

MyUserData userdata;
void HUGEP *pArray;
WCHAR szGUID[40];
```

(continued)

(continued)

```
INT64 iLowerBoundUSN;
HRESULT hr;
DWORD dwCount = 0;
VARIANT var;
BOOL bUpdate = TRUE;

// Validate input parameters.
if (!szPrevInvocationID || !szPrevHighUSN || !szDC) {
    wprintf(L"Invalid parameter.\n");
    return E_FAIL;
}

// If we have a DC name from the previous USN sync,
// include it in the binding string.
if (szDC[0]) {
    wcscpy(szServerPath, L"LDAP://");
    wcscat(szServerPath, szDC);
    wcscat(szServerPath, L"/");
} else
    wcscpy(szServerPath, L"LDAP://");

// Bind to root DSE.
wcscpy(szDSPath, szServerPath);
wcscat(szDSPath, L"rootDSE");
hr = ADsOpenObject(szDSPath,
                   NULL,
                   NULL,
                   ADS_SECURE_AUTHENTICATION,
                   IID_IADs,
                   (void**)&pRootDSE);
if (FAILED(hr)) {
    wprintf(L"failed to bind to root: 0x%x\n", hr);
    goto cleanup;
}

// Get the name of the DC we connected to.
hr = pRootDSE->Get(L"DnsHostName", &var);
if (FAILED(hr)) {
    wprintf(L"failed to get DnsHostName: 0x%x\n", hr);
    goto cleanup;
}
// Compare it to the DC name from the previous USN sync operation.
// If they aren't the same, do a full sync.
if (_wcsicmp(szDC, var.bstrVal)!=0)
```

```
{
    bUpdate = FALSE;

    // Save the DC name for next time.
    wcscpy(szDC, var.bstrVal);

    // Use the DC name in the bind string prefix.
    wcscpy(szServerPath, L"LDAP://");
    wcscat(szServerPath, szDC);
    wcscat(szServerPath, L"/");
}

// Bind to the DC's service object to get the invocationID.
// The dsServiceName property of root DSE contains the distinguished
// name of this DC's service object.
hr = pRootDSE->Get(L"dsServiceName", &var);
wcscpy(szDSPath, szServerPath);
wcscat(szDSPath, var.bstrVal);
VariantClear(&var);
hr = ADsOpenObject(szDSPath,
                   NULL,
                   NULL,
                   ADS_SECURE_AUTHENTICATION,
                   IID_IADs,
                   (void**)&pDCService);
if (FAILED(hr)) {
    wprintf(L"failed to bind to the DC's service object: 0x%x\n", hr);
    goto cleanup;
}

// Get the invocationID GUID from the service object.
hr = pDCService->Get(L"invocationID",&var);
hr = SafeArrayAccessData((SAFEARRAY*)(var.pparray), (void HUGEP* FAR*)&pArray);
if (FAILED(hr)) {
    wprintf(L"failed to get hugep: 0x%x\n", hr);
    goto cleanup;
}
BuildGUIDString(szGUID, (LPBYTE) pArray);
VariantClear(&var);

// Compare the invocationID GUID to the GUID string from the previous
// sync. If they are not the same, this is a different DC or the DC
// was restored from backup, so do a full sync.
if (_wcsicmp(szGUID, szPrevInvocationID)!=0)
```

(continued)

(continued)

```
{
    bUpdate = FALSE;
    wcscpy(szPrevInvocationID, szGUID);  // Save the invocationID GUID.
}

// If previous high USN is an empty string, treat this as a full sync.
if (szPrevHighUSN[0] == '\0')
    bUpdate = FALSE;

// Set the lower bound USN to zero if this is a full sync.
// Otherwise, set it to the previous high USN plus one.
if (bUpdate == FALSE)
    iLowerBoundUSN = 0;
else
    iLowerBoundUSN = _wtoi64(szPrevHighUSN) + 1;
// Convert string to integer.

// Get and save the current high USN.
hr = pRootDSE->Get(L"highestCommittedUSN", &var);
wcscpy(szPrevHighUSN, var.bstrVal);
wprintf(L"current highestCommittedUSN: %s\n", szPrevHighUSN);
VariantClear(&var);

// Get an IDirectorySearch pointer to the base of the search.
wcscpy(szDSPath, szServerPath);
wcscat(szDSPath, szSearchBaseDN);
hr = ADsOpenObject(szDSPath,
                   NULL,
                   NULL,
                   ADS_SECURE_AUTHENTICATION,
                   IID_IDirectorySearch,
                   (void**)&pSearch);
if (FAILED(hr)) {
    wprintf(L"failed to get IDirectorySearch: 0x%x\n", hr);
    goto cleanup;
}

// Set up the scope and page size search preferences.
arSearchPrefs [0].dwSearchPref = ADS_SEARCHPREF_SEARCH_SCOPE;
arSearchPrefs [0].vValue.dwType = ADSTYPE_INTEGER;
arSearchPrefs [0].vValue.Integer = ulScope;

arSearchPrefs [1].dwSearchPref = ADS_SEARCHPREF_PAGESIZE;
arSearchPrefs [1].vValue.dwType = ADSTYPE_INTEGER;
```

```
arSearchPrefs [1].vValue.Integer = 100;

hr = pSearch->SetSearchPreference(arSearchPrefs, 2);
if (FAILED(hr)) {
    wprintf(L"failed to set search prefs: 0x%x\n", hr);
    goto cleanup;
}

// The search filter specifies the objects to monitor
// and the USNChanged value to exceed.
swprintf(szSearchFilter,
        L"(&(objectClass=user)(objectCategory=person)(uSNChanged>=%I64d))",
        iLowerBoundUSN );

// Search for the objects indicated by the search filter.
hr = pSearch->ExecuteSearch(szSearchFilter,
                    pAttributeNames, dwAttributes, &hSearch );
if (FAILED(hr)) {
    wprintf(L"failed to set execute search: 0x%x\n", hr);
    goto cleanup;
}

// Loop through the rows of the search result. Each row is an object
// with USNChanged greater than or equal to the specified value.
hr = pSearch->GetNextRow( hSearch);
while ( SUCCEEDED(hr) && hr != S_ADS_NOMORE_ROWS )
{
    ZeroMemory(&userdata, sizeof(MyUserData) );

    // Get the distinguishedName.
    hr = pSearch->GetColumn( hSearch, L"distinguishedName", &col );
    if ( SUCCEEDED(hr) ) {
        wcscpy(userdata.distinguishedName, col.pADsValues->CaseIgnoreString);
        pSearch->FreeColumn( &col );
    }

    // Get the telephone number.
    hr = pSearch->GetColumn( hSearch, L"telephoneNumber", &col );
    if ( SUCCEEDED(hr) ) {
        wcscpy(userdata.phoneNumber, col.pADsValues->CaseIgnoreString);
        pSearch->FreeColumn( &col );
    }

    // Get the objectGUID.
```

(continued)

(continued)

```
    hr = pSearch->GetColumn( hSearch, L"objectGUID", &col );
    if ( SUCCEEDED(hr) ) {
        if (col.pADsValues->OctetString.lpValue) {
            BuildGUIDString(szGUID, (LPBYTE) col.pADsValues-
>OctetString.lpValue);
            wcscpy(userdata.objectGUID, szGUID);
        }
        pSearch->FreeColumn( &col );
    }

    // Write the data from Active Directory to the secondary storage.
    WriteObjectDataToStorage(&userdata, bUpdate);
    dwCount++;
    hr = pSearch->GetNextRow( hSearch);
}
wprintf(L"dwCount: %d\n", dwCount);

// If this is a full sync, we're done.
if (!bUpdate)
    goto cleanup;

// If it's an update, we need to look for deleted objects.

// Release the search handle and pointer so we can reuse them.
wprintf(L"Searching for deleted objects\n");
if (hSearch) {
    pSearch->CloseSearchHandle(hSearch);
    hSearch = NULL;
}
if (pSearch) {
    pSearch->Release();
    pSearch = NULL;
}

// Bind to the Deleted Objects container.
hr = pRootDSE->Get(L"defaultNamingContext",&var);
swprintf(szDSPath,
        L"%s<WKGUID=%s,%s>",
        szServerPath, GUID_DELETED_OBJECTS_CONTAINER_W, var.bstrVal);
VariantClear(&var);
hr = ADsOpenObject(szDSPath,
                NULL,
                NULL,
                ADS_SECURE_AUTHENTICATION | ADS_FAST_BIND,
```

```
                        IID_IDirectorySearch,
                        (void**)&pSearch);
if (FAILED(hr)) {
    wprintf(L"failed to get IDirectorySearch: 0x%x\n", hr);
    goto cleanup;
}

// Specify the scope, pagesize, and tombstone search preferences.
arSearchPrefs [0].dwSearchPref = ADS_SEARCHPREF_SEARCH_SCOPE;
arSearchPrefs [0].vValue.dwType = ADSTYPE_INTEGER;
arSearchPrefs [0].vValue.Integer = ADS_SCOPE_SUBTREE;

arSearchPrefs [1].dwSearchPref = ADS_SEARCHPREF_PAGESIZE;
arSearchPrefs [1].vValue.dwType = ADSTYPE_INTEGER;
arSearchPrefs [1].vValue.Integer = 100;

arSearchPrefs [2].dwSearchPref = ADS_SEARCHPREF_TOMBSTONE;
arSearchPrefs [2].vValue.dwType = ADSTYPE_BOOLEAN;
arSearchPrefs [2].vValue.Boolean = TRUE;

hr = pSearch->SetSearchPreference(arSearchPrefs, 3);
if (FAILED(hr)) {
    wprintf(L"failed to set search prefs: 0x%x\n", hr);
    goto cleanup;
}

// Set up the search filter.
swprintf(szSearchFilter,
        L"(&(isDeleted=TRUE)(uSNChanged>=%I64d))",
        iLowerBoundUSN );

// Execute the search.
hr = pSearch->ExecuteSearch(szSearchFilter,
                    pAttributeNames, dwAttributes, &hSearch );
if (FAILED(hr)) {
    wprintf(L"failed to set execute search: 0x%x\n", hr);
    goto cleanup;
}
wprintf(L"Started search for deleted objects.\n");

// Loop through the rows of the search result.
// Each row is an object that was deleted since the previous call.
dwCount = 0;
hr = pSearch->GetNextRow( hSearch);
```

(continued)

(continued)

```
while ( SUCCEEDED(hr) && hr != S_ADS_NOMORE_ROWS )
{
    ZeroMemory(&userdata, sizeof(MyUserData) );

    // Get the distinguishedName.
    hr = pSearch->GetColumn( hSearch, L"distinguishedName", &col );
    if ( SUCCEEDED(hr) ) {
        wcscpy(userdata.distinguishedName, col.pADsValues->CaseIgnoreString);
        pSearch->FreeColumn( &col );
    }

    // Get the objectGUID number.
    hr = pSearch->GetColumn( hSearch, L"objectGUID", &col );
    if ( SUCCEEDED(hr) ) {
        if (col.pADsValues->OctetString.lpValue) {
            BuildGUIDString(szGUID, (LPBYTE) col.pADsValues-
>OctetString.lpValue);
            wcscpy(userdata.objectGUID, szGUID);
        }
        pSearch->FreeColumn( &col );
    }

    // If the objectGUID of a deleted object matches an objectGUID in
    // our secondary storage, delete the object from our storage.
    DeleteObjectDataFromStorage(&userdata);
    dwCount++;
    hr = pSearch->GetNextRow( hSearch);
}
wprintf(L"deleted dwCount: %d\n", dwCount);

cleanup:

if (pRootDSE)
    pRootDSE->Release();
if (pDCService)
    pDCService->Release();
if (pDeletedObj)
    pDeletedObj->Release();
if (pSearch)
    pSearch->Release();
if (hSearch)
    pSearch->CloseSearchHandle(hSearch);
VariantClear(&var);
```

```
return hr;


}

//***************************************************************
// DeleteObjectDataFromStorage routine
//***************************************************************
VOID DeleteObjectDataFromStorage(MyUserData *userdata)
{
wprintf(L"DELETED OBJECT:\n");
wprintf(L"   objectGUID: %s\n", userdata->objectGUID);
wprintf(L"   distinguishedName: %s\n", userdata->distinguishedName);
wprintf(L"-------------------------------------------\n");
return;
}


//***************************************************************
// WriteObjectDataToStorage routine
//***************************************************************
VOID WriteObjectDataToStorage(MyUserData *userdata, BOOL bUpdate)
{
if (bUpdate)
    wprintf(L"UPDATE:\n");
else
    wprintf(L"INITIAL DATA:\n");
wprintf(L"   objectGUID: %s\n", userdata->objectGUID);
wprintf(L"   distinguishedName: %s\n", userdata->distinguishedName);
wprintf(L"   phoneNumber: %s\n", userdata->phoneNumber);
wprintf(L"-------------------------------------------\n");
return;
}


//***************************************************************
// WriteSyncParamsToStorage routine
// This example caches the parameters in the registry. In a real
// synchronization application, you must store the parameters in the
// same storage that you are keeping consistent with Active Directory.
// This ensures that the parameters and object data remain in sync if
// the storage is ever restored from a backup.
//***************************************************************
DWORD WriteSyncParamsToStorage(
            LPWSTR szPrevInvocationID, // Receives invocation ID
            LPWSTR szPrevHighUSN,      // Receives previous high USN
            LPWSTR pszDCName)          // Receives name of DC to bind to
```

(continued)

(continued)

```
{
HKEY hReg = NULL;
DWORD dwStat = NO_ERROR;

// Create a registry key under
//      HKEY_CURRENT_USER\SOFTWARE\Vendor\Product.
dwStat = RegCreateKeyExW(HKEY_CURRENT_USER,
            L"Software\\Microsoft\\Windows 2000 AD-Synchro-USN",
            0,
            NULL,
            REG_OPTION_NON_VOLATILE,
            KEY_ALL_ACCESS,
            NULL,
            &hReg,
            NULL);
if (dwStat != NO_ERROR) {
    wprintf(L"RegCreateKeyEx failed: 0x%x\n", dwStat);
    return dwStat;
}

// Cache the invocationID as a value under the registry key.
dwStat = RegSetValueExW(hReg, L"InvocationID", 0, REG_SZ,
                            (const BYTE *)szPrevInvocationID,
                            2*(wcslen(szPrevInvocationID)));
if (dwStat != NO_ERROR)
    wprintf(L"RegSetValueEx for invocationID failed: 0x%x\n", dwStat);

// Cache the previous high USN as a value under the registry key.
dwStat = RegSetValueExW(hReg, L"PreviousHighUSN", 0, REG_QWORD,
                            (const BYTE *)szPrevHighUSN,
                            2*(wcslen(szPrevHighUSN)) );//sizeof(INT64) );
if (dwStat != NO_ERROR)
    wprintf(L"RegSetValueEx for PreviousHighUSN failed: 0x%x\n", dwStat);

// Cache the DC name as a value under the registry key.
dwStat = RegSetValueExW(hReg, L"DC name", 0, REG_SZ,
                            (const BYTE *)pszDCName, 2*(wcslen(pszDCName)) );
if (dwStat != NO_ERROR)
    wprintf(L"RegSetValueEx for DC name failed: 0x%x\n", dwStat);

RegCloseKey(hReg);
return dwStat;
}
```

```
//********************************************************************
// GetSyncParamsFromStorage routine
// This example reads the parameters from the registry. In a real
// synchronization application, you must store the parameters in the
// same storage that you are keeping consistent with Active Directory.
//********************************************************************
DWORD GetSyncParamsFromStorage(
          LPWSTR szPrevInvocationID, // Receives invocation ID
          LPWSTR szPreviousHighUSN,  // Receives previous high USN
          LPWSTR pszDCName)          // Receives name of DC to bind to
{
HKEY hReg = NULL;
DWORD dwStat;
DWORD dwLen;

// Open the registry key.
dwStat = RegOpenKeyExW(
          HKEY_CURRENT_USER,
          L"Software\\Microsoft\\Windows 2000 AD-Synchro-USN",
          0,
          KEY_QUERY_VALUE,
          &hReg);
if (dwStat != NO_ERROR) {
    wprintf(L"RegOpenKeyEx failed: 0x%x\n", dwStat);
    return dwStat;
}

// Get the previous invocationID from the registry.
dwLen = 40*2; // size of buffer
dwStat = RegQueryValueExW(hReg, L"InvocationID", NULL, NULL,
                        (LPBYTE)szPrevInvocationID, &dwLen );
if (dwStat != NO_ERROR) {
    wprintf(L"RegQueryValueEx failed to get invocationID: 0x%x\n", dwStat);
    goto cleanup;
}

// Now get the previous high USN from the registry.
dwLen = 40*2;
dwStat = RegQueryValueExW(hReg, L"PreviousHighUSN", NULL, NULL,
                        (LPBYTE)szPreviousHighUSN, &dwLen );
if (dwStat != NO_ERROR) {
    wprintf(L"RegQueryValueEx failed to get previous high USN: 0x%x\n", dwStat);
    goto cleanup;
}
```

(continued)

(continued)

```
// Get the DC name from the registry.
dwLen = MAX_PATH*2;
dwStat = RegQueryValueExW(hReg, L"DC name", NULL, NULL,
                         (LPBYTE)pszDCName, &dwLen );
if (dwStat != NO_ERROR) {
    wprintf(L"RegQueryValueEx failed to get DC name: 0x%x\n", dwStat);
    goto cleanup;
}


cleanup:

RegCloseKey(hReg);
return dwStat;
}


//*********************************************************************
// BuildGUIDString
// Routine that makes the GUID a string in directory service bind form.
//*********************************************************************
VOID
BuildGUIDString(WCHAR *szGUID, LPBYTE pGUID)
{
    DWORD i = 0x0;
    DWORD dwlen = sizeof(GUID);
    WCHAR buf[4];

    wcscpy(szGUID, L"");
    for (i;i<dwlen;i++) {
        wsprintf(buf, L"%02x", pGUID[i]);
        wcscat(szGUID, buf);
    }
}


//*********************************************************************
// main
//*********************************************************************
int main(int argc, char* argv[])
{
DWORD dwStat;
HRESULT hr;

// attributes to retrieve
LPWSTR szAttribs[] = {
```

```
        {L"telephoneNumber"},
        {L"distinguishedName"},
        {L"uSNChanged"},
        {L"objectGUID"},
        {L"isDeleted"}
};
LPWSTR *pszAttribs=szAttribs;
DWORD dwAttribs = sizeof(szAttribs)/sizeof(LPWSTR);

// DC properties to cache for next synchronization run.
WCHAR szPrevInvocationID[40];
WCHAR szPrevHighUSN[40];
WCHAR szDCName[MAX_PATH];

CoInitialize(NULL);

if (argc>1)
{
    // Perform a full synchronization.
    // Initialize synchronization parameters to empty strings.
    wprintf(L"Performing a full read.\n");
    szPrevInvocationID[0] = '\0';
    szPrevHighUSN[0] = '\0';
    szDCName[0] = '\0';
} else
{
    // Perform a synchronization update.
    // Initialize synchronization parameters from storage.
    wprintf(L"Retrieving changes only.\n");
    dwStat = GetSyncParamsFromStorage(szPrevInvocationID,
                                      szPrevHighUSN,
                                      szDCName);
    if (dwStat != NO_ERROR) {
        wprintf(L"Could not get synchronization parameters: %u\n", dwStat);
        goto cleanup;
    }
}

// Perform the search and update the synchronization parameters.
hr = DoUSNSyncSearch(L"CN=Users,DC=twokay,DC=local",
                     ADS_SCOPE_ONELEVEL,
                     pszAttribs, dwAttribs,
                     szPrevInvocationID, szPrevHighUSN, szDCName);
if (FAILED(hr)) {
```

(continued)

(continued)

```
    wprintf(L"DoUSNSyncSearch failed: 0x%x\n", hr);
    goto cleanup;
}


// Cache the synchronization parameters in storage for next time.
wprintf(L"Caching the synchronization parameters.\n");
dwStat = WriteSyncParamsToStorage(
            szPrevInvocationID, szPrevHighUSN, szDCName);
if (dwStat != NO_ERROR) {
    wprintf(L"Error caching the synchronization params: %u\n", dwStat);
    goto cleanup;
}


cleanup:
CoUninitialize();
return 1;
}
```

Retrieving Deleted Objects

Synchronization programs that use the **uSNChanged** attribute must explicitly request that the search results include deleted objects. You can do this through ADSI by using **IDirectorySearch** with the ADS_SEARCHPREF_TOMBSTONE search preference. Alternatively, you can use the LDAP_SERVER_SHOW_DELETED_OID control with the LDAP search functions such as **ldap_search_ext**.

When an object is deleted:

- Its **isDeleted** attribute is set to TRUE. Objects with isDeleted == TRUE are called *tombstones.*
- Most of its attribute values are removed. The RDN, objectGUID, and objectSID (for security principals) are always retained.
- It is moved to the Deleted Objects container for its naming context, and its RDN is changed to ensure uniqueness within the Deleted Objects container.
- Its security-descriptor is set to a fixed value.

The tombstone lives for a configurable period of time (60 days by default), after which it is completely removed. To avoid missing deletions, an application must perform incremental synchronizations more frequently than the tombstone lifetime.

For sample code that retrieves deleted objects, see *Example Code to Retrieve Changes Using USNChanged.*

Synchronization programs that use the DirSync search do not need to explicitly request deleted objects, which are automatically included in the search results.

CHAPTER 16

Service Publication

Services advertise themselves using objects stored in Microsoft® Active Directory™. This is known as service publication. Clients query the directory to locate services of interest. This is called client-service rendezvous. This chapter discusses the types of directory objects used for service publication and explains how they are used for client-service rendezvous.

This chapter covers the following topics.

- An overview of service publication
- Security issues for service publication
- Connection point objects
- Publishing with service connection points (SCPs)
- What information to store in a service connection point
- Where to create a service connection point
- How to publish replicable, host-based, and database services using service connection points
- Creating and maintaining a service connection point
- How a client queries for an SCP and uses it to bind to a service instance
- Using the RPC name service (RpcNs) APIs to publish an RPC service
- Using Windows® Sockets registration and resolution (RnR) to publish a Windows Sockets service
- Publication of COM-based services in the COM+ class store

For additional information on programming issues for client/service applications, see the following topics:

- For information on how services and clients authenticate each other, see *Mutual Authentication Using Kerberos*.
- For information on service security contexts and logon accounts, see *Service Logon Accounts*.

About Service Publication

A *service* is an application that makes data or operations available to network clients. Often, a service is implemented as a formal Microsoft® Win32®-based service, but this is not required.

Service publication is the act of creating and maintaining information about one or more instances of a given service so that network clients can find and use the service. Publishing a service in Active Directory enables clients and administrators to move from a machine-centric view of the distributed system to a service-centric view.

In Microsoft® Windows NT® version 4.0 and earlier, a distributed system was a group of computers running various services. To access a service, an application needed to know which computers offered the service.

In Microsoft® Windows® 2000, services publish their existence using objects in Active Directory. The objects contain *binding information* that client applications use to connect to instances of the service. To access a service, a client does not need to know about specific computers: the objects in Active Directory include this information. A client queries Active Directory for an object representing a service (called a *connection point* object) and uses the binding information from the object to connect to the service.

The following table shows examples of bindings.

Service	Binding
File Service	UNC Name for a share.
	Example: \\MyServer\MyshareName
Web Service	URL.
	Example: http://www.Microsoft.com
RPC Service	RPC binding: special encoded information used to connect to the RPC server. RPC bindings can be converted to and from strings with the RPC APIs.
	Example: ncacn_ip_tcp:server.microsoft.com

In a distributed system, the computers are engines, and the interesting entities are the services that are available. From the user's perspective, the identity of the computer that provides a particular service is not important. What is important is accessing the service itself.

This is also the case with service management. The administrator of a given DNS zone is not interested in the computers running the DNS service; the administrator wants to administer DNS. There will likely be multiple instances of the DNS service, one of which (in classic DNS) will be authoritative. The computers that support the DNS service are *not important* to the DNS administrator. What is important is managing the service as a single distributed resource—not as individual processes running on different computers.

Security Issues for Service Publication

The system restricts the ability to create, modify, or delete connection point objects, which means you need to know about and cope with these restrictions when you publish a service.

Clients must be able to trust the information published in a connection point object in the directory. For this reason, permission to create a connection point object is typically restricted to privileged users, such as domain administrators. This prevents unauthorized users from deceiving clients by creating phony connection points for well-known services.

Services must not run with domain administrator privileges. This means that a service typically cannot create its own connection point. Instead, you provide a service installation or configuration program that creates the connection point. This installation program must be run by a user with the necessary privileges.

Although a service cannot typically create its connection point, it must be able to update the connection point properties at run time. The connection point properties contain the binding information used by clients to connect to the service. If the binding information changes, the service must update the connection point; otherwise, clients will not be able to use the service. This means that the installation program must also modify the security descriptor on the connection point object to enable the service to read and write the appropriate properties at run time. For sample code that does this, see *Enabling Service Account to Access SCP Properties*.

A service running under the LocalSystem account can create a connection point as a child object under its own computer object in the directory. Such a service is an exception to the rule of services not creating their own connection points. A LocalSystem service also has permission to modify the properties of connection point objects under its own computer object. Note that a service should run under the LocalSystem account only if absolutely necessary. For more information, see *Guidelines for Selecting a Service Logon Account*.

The program that creates a connection point object (or any object) must have *create child* permission for the object class to be created in the container where the object will be created. To remove an object, the process performing the operation must have *delete child* permissions for the object class to be deleted on the container holding the object, or have *delete* permission on the object itself. To update a connection point the process performing the operation must have write access to the properties to be updated on the object in question.

Connection Points

A *connection point* object contains information about one or more instances of a service available in the network. The **connectionPoint** object class is the abstract base class from which Active Directory objects representing connectable resources are derived. The following illustration shows some of the object classes derived from the **connectionPoint** object class.

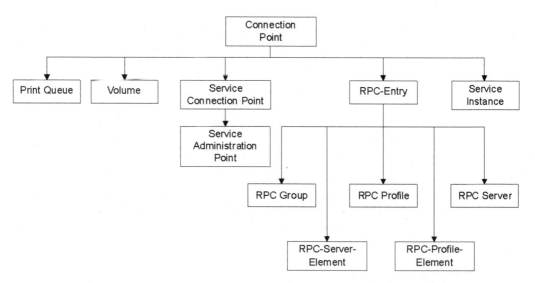

The following table describes the immediate subclasses of the **connectionPoint** class.

Object Class	Description
serviceConnectionPoint	Service connection point objects (SCP) for publishing information that client applications can use to bind to a service. See *Publishing with Service Connection Points (SCPs)*.
rpcEntry	An abstract class whose subclasses are used by the RPC Name Service (Ns), which is accessed through the **RpcNs*** functions in the Win32 API. See *Publishing with the RPC Name Service (RpcNs)*.
ServiceInstance	Connection point object used by the Windows Sockets Registration and Resolution (RnR) name service, which is accessed through the Windows Sockets **WSA*** APIs. See *Publishing with Windows Sockets Registration and Resolution (RnR)*.
printQueue	Connection point object used to publish network printers. See *IADsPrintQueue*.
volume	Connection point object used to publish file services.

Note that COM-based services do not use connection-point objects to advertise themselves. These services are published in the *class store*. The Windows 2000 class store is a directory-based repository for all COM-based applications, interfaces, and APIs that provide for application publishing and assigning. For more information, see *Publishing COM+ Services*.

Publishing with Service Connection Points

The Active Directory™ schema defines a **serviceConnectionPoint** (SCP) object class to make it easy for a service to publish service-specific information in the directory. Clients of the service use the information in an SCP to locate, connect to, and authenticate an instance of your service.

This section provides an overview of service connection points and code samples that show how a client/service application uses SCPs.

The example follows these steps to implement service publication with SCPs:

▶ **To create SCPs in the directory at service installation**

For sample code that performs these steps, see *Creating a Service Connection Point*.

1. Bind to the computer object for the host computer on which the service instance is being installed.
2. Create an SCP object as a child of the computer object, specifying the initial values for the attributes of the SCP.
3. Set access control entries (ACEs) in the security descriptor of the SCP object to enable the service to modify SCP properties at run time.
4. Cache the **objectGUID** of the SCP in the registry on the service's host computer.

▶ **To update the SCP attributes at service startup**

For sample code that performs these steps, see *Updating a Service Connection Point*.

1. Retrieve the **objectGUID** from the registry and use it to bind to the SCP.
2. Retrieve attributes, such as **serviceDNSName** and **serviceBindingInformation**, from the SCP. Compare these values to the current values and update the SCP if necessary.

▶ **To find and use an SCP by a client application**

For sample code that performs these steps, see *How Clients Find and Use a Service Connection Point*.

1. Bind to the global catalog and search for objects with a **keywords** property that matches the service's product GUID. Each object found is an instance of the service. Select an instance and retrieve the distinguished name of the SCP.
2. Use the distinguished name to bind to the SCP.
3. Retrieve the values of various attributes from the SCP, such as **serviceDNSName** and **serviceBindingInformation**. Use these values to connect to and authenticate the service instance.

For information on who can create and update an SCP, see *Security Issues for Service Publication*.

For information on where to create an SCP, see *Where to Create a Service Connection Point*.

For a discussion of the kind of information to store in an SCP, see *Service Connection Point Properties*.

For a discussion of how a service installation program and the service itself work together to keep up-to-date information in an SCP, see *Creating and Maintaining a Service Connection Point*.

Where to Create a Service Connection Point

When instances of your service are installed, your service installation program creates service connection point objects (SCPs) in Active Directory. Where in the directory should you create these objects? Your primary goals should be to minimize replication traffic and to make it easy to administer and maintain the objects.

Note that client applications find SCPs by searching the directory for keywords in the SCP. The **keywords** attribute of an SCP is included in the global catalog, so clients can simply search the global catalog to find SCPs anywhere in the forest. For this reason, the client does not influence where to publish SCPs.

Minimize Replication Traffic

To minimize replication traffic, create SCPs in the domain partition of the domain of the service's host computer. For example, you can create SCPs as child objects of the computer object on which the service is installed. A domain partition of Active Directory, sometimes called a domain naming context, contains domain-specific objects such as the objects for the users and computers of the domain. A full replica of all objects in the domain partition is replicated to every domain controller (DC) for the domain, but it is not replicated to DCs of other domains.

Do not create SCPs in the **Configuration** partition (also known as the configuration naming context), because changes to the **Configuration** partition are replicated to every DC in the forest. As noted above, clients throughout the forest can query the global catalog to find SCPs anywhere in the forest, so creating SCPs in the **Configuration** partition does not make them more visible to clients; it simply generates more replication traffic.

Ease of Administration

Consider the following guidelines in order to make administration easier:

- Place service-specific objects where administrators can control access to them using policy and inherited access permissions.
- Place the objects in intuitive locations where administrators can find them easily.

A good default location that satisfies both goals is to create SCPs and other service-specific objects under the computer object of the host computer of each service instance. See *Publishing Under a Computer Object*.

A good alternative for services that are not tied to a single host is to create a container for the service's objects under the **System** container in a domain partition. See *Publishing in a Domain's System Container*.

The following diagram shows part of the default container hierarchy for a domain partition to give you an idea of where these objects might be placed.

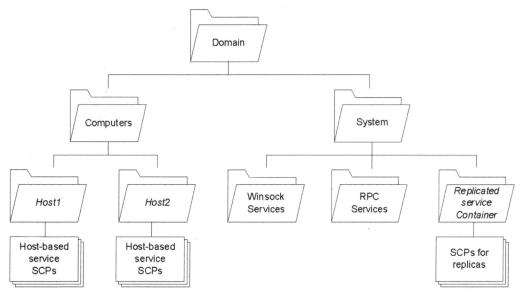

The diagram shows the default domain hierarchy that ships with Active Directory. However, many enterprises will create a hierarchy of organizational unit (OU) containers to group object classes (such as users and computers) together for purposes of administration. Administrators can then apply policy and inheritable access-control entries (ACEs) to an OU to delegate administrative authority for objects in the OU. This makes it easier for administrators to manage an enterprise, but it has a few consequences for service programmers.

- The computer object for a service's host might not be under the **Computers** container as shown in the diagram. For information on how to find the computer object for the local computer, see *Publishing Under a Computer Object*.

- Administrators may move objects as their organizational needs change. This means that you cannot depend on your objects remaining in a fixed location; that is, your service cannot depend on an object's distinguished name remaining the same over time. Instead, you should use an object's **objectGUID** attribute, which does not change if the object is moved or renamed. For sample code that creates an SCP, stores its **objectGUID**, and later retrieves the **objectGUID** to bind to the SCP, see *Creating and Maintaining a Service Connection Point*.

- All of the standard service-related object classes, as well as any subclasses of these classes, are valid children of the **computer** and **organizationalUnit** classes. If you extend the schema to define your own service-specific class, make sure that the **computer** and **organizationalUnit** classes are included in the possible superiors.
- Your service installation program determines the default location for creating SCPs, but you may want to allow the administrator who is installing your service to specify an alternate location better suited to the design of their enterprise.

Service-specific objects should not be created in the following areas:

- Services **should not** publish objects directly in the **Users** or **Computers** containers of a domain partition, nor should they create new containers in these containers. However, services can publish objects as children of a computer object, whether or not the computer object is stored in the **Computers** container.
- Services that use Microsoft® Windows® Sockets registration and resolution (RnR) or the RPC name service (RpcNs) APIs to advertise themselves automatically create the proper objects in the **WinsockServices** and **RpcServices** containers under a domain partition's **System** container. Do not explicitly create objects in these containers. Doing so will not cause direct harm, but it will be confusing for administrators.

Publishing Under a Computer Object

Typically, host-based services create SCPs under the computer object for their host computer. Host-based services are services closely tied to a single host computer.

▶ **To create SCPs under a computer object**

1. Call the **GetComputerObjectName** function to get the distinguished name (DN) in the directory of the computer object for the local computer.

2. Use that DN to bind to the computer object and create the SCP.

For sample code that does this, see *How Clients Find and Use a Service Connection Point*.

Note that only computers that are domain members have valid computer objects in the directory.

To get the DNS or NetBIOS name of the local computer, call the **GetComputerNameEx** function.

Publishing in a Domain's System Container

The **System** container of a domain partition holds per-domain operational information. This includes the default local security policy, file link tracking, network meetings, and containers for Windows Sockets registration and resolution (RnR) and RPC name service (RpcNs) connection points. The system container is hidden by default and provides a convenient place for storing objects that are of interest to administrators, but not to end users.

Services that are not tied to a single host may want to create their SCPs under the **System** container of a domain partition. This alternative can be useful for services with replicas installed on multiple hosts, each replica providing identical services to clients throughout the domain. It enables you to group all the objects for the replicated service under a single container.

Services that create service-specific objects in the **System** container must do the following:

1. Create a sub-container of object class **Container** as an immediate child of the **System** container. Give this sub-container a name that clearly identifies it as pertaining to the service.
2. Create the service-related objects in this sub-container. For example, NetMeeting uses the **Meetings** container to publish network meeting objects.

A vendor with multiple products can use a similar strategy to group service-related objects for all of its products. In this case, you could create a **Container** object with a name that clearly identifies the vendor; then create **Container** objects for each service as children of the vendor's container. Create the vendor-specific container as a child of the **System** container.

Service Connection Points for Replicated, Host-Based, and Database Services

When you publish your service using service connection points, you need to consider how clients will locate the SCP for your service. If multiple instances of the service exist, you must consider how clients will distinguish the service with the desired capabilities from similar services with different capabilities. If you are publishing a replicated service, you must consider how a client will choose a replica. This topic discusses these issues for various types of services.

Replicable services

For a replicable service there can be one or many instances (replicas) of the service, and clients don't care which replica they connect to because each provides the same service. Active Directory is an example of a replicated service: all domain controllers for a given domain hold identical data (subject to replication latency) and provide identical services.

Replicable services can store the SCPs and other service-specific objects for multiple replicas in a single container. The setup program for the first replica can create the container as a child of the local domain's **System** container, as described in Publishing in a Domain's System Container. Make sure that the security descriptor on your container allows the setup programs for subsequent replicas to create their objects in the same container. You should enable the installing administrator to specify the users or groups who are allowed to create or modify objects in the container.

One strategy for a replicable service is to create an SCP for each replica. When a client queries for the service's product GUID or other identifying keyword, it finds the SCP objects for all replicas and selects one at random or using some load-balancing algorithm. For example, an administrator could specify priority and load-balancing information for each replica, similar to the priority and weight fields of a DNS SRV record. The service's setup program can store this information in the **serviceBindingInformation** attribute of each replica's SCP. Clients retrieve the information from each SCP and use it to select a replica.

Another strategy is to create a single SCP for all replicas and set the SCP **serviceDNSName** attribute to the name of a DNS SRV record. Then the setup program for each replica simply registers a SRV record with that name. When a client finds the service's lone SCP, the client retrieves the name of the SRV record and uses the **DnsQuery** function to retrieve the array of SRV records for the replicas. Each SRV record contains the name of a host computer and additional information that the client can use to select a replica.

Database services

Different instances of a database service may contain entirely different data, even though they are all the same kind of service (usually called service class). To publish this kind of service, the **keywords** attribute of the SCP can identify both the service class and the specific database. A general-purpose client that knows only the GUID of the service class can query for all databases published by that service class, and then present a user interface to allow the user to select one. For a client that's designed specifically for the target database, you can hard-code the database GUID into the client's code.

Host-based services

Host-based services are services that are closely tied to a single host computer. You can install instances of the service class on many computers and each instance provides services that are identified with its host computer.

Each instance of a host-based service should create it's own SCP under the computer object of its host. Clients who use a product GUID to search for the SCP of a host-based service will typically find many instances of the service class throughout the enterprise forest. Clients can then use the **serviceDNSName** attribute of the SCPs to find the SCP for the service instance on the desired host computer.

Service Connection Point Properties

The attributes of the **serviceConnectionPoint** class are sufficient for the needs of most services. Active Directory does not define how the attributes are to be used, so the clients of your service must be able to interpret and use the information in your service's SCPs. Services that need to publish additional information about themselves can extend the Active Directory schema by creating a subclass of the **serviceConnectionPoint** class, giving the subclass a distinct name that makes it easily recognizable. For more information about schema extensions, see *Extending the Schema*.

The most important attributes of an SCP are **keywords**, **serviceDNSName**, **serviceDNSNameType**, **serviceClassName**, and **serviceBindingInformation**. Client applications search the directory for **keywords** values to locate your SCP. Having found your SCP, clients read the other attributes to retrieve information about your service.

keywords

The **keywords** attribute can contain multiple string values that identify your service. This attribute is included in the global catalog, which means that clients in any domain of an enterprise forest can search the global catalog for keywords associated with your service. This attribute is also indexed, which improves the performance of queries. The installation program that creates the SCP sets the values of the **keywords** attribute. Typically, these values are not modified by the service that is running.

The exact keywords you should include in your SCP depend on how clients will search for your service. The best keywords to use are GUID strings because GUIDs are guaranteed to be unique in a forest. Use the GUID string format returned by the **UuidToString** function in the RPC library. You can also include human-readable names, if clients may use them to search for your service. The keywords in an SCP should include GUID strings and/or names that identify the following information about your service:

- Your company or organization, for example, Microsoft.
- The product or service, for example, SQL Server. This enables client applications to find SCPs for services of that type.
- The specific version of the product or service, such as 7.5.
- For SCPs that publish a specific set of data or capabilities for a type of service, include a GUID string or name that identifies the specific instance. For example, a database service could publish an SCP for a specific database. In this case, the SCP would include a product GUID to identify the service and another GUID to identify the database.

serviceDNSName and serviceDNSNameType

Client applications use the **serviceDNSName** and **serviceDNSNameType** attributes to determine the service's host computer. The **serviceDNSNameType** value indicates the type of DNS name specified by **serviceDNSName**—usually "A" if **serviceDNSName** contains a host name or "SRV" if **serviceDNSName** contains a SRV record name.

The **serviceDNSName** value is typically the DNS name of the service's host computer. Your service installation program can call the **GetComputerNameEx** function to get the DNS name of the local computer.

For services that have DNS SRV records, **serviceDNSName** can be the name of the SRV record. A client application uses the DNS APIs to retrieve all the SRV records that match this name. The client then retrieves the DNS host name from one of the SRV records. This technique is useful for replicated services because SRV records also include information that enables the client to select the best replica.

serviceBindingInformation

A multi-valued property that contains string values that store information needed to bind to a service. This property is indexed and is replicated to the global catalog.

The content of **serviceBindingInformation** is specific to the service that published the SCP; clients must know how to interpret the binding information. In the simplest and most common case, the binding information consists of a port number on the service's host computer.

serviceClassName

A single-valued property that identifies the class of service represented by the SCP. This is a descriptive string specific to the service that published the SCP, for example SqlServer. For services that support mutual authentication, clients can use this property (along with the DNS name of the service's host computer) to form a service principal name (SPN). For more information, see *Mutual Authentication Using Kerberos.*

Creating and Maintaining a Service Connection Point

The guiding principle for publishing with an SCP is that it must contain up-to-date information about the service instance. Otherwise, clients who bind to the SCP will retrieve stale information. Your service installation program that creates an SCP specifies the initial values for the SCPs attributes. Then, when the service instance starts up, it must locate the SCP and update the attribute values, if necessary. In this way, interested clients are assured the most up-to-date information.

After creating the SCP, your service installation program performs two additional steps that enable your service to update the SCP.

- Set ACEs in the security descriptor of the SCP object to enable the service to modify SCP attributes at run time. For sample code that does this, see *Enabling Service Account to Access SCP Properties.*

- Cache the **objectGUID** of the SCP in the registry on the service's host computer. The service retrieves the cached GUID to bind to the SCP to verify and update its attributes.

The service installation program caches the SCP's **objectGUID** rather than its DN. The **objectGUID** never changes, regardless of whether the SCP is moved or renamed. The DN can change if an administrator moves or renames the SCP. For example, if you create an SCP as a child of a computer object, the distinguished name of the SCP changes if the computer is renamed or moved to a different domain or organizational unit.

When a service installation program creates an SCP, it must read the **objectGUID** of the newly-created object and cache it in the registry of the service's host computer. You can use the IADs::get_GUID method to get the **objectGUID** value in string format suitable for binding. Cache the GUID string as a value under the following registry key.

```
HKEY_LOCAL_MACHINE
    SOFTWARE
        <VENDOR-NAME>
            <PRODUCT-NAME>
```

Where <VENDOR-NAME> and <PRODUCT-NAME> identify the vendor and product.

When the service starts up, it retrieves the cached GUID string from the registry and uses it to bind to the SCP. The service reads the important SCP attributes and compares them to current values. If the SCP values are out of date, the service updates them. Values that the service might need to update include **keywords**, **serviceBindingInformation**, **serviceDNSName**, and **serviceDNSNameType**.

For sample code that creates an SCP, see *Creating a Service Connection Point*.

For sample code updates the SCP, see *Updating a Service Connection Point*.

Creating a Service Connection Point

The following sample code shows how to create and initialize a service connection point. The code performs additional steps that enable the service to update the SCP values at run time. Typically, a service installation program performs these steps as part of installing a service instance on a host computer.

This example creates the SCP object in Active Directory as a child of the computer object for the local computer. It uses the **GetComputerObjectName** function to get the DN of the local computer object. Then it uses the DN to bind to an **IDirectoryObject** pointer for the computer object. The **IDirectoryObject::CreateDSObject** method creates the SCP and specifies initial values for the important SCP attributes.

CreateDSObject returns a pointer to the new SCP, which the example uses to retrieve an **IADs** pointer for the SCP. The example uses **IADs** methods to retrieve the **objectGUID** and **distinguishedName** attributes of the SCP. It uses the **objectGUID** to compose a string that can be used to bind to the SCP, and then caches the GUID binding string in the local registry where it can be retrieved by the service at run time. The **distinguishedName** is returned to the routine's caller for use in composing a service principal name (SPN) for the service instance.

The sample code calls this routine as part of the basic steps of installing a directory-enabled service. See *Installing a Service on a Host Computer*.

```
// ScpCreate
//
// Create a new service connection point as a child of the local
// server's computer object.
//
DWORD
ScpCreate(
        USHORT usPort,          // Service's default port to store in SCP.
        LPTSTR szClass,         // Service class string to store in SCP.
        LPTSTR szAccount,       // Logon account that needs access to SCP.
        TCHAR *pszDN)           // Returns distinguished name of SCP.
{
DWORD dwStat, dwAttr, dwLen;
HRESULT hr;
IDispatch *pDisp;               // returned dispinterface of new object
IDirectoryObject *pComp;        // Computer object; parent of SCP
IADs *pIADsSCP;                 // IADs interface on new object

// Values for SCPs keywords attribute.
TCHAR       *KwVal[]={
        TEXT("937924B8-AA44-11d2-81F1-00C04FB9624E"),  // Vendor GUID
        TEXT("A762885A-AA44-11d2-81F1-00C04FB9624E"),  // Product GUID
        TEXT("Microsoft"),                             // Vendor Name
        TEXT("Windows 2000 Auth-O-Matic"),             // Product Name
};

TCHAR       szServer[MAX_PATH];
TCHAR       szDn[MAX_PATH];
TCHAR       szAdsPath[MAX_PATH];
TCHAR       szPort[6];

HKEY        hReg;
DWORD       dwDisp;

ADSVALUE cn,objclass,keywords[4],binding,classname,dnsname,nametype;

// SCP attributes to set during creation of SCP.
ADS_ATTR_INFO   ScpAttribs[] = {
{TEXT("cn"),ADS_ATTR_UPDATE,ADSTYPE_CASE_IGNORE_STRING,&cn,1},
{TEXT("objectClass"),ADS_ATTR_UPDATE,ADSTYPE_CASE_IGNORE_STRING,&objclass,1},
{TEXT("keywords"),ADS_ATTR_UPDATE,ADSTYPE_CASE_IGNORE_STRING,keywords,4},
```

```
{TEXT("serviceDnsName"),ADS_ATTR_UPDATE,ADSTYPE_CASE_IGNORE_STRING,&dnsname,1},
{TEXT("serviceDnsNameType"),ADS_ATTR_UPDATE,ADSTYPE_CASE_IGNORE_STRING,&nametype,1},
{TEXT("serviceClassName"),ADS_ATTR_UPDATE,ADSTYPE_CASE_IGNORE_STRING,&classname,1},
{TEXT("serviceBindingInformation"),ADS_ATTR_UPDATE,ADSTYPE_CASE_IGNORE_STRING,&binding,1},
};

BSTR bstrGuid = NULL;
TCHAR pwszBindByGuidStr[1024];
VARIANT var;

// Get the DNS name of the local computer
dwLen = sizeof(szServer);
if (!GetComputerNameEx(ComputerNameDnsFullyQualified,szServer,&dwLen))
    return GetLastError();
_tprintf(TEXT("GetComputerNameEx: %s\n"), szServer);

// Fill in the attribute values to be stored in the SCP.
keywords[0].dwType = ADSTYPE_CASE_IGNORE_STRING;
keywords[1].dwType = ADSTYPE_CASE_IGNORE_STRING;
keywords[2].dwType = ADSTYPE_CASE_IGNORE_STRING;
keywords[3].dwType = ADSTYPE_CASE_IGNORE_STRING;

keywords[0].CaseIgnoreString=KwVal[0];
keywords[1].CaseIgnoreString=KwVal[1];
keywords[2].CaseIgnoreString=KwVal[2];
keywords[3].CaseIgnoreString=KwVal[3];

cn.dwType                = ADSTYPE_CASE_IGNORE_STRING;
cn.CaseIgnoreString      = TEXT("SockAuthAD");
objclass.dwType          = ADSTYPE_CASE_IGNORE_STRING;
objclass.CaseIgnoreString = TEXT("serviceConnectionPoint");

dnsname.dwType           = ADSTYPE_CASE_IGNORE_STRING;
dnsname.CaseIgnoreString = szServer;
classname.dwType         = ADSTYPE_CASE_IGNORE_STRING;
classname.CaseIgnoreString = szClass;

_stprintf(szPort,TEXT("%d"),usPort);
binding.dwType           = ADSTYPE_CASE_IGNORE_STRING;
binding.CaseIgnoreString = szPort;
nametype.dwType          = ADSTYPE_CASE_IGNORE_STRING;
nametype.CaseIgnoreString = TEXT("A");

// Get the distinguished name of the computer object
```

(continued)

(continued)

```
// for the local computer
dwLen = sizeof(szDn);
if (!GetComputerObjectName(NameFullyQualifiedDN,szDn,&dwLen))
    return GetLastError();
_tprintf(TEXT("GetComputerObjectName: %s\n"), szDn);

// Compose the ADSpath and bind to the computer object
// for the local computer
_tcscpy(szAdsPath,TEXT("LDAP://"));
_tcscat(szAdsPath,szDn);
hr = ADsGetObject(szAdsPath, IID_IDirectoryObject, (void **)&pComp);
if (FAILED(hr)) {
    ReportError(TEXT("Failed to bind Computer Object."),hr);
    return hr;
}

//*****************************************************************
// Publish the SCP as a child of the computer object
//*****************************************************************

// Figure out attribute count.
dwAttr = sizeof(ScpAttribs)/sizeof(ADS_ATTR_INFO);

// Do the Deed!
hr = pComp->CreateDSObject(TEXT("cn=SockAuthAD"),
                           ScpAttribs, dwAttr, &pDisp);
if (FAILED(hr)) {
    ReportError(TEXT("Failed to create SCP:"), hr);
    return hr;
}

// Query for an IADs pointer on the SCP object.
hr = pDisp->QueryInterface(IID_IADs,(void **)&pIADsSCP);
if (FAILED(hr)) {
    ReportError(TEXT("Failed to QI for IADs:"),hr);
    pDisp->Release();
    return hr;
}
pDisp->Release();

// Set ACEs on SCP so service can modify it.
hr = AllowAccessToScpProperties(
        szAccount,      // Service account to allow access.
        pIADsSCP);      // IADs pointer to the SCP object.
```

```
if (FAILED(hr)) {
    ReportError(TEXT("Failed to set ACEs on SCP DACL:"), hr);
    return hr;
}


// Get the distinguished name (DN) of the SCP.
VariantInit(&var);
hr = pIADsSCP->Get(TEXT("distinguishedName"), &var);
if (FAILED(hr)) {
    ReportError(TEXT("Failed to get distinguishedName:"), hr);
    return hr;
}
_tprintf(TEXT("distinguishedName via IADs: %s\n"), var.bstrVal);

// Return the DN of the SCP, which is used to compose the SPN.
// Note that best practice is to either accept and return the buffer
// size or do this in a _try / _except block, both omitted here
// for the sake of clarity.
_tcscpy(pszDN, var.bstrVal);

// Retrieve the SCP's objectGUID in format suitable for binding.
hr = pIADsSCP->get_GUID(&bstrGuid);
if (FAILED(hr)) {
    ReportError(TEXT("Failed to get GUID:"), hr);
    return hr;
}


// Build a string for binding to the object by GUID
_tcscpy(pwszBindByGuidStr, TEXT("LDAP://<GUID="));
_tcscat(pwszBindByGuidStr, bstrGuid);
_tcscat(pwszBindByGuidStr, TEXT(">"));
_tprintf(TEXT("GUID binding string: %s\n"), pwszBindByGuidStr);


pIADsSCP->Release();

// Create a registry key under
//    HKEY_LOCAL_MACHINE\SOFTWARE\Vendor\Product.
dwStat = RegCreateKeyEx(HKEY_LOCAL_MACHINE,
          TEXT("Software\\Microsoft\\Windows 2000 Auth-O-Matic"),
          0,
          NULL,
          REG_OPTION_NON_VOLATILE,
          KEY_ALL_ACCESS,
          NULL,
```

(continued)

(continued)

```
              &hReg,
              &dwDisp);
if (dwStat != NO_ERROR) {
    ReportError(TEXT("RegCreateKeyEx failed:"), dwStat);
    return dwStat;
}


// Cache the GUID binding string under the registry key.
dwStat = RegSetValueEx(hReg, TEXT("GUIDBindingString"), 0, REG_SZ,
                        (const BYTE *)pwszBindByGuidStr,
                        2*(_tcslen(pwszBindByGuidStr)));
if (dwStat != NO_ERROR) {
    ReportError(TEXT("RegSetValueEx failed:"), dwStat);
    return dwStat;
}


RegCloseKey(hReg);

// TODO: cleanup should delete SCP and registry key if error.

return dwStat;
}
```

Updating a Service Connection Point

The following sample code shows how to update a service connection point. This code is typically executed by a service when it starts up.

This example retrieves the SCP's GUID binding string that the service installation program cached in the registry. It uses this string to bind to an **IDirectoryObject** pointer on the SCP object, and then calls the **IDirectoryObject::GetObjectAttributes** method to get the **serviceDNSName** and **serviceBindingInformation** attributes of the SCP. Note that your service may need to verify and update additional attributes.

The code compares the **serviceDNSName** value to the DNS name returned by the **GetComputerNameEx** function. It also compares the service's current port number to the port number stored in the **serviceBindingInformation** attribute. If either of these values have changed, the code calls the **IDirectoryObject::SetObjectAttributes** method to update the SCP attributes.

```
DWORD
ScpUpdate(USHORT usPort)
{
DWORD   dwStat, dwType, dwLen;
BOOL    bUpdate=FALSE;
```

```
HKEY      hReg;

TCHAR     szAdsPath[MAX_PATH];
TCHAR     szServer[MAX_PATH];
TCHAR     szPort[8];
TCHAR     *pszAttrs[]={
    {TEXT("serviceDNSName")},
    {TEXT("serviceBindingInformation")},
};

HRESULT            hr;
IDirectoryObject   *pObj;
DWORD              dwAttrs;
int                i;

PADS_ATTR_INFO  pAttribs;
ADSVALUE        dnsname,binding;

ADS_ATTR_INFO   Attribs[]={

{TEXT("serviceDnsName"),ADS_ATTR_UPDATE,ADSTYPE_CASE_IGNORE_STRING,&dnsname,1},

{TEXT("serviceBindingInformation"),ADS_ATTR_UPDATE,ADSTYPE_CASE_IGNORE_STRING,&bi
nding,1},
};

// Open the service's registry key.
dwStat = RegOpenKeyEx(
        HKEY_LOCAL_MACHINE,
        TEXT("Software\\Microsoft\\Windows 2000 Auth-O-Matic"),
        0,
        KEY_QUERY_VALUE,
        &hReg);
if (dwStat != NO_ERROR)
{
    ReportServiceError("RegOpenKeyEx failed", dwStat);
    return dwStat;
}

// Get the GUID binding string used to bind to the service's SCP.
dwLen = sizeof(szAdsPath);
dwStat = RegQueryValueEx(hReg, TEXT("GUIDBindingString"), 0, &dwType,
                            (LPBYTE)szAdsPath, &dwLen);
```

(continued)

(continued)

```
if (dwStat != NO_ERROR) {
    ReportServiceError("RegQueryValueEx failed", dwStat);
    return dwStat;
}


RegCloseKey(hReg);

// Bind to the SCP.
hr = ADsGetObject(szAdsPath, IID_IDirectoryObject, (void **)&pObj);
if (FAILED(hr))
{
    char szMsg1[1024];
    sprintf(szMsg1,
            "ADsGetObject failed to bind to GUID (bind string: %S): ",
            szAdsPath);
    ReportServiceError(szMsg1, hr);
    return dwStat;
}

// Retrieve attributes from the SCP.
hr = pObj->GetObjectAttributes(pszAttrs, 2, &pAttribs, &dwAttrs);
if (FAILED(hr)) {
    ReportServiceError("GetObjectAttributes failed", hr);
    return hr;
}

// Get the current port and DNS name of the host server.
_stprintf(szPort,TEXT("%d"),usPort);
dwLen = sizeof(szServer);
if (!GetComputerNameEx(ComputerNameDnsFullyQualified,szServer,&dwLen))
{
    pObj->Release();
    return GetLastError();
}

// Compare the current DNS name and port to the values retrieved from
// the SCP. Update the SCP only if nothing has changed.
for (i=0; i<(LONG)dwAttrs; i++)
{
    if (_tcscmp(TEXT("serviceDNSName"),pAttribs[i].pszAttrName)==0)
    {
        if (_tcscmp(szServer,pAttribs[i].pADsValues->CaseIgnoreString) != 0)
        {
            ReportServiceError("serviceDNSName being updated", 0);
```

```
                    bUpdate = TRUE;
            }
            else
                ReportServiceError("serviceDNSName okay", 0);


        }

        if (_tcscmp(TEXT("serviceBindingInformation"),pAttribs[i].pszAttrName)==0)
        {
            if (_tcscmp(szPort,pAttribs[i].pADsValues->CaseIgnoreString) != 0)
            {
                ReportServiceError("serviceBindingInformation being updated", 0);
                bUpdate = TRUE;
            }
            else
                ReportServiceError("serviceBindingInformation okay", 0);
        }
    }

FreeADsMem(pAttribs);

// The binding information or server name have changed,
// so update the SCP values.
if (bUpdate)
{
    dnsname.dwType            = ADSTYPE_CASE_IGNORE_STRING;
    dnsname.CaseIgnoreString  = szServer;
    binding.dwType            = ADSTYPE_CASE_IGNORE_STRING;
    binding.CaseIgnoreString  = szPort;
    hr = pObj->SetObjectAttributes(Attribs, 2, &dwAttrs);
    if (FAILED(hr))
    {
        ReportServiceError("ScpUpdate: Failed to set SCP values.", hr);
        pObj->Release();
        return hr;
    }
}

return dwStat;
}
```

How Clients Find and Use a Service Connection Point

The following sample code shows how a client application searches the global catalog for an SCP. In this sample, the client application has a hard-coded GUID string that identifies the service. The service's installation program stored the same GUID string as one of the values of the SCPs multi-valued **keywords** attribute.

This sample actually consists of two routines. The *GetGC* routine retrieves an **IDirectorySearch** pointer for a global catalog (GC). The *ScpLocate* routine uses the **IDirectorySearch** methods to search the GC.

The GC contains a *partial* replica of every object in the forest, but it does not contain all of the SCP attributes that the client needs. First, the client must search the GC to find the SCP and retrieve its DN. Then the client uses the SCP's DN to bind to an **IDirectoryObject** pointer on the SCP. The client then calls the **IDirectoryObject::GetObjectAttributes** method to retrieve the rest of the attributes.

```
DWORD
ScpLocate(
    TCHAR *pszDN,                   // Returns distinguished name of SCP
    TCHAR *pszServiceDNSName,       // Returns service's DNS name
    TCHAR *pszServiceDNSNameType,   // Returns type of DNS name
    TCHAR *pszClass,                // Returns name of service class
    USHORT *pusPort)                // Returns service port
{
HRESULT hr;

// Params for IDirectoryObject
LPOLESTR szSCPPath = new OLECHAR[MAX_PATH];
IDirectoryObject *pSCP = NULL;
ADS_ATTR_INFO       *pPropEntries = NULL;
DWORD dwNumAttrGot;

// Structures and Params for IDirectorySearch
IDirectorySearch    *pSearch = NULL;
DWORD               dwPref, dwAttrs;
TCHAR               szQuery[255];
ADS_SEARCH_COLUMN   Col;
ADS_SEARCH_HANDLE   hSearch = NULL;
ADS_SEARCHPREF_INFO SearchPref[2];

// Properties to retrieve from the SCP object.
TCHAR   *szAttribs[]={
        {TEXT("distinguishedName")},
        {TEXT("serviceClassName")},
```

```
            {TEXT("serviceDNSName")},
            {TEXT("serviceDNSNameType")},
            {TEXT("serviceBindingInformation")}
    };

// First, get an IDirectorySearch pointer for the global catalog.
// See the GetGC sample code below.
hr = GetGC(&pSearch);
if (FAILED(hr)) {
    ReportError(TEXT("GetGC failed"), hr);
    goto Cleanup;
}


// Set up the search. We want to do a deep search.
// Note that we are not expecting thousands of objects
// in this example, so we will ask for 1000 rows / page.
dwPref=sizeof(SearchPref)/sizeof(ADS_SEARCHPREF_INFO);
SearchPref[0].dwSearchPref =    ADS_SEARCHPREF_SEARCH_SCOPE;
SearchPref[0].vValue.dwType =    ADSTYPE_INTEGER;
SearchPref[0].vValue.Integer = ADS_SCOPE_SUBTREE;

SearchPref[1].dwSearchPref =    ADS_SEARCHPREF_PAGESIZE;
SearchPref[1].vValue.dwType =    ADSTYPE_INTEGER;
SearchPref[1].vValue.Integer = 1000;


hr = pSearch->SetSearchPreference(SearchPref, dwPref);
fprintf (stderr, "SetSearchPreference: 0x%x\n", hr);
if (FAILED(hr))     {
    fprintf (stderr, "Failed to set search prefs: hr:0x%x\n", hr);
    goto Cleanup;
}

// Search for an exact match on our product GUID.
_tcscpy(szQuery,
        TEXT("keywords=A762885A-AA44-11d2-81F1-00C04FB9624E"));

// Execute the search. From the GC we can get the distinguished name
// of the SCP. Use the DN to bind to the SCP and get the other
// properties.

hr = pSearch->ExecuteSearch(szQuery,
                            szAttribs,
                            1,
                            &hSearch);
```

(continued)

(continued)

```
fprintf (stderr, "ExecuteSearch: 0x%x\n", hr);
if (FAILED(hr)) {
    ReportError(TEXT("ExecuteSearch failed."), hr);
    goto Cleanup;
}


// Loop through the results. Each row should be an instance of the
// service identified by the product GUID.
// TODO: Add logic to select from multiple service instances.
hr = pSearch->GetNextRow(hSearch);
while (SUCCEEDED(hr) && hr !=S_ADS_NOMORE_ROWS)
{
    hr = pSearch->GetColumn(hSearch, TEXT("distinguishedName"), &Col);
    if (FAILED(hr))
        break;
    _tcscpy(pszDN, Col.pADsValues->CaseIgnoreString);
    pSearch->FreeColumn(&Col);
    hr = pSearch->GetNextRow(hSearch);
}


// Now bind to the DN to get the other properties.
wcscpy(szSCPPath, L"LDAP://");
wcscat(szSCPPath, pszDN);
hr = ADsGetObject(szSCPPath,
                  IID_IDirectoryObject,
                  (void**)&pSCP);
if (SUCCEEDED(hr))
{
    dwAttrs=sizeof(szAttribs)/sizeof(LPWSTR);
    hr = pSCP->GetObjectAttributes( szAttribs,
                                    dwAttrs,
                                    &pPropEntries,
                                    &dwNumAttrGot);

    if(FAILED(hr)) {
        ReportError(TEXT("GetObjectAttributes Failed."), hr);
        goto Cleanup;
    }

    // Loop through the entries returned by GetObjectAttributes
    // and save the values in the appropriate buffers.
    for (int i=0;i<(LONG)dwAttrs;i++)
    {
        if (_tcscmp(TEXT("distinguishedName"),
                pPropEntries[i].pszAttrName) ==0)
```

```
            {
                _tcscpy(pszDN,
                        pPropEntries[i].pADsValues->CaseIgnoreString);
            }

            if (_tcscmp(TEXT("serviceDNSName"),
                        pPropEntries[i].pszAttrName)==0)
            {
                _tcscpy(pszServiceDNSName,
                        pPropEntries[i].pADsValues->CaseIgnoreString);
            }

            if (_tcscmp(TEXT("serviceDNSNameType"),
                        pPropEntries[i].pszAttrName)==0)
            {
                _tcscpy(pszServiceDNSNameType,
                        pPropEntries[i].pADsValues->CaseIgnoreString);
            }

            if (_tcscmp(TEXT("serviceClassName"),
                        pPropEntries[i].pszAttrName)==0)
            {
                _tcscpy(pszClass,
                        pPropEntries[i].pADsValues->CaseIgnoreString);
            }

            if (_tcscmp(TEXT("serviceBindingInformation"),
                        pPropEntries[i].pszAttrName)==0)
            {
                *pusPort=(USHORT)_ttoi(
                        pPropEntries[i].pADsValues->CaseIgnoreString);
            }
        }
    }

Cleanup:
if (pSCP)
    pSCP->Release();
if (pPropEntries)
    FreeADsMem(pPropEntries);
if (hSearch)
    pSearch->CloseSearchHandle(hSearch);
return hr;
}
```

(continued)

(continued)

```
//**************************************************************
// GetGC
// Retrieves an IDirectorySearch pointer for a global catalog (GC)
//**************************************************************
HRESULT GetGC(IDirectorySearch **ppDS)
{
HRESULT hr;
IEnumVARIANT *pEnum = NULL;
IADsContainer *pCont = NULL;
VARIANT var;
IDispatch *pDisp = NULL;
ULONG lFetch;

// Set IDirectorySearch pointer to NULL.
*ppDS = NULL;

// First, bind to the GC: namespace container object. The "real" GC DN
// is a single immediate child of the GC: namespace, which must
// be obtained using enumeration.
hr = ADsOpenObject(TEXT("GC:"),
                NULL,
                NULL,
                ADS_SECURE_AUTHENTICATION, //Use Secure Authentication
                IID_IADsContainer,
                (void**)&pCont);
if (FAILED(hr)) {
    _tprintf(TEXT("ADsOpenObject failed: 0x%x\n"), hr);
    goto cleanup;
}

// Fetch an enumeration interface for the GC container.
hr = ADsBuildEnumerator(pCont, &pEnum);
if (FAILED(hr)) {
    _tprintf(TEXT("ADsBuildEnumerator failed: 0x%x\n"), hr);
    goto cleanup;
}

//Now enumerate. There's only one child of the GC: object.
hr = ADsEnumerateNext(pEnum, 1, &var, &lFetch);
if (FAILED(hr)) {
    _tprintf(TEXT("ADsEnumerateNext failed: 0x%x\n"), hr);
    goto cleanup;
}
```

```
if (( hr == S_OK ) && ( lFetch == 1 ) )
{
    pDisp = V_DISPATCH(&var);
    hr = pDisp->QueryInterface( IID_IDirectorySearch, (void**)ppDS);
}

cleanup:

if (pEnum)
    ADsFreeEnumerator(pEnum);
if (pCont)
    pCont->Release();
if (pDisp)
    (pDisp)->Release();
return hr;
}
```

Publishing with the RPC Name Service (RpcNs)

RPC services publish themselves in a namespace using the RPC name service (RpcNs) APIs. The RpcNs APIs in Microsoft® Windows® 2000 publish the RPC entries in Microsoft® Active Directory™. Services create RPC bindings and publish them in the namespace as named RPC Server entries with attributes including the unique interface ID, a GUID that is known to clients. Clients can then search for RPC Servers offering the desired interface, import the binding, and connect to the server.

Example Code for Publishing an RPC Service

The following C++ code fragment is called by a service installation program to publish an RPC service:

```
status = RpcServerUseProtseq((TCHAR *)TEXT("ncacn_ip_tcp"),
                             RPC_C_PROTSEQ_MAX_REQS_DEFAULT,
                             NULL);

//Register our interface with the RPC run time.

status = RpcServerRegisterIf(RpcExample_v1_0_s_ifspec,NULL,NULL);

//Collect the bindings provided by the RPC run time.

status = RpcServerInqBindings(&pBindingVec);
```

(continued)

(continued)

```
//Clear the endpoints out of the binding handles.
//This forces the clients through the Endpoint Mapper and
//reduces the volatility of the namespace entry for this
//service.

for (i=0; i < pBindingVec->Count; ++i) {
    RpcBindingReset(pBindingVec->BindingH[i]);
}

//Create the entry in the name service for this service.

status = RpcNsBindingExport(RPC_C_NS_SYNTAX_DEFAULT,
                            (TCHAR *)&szEntryName,
                            RpcExample_v1_0_s_ifspec,
                            pBindingVec,
                            NULL);
```

The following code is called by the service when it starts up to register with the endpoint mapper.

```
//Use TCP/IP as the protocol: max concurrent users 64,
//no NT Security Descriptor.


status = RpcServerUseProtseq((TCHAR *)TEXT("ncacn_ip_tcp"),
                             RPC_C_PROTSEQ_MAX_REQS_DEFAULT,
                             NULL);

//Register our interface with the RPC run time.

status = RpcServerRegisterIf(RpcExample_v1_0_s_ifspec,NULL,NULL);

//Collect the bindings provided by the RPC run time.

status = RpcServerInqBindings(&pBindingVec);

//Register the interface with the Endpoint Mapper.
//There are no Object UUIDs or Annotation string in this example.

status = RpcEpRegister(RpcExample_v1_0_s_ifspec,
                       pBindingVec,NULL,NULL);
```

```
//Start the server. When RpcServerListen returns, the server is
//shutting down.

if (status != RPC_S_OK)
    return;

//Handle calls from clients until we are shut down.

status = RpcServerListen(1,
                         RPC_C_LISTEN_MAX_CALLS_DEFAULT,
                         0);

//Remove this service from the endpoint map. We need to get a
//new binding vector since the old one has the endpoints removed
//and does not match what we registered.
//
//RpcBindingVectorFree(&pBindingVec);
//RpcServerInqBindings(&pBindingVec);
status = RpcEpUnregister(RpcExample_v1_0_s_ifspec,pBindingVec,
                         NULL);
```

Example Code for an RPC Client Locating a Server

The following code fragment locates a server with the example RPC service:

```
//Begin the import. We explicitly start with the a known
//entry, "ExampleRpcServiceEntry". The interface we are
//looking for is defined by RpcExample_v1_0_s_ifspec, which
//is generated by MIDL.

status = RpcNsBindingImportBegin(RPC_C_NS_SYNTAX_DCE,
                                 (TCHAR *)&szEntryName,
                                 RpcExample_v1_0_c_ifspec,
                                 NULL,
                                 &hNs);

//Abandon if we cannot find anything or get any errors.
if (status != RPC_S_OK)
    return;

//Now acquire the first available binding handle. In this
//example, implicit handles are used: the implicit handle
//"RpcExample_IfHandle" is generated by MIDL and defined in the
//MIDL-generated include file RpcExample.H.
```

(continued)

(continued)

```
//Loop through the bindings and try handles
//until one works.

while (status != RPC_S_NO_MORE_BINDINGS) {
    status = RpcNsBindingImportNext(hNs,
                                    &RpcExample_IfHandle);

    if (status != RPC_S_OK)
        continue;

    //Convert the binding to a string and display it to
    //the user/

    RpcBindingToStringBinding(RpcExample_IfHandle,&pszBind);
    _tprintf(TEXT("String Binding:%s\n"),pszBind);

    //Extract the service name, the host, in this case).

    ilen=_tcscspn((const TCHAR *)pszBind,TEXT(":"));
    _tcscpy(szServiceInstance,(const TCHAR *)(pszBind+ilen+1));

    RpcStringFree(&pszBind);

    //Make the RPC - Call the Server, then shut it down.

    RpcTryExcept {
        bResult = ServerProc((TCHAR *)TEXT("Text sent to server"));
        if (bResult)
            _tprintf(TEXT("ServerProc: Server accepted call\n"));
        else
            _tprintf(TEXT("ServerProc: Server rejected call\n"));

        bResult = Shutdown();
        if (bResult)
            _tprintf(TEXT("Shutdown: Server accepted call\n"));
        else
            _tprintf(TEXT("Shutdown: Server rejected call\n"));
        status  = RPC_S_NO_MORE_BINDINGS; //shut off the loop
    }
    RpcExcept(1) {
        ulCode = RpcExceptionCode();
        _tprintf(TEXT("RPC exception 0x%1x = %ld\n"), ulCode, ulCode);
    }
```

```
      RpcEndExcept;

      //Free the imported binding.

      RpcBindingFree(&RpcExample_IfHandle);
   }

   //Discard the Import handle, we don't need it any more.

   status = RpcNsBindingImportDone(&hNs);
```

Publishing with Windows Sockets Registration and Resolution (RnR)

Microsoft® Windows® Sockets services can use the registration and resolution (RnR) APIs to publish services and look up services so published. RnR publication occurs in two steps. The first step installs a service class that associates a GUID with a name for the service. The service class can hold service-specific configuration information. Services can then publish themselves as instances of the service class. Once published, clients can query the directory service for instances of a given class using the RnR APIs and select an instance to bind to. When a class is no longer useful, it can be removed.

Example Code for Installing an RnR Service Class

The following program installs an **RnR Service** class.

```
#include <winsock2.h>
#include <stdio.h>

#define BUFFSIZE 200

//{A9033BC1-ECA4-11cf-A054-00AA006C33ED}
static GUID SVCID_EXAMPLE_SERVICE =
{ 0xa9033bc1, 0xeca4, 0x11cf, { 0xa0, 0x54, 0x0, 0xaa, 0x0, 0x6c, 0x33, 0xed } };

HRESULT
main(void)
{


//Data structures for initializing Winsock.

WSADATA wsData;
```

(continued)

(continued)

```
WORD     wVer = MAKEWORD(2,2);


//Data structures for defining and installing a
//Winsock service class.


WSASERVICECLASSINFO    servinfo;
WSANSCLASSINFO         classinfo[2];


//Values for initializing the data structures.

WCHAR    wszServiceName[]=L"ExampleService";
WCHAR    wszParam1[]    =L"MaxConnections";
WCHAR    wszParam2[]    =L"Timeout";
DWORD    dwConn         = 64;
DWORD    dwTmo          = 1500;

//Miscellaneous variables for status, and so on.

DWORD    iLen;
WCHAR    buf[BUFFSIZE];
INT      status;

//Begin: Init Winsock2

status = WSAStartup(wVer,&wsData);
if (status != NO_ERROR)
    return -1;

//Set up the service class data structure.

servinfo.lpServiceClassId      = &SVCID_EXAMPLE_SERVICE;
servinfo.lpszServiceClassName  = wszServiceName;
servinfo.dwCount               = 2;
servinfo.lpClassInfos          = classinfo;

//This service has two items of class-specific data;
//set these up in the classinfo array.

classinfo[0].lpszName          = wszParam1;
classinfo[0].dwNameSpace       = NS_NTDS;
classinfo[0].dwValueType       = REG_DWORD;
```

```
classinfo[0].dwValueSize    = sizeof(DWORD);
classinfo[0].lpValue        = &dwConn;

classinfo[1].lpszName       = wszParam2;
classinfo[1].dwNameSpace    = NS_NTDS;
classinfo[1].dwValueType    = REG_DWORD;
classinfo[1].dwValueSize    = sizeof(DWORD);
classinfo[1].lpValue        = &dwTmo;

status = WSAInstallServiceClass(&servinfo);
if (status != NO_ERROR)
    printf("Install failed with status %d\n",WSAGetLastError());


//Read the class name back.

iLen = BUFFSIZE;

//Status = WSAGetServiceClassNameByClassId(&SVCID_EXAMPLE_SERVICE,
//                                          buf,&iLen);
//if (status != NO_ERROR) {
//        printf("GetServiceClassName failed with status %d\n",
//                WSAGetLastError());
//}


//Free resources and exit.

WSACleanup();
return 0;

}
```

Example Code for Implementing a Winsock Service with an RnR Publication

The following program implements the example Winsock service with RnR publication.

This sample calls the **serverRegister** and **serverUnregister** sample routines, which are documented in the *Example Code for Publishing the RnR Connection Point* section.

```
/*
** Simple Winsock Server
*/
#include <winsock2.h>
```

(continued)

(continued)

```
#include <stdio.h>


INT serverRegister(SOCKADDR *);
INT serverUnregister(SOCKADDR *);

HRESULT
main(void)
{


    //Data structures for initializing Winsock.

    WSADATA wsData;
    WORD    wVer = MAKEWORD(2,2);


    //Data structures for setting up communications.

    SOCKET      s, newsock;
    SOCKADDR    sa;
    struct hostent    *he;
    char    szName[255];

    struct sockaddr_in sa_in;

    INT         ilen;
    ULONG       icmd;
    ULONG       ulLen;

    //Miscellaneous variables

    INT status;
    WCHAR   wszRecvBuf[100];

    memset(wszRecvBuf,0,sizeof(wszRecvBuf));

    //Begin: Init Winsock2


    status = WSAStartup(wVer,&wsData);
    if (status != NO_ERROR)
        return -1;
```

```
//Create the socket.

s = socket(AF_INET,SOCK_STREAM,IPPROTO_TCP);
if (s == INVALID_SOCKET) {
    printf("Failed to create socket: %d\n",WSAGetLastError());
    WSACleanup();
    return -1;
}



//Disable non-blocking IO for purposes of this example.

icmd = 0;
status = ioctlsocket(s,FIONBIO,&icmd);


//Bind the socket to a dynamically assigned port.

sa.sa_family=AF_INET;
memset(sa.sa_data,0,sizeof(sa.sa_data));


status = bind(s,&sa,sizeof(sa));

//Note that we need to convert the port to the local
//host byte order.

ilen = sizeof(sa_in);
status = getsockname(s,(struct sockaddr *)&sa_in,&ilen);
if (status == NO_ERROR) {
    printf("Server: Bound to port %d\n",ntohs(sa_in.sin_port));
}
//Figure out our net address to fill in for registering ourselves
//in the directory service. Explicitly call the ANSI text version
//because gethostbyname does not understand UNICODE.

ilen = sizeof(szName);
GetComputerNameA(szName,&ulLen);
he = gethostbyname(szName);

//Put the address in the SOCKADDR struct. This is not
//as difficult as it looks.

sa_in.sin_addr.S_un.S_addr = *((long *)(he->h_addr));
```

(continued)

(continued)

```
//Listen for connections. SOMAXCONN tells the provider to queue
//a "reasonable" number of connections.

status = listen(s,SOMAXCONN);
if (status != NO_ERROR) {
    printf("Failed to set socket listening: %d\n",
            WSAGetLastError());
    WSACleanup();
    return -1;
}


//Register this instance with RnR.

status = serverRegister((SOCKADDR *)&sa_in);
if (status != NO_ERROR) {
    printf("Failed to register instance: %d\n",WSAGetLastError());
    WSACleanup();
    return -1;
}
printf("Server: Registered instance in the directory service\n");

//Block waiting for a connection. This example is single-threaded
//for simplicity. In a real service, spin off
//one or more threads here to call AcceptEx here and process the
//connections through a completion port.

ilen = sizeof(sa);
newsock = accept(s,&sa,&ilen);
if (newsock == INVALID_SOCKET)
{
    printf("Failed to create socket: %d\n",WSAGetLastError());
    status = serverUnregister((SOCKADDR *)&sa_in);
    WSACleanup();
    return -1;
}

printf("Server: There is a client connection\n");

//Receive a message from the client and shut down.

status = recv(newsock,(char *)wszRecvBuf,sizeof(wszRecvBuf),0);
if (status > 0)
        printf("Server: Received: %S\n",wszRecvBuf);
```

```
        //Unregister ourselves
        printf("Unregistering and shutting down.\n");
        status = serverUnregister((SOCKADDR *)&sa_in);

        WSACleanup();
        return 0;
}
```

Example Code for Publishing the RnR Connection Point

The following function is used by the example Winsock service above to register the
RnR connection point for the service.

```
/*
** Simple Winsock Service
*/
#include <winsock2.h>
#include <stdio.h>


//{A9033BC1-ECA4-11cf-A054-00AA006C33ED}
static GUID SVCID_EXAMPLE_SERVICE =
{ 0xa9033bc1, 0xeca4, 0x11cf, { 0xa0, 0x54, 0x0, 0xaa, 0x0, 0x6c, 0x33, 0xed } };


static WCHAR    ServiceInstanceName[] = L"Example Service Instance";
static WCHAR    ServiceInstanceComment[] = L"ExampleService instance registered
in the directory service through RnR";


INT
serverRegister(SOCKADDR * sa)
{
    DWORD           ret;
    WSAVERSION      Version;
    WSAQUERYSET     QuerySet;
    CSADDR_INFO     CSAddrInfo[1];
    SOCKADDR        sa_local;

    memset(&QuerySet,0,sizeof(QuerySet));
    memset(&CSAddrInfo,0,sizeof(CSAddrInfo));
    memset(&sa_local,0,sizeof(SOCKADDR));
    sa_local.sa_family = AF_INET;

    //Build the CSAddrInfo structure to contain address
    //information. This is what clients will use to make a connection.
    //
    //Note that we zeroed out the LocalAddr because we are using
```

(continued)

(continued)

```
    //dynamically assigned port numbers.
    //
    CSAddrInfo[0].LocalAddr.iSockaddrLength = sizeof( SOCKADDR );
    CSAddrInfo[0].LocalAddr.lpSockaddr = &sa_local;
    CSAddrInfo[0].RemoteAddr.iSockaddrLength = sizeof( SOCKADDR );
    CSAddrInfo[0].RemoteAddr.lpSockaddr = sa;
    CSAddrInfo[0].iSocketType = SOCK_STREAM;
    CSAddrInfo[0].iProtocol = PF_INET;

    QuerySet.dwSize = sizeof( WSAQUERYSET );
    QuerySet.lpServiceClassId = &SVCID_EXAMPLE_SERVICE;
    QuerySet.lpszServiceInstanceName = ServiceInstanceName;
    QuerySet.lpszComment = ServiceInstanceComment;
    QuerySet.lpVersion = &Version;
    QuerySet.lpVersion->dwVersion = 2;
    QuerySet.lpVersion->ecHow = COMP_NOTLESS;
    QuerySet.dwNameSpace = NS_NTDS;
    QuerySet.dwNumberOfCsAddrs = 1;
    QuerySet.lpcsaBuffer = CSAddrInfo;

    ret = WSASetService( &QuerySet,
                         RNRSERVICE_REGISTER,
                         SERVICE_MULTIPLE );

    return( ret );

}
```

Example Code for Removing the RnR Connection Point

The following function is used by the example Winsock service above to unregister the RnR connection point for the service.

```
/*
** Simple Winsock Service
*/
#include <winsock2.h>
#include <stdio.h>


//{A9033BC1-ECA4-11cf-A054-00AA006C33ED}
static GUID SVCID_EXAMPLE_SERVICE =
{ 0xa9033bc1, 0xeca4, 0x11cf, { 0xa0, 0x54, 0x0, 0xaa, 0x0, 0x6c, 0x33, 0xed } };

static WCHAR    ServiceInstanceName[] = L"Example Service Instance";
```

```
static WCHAR    ServiceInstanceComment[] = L"ExampleService instance registered
in the directory service through RnR";

INT
serverUnregister(SOCKADDR * sa)
{
    DWORD           ret;
    WSAVERSION      Version;
    WSAQUERYSET     QuerySet;
    CSADDR_INFO     CSAddrInfo[1];
    SOCKADDR        sa_local;

    memset(&QuerySet,0,sizeof(QuerySet));
    memset(&CSAddrInfo,0,sizeof(CSAddrInfo));
    memset(&sa_local,0,sizeof(SOCKADDR));
    sa_local.sa_family = AF_INET;

    //Build the CSAddrInfo structure to contain address
    //information. This is what clients will use to make a connection
    //
    //Note that the LocalAddr is zeroed out because
    //dynamically assigned port numbers are used.
    //
    CSAddrInfo[0].LocalAddr.iSockaddrLength = sizeof( SOCKADDR );
    CSAddrInfo[0].LocalAddr.lpSockaddr = &sa_local;
    CSAddrInfo[0].RemoteAddr.iSockaddrLength = sizeof( SOCKADDR );
    CSAddrInfo[0].RemoteAddr.lpSockaddr = sa;
    CSAddrInfo[0].iSocketType = SOCK_STREAM;
    CSAddrInfo[0].iProtocol = PF_INET;

    QuerySet.dwSize = sizeof( WSAQUERYSET );
    QuerySet.lpServiceClassId = &SVCID_EXAMPLE_SERVICE;
    QuerySet.lpszServiceInstanceName = ServiceInstanceName;
    QuerySet.lpszComment = ServiceInstanceComment;
    QuerySet.lpVersion = &Version;
    QuerySet.lpVersion->dwVersion = 2;
    QuerySet.lpVersion->ecHow = COMP_NOTLESS;
    QuerySet.dwNameSpace = NS_NTDS;
    QuerySet.dwNumberOfCsAddrs = 1;
    QuerySet.lpcsaBuffer = CSAddrInfo;

    ret = WSASetService( &QuerySet,
                         RNRSERVICE_DEREGISTER,
                         SERVICE_MULTIPLE );
```

(continued)

(continued)

```
    return( ret );

}
```

Example Code for a Winsock Client Locating a Service Using an RnR Query

The following program locates the example Winsock service and connects to it.

```
/*
** Simple Winsock Client
*/
#include <winsock2.h>
#include <stdio.h>

#define BUFSIZE 3000

/ {A9033BC1-ECA4-11cf-A054-00AA006C33ED}
static GUID SVCID_EXAMPLE_SERVICE =
{ 0xa9033bc1, 0xeca4, 0x11cf, { 0xa0, 0x54, 0x0, 0xaa, 0x0, 0x6c, 0x33, 0xed } };

static WCHAR    ServiceInstanceName[] = L"Example Service Instance";
static WCHAR    wszClientMessage[] = L"The directory service.";

HRESULT
main(void)
{

    //Data structures for initializing Winsock

    WSADATA wsData;
    WORD    wVer = MAKEWORD(2,2);


    //Data structures for searching

    HANDLE              hQ;
    WSAQUERYSET         QuerySet;
    PWSAQUERYSET        ResultSet;
    DWORD               dwResultSize;
    WCHAR               wBuffer[BUFSIZE];
```

```
//Data structures for setting up communications

SOCKET          s;


//Miscellaneous variables

INT status;
DWORD iAddr;
BOOL bConnected = FALSE;

//Clear out the data structures

ResultSet = (PWSAQUERYSET)wBuffer;
memset(&QuerySet,0,sizeof(QuerySet));
memset(ResultSet,0,sizeof(*ResultSet));


//Begin: Init Winsock2


status = WSAStartup(wVer,&wsData);
if (status != NO_ERROR)
    return -1;

//Create the socket

s = socket(AF_INET,SOCK_STREAM,IPPROTO_TCP);
if (s == INVALID_SOCKET)
{
    printf("Failed to create socket: %d\n",WSAGetLastError());
    WSACleanup();
    return -1;
}

//Set up the search

QuerySet.dwSize = sizeof(QuerySet);
QuerySet.lpServiceClassId = &SVCID_EXAMPLE_SERVICE;
QuerySet.dwNameSpace = NS_NTDS;
QuerySet.lpszServiceInstanceName = ServiceInstanceName;


printf("Client: querying the directory service for service instance...\n");
```

(continued)

(continued)

```
//Look up the service to use

status = WSALookupServiceBegin(&QuerySet,
                               LUP_RETURN_NAME |
                               LUP_RETURN_ADDR |
                               LUP_RETURN_TYPE,
                               &hQ);
if (status != NO_ERROR)
    {
    if (status == WSASERVICE_NOT_FOUND)
        {
        printf("The service was not found.\n");
        }
    else
        {
        printf("Query failed with error %d\n",WSAGetLastError());
        }
    WSACleanup();
    return -1;
    }

//Call LookupNext to collect an instance to use. Note that this
//can be called in a loop until WSA_E_NO_MORE is returned to get
//all the instances returned by the query. Try each instance
//until one works.


printf("Client: search successful. Trying to connect...\n");
dwResultSize = BUFSIZE;
while (WSALookupServiceNext(hQ,
                            0,
                            &dwResultSize,
                            ResultSet) == NO_ERROR)
{
for (iAddr=0;iAddr<ResultSet->dwNumberOfCsAddrs;iAddr++)
    {
    if (connect(s,
        ResultSet->lpcsaBuffer[iAddr].RemoteAddr.lpSockaddr,
        sizeof(SOCKADDR)) == NO_ERROR)
        {
        bConnected = TRUE;
        break;
        }
```

```
        else
            {
            printf("Connection failed %d. Error was
%d\n",iAddr,WSAGetLastError());
            }
        }
    if (bConnected)
        break;
    }

//Close out the search service found and connected to

status = WSALookupServiceEnd(hQ);


printf("Client: connected!\n");

//Send the service a message

printf("Client: Sending message to service...\n");
status = send(s,(char *)wszClientMessage,sizeof(wszClientMessage),0);

//Clean up

WSACleanup();
printf("Client: Finis!\n");
return 0;
}
```

Publishing COM+ Services

COM—based services provide an "application proxy" in the form of an MSI installation package. This MSI file contains the server name to be used and other "glue" like proxy/stubs and type libraries needed for marshalling. The Component Services snap-in automatically generates these application proxies for COM+ Server applications.

The application proxies are published into policy objects in Active Directory using the Group Policy Editor. No special intervention is required in the client application. The machine/user account on the client machine needs to be in an OU that is configured to use the policy object in which the application proxies are published. The COM binder will automatically locate the server via the directory when the client establishes an instance of the objects in question.

C H A P T E R   1 7

Service Logon Accounts

A service, like any process, has a primary security identity that determines the access rights and privileges that the service has to local and network resources. This security identity (or security context) also determines the potential the service has for doing damage to resources on the local computer and the network.

The security context for a Microsoft® Win32® service is determined by the logon account used to start the service. This chapter covers programming issues and best practices relating to the service logon account used by Win32 services, with a focus on directory-enabled services. This chapter includes the following topics:

- An overview of service logon accounts and security context programming issues for a Win32 service.
- Guidelines for selecting a logon account for a Win32 service.
- Setting up a service's user account.
- Installing a service on a host computer and specifying the service's logon account.
- Granting the service's user account the logon as a service right on the host computer.
- Detecting at installation time whether the service instance is being installed on a domain controller.
- Setting and maintaining ACEs and group memberships to ensure that the system will grant the running service access to the necessary local and network resources.
- Changing the password on a service's user account, and at the same time updating the password registered with the service control manager on each host server on which the service is installed.
- Maintaining service principal name (SPN) registration on the directory object associated with the logon account of each instance of your service. SPNs enable clients to authenticate a service using Kerberos mutual authentication. For more information, see Mutual Authentication Using Kerberos.
- Converting domain account name formats, for example, converting a distinguished name to *domain\username* format, and vice versa.

About Service Logon Accounts

When a Win32®-based service starts up, it logs on to the local computer. It can log on using one of the following:

- The credentials of a local or domain user account.
- The LocalSystem account.

The logon account determines the security identity of the service at run time, that is, the service's primary security context. And the security context determines the service's ability to access local and network resources. For example, a service running in the security context of a local user account would have no access to network resources. At the other extreme, a service running in the security context of the LocalSystem account on a Microsoft® Windows® 2000 domain controller, would have unrestricted access to Microsoft® Active Directory™. For a discussion of the tradeoffs between user accounts and LocalSystem, see *Security Contexts and Active Directoyr*.

Ultimately, administrators on the system where the service is installed have control over the service's logon account. For security reasons, many administrators will not allow you to install your service under the LocalSystem account (unless you can present convincing documentation why they should). This means that your service must be able to run under a domain user account. As a programmer, you can exercise some control over your service's logon account. Your service installation program specifies the service's logon account when it calls the **CreateService** function to install the service on a host computer. Your installation program can suggest a default logon account, but it should allow an administrator to specify the actual account.

Your installation program can also perform the following tasks relating to your service's logon account:

- If you are installing your service to run under a user account, the account must exist before you call **CreateService**. You can use an existing account or create one as part of the host-computer installation program. See *Setting up a Service's User Account*.

- If you want clients to use Active Directory support for Kerberos mutual authentication, you need to register the SPNs on the service's logon account. If the service runs under the LocalSystem account, the service's logon account is the computer account of the host computer. See *Service Principal Names*.

- Ensure that the service at run time has the access rights and privileges that it needs to perform its tasks. This can require setting ACEs in the security descriptors of various resources (directory objects, file shares, and so on) to allow the necessary access rights to the user or computer account. See *Granting Access Rights to the Service Logon Account*.

- Assign privileges to the specified logon account, such as the right to logon as a service to the host computer. See *Granting Logon as Service Right on the Host Computer*.

After a service is installed, there are maintenance tasks relating to your service's logon account. See *Logon Account Maintenance Tasks*.

- Password maintenance. For a service that runs under a user account, you need to periodically change the password and keep the password in sync with the password used by one or more local service control managers to start the service.

- SPN maintenance. If a service's logon account changes, you need to remove the SPNs registered on the old account and register them on the new account. Note that once a service is installed, a domain administrator can change the account under which your service runs (using Win32 functions or the user interface of the Computer Management administrative tool).
- ACE maintenance. If a service's logon account changes, you need to update ACEs and group memberships to ensure that the service can still access the necessary resources.

Guidelines for Selecting a Service Logon Account

A Win32®-based service can run in the security context of a local user account, a domain user account, or the LocalSystem account. How does an administrator decide which account to use? The guiding principal is that an administrator should install your service at the lowest "privilege level" that is sufficient to perform the service's operations. In a typical directory-enabled service, this means your service installation program should create a domain user account for the service and grant that account the specific access rights and privileges required by the service at run time. Your service should run under the LocalSystem account only if it needs administrative or act as part of the operating system privileges on the local computer.

Note that your service installation program should by default set up the service to run under a domain user account. If you need to run your service under the LocalSystem account, you must query the administrator for permission.

Local User Accounts

A local user account (name format: .\username) exists only in the SAM database of the host computer; it does not have a user object in Active Directory. This means that a local account cannot be authenticated by the domain. Consequently, the service does not have access to network resources (except as an anonymous user) and it cannot support Kerberos mutual authentication in which the service is authenticated by its clients. For these reasons, local user accounts are typically inappropriate for directory-enabled services. On the plus side, bugs in the service cannot damage the system. If your service can run under those limitations, it should.

Domain User Accounts

A domain user account enables the service to take full advantage of the service security features of Microsoft® Windows 2000 and Microsoft® Active Directory™. The service has whatever local and network access is granted to the account (or to any groups of which the account is a member). The service can support Kerberos mutual authentication.

The advantage of using a domain user account is that the service's actions are limited by the access rights and privileges associated with the account. Unlike a LocalSystem service, bugs in a user-account service cannot damage the system. This means that if the service is compromised by some sort of security attack, the damage is limited to the operations that the system allows the user account to perform. At the same time, clients running at varying privilege levels can connect to the service, which enables the service to impersonate a client to perform sensitive operations.

Note that a service's user account should not be a member of any administrators groups (local, domain, or enterprise). If your service needs local administrative privileges, run under the LocalSystem account. For operations that require domain administrative privileges, perform them by impersonating the security context of a client application.

A service instance that uses a domain user account requires periodic administrative action to maintain the account's password. The service control manager (SCM) on the host computer of a service instance caches the account's password for use in logging on the service. So when you change the account password, you must also update the cached password on the host computer where the service is installed. For sample code that shows how to do this, see *Changing the Password on a Service's User Account*. You could avoid the regular maintenance by leaving the password unchanged, but that would increase your vulnerability to a password attack on the service's account. Note that even though the SCM stores the password in a secure portion of the registry, it is nevertheless subject to attack.

A domain user account has two name formats that programmers need to deal with for various operations: the distinguished name of the user object in the directory and the *domain\username* format used by the local service control manager. For sample code that converts from one format to the other, see *Converting Domain Account Name Formats*.

The LocalSystem Account

The advantage of running under the LocalSystem account is that the service has complete unrestricted access to local resources. This is also the disadvantage of LocalSystem because a LocalSystem service can do things that would bring down the entire system. In particular, a service running as LocalSystem on a domain controller (DC) has unrestricted access to Active Directory. This means that bugs in the service, or security attacks on the service, can damage the system (or, if the service is on a DC, damage the entire enterprise network).

For these reasons, domain administrators at sensitive installations will be cautious about allowing services to run as LocalSystem. In fact, they may have policies against it, especially on DCs. If your service must run as LocalSystem, the documentation for your service should justify to domain administrators the reasons for granting the service the right to run at elevated privileges. Services should never run as LocalSystem on a domain controller. For sample code that shows how a service or service installation program can determine whether it is running on a domain controller, see *Testing Whether Running on a Domain Controller*.

When a service runs under the LocalSystem account on a computer that is a domain member, the service has whatever network access is granted to the computer account (or to any groups of which the computer account is a member). Note that in Windows 2000, a domain computer account is a service principal (just like a user account). This means that a computer account can be in a security group, and an ACE in a security descriptor can grant access to a computer account. Note however, that adding computer accounts to groups is not recommended for two reasons:

- Computer accounts are subject to deletion and re-creation if the computer leaves and then rejoins the domain
- If you add a computer account to a group, all services running as LocalSystem on that computer are permitted the access rights of the group. This is because all LocalSystem services share the computer account of their host server. For this reason, it is particularly important that computer accounts not be made members of any domain administrator groups.

Computer accounts typically have very few privileges and do not belong to groups. The default ACL protection in Active Directory permits minimal access for computer accounts. Consequently, services running as LocalSystem (on computers other than DCs) have only minimal access to Active Directory.

If your service runs under LocalSystem, you must test your service on a member server to ensure that your service has sufficient rights to read/write to Active Directory. A domain controller should not be the *only* Windows 2000 computer on which you test your service. Remember that a service running under LocalSystem on a Windows 2000 domain controller has complete access to Active Directory and that a member server runs in the context of the computer account which has substantially fewer rights.

Setting up a Service's User Account

Your service installation program can suggest a default logon account for a service instance and allow the administrator to select the default account or specify a different one. If the administrator selects a user account (rather than the LocalSystem account), the account must exist before you call the **CreateService** function to install an instance of the service on a host server. For sample code that creates a new domain user object in Active Directory, see *Creating a User*.

Ideally, each instance of a service, whether a host-based or replicable service, should have its own domain user account. Using separate accounts for each service instance is more secure than having multiple instances share the same account. Also, using separate accounts makes it possible to audit the activities of each service instance.

So when your installation program suggests a default logon account, it should specify the name of a new account to be created for the new service instance. The account name could be composed from the same elements used to compose a service principal name, such as the service class, host computer, and service name (see *Service Principal Names*). Typically, you would create the account in the Users container on the domain of the host computer.

You also need to generate a password for each account. For a discussion of how to write a tool that automates the task of updating service account passwords, see *Changing the Password on a Service's User Account*.

Installing a Service on a Host Computer

This sample code shows the basic steps of installing a directory-enabled service on a host computer. It performs the following operations:

- Calls the **OpenSCManager** function to open a handle to the service control manager (SCM) on the local computer.

- Calls the **CreateService** function to install the service in the SCM database. This call specifies the service's logon account and password, as well as the service's executable and other information about the service. **CreateService** fails if the specified logon account is not valid. However, **CreateService** does not check the validity of the password. It also does not check that the account has the logon as a service right on the local computer (see *Granting Logon as Service Right on the Host Computer*).

- Calls the service's *ScpCreate* subroutine (see *How Clients Find and Use a Service Connection Point*) that creates a service connection point object (SCP) in the directory to publish the location of this instance of the service. This routine also stores the service's binding information in the SCP, sets an ACE on the SCP so the service can access it at run time, caches the distinguished name of the SCP in the local registry, and returns the distinguished name of the new SCP.

- Calls the service's *SpnCompose* subroutine (see *Composing the SPNs for a Service with an SCP*) that uses the service's class string and the distinguished name of the SCP to compose a service principal name (SPN). The SPN uniquely identifies this instance of the service.

- Calls the service's *SpnRegister* subroutine (see *Registering the SPNs for a Service*) that registers the SPN on the account object associated with service's logon account. Registration of the SPN enables client applications to authenticate the service.

This sample works correctly regardless of whether the logon account is a local or domain user account or the LocalSystem account. For a domain user account, the *szServiceAccountSAM* parameter contains the *domain\username* name of the account, and the *szServiceAccountDN* parameter contains the distinguished name of the user account object in the directory. For the LocalSystem account, *szServiceAccountSAM* and *szPassword* are NULL, and *szServiceAccountSN* is the distinguished name of the local computer's account object in the directory. If *szServiceAccountSAM* specifies a local user account (name format is ".\username"), the sample code skips the SPN registration because mutual authentication is not supported for local user accounts.

Note that the default security configuration allows only domain administrators to execute this code.

Note that this code as written must be executed on the computer where the service is being installed. Consequently, it is typically in a separate installation executable from your service installation code, if any, that extends the schema, extends the UI, or sets up group policy. Those operations install service components for an entire a forest, whereas this code installs the service on a single computer.

```
void InstallServiceOnLocalComputer(
          LPTSTR szServiceAccountDN,    // distinguished name of
                                        // logon account.
          LPTSTR szServiceAccountSAM,   // SAM name of logon account.
          LPTSTR szPassword)            // Password of logon account.
{
SC_HANDLE   schService = NULL;
SC_HANDLE   schSCManager = NULL;
TCHAR szPath[512];
LPTSTR lpFilePart;
TCHAR szDNofSCP[MAX_PATH];
TCHAR szServiceClass[]=TEXT("ADSockAuth");

DWORD dwStatus;
TCHAR **pspn=NULL;
ULONG ulSpn=1;

// Get the full path of the service's executable.
// The sample assumes that the executable is in the current directory.
dwStatus = GetFullPathName(TEXT("service.exe"), 512, szPath, &lpFilePart);
if (dwStatus == 0) {
    _tprintf(TEXT("Unable to install %s - %s\n"),
             TEXT(SZSERVICEDISPLAYNAME), GetLastErrorText(szErr, 256));
    return;
}
_tprintf(TEXT("path of service.exe: %s\n"), szPath);
```

(continued)

(continued)

```
// Open the Service Control Manager on the local computer.
schSCManager = OpenSCManager(
                NULL,                       // computer (NULL == local)
                NULL,                       // database (NULL == default)
                SC_MANAGER_ALL_ACCESS       // access required
                );
if (! schSCManager) {
    _tprintf(TEXT("OpenSCManager failed - %s\n"),
                GetLastErrorText(szErr,256));
    goto cleanup;
}

// Install the service in the SCM database.
schService = CreateService(
            schSCManager,                   // SCManager database
            TEXT(SZSERVICENAME),            // name of service
            TEXT(SZSERVICEDISPLAYNAME),     // name to display
            SERVICE_ALL_ACCESS,             // desired access
            SERVICE_WIN32_OWN_PROCESS,      // service type
            SERVICE_DEMAND_START,           // start type
            SERVICE_ERROR_NORMAL,           // error control type
            szPath,                         // service's binary
            NULL,                           // no load ordering group
            NULL,                           // no tag identifier
            TEXT(SZDEPENDENCIES),           // dependencies
            szServiceAccountSAM,            // service account
            szPassword);                    // account password
if (! schService) {
    _tprintf(TEXT("CreateService failed - %s\n"),
                GetLastErrorText(szErr,256));
    goto cleanup;
}

_tprintf(TEXT("%s installed.\n"), TEXT(SZSERVICEDISPLAYNAME) );

// Create the service's Service Connection Point (SCP).
dwStatus = ScpCreate(
        2000,                   // Service's default port number
        szServiceClass,         // Specifies the service class string.
        szServiceAccountSAM,    // SAM name of logon account for ACE
        szDNofSCP               // Buffer returns the DN of the SCP.
        );
if (dwStatus != 0) {
```

```
        _tprintf(TEXT("ScpCreate failed: %d\n"), dwStatus );
        DeleteService(schService);
        goto cleanup;
}


// Compose and register a service principal name for this service.
// We do this on the install path because this requires elevated
// privileges for updating the directory.
// If a local account of the format ".\username", skip the SPN.
if ( szServiceAccountSAM[0] == '.' )
{
        _tprintf(TEXT("Don't register SPN for a local account.\n"));
        goto cleanup;
}


dwStatus = SpnCompose(
        &pspn,              // Receives pointer to the SPN array.
        &ulSpn,             // Receives number of SPNs returned.
        szDNofSCP,          // Input: DN of the SCP.
        szServiceClass);    // Input: the service's class string.

if (dwStatus == NO_ERROR)
    dwStatus = SpnRegister(
        szServiceAccountDN,  // Account on which SPNs are registered.
        pspn,                // Array of SPNs to register.
        ulSpn,               // Number of SPNs in array.
        DS_SPN_ADD_SPN_OP);  // Operation code: Add SPNs.

if (dwStatus != NO_ERROR)
{
        _tprintf(TEXT("Failed to compose SPN: Error was %X\n"),
                    dwStatus);
        DeleteService(schService);
        ScpDelete(szDNofSCP, szServiceClass, szServiceAccountDN);
        goto cleanup;
}

cleanup:
if (schSCManager)
    CloseServiceHandle(schSCManager);
if (schService)
    CloseServiceHandle(schService);
DsFreeSpnArray(ulSpn, pspn);
return;
}
```

For more information about operations performed in the previous example, see *Composing the SPNs for a Service with an SCP* and *Registering the SPNs for a Service*.

Granting Logon as Service Right on the Host Computer

If you install your service to run under a domain user account, the account must have the right to logon as a service on the local computer. Note that this logon right applies only to the local computer and must be granted in the local LSA policy of each host computer.

See the lsaprivs sample program in the Platform SDK for sample code that shows how to grant this right to a user account specified in *domain\username* format. You don't need to do this if your service runs as LocalSystem, which automatically has the right.

Testing Whether Calling Process is Running on a Domain Controller

The following code uses the **VerifyVersionInfo** function to determine whether the calling process is running on Windows 2000 domain controller. Your service installation program could use this test before installing a service under the LocalSystem account. If the test indicates that you are running on a domain controller, you either install the service to run under a user account, or display a dialog box warning of the dangers in running as LocalSystem on a domain controller (which are that the service would then have unrestricted access to Active Directory, a supremely powerful security context that has the potential to damage the entire network).

```
BOOL Is_Win2000_DomainController ()
{
    OSVERSIONINFOEX osvi;
    DWORDLONG dwlConditionMask = 0;

    // Initialize the OSVERSIONINFOEX structure.
    ZeroMemory(&osvi, sizeof(OSVERSIONINFOEX));
    osvi.dwOSVersionInfoSize = sizeof(OSVERSIONINFOEX);
    osvi.dwMajorVersion = 5;
    osvi.wProductType = VER_NT_DOMAIN_CONTROLLER;

    // Initialize the condition mask.
    VER_SET_CONDITION( dwlConditionMask, VER_MAJORVERSION,
        VER_GREATER_EQUAL );
    VER_SET_CONDITION( dwlConditionMask, VER_PRODUCT_TYPE,
        VER_EQUAL );

    // Perform the test.
```

```
    return VerifyVersionInfo(
        &osvi,
        VER_MAJORVERSION | VER_PRODUCT_TYPE,
        dwlConditionMask);
}
```

Granting Access Rights to the Service Logon Account

Part of installing a service instance is ensuring that the installed service will be able to access the necessary resources when it is running. To do this, you set ACEs in the security descriptors of objects that the service needs to access. An ACE can grant or deny access rights to a specified security principal, such as the service's user account (or the computer account for a LocalSystem service), or a group to which the service's account belongs. For more information about ACEs, security descriptors, and access control, see *Controlling Access to Active Directory Objects* and the *Access Control* chapter in the Platform SDK.

See *Enabling Service Account to Access SCP Properties* for a discussion and sample code of setting ACEs that allow the service to modify its service connection point (SCP).

You may also want to add your service's user account as a member of one or more security groups. For example, if you create an administrators group for your service, you might want to make the service itself a member of the group. Then you could simply grant access rights to the group rather than granting them explicitly to the service account. For more information about security groups, see *Managing Groups*.

Enabling Service Account to Access SCP Properties

The following sample code sets a pair of ACEs on a service connection point (SCP) object. The ACEs grant read/write access to the user or computer account under which the service instance will be running. Your service installation program calls this code to ensure that the service will be allowed to update its properties at run time. If you don't set ACEs like these, your service will get access-denied errors if it tries to modify the SCP's properties.

Typically, your service installation program would set these ACEs right after creating the SCP object. For sample code that creates an SCP and calls this function, see *How Clients Find and Use a Service Connection Point*. If the service is reconfigured to run under a different account, the ACEs would need to be updated. Note that this code needs to be run in the security context of a domain administrator.

The first parameter of the sample function specifies the name of the user account to be granted access. The function assumes the name is in *domain\account* format. If no account is specified, the function assumes the service uses the LocalSystem account, which means it must grant access to the computer account of the host server on which the service is running. To do this, the example calls the **GetComputerObjectName** function to get the *domain\account* name of the local computer.

Note that the code could be easily modified to grant the service full access to the SCP object. But the best practice is to grant only the specific access rights that the service might need at run time. In this case, it grants access to two properties:

ServiceDNSName
   The name of the host server on which the service is running.

ServiceBindingInformation
   Private binding information that the service updates when it starts up.

Each property is identified by the **schemaIDGUID** of the property's **attributeSchema** class. Every property in the schema has its own unique **schemaIDGUID**. The code uses strings to specify the GUIDs. The GUID strings have the following format:

```
hr = pACE1->put_ObjectType(
        L"{28630eb8-41d5-11d1-a9c1-0000f80367c1}" ); // serviceDNSName
```

Refer to the Active Directory Schema reference pages for the **schemaIDGUID** values assigned to the properties you want to grant or deny access to.

The code uses the **IADsSecurityDescriptor**, **IADsAccessControlList**, and **IADsAccessControlEntry** interfaces to do the following:

* Get the SCP object's security descriptor.
* Set ACEs in the DACL of the security descriptor.
* Set the security descriptor back on the SCP object.

```
HRESULT AllowAccessToScpProperties(
    LPOLESTR szAccountSAM,  // Service account to allow access.
    IADs *pSCPObject)       // IADs pointer to the SCP object.
{
TCHAR szServerSAMName[512];
DWORD dwLen;
LPOLESTR szTrustee;

VARIANT varSD;
HRESULT hr = E_FAIL;
IADsAccessControlList *pACL = NULL;
IADsSecurityDescriptor *pSD = NULL;
IDispatch *pDisp = NULL;
IADsAccessControlEntry *pACE1 = NULL;
IADsAccessControlEntry *pACE2 = NULL;
IDispatch *pDispACE = NULL;
long lFlags = 0L;
LPOLESTR szAttribute = L"nTSecurityDescriptor";
```

```
// If no service account is specified, service runs under LocalSystem.
// So allow access to the computer account of the service's host.
if (szAccountSAM)
    szTrustee = szAccountSAM;
else
{
    // Get the SAM account name of the computer object for the server.
    dwLen = sizeof(szServerSAMName);
    if (!GetComputerObjectName(NameSamCompatible,
                               szServerSAMName, &dwLen))
        return GetLastError();
    _tprintf(TEXT("GetComputerObjectName: %s\n"), szServerSAMName);
    szTrustee = szServerSAMName;
}


VariantClear(&varSD);

// Get the nTSecurityDescriptor
hr = pSCPObject->Get(szAttribute, &varSD);
if (FAILED(hr) || (varSD.vt!=VT_DISPATCH)) {
    _tprintf(TEXT("Get nTSecurityDescriptor failed: 0x%x\n"), hr);
    goto cleanup;
}

// Use the V_DISPATCH macro to get the IDispatch pointer from VARIANT
// structure and QueryInterface for an IADsSecurityDescriptor pointer.
hr = V_DISPATCH( &varSD )->QueryInterface(IID_IADsSecurityDescriptor,
                                          (void**)&pSD);
if (FAILED(hr)) {
    _tprintf(TEXT("Couldn't get IADsSecurityDescriptor: 0x%x\n"), hr);
    goto cleanup;
}

// Get an IADsAccessControlList pointer to the
// security descriptor's DACL.
hr = pSD->get_DiscretionaryAcl(&pDisp);
if (SUCCEEDED(hr))
    hr = pDisp->QueryInterface(IID_IADsAccessControlList,(void**)&pACL);
if (FAILED(hr)) {
    _tprintf(TEXT("Couldn't get DACL: 0x%x\n"), hr);
    goto cleanup;
}

// Create the COM object for the first ACE.
```

(continued)

(continued)

```
hr = CoCreateInstance(CLSID_AccessControlEntry,
                      NULL,
                      CLSCTX_INPROC_SERVER,
                      IID_IADsAccessControlEntry,
                      (void **)&pACE1);

// Create the COM object for the second ACE.
if (SUCCEEDED(hr))
    hr = CoCreateInstance(CLSID_AccessControlEntry,
                      NULL,
                      CLSCTX_INPROC_SERVER,
                      IID_IADsAccessControlEntry,
                      (void **)&pACE2);
if (FAILED(hr)) {
    _tprintf(TEXT("Couldn't create ACEs: 0x%x\n"), hr);
    goto cleanup;
}


// Set the properties of the two ACEs.

// Allow read and write access to the property.
hr = pACE1->put_AccessMask( ADS_RIGHT_DS_READ_PROP | ADS_RIGHT_DS_WRITE_PROP );
hr = pACE2->put_AccessMask( ADS_RIGHT_DS_READ_PROP | ADS_RIGHT_DS_WRITE_PROP );

// Set the trustee, which is either the service account or the
// host computer account.
hr = pACE1->put_Trustee( szTrustee );
hr = pACE2->put_Trustee( szTrustee );

// Set the ACE type.
hr = pACE1->put_AceType( ADS_ACETYPE_ACCESS_ALLOWED_OBJECT );
hr = pACE2->put_AceType( ADS_ACETYPE_ACCESS_ALLOWED_OBJECT );

// Set AceFlags to zero because ACE is not inheritable.
hr = pACE1->put_AceFlags( 0 );
hr = pACE2->put_AceFlags( 0 );

// Set Flags to indicate an ACE that protects a specified object.
hr = pACE1->put_Flags( ADS_FLAG_OBJECT_TYPE_PRESENT );
hr = pACE2->put_Flags( ADS_FLAG_OBJECT_TYPE_PRESENT );

// Set ObjectType to the schemaIDGUID of the attribute.
hr = pACE1->put_ObjectType(
        L"{28630eb8-41d5-11d1-a9c1-0000f80367c1}" ); // serviceDNSName
```

```
hr = pACE2->put_ObjectType(
        L"{b7b1311c-b82e-11d0-afee-0000f80367c1}" ); // serviceBindingInformation

// Add the ACEs to the DACL. Need an IDispatch pointer for each ACE
// to pass to the AddAce method.
hr = pACE1->QueryInterface(IID_IDispatch,(void**)&pDispACE);
if (SUCCEEDED(hr))
    hr = pACL->AddAce(pDispACE);
if (FAILED(hr)) {
    _tprintf(TEXT("Couldn't add first ACE: 0x%x\n"), hr);
    goto cleanup;
}
else {
    if (pDispACE)
        pDispACE->Release();
    pDispACE = NULL;
}

// Do it again for the second ACE.
hr = pACE2->QueryInterface(IID_IDispatch, (void**)&pDispACE);
if (SUCCEEDED(hr))
    hr = pACL->AddAce(pDispACE);
if (FAILED(hr)) {
    _tprintf(TEXT("Couldn't add second ACE: 0x%x\n"), hr);
    goto cleanup;
}

// Write the modified DACL back to the security descriptor.
hr = pSD->put_DiscretionaryAcl(pDisp);
if (SUCCEEDED(hr))
{
    // Write the ntSecurityDescriptor property to the property cache.
    hr = pSCPObject->Put(szAttribute, varSD);
    if (SUCCEEDED(hr))
    {
        // SetInfo updates the SCP object in the directory.
        hr = pSCPObject->SetInfo();
    }
}

cleanup:
    if (pDispACE)
        pDispACE->Release();
```

(continued)

(continued)

```
    if (pACE1)
        pACE1->Release();

    if (pACE2)
        pACE2->Release();

    if (pACL)
        pACL->Release();

    if (pDisp)
        pDisp->Release();

    if (pSD)
        pSD->Release();

    VariantClear(&varSD);

    return hr;
}
```

Logon Account Maintenance Tasks

There are two issues here.

- Updating the account password for a service instance that runs under a user account. See *Changing the Password on a Service's User Account*.

- Handling changes to the logon account of a service instance.

The latter is something that may never happen, but it could. The system provides the Computer Management administrative tool that makes it easy to change a service's logon account. In addition, other applications can use the **ChangeServiceConfig** function to specify a new logon account for an installed service. By default, you need local administrator privileges to change a service account. If this did happen, it could affect your service in two ways:

- If you have registered service principal names (SPNs), they would now be registered on the wrong account.

- If you set ACEs to grant access to the service, they would now grant access to the wrong account.

So what can you do? One approach is to have the service installation program store the registered SPNs for each service instance in the registry on the host computer. You could use the same registry key under HKEY_LOCAL_MACHINE that you used to store the binding string for the service's SCP. When the service starts up, it calls the **QueryServiceConfig** function to determine it's logon account and then queries Active Directory to determine whether the SPNs are registered on the directory object for that account. If the SPNs are not registered, or are registered on the wrong account, the service refuses to start and displays a message saying that a domain administrator must run the service's configuration program to update the logon account settings. Note that this reconfiguration needs to be done by an administrator because the service account should not have access to update its own SPN. Also note that SPNs must be removed from the old account, otherwise the SPNs will be useless for authentication because they aren't unique in the forest.

Changing the Password on a Service's User Account

For a service instance that logs on with a user account (rather than the LocalSystem account), the Service Control Manager (SCM) on the host computer stores the account password, which it uses to log on the service when the service starts up. As with any user account, you need to change the password periodically to maintain security. So when you change the password on a service's account, you also need to update the password stored by the SCM. The following code sample shows how to do both.

The samples uses **IADsUser::SetPassword** to set the password on the account. This method uses the distinguished name of the account. Then the sample opens a handle to the installed service on the specified host computer, and uses the **ChangeServiceConfig** function to update the password cached by the SCM. This function uses the SAM name (*domain\username*) of the account.

Note that this code must be executed by a domain administrator.

For a replicable service in which each replica uses a different logon account, you could update the passwords for all of the replicas by enumerating the service instances as shown in the sample code at *Enumerating the Replicas of a Service*.

```
DWORD UpdateAccountPassword(
        LPTSTR szServerDNS,    // DNS name of host computer
        LPTSTR szAccountDN,    // Distinguished name of service's
                               // logon account
        LPTSTR szAccountSAM,   // SAM name of service's logon account
        LPTSTR szNewPassword   // New password
        )
{
SC_HANDLE schService = NULL;
SC_HANDLE schSCManager = NULL;
```

(continued)

(continued)

```
DWORD dwLen = MAX_PATH;
TCHAR szAccountPath[MAX_PATH];
IADsUser *pUser = NULL;
HRESULT hr;

DWORD dwStatus=0;
SC_LOCK sclLock = NULL;

// First, set the password on the account.
// Use the distinguished name to bind to the account object.
_tcscpy(szAccountPath, TEXT("LDAP://") );
_tcscat(szAccountPath, szAccountDN);
hr = ADsGetObject(szAccountPath, IID_IADsUser, (void**)&pUser);
if (FAILED(hr)) {
    _tprintf(TEXT("Get IADsUser failed - 0x%x\n"), dwStatus = hr);
        goto cleanup;
}

// Set the password on the account.
hr = pUser->SetPassword(szNewPassword);
if (FAILED(hr)) {
    _tprintf(TEXT("SetPassword failed - 0x%x\n"), dwStatus = hr);
        goto cleanup;
}

// Now update the account and password in the SCM database.
// Open the Service Control Manager on the specified computer.
schSCManager = OpenSCManager(
                szServerDNS,            // DNS name of host computer
                NULL,                   // database (NULL == default)
                SC_MANAGER_ALL_ACCESS   // access required
                    );
if (! schSCManager) {
    _tprintf(TEXT("OpenSCManager failed - %d\n"), dwStatus = GetLastError());
    goto cleanup;
}

// Open a handle to the service instance.
schService = OpenService(schSCManager, TEXT(SZSERVICENAME), SERVICE_ALL_ACCESS);
if (! schService) {
    _tprintf(TEXT("OpenService failed - %s\n"), dwStatus = GetLastError());
    goto cleanup;
}
```

```
// Need to acquire the SCM database lock before changing the password.
sclLock = LockServiceDatabase(schSCManager);
if (sclLock == NULL) {
    _tprintf(TEXT("LockServiceDatabase failed - %d\n"), dwStatus =
GetLastError());
    goto cleanup;
}


// Now set the account and password that the service uses at startup.
if (! ChangeServiceConfig(
        schService,         // Handle of service
        SERVICE_NO_CHANGE,  // Service type: no change
        SERVICE_NO_CHANGE,  // Change service start type
        SERVICE_NO_CHANGE,  // Error control: no change
        NULL,               // Binary path: no change
        NULL,               // Load order group: no change
        NULL,               // Tag ID: no change
        NULL,               // Dependencies: no change
        szAccountSAM,       // Account name: no change
        szNewPassword,      // New password
        NULL) ) {           // Display name: no change
    _tprintf(TEXT("ChangeServiceConfig failed - %s\n"), dwStatus =
GetLastError());
    goto cleanup;
}
_tprintf(TEXT("Password changed for service instance on: %s\n"), szServerDNS);
cleanup:

if (sclLock)
    UnlockServiceDatabase(sclLock);
if (schService)
    CloseServiceHandle(schService);
if (schSCManager)
    CloseServiceHandle(schSCManager);
if (pUser)
    pUser->Release();

return dwStatus;

}
```

Enumerating the Replicas of a Service

This topic shows sample code that enumerates the installed instances of a replicated service on different host computers throughout an enterprise. To change the service account password on each instance of a replicated service, you could use this code in conjunction with the code sample in the *Changing the Password on a Service's User Account* topic.

The sample assumes that each service instance has its own service connection point (SCP) object in the directory. An SCP is an object of the serviceConnectionPoint class. This class has a **keywords** attribute, which is a multi-valued attribute that is replicated to all global catalogs (GCs) in the forest. The **keywords** attribute of each instance's SCP contains the service's product GUID. This makes it easy to find all of the SCPs for the various service instances by simply searching a GC for objects with a **keywords** attribute that equals the product GUID.

The example code gets an **IDirectorySearch** pointer to a GC, and uses the **IDirectorySearch::ExecuteSearch** method to search for the SCPs. Note that the GC contains a partial replica of each SCP. This means that it contains some of the SCP's attributes, but not all. In this example, we are interested in the **serviceDNSName** attribute, which contains the DNS name of the host server for that service instance. Because **serviceDNSName** is not one of the attributes that is replicated in a GC, the example uses a two step process to retrieve it. First it uses the GC search to get the distinguished name (DN) of the SCP, then it uses that DN to bind directly to the SCP to retrieve the **serviceDNSName** property.

```
HRESULT EnumerateServiceInstances(
        LPTSTR szQuery,                     // Search string filter
        TCHAR **pszAttribs,                 // Array of attributes to retrieve
        DWORD dwAttribs,                    // Number of attributes requested
        DWORD *pdwAttribs,                  // Number of attributes retrieved
        ADS_ATTR_INFO **ppPropEntries       // Returns pointer to
                                            // retrieved attributes

        )
{
HRESULT hr;
IEnumVARIANT *pEnum = NULL;
IADsContainer *pCont = NULL;
VARIANT var;
IDispatch *pDisp = NULL;
BSTR bstrPath;
ULONG lFetch;
IADs *pADs = NULL;
int iRows=0;
static IDirectorySearch *pSearch = NULL;
```

```
static ADS_SEARCH_HANDLE hSearch = NULL;
// Params for IDirectoryObject

TCHAR szSCPPath[MAX_PATH];
IDirectoryObject *pSCP = NULL;

// Structures and Params for IDirectorySearch
DWORD               dwPref;
ADS_SEARCH_COLUMN   Col;
ADS_SEARCHPREF_INFO SearchPref[2];

// First time through, set up the search.
if (pSearch == NULL)
{
    // Bind to the GC: namespace container object. The "real" GC DN
    // is a single immediate child of the GC: namespace, which we must
    // obtain via enumeration.
    hr = ADsGetObject(TEXT("GC:"),
        IID_IADsContainer,
        (void**) &pCont );
    if (FAILED(hr)) {
        _tprintf(TEXT("ADsGetObject(GC) failed: 0x%x\n"), hr);
        goto Cleanup;
    }

    // Fetch an enumeration interface for the GC container.
    hr = ADsBuildEnumerator(pCont,&pEnum);
    if (FAILED(hr)) {
        _tprintf(TEXT("ADsBuildEnumerator failed: 0x%x\n"), hr);
        goto Cleanup;
    }

    // Now enumerate. There's only one child of the GC: object.
    hr = ADsEnumerateNext(pEnum,1,&var,&lFetch);
    if (( hr == S_OK ) && ( lFetch == 1 ) )
    {
        pDisp = V_DISPATCH(&var);
        hr = pDisp->QueryInterface( IID_IADs, (void**)&pADs);
        if (hr == S_OK)
            hr = pADs->get_ADsPath(&bstrPath);
    }
    if (FAILED(hr)) {
        _tprintf(TEXT("Enumeration failed: 0x%x\n"), hr);
        goto Cleanup;
```

(continued)

(continued)

```
    }

    // At this point bstrPath contains the ADsPath for the current GC.
    // Now bind the GC to get the search interface.
    hr = ADsGetObject(bstrPath, IID_IDirectorySearch, (void**)&pSearch);
    if (FAILED(hr)) {
        _tprintf(TEXT("Failed to bind search root: 0x%x\n"), hr);
        goto Cleanup;
    }

    // Set up the search. We want to do a deep search.
    // Note that we are not expecting thousands of objects
    // in this example, so we will ask for 1000 rows / page.
    dwPref=sizeof(SearchPref)/sizeof(ADS_SEARCHPREF_INFO);
    SearchPref[0].dwSearchPref =    ADS_SEARCHPREF_SEARCH_SCOPE;
    SearchPref[0].vValue.dwType =   ADSTYPE_INTEGER;
    SearchPref[0].vValue.Integer =  ADS_SCOPE_SUBTREE;

    SearchPref[1].dwSearchPref =    ADS_SEARCHPREF_PAGESIZE;
    SearchPref[1].vValue.dwType =   ADSTYPE_INTEGER;
    SearchPref[1].vValue.Integer =  1000;

    hr = pSearch->SetSearchPreference(SearchPref, dwPref);
    it (FAILED(hr))    {
        _tprintf(TEXT("Failed to set search prefs: 0x%x\n"), hr);
        goto Cleanup;
    }

    // Execute the search. From the GC we can get the distinguished name
    // of the SCP. Use the DN to bind to the SCP and get the other
    // properties.
    hr = pSearch->ExecuteSearch(szQuery, pszAttribs, 1, &hSearch);
    if (FAILED(hr)) {
        _tprintf(TEXT("ExecuteSearch failed: 0x%x\n"), hr);
        goto Cleanup;
    }
}

// Get the next row.
hr = pSearch->GetNextRow(hSearch);

// Process the row.
if (SUCCEEDED(hr) && hr !=S_ADS_NOMORE_ROWS)
{
```

```
    // Get the distinguished name of the object in this row.
    hr = pSearch->GetColumn(hSearch, TEXT("distinguishedName"), &Col);
    if FAILED(hr) {
        _tprintf(TEXT("GetColumn failed: 0x%x\n"), hr);
        goto Cleanup;
    }

    // Bind to the DN to get the properties.
    wcscpy(szSCPPath, L"LDAP://");
    wcscat(szSCPPath, Col.pADsValues->CaseIgnoreString);
    hr = ADsGetObject(szSCPPath, IID_IDirectoryObject, (void**)&pSCP);
    if (SUCCEEDED(hr))
    {
        hr = pSCP->GetObjectAttributes(pszAttribs, dwAttribs,
                          ppPropEntries, pdwAttribs);
        if(FAILED(hr)) {
            _tprintf(TEXT("GetObjectAttributes Failed."), hr);
            goto Cleanup;
        }
    pSearch->FreeColumn(&Col);
    }
}

Cleanup:
if (pSCP)
    pSCP->Release();
if (pCont)
    pCont->Release();
if (pEnum)
    ADsFreeEnumerator(pEnum);
if (pADs)
    pADs->Release();
if (pDisp)
    pDisp->Release();

return hr;

}
```

Converting Domain Account Name Formats

The Microsoft® Win32® functions for working with the service control manager (SCM) on a host server use the *domain\username* format for service accounts. For example, if you call the **QueryServiceConfig** function to retrieve the user account under which your service runs, the function returns the name in *ArcadiaBay\jamess* format. To bind to the user account in the directory and change the account's password, you need the distinguished name of the account, which has the format like CN=*James Smith*,CN=*Users*,DC=*ArcadiaBay*,DC=*COM*.

To convert between the various name formats, use the **TranslateName** function, which can also be used to convert a name to other formats, such as a user principal name (UPN).

CHAPTER 18

Mutual Authentication Using Kerberos

Mutual authentication is a security feature in which a client process must prove its identity to a service, and the service must prove its identity to the client, before any application traffic is sent over the client/service connection.

Active Directory™ and Microsoft® Windows® 2000 provide support for service principal names (SPN), which are a key component in the Kerberos mechanism by which a client authenticates a service. An SPN is a unique name that identifies an instance of a service and is associated with the logon account under which the service instance runs. The components of an SPN are such that a client can compose an SPN for a service without knowing the service's logon account. This enables the client to ask the service to authenticate its account even though the client doesn't know the name of the account.

This chapter discusses the following topics:

- An overview of mutual authentication using Kerberos.
- How to compose a unique SPN.
- How a service's installation program registers SPNs on the account object associated with a service instance.
- How a client application uses a service instance's service connection point (SCP) object in Active Directory to retrieve information from which to compose an SPN for the service.
- How a client application uses a service's SPN in conjunction with the Security Support Provider Interface (SSPI) to authenticate the service.
- Example code of a Windows Sockets client/service application that uses an SCP and SSPI to perform mutual authentication.
- Example code of an RPC client/service that performs mutual authentication using the RPC name service and RPC authentication.
- How a Windows Sockets Registration and Resolution (RnR) service uses SPNs to perform mutual authentication.

This chapter focuses on using Active Directory for mutual authentication, in particular, the role that service connection points and service principal names play in mutual authentication. It is not intended to exhaustively document how to use SSPI for mutual authentication or the authentication and security support available for RPC and Windows Sockets applications.

About Mutual Authentication Using Kerberos

Mutual authentication is quite simple conceptually. The client and service must prove their respective identities to each other before performing any application functions. The central principal of mutual authentication is that neither party must "trust" the other before identity has been proven. What this means in practical terms is that the service must be able to determine who the client is *without asking the client* and the client must be able to determine who the service is *without asking the service*.

The value of a service being able to authenticate a client is well known. For example, a file service impersonates a client's identity to determine which files the client is allowed to access.

The value of a client being able to authenticate a service is less understood. Authenticating a service enables the client to trust the information it gets from the service and to feel secure in sending sensitive information to the service. The ability of a client to authenticate a service is particularly important in client/service applications that support delegation of the client's security context (in other words, the client authorizes the service to act as its delegate in accessing additional services or network resources).

A service authenticates a client as follows: The client establishes a local security context either by executing in a previously established context (for example, in the session of a logged-in user) or by explicitly presenting credentials to the underlying security provider. The service will not accept connections from any client that is not authenticated.

The Kerberos mechanism by which a client authenticates a service works as follows: When a service is being installed, a service installation program running with administrator privileges registers one or more unique SPNs for each service instance. The names are registered in Active Directory on the user or computer account object that the service instance will use to log in. When a client wants to connect to a service, it composes an SPN for a service instance, using known information or information provided by the user. The client then uses the SSPI negotiate package to present the SPN to the Key Distribution Center (KDC) for the client's domain account. The KDC searches the forest for a user or computer account on which that SPN is registered. If the SPN is registered on more than one account, the authentication fails. Otherwise, the KDC encrypts a message using the password of the account on which the SPN was registered. The KDC passes this encrypted message to the client, which in turn passes it to the service instance. The service uses the SSPI negotiate package to decrypt the message, which it passes back to the client and on to the client's KDC. The KDC authenticates the service if the decrypted message matches its original message.

Security Providers

The Security Support Provider Interface (SSPI) provides support for mutual authentication and is exposed directly through the SSPI APIs and services that are layered upon SSPI, including RPC.

Not all security packages available to SSPI support mutual authentication. To obtain mutual authentication, the application must request mutual authentication and a security package that supports it. For example, the sample code in *Mutual Authentication in a Windows Sockets Service with an SCP* uses the "negotiate" package in Secur32.dll, which ships with Microsoft® Windows® 2000.

Integrity and Privacy

Client/service communications that require mutual authentication must also take care to protect the traffic they exchange after successful authentication. It does no good to mutually authenticate at the time of the initial connection to the service if the traffic is later subject to modification by an attacker. SSPI, RPC, and COM all provide facilities for digitally signing and encrypting messages. Applying digital signatures prevents modified traffic from going undetected and discourages eavesdropping. Traffic can be intercepted of course, but decrypting the traffic is sufficiently difficult to deter most attackers.

Unless performance requirements are very stringent, use of both signing and encryption is highly recommended, especially for administrative functions. Even when performance is an issue, some customers choose tighter security over better performance. In such cases, make integrity and privacy configurable options with higher security the default and higher performance the option.

RPC clients can specify the level of integrity and privacy when they call the **RpcBindingSetAuthInfoEx** function to set the authentication information for the RPC binding. Use RPC_C_AUTHN_LEVEL_PKT_INTEGRITY for signing and RPC_C_AUTHN_LEVEL_PKT_PRIVACY for encryption. For sample code that shows the use of these flags, see *How a Client Authenticates an RpcNs Service*.

Services that use an SSPI package for mutual authentication can query the package to determine whether it supports the **MakeSignature**, **VerifySignature**, **EncryptMessage**, and **DecryptMessage** functions for signing and encrypting messages. For sample code that illustrates the use of these functions, see *Ensuring Communication Integrity During Message Exchange* in the SSPI documentation.

Limitations of Mutual Authentication with Kerberos

Both the client's account and the service's account must be in Windows 2000 native or mixed-mode domains because Kerberos services are not available in downlevel domains. In addition, both client and service accounts must be in the same forest because the client's KDC uses the global catalog to search for the service principal name.

Both service and client must be running on Windows 2000, ; otherwise mutual authentication with Kerberos will fail because earlier versions of Microsoft® Windows® do not support Kerberos.

Service principal names must include the DNS name of the host server on which the service is running. You must use the DNS name.

Service Principal Names

A service principal name (SPN) is the name by which a client uniquely identifies an instance of a service. If you install multiple instances of a service on computers throughout the forest, each instance must have its own SPN. A given service instance can have multiple SPNs if there are multiple names that clients might use for authentication. For example, an SPN always includes the name of the host computer on which the service instance is running, so a service instance might register an SPN for each name or alias of its host. For information on SPN format and composing a unique SPN, see *Name Formats for Unique SPNs*.

Before the Kerberos authentication service can use an SPN to authenticate a service, the SPN must be registered on the account object that the service instance uses to log on. A given SPN can be registered on only one account. For Microsoft® Win32® services, a service installation program specifies the logon account when an instance of the service is installed. The installation program then composes the SPNs and writes them as a property of the account object in Active Directory. If the logon account of a service instance changes, the SPNs must be re-registered under the new account. For more information, see *How a Service Registers its SPNs*.

When a client wants to connect to a service, it locates an instance of the service, composes an SPN for that instance, connects to the service, and presents the SPN for the service to authenticate. See *How Clients Compose a Service's SPN*.

Name Formats for Unique SPNs

An SPN must be unique in the forest in which it is registered. If it is not unique, authentication will fail. The SPN syntax has four elements: two required elements and two additional elements that you can use, if necessary, to produce a unique name.

```
ServiceClass/Host:Port/ServiceName
```

ServiceClass
A string identifying the general class of service; for example, "SqlServer". There are well-known service class names, such as "www" for a web service or "ldap" for a directory service. In general, this can be any string that is unique to the service class. Note that the SPN syntax uses a forward slash to separate elements, so this character cannot appear in a service class name.

Host
The name of the computer on which the service is running. This can be a fully-qualified DNS name or a NetBIOS name. Note that NetBIOS names are not guaranteed to be unique in a forest, so an SPN that contains a NetBIOS name may not be unique.

Port

An optional port number to differentiate between multiple instances of the same service class on a single host computer. Omit this component if the service uses the default port for its service class.

ServiceName

An optional name used in the SPNs of a replicable service to identify the data or services provided by the service or the domain served by the service. This component can have one of the following formats:

- The distinguished name or objectGUID of an object in Active Directory, such as a service connection point (SCP).

- The DNS name of the domain for a service that provides a specified service for a domain as a whole.

- The DNS name of an SRV or MX record

The components present in a service's SPNs depend on how the service is identified and replicated. There are two basic scenarios: host-based services and replicable services.

Host-based services

For a host-based service, the *ServiceName* component is omitted because the service is uniquely identified by the service class and the name of the host computer on which the service is installed.

```
ServiceClass/Host
```

The service class alone is sufficient to identify for clients the functionality that the service provides. You can install instances of the service class on many computers and each instance provides services that are identified with its host computer. FTP and Telnet are examples of host-based services. The SPNs of a host-based service instance can include the port number if the service uses a non-default port or there are multiple instances of the service on the host.

```
ServiceClass/Host:Port
```

Replicable services

For a replicable service there can be one or many instances of the service (replicas), and clients don't care which replica they connect to because each provides the same service. The SPNs for each replica have the same *ServiceClass* and *ServiceName* components, where *ServiceName* identifies more specifically the functionality provided by the service. Only the *Host* and optional *Port* components would vary from SPN to SPN.

```
ServiceClass/Host:Port/ServiceName
```

An example of a replicable service would be an instance of a database service that provides access to a specified database. In this case, *ServiceClass* identifies the database application and *ServiceName* identifies the specific database. *ServiceName* could be the distinguished name of a service connection point (SCP) containing connection information for the database. For example:

```
MyDBService/host1.example.com/CN=hrdb,OU=mktg,DC=example,DC=com
MyDBService/host2.example.com/CN=hrdb,OU=mktg,DC=example,DC=com
MyDBService/host3.example.com/CN=hrdb,OU=mktg,DC=example,DC=com
```

If clients will use the NetBIOS name to compose a service's SPN, each replica must also register an SPN containing the NetBIOS name.

```
MyDBService/host1/CN=hrdb,OU=mktg,DC=example,DC=com
MyDBService/host2/CN=hrdb,OU=mktg,DC=example,DC=com
MyDBService/host3/CN=hrdb,OU=mktg,DC=example,DC=com
```

Another example of a replicable service is one that provides services to an entire domain. In this case, the *ServiceName* component is the DNS name of the domain being served. A Kerberos KDC is an example of this type of replicable service.

Note that if the DNS name of a computer changes, the system automatically updates the *Host* element for all registered SPNs for that host in the forest.

How a Service Composes Its SPNs

There are two functions a service can use to compose its SPNs: **DsGetSpn** is a general-purpose function for composing SPNs and **DsServerRegisterSpn** is a specialized function for composing and registering simple SPNs for a host-based service.

A service installation program typically uses the **DsGetSpn** function to compose SPNs, which it then registers on the service's logon account using the **DsWriteAccountSpn** function. **DsGetSpn** can do any of the following:

- Create a simple SPN with the *ServiceClass*/*Host* format for a host-based service.
- Create a complex SPN that includes the *ServiceName* component used by replicable services or the *Port* component that distinguishes multiple instances of a service on a single host.
- Create a single SPN with the *Host* component set to either the name of a specified host or the name of the local computer by default.
- Create an array of SPNs for multiple service instances that will run on multiple hosts throughout the forest. Each SPN specifies the name of the host for a service instance.
- Create an array of SPNs for multiple service instances that will run on the same host. Each SPN specifies the name of the host and a port number for a service instance.

The array of names returned by **DsGetSpn** must be freed by calling the **DsFreeSpnArray** function.

Note that the **DsGetSpn**, **DsWriteAccountSpn**, and **DsServerRegisterSpn** functions do not check SPNs to ensure that they are unique. Because mutual authentication fails if a client presents an SPN that is not unique, you should check for uniqueness before registering an SPN. To do this, search the global catalog (GC) for **servicePrincipalName** attributes that match your SPN. For information about searching the GC, see *Searching Global Catalog Contents*.

How a Service Registers Its SPNs

Before a client can use an SPN to authenticate an instance of a service, the SPN must be registered on the user or computer account that the service instance will use to logon. Typically, SPN registration is done by a service installation program running with domain administrator privileges.

The service installation program that installs a service instance on a host computer typically performs the following steps.

▶ **To register SPNs for a service instance**

1. Call the **DsGetSpn** function to create one or more unique SPNs for the service instance. For more information, see *Name Formats for Unique SPNs*.

2. Call the **DsWriteAccountSpn** function to register the names on the service's logon account.

DsWriteAccountSpn registers SPNs as a property of a user or computer account object in the directory. **User** and **computer** objects have a **servicePrincipalName** attribute, which is a multi-valued attribute for storing all the SPNs associated with a user or computer account. If the service runs under a user account, the SPNs are stored in the **servicePrincipalName** attribute of that account. If the service runs in the LocalSystem account, the SPNs are stored in the **servicePrincipalName** attribute of the account of the service's host computer. The **DsWriteAccountSpn** caller must specify the distinguished name of the account object under which the SPNs are stored.

To ensure that registered SPNs are secure, the **servicePrincipalName** attribute cannot be written directly; it can only be written by calling **DsWriteAccountSpn**. The caller must have write access to the **servicePrincipalName** attribute of the target account. Typically, write access is granted by default only to domain administrators. However, there is a special case in which the system allows a service running under the LocalSystem account to register its own SPNs on the computer account of the service's host. In this case, the SPN being written must have the form *ServiceClass/Host* and *Host* must be the DNS name of the local computer.

DsWriteAccountSpn can also remove SPNs from an account. An operation parameter indicates whether the SPNs are to be added to the account, removed from the account, or used to completely replace all current SPNs for the account. When a service instance is uninstalled, you should remove any SPNs registered for that instance.

For sample code that registers or unregisters a service's SPNs, see *Registering the SPNs for a Service*.

Host-based services that use the simple SPN format, *ServiceClass/Host*, have the option of using the **DsServerRegisterSpn** function, which both creates and registers SPNs for a service instance. **DsServerRegisterSpn** is a helper function that calls **DsGetSpn** and **DsWriteAccountSpn**.

For more information, see *Service Logon Accounts*.

How Clients Compose a Service's SPN

To authenticate a service, a client application composes an SPN for the service instance to which it wants to connect. The client application can use the *DsMakeSpn* function to compose an SPN. The client specifies the components of the SPN using known information or information retrieved from sources other than the service itself.

The form of an SPN is as shown, where *ServiceClass* and *Host* are required, *Port* and *ServiceName* optional.

```
ServiceClass/Host:Port/ServiceName
```

Typically, the client "knows" the *ServiceClass* part of the name, and knows which of the optional components to include in the SPN. The client can retrieve components of the SPN from sources such as a service connection point (SCP) or user input. For example, the client can read the **serviceDNSName** attribute of a service's SCP to get the *Host* component. The **serviceDNSName** attribute contains either the DNS name of the server on which the service instance is running or the DNS name of SRV records containing the host information for service replicas. The *ServiceName* component, used only for replicable services, can be the distinguished name of the service's SCP, the DNS name of the domain served by the service, or the DNS name of SRV or MX records.

For sample code that a client program uses to compose an SPN for a service, see *How a Client Authenticates an SCP-based Windows Sockets Service*.

For a description of the SPN components, see *Name Formats for Unique SPNs*.

Mutual Authentication in a Windows Sockets Service with an SCP

This section provides sample code that shows how to perform mutual authentication with a service that publishes itself using a service connection point (SCP). The example is based on a Microsoft® Windows® Sockets service that uses an SSPI package to handle the mutual authentication negotiation between a client and the service.

The example on the next page follows these steps to implement mutual authentication.

▶ **To register SPNs in the directory at service installation**

1. Call the **DsGetSpn** function to compose service principal names (SPNs) for the service.

2. Call the **DsWriteAccountSpn** function to register the SPNs on the service account or computer account in whose context the service will run. This step must be performed by a domain administrator (except that a service running under the LocalSystem account can register its SPN in the form *ServiceClass/Host* on the computer account of the service's host).

▶ **To verify configuration at service startup**

Verify that the appropriate SPNs are registered on the account under which the service is running. See *Logon Account Maintenance Tasks*.

▶ **To authenticate the service at client startup**

1. Retrieve connection information from the service's connection point.

2. Establish a connection to the service.

3. Call the **DsMakeSpn** function to compose an SPN for the service. Compose the SPN from the known service class string, and the information retrieved from the service connection point. This information includes the host name of the server on which the service is running. Note that the host name must be a DNS name.

4. Use an SSPI security package to perform the authentication.

   a. Call the **AcquireCredentialsHandle** function to acquire the client's credentials.

   b. Pass the client credentials and the SPN to the **InitializeSecurityContext** function to generate a security blob to send to the service for authentication. Set the ISC_REQ_MUTUAL_AUTH flag to request mutual authentication.

   c. Exchange blobs with the service until the authentication is complete.

5. Check the returned capabilities mask for the ISC_RET_MUTUAL_AUTH flag to verify that mutual authentication was performed.

6. If the authentication was successful, exchange traffic with the authenticated service. Use digital signing to ensure that messages between client and service have not been tampered with. Unless performance requirements are very stringent, you should also use encryption. For sample code that illustrates the use of the **MakeSignature**, **VerifySignature**, **EncryptMessage**, and **DecryptMessage** functions in an SSPI package, see *Ensuring Communication Integrity During Message Exchange* in the SSPI documentation.

▶ **To authenticate the client by the service when a client connects**

1. Load an SSPI security package that supports mutual authentication.

2. When a client connects, use the security package to perform the authentication.

      a. Call the **AcquireCredentialsHandle** function to acquire the service's credentials.

      b. Pass the service credentials and the security blob received from the client to the **AcceptSecurityContext** function to generate a security blob to send back to the client.

      c. Exchange blobs with the client until the authentication is complete.

3. Check the returned capabilities mask for the ASC_RET_MUTUAL_AUTH flag to verify that mutual authentication was performed.

4. If the authentication was successful, exchange traffic with the authenticated client. Use digital signing. Use encryption as well, unless performance is an issue.

How a Client Authenticates an SCP-based Windows Sockets Service

This topic shows the code that a client program uses to compose an SPN for a service. The client binds to the service's service connection point (SCP) to retrieve the information needed to connect to the service. The SCP also contains information the client can use to compose the service's SPN. For sample code that binds to the SCP and retrieves the necessary properties, see *How Clients Find and Use a Service Connection Point*.

This topic also shows how a client uses an SSPI security package and the service's SPN to establish a mutually authenticated connection to the Windows Sockets service. Note that this code is almost identical to the code required in Microsoft Windows NT® 4.0 and earlier just to authenticate the client to the server. The only difference is that the client must supply the SPN and specify the ISC_REQ_MUTUAL_AUTH flag.

Client Code to Make an SPN for a Service

```
// Initialize these strings by querying the service's SCP.
TCHAR szDn[MAX_PATH],      // DN of the service's SCP
    szServer[MAX_PATH],    // DNS name of the service's server
    szClass[MAX_PATH];     // Service class

TCHAR szSpn[MAX_PATH];     // Buffer for SPN
SOCKET sockServer;         // Socket connected to service
DWORD dwRes, dwLen;
.

.

.
// Compose the SPN for the service using the DN, Class, and Server
// returned by ScpLocate
dwLen = sizeof(szSpn);
dwRes = DsMakeSpn(
```

```
        szClass,      // Service class
        szDn,         // DN of the service's SCP
        szServer,     // DNS name of the server on which service is running
        0,            // No port component in SPN
        NULL,         // No referrer
        &dwLen,       // Size of szSpn buffer
        szSpn);       // Buffer to receive the SPN


if (!DoAuthentication (sockServer, szSpn)) {
    closesocket (sockServer);
    return(FALSE);
}
    .
    .
    .
```

Client Code to Authenticate the Service

This code sample consists of two routines: *DoAuthentication* and *GenClientContext*. After calling **DsMakeSpn** to compose an SPN for the service, the client passes the SPN to the *DoAuthentication* routine, which calls the *GenClientContext* to generate the initial buffer to send to the service. *DoAuthentication* uses the socket handle to send the buffer and receive the service's response, which is passed to the SSPI package by another call to *GenClientContext*. This loop is repeated until the authentication fails or *GenClientContext* sets a flag that indicates the authentication was successful.

The *GenClientContext* routine interacts with the SSPI package to generate the authentication information to send to the service and process the information received from the service. The key components of the authentication information provided by the client are the following:

- The service principal name which identifies the credentials that the service must authenticate.

- The client's credentials. The **AcquireCredentialsHandle** function of the security package extracts these credentials from the client's security context which was established at logon.

- To request mutual authentication, the client must specify the ISC_REQ_MUTUAL_AUTH flag when it calls the **InitializeSecurityContext** function during the *GenClientContext* routine.

```
// Structure for storing the state of the authentication sequence.
typedef struct _AUTH_SEQ
{
    BOOL _fNewConversation;
    CredHandle _hcred;
```

(continued)

(continued)

```
    BOOL _fHaveCredHandle;
    BOOL _fHaveCtxtHandle;
    struct _SecHandle _hctxt;
} AUTH_SEQ, *PAUTH_SEQ;

/******************************************************************/
//    DoAuthentication routine for the client.
//
//    Manages the client's authentication conversation with the service
//    using the supplied socket handle.
//
//    Returns TRUE if the mutual authentication is successful.
//    Otherwise, it returns FALSE.
//
/******************************************************************/
BOOL DoAuthentication (
        SOCKET s,
        LPTSTR szSpn)
{
BOOL done = FALSE;
DWORD cbOut, cbIn;

// Call the security package to generate the initial buffer of
// authentication information to send to the service.
cbOut = g_cbMaxMessage;
if (!GenClientContext (s, NULL, 0, g_pOutBuf,
                       &cbOut, &done, szSpn))
    return(FALSE);

if (!SendMsg (s, g_pOutBuf, cbOut))
    return(FALSE);

// Pass the service's response back to the security package, and send
// the package's output back to the service. Repeat until done.
while (!done)
{
    if (!ReceiveMsg (s, g_pInBuf, g_cbMaxMessage, &cbIn))
        return(FALSE);

    cbOut = g_cbMaxMessage;
    if (!GenClientContext (s, g_pInBuf, cbIn, g_pOutBuf,
                           &cbOut, &done, szSpn))
        return(FALSE);
```

```
       if (!SendMsg (s, g_pOutBuf, cbOut))
           return(FALSE);
}


return(TRUE);
}


/***************************************************************/
//    GenClientContext routine
//
//    Handles the client's interactions with the security package.
//    Optionally takes an input buffer coming from the service
//    and generates a buffer of information to send back to the
//    service. Also returns an indication when the authentication
//    is complete.
//
//    Returns TRUE if the mutual authentication is successful.
//    Otherwise, it returns FALSE.
//
/***************************************************************/
BOOL GenClientContext (
            DWORD dwKey,        // socket handle used as key
            BYTE *pIn,
            DWORD cbIn,
            BYTE *pOut,
            DWORD *pcbOut,
            BOOL *pfDone,
            LPTSTR szSpn)
{
SECURITY_STATUS  ssStatus;
TimeStamp        Lifetime;
SecBufferDesc    OutBuffDesc;
SecBuffer        OutSecBuff;
SecBufferDesc    InBuffDesc;
SecBuffer        InSecBuff;
ULONG            ContextAttributes;
PAUTH_SEQ        pAS; // structure to store state of authentication

// Get structure containing the state of the authentication sequence.
if (!GetEntry (dwKey, (PVOID*) &pAS))
   return(FALSE);


if (pAS->_fNewConversation)
{
```

(continued)

(continued)

```
    ssStatus = g_pFuncs->AcquireCredentialsHandle (
            NULL,    // principal
            PACKAGE_NAME,
            SECPKG_CRED_OUTBOUND,
            NULL,    // LOGON id
            NULL,    // authentication data
            NULL,    // get key function
            NULL,    // get key argument
            &pAS->_hcred,
            &Lifetime
            );
    if (SEC_SUCCESS (ssStatus))
        pAS->_fHaveCredHandle = TRUE;
    else
    {
        fprintf (stderr,
                "AcquireCredentialsHandle failed: %u\n", ssStatus);
        return(FALSE);
    }
}

// Prepare output buffer
OutBuffDesc.ulVersion = 0;
OutBuffDesc.cBuffers = 1;
OutBuffDesc.pBuffers = &OutSecBuff;

OutSecBuff.cbBuffer = *pcbOut;
OutSecBuff.BufferType = SECBUFFER_TOKEN;
OutSecBuff.pvBuffer = pOut;

// Prepare input buffer
if (!pAS->_fNewConversation)
{
    InBuffDesc.ulVersion = 0;
    InBuffDesc.cBuffers = 1;
    InBuffDesc.pBuffers = &InSecBuff;

    InSecBuff.cbBuffer = cbIn;
    InSecBuff.BufferType = SECBUFFER_TOKEN;
    InSecBuff.pvBuffer = pIn;
}

_tprintf(TEXT("InitializeSecurityContext: pszTarget=%s\n"),szSpn);
```

```
ssStatus = g_pFuncs->InitializeSecurityContext (
                    &pAS->_hcred,
                    pAS->_fNewConversation ? NULL : &pAS->_hctxt,
                    szSpn,
                    ISC_REQ_MUTUAL_AUTH,        // Context requirements
                    0,                          // reserved1
                    SECURITY_NATIVE_DREP,
                    pAS->_fNewConversation ? NULL : &InBuffDesc,
                    0,                          // reserved2
                    &pAS->_hctxt,
                    &OutBuffDesc,
                    &ContextAttributes,
                    &Lifetime
                    );
if (!SEC_SUCCESS (ssStatus))
{
    fprintf (stderr, "init context failed: %X\n", ssStatus);
    return FALSE;
}

pAS->_fHaveCtxtHandle = TRUE;

// Complete token -- if applicable
if ( (SEC_I_COMPLETE_NEEDED == ssStatus) ||
     (SEC_I_COMPLETE_AND_CONTINUE == ssStatus))
{
    if (g_pFuncs->CompleteAuthToken)
    {
        ssStatus = g_pFuncs->CompleteAuthToken (&pAS->_hctxt,
                                                &OutBuffDesc);
        if (!SEC_SUCCESS(ssStatus))
        {
            fprintf (stderr, "complete failed: %u\n", ssStatus);
            return FALSE;
        }
    } else
    {
        fprintf (stderr, "Complete not supported.\n");
        return FALSE;
    }
}

*pcbOut = OutSecBuff.cbBuffer;
```

(continued)

(continued)

```
if (pAS->_fNewConversation)
    pAS->_fNewConversation = FALSE;

*pfDone = !((SEC_I_CONTINUE_NEEDED == ssStatus) ||
            (SEC_I_COMPLETE_AND_CONTINUE == ssStatus));

// Check for the ISC_RET_MUTUAL_AUTH flag to verify that
// mutual authentication was performed.
if (*pfDone && !(ContextAttributes && ISC_RET_MUTUAL_AUTH) )
    _tprintf(TEXT("Mutual Auth not set in returned context.\n"));

return TRUE;
}
```

Composing and Registering SPNs for an SCP-based Windows Sockets Service

The following code fragment shows how to compose and register the SPNs for a service. Call this code from your service's installation program after calling **CreateService** and creating the service's service connection point (SCP).

The following code fragment calls the *SpnCompose* and *SpnRegister* routines that compose and register the SPN. For the *SpnCompose* source code, see *Composing the SPNs for a Service with an SCP*. For the *SpnRegister* source code, see *Registering the SPNs for a Service*.

This example uses the service's class name and the distinguished name of its SCP to create its service principal name. For sample code that shows how the client binds to the service's SCP to retrieve these name strings, see *How Clients Find and Use a Service Connection Point*. Note that the code for composing an SPN varies depending on the type of service and the mechanisms used to publish the service.

The service registers its SPN by storing it in the *servicePrincipalName* attribute of the service's account object in the directory. If the service runs under the LocalSystem account instead of under a service account, it registers its SPN under the local computer account's object in the directory.

```
TCHAR szDNofSCP[MAX_PATH];    // DN of SCP. Initialize by querying SCP.
TCHAR szServiceClass[]=TEXT("ADSockAuth");
LPCTSTR szServiceAccountDN;   // DN of service's logon account.

DWORD dwStatus;
TCHAR **pspn = NULL;
ULONG ulSpn = 1;

// Compose the SPNs
```

```
dwStatus = SpnCompose(
        &pspn,                  // Receives pointer to the SPN array.
        &ulSpn,                 // Receives number of SPNs returned.
        szDNofSCP,              // Input: DN of the SCP.
        szServiceClass);        // Input: the service's class string.

// Register the SPNs
if (dwStatus == NO_ERROR)
    dwStatus = SpnRegister(
        szServiceAccountDN,     // Logon account to register SPNs on
        pspn,                   // Array of SPNs
        ulSpn,                  // Number of SPNs in array
        DS_SPN_ADD_SPN_OP);     // Add SPNs to the account

// Free the array of SPNs returned by SpnCompose.
DsFreeSpnArray(ulSpn, pspn);
```

You can use similar code to unregister your SPNs when your service is being uninstalled. Simple specify the DS_SPN_DELETE_SPN_OP operation instead of DS_SPN_ADD_SPN_OP.

Composing the SPNs for a Service with an SCP

The following code fragment composes an SPN for a service that uses a service connection point. The returned SPN has the following format:

```
ServiceClass/host/ServiceName
```

ServiceClass and *ServiceName* correspond to the *pszDNofSCP* and *pszServiceClass* parameters. In this example, *host* defaults to the DNS name of the local computer.

```
DWORD
SpnCompose(
    TCHAR ***pspn,              // Output: an array of SPNs
    unsigned long *pulSpn,      // Output: the number of SPNs returned
    TCHAR *pszDNofSCP,          // Input: DN of the service's SCP
    TCHAR* pszServiceClass)     // Input: the name of the service's class
{
DWORD   dwStatus;

dwStatus = DsGetSpn(
    DS_SPN_SERVICE,     // Type of SPN to create (enumerated type)
    pszServiceClass,    // Service class - a name in this case
    pszDNofSCP,         // Service name - DN of the service's SCP
    0,                  // Default: omit port component of SPN
```

(continued)

(continued)

```
    0,               // Number of entries in hostnames and ports arrays
    NULL,            // Array of hostnames. Default is local computer
    NULL,            // Array of ports. Default omits port component
    pulSpn,          // Receives number of SPNs returned in array
    pspn             // Receives array of SPN(s)
    );

return dwStatus;
}
```

Registering the SPNs for a Service

The following code fragment registers or unregisters one or more service principal names (SPNs) for an instance of a service.

The example calls the **DsWriteAccountSpn** function, which stores the SPNs in Microsoft Active Directory™ under the *servicePrincipalName* attribute of the account object specified by the *pszServiceAcctDN* parameter. The account object corresponds to the logon account specified in the **CreateService** call for this service instance. If the logon account is a domain user account, *pszServiceAcctDN* must be the distinguished name of the account object in Active Directory for that user account. If the service's logon account is the LocalSystem account, *pszServiceAcctDN* must be the distinguished name of the computer account object for the host computer on which the service is installed. For sample code that shows how to convert a *domain\account* format name to a distinguished name, see *Example Code to Convert a SAM Name to a Distinguished Name*.

```
// SpnRegister
// Register or unregister the SPNs under the service's account.
//
// The pszServiceAcctDN parameter is the distinguished name of the
// logon account for this instance of the service.
//
// If the service runs in LocalSystem account, pszServiceAcctDN is the
// distinguished name of the local computer account.
DWORD
SpnRegister(
    TCHAR *pszServiceAcctDN,    // DN of the service's logon account
    TCHAR **pspn,               // Array of SPNs to register
    unsigned long ulSpn,        // Number of SPNs in array
    DS_SPN_WRITE_OP Operation)  // Add, replace, or delete SPNs
{

DWORD dwStatus;
HANDLE hDs;
TCHAR szSamName[512];
```

```
DWORD dwSize = sizeof(szSamName);
WCHAR *pWhack = NULL;
PDOMAIN_CONTROLLER_INFO pDcInfo;

_tprintf(TEXT("SPN is:%s\n"), pspn[0]);
if (Operation == DS_SPN_ADD_SPN_OP)
    _tprintf(TEXT("SPN will be set for %s\n"), pszServiceAcctDN);
else
    _tprintf(TEXT("SPN will be removed from %s\n"), pszServiceAcctDN);

// Bind to a domain controller.
// Get the domain for the current user.
if ( GetUserNameEx( NameSamCompatible, szSamName, &dwSize ) )
{
    pWhack = wcschr( szSamName, L'\\' );
    if ( pWhack )
        *pWhack = L'\0';
} else
{
    _tprintf(TEXT("GetUserNameEx failed - %d\n"), GetLastError());
    return GetLastError() ;
}

// Get the name of a domain controller in that domain.
dwStatus = DsGetDcName(
                    NULL,
                    szSamName,
                    NULL,
                    NULL,
                    DS_IS_FLAT_NAME |
                    DS_RETURN_DNS_NAME |
                    DS_DIRECTORY_SERVICE_REQUIRED,
                    &pDcInfo );
if ( dwStatus != 0 )
{
    _tprintf(TEXT("DsGetDcName failed - %d\n"), dwStatus);
    return dwStatus;
}

// Bind to the domain controller.
dwStatus = DsBind( pDcInfo->DomainControllerName, NULL, &hDs );

// Free the DOMAIN_CONTROLLER_INFO buffer.
NetApiBufferFree( pDcInfo );
```

(continued)

(continued)

```
if ( dwStatus != 0 )
{
    _tprintf(TEXT("DsBind failed - %d\n"), dwStatus);
    return dwStatus;
}

// Write the SPNs to the service account or computer account.
dwStatus = DsWriteAccountSpn(
        hDs,            // handle to the directory
        Operation,      // Add or remove SPN from account's existing SPNs
        pszServiceAcctDN,       // DN of service account or computer account
        ulSpn,                  // Number of SPNs to add
        (const TCHAR **)pspn);  // Array of SPNs
if (dwStatus != NO_ERROR)
    _tprintf(TEXT("Failed to write SPN: Error was %X\n"),dwStatus);

// Unbind the DS in any case.
DsUnBind(&hDs);

return(dwStatus);
}
```

How a Windows Sockets Service Authenticates a Client

When a client connects to the Windows Sockets service, the service begins its side of the mutual authentication sequence, which is shown in the following code samples.

The *DoAuthentication* routine uses the socket handle to receive the first authentication packet from the client. The client buffer is passed to the *GenServerContext* routine, which, in turn, passes the buffer to the SSPI security package for authentication. *DoAuthentication* then sends the security package output back to the client. This loop is repeated until the authentication fails or *GenServerContext* sets a flag indicating the authentication was successful.

GenServerContext calls the following functions from an SSPI security package.

- **AcquireCredentialsHandle**, which extracts the service's credentials from the service's security context that was established when the service started.

- **AcceptSecurityContext**, which attempts to perform the mutual authentication using the service's credentials and the authentication information received from the client. To request mutual authentication, the **AcceptSecurityContext** call must specify the ASC_REQ_MUTUAL_AUTH flag.

- **CompleteAuthToken**, which is called, if necessary, to complete the authentication operation.

This sample uses the "negotiate" package from the secur32.dll library of security packages.

```
/****************************************************************/
//    DoAuthentication routine for the service
//
//    Manages the service's authentication conversation with the client
//    using the supplied socket handle.
//
//    Returns TRUE if the mutual authentication is successful.
//    Otherwise, it returns FALSE.
//
/****************************************************************/

BOOL DoAuthentication (SOCKET s)
{
DWORD cbIn, cbOut;
BOOL done = FALSE;

// Receive authentication information from the client and pass
// it to the security package. Send the package's output back
// to the client. Repeat until done.
do
{
    if (!ReceiveMsg (s, g_pInBuf, g_cbMaxMessage, &cbIn))
        return(FALSE);

    cbOut = g_cbMaxMessage;
    if (!GenServerContext (s, g_pInBuf, cbIn, g_pOutBuf,
                                &cbOut, &done))
        return(FALSE);

    if (!SendMsg (s, g_pOutBuf, cbOut))
        return(FALSE);
}
while(!done);

return(TRUE);
}

/****************************************************************/
//    GenServerContext routine
//
//    Handles the service's interactions with the security package.
```

(continued)

(continued)

```
//    Takes an input buffer coming from the client and generates a
//    buffer of information to send back to the client. Also returns
//    an indication when the authentication is complete.
//
//    Returns TRUE if the mutual authentication is successful.
//    Otherwise, it returns FALSE.
//
/******************************************************************/
BOOL GenServerContext (
            DWORD dwKey,
            BYTE *pIn,
            DWORD cbIn,
            BYTE *pOut,
            DWORD *pcbOut,
            BOOL *pfDone)
{
SECURITY_STATUS  ssStatus;
TimeStamp        Lifetime;
SecBufferDesc    OutBuffDesc;
SecBuffer        OutSecBuff;
SecBufferDesc    InBuffDesc;
SecBuffer        InSecBuff;
ULONG            ContextAttributes;
PAUTH_SEQ        pAS;

// Get structure containing the state of the authentication sequence.
if (!GetEntry (dwKey, (PVOID*) &pAS))
    return(FALSE);

if (pAS->_fNewConversation)
{
    ssStatus = g_pFuncs->AcquireCredentialsHandle (
                    NULL,    // principal
                    PACKAGE_NAME,
                    SECPKG_CRED_INBOUND,
                    NULL,    // LOGON id
                    NULL,    // authentication data
                    NULL,    // get key function
                    NULL,    // get key argument
                    &pAS->_hcred,
                    &Lifetime
                    );
    if (SEC_SUCCESS (ssStatus))
        pAS->_fHaveCredHandle = TRUE;
```

```
    else
    {
        fprintf (stderr, "AcquireCredentialsHandle failed: %u\n",
                ssStatus);
        return(FALSE);
    }
}

// Prepare the output buffer.
OutBuffDesc.ulVersion = 0;
OutBuffDesc.cBuffers  = 1;
OutBuffDesc.pBuffers  = &OutSecBuff;

OutSecBuff.cbBuffer   = *pcbOut;
OutSecBuff.BufferType = SECBUFFER_TOKEN;
OutSecBuff.pvBuffer   = pOut;

// Prepare the input buffer.
InBuffDesc.ulVersion  = 0;
InBuffDesc.cBuffers   = 1;
InBuffDesc.pBuffers   = &InSecBuff;

InSecBuff.cbBuffer    = cbIn;
InSecBuff.BufferType  = SECBUFFER_TOKEN;
InSecBuff.pvBuffer    = pIn;

ssStatus = g_pFuncs->AcceptSecurityContext (
                    &pAS->_hcred,
                    pAS->_fNewConversation ? NULL : &pAS->_hctxt,
                    &InBuffDesc,
                    ASC_REQ_MUTUAL_AUTH,  // context requirements
                    SECURITY_NATIVE_DREP,
                    &pAS->_hctxt,
                    &OutBuffDesc,
                    &ContextAttributes,
                    &Lifetime
                    );
if (!SEC_SUCCESS (ssStatus))
{
    fprintf (stderr, "AcceptSecurityContext failed: %u\n", ssStatus);
    return FALSE;
}
if (!(ContextAttributes && ASC_RET_MUTUAL_AUTH))
    _tprintf(TEXT("Mutual Auth not set in returned context.\n"));
```

(continued)

(continued)

```
pAS->_fHaveCtxtHandle = TRUE;

// Complete the authentication token -- if necessary.
if ((SEC_I_COMPLETE_NEEDED == ssStatus) ||
                    (SEC_I_COMPLETE_AND_CONTINUE == ssStatus))
{
    if (g_pFuncs->CompleteAuthToken)
    {
        ssStatus = g_pFuncs->CompleteAuthToken (&pAS->_hctxt,
                                            &OutBuffDesc);
        if (!SEC_SUCCESS(ssStatus))
        {
            fprintf (stderr, "complete failed: %u\n", ssStatus);
            return FALSE;
        }
    } else
    {
        fprintf (stderr, "Complete not supported.\n");
        return FALSE;
    }
}

*pcbOut = OutSecBuff.cbBuffer;

if (pAS->_fNewConversation)
    pAS->_fNewConversation = FALSE;

*pfDone = !((SEC_I_CONTINUE_NEEDED == ssStatus) ||
                (SEC_I_COMPLETE_AND_CONTINUE == ssStatus));

return TRUE;
}
```

Mutual Authentication in RPC Applications

RPC services can use service connection points to publish themselves, or they can use the RPC name service (RpcNs) APIs. This section provides sample code that shows how to perform mutual authentication with an RPC service that publishes itself using the RPC name service (RpcNs) APIs.

The steps for performing mutual authentication in an RPC application are shown on the next page.

▶ To register SPNs in the directory at service installation

1. Call the **DsGetSpn** function to compose service principal names (SPNs) for the service.

2. Call the **DsWriteAccountSpn** function to register the SPNs on the service account or computer account in whose context the service will run.

▶ To register with the RPC run time at service startup

1. Verify that the appropriate SPNs are registered on the account under which the service is running. See *Logon Account Maintenance Tasks*.

2. Call the **RpcServerRegisterAuthInfo** function to register the service's SPNs with the RPC authentication service, and specify RPC_C_AUTHN_GSS_NEGOTIATE as the authentication service to use.

▶ To authenticate the service at client startup

1. Extract the host name from the RPC Binding.

2. Compose the SPN for the service by calling **DsMakeSpn** with the service class, the DNS host name, and the service name (the distinguished name of the connection point in the case of RpcNs).

3. Set up an **RPC_SECURITY_QOS** structure to request mutual authentication.

4. Call the **RpcBindingSetAuthInfoEx** function to set the authentication information for the RPC binding. The client must request at least PKT_INTEGRITY to ensure that communications have not been tampered with. For greater security, the client should specify PKT_PRIVACY to request encryption.

5. Make the RPC call.

▶ To authenticate the client from the service at the start of each remote procedure call

1. Call the **RpcBindingInqAuthClient** function to check the authentication parameters specified by the client. If the client has not requested the desired level of authentication, reject the call. Note that an RPC service must verify the authentication level, authentication service, and client identity on every call to ensure that the client has been properly authenticated.

2. Call the **RpcImpersonateClient** function to impersonate the client.

3. Perform the requested operation.

4. Call the **RpcRevertToSelf** function to revert to the service's security context.

How a Client Authenticates an RpcNs Service

The following sample code shows the RPC client's side of a mutually authenticated connection. The client connects to the RPC name service to enumerate the bindings that match the RPC service's interface specification. For each binding handle in the enumeration, the client must call the **DsMakeSpn** function to compose the corresponding SPN.

```c
void main(void)
{
RPC_STATUS      rpcstatus;
boolean         bResult;
ULONG           ulCode;
TCHAR           szEntryName[] = TEXT("/.:/RpcExampleServiceEntry");
TCHAR           szDsEntryName[MAX_PATH];
BOOL            done=FALSE;
RPC_NS_HANDLE   hNs;  // Context for import operations
TCHAR           *pszBind;
int             ilen;

// Items for ADSI

IADs    *pRoot=NULL;
VARIANT varDSRoot;
HRESULT hr;

// Items for Mutual Auth, SPN

TCHAR    szServiceClass[]=TEXT("RpcExample");
TCHAR    szServiceInstance[MAX_PATH];
TCHAR    szSpn[MAX_PATH];
ULONG    ulSpn = sizeof(szSpn);

RPC_SECURITY_QOS     qos;

// To build an SPN for the RPC service, the DN of the
// service's entry in the RpcServices container is needed. To build
// that DN, retrieve the default naming context and combine it with
// the known strings for the RpcServices container and the service's
// entry in that container.
hr = CoInitialize(NULL);

hr = ADsGetObject(TEXT("LDAP://RootDSE"),
                  IID_IADs,
```

```
                    (void**)&pRoot);

hr = pRoot->Get(TEXT("defaultNamingContext"),&varDSRoot);
_tprintf(TEXT("\nDS Root :%s\n"),varDSRoot.bstrVal);

if (pRoot)
    pRoot->Release();

CoUninitialize();

// Compose the DN of the RPC service's connection point using
// "RpcExampleServiceEntry", which is the name of this service's
// entry in the RpcServices container.
_tcscpy(szDsEntryName,
        TEXT("cn=RpcExampleServiceEntry,cn=RpcServices,cn=System,"));
_tcscat(szDsEntryName,varDSRoot.bstrVal);

// Use the service's RPC name service entry to get a handle to
// enumerate the bindings that match our interface specification.
rpcstatus = RpcNsBindingImportBegin(RPC_C_NS_SYNTAX_DCE,
                                    (TCHAR *)&szEntryName,
                                    RpcExample_v1_0_c_ifspec,
                                    NULL,
                                    &hNs);
if (rpcstatus != RPC_S_OK)
    return;

// Loop through the bindings and try each handle until one works.
// In this example, implicit handles are used: the implicit handle
// "RpcExample_IfHandle" is generated by MIDL and defined in the
// MIDL-generated include file RpcExample.H.
while (rpcstatus != RPC_S_NO_MORE_BINDINGS)
{
    rpcstatus = RpcNsBindingImportNext(hNs,
                                       &RpcExample_IfHandle);

    if (rpcstatus != RPC_S_OK)
        continue;

    // Convert the binding to a string.
    RpcBindingToStringBinding(RpcExample_IfHandle,&pszBind);
    _tprintf(TEXT("String Binding:%s\n"),pszBind);

    // Extract the service name, the host, in this case.
    // Note that the DNS host name is used to compose the SPN.
```

(continued)

(continued)

```
ilen=_tcscspn((const TCHAR *)pszBind,TEXT(":"));
_tcscpy(szServiceInstance,(const TCHAR *)(pszBind+ilen+1));
RpcStringFree(&pszBind);

// Set up the authentication info for the call
//
// First make the SPN, which is composed of the service class,
// the DN of the RPC Service object in the DS, and the service
// instance name, which is the DNS name of the host,
// which was extracted from the RPC binding string.
rpcstatus = DsMakeSpn(
    szServiceClass,
    szDsEntryName,      // DN of the entry in RpcServices container
    szServiceInstance,  // DNS name of the host for the service
    0,                  // Use the default port
    NULL,               // No referral host
    &ulSpn,             // Size, in bytes, of the szSpn buffer
    szSpn               // buffer to receive the SPN
    );

_tprintf(TEXT("Client will present SPN %s\n"),szSpn);

// Set up the RPC_SECURITY_QOS struct for mutual authentication.
qos.Version             = RPC_C_SECURITY_QOS_VERSION;
qos.Capabilities        = RPC_C_QOS_CAPABILITIES_MUTUAL_AUTH;
qos.IdentityTracking    = RPC_C_QOS_IDENTITY_STATIC;
qos.ImpersonationType   = RPC_C_IMP_LEVEL_IMPERSONATE;

// Set the authentication information for this binding handle.
// Specify the service principal name and the QOS information.
// Ask for PKT_INTEGRITY to ensure that no-one has tampered
// with the traffic between the client and the authenticated
// service. Failure to ask for at least PKT_INTEGRITY renders the
// mutual authentication effectively worthless because an attacker
// can steal and re-issue compromised packets.
// For greater security, request PKT_PRIVACY which
// also encrypts the traffic. PKT_INTEGRITY is a good compromise
// between security and performance - an attacker can see the
// traffic but not tamper with it.
rpcstatus = RpcBindingSetAuthInfoEx(
                RpcExample_IfHandle,
                (TCHAR *)szSpn,
                RPC_C_AUTHN_LEVEL_PKT_INTEGRITY,
```

```
                        RPC_C_AUTHN_GSS_NEGOTIATE,
                        NULL,
                        NULL,
                        &qos);

    // Now that mutual authentication parameters have been set,
    // make RPC calls.
    RpcTryExcept
    {
        bResult = Shutdown();
        if (bResult)
            _tprintf(TEXT("Shutdown: Service accepted call\n"));
        else
            _tprintf(TEXT("Shutdown: Service rejected call\n"));

        // Stop looping through the bindings.
        rpcstatus  = RPC_S_NO_MORE_BINDINGS;
    }
    RpcExcept(1)
    {
        ulCode = RpcExceptionCode();
        _tprintf(TEXT("RPC exception 0x%lx = %ld\n"), ulCode, ulCode);
    }
    RpcEndExcept;

    // Free the imported binding
    RpcBindingFree(&RpcExample_IfHandle);
}

// Discard the Import handle.
rpcstatus = RpcNsBindingImportDone(&hNs);

return;
}
```

Composing SPNs for an RpcNs Service

The following sample code composes the service principal names (SPNs) for an RPC service that has an entry in the RpcServices container in the directory. An RPC service uses the **RpcNsBindingExport** function to create its RpcServices entry.

An RPC service uses this code to build the SPN or SPNs that identify an instance of the service. The service uses this routine at the following times:

- To register or unregister the SPNs in the directory, when the service is being installed or removed. For sample code, see *Registering the SPNs for a Service*.

- When the service is starting up: to register itself with the RPC authentication service. For sample code, see *How an RpcNs Service Authenticates a Caller*.

The code uses the distinguished name of the service's RpcServices entry to compose the SPN. So before calling this code, call the **RpcNsBindingExport** function to create the service's RpcServices entry.

The code calls the **DsGetSpn** function to build an SPN. The SPN is composed from service's class name and the distinguished name of the service's RpcServices entry.

```
DWORD
SpnCompose(TCHAR ***pspn, unsigned long *pulSpn)
{
DWORD   status;
TCHAR   szDsEntryName[MAX_PATH];

// Items for ADSI.
IADs    *pRoot=NULL;
VARIANT varDSRoot;
HRESULT hr;

hr = CoInitialize(NULL);

// First get the defaultNamingContext for the local domain.
hr = ADsGetObject(TEXT("LDAP://RootDSE"),
                  IID_IADs,
                  (void**)&pRoot);

hr = pRoot->Get(TEXT("defaultNamingContext"), &varDSRoot);
_tprintf(TEXT("\nDS Root :%s\n"), varDSRoot.bstrVal);

if (pRoot)
    pRoot->Release();

CoUninitialize();

// Compose the DN of the service's entry in the RpcServices container,
// which is created by a call to RpcNsBindingExport.
// The entry for an RPC service is in the System/RpcServices container
// in the defaultNamingContext of the local domain.
_tcscpy(szDsEntryName,
      TEXT("cn=RpcExampleServiceEntry,cn=RpcServices,cn=System,"));
_tcscat(szDsEntryName,varDSRoot.bstrVal);

// Build the SPN for this service using the DN and
```

```
// our service's class, "RpcExample".
status = DsGetSpn(
    DS_SPN_SERVICE,        // Type of SPN to create.
    TEXT("RpcExample"),    // Service class - a name in this case.
    szDsEntryName,         // DN of the RpcServices for this RPC service.
    0,                     // Use the default instance port.
    0,                     // Number of additional instance names.
    NULL,                  // No additional instance names.
    NULL,                  // No additional instance ports.
    pulSpn,                // Size of SPN array.
    pspn                   // Returned SPN(s).
    );

return status;
}
```

How an RpcNs Service Authenticates a Caller

For an RPC service, the RPC run time routine handles most of the details of mutual authentication. When the service starts up, it simply calls the **RpcServerRegisterAuthInfo** function to register its SPN and specify an authentication service. This example specifies the RPC_C_AUTHN_GSS_NEGOTIATE authentication service which performs the mutual authentication. The service then sets up the RPC bindings and waits for a client connection. When a client binds to the service, the RPC run time automatically performs the mutual authentication. If the client requests authentication and the client's credentials are invalid, the RPC run time does not dispatch the client's calls. Note, however, that if the client does not request the proper authentication level, the RPC run time dispatches the call without performing authentication. For this reason, your service must call the **RpcBindingInqAuthClient** function to verify the authentication parameters specified by the client.

The following code fragment composes the service's SPN and registers the service for authentication. For the *SpnCompose* source code, see *Composing SPNs for an RpcNs Service*.

```
RPC_STATUS      status;
DWORD           dwStatus;
TCHAR           **pspn;
ULONG           ulSpn=1;

dwStatus = SpnCompose(&pspn, &ulSpn);

// Register with the authentication service
status = RpcServerRegisterAuthInfo((TCHAR*)*pspn,
                                    RPC_C_AUTHN_GSS_NEGOTIATE,
                                    NULL,
                                    NULL);
```

If the client is authenticated, the service can call the **RpcBindingInqAuthClient** function to retrieve the security parameters specified by the client. This enables the service to enforce additional security requirements. For example, a service that uses mutual authentication should also require that communications between client and service be digitally signed and/or encrypted. The following code fragment calls the **RpcBindingInqAuthClient** function and rejects the client's call unless the client has specified the required authentication level.

```
boolean Shutdown()
{
RPC_STATUS          rpcStatus;
RPC_AUTHZ_HANDLE    hAuth;
TCHAR               *pszSpn;
ULONG               ulAuthnLevel;
ULONG               ulAuthnSvc;
ULONG               ulAuthzSvc;

_tprintf(TEXT("Shutdown called.\n"));

rpcStatus = RpcBindingInqAuthClient(
        0,
        &hAuth,
        &pszSpn,
        &ulAuthnLevel,  // Authentication level requested by client
        &ulAuthnSvc,
        &ulAuthzSvc);

if (rpcStatus != RPC_S_OK) {
    _tprintf(TEXT("RpcBindingInqAuthClient failed: %d\n"), rpcStatus);
    return false;
}

_tprintf(TEXT("Client SPN:%s\n"),pszSpn);
RpcStringFree(&pszSpn);

switch (ulAuthnLevel)
{
    case RPC_C_AUTHN_LEVEL_DEFAULT:
        _tprintf(TEXT("Client Auth Level: DEFAULT\n"));
        return false; // Keep running
    case RPC_C_AUTHN_LEVEL_NONE:
        _tprintf(TEXT("Client Auth Level: NONE\n"));
        return false; // Keep running
    case RPC_C_AUTHN_LEVEL_CONNECT:
```

```
            _tprintf(TEXT("Client Auth Level: CONNECT\n"));
            return false; // Keep running
    case RPC_C_AUTHN_LEVEL_CALL:
            _tprintf(TEXT("Client Auth Level: CALL\n"));
            return false; // Keep running
    case RPC_C_AUTHN_LEVEL_PKT:
            _tprintf(TEXT("Client Auth Level: PACKET\n"));
            break;  // Shutdown
    case RPC_C_AUTHN_LEVEL_PKT_INTEGRITY:
            _tprintf(TEXT("Client Auth Level: PACKET_INTEGRITY\n"));
            break;  // Shutdown
    case RPC_C_AUTHN_LEVEL_PKT_PRIVACY:
            _tprintf(TEXT("Client Auth Level: PACKET_PRIVACY\n"));
            break;  // Shutdown
    default:
            _tprintf(TEXT("Client Auth Level: UNKNOWN (%d)\n"),
                                ulAuthnLevel);
            return true;
}


// Shut down.
ReportStatusToSCMgr(
    SERVICE_STOP_PENDING,  // Service state
    NO_ERROR,              // Exit code
    3000);                 // Wait hint

_tprintf(TEXT("\nService shutting down by request.\n"));
RpcMgmtStopServerListening(NULL);
return true;
}
```

Mutual Authentication in Windows Sockets Applications

Microsoft® Windows® Sockets services can use the Registration and Resolution (RnR) APIs to publish services, or they can use service connection points.

For discussion and sample code that shows how to perform mutual authentication for a Windows Sockets service that publishes using a service connection point, see *Mutual Authentication in a Windows Sockets Service with an SCP*. This example uses an SSPI security package to manage the authentication negotiations between a client and the WinSock service.

Mutual Authentication for Windows Sockets RnR Services

A WinSock RnR service can use similar code to perform mutual authentication using an SSPI package. In this case, the service would compose its SPNs using the distinguished name of the service's entry in the WinsockServices container in the directory.

For example, if the service registers itself with the name "WinSockRnRSampleService", you could compose the service's SPN with the following code. A client could use similar code to construct an SPN to authenticate the service.

```
DWORD
SpnCompose(TCHAR ***pspn, unsigned long *pulSpn)
{
DWORD    status;
TCHAR    szDsEntryName[MAX_PATH];

// Items for ADSI.
IADs     *pRoot=NULL;
VARIANT varDSRoot;
HRESULT hr;

hr = CoInitialize(NULL);

// First get the defaultNamingContext for the local domain.
hr = ADsGetObject(TEXT("LDAP://RootDSE"),
                  IID_IADs,
                  (void**)&pRoot);

hr = pRoot->Get(TEXT("defaultNamingContext"), &varDSRoot);
_tprintf(TEXT("\nDS Root :%s\n"), varDSRoot.bstrVal);

if (pRoot)
    pRoot->Release();

CoUninitialize();

// Compose the DN of the entry in the WinsockServices container.
_tcscpy(szDsEntryName,
        TEXT("cn=WinSockRnRSampleService,cn=WinsockServices,cn=System,"));
_tcscat(szDsEntryName,varDSRoot.bstrVal);

// Build the SPN for this service using the DN and
// our service's class, "RpcExample".
status = DsGetSpn(
```

```
    DS_SPN_SERVICE,        // Type of. SPN to create.
    TEXT("RnRExample"),    // Service class - a name in this case.
    szDsEntryName,         // DN of the RpcServices for this RPC service.
    0,                     // Use the default instance port.
    0,                     // Number of additional instance names.
    NULL,                  // No additional instance names.
    NULL,                  // No additional instance ports.
    pulSpn,                // Size of SPN array.
    pspn                   // Returned SPN(s).
    );

return status;
}
```

CHAPTER 19

Backing Up and Restoring Active Directory

The Microsoft® Active Directory™ provides functions for backing up and restoring data in the directory database. This section describes how to back up and restore Active Directory programmatically. For information about backing up Active Directory using the utilities provided in Microsoft® Windows® 2000 Server, see the Windows 2000 Resource Kit.

Backup of Active Directory must be performed online and must be performed when the Active Directory Service is installed. Active Directory is built on a special Jet database and exports a backup interface similar to Microsoft Exchange 5.5. The primary difference is that Active Directory does not support incremental backups. A backup application binds to a local client-side DLL with entry points defined in ntdsbcli.h.

Restoration of Active Directory is always performed offline.

Although the topics in this section only describe how to back up and restore Active Directory, note that Windows 2000® has several "system state" components that must be backed up and restored together. These system state components consist of the following:

- Boot files including ntldr, ntdetect, all files protected by SFP, and performance counter configuration
- The Active Directory (domain controller only)
- SysVol (domain controller only)
- Certificate server (CA only)
- Cluster database (cluster node only)
- Registry
- COM+ class registration database

The system state can be backed up in any order. Restoration of the system state should replace boot files first and commit the system hive of the registry as the final step just before running the **DsRestore*** functions on the domain controller.

For information on restoring Certificate Services, see *Using the Certificate Services Backup and Restore Functions*.

For more information on the Microsoft Exchange backup and restore interface, see *Backing Up and Restoring Data* in the Microsoft Exchange Server Programmer's Reference.

Considerations for Active Directory Services Backup

Directory service information can be replicated. A recovery plan must be formulated prior to restoration. One option is to restore a replica of the directory and then propagate changes that occurred since the backup from other replicas in the domain.

In some cases you may want the restored replica to take precedence over the other replicas in the domain. For example, if an object is accidentally deleted and the deletion is replicated to all domain controllers, you could undelete the object by restoring one replica from a backup that was made before the object was deleted. Then you'd use the NTDSUtil utility to mark the undeleted object as authoritatively restored. The undeleted object will then be replicated to the other DCs, and the replica that was restored will receive the updates for all other objects that occurred since the time the backup was made. The end result for all the replicas is the same as that prior to the restore, except that the authoritatively restored object has been undeleted.

All changes occurring during backup are stored in a temporary log and added to the end of the backup set when the backup is complete.

Any recovery plan should ensure that the age of the backup should not exceed the Active Directory Tombstone Lifetime (default is 60 days). Restoration of a backup older than the tombstone lifetime may cause the restored domain controller to have objects that will not be replicated on other DCs. This occurs if an object is deleted after the backup is made and the restore occurs after the tombstone for the deleted object has been permanently removed. The restored DC would have the object as it existed before the deletion, and the other DCs would have no record that the object ever existed. In this case, an administrator will have to manually delete each unreplicated object on the restored domain controller.

Incremental backups of the Active Directory are not supported: a full backup is required.

Backing Up Active Directory

A backup of Active Directory requires backup of the database and backup of the transaction logs. This topic provides a walkthrough of how a backup application backs up Active Directory.

The caller of these backup functions must have the SE_BACKUP_NAME privilege. You can use the **DsSetAuthIdentity** function to set the security context under which the directory backup/restore functions are called.

▶ **To backup Active Directory**

1. Call the **DsIsNTDSOnline** function to determine if Active Directory is running.
2. If Active Directory is running, call the **DsBackupPrepare** function to initialize a backup context handle.
3. Call the **DsBackupGetDatabaseNames** function to get a list of files to back up. To release the memory returned by this function, call the **DsBackupFree** function.

4. For each name in the returned list of files, call the **DsBackupOpenFile** function followed by repeated calls to the **DsBackupRead** function until the entire file has been read. When you have finished reading the file, call the **DsBackupClose** function to close it.

5. After all database files are backed up, call the **DsBackupGetBackupLogs** function to get a list of transaction logs. This list is handled just like the list of database files.

6. When you have finished backing up the transaction log, call the **DsBackupTruncateLogs** function to delete all committed transaction logs that were backed up.

7. Finally, call the **DsBackupEnd** function to release all resources associated with the backup context handle.

Restoring Active Directory

Active Directory must be restored offline. The system must be rebooted in Directory Services Restore mode. In this mode, the operating system is running without Active Directory and all user validation occurs through the Security Accounts Manager (SAM) in the registry. To restore Active Directory, you must be a local administrator on the DC being restored.

The caller of the restore functions must have the SE_RESTORE_NAME privilege. You can use the **DsSetAuthIdentity** function to set the security context under which the directory backup/restore functions are called.

Note that when you restore Active Directory, you must also restore the other system state components.

▶ To restore Active Directory from backups

1. Call the **DsIsNTDSOnline** function to determine if Active Directory is running. If Active Directory is running, the application must fail the restore attempt.

2. Call the **DsRestorePrepare** function to get a backup context handle.

3. Call the **DsRestoreGetDatabaseLocations** function to determine the directories where the files are to be restored. If this function fails, restore the data back to the original backup source directory (the directory from which the data were backed up).

4. Once the restore is complete, call the **DsRestoreRegister** function to specify which database and which log files were restored.

5. Use standard Win32 functions to restore the files. First, delete all files in the destination directory; then copy the backup files to the destination directory.

6. Call the **DsRestoreRegisterComplete** function to indicate that the restore has been completed.

7. Call the **DsRestoreEnd** function to release any resources associated with the context.

After a restore in Directory Services Restore mode, the domain controller should be rebooted in normal mode. When the directory service starts, the domain controller will perform the normal consistency check and the restored directory will then be online.

Note that "restoring" an Active Directory is always a two-part operation. Part one is to restore the database up to the point in time when the backup was taken and not beyond. Part two is to replicate the directory, where the newly restored DSA replicates post-backup updates from other DSAs in the domain/enterprise.

Any Windows 2000® server that contains a replica of the Windows 2000® directory service is a domain controller (DC).

The **DsRestoreRegister** function adds a "Restore In Progress" key to the registry. If you commit the system hive of the registry after calling **DsRestoreRegister**, you need to move this key from the running hive to the restored hive. You can avoid this step by committing the system hive just before calling the DsRestore functions.

Part 3 – Glossary and Indexes

Part 3 of this volume provides a glossary of Active Directory terms, as well as a collection of indexes designed to make your life easier.

Rather than cluttering the TOCs of each individual volume in this library with the names of programming elements, I've relegated such per-element information to a central location: the back of each volume. These indexes point you to the volume that has the information you need, and organizes the information in a way that lends itself to easy use.

The only exception to this approach is the Active Directory Schema. Due to the specialized nature of the schema, the listing of Category 1 schema attributes and classes is only included in Volume 5, <u>Active Directory Schema</u>.

Also, to keep you as informed and up-to-date as possible about Microsoft technologies, I've created (and maintain) a live Web-based document that maps Microsoft technologies to the locations where you can get more information about them. The following link gets you to the live index of technologies:

www.iseminger.com/winprs/technologies

These indexes are in a constant state of improvement. I've designed them to be as useful as possible, but the real test comes when you use them. If you can think of ways to make improvements, send me feedback at *winprs@microsoft.com*. While I can't guarantee a reply, I'll read the input, and if others can benefit, I will incorporate the idea into future libraries.

Glossary

This glossary defines terms that you may encounter in Active Directory, ADSI, and LDAP information.

A

access-control entry (ACE)   An ACE is an entry in an access-control list (ACL). An ACE contains a set of access rights and a security identifier (SID) that identifies a trustee (such as a user or group) for whom the rights are allowed, denied, or audited.

access-control list (ACL)   An ACL is a list of access-control entries (ACEs) that define the security protections on an object. There are two kinds of ACLs that can appear in an object's security descriptor: a discretionary ACL (DACL) that controls access to the object, and a system ACL (SACL) that controls auditing of attempts to access the object.

ACE   *See* access-control entry.

ACL   *See* access-control list.

Active Directory Service Interfaces (ADSI) Active Directory Service Interfaces is a set of specifications for COM objects and interfaces. Administrators and developers can use ADSI objects to perform common administrative operations, such as adding new users or managing a print queue. See *ADSI Programmer's Guide*.

ADSI   *See* Active Directory Service Interfaces.

attribute   An attribute is a property of a directory object. A directory object is described by the values of its attributes; for example, a car can be described by its make, model, color, and so on. These are the attributes of the car. The term "attribute" is often used interchangeably with "property". Some attributes have a single value; others can have multiple values. See *Characteristics of Attributes*.

authoritative restore   When a replica of Active Directory is restored from backup, you can use the NTDSUTIL utility to mark selected objects as authoritatively restored. When replication occurs with other domain controllers, the authoritatively restored object replaces existing copies of the object on other DCs. Objects that are not authoritatively restored will be updated to reflect changes that occurred since the backup was made.

automation   Automation technology is a way to manipulate objects within a scripting environment. Methods within an Automation environment are typically accessed through the **IDispatch** interface.

B

backup domain controller (BDC)   In a Windows NT 4.0 or earlier domain, the backup domain controller is the server host computer that receives a copy of the domain's directory database, with all account and security policy information for the domain. The copy is synchronized periodically and automatically with the master copy on the primary domain controller (PDC). BDCs also authenticate user logons and can be promoted to function as PDCs as needed. Multiple BDCs can exist on a domain.

In a Windows 2000 domain, backup domain controllers are not required; all domain controllers are peers, and all can perform maintenance on the directory. Windows NT 4.0 and 3.51 backup domain controllers can participate in a Windows 2000 domain when it is running in mixed mode.

BDC   *See* backup domain controller.

C

canonical name   The canonical name of a directory object is the distinguished name, rendered in a more friendly way, namely, root first, "/" delimited, and without the LDAP attribute tags (CN=, DC=).

For example, the following distinguished name:
CN=Foo,OU=MyOU,DC=Microsoft,DC=Com
is rendered as
Microsoft.Com/MyOU/Foo
in canonical form.

class   In ADSI, a class is a formal description of a discrete, identifiable type of object that can be stored in a directory service. For example, User, Print-Queue, and Group are all *classes* in Active Directory. The definition of a class is stored in a directory service's schema, and acts as a template for instances of the class.

class instance   A class instance is a specific occurrence of a class defined in a directory service schema. For example, **user** objects with the attributes "James Smith" or "Martha Dale" would represent instances of the user class.

client (directory client)   A directory client is a server, workstation, or application that accesses a directory service using the LDAP protocol to query the directory for objects of interest.

collection   A collection is an arbitrary set of directory objects that can be represented using the same data type. In ADSI, you can use the **IADsCollection** interface to work with collections.

COM   *See* Component Object Model.

common name (CN)   Every object in Active Directory has a naming attribute from which it's relative distinguished name is formed. For most object classes, the naming attribute is the Common-Name (**cn**). For example, a user object with its **cn** set to "John Smith" might have a distinguished name of CN=John Smith,CN=Users,DC=Microsoft,DC=com.

Component Object Model (COM)   COM is a programming model that defines the way in which software components communicate with and provide services to one another, regardless of where the components reside. ADSI defines a set of COM interfaces (and related APIs) for working with directory service objects. For more information, see the COM SDK.

configuration partition   A configuration partition is a directory partition that contains replication topology and other configuration information that must be replicated throughout the forest. Every DC in an enterprise forest has a replica of the same configuration partition.

container   A container is a directory object that can contain other directory objects. In Active Directory, the schema definition of each object class determines the types of objects that can be containers of instances of the class. See *Containers and Leaves* and **IADsContainer**.

content rules   Content rules define the possible attributes of the class instances stored in a directory service. In Active Directory, the schema definition of each class specifies the mandatory (**mayHave**) and optional (**mustHave**) attributes for instances of the class. See *Characteristics of Object Classes*.

cross-reference   Active Directory stores knowledge information about the naming contexts in cross-reference objects. A cross-reference provides information to the directory system agent (DSA) to use to generate referrals.

Cross-references can refer to naming contexts that are part of the local forest, or that are external. An example of an external naming context is a separate Lightweight Directory Access Protocol (LDAP) directory used in an enterprise that also has Windows 2000 installed. By creating a cross-reference for the separate LDAP directory, Active Directory DSA can generate referrals to the external directory when client queries reference it.

D

DACL   *See* discretionary access-control list.

data model   Active Directory data model is derived from the X.500 data model. The directory holds objects that represent various things described by attributes. The types of objects that can be stored in the directory is defined in the schema. For each object class, the schema defines what attributes an instance of the class must have, what additional attributes it may have, and which object classes can be a parent of the current object class.

delegation   Delegation is one of the most important security features of Active Directory. Delegation allows a higher administrative authority to grant specific administrative rights for containers and subtrees to individuals and groups. This eliminates the need for domain administrators with sweeping authority over large segments of the user population. Access-control entries (ACEs) can grant specific administrative rights on the objects in a container to a user or group. Rights are granted for specific operations on specific object classes using ACEs in the container's access-control list (ACL).

directory   A directory is an information source used to store information about objects. A telephone directory stores information about telephone subscribers. In a file system, the directory stores information about files. In a distributed computing system or a public computer network like the Internet, there are many objects, such as printers, fax servers, applications, databases, and users.

directory partition   A directory partition (also called a naming context) is a contiguous Active Directory subtree that is replicated on one or more Windows 2000 domain controllers (DCs) in a forest. Each DC has a replica of three partitions: the schema partition, the configuration partition, and a domain partition.

directory service (DS)   A directory service differs from a directory in that it is both the directory information source, and the services making the information available and usable to the users.

A directory service is one of the most important components of an extended computer system. Users and administrators frequently do not know the exact name of the objects they are interested in. They may know one of more attributes of the objects and can query the directory to get a list of objects that match the attributes. For example, "find all duplex printers in Building 26." A directory service allows a user to find any object given one of its attributes.

A directory service can:

- Enforce security defined by administrators to keep information safe from intruders
- Distribute a directory across many computers in a network
- Replicate a directory to make it available to more users and resistant to failure
- Partition a directory into multiple stores to allow the storage of a very large numbers of objects

A directory service is both a management tool and an end user tool. As the number of objects in a network grows, the directory service becomes essential. The directory service is the hub around which a large distributed system turns.

directory system agent (DSA)   The directory system agent is the process that provides access to the physical storage for Active Directory.

discretionary access-control list (DACL)
A discretionary access-control list is a list that is controlled by the owner of an object and that specifies the access that particular users or groups can have to the object. See access control list.

distinguished name (DN)   A distinguished name is a name that identifies an object by indicating its current location in the directory hierarchy. The name is formed by concatenating the relative distinguished names of the object and each of its ancestors up to the root of the directory partition. An object's distinguished name is unique across the entire directory, but it changes if the object is moved or renamed. For example, "CN=John Smith, CN=Users,DC=Microsoft,DC=com" is the distinguished name of the John Smith object in the Users container on the Microsoft.com domain.

domain   A domain is a single security boundary of a Windows NT/Windows 2000 computer network. On a standalone workstation, the domain is the computer itself. A domain can span more than one physical location. Every domain has its own security policies and security relationships with other domains. When multiple domains are connected by trust relationships and share a common schema, configuration, and global catalog, you have a tree. Multiple trees can be connected together into a forest.

domain component (DC)   A domain component is used in distinguished names (DNs) to indicate an identifier for a part of an object's network domain. For example, /O=Internet/DC=COM/DC=Microsoft/ CN=Users/CN=John Smith contains the Domain Components "COM" and "Microsoft".

domain controller   A domain controller (DC) is a server computer that holds Active Directory replicas of the domain partition for the local domain, as well as replicas of the schema and configuration partitions for the enterprise forest. A DC can also hold a replica of the global catalog.

domain local group   A domain local group can be used on access-control lists (ACLs) only in its own domain. A domain local group can contain users and global groups from any domain in the forest, universal groups, and other domain local groups in its own domain.

domain name service (DNS)   A domain name service (DNS) is used in Internet routing to convert an IP address to a friendlier text address.

domain partition   A domain partition is a directory partition that contains the objects, such as users and computers, associated with the local domain. A domain can have multiple DCs; a forest can have multiple domains. Each DC stores a full replica of the domain partition for its local domain, but does not store replicas of the domain partitions for other domains.

DSA   *See* directory system agent.

E

enumerator   An enumerator is an object that supports the **IEnumVARIANT** interface, which provides a **Next** method to enumerate objects in a collection.

F

forest   A forest is a set of one or more trees that do not form a contiguous namespace. All trees in a forest share a common schema, configuration, and global catalog. All trees in a given forest trust each other using transitive hierarchical Kerberos trust relationships. Unlike trees, a forest does not need a distinct name. A forest exists as a set of cross-reference objects and Kerberos trust relationships known to the member trees. Trees in a forest form a hierarchy for the purposes of Kerberos trust; the tree name at the root of the trust tree can be used to refer to a given forest.

G

global catalog (GC)   An Active Directory forest consists of several directory partitions. Often, the user or application does not know what partition contains a desired object. The global catalog (GC) servers enable users and applications to find an object in a forest, given one or more attributes of the target object.

A global catalog server is a domain controller that contains a full replica of its own domain and a partial replica of every other domain in the forest. Like all domain controllers, it contains the schema and configuration partitions as well. This means that a GC server holds a replica of every object in Active Directory, but most replicas contain only a small subset of attributes. The attributes in the partial replicas are those most frequently used in search operations (such as a user's first and last names, login names, and so on)—attributes that are most useful to locate a full replica of the object. A GC search yields the distinguished name (DN) of the desired object; given the DN, an application can connect to a domain controller holding a full replica of the object.

Administrators specify which domain controllers are global catalog servers. The Active Directory replication system automatically maintains partial replicas held on global catalog servers. The properties replicated into the global catalog include a base set defined by Microsoft. Administrators can specify additional properties to meet the needs of their installation.

global catalog server   The global catalog server is a Windows 2000 domain controller that holds a copy of the global catalog for the forest.

global group   A global group can appear on access-control lists (ACLs) anywhere in the forest. A global group can contain users and other global groups from its own domain.

GPE   *See* Group Policy Editor.

GPO   *See* group policy object.

group   The three group types (global, domain local, universal) provide a rich and flexible access-control environment, while reducing replication traffic to the global catalog (GC) when group membership changes. A universal group appears in the GC, but will contain primarily global groups from domains in the forest. Once the global groups are established, the membership in the universal group will change infrequently. Global groups appear in the GC, but not their members. Membership changes in global groups are not replicated outside of the domain where they are defined. Domain local groups are valid only in the domain where they are defined and do not appear in the GC at all.

group policy   Group policy is an extensible framework that refers to applying policy to the "groups" of computers and/or users contained within Active Directory containers. This type of policy includes not only registry-based policies, but many types of policy data, such as file deployment, application deployment, logon/logoff scripts and startup/shutdown scripts, domain security, IPSEC, and so on.

The "blobs of policy" are referred to as group policy objects (GPO).

This new infrastructure works with a document-centric approach. In addition to the enhanced polices that are available, the directory hierarchy allows group policy to affect computers and users in sites, domains, or organizational units (SDOU), as well as filtering effective policy based on security group membership. GPO(s) are associated (linked) with these Active Directory containers: sites, domains, organizational units (SDOU). This is analogous to Microsoft Word permitting multiple .dot templates to specify the formatting of a .doc file.

Group Policy Editor   The Group Policy Editor is a tool that is used for configuring policy. The Group Policy Editor (GPE) has a relationship to group policy objects (GPO) that is similar to the one that Microsoft Word has to .dot (template) files.

group policy object (GPO)   A group policy object (GPO) is a virtual collection of policies. It is given a unique name, such as a GUID. GPOs store group policy settings in two locations: a group policy container (GPC) (preferred) and a group policy template (GPT). The group policy container is an Active Directory object that stores version information, status information and other policy information. The group policy template is used for file-based data, and stores software policy, script, and deployment information. The group policy template is located on the system volume folder of the domain controller.

A GPO can be associated with one or more Active Directory containers, such as a site, domain, or organizational unit. Multiple containers can be associated with the same GPO, and a single container can have more than one associated GPO.

In addition, by default every computer receives a local group policy object (LGPO) that contains only policies specifically for security. It is also possible for the administrator to set and apply different local group policies on individual computers. This is useful for computers that are not members of a domain, or computers that the administrator wishes to exempt from group policy inherited from the domain.

I

inheritance   Inheritance in the Active Directory schema is the ability to define new object classes from existing object classes. See *Class Inheritance in the Active Directory Schema*.

Active Directory also supports inheritance of security protections, which enables an administrator to specify access control settings on a directory object such that the settings can be inherited by child objects below the parent object in the directory hierarchy. See *Inheritance and Delegation of Administration*.

interface   In ADSI, interface refers to a COM interface. Each COM interface defines a set of related member functions that provide access to COM objects. ADSI defines and implements a set of COM interfaces and related APIs for providing access to directory service objects.

Internet Engineering Task Force (IETF)
See *www.ietf.org* for information on the IETF and its activities.

Intersite Messaging Service (ISM)
ISM supports pluggable transports for asynchronous, site-to-site messaging. Each transport serves two major roles: to send and receive messages, and to make topology queries (such as what are the various sites connected by this transport, and at what cost?).

Two ISMs are shipped in Windows 2000, remote procedure call (RPC), and simple mail transfer protocol (SMTP).

ISM *See* Intersite Messaging Service.

L

latency Latency is an intrinsic characteristic of Active Directory replication. Latency is the delay between the time an update is applied to a given replica and the time that the update is propagated to some other replica. Latency is sometimes referred to as propagation delay.

The replication model used in Active Directory is called multi-master loose consistency with convergence. In this model, the directory can have many replicas; a replication system propagates changes made at any given replica to all other replicas. The replicas are not guaranteed to be consistent with each other at any particular point in time ("loose consistency"), since changes can be applied to any replica at any time ("multi-master"). If the system is allowed to reach a steady state, in which no new updates are occurring and all previous updates have been completely replicated, all replicas are guaranteed to converge on the same set of values ("convergence").

LDAP *See* Lightweight Directory Access Protocol.

Lightweight Directory Access Protocol (LDAP) LDAP the standard Internet communications protocol used to communicate with Active Directory. Both versions 2 and 3 of LDAP are supported.

local group As in earlier versions of Windows NT, administrators on member servers and workstations can create local groups. These remain strictly local to the machine where they are created, and do not appear in the directory.

Windows 2000 introduces the domain local group which does appear in the directory. Domain local groups provide the functionality of local groups defined on domain controllers in earlier versions of Windows NT.

M

MAPI *See* Messaging API.

Messaging API (MAPI) Active Directory provides MAPI support for backwards compatibility with Exchange applications. New applications should use ADSI for accessing the directory.

Microsoft Management Console (MMC) The MMC is the Windows 2000 user interface for managing networks.

mixed mode Windows 2000 domains are installed in mixed mode, by default. In mixed mode, the domain may have Windows NT 4.0 backup domain controllers present. Nested groups are not supported in mixed mode. *See* native mode.

MMC *See* Microsoft Management Console.

N

name resolution Name resolution is the process of translating a name into some object or information that the name represents.

namespace A namespace is a directory service that uses a particular syntax for naming conventions. Examples are:

LDAP

WinNT

"//MyWorkstation/MyName"

"//MyServer/C=US/O=MS/CN=MyName"

NDS

"//Planets/O=Mars/OU=DEV"

Novell NetWare 3.x

"//Docs/MyNw3xPrinter"

naming context (NC)   A naming context (also called a directory partition) is a contiguous Active Directory subtree that is replicated on one or more Windows 2000 domain controllers (DCs) in a forest. *See* directory partition.

native mode   A Windows 2000 Domain is in native mode when:

- All domain controllers in the domain have been upgraded to Windows 2000
- An administrator has enabled the native mode operation using the domain property page in the Active Directory Users and Computers snap-in

Domains must be operating in native mode for nested groups to be supported. *See* mixed mode.

NDS   NDS refers to NetWare Directory Services.

O

object   In ADSI, an object refers to a COM object that implements one or more interfaces. For more information, see *The Component Object Model.*

In Active Directory, an object is the basic named unit of storage. A directory object is an instance of an object class, which is defined in the Active Directory schema.

object class   An object class is a formal definition of a specific kind of object that can be stored in the directory. An object class is a distinct, named set of attributes that represents something concrete, such as a user, a printer, or an application. The attributes hold data describing the thing that is identified by the directory object. Attributes of a user might include the user's given name, surname, and e-mail address. The terms object class and class are used interchangeably.

object class instance   An object class instance is an object with a given object class. This term is used to distinguish between the definition of a class and a discrete occurrence of the class. For example, storing a **user** object for "James Smith" in the directory service creates an instance of user. Typically, you'd just say "object" rather than "object class instance."

object identifier (OID)   An OID is a numeric value that unambiguously identifies an object class, attribute, or syntax in a directory service. An OID is represented as a dotted decimal string (for example, "1.2.3.4"). Enterprises (and individuals) can obtain a root OID from an issuing authority and use it to allocate additional OIDs. See *Object Identifiers (OIDs).*

OID   *See* object identifier.

operation policy   An operation is the interaction that a subject wants to have with an object. For example, when a user (the subject), wants to access (the operation), a given server (the object), over the network, a policy determines whether that access will be allowed.

operational attribute   An operation attribute is an attribute implemented internally by a particular directory implementation. Operational attributes do not appear in the schema and must be requested explicitly. Operational Attributes occurred originally in the X.500 specifications for a directory service and have been carried over into the LDAP version 3 specifications (RFC 2251). RFC 2251 requires support for certain operational attributes; a given directory implementation may implement any number of others.

P

partial update   A partial update can occur while replication is in progress if an application reads an object during a brief interval when some, but not all, of an update has been replicated to the DC from which the application is reading.

PDC   *See* primary domain controller.

primary domain controller (PDC)   A primary domain controller is a computer that runs a Windows NT Server that authenticates logons and maintains the directory database for a Windows NT 4.0 domain. A PDC is not used in Windows 2000. Instead, one domain controller is designated as the PDC for backwards compatibility.

property   A property is a value that can be read or written. Properties are associated with specific interfaces on an object.

provider   A provider is a vendor who supplies an implementation of the ADSI objects for a particular namespace.

Q

query   A query is a request to a directory service to return the location of one or more specified directory service objects.

R

referral   A referral is returned to an LDAP client by a directory system agent (DSA) when the query presented by the client cannot be serviced locally, and the DSA has "knowledge information" about other DSAs that can handle the query.

remote procedure call (RPC)   A remote procedure call is a system for calling software procedures on a different machine using a

network. For more information, see *Microsoft RPC Model*.

replication   Active Directory provides multi-master replication. Multi-master replication means that all replicas of a given partition are writeable. This allows updates to be applied to any replica of a given partition. Active Directory replication system propagates the changes from a given replica to all other replicas. Replication is automatic and transparent.

RPC   *See* remote procedure call.

S

SACL   *See* system access-control list.

schema   The Active Directory schema contains formal definitions of every object class that can be created in an Active Directory forest. The schema also contains formal definitions of every attribute that can exist in an Active Directory object. See *Active Directory Schema*.

In ADSI, the schema management interfaces supply a means of reading and setting the information associated with class, attribute, and syntax definitions. You can use these interfaces with the Active Directory schema as well as with the schemas of other directory services.

schema partition   A schema partition is a directory partition that contains the **classSchema** and **attributeSchema** objects that define the types of objects that can exist in the Active Directory forest. Every DC in an enterprise forest has a replica of the same schema partition.

security identifier (SID)   A security identifier is a variable length value that uniquely identifies a security principal (such as a user or group). SIDs are used in security descriptors and access-control entries.

service principal name (SPN)   A service principal name (SPN) is the name by which a client uniquely identifies an instance of a service. See *Service Principal Names*.

site   A site is a location in a network where Active Directory servers are held. A site is defined as one or more well connected TCP/IP subnets. "Well connected" means that network connectivity is highly reliable and fast. Defining a site as a set of subnets allows administrators to quickly and easily configure Active Directory access and replication topology to take advantage of the physical network. When users log in, Active Directory clients find Active Directory servers in the same site as the user. Since machines in the same site are close to each other in network terms, communication among machines is reliable, fast, and efficient.

structure rules   Structure rules define the possible tree structure of Active Directory, that is, which object classes can contain which object classes. In Active Directory, the **possSuperiors** and **systemPossSuperiors** attributes in the schema definition of each object class specifies the object classes that can contain instances of the class. See *Characteristics of Object Classes*.

system access-control list (SACL) A system access-control list controls the generation of audit messages for attempts to access a securable object. The ability to get or set an object's SACL is controlled by a privilege typically held only by system administrators.

T

Top   In the Active Directory schema, *Top* is the object class from which all other object classes are ultimately derived.

trustee   In Windows NT security, a trustee is the user account, group account, or logon session to which an access-control entry (ACE)

applies. Each ACE in an access-control list (ACL) applies to one trustee.

U

universal group   A universal group can appear in access-control lists (ACLs) anywhere in the forest, and can contain other universal groups, global groups, and users from anywhere in the forest. Enterprises with a single domain should not use universal groups. Typically, the members of a universal group are global groups rather than individual users. See *What Type of Group to Use*.

update sequence number (USN)   An update sequence number is a 64-bit number that each Active Directory server maintains to indicate the sequence of changes on the local DC. Each DC increments its USN whenever it modifies a directory object. The DC assigns the incremented USN to the **uSNChanged** attribute of the object that changed. The **uSNChanged** attribute is not replicated, so an object's **uSNChanged** value can be different on different DCs.

user principal name (UPN)   A user principal name is a "friendly" name for a user or group, shorter than the distinguished name, and easier to remember. It is composed of a shorthand name for the user and the domain name service (DNS) name of the tree where the user object resides. For example, someone in the microsoft.com tree might have the UPN *someone@microsoft.com*.

USN   *See* update sequence number.

X

X.500   X.500 is a set of standards that define a distributed directory service, developed by the International Organization for Standardization (ISO).

INDEX 1

Active Directory Programmer's Guide Coverage

INDEX 2

Active Directory Reference – Alphabetical Listing

Active Directory Programming Elements

Active Directory Programming Elements, *(continued)*

O

LDAP Programming Elements

B

C

L

Q

V

INDEX 3

ADSI, ADSI Exchange, and Group Policy Programmer's Guides Coverage

ADSI Programmer's Guide Coverage

ADSI Programmer's Guide Coverage *(continued)*

ADSI Exchange Programmer's Guide Coverage

Group Policy Reference

INDEX 4

ADSI Reference – Alphabetical Listing

MICROSOFT LICENSE AGREEMENT

Book Companion CD

IMPORTANT—READ CAREFULLY: This Microsoft End-User License Agreement ("EULA") is a legal agreement between you (either an individual or an entity) and Microsoft Corporation for the Microsoft product identified above, which includes computer software and may include associated media, printed materials, and "online" or electronic documentation ("SOFTWARE PRODUCT"). Any component included within the SOFTWARE PRODUCT that is accompanied by a separate End-User License Agreement shall be governed by such agreement and not the terms set forth below. By installing, copying, or otherwise using the SOFTWARE PRODUCT, you agree to be bound by the terms of this EULA. If you do not agree to the terms of this EULA, you are not authorized to install, copy, or otherwise use the SOFTWARE PRODUCT; you may, however, return the SOFTWARE PRODUCT, along with all printed materials and other items that form a part of the Microsoft product that includes the SOFTWARE PRODUCT, to the place you obtained them for a full refund.

SOFTWARE PRODUCT LICENSE

The SOFTWARE PRODUCT is protected by United States copyright laws and international copyright treaties, as well as other intellectual property laws and treaties. The SOFTWARE PRODUCT is licensed, not sold.

1. **GRANT OF LICENSE.** This EULA grants you the following rights:

    a. **Software Product.** You may install and use one copy of the SOFTWARE PRODUCT on a single computer. The primary user of the computer on which the SOFTWARE PRODUCT is installed may make a second copy for his or her exclusive use on a portable computer.

    b. **Storage/Network Use.** You may also store or install a copy of the SOFTWARE PRODUCT on a storage device, such as a network server, used only to install or run the SOFTWARE PRODUCT on your other computers over an internal network; however, you must acquire and dedicate a license for each separate computer on which the SOFTWARE PRODUCT is installed or run from the storage device. A license for the SOFTWARE PRODUCT may not be shared or used concurrently on different computers.

    c. **License Pak.** If you have acquired this EULA in a Microsoft License Pak, you may make the number of additional copies of the computer software portion of the SOFTWARE PRODUCT authorized on the printed copy of this EULA, and you may use each copy in the manner specified above. You are also entitled to make a corresponding number of secondary copies for portable computer use as specified above.

    d. **Sample Code.** Solely with respect to portions, if any, of the SOFTWARE PRODUCT that are identified within the SOFTWARE PRODUCT as sample code (the "SAMPLE CODE"):

        i. **Use and Modification.** Microsoft grants you the right to use and modify the source code version of the SAMPLE CODE, *provided* you comply with subsection (d)(iii) below. You may not distribute the SAMPLE CODE, or any modified version of the SAMPLE CODE, in source code form.

        ii. **Redistributable Files.** Provided you comply with subsection (d)(iii) below, Microsoft grants you a nonexclusive, royalty-free right to reproduce and distribute the object code version of the SAMPLE CODE and of any modified SAMPLE CODE, other than SAMPLE CODE, or any modified version thereof, designated as not redistributable in the Readme file that forms a part of the SOFTWARE PRODUCT (the "Non-Redistributable Sample Code"). All SAMPLE CODE other than the Non-Redistributable Sample Code is collectively referred to as the "REDISTRIBUTABLES."

        iii. **Redistribution Requirements.** If you redistribute the REDISTRIBUTABLES, you agree to: (i) distribute the REDISTRIBUTABLES in object code form only in conjunction with and as a part of your software application product; (ii) not use Microsoft's name, logo, or trademarks to market your software application product; (iii) include a valid copyright notice on your software application product; (iv) indemnify, hold harmless, and defend Microsoft from and against any claims or lawsuits, including attorney's fees, that arise or result from the use or distribution of your software application product; and (v) not permit further distribution of the REDISTRIBUTABLES by your end user. Contact Microsoft for the applicable royalties due and other licensing terms for all other uses and/or distribution of the REDISTRIBUTABLES.

2. **DESCRIPTION OF OTHER RIGHTS AND LIMITATIONS.**

    - **Limitations on Reverse Engineering, Decompilation, and Disassembly.** You may not reverse engineer, decompile, or disassemble the SOFTWARE PRODUCT, except and only to the extent that such activity is expressly permitted by applicable law notwithstanding this limitation.

    - **Separation of Components.** The SOFTWARE PRODUCT is licensed as a single product. Its component parts may not be separated for use on more than one computer.

    - **Rental.** You may not rent, lease, or lend the SOFTWARE PRODUCT.

- **Support Services.** Microsoft may, but is not obligated to, provide you with support services related to the SOFTWARE PRODUCT ("Support Services"). Use of Support Services is governed by the Microsoft policies and programs described in the user manual, in "online" documentation, and/or in other Microsoft-provided materials. Any supplemental software code provided to you as part of the Support Services shall be considered part of the SOFTWARE PRODUCT and subject to the terms and conditions of this EULA. With respect to technical information you provide to Microsoft as part of the Support Services, Microsoft may use such information for its business purposes, including for product support and development. Microsoft will not utilize such technical information in a form that personally identifies you.

- **Software Transfer.** You may permanently transfer all of your rights under this EULA, provided you retain no copies, you transfer all of the SOFTWARE PRODUCT (including all component parts, the media and printed materials, any upgrades, this EULA, and, if applicable, the Certificate of Authenticity), **and** the recipient agrees to the terms of this EULA.

- **Termination.** Without prejudice to any other rights, Microsoft may terminate this EULA if you fail to comply with the terms and conditions of this EULA. In such event, you must destroy all copies of the SOFTWARE PRODUCT and all of its component parts.

3. **COPYRIGHT.** All title and copyrights in and to the SOFTWARE PRODUCT (including but not limited to any images, photographs, animations, video, audio, music, text, SAMPLE CODE, REDISTRIBUTABLES, and "applets" incorporated into the SOFTWARE PRODUCT) and any copies of the SOFTWARE PRODUCT are owned by Microsoft or its suppliers. The SOFT-WARE PRODUCT is protected by copyright laws and international treaty provisions. Therefore, you must treat the SOFTWARE PRODUCT like any other copyrighted material **except** that you may install the SOFTWARE PRODUCT on a single computer provided you keep the original solely for backup or archival purposes. You may not copy the printed materials accompanying the SOFTWARE PRODUCT.

4. **U.S. GOVERNMENT RESTRICTED RIGHTS.** The SOFTWARE PRODUCT and documentation are provided with RESTRICTED RIGHTS. Use, duplication, or disclosure by the Government is subject to restrictions as set forth in subparagraph (c)(1)(ii) of the Rights in Technical Data and Computer Software clause at DFARS 252.227-7013 or subparagraphs (c)(1) and (2) of the Commercial Computer Software—Restricted Rights at 48 CFR 52.227-19, as applicable. Manufacturer is Microsoft Corporation/One Microsoft Way/Redmond, WA 98052-6399.

5. **EXPORT RESTRICTIONS.** You agree that you will not export or re-export the SOFTWARE PRODUCT, any part thereof, or any process or service that is the direct product of the SOFTWARE PRODUCT (the foregoing collectively referred to as the "Restricted Components"), to any country, person, entity, or end user subject to U.S. export restrictions. You specifically agree not to export or re-export any of the Restricted Components (i) to any country to which the U.S. has embargoed or restricted the export of goods or services, which currently include, but are not necessarily limited to, Cuba, Iran, Iraq, Libya, North Korea, Sudan, and Syria, or to any national of any such country, wherever located, who intends to transmit or transport the Restricted Components back to such country; (ii) to any end user who you know or have reason to know will utilize the Restricted Components in the design, development, or production of nuclear, chemical, or biological weapons; or (iii) to any end user who has been prohibited from participating in U.S. export transactions by any federal agency of the U.S. government. You warrant and represent that neither the BXA nor any other U.S. federal agency has suspended, revoked, or denied your export privileges.

DISCLAIMER OF WARRANTY

NO WARRANTIES OR CONDITIONS. MICROSOFT EXPRESSLY DISCLAIMS ANY WARRANTY OR CONDITION FOR THE SOFTWARE PRODUCT. THE SOFTWARE PRODUCT AND ANY RELATED DOCUMENTATION ARE PROVIDED "AS IS" WITHOUT WARRANTY OR CONDITION OF ANY KIND, EITHER EXPRESS OR IMPLIED, INCLUDING, WITHOUT LIMITA-TION, THE IMPLIED WARRANTIES OF MERCHANTABILITY, FITNESS FOR A PARTICULAR PURPOSE, OR NONINFRINGEMENT. THE ENTIRE RISK ARISING OUT OF USE OR PERFORMANCE OF THE SOFTWARE PRODUCT REMAINS WITH YOU.

LIMITATION OF LIABILITY. TO THE MAXIMUM EXTENT PERMITTED BY APPLICABLE LAW, IN NO EVENT SHALL MICROSOFT OR ITS SUPPLIERS BE LIABLE FOR ANY SPECIAL, INCIDENTAL, INDIRECT, OR CONSEQUENTIAL DAM-AGES WHATSOEVER (INCLUDING, WITHOUT LIMITATION, DAMAGES FOR LOSS OF BUSINESS PROFITS, BUSINESS INTERRUPTION, LOSS OF BUSINESS INFORMATION, OR ANY OTHER PECUNIARY LOSS) ARISING OUT OF THE USE OF OR INABILITY TO USE THE SOFTWARE PRODUCT OR THE PROVISION OF OR FAILURE TO PROVIDE SUPPORT SERVICES, EVEN IF MICROSOFT HAS BEEN ADVISED OF THE POSSIBILITY OF SUCH DAMAGES. IN ANY CASE, MICROSOFT'S ENTIRE LIABILITY UNDER ANY PROVISION OF THIS EULA SHALL BE LIMITED TO THE GREATER OF THE AMOUNT ACTUALLY PAID BY YOU FOR THE SOFTWARE PRODUCT OR US$5.00; PROVIDED, HOWEVER, IF YOU HAVE ENTERED INTO A MICROSOFT SUPPORT SERVICES AGREEMENT, MICROSOFT'S ENTIRE LIABILITY REGARDING SUPPORT SERVICES SHALL BE GOVERNED BY THE TERMS OF THAT AGREEMENT. BECAUSE SOME STATES AND JURISDICTIONS DO NOT ALLOW THE EXCLUSION OR LIMITATION OF LIABILITY, THE ABOVE LIMITATION MAY NOT APPLY TO YOU.

MISCELLANEOUS

This EULA is governed by the laws of the State of Washington USA, except and only to the extent that applicable law mandates govern-ing law of a different jurisdiction.

Should you have any questions concerning this EULA, or if you desire to contact Microsoft for any reason, please contact the Microsoft subsidiary serving your country, or write: Microsoft Sales Information Center/One Microsoft Way/Redmond, WA 98052-6399.

Proof of Purchase

0-7356-0992-6

Do not send this card with your registration.
Use this card as proof of purchase if participating in a promotion or
rebate offer on *Active Directory™ Developer's Reference Library*. Card must be used in conjunction with
other proof(s) of payment such as your dated sales receipt—see offer details.

Active Directory™ Developer's Reference Library

WHERE DID YOU PURCHASE THIS PRODUCT?

CUSTOMER NAME

Microsoft®

mspress.microsoft.com

Microsoft Press, PO Box 97017, Redmond, WA 98073-9830

OWNER REGISTRATION CARD   *Register Today!*   0-7356-0992-6

Return the bottom portion of this card to register today.

Active Directory™ Developer's Reference Library

FIRST NAME   MIDDLE INITIAL   LAST NAME

INSTITUTION OR COMPANY NAME

ADDRESS

CITY   STATE   ZIP

                                                (   )
E-MAIL ADDRESS   PHONE NUMBER

U.S. and Canada addresses only. Fill in information above and mail postage-free.
Please mail only the bottom half of this page.

For information about Microsoft Press®
products, visit our Web site at
mspress.microsoft.com

Microsoft®

Into the Unknown

The Story of Exploration

Into the Unknown
The Story of Exploration

Published by
The National Geographic Society

Gilbert M. Grosvenor
President and Chairman of the Board

Owen R. Anderson
Executive Vice President

Robert L. Breeden
Senior Vice President, Publications and Educational Media

Prepared by
National Geographic Book Service

Charles O. Hyman
Director

Ross S. Bennett
Associate Director

Margaret Sedeen
Managing Editor

Susan C. Eckert
Director of Research

Staff for this book

Jonathan B. Tourtellot
Editor

Lynn Addison Yorke
Assistant Editor

Lise Swinson Sajewski
Chief Researcher

Mary B. Dickinson
Edward Lanouette
Elizabeth L. Newhouse
Robert M. Poole
David F. Robinson
Margaret Sedeen
Editor-Writers

Jennifer Gorham Ackerman
Paulette L. Claus
Susan C. Eckert
Lydia Howarth
Mary P. Luders
Melanie Patt-Corner
Jean Kaplan Teichroew
Penelope A. Timbers
Editorial Researchers

Kerry J. Kreiton
Brian L. McKean
Geography Interns

Leah Bendavid-Val
Illustrations Editor

David Ross
Illustrations Researcher

D. Samantha Johnston
Illustrations Assistant

Karen F. Edwards
Traffic Manager

Lydia Howarth
Jean Kaplan Teichroew
Map Coordinators

Maps by
John D. Garst, Jr.
Judith F. Bell
Donald L. Carrick
Marguerite S. Dunn
Hildegard B. Groves
Sharon J. Hongell
Gary M. Johnson
Joseph F. Ochlak
Susan Sanford
Nancy S. Stanford
Alexander M. Tait
Tibor G. Toth

R. Gary Colbert
Administrative Assistant

Teresita Cóquia Sison
Editorial Assistant

Teresa P. Barry
James B. Enzinna
Susan G. Zenel
Indexers

David M. Seager
Art Director

Charlotte Golin
Design Assistant

John T. Dunn
Technical Director

Richard S. Wain
Production Manager

Andrea Crosman
Production Coordinator

Leslie A. Adams
Production Assistant

David V. Evans
Engraving and Printing

Ratri Banerjee
Gretchen C. Bordelon
Cathryn P. Buchanan
Jean Shapiro Cantu
Michael Frost
Valerie Mattingley
Anne Meadows
Tom Melham
Jennifer Moseley
Suzanne Kane Poole
Shirley L. Scott
Anne E. Withers
Contributors

Color enhancement of engravings and selected photographs by Michael A. Hampshire

First edition: 170,000 copies 336 pages, 266 illustrations, plus 23 maps.

Page 2: A model of Henry Hudson's 17th-century ship, *Half Moon*, crests the globe. The hourglass, compass, calipers, and globe are all from the 18th and early 19th centuries. The map is a reproduction of an 18th-century original. Photography by Kan.

Contents

Foreword

"Is there anything left on Earth to explore?" It's one of the questions people most often ask me. In the sense of finding unknown lands or oceans, as Columbus or Balboa did, the answer is no. But in another sense, the story of exploration has just begun.

Into the Unknown chronicles that story from the first explorers to push back the edge of the known world. Egyptians, Greeks, Arabs, and Chinese left records of their visits to new lands; sadly, others—Polynesians, native Americans, Malays—did not. The widest-ranging explorers were the Europeans and their progeny, who began to fan out over the globe in the 15th century. Great though these explorers were, theirs was often a parochial "unknown"; the lands they discovered had been long occupied by other people. Some explorers just followed local guides.

Today, explorers not only press on to realms beyond human habitation—ice caps, ocean deeps, and the reaches of space—they seek also to understand the world we have now encompassed, including its past and, in some ways, its future.

Sometimes present and past collide. In 1986 National Geographic writer Thomas Abercrombie, having used satellite images to pinpoint the source of the Indus River in a remote corner of China, obtained government permission to approach by land—only to find his expedition barred by a hazard of Marco Polo's era: warlords who did not acknowledge the authority of Beijing.

Explorers of both past and present ventured forth, ideally, to seek knowledge. James Cook perhaps epitomizes that "pure" explorer. But many went forth for other reasons—trade, fame, gold, God, conquest, safety from conquest. Missionaries went to convert; pioneers to colonize. Conquistadores set courses of greed, and left wakes of blood. Were they all explorers? This book counts them so if they fit its title, if they did go "into the unknown"—unknown as they saw it—however honorable or heinous we judge their motives.

They did share one thing—the discoverer's thrill. Can it still happen? In 1979 I joined a party that cut through the Arctic Ocean ice pack and dived beneath it. We were only a few miles from the North Pole, goal of famous explorers like Peary and Nansen, who struggled for months across jagged pressure ridges formed by this ice. From below, with the cold seeping into our insulated wet suits and the hollow whoosh of the breathing hoses in our ears, we could look up at those pressure ridges to see how the clear ice had been folded and twisted into fantastic structures—cathedrals of ice atop a darkling sea. "No one has ever seen this before," I thought, and in that moment knew, just a little, that thrill the great explorers knew.

What were these explorers like? After each chapter in *Into the Unknown* you will find a story about one or two of them. Some were famous,

Destination: the Pole. Struggling to heave a dogsled over cracked, jumbled Arctic Ocean ice, the Steger International Polar Expedition drives northward in 1986, much as Robert Peary's expedition did in 1909. Steger crossed nearly 500 miles of ice to reach the Pole, one of the few to succeed among the hopefuls who now make the attempt each year, by sled, ski, snowmobile, helicopter, even motorcycle.

some less so. To convey more vividly the nature of their adventures, our writers have sometimes used dramatic devices—an imaginary trial, some correspondence, a companion's viewpoint, a re-created scene. You'll find the stories enjoyable to read and, unlike many television docudramas, accurate; National Geographic's researchers have verified every event.

Some explorers you'll meet in this book—Peary, Beebe, Rock, Cousteau, Ballard, and others—received National Geographic support. That support continues today, for explorers you will read about tomorrow.

What's left to discover? In *Into the Unknown* you will learn how ocean floor exploration has revolutionized our ideas of geology and biology, how rain forest explorers find new medicines, and how space travel has changed our view of our own planet.

Today we explore our past, too. Archaeologist-divers in the Mediterranean seek traces of ancient civilizations—and perhaps of *their* explorers—in shipwrecks on the seafloor.

And we explore our future. Scientists in Antarctica have discovered remnants of forests that flourished about three million years ago; some of the wood can still burn. If Antarctica was that free of ice, that recently, what does today's global greenhouse effect portend for tomorrow?

The story is far from over.

Gilbert M Grosvenor

Early Quests

By Ian Cameron

Monument to a monarch and her passion for exploration, the mortuary temple of Egypt's Queen Hatshepsut cascades from the Deir el Bahri cliffs near ancient Thebes. Relief carvings on the colonnades trace a reign crowned by a 15th-century B.C. sea expedition to the distant land of Punt on the east coast of Africa. These detailed pictures, which show African natives, reed houses on stilts, and long-tailed apes, are among the earliest known records of geographical discovery.

Two *Homo erectus* hunters stood before a fresh kill. It was their first for many days, and not enough to feed all 34 men, women, and children in their group. Hunting had been bad during the dry season and the group was desperate for food. They decided to move on—into the unknown. They climbed the mountains that rimmed the horizon, crossed a vast plain covered in shrub, then came to a slow-flowing river. Here at last they found water and an abundance of game. Here they would stay until food once again became scarce.

Human beings had discovered another part of their planet.

Such scenes were commonplace half a million to a million years ago, as our ancestors fanned out from Africa to populate the Earth. What journeys they must have made! Stone Age hunters gazed in wonder at lakes and mountains no human had set eyes on before. These were surely among the greatest moments in the exploration of our planet, for few people have ever journeyed into so vast an unknown.

Like their Stone Age ancestors, people of ancient civilizations around the globe no doubt traveled remarkable distances and made great discoveries. But scant records—or no records at all—remain to tell the tale of these fantastic voyages. Most of them are lost to us.

The Egyptians were the first people to make any records of their travels. From hieroglyphics and temple reliefs we can put together accounts of their voyages to a distant and mysterious land they called Punt.

The story began on the River Nile, around 3500 B.C. The Nile is an ideal river for waterborne traffic because it flows from south to north, while the prevailing wind blows up it from north to south. By 3500 B.C. the Egyptians were building long low ships they could row downstream with the current and sail upstream with the wind. These boats were excellent for river work but useless on the open sea, as they were built from papyrus—abundant in Egypt but unsuitable for oceangoing vessels. Before the Egyptians could leave the Nile or venture out of coastal waters they needed timber that could stand the pounding of waves. In 2600 B.C. King Snefru sent ships to Byblos, in Lebanon. From the Phoenicians who lived there on the shores of the Mediterranean, the Egyptians obtained cedar.

With the cedar the Egyptians built seaworthy ships, and around 2500 B.C. Pharaoh Sahure sent his new fleet to search for Punt, the legendary Land of the Gods—so called because Egyptians believed it was the home of their earliest ancestors, and because it was said to abound in all those treasures Egypt longed for: ebony and ivory, silver and gold, and incense to burn on its altars.

We cannot be certain exactly where Punt was, but we can make an

King Snefru 2600 B.C.
Egyptians:
    King Sahure 2500 B.C.
    Hennu 2000 B.C.
    Queen Hatshepsut 1493 B.C.
King Necho II 600 B.C.
Hanno 450 B.C.
Alexander the Great 334-323 B.C.
Nearchus 325-324 B.C.
Pytheas 325 B.C.
Eudoxus 120 B.C.

Long on legends and short on facts, the accounts of early explorers make guessing games of their exact routes and destinations. Egyptian mariners sailed many times to the place they called Punt, but forgot in the centuries between trips where they had gone; we still cannot be sure of its location on the map. Did a Phoenician crew hired by Egypt's King Necho II really circumnavigate Africa in 600 B.C. as Herodotus reports? No other ancient historian concurs—yet contemporary

Greek maps correctly depicted Africa as an island joined to Asia. And what of the Greek astronomer Pytheas, who described voyaging beyond Britain to Ultima Thule—the edge of the Arctic? Although early chroniclers deride him as a charlatan, modern scholars consider his voyage real, and as remarkable as the better recorded campaigns that took Alexander the Great from the Mediterranean to the Indus River.

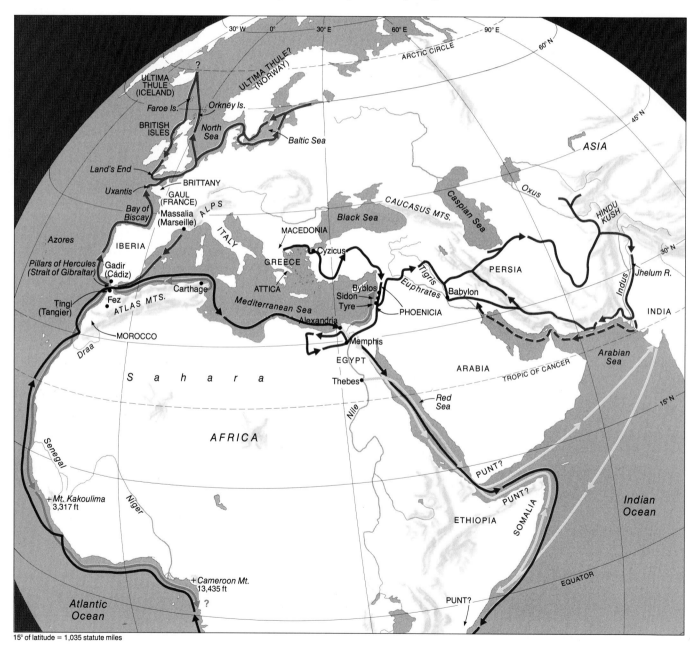

15° of latitude = 1,035 statute miles

Timeless beasts of burden, camels continue to work in modern Ethiopia, a possible site of Punt. Queen Hatshepsut's retinue, frozen in relief in her temple at Deir el Bahri (below), appears on another wall marching to Punt with gifts for Eti, its queen (lower).

informed guess. When Sahure's fleet returned, the ships were laden with 80,000 measures of myrrh; 6,000 bars of electrum, a gold-silver alloy; and 2,600 logs of wood—probably ebony. The state records that list this cargo contain no reference to Punt's whereabouts, but the freight suggests a distant location, possibly on the east coast of Africa.

Around 2000 B.C. Pharaoh Mentuhotep sent a court official named Hennu on another expedition to Punt. The words inscribed on Hennu's tomb record how Mentuhotep "sent me to dispatch a ship to Punt to bring him fresh myrrh. . . . I went with three thousand men. I made the road to be even as a river, and the desert even as a sown field. To each man I gave a leather bottle, a carrying pole, two jars of water, and twenty loaves of bread. . . . I dug two wells in the wasteland and three more in Idahet. I reached the Red Sea. I then built this ship. I dispatched it laden with everything. . . ."

The inference is that the ship was manhandled across the desert in sections—hence the large number of men, the water rationing, and the digging of wells—then assembled and launched on the Red Sea. Again the east coast of Africa seems a likely location for Punt.

The Egyptians' last recorded voyage to Punt is better documented. In 1493 B.C. Queen Hatshepsut sent five ships commanded by Nehsi to search again for the Land of the Gods—it would seem that Punt was so far distant and sporadically visited that its whereabouts had either been forgotten or were still a matter of conjecture. Nehsi's ships were probably built on the shore of the Red Sea and then launched, heading south. After a couple of years they came back, bringing the "marvelous things of the land of Punt." Queen Hatshepsut had Punt's exports carved in relief and enumerated in hieroglyphic inscriptions on the walls of her mortuary temple at Deir el Bahri near Thebes. Incense trees in tubs, ebony, ivory, cinnamon, monkeys, dogs, panther skins— "Never was the like of this brought for any king since the beginning," declare the inscriptions.

The same carvings provide clues to the whereabouts of Punt. One bas-relief shows Nehsi's five ships with their small square sails and their 30 or so rowers setting out on the Red Sea, laden with merchandise for trading. We next see them anchored off a village of reed huts built on stilts. Finally we see Nehsi's crews carrying their precious burden up the ships' gangplanks. The animals and the village of huts suggest a location in southern Africa.

Another carving shows an Egyptian official receiving the king and queen of Punt with their retinue. Some people think that the sturdy limbs and buttocks of the queen suggest she was deformed. There is, however, a simpler explanation: She displayed a racial characteristic of

11

the Khoikhoi, or Hottentots—people who in prehistoric times inhabited much of the coast of southern Africa. If this was so, Punt might well have been in the neighborhood of present-day Mozambique.

We know, too, that Nehsi's cargo included antimony, an essential ingredient of the rouge found in cosmetic boxes in Egyptian tombs. One of the few antimony deposits known to have been mined in the ancient world lay in Mozambique.

So although the exact position of Punt cannot be pinpointed, it may well have been in southern Africa—a long way from the Nile. Egyptians who traveled there and back would have had to cover almost 8,000 miles: an amazing journey indeed.

Yet Egyptian voyages were far surpassed by those of the Phoenicians.

Around 3000 B.C. a dark-skinned Semitic people moved into the coastal region of what is now Israel and Lebanon. The territory these Phoenicians occupied, though small, was fertile. But it was soon overcrowded, for mountains and hostile neighbors kept the Phoenicians from expanding eastward. So the Phoenicians became sea traders, redistributing by ship the treasures that had reached them by caravan. Gradually they cornered the seaborne traffic of the Mediterranean Sea, and built up the world's first maritime empire.

It is difficult to generalize about the Phoenicians for they were a loosely knit network of self-governed

trading posts. Determined to preserve their monopoly, they were also obsessively secretive. They falsified sailing orders in case they should fall into the wrong hands; destroyed cargo ledgers; and, to discourage competitors, disseminated fo'c'sle yarns of sea serpents that ate vessels and gales that blew ships off the rim of the world. The story goes that one Phoenician captain, rather than allow a foreign vessel to follow him on a trading expedition, deliberately ran his ship aground.

What we do know is that the Phoenicians built seaworthy ships, and that in these ships they could go virtually anywhere, trading with places as far apart as the British Isles and the coast of Africa.

Africa was the setting for two of the Phoenicians' greatest feats of exploration—the voyage of Hanno and an expedition sponsored by the Egyptian king Necho II.

Around 450 B.C. Hanno, a sailor from the Phoenician city of Carthage, traveled down the west coast of Africa with a fleet of 60 ships carrying settlers. He established colonies along the coast of present-day Morocco and Western Sahara, and some of the sites he described still exist. The place where he "founded a temple of Poseidon" was Cape Cantin; his "lagoon full of high and thick-grown cane . . . haunted by elephants and multitudes of other grazing beasts" was the mouth of the Tensift River; and his land of "the Troglodytes who . . . are said to run

The Phoenicians (opposite) were first to rove the entire Mediterranean— and first to navigate by the North Star. Commerce, not conquest, spurred their daring voyages, as they continually sought new markets and new sources of trade goods. Starting with Cyprus, Sicily, Carthage, and Malta, they had built by 800 B.C. a network of trading posts around the Mediterranean. As middlemen, the Phoenicians busily purveyed raw materials and finished goods: linen and papyrus from Egypt, ivory and gold from Nubia, grain and copper from Sardinia, olive oil and wine from Sicily, perfume and spice from the East.

Eventually these international traders, driven by insatiable curiosity, ventured beyond the Mediterranean. They reached England and perhaps the Azores, and possibly the stormy waters (below) around Africa's Cape of Good Hope—more than 2,000 years before Vasco da Gama dazzled Europe with the same feat.

14

faster than horses" was part of the Atlas Mountains.

Hanno's southernmost colony was "an island we called Cerne." We do not know where Cerne was; but after leaving the last of his colonists there, Hanno headed south, exploring the unknown coast of Africa.

"We sailed away in fear, and in four days' journey saw the land ablaze by night. In the centre a leaping flame towered above the others and appeared to reach the stars. This was the highest mountain which we saw: it was called the Chariot of the Gods."

They came to an island that "was full of wild people. By far the greater number were women with hairy bodies. Our interpreters called them Gorillas. We gave chase to the men, but could not catch any, for they all scampered up steep rocks and pelted us with stones."

Where was this "Chariot of the Gods"? Obviously it was a volcano. Some say it was the 3,317-foot Mount Kakoulima in the Republic of Guinea, and that Hanno's "gorillas" were really chimpanzees. Others claim that Hanno sailed almost as far as the Equator, and sighted the great volcanic peak of Mount Cameroon. Today this mountain is one of the last strongholds of the gorilla and, at 13,435 feet, could easily have been the highest any of his crew had seen. Not for another 2,000 years were Europeans to penetrate so far south along the coast of Africa.

The Phoenician voyage sponsored by King Necho II took place about 150 years before Hanno sailed, and in some ways was even more remarkable. The only account we have of it is by the Greek historian Herodotus, who writes: "Libya [Africa] shows that it has sea all round except the part that borders on Asia, Necho a king of Egypt being the first within our knowledge to show this fact. . . . He sent forth Phoenician men in ships, ordering them to sail back between the Pillars of Heracles [the Strait of Gibraltar] until they came to the Northern [Mediterranean] Sea and thus to Egypt. The Phoenicians therefore setting forth from the Red Sea sailed in the Southern Sea [Indian Ocean] and whenever autumn came, they each time put ashore and sowed the land wherever they might be in Libya. . . . After the passing of two years they doubled the Pillars of Heracles in the third year and came to Egypt. And they told things believable perhaps for others but unbelievable for me, namely that in sailing round Libya they had the sun on the right hand."

Herodotus' story is creditable on many counts. He describes the voyage as being made from east to west, which is the route by which winds and currents are most favorable. His words about the sun ring true because, incredible as it must have seemed to the ancients, when Necho's ships rounded the Cape of Good Hope the crews, being in the Southern Hemisphere, would indeed have seen the midday sun on their right. Also, Greek maps drawn between 450 B.C and A.D. 43 all show Africa surrounded by sea, and how could the Greeks have known that the continent was a virtual island

After defeating Persian king Darius III, Alexander the Great confronts his archenemy's family, fancifully shown in 16th-century Italian brocades before a neoclassic facade. An enlightened ruler, Alexander aimed to unite West with East rather than to subjugate the vanquished. He encouraged his soldiers to marry into conquered tribes; Alexander himself wed Stateira, one of Darius's daughters.

unless someone had sailed round it?

Herodotus was a historian, not an explorer. But he was Greek, and he shared with other Greeks a lust for knowing the unknown. Greeks like Pytheas of Massalia, who voyaged north to the edge of the known world and kept copious records that have, unfortunately, been lost to us. Greeks like Eudoxus of Cyzicus, who disappeared trying to circumnavigate Africa. Or Greeks like Alexander of Macedonia—Alexander the Great—who was an explorer truly worthy of that name.

More than a warlord, Alexander was a seeker of truth. He took with him on his campaigns geographers, engineers, architects, botanists, historians, and "steppers" to count their paces as they traveled, and thus judge the distances of their journeys.

In 334 B.C. Alexander, in pursuit of the Persians, led his troops into the unknown regions of Asia. Two of his many momentous achievements were crossing the Hindu Kush and navigating the Indus River.

The bleakly beautiful mountains of the Hindu Kush, along with the Himalayas and the Pamirs, create a formidable barrier between the subcontinent of India and the rest of Asia. Alexander, eager to mount a surprise spring offensive against the Persians in Afghanistan, led his army through the mountains on a 1,700-mile march. Autumn passed; the winter brought bitter winds, ice, and snow. The men struggled on until snow blocked their passage, then

A stone arch venerating the third-century A.D. Roman emperor Caracalla still stands triumphant amid the ancient ruins of Volubilis, a center of Greco-Roman culture that flourished in Morocco two centuries after Alexander's death. Morocco then stood at the western edge of the mapped world, beyond which only the most daring of Greek sailors, like Pytheas, ventured.

camped until the spring of 329 B.C., when they made their way through an 11,000-foot pass to cross the Hindu Kush. Reaching the Oxus River, swollen with spring's melting snow, they filled their leather tents with straw and used them as rafts to float across. It had never occurred to the Persians that a scouting party, let alone an entire army, would attempt to cross the Kush in early spring. They fled, but were soon captured.

Lured now by the unknown regions of India, Alexander and his troops in 327 B.C. marched east to the upper Indus River. Here they found crocodiles, and since the only others he had seen were in the Nile, Alexander wrote to his mother that he had discovered its source—a mistake he subsequently admitted.

Halfway to the sea the Rivers Indus and Jhelum converge. "Here," the Roman historian Arrian tells us, were "swift currents through a narrows and terrific whirlpools where the water surges and boils. So great was the roar of the rapids that the oarsmen . . . were struck dumb with amazement. . . .Many ships were in trouble, and two actually collided and were wrecked, with the loss of many of their crews."

Near the mouth of the Indus lay even greater peril. "There ensued the ebbing of the tide," writes Arrian, "with the result that the entire fleet was left stranded. Now this was something of which Alexander's company had no previous knowledge, so that it caused them great be-

wilderment. But they were yet more surprised when after the normal interval the sea advanced again and the ships were floated. As the tide rushed in all at once . . . the ships . . . were knocked together or hurled against the land and staved in." But nothing could stop Alexander. He rebuilt his fleet, explored the Indus Delta, then sent his officer Nearchus to the Persian Gulf while he marched back to Babylon.

It was not the least of Alexander's achievements that he brought to his travels an inquisitive mind and a desire to record and disseminate the knowledge he gained. His are among the first truly detailed accounts of exploration.

Europe's Great Age of Discovery had yet to dawn when the Egyptians, Phoenicians, and Greeks struck out into the unknown. And even as these ancient civilizations explored their worlds, other journeys of discovery were underway. In the Pacific the Polynesians sailed thousands of miles through unknown seas to build their island kingdoms. Chinese merchants trekked thousands of miles across China and Tibet to establish a trade route for silk. Arab traders in their sailing ships voyaged thousands of miles across the Indian Ocean to trade in India and China.

The Earth's first people were true discoverers, but detailed stories of only a few survive. We see the ancient explorers as "through a glass, darkly," and in the end can only guess at their greatness.

21

APOLLO

POSEIDON

PYTHEAS

Pytheas

By Ian Cameron

I magine, if you will, a trial, with you the jury. Imagine that what is on trial is a man's historical reputation: Was he or was he not a charlatan and a liar?

The judge of our imagined court has been able to reach back across the ages to classical times, to summon the defendant and witnesses. These witnesses—eminent historians and geographers of the ancient world—have testified, and they have branded the man in the dock "an arch-falsifier," "that charlatan Pytheas," "the greatest of liars." For it is obvious, these learned men say, that the stories Pytheas of Massalia brought back of his travels in the Atlantic around 325 B.C. are tall tales, the sort of yarns that seamen indulge in when their tongues are loosened by wine.

The judge now asks Pytheas if he can produce evidence to refute his critics, and the Massalian steps into the witness-box. "My books vindicate me," he cries. "In *On the Ocean* and *Description of the Earth* you will find all the evidence you need."

"But not a page of these books has survived," the judge says. "All that has come down to us are a few fragments quoted by later writers."

Pytheas is indignant: "Must I be judged by those fragments alone? What of my scientific background? My astronomical discoveries? I invented a calibrated sundial which enabled me to determine latitude accurately. I discovered the exact direction of true north. I discovered—"

The judge cuts him short. "We have no doubt you were a bona fide scientist. The question is, were you also a bona fide explorer? Did you or did you not tell the truth about your expedition into the North Atlantic, and in particular about a land you claim to have discovered on the rim of the world, next to a 'jellyfish' sea? Suppose you take us with you on this expedition, step by step. And at each step prove—if you can— that it is you and not your critics who speak the truth. But remember, this investigation is for history, so you must limit yourself to evidence from the written record."

The court becomes suddenly silent. What hope, all are thinking, has this solitary man of refuting his many eminent accusers?

"The Greek geographer Strabo," the judge is saying, "quotes you as

Sailors loading wine and figs as the Mediterranean astronomer Pytheas asks protection from the gods for a voyage in search of tin and amber. In this modern painting, his fourth-century B.C. expedition reaches the land of the midnight sun, but the Greek's claim to have rounded "the farthest of all known islands"—probably Iceland— was not credited until the 20th century.

Ancient Britons as Pytheas may have seen them. The engravings are based on Caesar's Commentaries.

claiming that after passing through the Pillars of Hercules, you took 'five days to sail from Gadir'—that's Cádiz—'to the Sacred Cape,' Cape St. Vincent. But Strabo points out that five days is a ridiculously long time to cover the hundred or so miles in question. Others have claimed that the Carthaginian warships patrolling the Strait of Gibraltar would never have allowed you, a Massalian, to pass through; that their blockade was intended to keep Greeks like yourself from finding out about their lucrative Atlantic trade."

"This is easily answered. To avoid the Carthaginian warships I sailed close inshore, and by night, as later historians have conjectured. For this reason the voyage took much longer than it should have."

The judge makes a note. "Next, the Greek geographer Artemidorus quoted you as observing that northern Iberia 'is more readily accessible by way of the Celtic land'—France—'than in sailing by way of the Atlantic'; and this, he says, is another instance of your falsehoods."

Pytheas smiles. "Look at a modern map, and you will see who deals in falsehood. It is more than 2,000 miles from Massalia to the Bay of Biscay by sea and less than 500 by land."

"Then consider your description of France," responds the judge. "You describe that great 'bulge of Europe . . . opposite Iberia and projecting toward the west for more than 3,000 stades'—almost 400 miles—'likewise the various headlands . . . and islands there along, the last of which is Uxantis.' Yet maps of Strabo's time show the coast of France running not west but north, and he says that 'all these places . . . in the north . . . are mere inventions of Pytheas.'"

"When I returned to Massalia," the explorer explains, "my description of France was at first believed, and the maps of Europe were drawn correctly. It was only later, after my death, when cartographers listened to the jibes of men like Strabo—who wrote 300 years after my voyage!—that the maps of Europe were redrawn. And redrawn incorrectly,

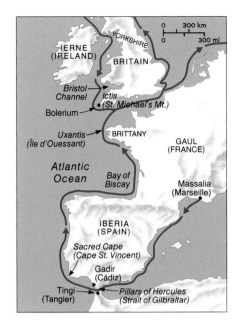

with the coast of France running due north. Yet later geographers found that the French coast does indeed curve to the northwest, exactly as I described, to Brittany and the Île d'Ouessant—my Uxantis."

The judge acknowledges the point. "But," he adds, "it is now as we leave the world known to the Mediterranean that you stretch credulity too far. Can you *prove* that you visited Bolerium—Land's End?"

"Why, surely! I wrote a description of it that is quoted by the Sicilian Diodorus: 'The natives of Britain by the headland of Bolerium . . . extract the tin from its bed by a cunning process. The bed is of rock, but contains earthy interstices along which they cut a gallery. Having smelted the tin and refined it, they hammer it into knuckle-bone shape and convey it to an adjacent island named Ictis'—St. Michael's Mount. 'They wait till the ebb-tide has drained the intervening frith, and then transport whole loads of tin on wagons.' For confirmation you need no written record, for even after 2,000 years, you can still see the remains of a smelting pit and the refuse of smelted ores."

The judge looks at Pytheas with new interest. Could it be that the man has been misjudged by the ancient scholars, that he is *not* a charlatan?

"Even if we accept that you *did* land in Bolerium," the judge presses on, "what of your stories of Britain? You claim to have seen tides north of Britain swell to 120 feet."

"I kept detailed accounts of what I saw there," says Pytheas, growing annoyed. "I wrote: 'Britain is triangular in shape, like Sicily, but its sides are not equal; It stretches out along Europe slantwise.'" Pytheas cites some detailed measurements, and continues. "Since the size and shape of Britain were previously unknown, my detailed description is surely evidence that I sailed around it. I landed in several places, and over a period of 3 years I observed that the longest day was exactly 18 hours near Inverness, and 17 hours in Yorkshire. And I observed the inhabitants of this island. I described their habits: 'They do not drink wine, but a fermented liquor made from barley.'

"I did indeed report great tide ebbs and waves, and to the people of our almost tideless Mediterranean this must have seemed incredible. Yet modern British observers have recorded an ebb of over 50 feet in the Bristol Channel, occasional waves of 60 feet between Scotland and the Orkneys, and one remarkable wave that climbed the 200-foot cliffs of Stroma and swept clean over the island. So you see once again I reported nothing but the truth."

The judge ponders all he has heard. "In the opinion of this court," he says, "you have gone far toward salvaging your reputation. But what of this amazing island on the rim of the world where the sun never sets and where your ship and crew were brought up short by a strange 'jellyfish' sea, where land and sea and air merge?"

"I first heard of Ultima Thule," Pytheas tells us, "when I was in northern Britain. It was said to be an island, six days' sail to the north of Britain. When we arrived, we found the sun was above the horizon

Any man who has told such great falsehoods about the known regions would hardly, I imagine, be able to tell the truth about places that are not known to anybody.
STRABO

for 20 hours out of 24, and that even at midnight there was sufficient light to read by. We would have sailed farther, but a day to the north of Thule our ship was stopped by a strange metamorphosis of the sea. It seemed to combine with the air to form a mass like jellyfish, which could be crossed neither on foot nor by boat. The fishermen told us that this was the end of the world, and no man could go farther. We therefore returned home via the Baltic Sea, visiting an island where each spring the waves wash amber up onto the shore."

"We know of Baltic amber, but a sun that gives light at midnight," the judge says, "sounds almost past belief to people of the ancient Mediterranean—though astronomers might concede it possible. But sea and

A modern artist's vision: Pytheas trading spear blades and wine for amber beads scooped from the sea by natives of an island in northeast Europe. Greek myth held the prized beads to be the hardened tears of the Heliades, sisters turned to poplar trees by Zeus. Returning home, Pytheas orders a bull sacrificed to the sea god, Poseidon, in thanksgiving for his successful voyage.

air combining into a mass like jellyfish! How can anyone credit this?"

"Yet explorers of later centuries have seen this phenomenon. Scientists and scholars. Will you believe *their* evidence?"

"Let us hear who these men are, and what they say."

"The first man I would have as my witness is Fridtjof Nansen, Norwegian explorer at the turn of the 20th century. He has written: 'What Pytheas himself saw may have been the ice-sludge . . . which is formed . . . along the edge of the drift ice, when this has been ground to a pulp by the action of waves. The expression "can neither be traversed on foot nor by boat" is exactly applicable to this ice-sludge. If we add to this the thick fog, which is often found near drift ice, then the description that the air is also involved . . . and that land and sea and everything is merged in it, will appear very graphic.'

"My second witness is Frank Debenham, polar explorer and Emeritus Professor of Geography at the University of Cambridge. The professor has written: 'When ice forms on sea water it forms a thin flexible skin and is immediately broken up by the wave motion into small cakes of ice, the edges jostled into a thicker rim so that we call it pancake ice.

'It is a curious thought that if Pytheas had used the pancake . . . simile instead of . . . jelly-fish he might have been believed and his narrative might have been preserved to posterity.' My third witness—"

The judge raises his hand. "Enough. You have said enough to convince this court that what once seemed unbelievable can be accepted as fact. One question only remains. Why did you do it? Why did you spend so many years exploring these regions on the edge of the world?"

"We Greeks of Massalia were of course interested in learning whence came the Carthaginian wealth from beyond the Pillars of Hercules. But I, a scientist, had other goals. Before we left, I spent many hours with

my calibrated sundial calculating Massalia's exact latitude on the Earth's surface. In the countries we visited I again worked out our position. This enabled me—albeit imperfectly—to map our route, to define and to learn what lay beyond our Mediterranean horizon." Pytheas pauses, then says thoughtfully, "After our return, the Carthaginian hold on the Strait of Gibraltar tightened. No further Greek expeditions ever penetrated the blockade to confirm my reports. Perhaps that is why so many scholars thereafter questioned my veracity."

Pytheas of Massalia, one of the world's least known explorers, stands down. Was he also one of the least appreciated? You, the jury, decide.

Today scholars continue trying to reconstruct Pytheas's route from such fragments of evidence as those cited in our imaginary trial. Modern geography has vindicated many of Pytheas's claims, but the location of Ultima Thule remains uncertain—some say Iceland, others Norway or the Faroe Islands. For more on Pytheas and other ancient explorers, see Beyond The Pillars of Heracles *by Rhys Carpenter.*

To Cross the Seven Seas

By David F. Robinson

Billowing sails recall exploration's golden age—the 15th and 16th centuries—when bold mariners probed beyond the limits of the known world. Here a recreation of Sir Francis Drake's Golden Hind completes a trial run off England's coast after its launching in 1973. In 1580, half a century after Ferdinand Magellan circled the globe, Drake plundered Spanish treasures in South America and reconnoitered western North America from California to Oregon and perhaps beyond.

It was but a puny glimmer, like the light of a wax candle moving up and down. But the admiral says he saw it earlier this evening, far across the jostling waves. And now he promises a silken jacket to him who first spies the land on which the light must have burned.

Ah, but this sea captain from Genoa, this Christopher Columbus, has told his Spanish seamen many things to lure them on toward his vision of Cathay just over the rim of the horizon. That seabird, this floating weed, those clouds, all tell of land out here in the empty waters. So he says. More than a month at sea, and this square-rigged nao and its two companion caravels will nose into a snug harbor on the morrow. So he says. So he has said for weeks.

Still, what is there to do but hope? Eyes bleary from the midnight watch peer anxiously from the ship's fo'c'sle at the empty seam where sea meets sky. Hands raw from wrestling with the lurching rudder keep a straight wake by the feel of the tiller. Great squares of canvas bulge with the wind like hide over muscle. Spars groan, planks creak, halyards whack the masts, grains crawl through the *ampolleta*, the sandglass that binds a weary man to his duty station until the last grain falls. Eight times the grains must run through until a four-hour watch is done. It is 2 a.m.; one dreary hour to go. How great the temptation to hang the infernal ampolleta above the lantern so the heat will expand the glass and the grains will hurry through faster!

Listen—from the *Pinta,* the lead ship of this little fleet of three, a cry splits the night, a cry that soon will awaken Europe to a New World.

"Tierra! Tierra!" bellows the lookout. "Land! Land!"

Spanish words. But they could have been Chinese.

Why weren't they? China had the ships, the men, the money for such an expedition long before Columbus was born. And so did other nations, for that matter; some had explored far and wide by the time he set sail. So why didn't China or one of these other nations discover America?

Europe in the 15th century had awakened from a millennium of feudalism, stretched, and found its arms spanning not just a Mediterranean world but a whole globe. In the blink of a lifetime, daring sea captains would round the tip of Africa and fetch home the riches of the Orient . . . breast the uncharted Atlantic and butt into land . . . traverse the land and glimpse another ocean beyond . . . struggle down the endless coast of South America, find its end at last, and limp across the Pacific, leaving a wake around a globe whose surface is but two-sevenths dry land. Their names are firmly anchored in the history of this Great Age of Discovery: da Gama, Cabral, Columbus, Dias, Magellan, names known to any schoolchild. But who ever heard of Cheng Ho?

Half a century before Columbus

From a realm of fantasy to a world of reality—such was the leap of the Great Age of Discovery. Beginning with Portuguese voyages down the west coast of Africa, the century-long outburst of exploration erased medieval notions of a flat Earth populated by monsters and mythical beings. Columbus himself reckoned the distance between Europe and Cathay at 4,000 miles—about 9,000 short. By the 1500s, explorers had added to their charts Earth's largest feature: the Pacific Ocean.

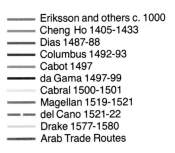

———	Eriksson and others c. 1000
———	Cheng Ho 1405-1433
———	Dias 1487-88
———	Columbus 1492-93
———	Cabot 1497
———	da Gama 1497-99
———	Cabral 1500-1501
———	Magellan 1519-1521
– – –	del Cano 1521-22
———	Drake 1577-1580
———	Arab Trade Routes

was born, a new emperor seized the throne of China. This haughty demigod had little use for the rude wares of barbarians beyond his Great Wall. He wanted only their profound respect. And so in 1405 began a series of sea voyages like none before. The emperor's trusted admiral, the eunuch Cheng Ho, coursed the seas from Japan to Zanzibar with flotillas numbering up to 317 ships.

On one mighty vessel a forest of 9 masts sprouted from a hull 444 feet long by 180 feet wide. This was the treasure ship, from whose hold poured gifts to dazzle petty potentates at every port of call. Smaller vessels schooled about this great whale: horse ships, supply ships, billet ships, and the little combat ships.

Little? At 180 feet end to end, with 68-foot beam and 5 masts, they dwarfed anything Europe would launch for the next 100 years. Surely Cheng Ho could have captained even the smallest of his ships across an ocean, financed by the wealth of his emperor and guided by a magnetic compass that Europe's mariners disdained as a tool of fortune-tellers.

But the Chinese were too advanced to go grubbing for commerce. Their fleets sailed to neighbor nations seven times, not to trade or conquer, but to impress. Having done that, the ships sailed home to rot as the lotus of China slowly closed back into itself.

Tierra! Electrified by the realization that they have sailed into the unknown and made it to the other

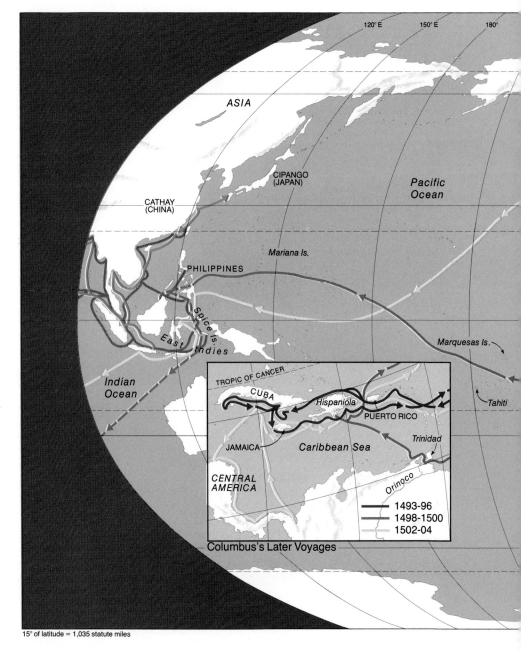

15° of latitude = 1,035 statute miles

A slithering sea serpent snatches a hapless seaman from the deck of his ship in this 1555 woodcut by Swedish map maker Olaus Magnus. Fear of such terrors kept most mariners sailing close to shore until the era of Columbus.

OVERLEAF: Summer ice clots the harbor of a fishing village in southern Greenland. Along these shores slumber the ruins of Viking colonies that defied such seas and coastlines and served as stepping-stones to the New World.

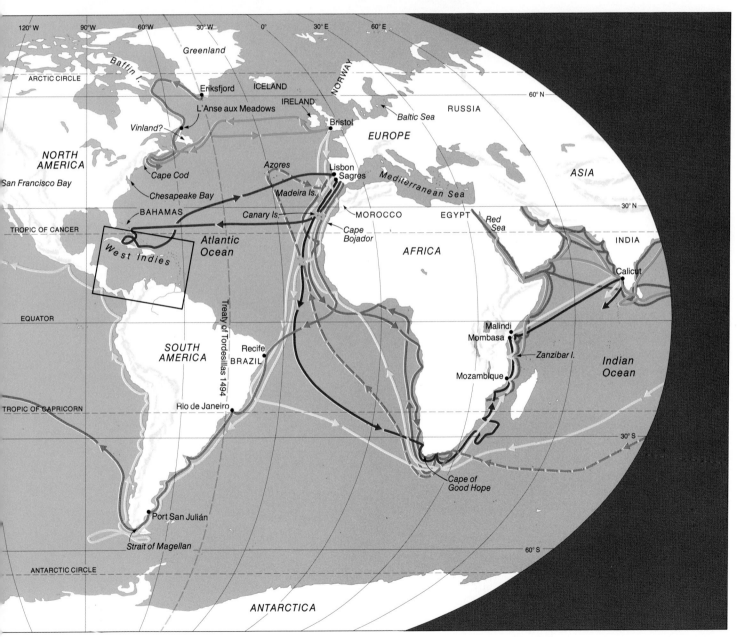

Relics of a Nordic past evoke daring sea voyages across the North Atlantic to the New World. The finely wrought warrior's helmet, found in a ship burial near Stockholm, dates from the seventh century. A tenth-century Anglo-Saxon drawing caricatures the dreaded dragon ships of Viking sea rovers who raided and traded throughout Europe from the Baltic to the Mediterranean. Such vessels, built of overlapping planks, were among the most seaworthy ever built. Lithe and supple longships probed the brawling reaches of the northern seas as early as the ninth century A.D., bringing raiders and settlers to outposts from Ireland to Russia. A bulkier, beamier ship known as a knarr carried settlers to Iceland and Greenland—and may have coasted North America's shores as early as A.D. 986.

side, the crewmen of Columbus's nao scramble to the deck. Columbus speaks an order, and the helmsman below decks hauls the long tiller arm hard alee. The deep, narrow rudder swings like a cathedral door, and the wind spills from the sails. Now they thrash and flap, and the sheets and clew lines bound to their corners crack like whips as deckhands lunge for the flailing lines.

Square sails let a ship run before the wind, but the new, triangular lateen sail on the mizzenmast makes a ship more maneuverable and helps her beat into the wind. Thus could Columbus's ships, the *Santa Clara* (*Niña* was only her nickname), the *Pinta*, and the *Santa María* win the confidence of these sailors who have driven them down the wind into oblivion: They held the promise of bringing their sailors back home.

Spanish sailors. But they could have been Arab.

It was, after all, the Arab traders who most likely invented that lateen sail. Under its bellying triangle they had sailed the Indian Ocean for generations. In the marts of India and the Spice Islands they filled their holds with silks, medicines, jewels, and spices—especially pepper for the taste buds of Europe.

Not that Europeans were such gourmets; the spice trade sprang from much humbler roots. By a quirk of geography, Europe had little that it could use for fodder to feed its cattle over the winter. Thus stockmen had to butcher many of their animals in the fall and salt the meat so it would keep. If it didn't, well, it would likely be eaten anyway. In either case, pepper made it palatable.

And made the Venetians rich. Venice's merchants had cornered the market on the spice trade from the islands of the Indian Ocean. A hundredweight of pepper was worth 3 ducats in Calicut—but by the time it crossed the Indian Ocean under lateen sails, jounced by camel caravan through the deserts of Egypt, and thudded onto the warehouse floors of Venice, the price had zoomed to 80 ducats. Egypt's sultans restricted the annual tonnage, keeping pepper precious by keeping it rare.

In the lucrative spice trade, the Arab sailors were the deliverymen, riding the northeast monsoons to Africa and the Red Sea in the fall and the southwest monsoons back to India in the summer. It was a trade route; why struggle off into nothingness when there was commerce

35

Under a cloud of canvas, a full-scale re-creation of Lord Baltimore's Dove furrows the waters of Chesapeake Bay. Square-riggers such as this pinnace ran well with the wind, but to make good headway against the wind on a return voyage took another sail—the triangular lateen used by Arab seamen. Navigators of the time used a sandglass and "log" line (below) to measure speed and a compass to gauge direction.

aplenty right here? Father, son, and grandson commuted across the Indian Ocean under a sail that could have taken them around the world.

As spices reached the Mediterranean, so too did the sail that brought them. Medieval knights from western Europe had seen tricornered sails dotting the harbors and seaways as they journeyed along the eastern Mediterranean on their Crusades. They called the rigs lateen after the Latin countries whose sailors hoisted them aloft on long spars held by stout, raked masts.

The wonder is not only in the cleverness of the fore-and-aft rig but in the slowness of western Europe to adopt it. Not until the 1400s did the Portuguese develop a ship with full lateen rig—the oceangoing caravel, fast, nimble, able to tack well upwind. The caravel was the high-tech space shuttle of its day, a capsule fit for crossing the seven seas. Yet Columbus, pausing in the Canary Islands on his first voyage of discovery, stripped down the two-masted caravel *Niña*, gave her a lateen mizzen, and rerigged main and fore with the old reliable square sails for better downwind speed in the open sea.

Tierra! But which land? Columbus is certain it's the Orient, so the Orient it must be. An offshore island, surely. A dot off the coast of Cipango, the island realm told of by Marco Polo. The Indies, at last.

In his stuffy little cabin aft, the admiral thumbs his logbook. October 12, 1492. Thirty-three days out of the Canary Islands. A crude magnetic compass has guided him westward. Mariners to come will speak of him as a consummate dead-reckoning navigator, for he can watch the water hiss past his hull and estimate his speed within a tenth of a knot.

Each day he tells his men how far they have sailed. And they believe him. But he lies. When they make 59 leagues he tells them 44, lest they despair at sailing so far into the void.

A liar, but a pious one. In gratitude for safe passage, the devout Columbus names his landfall after his Holy Savior. San Salvador.

A Spanish name. But it could have been Norse.

It probably *was* through the eyes of Norsemen that Europe first beheld

Embarking on his grand adventure from Palos, Spain, Christopher Columbus bids farewell to King Ferdinand and Queen Isabella. A 19th-century artist has romanticized the scene; the royal pair did not attend the pre-dawn sailing on August 3, 1492. Columbus's three ships made landfall in the Bahamas early on October 12. Historians ever since have debated which island he sighted. Aided by computers, a National Geographic study in 1986 traced his wake to tiny Samana Cay.

OVERLEAF: *The island of Dominica remains much as Columbus found it on November 3, 1493, during the second of his four voyages to the New World. Its name in Spanish means "sabbath," for he sighted it on a Sunday. The island, wrote one adventurer, "is notable for the beauty of its mountains and the charm of its verdure."*

At a banquet following his first voyage of discovery, Columbus stands an egg on end—by crushing its base. His companions, who had scorned the uniqueness of his sea exploit, take the point: After a deed is done, everybody knows how to do it. The pleasant fable shows the value of unorthodoxy—in Columbus's case, sailing west to arrive in the East. Not so pleasant for Columbus was his return to Spain in chains in 1500, after his third voyage (right), in disgrace for hanging rebellious settlers.

North America. Half a millennium before that lookout's cry, graceful ships with single square sails and a bristle of oars were pouring out of the rock-walled fjords of Scandinavia. Neighboring peoples saw little grace in those slender warships with their dragon figureheads, for they brought warriors to pillage and burn.

What plunder could be richer, what victims easier, than the gentle monks of Ireland in their monasteries filled with gold chalices and bejeweled reliquaries? The fearsome dragon ships became a plague upon the shores. And when the Vikings prowled westward to Iceland, they found Irish monks there too—mostly hermits with little to steal. But the brothers knew only too well what "viking" meant; the Norseman's word for "raiding" had become the name for all his kind. The panicky monks had but two choices: stand fast and die, or flee.

And so the Irish monk became an unlikely seafarer in an even more unlikely ship of skin—the curragh, a sailing skiff made of leather stretched over a wicker frame. Through the treacherous northern seas the brothers plowed a path to Greenland with the dreaded longships almost in their wake. Did Irish monks make it even farther—to mainland North America, or even to the same Caribbean islands that Columbus knelt upon and named? The chronicles of a sixth-century saint named Brendan speak vaguely of a 40-day voyage westward, of a flat and treeless island like those of the Bahamas, of grapes as big as apples on a perfumed isle some say might be Jamaica. We can only read the chronicles and wonder.

But the Vikings surely beached their admirable *knarrs* in the New World. Like stepping-stones, the remains of their colonies cross the North Atlantic: Iceland . . . Greenland . . . and finally L'Anse aux Meadows in Newfoundland. There we see their imprints today—here a longhouse foundation, there a cookhouse with a slate-lined cooking pit.

In their sagas we read of another place, an evanescent paradise, a Vinland the Good with wonderful berries for making wine. Surely this was not rocky, cold Newfoundland. Where then? Cape Cod? Again, we

39

can only read the sagas and wonder.

In time the *skraelings*—native Americans whom Columbus will stubbornly call Indians; after all, this *is* the Indies!—turned the Norsemen back toward Greenland and Iceland. A spindle whorl, a posthole, a bronze pin—the Norse saga is written in the dirt of a New World that, to them, was just another settlement that didn't work out.

Tierra! By morning light Columbus and his captains clamber over the ships' gunwales into a boat, prudently armed, and soon the oarsmen crunch its prow onto the sandy shore. Feet that staggered on pitching decks for more than a month must now learn again the feel of firm ground. And so must stomachs that now turn landsick on a footing that seems to roll but does not.

The men seek fresh water to replace the rancid broth now stinking in the water casks. They seek fruits and meats and vegetables for crews weary of leathery salt beef and beans turned to cannon shot and biscuits like bricks. They seek human contact, for a ship is small and a voyage long and a gang of seamen rounded up on a sordid waterfront not the most enchanting of societies. But above all, Columbus seeks the Great Khan of Cathay.

In his zeal to make this place fit into the world where it ought to, Columbus identifies plants and birds and animals as species found in Asia. Humans dwell here too—naked, copper skinned, shy at first, then gleeful over the red cloth caps and glass beads the strangers give them.

But no Great Khan. Columbus will voyage to these waters three times more before his death, yet never will he heed a rising chorus of scoffers nor know that the Great Khan sits 9,000 miles farther west.

Columbus steps from the boat, clutching the royal standard. Two captains each carry a banner of the green cross bearing the initials of the king and queen, the sovereigns who dithered six years before agreeing to fund what Columbus so grandly called his Enterprise of the Indies. Ferdinand and Isabella.

Spanish sovereigns. But they might have been Portuguese.

It took Columbus more than a decade of lobbying, wheedling, and string pulling before he finally found a sponsor. Much of that time he cajoled the royal councils not of Spain but of Portugal. And what better choice? It was Portugal's Prince Henry the Navigator who had set up a kind of Renaissance Cape Canaveral at Sagres and sent ship after ship down the fearsome coast of Africa.

There at Sagres the prince who never went to sea prodded his captains to sail farther south while his naval architects perfected the nimble caravel. They had to. There were no steady tail winds to blow a square-rigger around the western shoulder of Africa, down the long coastline, around the southern tip, and up across the Indian Ocean. Only a lateener could make good headway

against that mishmash of winds.

League by league, voyage by voyage, Henry's captains groped down
the continent's interminable flank,
planting stone pillars called *padrões*
on shore to mark their progress and
reassure the ships that followed. In
1434 Gil Eannes rounded the dreaded Cape Bojador, once considered
impassable. He dodged its shallows
by sailing many days out to sea and
around the long, lurking shoal. His
breakthrough heartened others to
sail in his wake. Farther and farther
south the padrões marched.

Then in 1488 Bartholomeu Dias,
exasperated by weeks of ornery head
winds far down the coast, turned
south-southwestward and ran out
into the South Atlantic for 13 days

in search of better breezes. When he
found them he rode them eastward—and rounded the continent's
rock-toothed tip at long last. To Portugal's sovereign, John II, Dias
brought back tales of a tempestuous
promontory. One account says he
called it the Cape of Storms, but
John had another name: the Cape of
Good Hope. And the hope would be
fulfilled, for Portugal had made an
end run around the empire of Islam
and the Venetian spice cartel.

The Portuguese crown in 1497
sent the steel-willed nobleman Vasco da Gama to inaugurate trade on
the route blazed by Dias. Da Gama
sailed from Portugal with two square-
riggers, a caravel, and a fat storeship
heavy with trade goods and provi-

Amerigo Vespucci drops in on America, an allegorical figure who stares from her hammock at the overdressed visitor as natives roast a human leg nearby. Her guest holds an astrolabe, used to navigate by star sights. He was first to call this a "new world," but a 1507 pamphlet gave it his name: "Let it be named America." Two continents now bear the name—but where or how often he landed, no one knows.

sions for a three-year expedition.

All boded well as the fleet sailed across the Indian Ocean in a mere 22 days. But a rude reception awaited them on the Malabar coast. Sultans and merchants used to trafficking in gems by the handful guffawed at the newcomers' chintzy beads and caps.

After weeks of dickering the fleet slunk away, ill prepared for bucking the Indian Ocean's head winds. The crossing now took three months—and many lives, as scurvy and malnutrition wrought their full horror.

Two years after leaving Portugal a remnant of the fleet staggered home. Da Gama could present his king with only a few gems and a sprinkle of spice—a modest profit to show for a voyage of 27,000 miles, but reason enough for joyous celebration. Portuguese merchant seamen soon were swarming around the cape, well provisioned for trading in the sumptuous bazaars of the Indies.

The princes of Portugal had spent heavily for half a century to pioneer this hard-won path to profit. Why bankroll a Genoese dreamer to sail in the opposite direction for another route to the same place?

The dreamer had sailed anyway, financed by Spanish monarchs seeking their own end run around both Venice's monopoly on land trade and Portugal's hammerlock on the sea route around Africa. How the scoffing Portuguese monarch must have squirmed on his throne when Columbus sailed back to Europe with news that he had fetched the Indies

Ioan. Stradanus inuent.
Theodor Galle sculp.   Phls Galle exud.

in a single voyage! And how Columbus must have squirmed when, clawing his way homeward through a murderous tempest, he found himself limping into a Portuguese port only four miles from Lisbon!

Two rival Catholic powers had apparently reached the same lands by opposite tracks. Which had the right to colonize where? Pope Alexander VI finally drew a line down the middle of the Atlantic; westward was Spain's domain, eastward was the rest of Europe's. Portugal objected— and, by the Treaty of Tordesillas in 1494, moved the line nearly a thousand miles west and claimed any new lands to the east of it, ignoring the rest of Europe entirely. It was a momentous coup, for it enabled the courtly Pedro Álvares Cabral to take his fleet of 13 ships far to the west on his voyage to India in 1500—so far west that he sighted land, a shore that was now his right to claim for Portugal. A shore we call Brazil.

Down that shoreline 19 years later Ferdinand Magellan would sail. By then most of the learned world would know that this was not the Indies but a barrier of land. Magellan came to take the measure of that barrier and find a chink in it, if chink there be. Through a storm-lashed strait he would grope at last, only to find another trackless ocean—and a berth in history as the first to lead an expedition that circled the globe.

Tierra! Shouted in triumph, the cry now hangs like a curse as Columbus leans on the rail and scans the

47

"They are a people of a tractable, free, and loving nature, without guile or treachery," wrote Francis Drake of the natives he met along the California coast in the summer of 1579. Drake and his men put into a "convenient and fit harborough"—probably in the San Francisco Bay area—for ship repairs after seven months of sailing and raiding along the western coasts of the Americas. He claimed the land for his queen and named it Nova Albion because of "the white bancks and cliffes, which lie toward the sea." On July 23, after more than a month ashore, Drake set out across the broad Pacific—the first Englishman to circle the globe.

Young sailors still take to the sea under square sails. Argentine cadets lay aloft on the training ship Libertad (opposite)—at first fearfully, then with confidence. So the sailors of centuries past dared the empty oceans and found them filled with discovery.

heaving sea. It is 1504. His bows aim homeward after his fourth voyage to lands he still calls the Indies. But where are those accursed bazaars?

The fourth voyage has borne no more fruit than his first three. Still no bustling marketplaces, no dazzling cities, no steely-eyed merchants proffering baskets of pearls. Mostly he has met only naked inhabitants who sleep in nets of string and drink the smoke from a rolled-up leaf they call *tabaco*. But they can fight. Pitting their wooden spears against his thundering bombards and swivel guns, they have sometimes attacked the colonies he has tried to plant and slain his shipmates.

Other times it has been his shipmates who have turned against him, disobeying his orders, fomenting mutiny—and even costing him his old flagship, the *Santa María*, on Christmas Day of the first voyage.

How that big, beamy nao would wallow in following seas like these, he recalls. She'd slide down each hill of water, then fishtail until the next roller buoyed her stern again. But the *Santa María* was his flagship, and there was no excuse for her loss. Did he not make it clear that no cabin boy should ever steer, "come wind, come calm"? Yet, while he slept below—minus his bed canopy, which he had given to a minor nabob on one of those interminable islands—a weary helmsman gave the tiller to a cabin boy, and the ship struck a reef and was lost. A cabin boy!

The admiral squints ahead at the empty Atlantic. No more will he pass this way, returning to skeptical sovereigns with reports of the Indies while they listen instead to wild theories about a whole New World. Someone else will command the armies that plunder these lands of their gold and skew Europe's economy into disarray. The English corsair Francis Drake will grow rich on the gold and silver of this vast new realm, then scout its sunset coast on his way around the world. And other sea captains will plant lasting settlements on the continent north of the Indies, from which a mighty nation will spring.

English settlements. But they might have been Spanish. For the saga of discovery by sea is a story not only of what was but of what might have been. Columbus's voyage was the first sponsored attempt to cross the Ocean Sea to the Orient, but instead it ran into a wall of land. Later explorers would round that wall and sail another ocean that few Europeans knew was even there. In a single generation the sea explorers jarred the mind of Europe out of its Mediterranean mind-set and put it to pondering a whole stupendous sphere.

Leif Eriksson and Clan

By Edwards Park

T he Viking flame barely flickered in Bjarni Herjolfsson. A good sailor? Of course. Look at how he prospered, trading between Iceland and Norway. But where was the lust to conquer and explore? Where was the good old berserker spirit that had driven Svein Forkbeard to skip along the oar shafts, yelling murderous oaths as his crew rowed to the attack? Bjarni never shrieked bloody threats at cowering abbots, or sprang at French castles with flashing battle-ax. His passions ran to the mundane: like getting to port at the right time with the right cargo.

Bjarni was master of a sturdy *knarr*, beamier and more seaworthy than the longships of his Viking forebears. And in the 986th year of the Christian Lord, he sailed her straight toward glory. Then, at the last minute, this stolid captain came about and sailed her straight away again, taking with him only a tale of strange shores and a voyage gone awry.

But what a tale to stir a Viking lad! It begins with Bjarni sailing to his Iceland home with cargo in the hold. Before he could unload, he heard that his father, Herjolf, had sailed with the notorious Erik the Red to a western land that Erik had found and was touting as a "green land."

What in the world, thought Bjarni, was a nice old man like his father doing with a rascal like Erik? Beard as fiery as the great god Thor's, Erik had been in trouble all his life. Ousted from Norway for murder, then from Iceland for killing again, he had sailed off into the sunset. Many in Iceland had sighed with relief that this was probably the last of him.

Incredibly, he had returned, bragging of making a landfall, of following a bleak coast west below mountains of ice, of finding deep fjords cut into lush green hills. In one he built his hall and dubbed himself a jarl, second only to a king. With him settled a brawling brood: his formidable daughter Freydis . . . his wife Thjodhild, daughter of that obviously splendid woman, Thorbjorg Ship-bosom . . . a youngster thirsty for

A Viking raid, depicted in a medieval manuscript. Such fleets drove monks of western Europe to their knees in a common prayer: "From the fury of the Northmen deliver us, O Lord!"

adventure—his eldest son Leif. But family was not enough; Erik wanted settlers for Greenland. He got them, too, for Iceland was overcrowded.

"Insanity!" snorted Bjarni at the idea of 25 ships and 300 or 400 people, including Herjolf, sailing for Greenland. He nodded wisely when told that many had hastily returned, weary of steep seas that even oceangoing knarrs couldn't weather. Some settlers may have gotten through, but was Herjolf among them? Bjarni had to find out.

Bjarni took a bearing on an Icelandic mountain and sailed west. When the land slid below the horizon he checked his latitude by the sun's shadow at midday. At night he used his outstretched palms to gauge the height of the North Star. When a brisk breeze filled the single sail, the big vessel slid along at a good seven knots. She was built the old way, her lower strakes lashed to the oaken ribs and keel with vines. This allowed the planking to work, the hull to writhe and twist. That flexing, Bjarni knew, gave knarrs their durability in the open sea.

Bjarni's simple navigation forsook him when, as the old Norse sagas say, "the fair wind failed and northerly winds and fog set in, and for many days they had no idea what their course was." One thing was certain: They had fallen too far south and missed Greenland altogether.

They were groping northwestward when they sighted a low shore with forested hills. The crew grinned at the land and cracked each other on the back for having beaten the odds. Not Bjarni. He had never seen Greenland, but he'd been told what to expect—and this wasn't it.

"Leaving the land on their larboard with their sail swung over toward it, they sailed for two days before they sighted another land." It was flat and wooded, no more like Greenland than the first landfall. No matter; the crew wanted to land, refresh the water supply, and collect firewood. Bringing buckets on deck, they eyed the captain anxiously: "Well, sir?"

But Bjarni had not completed his passage. He growled something to his helmsman and waved his disgusted crew back to work. And the knarr, slapping through light waves, headed purposefully away.

Still too far south. He sailed northward, and a third time the lookout yelled, and the crew poured on deck, and they all craned at wild, ice-clad hills above a barren shore. This time the men grumbled little when Bjarni gestured to the helm to swing the bow toward the open sea.

Now they ran east with the wind, and in four days made land again, high mountains with a flash of distant ice, but with lush green fringing the sea. Here at last was the jarldom of Erik the Red. Now the skipper smiled, not for sighting a new world but for finally making port.

Bjarni's story stirred the Greenlanders. All that land for the taking! All those forests! All that adventure! They scoffed at good old Bjarni for ignoring it. And the sagas wrote him a bit part and forgot him, a dependable, coolheaded sea captain, but not much of a Viking.

Erik's sons, Leif, Thorvald, and Thorstein, grew up on Viking tales. Bjarni's story set Leif to daydreaming. Someday he would explore and

Blood feud: Erik the Red slays a rival settler in Iceland, circa 980.

conquer Bjarni's mysterious lands, and the sagas would laud him forever. And so, at about 25, "a big, strapping fellow, handsome to look at, thoughtful and temperate in all things," Leif Eriksson went to see old Bjarni, bought his ship, and hired a crew of 35. He was off to see what Bjarni had found.

Leif offered his sire a leading role in the expedition. But as Erik rode to the ship, the horse stumbled and he fell off. An evil omen. Said Erik, "I am not meant to discover more countries than this one we now live in. This is as far as we go together." Leif boarded without him, eased the knarr down the long stretch of Eriksfjord, and headed for the unknown.

Blessed with decent weather, Leif sailed to Bjarni's last landfall. As his shipmates clambered onto the layered rock of the coast, Leif crowed of outdoing Bjarni in this new country: "We at least have set foot on it." They named it Helluland ("flat-stone land"), and shoved off.

Coasting southward, they reached a stretch of low forest which Leif named Markland ("forest land"). White beaches rimmed the coast, and the men strode along the sand, found no sign of humans, and sailed away, huddled in their warm, hooded robes against a chilly nor'easter.

Landfall again; an island under a fair sky. The men climbed to its high point for a look around. And here the oft-embroidered sagas preserve one exquisitely real moment. "There was dew on the grass, and the first thing they did was to get some of it on their hands and put it to their lips, and to them it seemed the sweetest thing they had ever tasted." Here stand Leif Eriksson and his crew—real people with sweet dew on their lips—on the coast of North America a millennium ago.

The land to the south looked inviting, so they sailed to it. Rounding a cape, the ship headed close to shore. The men rowed a boat up a stream to a lake. At high tide they towed the knarr in and unloaded their sleeping bags of hide. Being Norse and fond of baths, they likely swam in the river, then dried out in the sun, lolling naked on the warm grass. "There was no lack of salmon in the river or the lake. . . . The country seemed to them so kind that no winter fodder would be needed for livestock." Leif decided to build shelters and stay the winter.

They explored all winter, and on one foray an old German in the group found grapes that he swore would yield wine. "Is that true, foster father?" Leif asked. "Where I was born there were plenty of vines and grapes," he answered. "And Leif named the country after its natural qualities," adds the saga, "and called it Vinland."

At last, with a sou'westerly astern, they sailed for home. Just off Greenland they rescued some shipwrecked mariners clinging to a reef. A woman was among them, the captain's wife, Gudrid. Leif's men eyed her hungrily, for even wet and bedraggled, she was a Norse beauty.

Reaching home, Leif told of Vinland to eager listeners. Old Erik soon died, and, as oldest son and heir, Leif the Lucky settled down to run the farm. But Leif's brother Thorvald was not so lucky. He set out for Vinland with a crew of 30, found Leif's houses, and moved right in. From

Leif Eriksson sighting America, circa 1000.

there on the venture was a disaster. One day Thorvald and his men saw three skin boats overturned on a beach. Under each, three men slept—small, fierce men with coarse hair and broad cheekbones. Thorvald's men dubbed them *skraelings* (wretches) and quickly slew eight of them. But the one that got away returned with a war party, shrieking and brandishing wooden bows. Thorvald died when an arrow struck home.

Now it was Leif's brother Thorstein who saw good luck turn bad. He won the fair widow Gudrid, and set out with her for Vinland to fetch Thorvald's body. But storms blew him about the ocean all summer, and his battered knarr finally staggered to Greenland a week before winter began. There he and many of his crew fell sick with fever and died.

Widowed again, Gudrid soon wed Thorfinn Karlsefni, a Norwegian seafarer. And when adventure beckoned, they sailed to Vinland with crews of Greenlanders and "all kinds of livestock."

But Leif's Vinland wasn't easy to find. At the first landfall, scouts found some grapes. That boded well. The passengers chattered happily as the two ships continued along the coast. In a series of bays and inlets the explorers found good land and deep water, and they eased the ships right into shore where they could at last off-load the livestock. The grass was tall, and the cattle grazed at will. And the people cleaned themselves, and the reeking ships, and set up camp.

They saw no sign of Leif's shelters, but the spot seemed hospitable enough for wintering over. In the fall Gudrid bore a son, Snorri—if the sagas be true, the first child of European lineage born in the New World. But a savage winter followed, and food ran short. When Thorhall the Hunter found a dead whale, he bragged that his incantations to Thor had washed it up. Most of the people refused to eat it, for they were Christians and wanted no favors from a pagan god. Perhaps a whiff of its putrid flesh stiffened their righteous resolve.

Things looked better by winter's end. One day Thorfinn and his explorers met with many skraelings, and began to trade peacefully. Then a bull from the Viking herd charged out of the woods. The skraelings fled. Three weeks later they replied with a howling attack of their own.

The Vikings fell back. Suddenly from their midst rang a woman's strident yell. "Why do you flee from such pitiful wretches, brave men like you?" bellowed Leif's sister, Freydis. Her blood ran rich with that old berserker fire: She seized a sword and faced the foe. Did she know that, in battle, skraelings never smote a woman? Or was it to make a splendid Viking gesture that she tore open her clothes and slapped the blade on her bared breast? They fled her shrieking charge, and no wonder.

Yet in the end, the skraelings won. Eventually, the harried Norse pulled out—but not before the doughty Freydis all but took over the expedition and carved out one more blazing episode for the sagas.

A group from Iceland had a larger boat than hers, and she wanted it. So she told her husband that they had maltreated her. "But you, spineless man that you are, will not avenge my shame or your own!"

Now we have done better than Bjarni where this country is concerned—we at least have set foot on it.
LEIF ERIKSSON

56

Leif Eriksson's arrival in the New World, as shown in a fanciful American painting of the early 20th century.

The henpecked husband "could endure her upbraidings no longer." He and his men slew the boatmen from Iceland. But no one would kill their women. No one? Seizing an ax, Freydis charged upon the five women and hacked them apart herself.

Freydis warned her crew that she would kill any man who peeped a word of her "damnable deed." But when the Norse abandoned Vinland and returned to Greenland, the story leaked out. Leif, like a true Viking, "took three men who had been with Freydis and tortured them to confess the whole affair."

But he couldn't bring himself to punish her. After all, she was family.

The Norse sagas blend history with storytelling, a mix that entertains but also distorts. The Grænlendinga Saga and the less accurate Eirik's Saga, written in Iceland in the 12th and 13th centuries respectively, chronicle the Norse discovery of North America long after the fact. From their vague and sometimes conflicting details, this story has been woven. Some scholars place Helluland in Baffin Island. Most think Vinland was Newfoundland, where the ruins of a Norse settlement dot the grass at L'Anse aux Meadows.

Ferdinand Magellan

By James A. Cox

Ferdinand Magellan. "So valiant and noble a captain," wrote chronicler Antonio Pigafetta. "No other had so much natural wit, boldness, or knowledge to sail . . . round the world."

I do not deny that I plotted to kill my master's Spanish captains. Why should I not want to kill them? I was his slave, not theirs. He, the Captain-General Fernão de Magalhães, whom you know as Ferdinand Magellan, wrote in his will that when he died I would be free. He often told me about it. But when he died, in that calamitous battle on Mactan Island in the Philippines, his captains refused to free me. But that is not the only reason I decided to kill them.

I was with Magellan when he died. I fought by his side against Chief Lapulapu's 3,000 warriors, and fled only when they gathered around my fallen master like flies on a lump of sugar, plunging their bamboo spears into his body. Where were the Spanish captains then? Safe on their ships, licking their mustaches and winking at each other. Even when Humabon, the Filipino raja whom Magellan had converted to Christianity, went from ship to ship with tears in his eyes, pleading with them to save his blood brother and their leader, they did nothing. Nothing until Humabon, in desperation, sent two canoes to snatch the survivors to safety. Then Carvalho of the *Concepción* loaded his carronades and sank Humabon's canoes. You cannot believe that? Believe it. I was with my beloved master from the beginning of the expedition, and I saw how they schemed to get rid of him.

I am Enrique de Malacca, sometimes called Black Henry. Magellan named me when I was 13 and a miserable slave in the Malay city of Malacca. That was in the year 1511. The Portuguese sacked the city, and Magellan, captain of a caravel, purchased me. I was fortunate. He was a good master, firm but considerate. I loved him like a father, and he taught me many things.

I sailed with him everywhere—eastward from Malacca until we stumbled on islands we took to be the Philippines . . . to Morocco and battles with the Moors, where a lance thrust behind the knee gave him a limp for life . . . back to Portugal, where his king insulted him, humiliated him, and cast him aside like an old shoe . . . to Seville, in Spain, where he married Beatriz Barbosa and fathered his son, Rodrigo . . . and on to Valladolid, where we entered the service of Spain's King

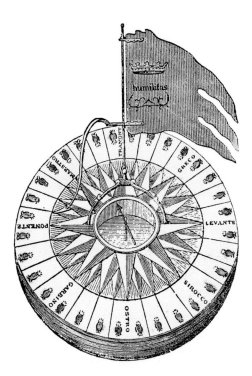

Magellan's compass, from a drawing by Pigafetta.

We ate only old biscuit turned to powder, all full of worms. . . . We ate also ox hides. . . . And of the rats . . . some of us could not get enough.

ANTONIO PIGAFETTA

Charles. For a score of years and more, Portugal had owned the eastward sea route around Africa to the Moluccas, the Spice Islands. My master now would seek a route for Spain by sailing west and finding *el paso,* the passage through the wall of land that blocked and deluded the great Christopher Columbus. So began that terrible voyage that the gods frowned on from the start.

I was Magellan's servant, his loyal and faithful friend, and his interpreter when we reached the islands. And always the ears that listened when he was angry or overflowing with excitement about some new chance at fame and riches.

Never was his excitement greater than in the spring of 1518. With the backing of influential men, he had gained approval for the expedition. As captain-general, he was assigned five rotting old naos—*Trinidad,* his flagship, *San Antonio, Concepción, Victoria,* and *Santiago.*

Soon the smiling men of influence became predators. Most powerful was Bishop Juan Rodríguez de Fonseca. While Magellan was at the docks, refitting his ships and poring over nautical charts, Fonseca was busy replacing good Portuguese seamen with incompetent Spanish dandies. Juan de Cartagena, the bishop's natural son—though referred to as his nephew—was named second-in-command and captain of *San Antonio.* Luís de Mendoza and Gaspar de Quesada were given *Victoria* and *Concepción.* Only João Serrão, Magellan's cousin, kept his command—*Santiago,* smallest in the fleet.

On August 10, 1519, the crewmen—all 270 or so—assembled at dawn for a solemn Mass of farewell. Magellan received the silken royal standard and vowed to claim any lands he discovered in the name of King Charles. Then his captains, pilots, and masters knelt before him and swore to obey him in all things. Antonio Pigafetta, a young Venetian nobleman who was keeping a diary of all that befell us, whispered, "It seems these captains hate your master exceedingly. Can it be merely because he is Portuguese and they are Spanish?" I held my tongue.

Our sorrows began only six days out of Spain. As we anchored off the Canary Islands to take aboard fresh vegetables, a fast caravel arrived from Spain with a secret message for my master: The Spanish captains and two treacherous Portuguese pilots, Estevão Gomes and João Carvalho, were planning to kill the captain-general and replace him with Cartagena.

Magellan called a meeting in his cabin. The conspirators arrived, biting their lips nervously. My master let them insult him, and even gave in when they demanded that he change his sailing plans. His meekness made them bolder—but gave them no excuse to strike.

Weeks at sea went by. Terrible gales hurled us about among towering breakers. Then we drifted becalmed near the Equator while the sun roasted our flesh and gagging stenches boiled up from the bilges. We had been at sea twice as long as Columbus on his first crossing, and tempers began to flare. The captains complained about every decision the

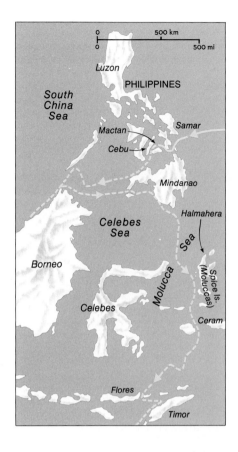

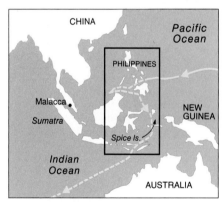

Site of Magellan's death on Mactan Island; subsequent route of the Victoria *under a minor Spanish mutineer, Juan Sebastián del Cano, who completed the voyage of circumnavigation.*

captain-general made. Even the seamen began to doubt his wisdom.

At a meeting aboard the flagship in November, the captains once again tried to provoke a quarrel. As before, my master accepted their taunts meekly, even when Cartagena, strutting about the cabin like an overweening cockerel, lectured him on navigation and accused him of endangering the fleet. Then the Spaniard went too far. "No longer am I prepared," he blurted, "to follow a hazardous course set by a fool!"

It was the moment Magellan had been waiting for. He seized Cartagena's doublet, roaring, "This is mutiny! You are my prisoner!"

"Stab him!" Cartagena screamed. But his henchmen dared not move, for the cabin was suddenly filled with *Trinidad*'s marines.

Magellan could have beheaded Cartagena on the spot. Instead, he sent him to *Victoria* as Mendoza's prisoner and gave the captaincy of *San Antonio* to Antonio de Coca, another "nephew" of the all-powerful bishop, instead of to one he could trust.

We sailed on. In December we raised the coast of Brazil. This was Portuguese territory, but no fleet guarded its shore. So we turned past a cone-shaped mountain into a beautiful, secluded bay; you know it as Rio de Janeiro. The natives were joyous at seeing us. They had been suffering a drought, and we arrived on the wings of thunderstorms—strange gods bearing the precious gift of rain. We stayed for 13 days, trading combs and little bells and playing cards for chickens, suckling pigs, and more fish than we could eat, and knives and hatchets for young women, who were comely and wore nothing but their hair.

This distressed my honorable master. He arrested his own brother-in-law, Duarte Barbosa, for carousing, and ordered the fleet to sail. Coca heard the crew grumble about leaving this paradise, so he released Cartagena, and the two illegitimate Fonsecas tried to stir up a mutiny. My master merely demoted Coca, put Cartagena back in irons, and named his own cousin, Alvaro de Mesquita, captain of *San Antonio*.

We could not linger in the realms of Spain's rival. Southward we drove, probing every inlet. The days grew shorter and the weather became bitter cold. Icy winds raged along a bleak, treeless coast. We were past latitude 40°, farther south than any explorer had ever been. We saw strange black-and-white geese that waddled upright and dived beneath the waves but could not fly. Who knew what terrors lay ahead?

Magellan sent the fleet into winter quarters in a bay he named Port San Julián. He had us build huts on the sandy shore, and reduced our daily rations. Again the air reeked of mutiny.

On Easter Sunday, Quesada of *Concepción* and 30 men stole aboard *San Antonio* and overpowered bumbling old Mesquita. When an officer yelled "Treason!" Quesada frantically stabbed him, then proclaimed himself captain of *San Antonio*. Mendoza of *Victoria* released the arrogant Cartagena, who took over *Concepción*. Next day, Quesada demanded the captain-general join him and the other captains on *San Antonio* to decide the expedition's future. An invitation to death.

Muffled in fog, Gonzalo Gómez de Espinosa, the fleet's master-at-arms, clambered aboard *Victoria* at dusk and handed Mendoza a letter

Magellan in the strait that bears his name, ushered by gods, demons, and nymphs.

from Magellan ordering him to the flagship. Mendoza laughed scornfully and crumpled the letter. Espinosa seized him by the beard and plunged a dagger into his throat. Before *Victoria*'s crew could react, Barbosa and a squad of armed men swarmed over the gunwale from a boat alongside. Barbosa weighed anchor, ranging *Victoria* near *Trinidad* and *Santiago.* Now the advantage was Magellan's, in numbers and position; his ships blocked the harbor. The mutineers laid down their arms.

This time there was a court-martial. Quesada paid with his head. Cartagena and Pedro Sanchez de Reina, the bawdy priest who was his advisor, would be marooned in that desolate land when we sailed in the spring. So it was done. I can but hope they were heard from no more.

But our troubles were by no means over. We left winter quarters in October, spring in that clime, in four ships, *Santiago* having been wrecked on a scouting mission. In a forbidding inlet only a few hundred miles south we at last found el paso—a series of deepwater channels and bays as far as the eye could see. My master was ecstatic, and so were the officers and crew at first. But they had been on short rations all winter. We were suffering the plague that afflicts sailors, swelling the gums and wasting the body. They looked at the harsh cliffs and snowcapped peaks and feared what lay ahead. Gomes, pilot of *San Antonio*, argued sourly that we should chart el paso and return home. Even Barbosa and Mesquita agreed. But Magellan did not. "Though we have nothing to eat but the leather wrappings from our masts," he cried, "we shall go on!"

We felt our way through the strait. One day *San Antonio* sailed behind an island and never rejoined us. Gomes had persuaded Mesquita— or overpowered him—and sailed for Spain.

The rest is short in the telling, though desperately long in the doing. We left el paso on November 28, 1520, on the bosom of a sea so calm Magellan named it Pacifico—"peaceful," in hopes it would always be so. We expected to anchor off the Spice Islands in a few days. All the chart makers in Europe agreed that this new sea was no wider than the Mediterranean was long. But the world was much bigger than they knew, and this endless ocean was the biggest thing on it.

One cloudless day followed another. Days became weeks. The sun burned hotter as we moved steadily north and west, but no sign of land did we see. Meat putrefied in the holds. Green scum fouled the water casks. We ate the last of our worm-filled biscuits, and hunting parties scoured the bilges for rats. Sharks circled the ships, growing fat on the bodies of our dead. And still there was no end to the emptiness.

Twice the gods pitied us, guiding us to islands where we found food and water. Over three months from el paso, more hollow-eyed skeletons than men, we finally reached the isles known as the Philippines. Somewhere in these isles, my master thought, he and I had made landfall many years before. If so, he and I became the first men to circle the globe completely, although not on a single voyage. It was a sweet triumph for the captain-general, for after some 550 days of hard sailing over thousands of miles of unknown seas, he had led us to the portals of our goal—the Spice Islands lay only a few days to the south.

But the gods of misfortune were not finished with Ferdinand Magellan. Our men had recovered from the terrible ordeal and were chafing to move on to the Spiceries and to fame and fortune in Spain. But the pious captain-general was obsessed with moving from island to island, persuading the natives to burn their idols and kiss the Cross of Christ. On Cebu he and the Filipino raja Humabon performed the native blood-mingling rite, and thousands eagerly embraced the new faith. My master came to see himself as an invincible instrument of his God.

So it was that, when Lapulapu scorned Humabon and Christ, Magellan, though never a bloodthirsty man, vowed to make an example of him. His officers pleaded to stay out of the matter and urged him to sail. But the captain-general would not be swayed. Since they were all against him and God's work, he said, he would lead the raid himself, taking only 60 volunteers from the crew. Humabon was appalled and offered a thousand trained warriors, but my master refused, saying that God would lead the soldiers of Christ to victory.

The outcome of that sad battle you know. Pigafetta, that man of words, spoke for those who grieved: "They slew our mirror, our light, our comfort, and our true guide." But I, who was like a son to him, was not allowed to mourn. The captains kicked and beat me when I told them I was a free man, and sent me ashore to collect provisions.

I sought out the disillusioned Humabon. I did not have to tell him how valuable the three ships would be in helping him subdue his rivals, or how valuable the trade goods in their holds. Back to the ships I went with Humabon's invitation for the Spanish officers to come to a farewell banquet and receive gifts of jewels and gold nuggets that the chief had promised to his lamented blood brother.

Like greedy, foolish sheep, 29 officers came ashore to gorge themselves with food and wine and the favors of Humabon's women. Something must have alerted Carvalho and Espinosa, for they slipped away to their ships. Otherwise, my vengeance would have been complete in the massacre that followed.

I watched the ships weigh anchor, pour a broadside into the native huts, and sail away for the Spiceries, leaving their officers for dead. I neither know nor care what befell them under their new leaders. I do miss Pigafetta and a few of the others, but I am serene in the knowledge that I have properly honored the memory of my beloved master, the Captain-General Ferdinand Magellan.

The facts of Black Henry's story are true, as best we can reconstruct it from the journals of Antonio Pigafetta and the various pilots' logs (Magellan's own were destroyed). Black Henry himself was never heard from after the ambush of the Spanish captains, and, so far as we know, he wrote no chronicle. But history should not forget him, for if one of Magellan's early, unrecorded voyages did go far enough east of Malacca, then Fernão de Magalhães and Enrique de Malacca were indeed the first men to circle the world.

I believe that nevermore will any man undertake to make such a voyage.
ANTONIO PIGAFETTA

April 27, 1521: Magellan falls in a skirmish on Mactan Island.

The Golden Americas

By Loren McIntyre

Christopher Columbus *did* reach an outpost of China—in a way.

On that morning in 1492 when the admiral supposed that he had landed on an outer island of the Celestial Empire and asked the naked inhabitants if they were subjects of the Great Khan, he was not altogether mistaken.

Some 20 millennia earlier, when oceans were lower and ice lay thick upon the land, wanderers from northern China began to spread across a thousand-mile-wide isthmus into Alaska. They and their descendants explored all the way to Cape Horn. Then the ice melted, the oceans rose, and the first Americans had two continents to themselves.

Before Europeans had learned to tack against the wind, those Americans had created great cities and civilizations. They adorned their temples and themselves with gold, and fashioned fountains and figures of the metal. Since its value was largely aesthetic, they never imagined that gold would bring alien armies crashing into their realms.

For a quarter century after Columbus's first voyage, Spanish explorers saw little more than the West Indies and failed to realize a new world lay beyond. The early colonists never got far enough inland to encounter the empires of Aztec and Inca.

Travelers returned to Spain with monkeys, slaves, and trinkets. But it was their talk of treasure that aroused the aspirations of unemployed swordsmen who had drifted to the seaports after driving the Moors from Spain in 1492. For almost eight centuries this breed had fought a holy war against the Muslims. These Spanish soldiers were quick to anger and quicker to attack. They hungered to become *hidalgos*, "somebodies" by means of force or wealth—and, if the Virgin smiled, in the New World one begot the other.

The promise of pearls drew one of them, Vasco Núñez de Balboa, to the West Indian colonies in 1501. Settling in Hispaniola, he found no treasure and got deeply into debt. To escape, he stowed away in a ship's cask, emerged in a settlement near the Gulf of Urabá, between Colombia and Panama, and tried to make a new life. The settlement failed. Its colonists—with stomachs empty and poison arrows whistling around them—left for safer ground, led by Balboa and Francisco Pizarro, an Indies veteran since 1502. Balboa then founded Darién, the first stable colony on the American mainland.

With astonishing energy, considering the depressing humidity, Balboa spent years exploring both rain-lashed sides of the Gulf of Urabá. On one campaign with Francisco Pizarro, Balboa sighted the Pacific Ocean and took possession of the "South Sea" for his Spanish sovereigns.

A picture of the New World was emerging. Maps now showed a continuous coastline from the mouth of the Rio Grande to beyond the mouth

Grim warriors of basalt guard the ruins of Tula, capital of a pre-Aztec empire that flourished in Mexico from about A.D. 900 to 1200. From Tula sprang the legend of Quetzalcoatl, a bearded, light-skinned god banished by a rival. Sailing eastward on a giant raft, Quetzalcoatl vowed to return. His prophecy, and others like it, helped set the stage for the conquest of Mexico and Peru five centuries later, when ships brought bearded, fair-skinned strangers—the Spanish conquistadores.

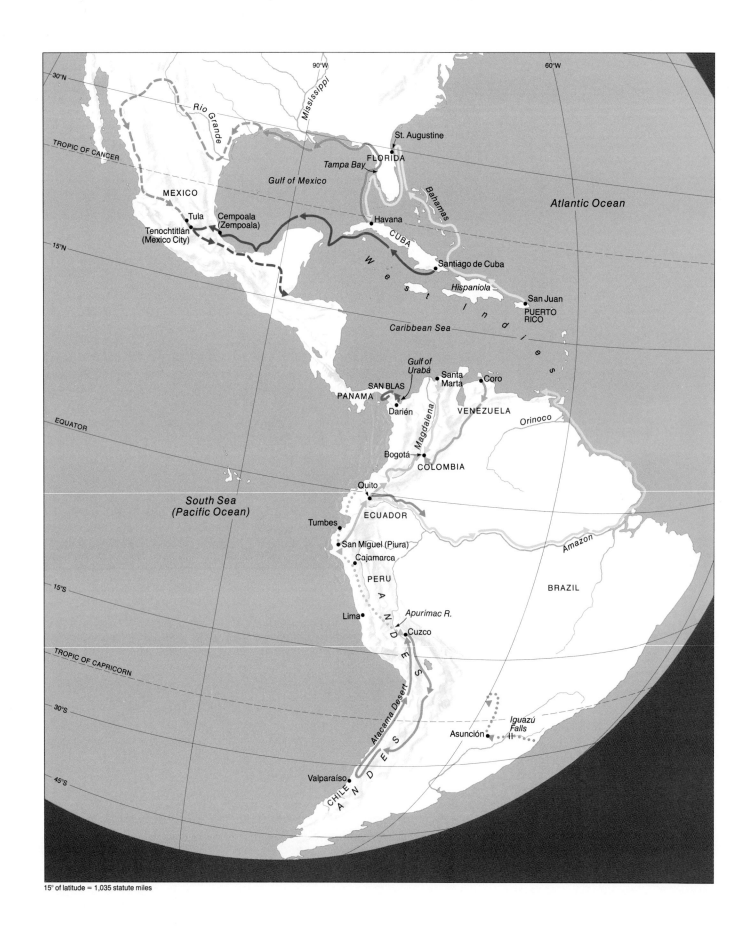

30°N

90°W   60°W

Río Grande

Mississippi

TROPIC OF CANCER

St. Augustine

Tampa Bay

FLORIDA

Gulf of Mexico

Bahamas

MEXICO

Atlantic Ocean

Tula
Cempoala
(Zempoala)

Havana

CUBA

Tenochtitlán
(Mexico City)

W e s t

15°N

Santiago de Cuba

San Juan

Hispaniola

PUERTO
RICO

Caribbean Sea

I n d i e s

*Gulf of
Urabá*

Santa
Marta

Coro

SAN BLAS

PANAMA

Darién

Magdalena

VENEZUELA

Orinoco

EQUATOR

Bogotá

COLOMBIA

Quito

ECUADOR

*South Sea
(Pacific Ocean)*

Tumbes

San Miguel (Piura)

Cajamarca

Amazon

BRAZIL

PERU

15°S

A

Lima

Apurímac R.

Cuzco

N

TROPIC OF CAPRICORN

D

30°S

E

*Iguazú
Falls*

Atacama Desert

S

Asunción

45°S

Valparaíso

CHILE

A   N   D   E   S

15° of latitude = 1,035 statute miles

Sixteenth-century dreams of gold and glory fueled one of the greatest outbursts of exploration, conquest, and colonization the world had yet seen. In less than half a century, Spaniards had reconnoitered and conquered vast regions of the New World. The widely heralded successes of Hernán Cortés in Mexico and Francisco Pizarro in Peru lent credence to tales of fabulous riches. Both men found gold treasures, like those shaped by Colombia's Tairona Indians (lower), but Cortés's luck

eventually ran out. Restless for new riches, he left Tenochtitlán three years after conquering the Aztec capital, and struck southward on a fruitless two-year campaign through the jungles, where he found only illness and despair. Many others came in search of El Dorado, the fabled gilded man, said to be a chieftain whose subjects anointed him from head to toe with gold dust on ceremonial occasions (below).

of the Amazon River. And probes into Mexico in 1517 and 1518 suggested that it was not an island, as originally thought, but part of a mainland. The Indians living there were better dressed and housed than natives in Cuba. The Cuban governor could not authorize conquest and settlement, but he sent Hernán Cortés, a 33-year-old farmer, to "engage in discovery and trade" while scouting the Mexican shore for lost ships and sailors.

Cortés had something more in mind. He fitted out a force of 11 ships and 600 men, and put to sea before the governor could move to restrain him. The conquest of Mexico was underway.

Tales reaching Spain of his successful invasion—the smoking volcanoes, the plumed priests, the Indian mistress, the victims' screams—struck the European imagination like an Amadís exploit come true.

Amadís de Gaula was "the one knight errant above all others," a fictitious superman of chivalric romances. Spawned by medieval holy wars, the Amadís stories were perhaps the most popular printed matter in Spain. To gain gold and glory or rapturous love, Amadís fought pagan kings against astounding odds—just as Cortés attacked armies of real heathens in distant Mexico.

Cortés's success set off a rush to find more Mexicos. The king commissioned Pánfilo de Narváez to conquer and settle Florida. As with so many expeditions in the decade to

With sword and buckler raised to the heavens, Vasco Núñez de Balboa lays claim to the Pacific Ocean "for the royal Crown of Castile" on the evening of September 29, 1513. His dog, Leoncico—Little Lion—was one of a specially trained pack that tore Indians to pieces; Leoncico frolics on the beach in this 17th-century engraving. Two days earlier, from "a peak in Darién," Balboa had gazed upon the broad waters of the "South Sea"—the first European to do so. Friendly Indians, promising the riches that lay beyond, guided him across the narrow Isthmus of Panama on a 22-day march through the jungle. Today their descendants, the Cuna Indians of San Blas, inhabit villages (opposite) much like those visited by the explorer. Balboa did not long survive his triumph. A few years later he was arrested, tried, and beheaded on trumped-up treason charges brought by the governor of Panama.

Vasco Nuñe del Sur

come, Narváez's plans were scuttled by desertions, storms, starvation, Indian attack, and death. The expedition set out with hundreds of men, but only four survived. One of those four, Álvar Núñez Cabeza de Vaca, proved to be an explorer's explorer, working on two continents.

Shipwrecked off the Texas coast, Cabeza de Vaca wandered through southwestern North America, where Indians enslaved him. In 1536, eight years after his journey began, Cabeza de Vaca and his companions reappeared in Mexico, describing how they had seen bison and repeating rumors about rich Indian pueblos. The rumors became legend: the Seven Golden Cities of a land called Cíbola. Eager listeners went to search for them. Cabeza de Vaca turned to South America and there discovered the world's widest waterfall, Iguazú.

An explosive decade of discovery in South America was dominated by Francisco Pizarro, Balboa's companion at the discovery of the South Sea. Hearing of a rich realm to the south, Pizarro in 1524 began to probe the Pacific coast from Panama, sailing farther each time. Unlike Cortés, he returned to Spain for royal approval of his plans—and for a coat of arms displaying a llama and a title: governor and captain-general of Peru—wherever that might be. He sailed back to America with his four half brothers from Extremadura, the harsh frontier of west-central Spain where many conquistadores were born.

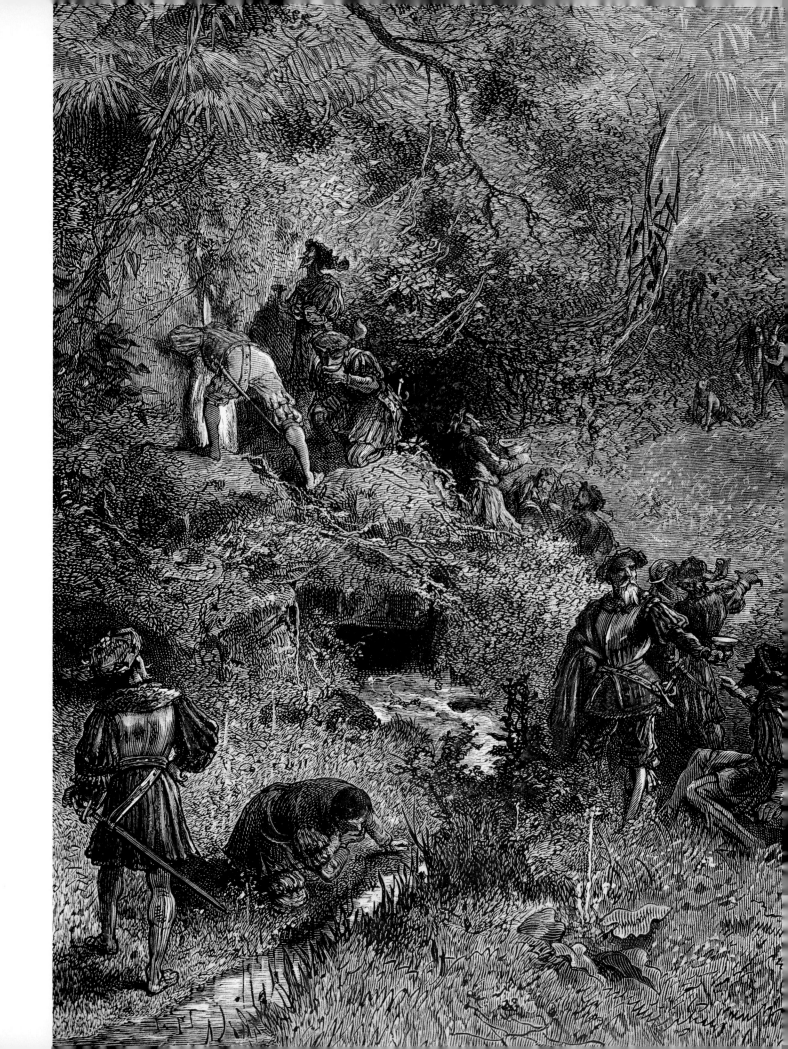

Early in 1531 Pizarro, then in his fifties, sailed on a final voyage from Panama. He landed inside the Inca Empire, near the Equator, and fought his way down the coast with a ridiculously small force of less than 200 soldiers. They were a thousand miles from Panama—and even farther from Cuzco, the Inca capital in the Andes. "The daring of the Spaniards is so great that nothing in the world can daunt them," wrote Pedro de Cieza de León, a soldier who came later with paper and ink in his saddlebags. "No other race," he wrote, "can penetrate through such rugged lands . . . solely by the valor of their persons . . . without bringing with them wagons of provisions, nor great store of baggage, nor tents in which to rest." But they always brought along a few firearms, and the cherished horses that vastly extended each rider's mobility and power.

Luckily for Pizarro the Inca realm was too disrupted by plague and civil war to pay him much heed. He recruited a force of dissident Indians to help him. The Indians, in turn, felt that *they* had enlisted Pizarro to fight their hated Inca overlords, who plucked whole populations from their homelands and exchanged them with others in distant parts of the empire—a device that restrained rebellion. Local tribes were often willing to collaborate with the Spaniards. When Pizarro heard that Atahuallpa, the ruling Inca, was camped

Showdown at Cempoala: Pánfilo de Narváez, fettered, and wounded in the eye, stands before a victorious Cortés. At the behest of Cuba's governor, Narváez had come to arrest Cortés, who had exceeded his authority in Mexico. But the sly Cortés turned the tables: With a handful of trusted troopers, he struck at Narváez with lightning speed on a rainy night, routing his rival's much larger force. Narváez eventually returned to Spain and in 1527 mounted an expedition with hundreds of men to explore and conquer Florida, a place barely touched by Ponce de León and previous visitors. Landing near Tampa Bay, Narváez encountered stiff Indian resistance. The expedition soon disintegrated. One of its four survivors, Álvar Núñez Cabeza de Vaca (seated at center, below), returned to Mexico—but only after an agonizing eight-year trek through southwestern North America.

with his army at Cajamarca, he led his Indian allies, 62 cavalrymen, 105 foot soldiers, and a priest into the high Andes of Peru. His daring act abruptly changed the lives of the six million people who dwelt there.

Atahuallpa, protected by 30,000 to 80,000 Inca warriors, was bemused by the approach of the band of bearded strangers, their beasts, and their magic staves that spoke thunder. He withdrew his people from Cajamarca and let Pizarro's army occupy the town.

On the next day, November 16, 1532, Atahuallpa, surrounded by thousands of chanting courtiers, swept royally into Cajamarca to dine with the crafty Pizarro. At the sight of all these heathens, "many Spaniards wet their pants from terror," wrote an eyewitness. But then the conquistadores sprang their trap, charging out of the shadows of Cajamarca's doorways. Guns thundered. Horses' hooves clattered. Lances and swords thrust and slashed at feathered warriors who cowered as if attacked by supernatural forces. Thousands of Indians died, while Pizarro captured Atahuallpa without losing a single Spaniard.

For ransom, the Inca chief agreed to fill a 17-by-22-foot room once with gold and twice with silver as high as he could reach. Francisco Pizarro's half brother Hernando rode south with 20 horsemen to speed the flow of treasure. For three months Hernando gathered loot along a thousand miles of Inca highway,

An Inca-style footbridge made of twisted grasses sways above the gorge of the Apurímac River in Peru. At the time Francisco Pizarro was putting an end to the Inca Empire, hundreds of such spans linked more than 14,000 miles of roadways that reached from Chile to Ecuador. To cross the Huaca-chaca, or Holy Bridge, over the raging Apurímac was, in the words of one conquistador, "no small terror."

beneath lofty cordilleras heavy with ice and along deserts where rain falls once a generation. He paused in 40 towns, where time stood still: While Atahuallpa was captive, no Indian dared lift a weapon. By mid-1533 more than 24 tons of exquisite treasure had been melted down. Each common soldier got 45 pounds of gold and 90 of silver.

Hernando took the royal fifth of the booty to Spain, pausing long enough in the Indies to tell his story. Such was the ensuing gold rush to Peru that the governor of Puerto Rico cut off some settlers' feet to deter others and slow the exodus.

Meanwhile, Francisco's partner, Diego de Almagro, brought reinforcements to Cajamarca too late to share the ransom. The Spaniards executed Atahuallpa and set out for Cuzco. Pizarro sacked and occupied the Inca capital late in 1533.

In 1535 Almagro left Cuzco with 570 Spaniards and 12,000 Indians to explore lands to the south, awarded him by the king of Spain. On a year-and-a-half march into Chile, Almagro left a horrifying trail of dead and mutilated Indians. He found no golden cities, only terrain so arid that even 20,000-foot volcanoes held no snow. His "Men of Chile," disillusioned by their barren journey, later murdered Francisco Pizarro.

Sebastián de Benalcázar, who captured Quito for Pizarro in 1534, turned his attention northward to the gold-rich tribes of Colombia. Many adventurers had heard of such wealthy Indians, which led to the most astonishing coincidence in South American exploration: When Benalcázar finally reached the gold-smithing Muisca Indian homeland around present-day Bogotá, he found it already occupied—by Spaniards dressed like Muiscas, their European clothes long since rotted away. They were the remnants of a large expedition from the Caribbean led up the Magdalena River by a lawyer, Gonzalo Jiménez de Quesada. Within weeks of the wary meeting of conquistadores from north and south on the Muisca plain, yet a third group of explorers in sorry state appeared from the east, led by Nikolaus Federmann, a German whom the Spanish king had authorized to explore Venezuela. Federmann was hollow eyed from a fruitless two-year search for gold in the llanos—a grassland the size of California.

Other adventurers were drawn to the mountains near Bogotá, where a huge lake had been formed by a meteorite. Tribal memory held that a chieftain used to be ritually dusted with gold, rafted out, and rinsed in the lake to send a golden rain to the bottom—perhaps to propitiate a fiery god who had fallen to the Earth.

The mystique of El Dorado, The Gilded Man, had caught on in Quito by 1541. The first to search for him was the governor, Gonzalo Pizarro, Francisco's youngest brother. With 220 Spaniards, 4,000 Indians, and thousands of hogs, llamas, and dogs, Gonzalo marched into the steaming

79

"Santiago, and at them!" cry Francisco Pizarro's soldiers, invoking the aid of St. James in their fight for the Inca capital of Cuzco (below). The war whoop, used when Spaniards drove the Moors from their homeland, inspired the slaughter of countless American infidels as well. In just one year, Pizarro brought the mighty Inca Empire to its knees. The Incas' hand axes and clubs proved but a crude match for the sword-swinging horsemen of Spain and their Indian allies. When Pizarro's weary army finally captured Cuzco on November 15, 1533, a proud soldier described the prize in a letter to King Charles V: "We can assure Your Majesty that it is so beautiful and has such fine buildings that it would be remarkable even in Spain."

The conquistadores' bold campaign left a trail of carnage in the New World, recalled in a plundered burial site near Lima, Peru (opposite).

jungle east of the snowcapped Andes to claim the Land of Cinnamon and the Lake of El Dorado, as he called it. "Passing through great marshes and crossing many streams," he ran short of food, and was forced to eat his priceless horses.

Gonzalo sent a foraging party downriver under Francisco de Orellana, but the gathering waters swept Orellana's ship east into a huge river where skirted warriors fired arrows from the banks. "There was one woman among them who shot an arrow a span deep into one of the brigantines," wrote a chronicler, "and others less deep, so that our brigantines looked like porcupines." Orellana survived the 2,800-mile odyssey down the Amazon. He had explored Earth's largest river—so extensive that its ultimate source was unknown until the 20th century.

Meanwhile, Gonzalo Pizarro had slogged home to find Francisco murdered. He later met his own death on the block, for making himself dictator of Peru without royal approval.

Soon the tale of El Dorado grew into a legend that lured expeditions into humid undergrowth and frigid heights, and speeded the conquest of both continents. Retelling by chroniclers transformed The Gilded Man into a rich city "resplendent in the beaming sun" that passed into European literature and found its way onto maps of the Orinoco, the Amazon, and the Andes. In time, El Dorado came to symbolize splendors forever sought yet unattainable.

Hernán Cortés

By Elizabeth L. Newhouse

Allies against Moctezuma: A Tlaxcalan chief agrees to aid Hernán Cortés. Between them Marina, Cortés's Indian mistress, waits to translate. "Beautiful as a goddess," the chronicles said.

istory notes that Marina, also called Malinche, was born near Aztec lands and sold into slavery as a child. We do not know if she ever sent Charles V a letter such as this, but we do know what it might have said—

Most High Mighty and Catholic Prince, Invincible Emperor and Sovereign:

Most humbly I write on behalf of my lord and master, Hernán Cortés, Marquess of the Valley of Oaxaca, Captain-General of New Spain, in support of his petition to be reinstated as governor of that same great dominion, which through constancy and valor he delivered unto your realm some ten years past. To his heroic service and unswerving loyalty I can attest, for from his arrival in this land until its conquest, I rarely left his side.

In the Year of Our Lord 1519, I was residing in a coastal town in the region of Tabasco, the slave of a Maya chief. One day 11 ships arrived; "temples in the sea," the people said. Thousands of our warriors shot arrows and hurled javelins and stones at the bearded white men. Over several days they furiously fought; the Spaniards' cannon and musket fire cut down hundreds but could not drive them off. Then from behind us came a terrifying surprise, snorting, racing creatures never before seen by our people. Our warriors, believing each horse and rider to be one animal, turned and fled, and the battle was lost.

In homage to the white lords, our Indian chieftains brought gifts of fowl and maize cakes, gold ornaments and cloth. And 20 women, including your most humble servant, myself. The Spaniards called us pagan idolaters and would not cohabit with us until we had been baptized into the True Faith, and so we were among the first native Christians of New Spain. I was christened Marina and given to Alonso Hernández Puertocarrero. Later the great Cortés would take me for his own, and I would bear him a son. But first I had a greater service to perform.

83

My understanding of both Maya and Aztec languages allowed me to interpret for Cortés through a Maya-speaking Spaniard he had found shipwrecked down the coast. The captain treated me kindly for he was well pleased; his ambitions on behalf of Your Sacred Majesty required communication with my countrymen. No other man has shown such zeal in Your Majesty's service. Fie on those rivals and enemies who now slur Cortés's name by falsely accusing him of squandering treasure and seeking the independent sovereignty of New Spain!

No hardship, no obstacle would divert him from his glorious cause: securing Moctezuma's empire for Your Majesty's Crown.

We met Moctezuma's emissaries on Good Friday, some leagues up

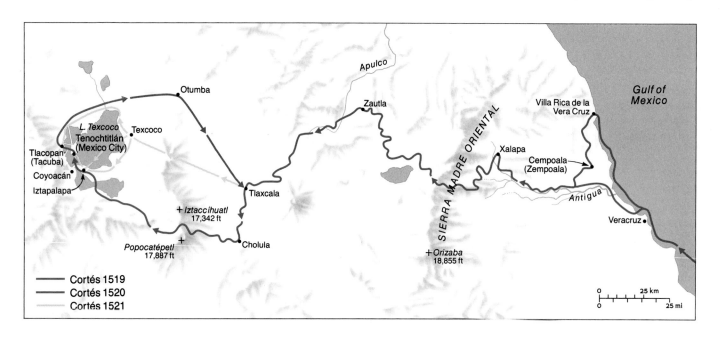

the coast from Tabasco. Cortés gave them blue beads and told them we were vassals of the greatest Emperor on Earth and that we had come in friendship to meet their prince. Artists made pictures of the Spaniards and their ships to send by runners to Moctezuma. The messengers described the horses as "deer" and showed him thundering cannon that could pulverize a tree, and dogs with "blazing eyes," an Aztec later said. "And when Moctezuma so heard, he was much terrified."

The emissaries returned with gifts astonishing to the Spaniards: a turquoise mask, gold ornaments in the shapes of animals, and two disks representing the sun and moon, one of gold, one of silver. They also brought food soaked in human blood, which nauseated the Spaniards on beholding. All this, Moctezuma's message said, for the *teules*—gods—who have come in fulfillment of a prophecy. But, he implored, venture no farther toward my capital, Tenochtitlán. Later he ordered his magicians to "cast a spell over them . . . cast stones at them . . . utter an incantation over them, so that they might take sick, might die, or else because of it turn back."

Cortés the conqueror in 1530, as captain-general of New Spain.

The gifts of gold made my brave captain ever more determined to proceed inland. "It is probable that this land contains as many riches as that from which Solomon is said to have obtained the gold for the temple," he exclaimed. But first there was a political matter to attend to.

The governor of Cuba had sent Cortés to trade and explore the coast of New Spain. Now the governor's officers accused my master of exceeding instructions and demanded his return to Cuba. Abandon Your Majesty's holy work? Not Cortés! He established a settlement, Villa Rica de la Vera Cruz, in Your Majesty's name and made himself captain-general, thus to renounce the governor's authority and serve directly Your Sovereign Majesty. Later he destroyed all his ships, lest they tempt the weakhearted into rebellion. An audacious move, but audacity came easily to Cortés in pursuit of Your Majesty's sacred interests.

Cortés had learned that Moctezuma had enemies too, important ones like the Totonacs, who would aid Your Majesty's cause. At Cempoala, their admirable capital, the fat chieftain told us how cruelly Moctezuma had subjugated and oppressed his people. Every year the prince demanded their sons and daughters for servitude or sacrifice. And his tax collectors kidnapped and ravished whatever women struck their fancy.

To prove his helpfulness, my captain ordered five of Moctezuma's tax collectors imprisoned. He told the quaking Totonacs: You and your allies should pay Moctezuma no more tribute or obedience. While saying these things, Cortés secretly arranged for the tax collectors to escape to Moctezuma with messages of friendship. Ah, the intrigues we concocted in Your Majesty's royal service!

The service of the Almighty Father was also on my pious master's mind. "How can we ever accomplish anything worth doing if for the honor of God we do not first abolish these sacrifices made to idols?" Cortés demanded. Every day at Cempoala he saw priests tear throbbing hearts from the chests of human victims and offer them to idols. When the Totonacs made clear they would not destroy the evil images, Cortés sent his soldiers to do it for them. Then he ordered lime to cleanse the temple of blood and had an altar built to the Virgin.

In August we sallied forth again, with 200 Totonac bearers and 40 chieftains to guide us. Our route led through the land of Moctezuma's bitter enemies, the Tlaxcalans, fierce warriors whom Cortés hoped to enlist as allies. From the tropical coast we crossed mountains and a high plateau, with cold, rain, and hunger our constant companions.

In the plaza of one town, we found more than 100,000 human skulls in piles. "Desist from your sacrifices, and no longer eat the flesh of your own relations, and the other evil customs which you practice," demanded staunch Cortés of the chieftains. He set about raising a cross when a priest stayed his hand: "It seems to me, sir, that the time has not yet come to leave crosses in the charge of these people for they are somewhat shameless and without fear."

Soon after we crossed into Tlaxcala Province the full force of an army, 40,000 Indians in feathery dress, came down upon our meager company of 400 soldiers and several hundred Indian allies. With bows

The meeting of Cortés and Moctezuma: November 8, 1519.

and arrows, clubs, and obsidian-pointed javelins the Tlaxcalans struck. Four times they charged. Four times our cannon, crossbows, and armored horsemen sent them fleeing. Finally, as God was on our side, they yielded. But the damage to our force and spirit was great. Cortés later wrote: "There was not one amongst us who was not heartily afraid at finding himself so far in the interior of the country among so many and such warlike people." But turn back? Many suggested it, but our captain exhorted them onward, reminding them of their opportunity to gain for Your Majesty the greatest dominions in the world.

And this is the man whom foes now call disloyal!

Forty-five Spaniards died in battle here. While others tended their vicious wounds, my valiant master commanded me to send messengers to the Tlaxcalans, saying if you do not come and make peace within two days, we will destroy you. Finally a large group of chieftains arrived and offered themselves as vassals of Your Majesty. We accepted entreaties to come to their capital, even while receiving emissaries from Moctezuma, who implored us not to go there, fearing an alliance. "I

86

continued to treat with both one and the other," wrote the shrewd captain, "thanking each in secret for the advice . . . and professing to regard each with greater friendship than the other."

In Tlaxcala Cortés found much to praise. "The city is indeed so great and marvelous . . . much larger than Granada and much better fortified." We concluded a most excellent alliance with the Tlaxcalans and left for Cholula. Our new allies had warned us that the Cholulans were vassals of Moctezuma. But by now the Aztec prince, desperate to separate us from Tlaxcala, had invited us to his capital by this swift route. A thousand Tlaxcalan warriors accompanied us to Cholula's outskirts.

There, we were told, 20,000 of Moctezuma's warriors lay in ambush, and already pots with salt and peppers and tomatoes had been prepared to cook our flesh in. But bold Cortés moved first. "We fell upon the Indians in such fashion that within two hours more than three thousand of them lay dead," my captain wrote. He sent word to Moctezuma: Though the Cholulans blame you for the provocation, I do not believe so great a prince, a professed friend, could be capable of such treachery.

Ah, pity Moctezuma; surely he saw his match in Your Majesty's steadfast servant. The prince's emissaries brought gifts of gold to the Spaniards, who "lusted for it like pigs," an Aztec remarked. But pleas to advance no farther could not stay our captain.

We climbed over a high pass close by a smoking mountain—the first the awestruck Spaniards had ever seen. We proceeded through a valley and soon reached the shores of a vast lake. A league farther on, a causeway led us to an island city called Iztapalapa with fine stone houses, floating flower gardens, and pools of fresh water.

About two leagues down the causeway, we saw the glistening temples and palaces of the great Aztec capital, Tenochtitlán, rising like a vision in the lake's center. Thousands of people, many paddling canoes, came out to look at us; never had they seen horses or such as Spaniards. Though the day was hot, our foot soldiers walked in close formation. "As we are but human and feared death, we never ceased thinking about it. . . . we made short marches, and commended ourselves to God and to Our Lady. . . ." one said later, for they knew not what to expect.

Most Sovereign Lord, the rest of the story you know well: How Moctezuma, richly attired and borne on a litter, came to welcome Cortés and bow down in greeting; how he lodged us in great apartments, fed us sumptuously, and gave us splendid gifts of featherwork, embroidered cloth, and gold. How Moctezuma and Cortés exchanged all manner of flattery, and how Moctezuma pledged obedience, repeating the prophecy that a great lord would come and conquer this land. And how Your Majesty's servants discovered the city's awesome wealth—the fine buildings, the system of canals, the sweet gardens, the market where thousands traded foods, gold ornaments, and other manner of finery. And the stink and horror of the blood-encrusted temples.

When rumors started that the Aztecs schemed to cut the bridges and trap us, Cortés took Moctezuma hostage to ensure our safety. Unable by plea and reason to turn Moctezuma from his gods, our leader then had the prince's favored idols thrown from the temples and replaced them with our holy Christian images. Moctezuma, emboldened by this effrontery, warned us to leave before his people killed us.

Cortés did have to leave the capital, to battle a force under Pánfilo de Narváez that the Cuban governor sent to relieve Cortés of power, and it sorely cost Your Majesty's cause. The impetuous captain left in charge attacked a group of Aztec holidaymakers, provoking a general uprising against us. Although Cortés marched back and tried to make peace, the Aztecs fought on. Among the casualties was the great Moctezuma, stoned by his own people because they felt he had betrayed them.

We fled the city under darkness, but as we struggled down the causeway, the Aztecs caught part of our rear guard, dragged them to the temple, and slashed open their chests and offered their pulsing hearts to the gods. Hundreds of Spaniards and thousands of Tlaxcalans died on this sad night, *la noche triste*, June 30, 1520. But, Most Sovereign Lord, take pride, for as a survivor averred: "All the Spaniards who that day saw Hernán Cortés in action swear that never did a man fight as he did, or lead his troops, and that he alone in his own person saved them all."

Bowed, yes, but abandon the holy cause? Not Cortés. Six months later, his army reinforced by artillery, Spanish troops, and thousands of Tlaxcalans and other allies, he set out from Tlaxcala to reconquer Tenochtitlán. Bearers brought 13 brigantines in pieces across the mountains and began to assemble them by the lake. Your Majesty's shrewd captain laid siege to the city and cut off its fresh water. By May he sent assault parties down the causeways from Tlacopan, Coyoacán, and Iztapalapa, and he himself set sail across the lake. After almost 80 days, the capital lay in ruins, and the dead bodies of tens of thousands of Indians clogged the city. On the 13th of August in Our Lord's Year 1521, Spaniards seized the new ruler, Cuauhtémoc, and the Aztecs surrendered.

In the name of Your Most Excellent Prince, Cortés had secured Moctezuma's empire; now he would go on to rebuild the city and conquer more lands for Your realm. The deeds I have recounted here, Most Catholic Lord, bear witness to his invincible courage and steadfast loyalty. I close now in the humble expectation that Your Royal Person will see fit, in all justice, to restore the favors and honors so richly due Your Majesty's servant, the greatest of your conquistadores, Hernán Cortés.

On the 6th of December in the year of Our Lord 1530, Your Sacred Majesty's very humble slave and vassal who kisses the royal hands and feet of Your Highness,

Marina

The chronicles of Bernal Díaz del Castillo, one of Cortés's soldiers, document the events we have put in Marina's letter, as well as her devotion to her master and lover; Friar Bernardino de Sahagún recorded the Aztec side of the story. Perhaps a plea like this would have helped Cortés, for despite his own best efforts, he was never reinstated and died in Spain a bitter man.

CONQVISTA DE MEXICO POR CORTES. N.7

Cortés and his troops storming the Aztec capital: May 1521.

By Trail and Stream

By Ernest B. Furgurson

Cypress stumps in Louisiana's Atchafalaya swamp exemplify the forbidding terrain Hernando de Soto explored on his gold hunt through southeastern North America. The successes of Pizarro and Cortés brought on a rampaging gold fever that sent would-be conquistadores hacking and battling their way into North America's wilds. De Soto's extensive 1539-1542 expedition discovered the Mississippi River, but left him dead on its banks 50 miles from the Atchafalaya's northern end.

Some Americans have it all wrong.

It would be understandable for a visitor brainwashed in the many-layered historyland of the East Coast to arrive in Washington, focal point of American history, and stand beside the Potomac River and imagine out there one of our fabled explorers. Instead of monuments and jets and busy bridges, he might see brave Capt. John Smith of Virginia heading upstream nearly 400 years ago into the rich interior of the continent.

But it didn't happen that way.

We tend to forget that the continent was not seen first by Virginia cavaliers or Massachusetts Pilgrims, nor opened by hunters in raccoon caps and pioneers in covered wagons pressing west. In time they did move across the land and people our folklore, but long before Smith was born or the idea of Virginia conceived, the Spaniards and French were making bold flanking movements that left the English far behind on the Atlantic shore for most of the 1600s.

In western New Mexico you can still see reminders of that bygone Spanish presence. Here, where cloud shadows race across the juniper and rabbitbrush, the land is so big and empty it absorbs the modern marks of man just as it has enfolded the old.

The most poignant of those may be at Kyakima, easternmost of the Zuni pueblos, which rises against the towering, red and pale ocher Dowa Yalanne mesa. Ravens and sometimes golden eagles soar on thermals up the face of the mesa. At its base, above the ruins, are graffiti left by disrespectful visitors of modern times. And beneath those, worn but clear to anyone who knows where to look, are centuries-old Indian petroglyphs. One, crude and eloquent, is the angular outline of a man on a horse, carrying a lance. It has been there, facing the constant wind, for almost 450 years, since the first horsemen rode up with Francisco Vásquez de Coronado, a great conquistador who, like many others, came in pride and left in humility.

The Spanish lust for gold and empire was heightened by the account of explorer Álvar Núñez Cabeza de Vaca, who in 1536 began repeating Indian tales of rich cities, the seven cities of Cíbola, somewhere north of the Mexican mountains. To the Spaniards, eager to plunder another Peru, this was new evidence that their favorite legend was true.

The legend of seven golden cities was a prime motivator for the Spaniards in ripping open the New World. It originated back in the mists of Moorish occupation of Spain, in a tale of how a Christian archbishop and six bishops led their people to escape into the Atlantic Ocean, to an island where each of the prelates created a flourishing city. In retelling, the cities grew and turned to gold and shifted about with the flow of Spanish history, always

91

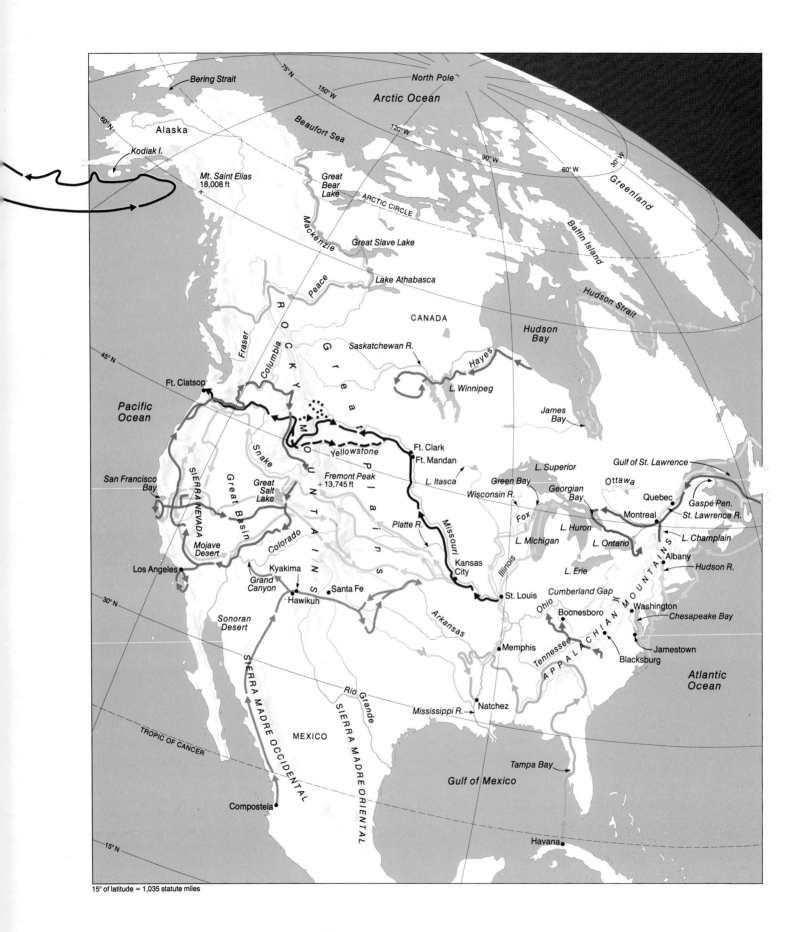

Bering Strait · North Pole · Arctic Ocean · 75° N · 150° W · 120° W · 90° W · 60° W · 30° W

60° N · Alaska · Beaufort Sea · Greenland

Kodiak I. · Mt. Saint Elias 18,008 ft + · Great Bear Lake · ARCTIC CIRCLE · Baffin Island

Mackenzie · Great Slave Lake · Hudson Strait

Peace · Lake Athabasca · CANADA · Hudson Bay

45° N · Fraser · R O C K Y · Saskatchewan R. · Hayes · L. Winnipeg

Ft. Clatsop · Columbia · G r e a t · James Bay

Pacific Ocean · Snake · M O U N T A I N S · Yellowstone · Ft. Clark · Ft. Mandan · L. Superior · Gulf of St. Lawrence

San Francisco Bay · SIERRA NEVADA · Great Salt Lake · Fremont Peak + 13,745 ft · L. Itasca · Green Bay · Wisconsin R. · Ottawa · Quebec · Gaspé Pen.

Great Basin · Platte R. · P l a i n s · Fox · Georgian Bay · Montreal · St. Lawrence R.

Colorado · Missouri · L. Michigan · L. Huron · L. Ontario · L. Champlain

Los Angeles · Mojave Desert · Kansas City · Illinois · L. Erie · Albany · Hudson R.

30° N · Kyakima · Santa Fe · Arkansas · St. Louis · Cumberland Gap · Washington · Chesapeake Bay

Grand Canyon · Hawikuh · Ohio · Boonesboro · APPALACHIAN MOUNTAINS

Sonoran Desert · Tennessee · Memphis · Jamestown · Blacksburg

SIERRA MADRE OCCIDENTAL · Rio Grande · SIERRA MADRE ORIENTAL · Mississippi R. · Natchez · Atlantic Ocean

TROPIC OF CANCER · MEXICO

Tampa Bay · Gulf of Mexico

Compostela · 15° N

Havana

15° of latitude = 1,035 statute miles

Lust for riches enticed the Europeans to penetrate deep into North America. Spanish conquistadores—de Soto and Coronado—sought gold in the South and West, as the French led by Cartier vainly sought a northwest route to China's treasures. But fur in the Great Lakes region proved a valuable consolation; for nearly 150 years the French competed with the British in northern Canada to explore and claim new fur-bearing lands. After American inde-pendence, coastal settlers began to move inland and over the Appalachians. Lewis and Clark explored the Northwest, revealing the West's potential for trading and settlement and befriending Hidatsa warriors like the richly attired Pehriska-Ruhpa below. In Lewis and Clark's wake came land speculators, army surveyors, fur traders, and scientists—explorers all.

just beyond the last conquest, pulling men on and on.

Cabeza de Vaca's stories made the legend glow anew. Would-be conquistadores begged for royal permission to lead expeditions north from New Spain into the unexplored continent. One of these, Hernando de Soto, was appointed governor of Florida. To Spaniards that included everything running north and west from the Florida peninsula. Earlier excursions had been mounted by Juan Ponce de León and others, but none were on the scale of de Soto's. He gathered 622 men, horses, a herd of pigs for food on the march, and landed at Tampa Bay in May 1539.

From there, he led a cruel, courageous, and desperate campaign up through the Florida jungle and westward. He attacked tribe after tribe, taking hostage their chiefs for provisions and safe passage. Choctaws, then Chickasaws cut down his force.

De Soto and his dwindling army pushed onward until May 1541, when just below today's Memphis they came to the Mississippi. They called it Rio Grande. Crossing it, they still followed rumors of gold, but increasingly their aim became escape. Then de Soto fell ill, and on the Mississippi's bank near Natchez, he died. His survivors, who eventually made it back half dead to Mexico, weighted his body to the river bottom. On the map de Soto's journey left impressive curls and loops, but in the king's coffers, nothing.

While de Soto marched around

93

Though Missouri River fur traders sometimes encountered hostile Indians, peace usually prevailed during the lucrative bartering that spurred white exploration of North America. In their pursuit of red fox (upper) and other pelts, traders found the flat-bottomed keelboat ideal for midwestern rivers, while Hudson's Bay Company trappers (lower) adopted the Indian canoe for navigating rapids of the far north.

OVERLEAF: *"Remote and malign, devoid of resources," reported Spanish explorer Cabeza de Vaca of the desert land north of Mexico. But the Indian tales he repeated of gold-filled cities helped launch Francisco de Coronado's expedition from New Spain. Though Coronado found humble pueblos instead of cities, the expedition made another momentous discovery, the Grand Canyon.*

the Southeast, the viceroy of Mexico sent Coronado, an ambitious young soldier, northward up Mexico's west coast. Coronado led 336 men with some 1,500 horses and mules, plus nearly 1,000 Indians as helpers.

In the summer of 1540 Coronado reached Hawikuh, a Zuni pueblo. Today Hawikuh is a mound of rubble, dotted with shards of painted pottery. Some rough Indian sheep camps beside cottonwood-lined gullies have TV dish antennas, and now and then a pickup truck coils dust behind as it heads toward town.

For Coronado the living pueblo looked almost as bleak. The uninspiring huddle of adobe and stone was nothing remotely like the fairytale cities of Cíbola. Could the gold be hidden inside? Coronado tried to move in peaceably. The Zunis responded with arrows. Coronado's men charged; he himself narrowly escaped death. When Hawikuh fell, he found only beans, maize, and squash. After he took Kyakima and the other Zuni pueblos, he had conquered the alleged cities of gold, and he was not a peso richer.

When Indians pointed him and his predecessors to fantastic riches, they were not necessarily lying. To them, the humble pueblos were grand cities; the plenteous food, riches. And besides, it would be unfriendly not to tell the Spaniards what they wanted to hear. From the Sonora River, Coronado sent out patrols, one of which discovered the Grand Canyon. Indians told him of a

An idealized Coronado raises the cross during another fruitless gold chase that took him through Texas and Oklahoma into Kansas. "It was God's pleasure that these discoveries should remain for other peoples," the conquistador lamented. The expedition headed home "very sad and . . . completely worn out and shamefaced," taking cold comfort in the prize it could claim: the whole of southwestern North America.

A dashing de Soto astride prancing horse arrives at an Indian village on the Mississippi's bank, in this romantic portrayal. In reality the expedition's two-year trek from Florida, marked by the wanton killing and torture of Indians, had left the conquistador and his army wasted and bedraggled. The Mississippi Indians showered them with arrows as they built barges to cross the river and get on with the gold search.

wonderland to the east, named Quivira, where plates were made of gold.

Ever hopeful, Coronado set out the next spring across the Texas Panhandle, wandered southeast and back north. In Kansas he met the Quivira Indians, but found no gold, not even pueblos. The riches of Quivira were tallgrass and buffalo herds. Coronado staked a claim to the land for the king of Spain. Later the world realized that de Soto and Coronado had come within about 350 miles of linking a belt of Spanish exploration across the continent.

Even before the Spaniards beat their way toward the center of what is now the United States, a long arm of French exploration reached inland from the North Atlantic. Navigator Jacques Cartier, on his 1535 voyage, found a breach west of Newfoundland that he hoped would lead to the Pacific. But it was a river, not a strait. Later named the St. Lawrence, it was the route by which the French drove deep into America.

Cartier pressed upstream until he struck rapids around a river island almost a thousand miles from the ocean. Indians led him up a high hill, and he named the place Mount Royal. From the peak they pointed toward the west, where lay a series of inland seas—the farthest of them said to be on the world's edge. The prospect was grandiose enough to raise Cartier's hopes of the long-sought passage to the Orient.

That was the way visionary explorers insisted on thinking: There

must be a water route westward to Asia. The rich Americas could not be seen as a goal in themselves, but rather a barrier to greater wealth beyond. Only slowly did the truth dawn. As gold from Peru and Mexico continued to pour back across the Atlantic through the 1500s to finance Spain's century of dominance in Europe, France began to see that a different kind of gold might be at the end of its New World route: fur. A vogue for furs in Europe had created such an intense demand that the continent's supply of fur-bearing animals had nearly been depleted.

Some 70 years after Cartier, the quest for furs brought Samuel de Champlain to Mount Royal, today's Montreal, and for decades he was the driving force of French exploration.

Three things distinguished this French push: It was motivated by trade with the Indians, rather than the search for gold. It developed Indian diplomacy to such a high state that some northern tribes became France's major allies in the struggle for the continent. And finally, the French, through luck at choosing their main route of entry, stayed on the water as they drove inland.

South past Mount Royal, Champlain in 1609 accompanied a war party of Indians down a St. Lawrence tributary he called the Iroquois, today's Richelieu. As he crossed the future U. S.-Canadian border, he entered a lake "of great extent, say eighty or a hundred leagues long."

Lake Champlain, lying between

98

the Green Mountains of Vermont and New York's Adirondacks, is only 125 miles long, less than half his estimate. Its rocky shores are still green with pines and cottonwoods. From a ferry crossing between Port Kent and Burlington, it is easy now to imagine Champlain and the war party slipping silently down the western side, crossing the mouths of cove after cove, leaving no trace after the wakes of their canoes rippled away.

The birchbark canoe helped make the 1600s the French century, as horses made the 1500s the Spanish. The French and their Indian allies would glide into the continent across wind-chopped lakes and weed-choked shallows, portaging around rapids and over watershed ridges. Champlain pointed the way.

In 1673 Louis Jolliet and the Jesuit Jacques Marquette paddled canoes down the Fox and Wisconsin Rivers to the Mississippi and on south almost to the mouth of the Arkansas.

Jolliet, born in Canada, was the first white native North American to become a great inland explorer. Marquette, the zealous priest, was driven to spread the word to pagan Indians. Their expedition of almost 2,000 miles opened the way for France's claim to the Mississippi Valley. Nearly a decade later René-Robert Cavelier de La Salle would reach the Gulf of Mexico. Near the Mississippi's mouth he took possession in his king's name of the river and all the lands it drained, however far they might stretch.

From its Minnesota headwaters at Lake Itasca, the Mississippi River loops and winds on its 2,348-mile course to the Gulf of Mexico. Indians knew the river as the Father of Waters—Missi Sipi. French explorers Louis Jolliet and Jacques Marquette in 1673 traced its upper reaches from near Lake Superior to present-day Arkansas. Nine years later René-Robert Cavelier de La Salle journeyed to its mouth and claimed the Mississippi basin for France. But his haughty, hard-driving manner stirred ill will among disgruntled followers. On a subsequent expedition in 1687, they lured him into ambush along the Trinity River in Texas (below, right) and put a bullet through his head.

In 1687 La Salle was murdered by mutineers—not a unique fate for great explorers. Leading expeditions farther, ever farther demands a determination that followers, often sick, hungry, and demoralized, may consider madness. One of those who dared too long was Henry Hudson, who took the British flag deep into North America.

Hudson and other English navigators had tested the northern waters repeatedly in search of a sea passage to China, but they were turned back by ice. The Dutch, also eager to reach the magical East, hired Hudson to try again. He sought first to loop across the top of Europe, then reversed course and worked down the American coast from Maine to the Chesapeake Bay before testing the broad river that is named after him. Pushing past the stony island that now anchors the towers of Manhattan, Hudson sailed as far north as Albany before turning back. The following year, 1610, under the English flag, he set out northwestward, past Greenland. Through fog and ice, he drove his surly crew beyond Hudson Strait. When the shores fell away before them he was confident that he had found the far ocean at last.

Hudson was instead beating down the forbidding east coast of the immense inland sea that would be known as Hudson Bay. When he reached the southern tip of James Bay this truth dawned, but by the time he had tacked uncertainly back and forth it was late fall, and ice had locked in his ship *Discovery*. After wintering in James Bay, Hudson debated whether to press on but wavered once too often before his starving, mutinous crew, who set him and his son and a handful of sick men adrift in a small boat to die. Still, he had given England a new frontier on the edge of one of the world's greatest fur forests.

Other English captains sailed after Hudson for the Northwest Passage, but none could force his way through the ice. And so for the British, too, the immediate riches of the fur trade began to push aside the dream of the distant Orient.

English king Charles II sent two French brothers-in-law, Médard Chouart des Groseilliers and Pierre Esprit Radisson, to bypass the Dutch and French fur operations below the Great Lakes and open the vast Canadian wilderness to the northwest. Their first winter at James Bay was such a success that in 1670 "The Governor and Company of Adventurers of England trading into Hudson's Bay" were granted a charter for an enterprise called the Hudson's Bay Company. The extent of its lands was as vaguely comprehended as La Salle's claim to Louisiana and Coronado's claim in the Southwest.

By now the English, bogged down so long on the middle Atlantic coast, had at last gathered strength to pierce the mountains. Their first, earlier attempt had failed. John Smith had arrived with the Virginia colonists to settle at Jamestown in

1607, almost a quarter century after Sir Walter Raleigh's colony on the North Carolina shore had disappeared. Smith believed that somewhere tantalizingly close lay the passage to the Orient. Hardly had the Jamestown English settled when Smith started looking for that passage, poking up the Chesapeake Bay and its rivers. On one trip he reached the falls of the Potomac, but the 14 men in his shallop were exhausted, their bread sodden, their spirits unresponsive to his cajoling. They returned to Jamestown.

There malaria, dysentery, famine, and Indian massacres kept the Virginians clinging to life by their fingernails. Hundreds of miles southwest, west, north and northwest, other nations were striking into the heart of North America, but some 60 years would pass before the English made their first recorded expedition into the Blue Ridge Mountains.

In 1669 Virginia governor Sir William Berkeley sent a German physician, John Lederer, to find a way through the mountains. He became the first white person to see the Shenandoah Valley, from near Manassas Gap in the Blue Ridge.

Interstate 66 runs through that gap now. Travelers flashing past do not see the state marker that notes Lederer's accomplishment beside the old parallel road. They do see the ancient rounded mountains, many of them as thickly forested as they were in the 1600s. Beneath the Virginia pines, tulip poplars, and red oaks,

Highway to the interior, Canada's Mackenzie River mirrors the midnight sun on its 1,120-mile run to the Arctic Ocean. Alexander Mackenzie explored the river for Britain in 1789, opening extensive hinterlands to the fur trade—the region's economic mainstay into the 20th century.

A Hudson's Bay Company trader gripping his beaver hat runs the Fraser River (below). His birchbark canoe, a 25-foot canot du nord, could haul 1½ tons of pelts and trade goods.

undergrowth covers the slopes. Catbriers, poison ivy, and brambles clutch at passing legs, and the roller coaster ridges stretch one behind another toward the sunset horizon. Lederer, after his grueling trips through here, reported back with a perception few before him had had: "They are certainly in a great errour," he wrote, "who imagine that the Continent of North America is but eight or ten days over from the Atlantick to the Indian Ocean."

Not until a forceful frontier commander named Abraham Wood sent a horseback party up the north branch of the Roanoke in 1671 did Virginians cross the eastern divide. Near today's Blacksburg a rough ridge separates the uppermost fingers of the Roanoke and the creeks feeding the New River, which runs northwest into the Kanawha, thence to the Ohio, the Mississippi, and the Gulf. The explorers, Thomas Batts and Robert Fallam, dismounted to scramble over the ridge. They followed the New River three days and ran out of food. As they started to turn back, they saw beyond the mountains "a fog arise and a glimmering light as from water. We supposed there to be a great Bay."

There was not, of course, as James Needham, another explorer sent by Wood, found when he reached the Cherokee nation along the upper Tennessee River two years later. Those Cherokees had never seen a great bay, white man, or horse, but they did have Spanish trade goods.

Shipwrecked and ravaged by scurvy, Vitus Bering and his crew make a desperate push for a rocky island off Kamchatka, in this romanticized painting. Here Bering would die of the disease along with many of his men. On this voyage in 1741 the Danish navigator, commissioned by the Russian navy, had set off from Siberia with two ships to explore the North Pacific. The vessels sailed parallel to the Aleutian Islands and then separated. Bering went on to sight Alaska's Mount Saint Elias, thus discovering America from the west, and met his death returning home. The second ship had sailed home independently, contrary to what this painting shows.

The survivors among Bering's crew rebuilt their ship and returned to Siberia. The luxurious sea otter pelts they carried led to a fortune in fur trading for Tsar Peter the Great and, eventually, to a Russian settlement in Alaska.

So among the English on the coast, still bedazzled by the glimmering light of illusory seas beyond the mountains, awareness grew that the Spaniards down that way and the French up the other way were not stories, but real. These metal hatchets and glass beads said so. By 1689 the Virginians and their coastal countrymen were struggling with the French in an off-and-on frontier war that would last nearly 75 years longer. For many of those years, the French and Spaniards were also contending for the great spaces between the Mississippi and the still elusive western sea.

Farther north, the British were looking in the same direction. In 1690 the Hudson's Bay Company sent west a young man who had learned Indian ways. Henry Kelsey pushed across the head of Lake Winnipeg to the Great Plains. In the journal of his two-year trip he recorded seeing "a great sort of bear . . . neither white nor black but silver haired like our English rabbit"— the grizzly. He probably was the first European to see the musk-ox. He had blazed what would become Canada's historic route west.

A century later Britain's Alexander Mackenzie left the Great Slave

An outcrop now dubbed Rebel's Rock looms over the Kentucky region that Daniel Boone explored in 1769. Having heard tales of wondrous, game-rich lands beyond the Appalachians, Boone and a few companions crossed through the Cumberland Gap into the forests of eastern Kentucky. A path he cleared six years later became the Wilderness Road, which served pioneering settlers for many years as the gateway to the West. Seen here with dog and rifle in his later years, Daniel Boone lived to become a new nation's quintessential frontiersman—celebrated as much in folklore as in fact.

The hazards of frontier life—as dramatized below—included the abduction by Shawnee Indians and rescue of Boone's daughter Jemima and two of her friends in the summer of 1776, soon after the establishment of a permanent settlement at Boonesboro.

Lake to trace the river that has his name, expecting to reach the Pacific. Instead it curved north, and he followed it to where it spills into the Beaufort Sea and the Arctic Ocean. In 1793 he paddled up the Peace River into the Rocky Mountains, crossed them, and then ran down the Bella Coola to the Pacific. He thus became the first European to traverse the continent north of Mexico.

Back East, population pressure was building that would eventually explode in a broad movement across North America. In 1775 frontiersman Daniel Boone, born in Pennsylvania and brought up there and in the mountains of North Carolina, led the band that blazed the Wilderness Road. He took them through the mountains at Cumberland Gap to open the way into Kentucky. Land agent Thomas Walker had discovered that gap, an old Indian trail, a quarter century earlier while probing the Tennessee Valley.

Boone is well known in legend for fighting Indians, but his raptures over the land he opened inspired others to poetry on his behalf. At first, his ghostwriter penned, Boone might have been seized with melancholy without his family, but the land's beauty "expelled every gloomy thought." He did not return to his family till the next year, "with a determination to bring them as soon as possible to live in Kentucke, which I esteemed a second paradise."

Settlers poured through the gap into Boone's paradise, and looked

beyond it to the Mississippi River and French Louisiana. Americans were following Alexander Hamilton's advice: "Learn to think continentally." In 1803 President Thomas Jefferson bought that vast French domain and determined to make it American. He sent Virginians Meriwether Lewis and William Clark on an epic venture up the Missouri, across the Rockies, and down the Columbia River to the western sea.

Except for Alaska and the Arctic, the broad geography of North America was settled. But a large part of it still had to be filled in. The Great Basin, between the Rockies and the Sierra Nevada, was not explored until 1826 when an indomitable fur trader named Jedediah Smith set out to find a link between the Great Salt Lake and the Pacific—the legendary Rio Buenaventura. He found no river, but he crossed the Mojave Desert, becoming the first American to enter California from the east, and returned over the Sierra Nevada. He later traveled the California coast to Oregon. Smith's small parties of explorers were repeatedly attacked by Indians, but he kept going out again. Once he was half-scalped by a grizzly and calmly instructed his comrade how to sew his head back together.

Almost two decades after Smith's determined journeys, the flamboyant soldier-surveyor John Charles Frémont went on his first western expedition, to establish American claims in Oregon. On the way he met the famous Indian agent Kit Carson, who signed on as guide. Frémont's three major expeditions earned him the nickname The Pathfinder. A zealous expansionist, he mapped much of the land between the Mississippi Valley and the Pacific, methodically recording temperatures, geological structures, topography. His third journey in 1845 took him over the Sierra at the outset of the Mexican War, in which he aided in the conquest of California.

The westward sweep of settlers after the war left only a few places to be explored. The formidable valley of the Colorado River was one of them.

John Wesley Powell, who had lost his right arm at Shiloh but fought on through the Civil War, was a professor of geology when he and his nine assistants put four heavily laden boats into the water at Green River, Wyoming, on May 24, 1869. Propelled by a swift current, his boats plunged south, leaping like "herds of startled deer bounding through forests beset with fallen timber." That was only a suggestion of what lay ahead. The evening before tackling the Canyon of Lodore, Powell wrote of black shadows creeping downward, making the canyon "a dark portal to a region of gloom—the gateway through which we are to enter on our voyage of exploration tomorrow. What shall we find?" They found dangerous rapids that had to be portaged, but one of his boats missed his signal from shore and shot into the maelstrom, to be smashed into splinters. Other deadly chutes

Tumbling rapids hurtle John Wesley Powell and his crew through the Grand Canyon in 1869. On this 1,000-mile journey down the Green and Colorado Rivers, the men suffered near starvation and arduous portages to explore the unknown region Coronado's men found more than 300 years before. Geologist Powell wrote: "All these canyons unite to form one grand canyon, the most sublime spectacle on earth."

roared downstream, day after day, with few stretches of calm.

Eleven weeks of this, and Powell was only then heading into the Grand Canyon itself. He wrote, "What falls there are, we know not; what rocks beset the channel, we know not; what walls rise over the river, we know not. . . . The men talk as cheerfully as ever; . . . but to me the cheer is sombre." Pressing on, they plunged over rapids where the canyon walls were so high there was no way to portage around. They made it, and another, and another, until a smooth run enabled Powell to write, "a few days like this, and we shall be out of prison."

He was too optimistic. There was more. To traverse the gorge where sightseeing planes and helicopters flash today, the expedition endured murderous portages, capsizings, near starvation. Three men deserted; after climbing up to the plateau, they were killed by Indians. Eventually Powell brought his surviving crewmen out of the Grand Canyon 98 days and some 1,000 miles below his entry. He became a national hero.

John Wesley Powell was one of the last of his premechanized kind. Through more than 300 years, these men risked their lives to slash across North America. Spaniards, French, English, and Americans, they opened the land of the Indians and buffalo. They died not knowing that their legacy to us—a land once considered a barrier to riches—would turn out to be the richest in history.

114

Meriwether Lewis
William Clark

By Margaret Sedeen

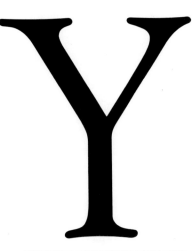

May 26, 1805: Capt. Meriwether Lewis, near the source of the Missouri River, feels "a secret pleasure" at his first view of the Rocky Mountains.

Y*our mission is to explore the Missouri river, & such principal stream of it, as*—today the ink on the yellowed paper is faint, the writing here and there almost illegible—*by it's course & communication with the waters of the Pacific Ocean, may offer the most direct & practicable water communication across this continent, for the purposes of commerce.* The date, *this 20th day of June 1803,* and the signature, *Th. Jefferson Pr. U. S. of America.*

A year later Jefferson's Corps of Discovery set out. The place they went, by pirogue and canoe, by horseback and bleeding, aching feet, was an unimaginable other world from the tidy frontier of coastal plain and round-shouldered Appalachians. For months they were given up for dead, long before they set their downstream oars in the mighty Missouri. They were Virginians and Kentuckians, Georgians and Pennsylvanians, Tarheels and Yankees. From St. Louis they paddled and poled, towed and rode, and walked 1,610 miles, to build themselves a log fortification surrounded by the earthen lodges of Mandans, Arikaras, and Hidatsas, in the midst of bleak Dakota hills, in a winter so cold the whiskey froze, on a bend along the north bank of the Missouri River.

Come spring, they would paddle and pole, ride and tow, and walk in the end 8,000 miles—almost a third of the way around the world—in hardscrabble pursuit of the destiny of the United States of America.

Meriwether Lewis and William Clark, wilderness soldiers and Virginia gentlemen, led the search for trade routes and trading partners among the Indian nations. Lewis, secretary to President Jefferson, was 29 years old. From the age of 18, he'd seen this mission as a "da[r]ling project." Others had almost gotten it, but now it was his.

And Clark's. William Clark, draftsman, geographer of genius, and cocaptain, was 33 years old. Among the corps Patrick Gass and Nathaniel Hale Pryor were carpenters; the smiths were John Shields (kin

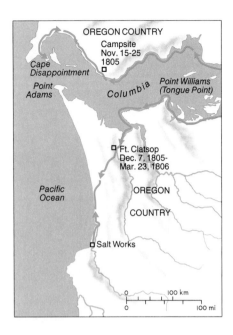

to Daniel Boone), William Bratton, and Alexander Hamilton Willard; Joseph Whitehouse was a hide curer and tailor; Pierre Cruzatte knew the hand signs that made a common language across the plains; several men were expert hunters whose game fed the explorers and multitudes of Indian friends. Lewis's Newfoundland, Scannon, pulled fowl out of the rivers. Clark's servant and companion since childhood, a large black man called York, delighted in the consternation of Indians who judged his mysterious color "big medicine."

They named their Dakota camp Fort Mandan and placed it at an ancient crossroads of Plains Indian traders. While men of the corps scouted for timber, hewed logs, and built the stockaded cabins, Indians milled about day and night. Along the riverbanks between villages, women in buckskin dresses, with vermilion-painted faces, filled their braided willow baskets with firewood, fish from the weirs, or corn harvested from the rich bottomlands. Some ferried their burdens across the river in coracles made of a buffalo skin with the tail still on, stretched on a willow frame. Men, women, and children dived into the river, bathing, swimming, and splashing. Haughty warriors, wrapped in painted buffalo robes and adorned with necklaces of three-inch, white-tipped grizzly claws, wheeled their spirited horses and galloped up and down flourishing muskets, bows, and battle-axes.

Captains Lewis and Clark planned a winter of diplomacy and accordingly had packed $669.50 worth of Indian presents, the largest item in their budget. They held official meetings with Indian leaders to remind any and all that by virtue of the Louisiana Purchase this was now American territory. Amidst much ritual handing around of medicine pipes, solemn puffing for the success of the councils, and speechifying on all sides, the captains "made chiefs." One was Black Moccasin, the Hidatsa who nicknamed Lewis "Long Knife," for his sword, and Clark "Red Hair," so strange was such a thing.

In deference to Indian protocol, they presented to first-rank chiefs hollow, silver medals imprinted with Jefferson's likeness; to less important chiefs medals with motifs of farm and home. All received American flags and clothing: cocked hats with red feathers, belts, garters, calico shirts, and especially, gaudy frock coats.

On one windy October day Lewis and Clark ratified 21 Indian chiefs, all of them chiefs already well made by feats of bravery, by largesse, by the acclaim of their own people, in a land where their culture had ripened over seven centuries. Probably Black Moccasin and his fellows thought they were joining a chiefdom of commerce, since the coats and other symbols were the same as they'd already received from British and French fur traders. Jefferson had supplied the captains with printed forms that declared in lawyers' English the confidence of the United States government in the friendship of the particular Indian leader. Each certificate had a dotted line where the chief's or the warrior's name was written in: *Sha-ha-ka* or *Min-nis-sur-ra-ree* or *Omp-se-ha-ra*

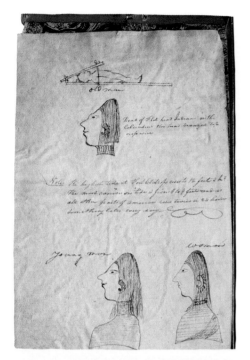

Clark's journal sketches: Clatsop Indians beautifying the skulls of their infants; a sage grouse, discovered by Lewis on the Marias River in northwest Montana.

(Black Moccasin). Then the two captains dated and signed each page.

The Indians reciprocated with social calls—"as usial Stay all Day," complained Clark—and gifts of food. Some brought dried pumpkin and pemmican. All winter of 1804 and 1805 they came with corn in payment for the labor of the corps' hardworking smiths, who fixed tools and guns and made iron battle-axes.

In March the river ice broke up. The water rose in the banks. Ducks and geese flew north, and the Indians began to set the prairie fires that would bring rich green grass for the buffalo. By the dim light of April dawns, Indians on the Missouri bluffs watched two pirogues and six canoes point their prows upstream, seeking the western ocean. The 31 corpsmen viewed their "little fleet" with as much pride as Columbus or Cook had theirs. Two thousand miles of unknown terrain lay ahead, and "the good or evil it had in store," Lewis somberly observed, "was for experiment yet to determine, and these little vessells contained every article by which we were to . . . subsist or defend ourselves."

In camp the captains shared their buffalo-skin tepee with the interpreters George Drouillard and Toussaint Charbonneau, and Charbonneau's 17-year-old wife and infant son. That the woman, Sacagawea, was Shoshoni was a happy accident, for it was the Shoshoni from whom captains Lewis and Clark hoped to buy horses to span the trail between navigable water at the head of the Missouri and the western river they sought to the Pacific. Sacagawea would be useful as an interpreter, they hoped, and as a sign of friendship to Indians they met, for no war party ever traveled with a woman and a baby.

With a good wind, the pirogues went under sail. In deep water the oarsmen rowed. In shallow, the men lined up on each side of the boat, poles in hand. One by one, each man at the head of the line thrust his pole into the riverbed, then walked aft. When he reached the stern, he pulled out the pole and took his place at the end of the line.

Early May was cold, with snow squalls and morning frosts, and ice on the oars. One of the captains usually walked on shore, often exploring miles into the countryside, hunting game and feeding a boundless curiosity about the stretches of the great continent where, they told themselves, "the foot of civilized man had never trodden." The river bluffs were high now, the current swift, and the bottom rocky. Sails, oars, and poles gave way to towropes—the best were of braided elk skin—man-handled by heaving crews sometimes up to their armpits in water, or barefoot on the slippery slopes. Not that moccasins lasted anyway. Two days was their lifespan, one day new, one day patched.

By the end of May, they'd made 2,500 miles upriver. Lewis thought the sandstone bluffs of the Missouri Breaks, "most romantic." They reminded him "of those large stone buildings in the U. States." But the perpendicular walls made the towing so painful that the captain called a halt one noon and gave a dram to his "faithful fellows."

Mindful of their duty, both Clark and Lewis recorded everything they saw, with an eye to its use to a young nation. What they took to be good coal was only lignite. The plains seemed fertile. And the game!

Clark and Lewis, with Sacagawea and Toussaint Charbonneau at Three Forks of the Missouri.

Elk, deer, antelope, buffalo by the thousand and tens of thousands, buffalo in "gangs." One bull, swimming the river in the middle of the night, clambered across a pirogue and charged up the riverbank, thundering inches from the heads of the sleeping men.

One day they came to an Indian buffalo jump, the stampeded carcasses in heaps at the foot of the cliff. Wolves prowled about so "verry gentle" that Clark killed one with his sword. Sergeant Ordway complained, "the Game is gitting so pleanty and tame in this country that Some of the party clubbed them out of their way."

Even so, the entire contingent of buckskinned hunters, pouring water down prairie dog holes, needed several hours to capture a single specimen of the intriguing species new to American science. The expedition also introduced to naturalists back East the pronghorn, mule deer, coyote, jack rabbit, and the grizzly, of which Lewis soon admitted that he'd rather fight two Indians than one of these "gentlemen."

A third of a ton, eight feet from nose to tail, and "so hard to die," the grizzly bear seemed an almost invincible spirit of the wilderness. The mountain men had a rule: Never fight a grizzly except in self-defense. But the animal held a fascination for the men of the corps that time and again almost cost them their lives. Grizzlies preyed among the swarms of game, and whenever Lewis or Clark or one of the men saw a bear, they shot. And usually had to flee from its rage, and shoot again and again— ten musket balls went into one—until the bear fell.

Early in June a critical question presented itself. The river split, one stream flowing from the north, another from the south. Which fork was the Missouri? Which the way to the Columbia? A mistake now would lose the rest of the season and jeopardize the enterprise. Men went investigating. All were asked an opinion; most voted for the north fork, with its muddy resemblance to the Missouri they knew. But it was on the south fork that Lewis found the magnificent Great Falls the Indians had told them about.

A nasty portage lay ahead. Clark surveyed it and found a 10-mile stretch where the river dropped 400 feet. In camp, Lewis supervised the construction of "four sets of truck wheels with couplings, toungs and bodies" for carrying baggage and canoes. In the whole neighborhood they found only one tree, a 22-inch cottonwood, large enough to make wheels. They'd left one pirogue behind long ago. Now they unloaded and cached the other. Clark staked out the best route he could find but it took the men 11 days and 18 miles of moccasin-piercing torture, cutting a riverside road as they went.

Stroke by stroke they were nearing the end of navigable water. Even now they spent more time dragging the boats through canyons than rowing. If they were to cross the Rocky Mountains before winter, they must find Shoshonis with horses. Sacagawea began to recognize the country. One August night they camped on the spot where she'd been captured by Hidatsa raiders five years before, to be carried off to the Dakotas and bought by Charbonneau for a horse or two, a gun or some blue beads, and maybe a gallon of whiskey.

Le Borgne, the fierce, one-eyed Hidatsa chief, baffled by a black man. A wet finger tries to rub away the "paint," as Le Borgne would stripe himself for war.

The captains split the group in order to widen the search. As bald eagles and ospreys soared overhead, and rattlesnakes and prickly pear lurked underfoot, both groups of explorers combed the countryside for nine days, hoping that from behind a clump of willows or out of a ravine would step the Indians they knew must be watching the approach of the strange people—obviously poor—who wore no blankets. When separated, the captains often left notes for each other on branches, white men's words fluttering in a wilderness that until now knew neither writing, nor paper, nor ink. When Lewis headed up a river fork, he posted the news on a green willow pole by the riverbank. Clark never found the message because a beaver appropriated the signpost.

But Sacagawea's message was clear. As they approached some Shoshoni horsemen, she began to skip and dance, joyously sucking on her fingers in sign language to Clark, "Here are the people who suckled me!" The Indian girl, by a small gift of grace, had come home.

Soon Indians were embracing the explorers in a bear-greasy, squeezing cheek-to-cheek. Lewis grew "heartily tired of the national hug." Before they could council, they must smoke a pipe, and as a sign of

122

trust, remove the moccasins—Lewis, Clark, the braves, and the chief, Cameahwait, "a man of Influence Sence & easey & reserved manners," though hard times had made him lank jawed from hunger. Barefoot, the councils began, with Sacagawea interpreting. It was unusual enough to have a woman present, but this one broke all decorum by jumping up, bursting into tears, and throwing her blanket around Chief Cameahwait, whom she had suddenly recognized as her brother.

"We made [the Indians] sensible of their dependance on the will of our government," said Lewis and Clark through their sobbing interpreter, "for every species of merchandize as well as for their defence & comfort." They went on: "We also gave them as a reason why we wished to pe[ne]trate the country as far as the ocean to the west of them was to . . . find out a more direct way to bring merchandize to them." The captains distributed certificates, medals, coats, scarlet leggings, tobacco, knives, awls, beads, and looking glasses. With more presents they bought horses and guides.

Back in Virginia, early autumn meant cool mornings, hot sunny afternoons, red and gold leaves, and a dawdling summer. But to the men, and the Indian girl and her baby, who slogged along the Salmon and the Lehmi, high in the Bitterroot range of the Rockies, tracing the ridges of the Nez Perce buffalo road, September brought frost on their blankets, sleet, and eight inches of snow on the trail. Game was scarce and shy. Horses slipped and rolled down the mountainsides. Hungry, shivering in their brittle, heavy buckskins, the men stumbled over fallen timber, finding their way by the line of tree branches broken when the Indian horses packed buffalo meat back from the plains.

"High ruged mountains in every direction as far as I could see." On the sixth day of the climb, his feet freezing in thin moccasins, Clark forged ahead of the main party to get fires going and cook the "fine meat" of the second colt they'd eaten that week. Two days later, with a few men and no baggage, he descended rapidly toward the Nez Perce camp on the Clearwater, and food. The generosity of these Indians was a mixed blessing. Almost the entire corps fell ill with dysentery, probably from the dried salmon and camas root given them by the chief, Twisted Hair. But they wanted to press on. They had crossed the Rockies. The current that ran beside them now would lead to the Pacific.

They found some good stands of pine, and in eleven days the men who could work had made five dugouts. The swift flow of the Clearwater and the Snake led to the Columbia. They tackled rapids, shoals, rocks, cascades, portages, and a diet of rotting elk meat, dried salmon, dogmeat, acorns, and, with infrequent luck, "blue wing Teel," and Private Collins's delicious beer of camas root. Each day they met more Indians, people who had brass teakettles, scarlet and blue cloth, sailor jackets, and weapons—goods from traders on the coast. They also had fleas, as the explorers discovered in portaging by Indian campsites. "Every man of the party was obliged to Strip naked dureing the time of take-

Had I these white warriors in the upper plains, my young men would do for them as they would for so many wolves, for there are only two sensible men amongst them, the worker in iron and the mender of guns.
LE BORGNE, HIDATSA CHIEF

123

ing over the canoes, that they might have an oppertunity of brushing the flees of[f] their legs and bodies."

As the river widened and the fine-furred seals somersaulted among the rocks, the fare improved, and the corps ate deer, grouse, fish, and roots and vegetables gathered by Sacagawea. But they had learned to like dog, and bought it from the Indians when they could.

Early in a stormy November, they began riding the tide. At every flood, great swells dashed drift logs against the rocks. Flea-bitten and miserable, the men wore sodden, rotted clothes, and would have no better until they could hunt and dress skins, and sew during winter camp. But in their ears roared the breakers of the 20-mile-wide estuary.

"Ocian in view! O! the joy." Later a jubilant Clark led his men to a promontory above the Pacific, where they seemed "much Satisfied with their trip." Then they carved their names on the tree trunks.

Again the captains consulted their corps. Where to build the winter quarters? They explored the north bank of the river but chose the south, where they could make themselves salt from the seawater, and keep a watch for trading vessels that might call. None did. There were calls from Clatsops and Chinooks, including a chief and "six women of his nation which the old baud his wife had brought for market." During the five-months' winter they saw the sun only six days. In a windy, rainy spring, 1806, they turned their eyes to the east.

They would report to Thomas Jefferson that they had found a way: "Fur trade may be carried on . . . much cheaper than by any [other] rout by which it can be conveyed to the East indias." The Northwest Passage turned out to be the American frontier.

That they knew as they pulled their oars homeward. They prophesied that trading posts would rise at the mouth of the Yellowstone and the Marias; recommended that they be built on the Columbia. When Lewis and Clark rowed homeward past Fort Mandan, they might have guessed that their Hidatsa and Mandan friends would meet big medicine—the great thunder canoe—when steamboats came up the Missouri, and the biggest, when the smallpox that traveled with the white men killed the red men.

But they could never have known that by their success railroads would obliterate their footsteps along the Clearwater and the Columbia; that dams would drown their campsites; that the buffalo and the grizzly were not, after all, so hard to die. Going home in triumph, they made sometimes 70 downstream miles a day, in their wake the road now open. On the afternoon of September 20, 1806, just above St. Charles, Missouri, they rowed past a field of grazing cows, and raised a cheer.

To know Lewis and Clark is to know America, so well does their story embody our national icons. To know them best, read their journals in the original or in the classic one-volume edition by Bernard de Voto. The journals of George Catlin and Prince Maximilian of Wied, with the magnificent paintings of Catlin and Karl Bodmer, portray the Plains Indian life that Lewis and Clark knew on the eve of its demise.

The Corps of Discovery greeting Chinooks near the mouth of the Columbia, November 1805.

West Meets East

By Elisabeth B. Booz

Muslim Uygurs drive a traditional cart with donkey outriders past weathered mud-brick ruins of Turfan in the Gobi of northern China. Empires and religions swept across this region through many centuries. The hollows in a man-made hillside housed princes, merchants, scholars, and Buddhist monks when Turfan's wealthy oasis formed a vital link in Asia's fabled Silk Road. Mongol conquerors had occupied Turfan when the Polo brothers visited about 1265 en route to Cathay.

The goatskin water bottles were dry. Camels, horses, and two score men plodded down the edge of the shimmering, wind-ridged Kyzyl Kum, one of west-central Asia's bleakest deserts. Anthony Jenkinson, the young English merchant-adventurer who had hired them, could only trust the word of his Muslim guides that a river, the Oxus, was near.

Bandits attacked the next morning, December 15, 1558. Shots from Jenkinson's four harquebuses held the intruders off until nightfall. Bales of woolen cloth made a fortress, but the bandits, encamped at arrow range, blocked the way to the river. Their price was the surrender of any Christians. A brave Muslim holy man from the caravan stepped out to vow that there were none. The bandits roughed him up and took a loaded camel as tribute, then vanished into the desert. That next evening the caravan reached the Oxus River and men and animals drank for the first time in three days.

One week later, Anthony Jenkinson sighted the great minaret of Bukhara on the horizon, a beacon to Cathay. If his luck held, an Englishman would at last find a shortcut to the wealth of the East.

That search had engrossed England since John Cabot failed to navigate a northwest passage through Canada's arctic seas in 1497. Cabot's son, Sebastian, sent

mariners in 1553 to seek a northeast passage to the "backe side" of Cathay. They found Russia and forged a friendship. Young Ivan IV, the tsar, who had not yet earned his nickname, the Terrible, welcomed the English to his gaudy court in Moscow and agreed to trade with them through the White Sea. Anthony Jenkinson, captain-general of the new Muscovy Company, dreamed of taking England's trade to Cathay. He set out, with the tsar's blessing, to find a route through Russia.

Bukhara's twinkling turquoise domes, capped with lopsided storks' nests, greeted Jenkinson. The aroma of grilled mutton, yellow dust in the eyes, the babble of strange languages rose as he shoved his way through the city's massive gateway. Domed malls straddled intersections, enclosing a hubbub of bargaining for pungent cloves and cardamom, rugs, jewelry, a rare bolt of silk.

This small khanate was long past its 6th-century heyday on the Silk Road. Muslim invaders from Arabia had taken it in the 7th century; nomads from Mongolia under Genghis Khan did so again in the 13th. The Mongols welded Eurasia into the biggest empire the world has ever seen and stopped only after slaughtering all the way into Eastern Europe.

The Pope, much shaken, composed a letter in 1245 to the Great Khan protesting further invasions and suggesting he convert to Christianity. John of Plano Carpini and a companion friar carried the letter

Hsuan-tsang, a Buddhist monk and one of Asia's first recorded explorers, returns to China in A.D. 645 carrying scriptures from India in his backpack. The advanced civilizations of China and India, separated by central Asia's formidable terrain, remained mysteries to one another. Europeans explored complex societies on the continent's periphery, and gradually penetrated interior deserts and mountains until Tibet, at the center, was opened to Western influences in the 20th century.

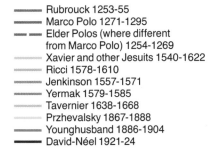

Rubrouck 1253-55
Marco Polo 1271-1295
Elder Polos (where different from Marco Polo) 1254-1269
Xavier and other Jesuits 1540-1622
Ricci 1578-1610
Jenkinson 1557-1571
Yermak 1579-1585
Tavernier 1638-1668
Przhevalsky 1867-1888
Younghusband 1886-1904
David-Néel 1921-24

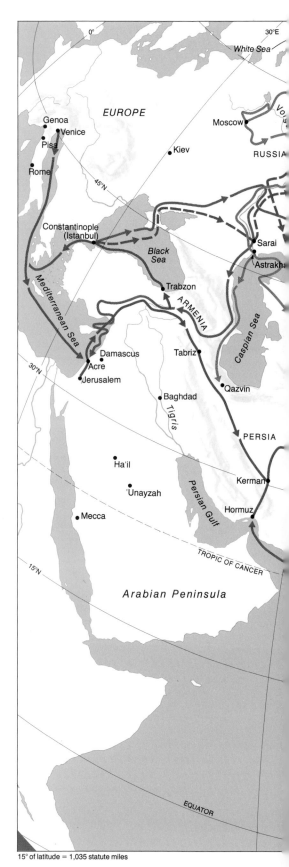

some 5,000 miles across deserts and mountains to Karakorum, a sprawling city of gold-embroidered tents glittering on Mongolia's grassy plain. Thus the friars became the first western Europeans to explore Mongolia and write about it. They marveled at the khan's elaborate throne, the silks and furs of his cosmopolitan courtiers. The khan, however, scoffed at the Pope's overture, offered without tribute.

Europe's scholars pored over the report the monks brought back, and the journal of William of Rubrouck, a friar who reached Karakorum a decade later. Like many who would venture into Asia, Rubrouck and Plano Carpini were not wilderness adventurers so much as social explorers, strangers in strange lands. When West met East, when European faced Asian, often the arena was religion, commerce, or military conquest, or a tangle of all three.

Europe had long gazed at Asia through a haze of fantasy that included a land of dogheaded humans. In 1298 a new account seized European imaginations, that of a young Venetian who accompanied his father and uncle, merchants Niccolò and Maffeo Polo, on their second trip to Cathay. Marco Polo's book amused readers, and in time was recognized as truth. In 1558 Anthony Jenkinson wanted to follow the Polos' footsteps to Cathay.

In Bukhara, Jenkinson's luck ran out. No traders had come from Cathay for years and he learned that the

128

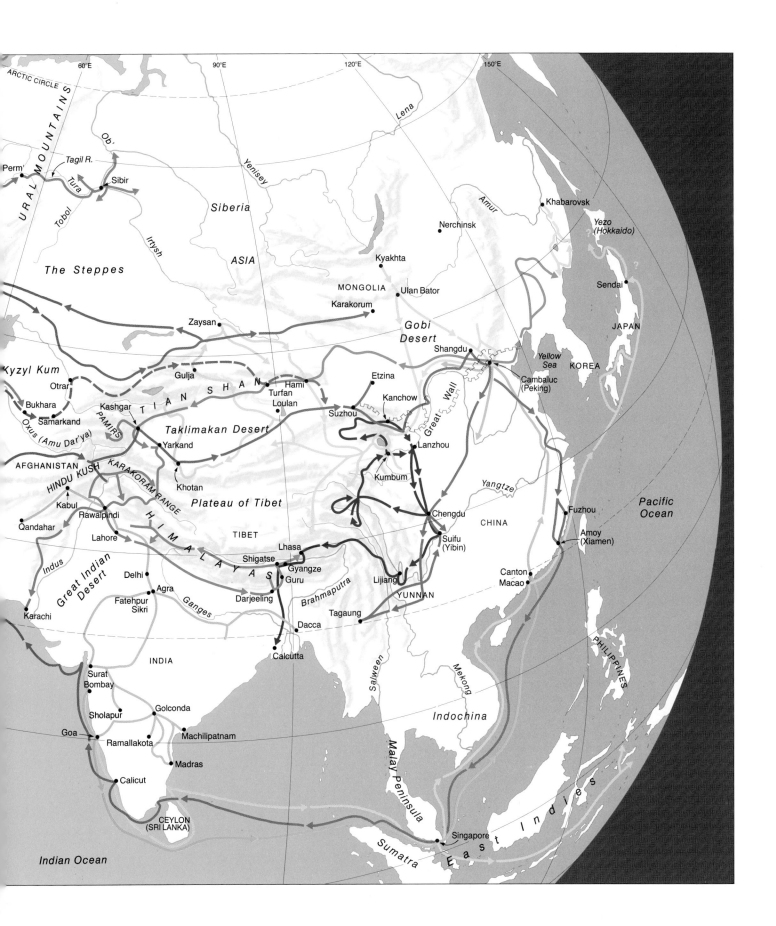

ARCTIC CIRCLE

URAL MOUNTAINS

Perm'

Tagil R.

Ob'

Tura

Sibir

Tobol

Irtysh

Yenisey

Lena

Amur

Khabarovsk

Nerchinsk

Yezo (Hokkaido)

Siberia

ASIA

Sendai

JAPAN

The Steppes

Kyakhta

MONGOLIA

Ulan Bator

Karakorum

Gobi Desert

Shangdu

KOREA

Yellow Sea

Cambaluc (Peking)

Zaysan

Kyzyl Kum

Otrar

Gulja

T I A N   S H A N

Hami

Turfan

Loulan

Etzina

Kanchow

Great Wall

Bukhara

Kashgar

Suzhou

Samarkand

PAMIRS

Taklimakan Desert

Lanzhou

Oxus (Amu Dar'ya)

Yarkand

Kumbum

Yangtze

Fuzhou

Pacific Ocean

AFGHANISTAN

HINDU KUSH

KARAKORAM RANGE

Khotan

Plateau of Tibet

Chengdu

CHINA

Amoy (Xiamen)

Kabul

Rawalpindi

H I M A L A Y A S

Suifu (Yibin)

Canton

Macao

Qandahar

Lahore

TIBET

Lhasa

Indus

Shigatse

Gyangze

Lijiang

Great Indian Desert

Delhi

Guru

YUNNAN

Agra

Darjeeling

Brahmaputra

Fatehpur Sikri

Ganges

Dacca

Tagaung

Karachi

Salween

Mekong

PHILIPPINES

INDIA

Calcutta

Surat

Bombay

Golconda

Sholapur

Indochina

Goa

Ramallakota

Machilipatnam

Madras

Calicut

Malay Peninsula

CEYLON (SRI LANKA)

East Indies

Singapore

Indian Ocean

Sumatra

129

Beehive houses constructed of mud and stone cluster in remote Harran, an ancient crossroads city halfway between the Tigris and the Mediterranean Sea. Reflecting western Asia's succession of cultures, this strategic citadel welcomed the biblical patriarch Abraham, thrived under Babylonians and Assyrians, battled with Romans, Muslims, and crusaders. Armies of the Mongol Empire snuffed out the life of old Harran in the 13th century. On his quest in 1253 to learn about the Mongols, William of Rubrouck, a French Franciscan friar, kneels before Batu, Khan of the Golden Horde (below), at his encampment on the lower Volga River. An 18th-century French artist drew his interpretation of yurts from Rubrouck's description. The missionary rode onward 3,000 miles to Karakorum, the capital of Mongolia, through a land "where stones and trees are split by the cold." On his return, he wrote the most thorough report on the Mongols that scholars had yet seen.

dangerous journey there took nine months; it was farther than anyone in England imagined. And the only customer for his cloth was Bukhara's crafty khan, who failed to pay.

Jenkinson retraced his way across the desert and the Caspian Sea, shepherding six Asian ambassadors to the tsar of Russia. His journey was not as fruitless as he believed. His observations provided a base for later European explorers. And by delivering the ambassadors to Tsar Ivan, he introduced the khanates of central Asia to modern Russia.

Ivan was to have another, less courtly Asian encounter. Near the Ural Mountains his vassals the Stroganovs ran a huge fur enterprise protected by Cossacks. Ivan depended on fur to pay his debts. So he shook with anger on hearing that the Stroganovs had left their lands unprotected. They had urged an outlaw Cossack named Yermak to cross the Urals and battle Kuchum Khan, a Tatar warlord who was terrorizing western Siberia.

It was 1581. Yermak Timofeyevich led into the mountains a Cossack army carrying muskets provided by the Stroganovs and banners embroidered with images of Russian saints. From there melting snow carried them in rough-hewn boats down the little Tagil River through silent, misty birch forests into Siberia. The silver treetops of winter dissolved into golden-green leaf as their stream joined the bigger Tura River and

A Siberian tribesman drives his reindeer herd through a snowbound valley. Seminomadic tribes once counted their two million reindeer as Siberia's greatest treasure, but outsiders coveted the land's wealth of fur: sable, ermine, and beaver. Mongol conquerors imposed a fur tax on Siberians in the 14th century. Yermak Timofeyevich, a Russian Cossack, crossed the Ural Mountains from Europe in 1581, subdued tribes, plundered their fur, and captured Sibir, an outpost of the Mongol Empire. Folklore glorified Yermak after his death. According to legend, his body bled fresh blood for weeks. A 17th-century chronicle shows awestruck Tatars stabbing his miraculous corpse (below) to see the phenomenon. Cossacks and other Russians completed the conquest of Siberia by following its vast, unexplored river network.

flowed to the Tobol, the Irtysh, the Ob'. The Cossacks were entering one of the immense river systems that connect most of Siberia.

Kuchum Khan heard of their approach. He ordered an iron chain stretched across the lower Tura River and placed hundreds of bowmen out of sight on its overgrown banks. Yermak's boat, well ahead of the rest, met a hail of arrows but escaped upstream. When the hidden Tatars saw the main flotilla riding the swift current toward the chain, they realized too late that the "boatmen" were birch branches dressed in Cossack shirts. Yermak's men had sneaked ashore to attack them from the rear.

On the Irtysh a Tatar army waited to defend Kuchum Khan's log-built capital, Sibir—"sleeping land." Cossacks plunged into battle. When Kuchum's commander fell, the khan of Sibir retreated into the forest.

Winter assaulted the Cossack remnants. Kuchum Khan menaced, invisible. Yermak, the outlaw, took a bold gamble. He sent a ragged squad on snowshoes to Moscow, their sleds piled high with sable, black fox, beaver—tribute from Siberian tribes. Yermak was offering the conquered lands to the tsar in return for help.

A joyful Ivan embraced the exhausted messengers and set church bells pealing. He promised troops, and to Yermak himself he sent two suits of richly worked body armor and his own fur mantle.

A camphorwood torii gate rises above Japan's Hiroshima Bay, demarcating the holy space that extends from a Shinto shrine on shore. Japan's native religion espoused nationalistic values. Religious ceremonies were the foundation of the government. Shintoism would prove unfertile ground for some of the ideas imported by European traders and missionaries who arrived on Japan's shores in the 16th century.

A folding rice-paper screen painted around 1600 (below) shows a Portuguese ship embarking on a trading voyage to the Far East. The foreign port, possibly Goa, imagined by Japanese artist Kano Naizen teems with Europeans in exaggerated pantaloons.

Yermak held Sibir fast, but Kuchum Khan lurked in the forests. In late summer, 1585, out along the Irtysh, the Tatars attacked at night and butchered many Cossacks. Yermak made a run for his boat but the leap fell short. Dragged down by the tsar's splendid armor, he drowned.

Yermak's life and death lived on in legend. His feats had given Russia the foundation of its great Asian power. Explorers, followed by traders and soldiers, pressed on toward the Pacific. Eventually, Russians were confronting Chinese along the Amur River. In 1689 the two sides met at a small Siberian town.

They had no common tongue. To the Russians' amazement, western Europeans in Chinese clothing, speaking half a dozen languages, negotiated an agreement. The Treaty of Nerchinsk was written in three languages: Russian, Manchu, and Latin, the language of these indispensable Jesuit priests.

Jesuits had been in Asia for well over a century. Members of this quasi-military Society of Jesus fanned out to convert the heathen of newly discovered lands overseas. In 1542 Francis Xavier set up Asian headquarters at Goa, on India's west coast. Xavier went to Japan in 1549. The honesty and good manners of the Japanese people delighted him. In a letter to Goa he wrote, "We shall never find among heathens another race to equal the Japanese."

Xavier found that in Japan feudal lords, or daimyos, ruled fiefdoms as they pleased. Jesuits and other Christians who came after Xavier saw that if they could befriend and convert a daimyo, his retinue would follow. By 1614 there were 300,000

135

A Japanese Buddhist priest burns prayer sticks in a sacred ritual of the Tendai sect (opposite). Buddhism first flourished in India around 500 B.C. A thousand years later Koreans brought it to Japan, where it took root because it adapted to native customs and beliefs. Catholic missionaries from the militant Society of Jesus, called Jesuits, reached Japan in 1549, initiating what was called a Christian Century. But the European faith demanded obedience to a foreign God. This allegiance threat-ened a growing political unity in Japan, and rulers outlawed Christianity.

Expelled in 1614, Diogo Carvalho joined other Jesuits returning in disguise. Most were captured. A 17th-century engraving depicts Carvalho's slow execution by freezing in a river. The figure on the bank is the European artist's idea of a Japanese soldier.

Christians in Japan. European customs became fashionable. Daimyos wore imported hats and crucifixes, and sat sipping sherry from goblets.

The Jesuits became part of Japanese society. They made themselves indispensable to the daimyos as agents to the Portuguese merchants who for half a century had carried the lucrative silk trade from China. More than one daimyo may have embraced Christianity for the commercial opportunities it offered.

In 1600 a new ruler, Ieyasu, seized power in Japan, bringing the daimyos under his control. Wary of the growing Christian strength, Ieyasu banned Christianity in 1614.

Several Jesuits stayed, as outlaws. They traced clandestine Christian groups who had scattered northward into unknown regions. Girolamo de Angelis mapped part of Hokkaido, where he discovered Caucasoid aborigines known as Ainu. The men's stocky bodies were covered with thick hair, like the bears they sacrificed; the women wore tattooed moustaches. De Angelis began a glossary of their language.

Ieyasu's son captured de Angelis in 1622 and burned him at the stake. Other Jesuits, betrayed or discovered, also met death by torture. Japan snapped shut, to live in feudal isolation until American gunboats reopened the country in 1854.

Jesuits faced problems of a different kind with China's Ming emperors. The mandarins who ran China's bureaucracy on the principles of

China's Great Wall (opposite) winds from the Yellow Sea deep into central Asia. Conceived in the 3rd century B.C. as a barrier to fierce nomadic tribes, it came to represent China's voluntary isolation from the world. Haughty mandarins believed their land was the center of the Earth and all foreigners were barbarians.

When Jesuit Matteo Ricci showed mandarins a map of China's relationship to the rest of the world, they were so offended that he drew a new one,

placing the Middle Kingdom closer to the center (below). "The Great Map of Ten Thousand Countries," produced in the 1580s, carried copious notes by Ricci in Chinese. A handpainted copy, six feet by twelve on silk panels, was presented to the emperor in Peking. Woodblock copies sent to Europe gave scholars their first comprehensive view of the Far East. Ricci helped prove that the legendary Cathay—thought by some Europeans to be near India—was in fact China.

Confucian morality and filial piety were not unlike the Jesuits themselves—disciplined scholars, careful record keepers. Contemptuous of foreigners, they believed China was the center of the earth, the superior Middle Kingdom.

The Jesuits selected Matteo Ricci as their spearhead. Ricci was an Italian, skilled in mathematics, astronomy, literature, and languages, with a phenomenal memory and boundless patience. He, if anyone, could crack China's proud isolation.

Ricci slipped into China from Macao in 1583. At first he dressed as a Buddhist monk. In a mission house near Canton, he displayed European inventions—prisms, chiming clocks, oil paintings, astronomical instruments—to persuade visitors that foreigners were not barbarians.

He befriended mandarins, learned their etiquette, studied their literature, and found that classic Confucianism did not clash with Christianity. When he saw that intellectuals disdained his Buddhist guise he adopted a long silk gown and the cap of a Confucian scholar.

In Ricci's lifetime some 2,000 influential Chinese were converted, but the Jesuits' success in China depended far more on their skill as engineers, metallurgists, military technicians, and astronomers. When Manchus overthrew the Ming Dynasty in 1644, Jesuits served them as diplomats, too. In their most ambitious project they surveyed and mapped the whole of China—more

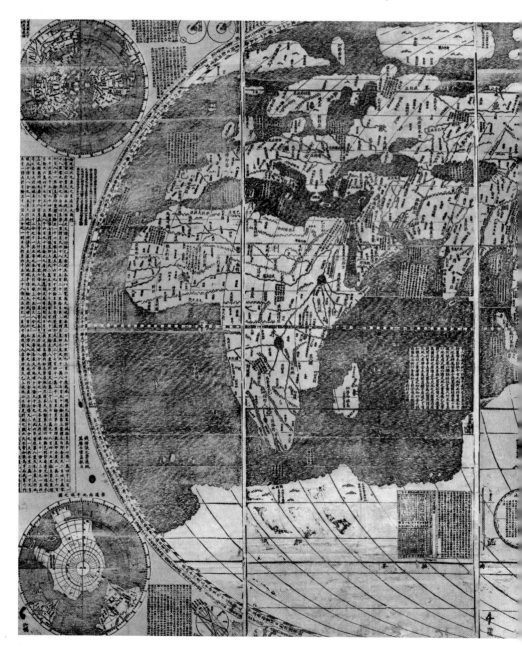

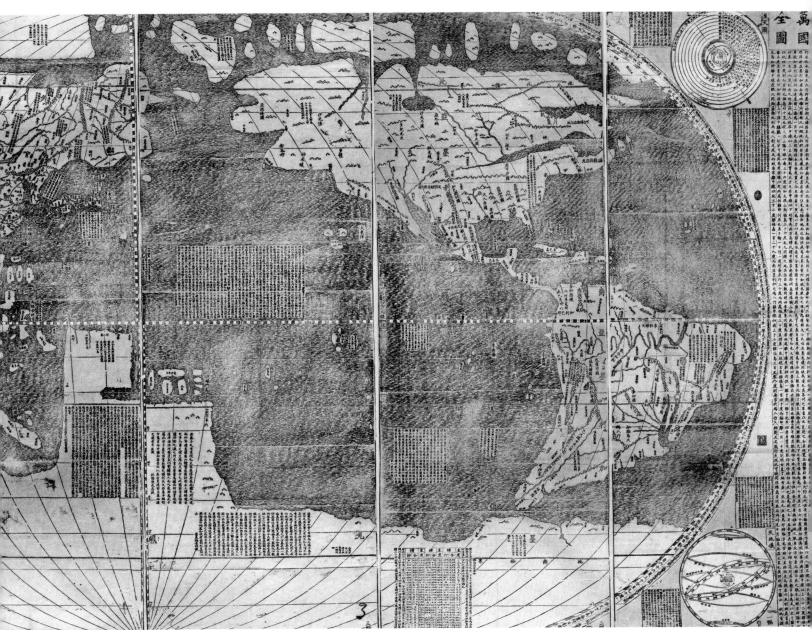

Francis Xavier (left) brought Roman Catholic zeal to Asia in 1542. He established Jesuit headquarters in the Portuguese enclave of Goa, on India's west coast. Jesuit priests spread through Asia hoping to convert its peoples by first converting their rulers. Emperor Akbar of India, a liberal Muslim, kept Jesuits like pets at his magnificent court in Fatehpur Sikri. Seated under a canopy, Akbar umpires a religious debate (opposite) pitting Father Ridolfo Aquaviva and a companion against Muslim mullahs. Though Jesuits failed to convert the emperor or his court, missions gained footholds in Delhi, Agra, and Lahore. Aquaviva and four fellow priests (below) were killed in 1583 by a mob near Goa, far from Akbar's personal protection.

than a million square miles, a task of over a decade. This Jesuit map of 1717 remained a standard for the world until the late 1800s.

But by the 18th century the Jesuits' time was ending. Jealousy inside China led to persecution, and their respect for Chinese customs drew fire from the Church in Europe, which condemned them for such practices as painting shoes on images of Christ to appease Chinese distaste for bare feet and, worse, for letting their converts perform ancient rites venerating ancestors. But their reports fueled a fascination with the East. European philosophers idealized the Jesuit picture of the rationally ordered government of China. Voltaire imagined that the Chinese had "perfected moral science."

Asia was curious about the West, too. In 1580, on the invitation of India's emperor, Akbar the Great, a group of Jesuits led by Ridolfo Aquaviva, a shy young Italian aristocrat, traveled to Fatehpur Sikri, Akbar's red stone city. The dazzled priests found themselves in debate with Hindus, Zoroastrians, Muslims, and Jews, while the emperor himself refereed, tossing gold coins to the winners. The Jesuits' letters about India's wealth and variety tempted a type of European traveler concerned not with Christianizing but with exploring to make money.

Jean-Baptiste Tavernier was a plump little Parisian gem merchant whose curiosity took him on five different trips to India between 1638 and 1668. Traveling like a gentleman, he often rode in a palanquin shaded by a parasol. Tavernier let jewels lead the way—from the diamond mines of Golconda, through caravansaries and village huts to the palaces of princes, where he found the nabobs would accept only "gold of the best sort" in trade for his gems.

Tavernier wrote a book about India's caste system, the tricks of money changers, and the wiles of fakirs, the itinerant Hindu ascetics. He described one fakir who "drags a heavy iron chain attached to one leg. . . . When he prays it is with a great noise . . . [and] an affected gravity which attracts the veneration of the people." Some fakirs summoned scores of disciples with drums and horns. "Vagabonds and idlers," judged Tavernier.

His book reinforced Europe's perception that Asia was too inviting to be left to freelancers. Nations followed their citizen explorers. England's East India Company took over India and parts of southeast Asia; Holland's turned the East Indies into a spice empire. France appropriated ore-rich Indochina, and by the mid-1800s Russia was thinking of a railway across Siberia.

Among the few regions still unmapped was the formidably inhospitable Arabian Peninsula, barred to all but Muslims. Unknown and forbidden, it lured Victorian romantics and scientists such as Charles Montagu Doughty. Unlike daredevils who courted death by penetrating

sacred Mecca disguised as Muslim pilgrims, Doughty lived openly as a Christian. Moving among Arabs of town, court, and caravan from 1876 to 1878, he often endured Muslim scorn and abuse but made friends with his medicinal skills. His landmark book *Travels in Arabia Deserta* presents, in prose as mannered and intricate as a Persian carpet, a panorama of life little known to the West: The nomad camp under "the blue night and clear hoary starlight," with the tethered camels who have "wandered all day upon the droughty face of the wilderness"; the supper of buttermilk and bread freshly baked on the campfire; the "sweet reek" of smoldering frankincense, passed beneath robes as live perfume; sandals made of "old camel sack-leather, moisty with the juice of the dates."

In the town of 'Unayzah, in central Arabia, Doughty watched the daily round of shopping in the souk, the calls to prayer, the endless talk among the idle, favored males of Arabian society—the "coffee-lords" —and the women as "veiled forms flitting to their gossips' houses," creeping home when the men go for late prayers to the mosque.

Doughty became legend in the desert. T. E. Lawrence—Lawrence of Arabia—said Doughty "broke a road" for other Westerners, among them Lady Anne Blunt and her husband, Wilfred. The Blunts crossed central Arabia from Damascus to the Persian Gulf in 1878.

In the depth of the desert one day,

II.ᵉ Partie fol. 376

12

13

Penitents and fakirs under a banyan tree appeared in a popular 17th-century guidebook for adventurers in India. Numbers 2 through 5 identify shrines. Penitents display painful, life-long postures, maintained day and night in hopes of rewards in a future life. The book's French author, Jean-Baptiste Tavernier, made five trips to India, where he amassed a fortune as a gem dealer. Curiosity led him to study Indian customs on his excursions.

Niccolao Manucci (below), a Venetian soldier of fortune, lived by his wits in India for 54 years. Masquerading as a doctor, he grew rich applying commonsense remedies to wealthy patients. To embellish his memoirs Manucci commissioned the miniature showing him in upper-class dress.

the Blunts rode out with their Bedouin companions, spurring swift mounts between towering red sand dunes toward Ha'il, a distant oasis city where Emir Ibn Rashid had a renowned stable of horses.

The emir could have beheaded these infidels at a whim. But perhaps because he had spent many hours with Doughty, he instead shared with them his love of horses. The Blunts brought to England a sheaf of Lady Anne's evocative paintings of desert life and several magnificent Arabian horses that made their stud world famous.

Only Tibet, girded by deserts and the world's highest mountains, surpassed Arabia in hostile remoteness. The Dalai Lama, Tibet's ruler, enforced its isolation to guard the power of the maroon-robed monks and the colorful pantheon who shaped its life. Expulsion or execution faced foreigners who trespassed, and death awaited Tibetans who were found to have helped them.

Spheres of influence became deadly rivalries as Britain and Russia pressed toward Tibet, then under the political control of China. To map Tibet as a step toward control, the British used ingenious ruses. In the 1860s Indians, trained as surveyors and spies, entered Tibet posing as merchants or Buddhist pilgrims. They counted their footsteps on prayer beads to calculate distances, took secret measurements with hidden instruments, and figured out latitudes and altitudes.

145

Caravans ply the Silk Road's southern branch through the Pamirs. Empires clashed here in the 19th century as Russia and Britain pressed toward eastern central Asia, a little-known region nominally ruled by China.

Col. Nikolay Przhevalsky, Russia's foremost explorer, made four expeditions into the deserts and mountains south of Siberia in the 1870s and 1880s, aided by a retinue of guides, interpreters, and sharpshooting Cossacks (below). Camel loads of scientif-

ic instruments yielded route surveys, maps, botanical collections, and new knowledge about the area. Though Przhevalsky failed to reach his goal —Lhasa, Tibet's capital—he is remembered for other discoveries, including the world's last wild horse, which bears his name (Equus caballus przewalskii).

The Russians openly backed their brilliant explorer, Colonel Nikolay Przhevalsky. Geographer, botanist, zoologist, and crack marksman, he longed to find Lhasa. In 1872 he climbed from the Gobi into northern Tibet. When he faced down both Tibetan bandits and bandit-hunting Chinese cavalry, villagers regarded his lack of fear as saintly magic. But winter and short supplies kept him from striking on toward the capital.

Expeditions in the Gobi led to a second try six years later. Camped on Tibet's soaring, treeless plateau, Przhevalsky and his Cossack escort were barely a week's march from Lhasa. Rumors raced through the capital that a Russian force was bent on kidnapping the Dalai Lama. Mobs of burly Tibetan guards in sheepskins blocked Przhevalsky's path. Przhevalsky's 13 men were so far outnumbered that he turned back, bitterly disappointed. They

were only 160 miles from their goal.

An unlikely group from England almost succeeded. Mr. and Mrs. St. George Littledale, with their nephew and their fox terrier, took a caravan onto Tibet's plateau in 1895. Their caravan leader was Rassul Galwan, a Ladakhi with an appetite for adventuring with sahibs.

The Littledale pack animals died from altitude sickness and exposure, Mrs. Littledale became ill, but the caravan struggled on. Eight days' ride from the forbidden city, some 300 Tibetans tried to force the tattered party to halt. Rassul boasted, "These two are English sahib, and the other one are very big lady, relative of queen of English." That claim gained them only a brief advantage. Then Rassul had to threaten: "In these boxes we have enemy-killing thing. If put fire to a box, then burn all men of country." The gullible locals, scoffed Rassul, were "jungly

men, believe to that matter."

They marched on, but Mrs. Littledale's illness worsened, and they had to give up and return to India. Rassul wrote a book about his travels, with an introduction by Col. Francis Younghusband, the self-confident star of British imperialism who would finally force Lhasa open.

As a young army officer Younghusband had crossed Asia from Peking to India, and explored the Karakoram Range and the Pamirs. He dreamed of entering Lhasa in disguise. When India's viceroy panicked over rumors of a Russian pact with Tibet, the British government authorized Younghusband to "show the flag" and compel exclusive agreements with Britain.

Younghusband led a small army across the Himalayas in December snow, 1903, accompanied by a caravan of thousands of mules and yaks, six camels and several correspon-

Soaring high above Lhasa, the Potala embodies the religious and political power of Tibetan Buddhism. Thirteen labyrinthine stories rising a thousand feet from the valley floor conceal storerooms, offices, dungeons, apartments, thousands of altars, and the sumptuous gilded tombs of past rulers. In the 19th century, explorers from four western nations grasped for the glory of reaching forbidden Lhasa. All courted death from exposure, altitude sickness, or hostile Tibetans. Col. Francis Young-

husband (below), leads soldiers into Tibet in early 1904 to force alliances with Britain. Battles left 2,700 Tibetans dead; the British lost only a few men. In Lhasa Younghusband established trade and political relations for Britain, thus breaching Asia's last bastion against European intruders.

dents from newspapers in London.

Tibetans armed with swords, muskets, and magic charms gathered at Guru. Shooting began by mistake. Horrified, Younghusband watched a four-minute massacre that left 700 Tibetans dead or dying. An ancient superstition held that if the fortress at nearby Gyangze ever fell to invaders, Tibet would be lost. Younghusband took the fortress, then marched on to Lhasa. The Dalai Lama had fled, and the regent signed England's treaty. London set up a flourishing trade mission in Gyangze and, with Tibetan cooperation, banned foreigners—except for the English and the Chinese.

Infuriated, a French Orientalist named Alexandra David-Néel entered Tibet without permission. Her books about this strange land, where nomads lived on neighborly terms with demons and a cranky sorcerer might bombard his enemies with flying barley cakes, encouraged the new field of Tibetology.

With Tibet, Asia was yielding its last secrets to Europeans. For 700 years, gate-crashers seeking wealth, souls, power, and knowledge had brought tales of Asia's startling ways back to Europe. Now Europeans would try to coerce the one continent to serve the desires of the other. But as Jesuit explorers had learned, Asia would receive the touch of the West on Asia's own terms. Generations later, many an Asian businessman would wear a gray flannel suit— and worship at a Buddhist shrine.

Cy apres commence le liure de marc pol des merueilles dice la grant et dm
de la mineur et maieur.

Et des diuerses regions du monde.

Our sauoir la pure verite de diuerses regions du mon
de. Si prenes ce liure cy et le faictes lire. si y trouueres les
grandismes merueilles qui y sont escriptes. De la grãt
ermenie. et de perse. et des tartars. et dinde et de main
tes autres prouinces. si comme nře liure comptera p
ordres appertement. de quoy messire marc pol. sages z
nobles de venisse racompte pour ce que il le

with highly developed land communications by postriders; paper money accepted as legal currency; and . . .

"black stones existing in beds in the mountains, which they dig out and burn like firewood. If you supply the fire with them at night, and see that they are well kindled, you will find them still alight in the morning. Oh, Marco, Marco, for the sake of your soul. . . ."

The old man ignored the interruption. He was back in the southern regions of the Khan's empire, where he came upon primitive people tattooed from head to toe; crocodiles with mouths big enough to swallow a man at one gulp; tribes that were addicted to eating human flesh, deeming it more delicate than any other. He sailed to Ceylon in a fleet of four-masted junks under orders to purchase for the Khan the world's largest ruby and a begging bowl said to have belonged to the Buddha himself. On the way, stopping off at Sumatra, he had made a discovery that would, he knew, generate intense interest in the mercantile centers of Europe. Spices! "All the precious spices that can be found in the world," he mumbled, remembering the words in his book.

Now he thought of the Khan's winter palace at Cambaluc, an immense marble structure set in a maze of walls, parks, gardens, copses, grazing lands, and game preserves, all surrounded by outer ramparts. It was the time of the Mongol New Year, early in February. The Khan and his subjects, all dressed in white, the color of good luck, were attending a parade of 5,000 royal elephants, each piled high with samples of the royal treasure. Later, the Khan entertained 6,000 guests at a huge celebration and feast in the grand hall of the palace, and graciously accepted gifts to the crown. There were jewels, jade vases, pelts of sable and ermine from the north, silver and gold. . . .

"On that day, I can assure you, among the customary presents there shall be offered to the Khan from various quarters more than 100,000 white horses, beautiful animals, and richly caparisoned. Ah, Marco, your time is so short—why won't you retract these exaggerations?"

Lips pursed stubbornly, Marco continued his journey through the past. When the snows melted, the Khan and his court, a vast assemblage of men and women, left Cambaluc on the great spring hunt, a leisurely tour of the provinces. Kublai Khan rode on four elephants in a howdah covered with tiger skins and gold leaf, while his barons rode horses and the ladies reclined in palanquins. They were accompanied by huntsmen, beaters, falconers, hounds, and birds, with servants at everyone's beck and the whole guarded over by troops of soldiers.

Then it was on to the summer court at Shangdu, in the cool western hills. Shangdu was a walled park with winding waterways, meadows, wild animals, and a stable of pure white mares whose milk was drunk only by the Great Khan and his family and favorites. In the park were two palaces. One was marble, decorated with gilded paintings of trees and flowers, birds and beasts. The other was a marvel of construction made of polished bamboo canes embellished with gilt and brilliant lacquers, and carved dragons clad in gold. . . .

"The construction of the Palace is so devised that it can be taken down and

155

Dragons of Yunnan from a 14th-century French version of Marco Polo's book.

In Xanadu did Kubla Khan
A stately pleasure dome
*   decree:*
Where Alph, the sacred
*   river, ran*
Through caverns measureless
*   to man*
Down to a sunless sea.

SAMUEL TAYLOR COLERIDGE
"KUBLA KHAN"

put up again with great celerity; and it can all be taken to pieces and removed whithersoever the Emperor may command. When erected, it is braced by more than 200 cords of silk.

"Your soul, Marco. Think of your soul!"

The old man kept his eyes closed. After 17 years in the service of the Khan, the Polos had begun to think wistfully of home. Niccolò and Maffeo were showing their age and so was Kublai Khan, now well into his 70s. He would be joining his ancestors soon enough, and who knew what the new ruler would think of the white men from the West?

At first, the Khan would not hear of their leaving. But fate intervened. Ambassadors arrived with a request from Arghun, King of Persia, that the Great Khan send him a new wife from the same Mongolian family as his favored queen who had died. A 17-year-old beauty named Cocachin was selected, but fighting among princes in the western provinces had closed the overland route back to Persia. Reluctantly, the Khan agreed to let the Venetians, excellent mariners, deliver the bride by sea in return for the privilege of regaining their homeland.

A fleet of 14 four-masted junks was prepared for the voyage, while the Polos converted their considerable holdings into gems and jewelry, which they carefully sewed into the linings of their woolen garments. The old man in the bed was too weary now to linger on the two years of that arduous trip to Persia, through uncharted seas, with many stops

Rustichello in a Genoese prison, recording the fabulous adventures of his cell mate, Marco Polo.

along the way—Sumatra, Java, Malaya, Ceylon, India. They delivered Cocachin to her queenship and sailed on to Venice.

They arrived in 1295, after an absence of 24 years, in queer Oriental clothes, travel stained and tattered, stray dogs yapping at their heels. At first they were denied entrance to their ancestral home, now occupied by relatives who believed them long dead. Marco remembered how remarkably they had returned to life when, having argued themselves inside and donned fresh silken robes of crimson hue, they tore open the linings of their rags and dumped forth diamonds, pearls, sapphires, emeralds, and rubies.

Jewels that could be held in the hand were proof enough that the three wandering Polos had indeed done something out of the ordinary. But the stories they told—especially Marco—stretched belief. Great wealth can make all sorts of eccentricities acceptable, so the relatives did nothing foolish. But Marco knew how they shook their heads among themselves and shuddered when some of his tales began to be repeated along the Rialto.

Matters went from bad to worse when hand-transcribed copies of his book appeared. As fast as words can travel, much of the Western world was laughing its incredulity. Once again, the old man marveled at it: People so willing to believe that alchemists could transmute base metals into gold, that an infinite number of angels could dance on the head of a pin, that fire-breathing monsters gobbled ships as they tumbled over the edge of a flat Earth, such people could not accept a Mongolian emperor rich and powerful enough to command a gift of 100,000 white horses. Or paper money. Or trees that grew nuts as big as a man's head.

The old man hoped that not everybody disbelieved. There were some—better educated, perhaps, or more worldly, or blessed with greater imagination—who lusted after islands where all the world's spices grew. Perhaps there would be men who would carry his book with them on voyages of exploration across unknown seas.

It would be vindication, of sorts. But too late now, in 1324, as he lay on his deathbed, listening to friends and relatives, with sneers or pious horror in their voices, importune him to admit that the things he had seen with his own eyes, heard with his own ears, were all lies.

"The end is near, Uncle Marco! For your soul, tell the truth at last!"
The old man opened eyes filled with memory, and whispered back:
"I have not told half of what I saw!"

Europe had received Marco Polo's book with enthusiasm, but to readers it seemed more like enjoyable fiction than fact. Scribes who hand copied the book sometimes added their own embellishments. Nevertheless, later explorers, including Columbus and Magellan, read Marco Polo's book with care. Marco's friends and relatives may not have quoted from it at his bedside as we have conjectured, but the story goes that they did gather there to implore him to recant and so provoked his famed deathbed response.

157

Alexandra David·Néel

By Elisabeth B. Booz

The British Trade Agent in Gyangze was taking his afternoon nap. It was April 1924 in southern Tibet. An agitated servant tapped at his bedroom door: Sorry to disturb him but two common-looking Tibetans, a man and a woman, were outside. The woman was asking to see the sahib, in a peremptory tone. She behaved just like a European.

"Oh, God," groaned David Macdonald. "Send her in here."

His nine children took glee in practical jokes. He was not about to be taken in. When he heard footsteps, he rolled over and pretended to snore. Without turning, he said crossly, "I know perfectly well who you are! Now get out of here and stop acting the fool!"

He sensed a shocked silence. A voice with a French accent replied, "You are speaking to Madame Alexandra David-Néel!"

His Majesty's Trade Agent jumped out of bed. The owner of that name, a thorn in the side of the British Raj for the past decade, was a tiny, frail woman in Tibetan dress, barely five feet tall and 55 years old. In a flurry of apologies, Mr. Macdonald summoned the family and escorted her to the drawing room, where tea was served.

Eight years earlier the British had deported Alexandra David-Néel for illegally entering Tibet. She had vowed then and there to reach its heart, Lhasa. The capital was so inaccessible and so tightly sealed against foreigners, under pressure of world politics, that only a handful of men from the West had ever seen it—and never a woman. Outrage motivated her as much as her aim to discover the mysterious life of the Tibetan people by living as one of them. This was a startling idea in 1916. No outsider had ever attempted it.

David-Néel had the resources she needed. She had gained acceptance in France as a serious Orientalist. As a former actress, she could disappear into the scenery. She had a journalist's sharp eye. And she

Visions of the high lamas: Grotesque masks worn by Tibetan Buddhist dancers depict mythological fairies and demons that inhabit spiritual trances.

159

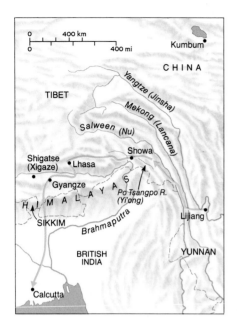

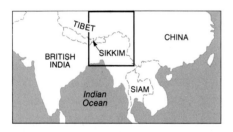

had enough money. At age 36 Alexandra David had married Philippe Néel, a distant cousin. They rarely lived together, but he supported her financially and they remained intimate friends through a lifelong exchange of letters—the material of her books.

In 1911 David-Néel left for India, hoping to write articles for the French press. Tibet's Dalai Lama, in exile there, granted her his first interview with a foreign woman. After a learned discussion of Buddhist doctrine he advised, "Learn the Tibetan language."

In Sikkim David-Néel hired her indispensable companion-servant, a 15-year-old Sikkimese monk named Aphur Yongden, who practiced Tibetan Buddhism. She deepened his understanding of the doctrines and eventually became his adoptive mother. Yongden never left her side until his death, in France, 40 years later.

Her clandestine excursions into Tibet began in 1914. With camera and notebook, David-Néel reached Chorten Nyima, a tiny, ruined monastery just over the border from Sikkim, inhabited by three nuns. Their spiritual insight led her to seek a tutor like theirs, a hermit who lived in Sikkim's mountains. Throughout one winter she stayed as his apprentice in a cave at 13,000 feet. The anchorite shared secret knowledge and taught her Tibetan.

At Shigatse, deep in Tibet, Alexandra David-Néel met the Panchen Lama, Tibet's second most revered figure. He heard her debate with erudite monks and conferred on her the robes of a graduate lama, a sort of Tibetan Ph.D. Wearing the yellow silk bonnet of an abbess, she wrote to her husband, "I feel completely at home in this central Asian character." The British Raj got wind of it and deported her.

Two years later David-Néel struggled across China from Peking to Kumbum, a Tibetan monastery in the undefined borderlands. She and Yongden remained among its 3,800 monks for three years. Throughout these highlands, the lady lama traveled with a small caravan of mules, in local style. She blessed villagers and nomads while she learned their customs. One winter, on China's tea-trade route, she met an English geographer, who lent her his maps and pointed out an unexplored route into Tibet up the Salween River from China's Yunnan Province. The way continued through wild territory along the Po Tsangpo River to Tibet's main east-west caravan route—and on to Lhasa.

David-Néel prudently "disappeared" to the Gobi, to let border officials forget her. The mules and servants, her camera, her comfortable tent and zinc bathtub would all have to go. She and Yongden, in disguise, would risk it alone.

In late October 1923, two beggars joined the thousands of pilgrims who continually circulated throughout Tibet, visiting its sacred places. The poor young lama and his aged mother appeared to be the lowest of the low. But their knapsacks contained two compasses, a tiny tent, rope, and other necessities. Rough copies of the Englishman's maps lined David-Néel's boots. Under their clothing both pilgrims wore

Mme. Alexandra David-Néel with a Nepalese servant: In 1912 she traveled the jungle of Nepal on pilgrimage to the birthplace of Siddhartha Gautama, the founder of Buddhism.

revolvers and money belts with silver and gold. Because surveying instruments were out of the question, David-Néel guessed at altitudes. Where possible she followed rivers. Many times, when snow blotted out landmarks and trails, she was completely lost.

Discovery as a foreigner could mean death at the hands of superstitious Tibetans. At the very least it meant capture and an end to exploring. She blackened her hair with ink and lengthened it with skinny yak-hair braids. She darkened her skin with cocoa and soot. A dirty old fur bonnet found on the path completed her peasant's outfit. Filth was essential to the disguise, as Tibetans rarely washed. When chance brought them to a hot spring and a yearned-for bath, Yongden implored her not to wash her face, which finally had the right color.

Once, rinsing her cooking pot in a stream, she heard a woman whisper, "Her hands are like a foreigner's!" Washed clean, they were startlingly white. While frantically blackening them with soot from the pot, she overheard the general reprieve: She must be Mongolian.

They preferred to sleep in the open and cook their own food—barley

A tea porter on the main trade route of China-Tibet borderlands.

gruel and brick tea with butter. But as winter deepened, they accepted hospitality, usually in hovels at a level of society unknown even to many Tibetans. As a lama, Yongden was always welcome, badgered to give blessings and prophecies. In an ironic exchange of roles, Yongden sat on cushions by the fire while the worthless old woman was relegated to an icy corner on the dirt floor. She was gathering anecdotes for books, but the raw material was sometimes hard to live through.

They sometimes used people's superstition to good effect. When Yongden told fortunes, he prescribed cleanliness or an act of kindness as an antidote to demons. After crossing lonely passes into the kingdom of Po on the Po Tsangpo, they met robbers. Yongden was forced to surrender a couple of coins and would have had his money belt discovered had David-Néel not taken over. She screamed and howled at the theft of her son's fortune and called down vengeance from the most dreaded Tibetan deities whose names no common person dared pronounce. She later wrote, "I am a tiny woman with nothing dramatic in my appearance; but at that moment I felt myself rising to the height of a powerful tragedienne." She petrified even herself with the supernatural aura she had created. The terrified robbers begged her to stop, returned the stolen money, and retreated with a blessing from Yongden.

On a 19-hour march across uninhabited mountains, with winter snow closing the passes behind them, Tibetan lore came to the rescue. Exhausted and half-frozen, David-Néel tried to make a fire by moonlight—only to find that the flint and steel were wet. Without fire, in their sodden clothes, they would freeze to death. Yongden urged David-Néel to try *thumo reskiang* to raise her body heat. Not unlike modern biofeedback, this art had been used by Tibetan hermits for centuries to survive at high altitudes with the scantiest of clothing.

She put the flint, steel, and a pinch of kindling under her dress and began to concentrate. Imagining fire blazing around her, flames curling over her head, she became semiconscious until the loud snap of ice cracking on a nearby stream jolted her awake. She found herself feverishly hot and deliciously comfortable. She lit a fire with ease, and awoke the next morning, refreshed.

David-Néel and Yongden approached the big caravan route with dread, knowing they must obtain travel permits at a toll bridge. But their disguises held up. Yongden dealt with officialdom while his old mother, muttering prayers by the doorstep, went unnoticed. Luck stayed with them all the way. When they reached Lhasa among throngs of pilgrims for the New Year celebrations, nature supplied a sandstorm to cloak their entrance into the holy city.

Alexandra David-Néel must have mentally thumbed her nose at the British as she followed other pilgrims to the roof of the Potala, the Dalai Lama's magnificent fortress. Panic struck when an officious palace monk made her take off the dirty fur bonnet, exposing brown hair from which the ink had long worn off—but she passed as a Ladakhi, from India's borderland. Under the full moon of the New Year, David-Néel and Yongden joined the festival crowds around Lhasa's ancient Bud-

A ruined shrine, three Buddhist nuns, and Alexandra David-Néel, who admired the independence of these women in their mountain isolation.

dhist shrines. Larger-than-life-size images of animals, men, and gods, sculptured of butter and vividly colored, lined the streets. Nomads burst through the excited throng, "sturdy giants, cowmen clad in sheepskin, holding on to one another, ran for joy. . . . Their big fists belaboured the ribs of those whom bad luck had placed in their way."

David-Néel and Yongden stayed in Lhasa for two months. Then they changed disguise, adopting the dress of the lower middle class. David-Néel bought books and manuscripts to delight Oriental scholars in Europe, and a horse to carry her and Yongden on to Gyangze.

As she told it afterwards in the drawing room of His Majesty's Trade Agent, the whole trip had been a splendid adventure of "wanderings truly wonderful." It seemed hardly possible to her astonished audience that this small Frenchwoman could have crossed unexplored parts of Tibet in the middle of winter and lived in Lhasa, undetected. David Macdonald, a rare Tibet hand, could not hide his admiration.

Only in letters to Philippe did she admit that she had arrived in Lhasa "reduced to a skeleton . . . my skin hung from my bones in long folds, like a deflated balloon. . . ." and that nothing could ever induce her to repeat such madness again. But she had accomplished her goal. From lofty philosopher to squalid villager, Alexandra David-Néel had experienced Tibet. And told the world.

Alexandra David-Néel recounted her adventures in My Journey to Lhasa, Magic and Mystery in Tibet, *and other books.*

A Sea So Vast

By Robert M. Poole

Captain James Cook lay facedown in the Pacific Ocean. He was dead. A Hawaiian, part of a mob assembled on the shore at Kealakekua Bay, had clubbed him from behind. He fell from the black lava beach into the turquoise water, and two or three assailants splashed in after him. They stabbed him and beat him until he ceased struggling.

Silence spread from the shore, like the rain clouds that boil up daily from Mauna Loa and fan across the huge green island of Hawaii. Nothing about Cook's death on this day—February 14, 1779—made sense. He was revered throughout much of the world, a Briton sailing under the protection of the French, Spanish, and American governments.

On three voyages in ten years, he touched the ice of both Poles, explored the western shores of Canada and Alaska, and filled the vast blue spaces of Europe's maps with islands and peoples that were unimagined before he made them known.

Earth's largest ocean, the Pacific, stretches some 10,000 miles from east to west and 10,000 miles from north to south. All seven continents could fit within its boundaries.

That expanse of water, with so little land sprinkled through it, would defeat more than one explorer. In this emptiness a ship could sail for months without finding land, as Ferdinand Magellan learned on his frightful crossing. Those who fol-

lowed also would suffer from starvation and scurvy—once the bane of Pacific exploration. If sailors survived these hazards, they might face death in a fight on a lonely shore, as Cook and Magellan had done.

But nothing that the Europeans endured compared to the sufferings they inflicted, deliberately or not, on Pacific peoples. For each European who died, many thousands of Polynesians fell victim to the guns and diseases the visitors brought.

The Polynesians, called savages by Europeans, had themselves settled the Pacific long before Magellan nosed his *Trinidad* into the Great South Sea. By then, Polynesians were scattered over a larger area than any other people on Earth.

They had settled island after island in the Polynesian triangle, defined by the Hawaiian Islands, New Zealand, and Easter Island. Living in a region of seventy parts water to one part land, the Polynesians naturally developed a mastery at sea. They navigated without compass or sextant, setting their course by the stars, by wind direction, by the pattern of ocean swells. A Polynesian sailor could dip his hand in the water and by its temperature detect a change of current. To his eye cloud formations reflected the shimmering waters of a lagoon, and thus announced the position of an atoll long before its palm trees appeared on the horizon.

What prompted the Polynesians to scatter? Perhaps a family had to flee for breaking *tapu*, the sacred

Besieged by the immense Pacific, spindly islands of the Tuamotu group shimmer in a relentless surf. Polynesian voyagers settled the far-flung lands in Earth's largest ocean, bringing coconuts, bananas, taro, and other food plants with them from other islands.

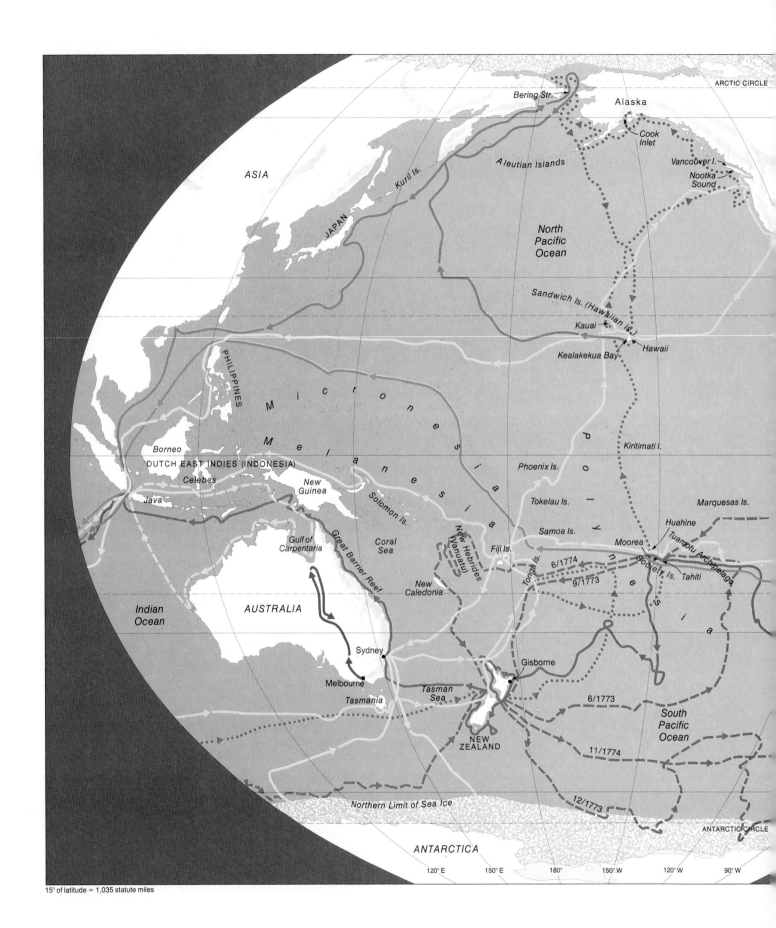

ARCTIC CIRCLE

Bering Str.

Alaska

Cook
Inlet

ASIA

Kuril Is.

Aleutian Islands

Vancouver I.

Nootka
Sound

JAPAN

North
Pacific
Ocean

PHILIPPINES

Sandwich Is. (Hawaiian Is.)

Kauai

Hawaii

Kealakekua Bay

M
i
c
r
o
n
e
s
i
a

P
o
l
y
n
e
s
i
a

Borneo

DUTCH EAST INDIES (INDONESIA)

M
e
l
a
n
e
s
i
a

Kiritimati I.

Celebes

New
Guinea

Phoenix Is.

Marquesas Is.

Java

Solomon Is.

Tokelau Is.

Huahine

Tuamotu Archipelago

Gulf of
Carpentaria

Great Barrier Reef

Coral
Sea

New
Hebrides
(Vanuatu)

Fiji Is.

Samoa Is.

Moorea

Society Is. Tahiti

Indian
Ocean

AUSTRALIA

New
Caledonia

Tonga Is.

6/1774

9/1773

Sydney

Gisborne

Melbourne

Tasmania

Tasman
Sea

6/1773

South
Pacific
Ocean

NEW
ZEALAND

11/1774

Northern Limit of Sea Ice

12/1773

ANTARCTIC CIRCLE

ANTARCTICA

120° E   150° E   180°   150° W   120° W   90° W

15° of latitude = 1,035 statute miles

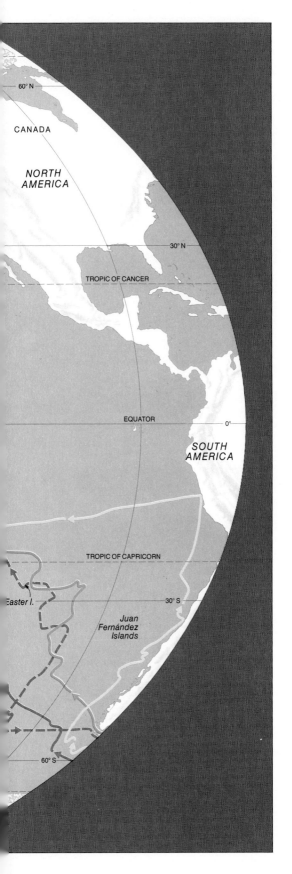

"He left nothing unattempted," said King George III of James Cook (below, right), who changed the map of the world, filling in blanks from the Antarctic to Alaska. On three historic Pacific voyages, Cook built upon earlier discoveries by Abel Janszoon Tasman, the Dutchman who first saw New Zealand, and Samuel Wallis, the English captain who found Tahiti. After Cook came Charles Wilkes, who confirmed Antarctica's existence while on the U. S. Exploring Expedition. On

land, explorers Robert O'Hara Burke and William John Wills first crossed Australia from south to north.

But long before Europeans entered the Pacific, Polynesians set out on their early voyages of settlement. By A.D. 800 they occupied an area nearly twice the size of the continental U. S.

OVERLEAF: *Polynesians glide an outrigger past Moorea's peaks. The stability of larger, seagoing outriggers enabled early voyagers to travel vast distances.*

Polynesian Discovery

(map labels)
Hawaii A.D. 500
Marquesas Is. A.D. 300
Samoa Is.
Fiji Is.
Society Is. A.D. 600
Tonga Is.
Easter I. A.D. 400
NEW ZEALAND A.D. 800

Tasman 1642
Tasman 1644
Wallis 1766-68
Cook 1768-1771
Cook 1772-75
Cook 1776-79
Voyage after Cook's death 1779-1780
Wilkes 1838-1842
Burke and Wills 1860-61
Early settlement
Dispersal

code. Perhaps others lost at war and sought peace elsewhere. Or perhaps a sailor wondered, as sailors will, what lay beyond the horizon.

Less mystery surrounds the motivations of the Europeans who first sailed into the Pacific. They wanted dominion and gold.

The Spaniards who came in the 16th century sought a quick route from the Americas to the Philippines, the center of what they hoped would be their eastern empire. The 17th century brought a wave of Dutch explorers searching for new trade routes to the East Indies. In the

process, those first European sailors discovered an island here and there, but it was largely a matter of luck.

Both Spanish and Dutch explorers sought in vain for a rich continent known as Terra Australis Incognita, the unknown southern landmass that had loomed large in human imagination since ancient times, when Greeks reasoned that huge landforms existed in the Southern Hemisphere to counterbalance the lands that spread through the north. In the absence of fact, later travelers filled the unknown region with fantasy: It was rich in gold, with a mild climate and docile natives. Pedro Fernandez de Quiros, sailing under the Spanish flag in 1606, mistook an island of the New Hebrides for the continent and staged a High Mass and fireworks to commemorate his "discovery." Others glimpsed the continent's ghostly outlines in the

distance, only to see it vanish in clouds or turn into an island.

Still the legend of the Great South Land became an obsession of Europe, one that inspired the greatest era of Pacific discovery.

When James Cook turned toward that ocean in 1768, he had two sets of orders: He was to solve the continental question, once and for all. And he was to visit Tahiti to watch Venus pass before the sun. By observing the planet's transit, the Royal Navy could calculate Earth's distance from the sun, which would aid celestial navigation.

Cook was a natural choice as expedition leader: He was a masterful navigator, trained on the rough waters of the North Sea. There he had served on a merchant coal ship, or collier, before joining the Royal Navy for the Seven Years' War.

The North Sea experience prompted Cook to request a collier for his worldwide expedition. At 368 tons, the *Endeavour* was slow and homely, with the stout lines of a tugboat, but her flat bottom reduced the risk of running aground in unknown waters, and her vast hold could store provisions for a long voyage. Plain and practical, like James Cook.

The same could not be said of Joseph Banks, a wealthy young dilettante and amateur botanist who accompanied Cook as an unofficial observer. Other gentlemen would tour Europe to finish their educations, but not Joseph Banks. "Every blockhead does that," he scoffed. "My

Grand Tour shall be one round the whole globe."

For such a person, what better place to explore life, in all its raw beauty and variety, than Tahiti? Here was a place scarcely affected by civilization, an isolated society that had seen European ships on only two previous occasions.

When Samuel Wallis, an Englishman, discovered the island in 1767, Tahitians met him with a shower of stones—a common greeting for the first Europeans landing on many Pacific islands. Most natives assumed that strangers came to conquer, not to befriend. When the Tahitians resisted Wallis, he shot two natives, killing one. The Tahitians eventually yielded, and established friendly relations with the British.

Several months later, the Frenchman Louis-Antoine de Bougainville arrived at Tahiti, which he described as paradise on Earth: "Nature has placed it in the best climate of the universe, embellished it smilingly, enriched it with all its gifts, covered it with handsome inhabitants...; she herself has dictated their laws," wrote Bougainville, thus beginning the romantic myth of Tahiti.

For a weary sailor who had been months aboard ship, Tahiti *was* a paradise, where coconut palms leaned to soft breezes and black sand beaches shimmered like polished onyx. Tahiti smelled of the sea, mingled with the fragrance of jasmine and gardenia. Fruits and other fresh foods abounded, and the Tahitian

"The face of the Country is of a hilly surface and appeares to be cloathed with wood and Verdure," Cook wrote in 1769, when he first glimpsed New Zealand. He thought it might serve well as a colony. But he misjudged the native Maori, whom he thought too divided to oppose colonization. They did resist European settlement, in bloody wars that shook New Zealand during the 19th century.

people were willing to share them.

Cook and Banks arrived a year after Bougainville. While Cook made preparations to observe Venus, Banks plunged into island life. He got a tattoo, collected plants, noted how people worshiped, and how they cooked a dog (suffocate it, singe its hair, and roast it for two hours). When Banks heard about a mourning ceremony, he stripped off his clothes (including his white waistcoat with silver frog clasps) and participated, allowing the Tahitians to blacken him with charcoal. Reduced to a loincloth, the gentleman botanist marched around with the funeral party, stopping to pray here and there. He wrote about it, as he did everything, often without slowing for commas and the other impediments of punctuation.

Banks and his entourage of scientists examined all aspects of island life—animal, vegetable, and mineral—and thus began a new age of exploration that set high standards for later voyages by Charles Wilkes, Charles Darwin, and Jean-François de Galaup, Comte de La Pérouse.

Looking over Banks's botanical collections, the practical Cook wondered whether they served any purpose. Could his men eat them? Banks assured the captain that they could not. Like Banks, Cook recorded all he saw and tasted. This included Tahitian pudding, a concoction of breadfruit, plantain, nuts, and coconut, for which he carefully copied the recipe. "I seldom or never dined

without one when I could get it," wrote the great navigator.

That attention to detail, reflected in the writings of Cook and Banks, exploded the myths of idyllic Tahitian life that Bougainville and others had promoted. In fact, Cook wrote, Tahiti's natives stole anything that glittered, often warred with their neighbors, and practiced human sacrifice—hardly the stuff of paradise.

Still, Cook much admired the people. He later worried about how Europeans would ruin Tahiti. "It would have been far better for these poor people never to have known our superiority," Cook wrote in sorrow. Less than a century later, the island's culture was a shambles. First came disease, then missionaries who sacked temples and banned native dancing and religion. Then the settlers came, leaving only the Tahitian language as a cultural vestige.

Leaving Tahiti, Cook turned the *Endeavour* westward toward the neighboring islands, which he named the Society Isles "as they lay contiguous to one another." Here as elsewhere, Cook took on fresh fruits and meat, part of his campaign against scurvy, the crippling disease now known to be caused by a deficiency of vitamin C.

Cook recognized the importance of diet and cleanliness on long voyages. He kept the men's sleeping quarters scrubbed and aired. The *Endeavour* sailed crammed with experimental antiscorbutics, including malt, sauerkraut, and soup. Cook

used them all, and though he once whipped those men who would not eat their allotment of fresh food, he preferred subtler methods of persuasion. "Such are the Tempers and disposissions of Seamen," Cook wrote, "that whatever you give them out of the Common way . . . will not go down with them and you will hear nothing but murmurings gainest the man that first invented it; but the Moment they see their Superiors set a Value upon it, it becomes the finest stuff in the World and the inventer an honest fellow."

So when the men balked at sauerkraut, Cook had heaps of it served at his table. He instructed his officers to eat it with enthusiasm. Suddenly the crew craved sauerkraut. In less than a week, Cook had to ration it.

He had solved the problem of scurvy. Through ten years of hard sailing, not one man under Cook's direct command died from scurvy—a remarkable achievement for an age in which the disease had been the major obstacle to long voyages.

From the Society Islands, Cook ordered the *Endeavour* southwest, in search of the southern continent, and came upon New Zealand. He landed on North Island, near the present-day city of Gisborne, and anchored in a horseshoe bay. Buff-colored cliffs protected the waters, and steep green mountains rose in the interior. Land breezes carried the scent of black pine and rippled the bay: A quiet place and a good refuge—so it seemed.

Within hours, the British faced angry Maori natives who stood their ground on the gray beach. They hit the British with stones and swatted at them with war clubs, and one native was killed by gunfire. Next day, Cook resolved to capture a few Maori, take them to his ship "and by good treatment and presents endeavour to gain their friendship."

But the Maori resisted, and four or five more natives fell to the guns. Cook wisely turned away, naming the place Poverty Bay, "because it afforded us no one thing we wanted."

In retrospect, however, the experience proved valuable. Cook was remorseful. "Had I thought that they would have made the least resistance I would not have come near them," he wrote. Henceforth, he would approach unknown peoples gingerly, and he would insist on honest dealing with the local folk, even whipping one of his own men who stole a native's hatchet. Cook prevented his crew from felling a single coconut tree in New Guinea, for fear of offending the owners. And he ordered his men to fire wide of their attackers, to frighten, not to kill.

It is one thing to bump up against a new land and proclaim that you have discovered it, another to disprove the existence of a land, such as the illusory southern continent. To do that, you had to go to all the places the myth was thought to be, and discover that it was not there.

Now James Cook had to see whether New Zealand was part of the

"Our faithfull guide through all the vicissitudes of climates," said Cook in praise of the chronometer (left) he tested on his second voyage. The timepiece opened new possibilities for mariners, who could now calculate almost exactly their position at sea. Using the new clock, Cook compared Greenwich time to his local time, and thus pinpointed his longitude, the distance east or west of the Greenwich meridian. Before the invention of the chronometer, sailors judged longitude by complicated guesswork that sent many a ship wide of its target, often by hundreds of miles.

Less than a century after Cook, Americans explored Antarctica's fringes. An engraving, based on a sketch by expedition leader Charles Wilkes, shows some members of the Vincennes's crew skidding down an "ice island." Wilkes's dog, Sydney, lies in the foreground. "The icebergs were covered with penguins," wrote Wilkes, whose scientists collected more than 500 species of birds.

great continent, as Abel Janszoon Tasman, a Dutch explorer, had postulated more than 120 years before.

So Cook set out on a punishing six-month voyage to circumnavigate New Zealand. Gales and heavy surf pushed him away. He fought back, only to have the *Endeavour* buffeted away again, like a toy. Cook kept at it, sails split and rigging slipping, determined to complete his work. Inch by inch, a chart of New Zealand gradually appeared under Cook's hand, all 2,400 miles of ragged coastline. Tasman was wrong: The lands were not part of a great continent.

Terra Australis retreated a bit more, and Cook turned westward, sailing toward the eastern coast of Australia. There he stopped to take on fresh water and wood near the present site of Sydney.

In the baking sunlight of the beach, Aboriginals shook their spears and attempted to wave the newcomers away. The British landed anyway, and the natives vanished into the muffled gloom of the woods, where burrawangs and scribbly gums choked out the sun and parrots jabbered in the treetops.

That scene would be often repeated in Australia over the next century. As British settlers came, the Aboriginals retreated before them; thousands were killed in Tasmania, where the entire native population was almost exterminated. The people of this continent were not the main obstacle to exploration; the land was. Colonists began settling

Australia from the outside in, tentatively probing the continent's harsh interior. Charles Sturt explored the Murray-Darling river system in 1828 and 1829. In 1840 Edward John Eyre struggled toward the Sahara-like center until the barrenness deterred him. Twenty years later, that wasteland would doom Robert O'Hara Burke and William John Wills.

The continent's coastal fringes almost did in James Cook. Leaving the mainland, Cook made northward to chart Australia's eastern coast, not realizing that he was sailing inside the Great Barrier Reef, a 1,250-mile-long coral maze. Threading through this trap, the *Endeavour* ran aground, and was barely saved.

She arrived home three years after her voyage had begun. Though Cook's first voyage achieved much, the question of the southern continent remained. So in 1772, he set out again with two rebuilt colliers, the *Resolution* and *Adventure*. In three years he covered 70,000 miles, making a bold circumnavigation of the globe that took him as far south as 71° 10'. He proved that a habitable Terra Australis did not exist.

Cook crossed the Antarctic Circle on January 17, 1773—the first person to do so—and slowly worked his way around the pack ice.

"Excessive Cold," wrote Lt. Richard Pickersgill on the *Resolution*, "the people Numb'd, y^e Ropes all froze over with Ice & y^e Rig^g and Sails all covered with Snow."

Cook came close to Antarctica,

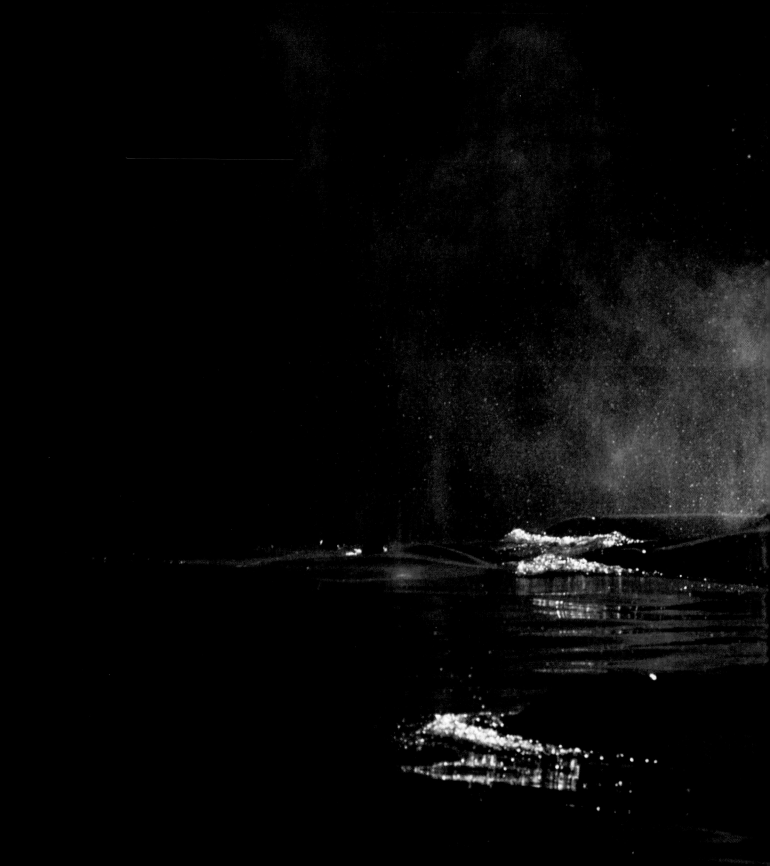

The forested slopes of Vancouver Island at Nootka Sound proved a welcome refuge on Cook's North Pacific voyage. Here the British found much needed drinking water, and timber to replace the Resolution's fore-topmast.

Nootka's Indians proved astute traders who demanded that the visitors pay them with buttons, candlesticks, kettles, and other brass items, rather than the usual beads and trinkets.

"Before we left the place," wrote an exasperated Cook, "hardly a bit of brass was left in the Ship. . . ."

Dressed for the damp weather, the Nootkas wore robes of woven bark or fur, made partly of "the hair of the white bair" Cook mistakenly thought; in fact, the white fur in the garments came from mountain goats. Cook's crew first saw polar bears in the Arctic, long after the stop at Nootka Sound.

but saw no land. He guessed that the continent was the source of huge ice floes that threatened his ships. Near the end of his second voyage, Cook wrote: "The risk one runs in exploring a coast in these unknown and Icy Seas, is so very great, that I can be bold to say, that no man will ever venture farther than I have done."

For once, Cook was wrong.

Less than a century later, American sailors spied the mountains of the seventh continent and confirmed its existence. It was January 16, 1840. The squadron of six Navy vessels were sailing under Lt. Charles Wilkes. Self-righteous and aloof, Wilkes shared none of James Cook's generous spirit. But difficult as Wilkes was, his determination, scientific ability, and thorough professionalism made his voyage one of the most revealing in Pacific history.

Wilkes delved into a part of the Pacific that Cook had scarcely examined. This was Melanesia, a group of Pacific islands northeast of Australia. Melanesian lands were poor, with the meager food supply constantly threatened by hurricanes and the demands of other tribes. Little wonder that the Melanesians resisted when boatloads of hungry Europeans descended on them.

Fiji, part of Melanesia, was well known for its fierce inhabitants. And navigation was a nightmare among the three hundred islands of the Fiji group, where the ocean bottom could go from fifty fathoms to three without warning. As the U. S.

Serenity reigns in the Place of Refuge of Hōnaunau on Hawaii, as ukulele players greet the sunset. When Cook visited the island, strict taboos governed daily life: Commoners could not touch the chief's possessions; women could not eat with men; fishing seasons were limited. Executioners killed taboo violators, often by strangling, unless the offender escaped to one of these Hawaiian sanctuaries. There a priest would absolve the accused, who could return safely home.

expedition approached the Fijian maze in 1840, some of the officers began to write their wills.

The Americans found the inhabitants of Ovalau in an ugly mood, as if preparing for war. Fortresses and stockpiles choked the streets of its port, Levuka. The local people, their black skin daubed with soot and red paint, presented a "spectacle of mingled hideousness & ferocity," according to an awed visitor. One Fijian carried a cooked human head, from which he took an eye and ate it, "smacking his lips at the same time, with the greatest possible relish," wrote an American.

A few weeks later, the Americans displayed their own brand of savagery. On the island of Malolo to purchase food, a party of Wilkes's men came upon a group of natives. The Americans, thinking to ensure their safety, took a local man hostage. A crowd gathered, a struggle began, and two Americans were clubbed and stabbed to death.

In retaliation, Wilkes ordered his troops to storm Malolo's villages. Supported by rocket fire, the Americans went in with muskets blazing. In half an hour, about 80 Fijians were dead. A calm descended, disturbed only by the moans of the injured and the crackling of flames. Into the fire Wilkes's men piled spears, bows, arrows, and clubs. Then to mock the natives' cannibalism, they tossed in a warrior's corpse, along with some yams.

Some of the Americans seemed shocked by their own behavior. "I hope I am not a savage in disposition," wrote one, "but . . . I felt a degree of savage like satisfaction every time I did or thought I had Killed one of those Miscreants." The travails of a long expedition, piled one upon the other, could transform the most humane of people.

Even James Cook was not immune. He rested for just a year after his second expedition before the Admiralty called on him again, this time to search for a northern passage between the Pacific and Atlantic.

In the process, he discovered Hawaii, mapped the northwest coast of North America, charted unknown parts of Canada and Alaska, and crossed the Arctic Circle. He reached northward to 70° 44'. Here he found no passage between the oceans—just a 12-foot-high barrier of ice, stretching across the horizon "compact as a Wall," wrote Cook. He turned southward, for Hawaii.

Despite his achievements, Cook had been in no condition for another worldwide voyage. Although still shy of 50 when selected for the third expedition, he was worn down by the unending stress of exploring. Day after day, he faced unknown waters or unknown lands. One misjudgment could doom ship and crew. His men, as always, were a hard-drinking, hardheaded lot plucked from the dregs of society. They had to be watched, cajoled, and outmaneuvered. And on this last voyage, Cook's *Resolution* was a constant

Serrated mountains plunge to the sea on the coast of Kauai, one of the Hawaiian Islands discovered by James Cook in 1778. The "prodigious surf," he wrote, "broke so high against the shore that we could not land. . . ."

In more than a decade of Pacific voyaging, Cook's masterful seamanship saved his ships from disaster. But even this great navigator could not steer clear of the cultural misunderstandings that bedeviled many explorers in this region: Hostile Hawaiians stabbed and *clubbed Cook in an argument over a stolen boat at Kealakekua Bay, where just weeks before the captain had received a god's welcome.*

Cook's wide-ranging travels opened the Pacific to a tidal wave of change. After him came whalers, missionaries, and colonists who remade most aspects of native life—including diet, religion, work, and language—forever altering this once secluded ocean realm.

problem. Though she had performed nobly on the second voyage, she was hastily and improperly refitted for this one. She leaked steadily, prompting an officer to write home: "If I return in the *Resolution,* the next trip I may Safely Venture in a Ship Built of Ginger Bread."

Finally, there were the thefts. Everywhere Cook landed, it seemed, the native people stole from him. A sextant vanished in Huahine, a goat at Moorea, a 20-pound anchor hook in Nootka Sound. One light-fingered Indian even managed to pinch Cook's gold watch—while his cabin was under guard. Pacific cultures did not cherish private property as Europeans did. Usually the thieves meant no harm; stealing

from Englishmen was largely a matter of sport.

For a weary Cook, the thieving was a final insult. He ordered floggings. He jailed offenders. He slashed their arms. He sacked a village and burned canoes to punish one thief, and cut off another man's ears to make an example of him.

Was this the same Cook who had worked so hard to prevent bloodshed on earlier voyages?

The answer came at Kealakekua Bay, where Cook called after his arduous northern passage of 1778 and 1779. Learning that Hawaiians had stolen one of his ship's cutters, Cook went ashore to take a local chief as hostage, thinking this would secure the boat's return.

Cook found the chief and began walking him toward the shore. The old chief's wife and others rushed out to protest, and a crowd gathered, menacing the British with stones, spears, and taunts. Cook the humanitarian spoke: "We can never think of compelling him to go on board," he told a marine, "without killing a number of these People."

Too late. Someone threatened Cook with a dagger and a stone, and Cook answered with a load of shot from his musket. The crowd advanced. Now Cook fired with ball, and a Hawaiian fell. For the last time, the captain turned toward his ship—perhaps to retreat, perhaps for reinforcements—but by then, the mob was already upon him.

Robert O'Hara Burke
William John Wills

By Edwards Park

Last day's trek to the false promise of safety: Weak from hunger, Burke, Wills, and King struggle toward Cooper's Creek and the end of their journey across Australia.

In Melbourne in the late 1940s, you could see their giant statue from the lawns outside the old Parliament House of the state of Victoria. You could eat lunch and look at them.

Burke stood, bearded and gaunt, beside the seated Wills, his hand on the other's shoulder. Both looked away as though searching. For what? The way across the wild, unknown continent? The way back?

Melbourne perches on the very fringe of a vast and still relatively empty landmass. Drive northwest past the suburbs, and you can see the green ridge of the horizon. Climb it, and you see another ridge beyond, and then another, and another. And hundreds of miles beyond them, the green turns to the brown-yellow plains and downs of the Outback. And much farther beyond that, cracked claypans and stone deserts shimmer in blazing heat: the Never-Never, where the crystalline air makes nameless hilltops and rock formations on the horizon seem close enough to touch. And still farther north, the tropics wait, breathless, dank, soul rotting.

Many Australians have never seen this—just the first part. Burke and Wills saw it all, struggled through it on an epic journey, a journey you could envy, except for the end.

Robert O'Hara Burke, originally a Galwayman, was a police superintendent in the mining district of Castlemaine in the 1850s. He was a strangely driven man—a little fey. Sturdy, black-bearded, he had pale, brooding eyes. He cared little for his own appearance. His trousers sagged around his heels, and often saliva dribbled down his beard.

Though Burke ran his police station well, he made his neighbors wince by sitting stark naked, except for his helmet, reading a book in the wading pool behind his house. Notoriously apt to get lost in the bush, he nonetheless would gallop hell-for-leather through the woods, 30 miles, just to swing on the front gate of a certain magistrate who danced with rage if anyone swung on his front gate.

At 39, Burke was unmarried. When he cleaned himself up, however, he could charm the ladies with small gallantries and Irish wit. He had, recalled a Melbourne hostess, "such a daring, reckless look about him."

187

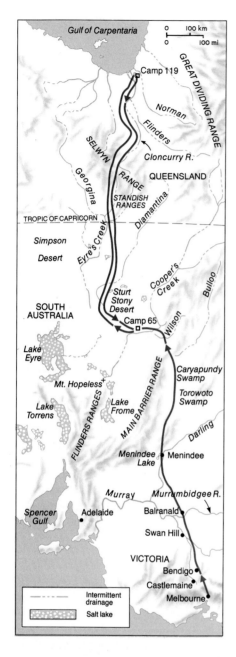

Gulf of Carpentaria

0   100 km
0   100 mi

Camp 119

GREAT DIVIDING RANGE

Norman

Flinders

Cloncurry R.

SELWYN RANGE

Georgina

QUEENSLAND

STANDISH RANGES

Diamantina

TROPIC OF CAPRICORN

Eyre's Creek

Simpson Desert

Cooper's Creek

Bulloo

Sturt Stony Desert

SOUTH AUSTRALIA

Camp 65

Wilson

Lake Eyre

Caryapundy Swamp

Mt. Hopeless

Torowoto Swamp

Lake Frome

Lake Torrens

MAIN BARRIER RANGE

FLINDERS RANGES

Darling

Menindee Lake

Menindee

Murray

Murrumbidgee R.

Spencer Gulf

Adelaide

Balranald

Swan Hill

VICTORIA

Bendigo

Castlemaine

Melbourne

- - - - Intermittent drainage

Salt lake

AUSTRALIA

Gold had made Melbourne prosperous at mid-century. A new Royal Society determined to explore the great unknown to the north. Plans were laid. It would be a big expedition, using camels, and would be the first to traverse the country northward to the Gulf of Carpentaria. To find a leader, the Exploration Committee scanned 14 applications and chose the ingratiating policeman from Castlemaine, Robert Burke.

On August 20, 1860, Burke led a small army out of Melbourne town while the crowd cheered and little boys ran beside the caravan. With him rode 3 scientists and 14 assistants, followed by 27 camels and several horse-drawn wagons bearing 21 tons of supplies.

The winter month of August brings rain to Victoria, and the expedition inched north through black mud. But in every town and mining camp, settlers turned out to cheer the explorers, who took almost three weeks to reach the little settlement of Swan Hill near the Murray River.

Burke's second-in-command, George James Landells, had earned his position by selecting the Indian camels and shipping them to Melbourne. But he had insisted on lacing their rations with rum, for the salubrious effect it would have, so the expedition lugged 60 gallons of it. News of the rum reached some sheepshearers on a remote station near the Darling River. They broached the supply and got howling drunk.

That was enough for Burke. Out went the rum—and Landells. The camels were taken over by his assistant, a former soldier in India named John King, a capable and biddable man. For his new second-in-command, Burke chose the youngest of the scientists, William John Wills.

He was a handsome athlete of 26, son of an English doctor who had come out to the goldfields. Young Wills worked on a sheep station, helped his father in medicine, and finally got a job at the Melbourne observatory. Fond of mathematics, he had taught himself surveying and delighted in astronomy. Burke thought the world of him, and Wills complemented his leader with his careful work and undeviating loyalty.

The party stopped at Menindee, then an outpost of civilization. Beyond it lay the Never-Never. Here Burke picked up William Wright, a local character who offered to guide the group on the next leg of the journey, a 400-mile hike to Cooper's Creek (now Cooper Creek), which previous explorers had found to be a reliable oasis.

Burke split the party. Eight men, 15 horses, and 16 good camels would go ahead to set up a supply depot at Cooper's Creek. The rest would hole up at Menindee, await the lagging supply train, and continue to the Cooper. On October 19, Wright led Burke, Wills, King, the foreman William Brahe, and three assistants northward.

October is a bad time to head toward the Australian center, for the sun sends the mercury out of sight. Through the fierce heat the party struggled, finally reaching the Torowoto Swamp with its reliable water. Burke sent Wright back to Menindee, where he was to gather the supplies and bring them up to the depot at the Cooper.

Wright headed south and the other seven plodded through rocky

An Aboriginal guide, known only as Dick, who led a search party in a futile hunt for Burke and Wills.

Portrait of Dick,
the brave and gallant native guide.
Darling Depôt Dec 21. 60.

He was a wild, eccentric daredevil. . . . Either he did not realise danger or his mind was so unhinged . . . that he revelled in it.

A CONTEMPORARY, SPEAKING OF BURKE

plains, from water to water. Each distant cluster of trees marked a creek bed—often, in that wet year, a series of water holes, or billabongs, where they could camp.

Cooper's Creek was the largest of these, a string of splendid billabongs shaded by trees. The party arrived on November 11, were driven from their first camp by a plague of rats, then settled comfortably beside a large billabong near an old coolabah tree. Here they built their depot. They also rested, prepared supplies for the long push to the gulf, and waited for Wright to return with the reserves. Young Wills, feeling wonderfully fit, explored the area, looking for various routes north.

By mid-December, Burke was ready to go. Wright must show up any day now, and the leader felt his men were capable of a mighty effort— nearly 1,500 miles to the gulf and back. Burke split the group again. With Wills, King, and one assistant, an ex-sailor called Charley Gray, he would make the dash north. He would take his own horse, Billy, and the six best camels. Brahe and the others would man the depot at Cooper's Creek. "It is my intention," Burke optimistically wrote to the committee, "to return here within the next three months at latest."

"Sunday, Dec. 16, 1860," begins an entry in the journal that William Wills kept. "The two horses having been shod, and our reports finished, we started at forty minutes past six a.m. for Eyre's Creek." Brahe rode with them to their first camp, then headed back to Cooper's Creek. He turned and called out his own estimate to his friend, "Goodbye, King, I do not expect to see you for at least four months."

Burke's diary is a scrappy, messy collection of notes—some of them merely tantalizing: "Made a creek where we found a great many natives. They presented us with fish, and offered their women." Wills's more detailed journal fills in facts and figures, as well as descriptions of the countryside and its life: " . . . red-breasted cockatoos, pigeons, a crow, and several other birds . . . two wild plants of the gourd or melon tribe;

189

one much resembling a stunted cucumber, and other . . . very similar to a small model of a water melon. . . ." He reflects the then current attitude—haughty yet fearful—of white settlers toward the natives: "A large tribe of blacks came pestering us to go to their camp and have a dance, which we declined. They were very troublesome, and nothing but the threat to shoot them will keep them away. . . ."

At first the going was faster than they'd dared hope, the country better watered. Of western Queensland Wills noted, "fresh plants met our view on every rise; everything green and luxuriant. The horse licked his lips, and tried all he could to break his nose-string and get at the food."

Gradually the land changed. They came among giant anthills, then the Standish and Selwyn Ranges. Here, Wills noted, "Pieces of iron ore, very rich, were scattered in great numbers over some of the hills."

Unluckily, the party arrived in the tropics at the same time as "the wet." During this rainy season the flat land turned into huge marshes, and the camels slid and plunged in the mud. Camp 119 (the 119th since leaving Melbourne) was about 30 miles from the sea. Burke and Wills

left the other two there and slogged on toward the northern coast.

They waded through a bog, then found a streambed and followed it. "We passed three blacks, who, as is universally their custom, pointed out to us, unasked, the best part down. This assisted us greatly. . . ." When they camped for the night, that Sunday, February 10, they tasted the water. Brackish. They noted an eight-inch tide. They were at the Gulf of Carpentaria. Mangrove swamps barred them from the shore, but they had made it.

"It would be well to say that we reached the sea," wrote Burke, "but we could not obtain a view of the open ocean." Still they were the first white men to link the north and south coasts of Australia.

Weary but proud, the two rejoined King and Gray. However, there was no time for celebration. Terribly short of food, they knew they must head straight back south. So, with the rain pelting them and the ground giving way underfoot, they began their laborious back track.

Fatigue began turning Wills's entries to short scraps—sometimes the bare mention of a camp. Often, now, he gave the camps names instead of numbers: Recovery Camp, Saltbush Camp. At Eureka Camp they stumbled across a huge snake, killed it, and ate it. Burke promptly came down with dysentery. The others didn't feel too well, either.

Through the first three weeks of March it rained almost steadily, and their going was painful. The tough Gray began to complain of headaches. By the end of March they were back at last in the dry country, but all were weakened by lack of food. On April 8, they were held up by Gray, "who gammoned he could not walk." On the tenth, they had to kill Billy the horse and cut him up for meat. "We found it healthy and tender, but without the slightest trace of fat. . . ."

Only two camels remained, and since Gray now couldn't walk, they strapped him to a saddle. On April 17 Wills made a terse entry: "This morning, about sunrise, Gray died." They buried him as deep as they could dig—three feet. And only seventy miles from safety.

Safety? At the depot at Cooper's Creek, Brahe was at his wit's end. Wright had never arrived from the south with the supplies that he was supposed to have delivered almost six months ago. Burke and Wills and the others had never returned from the north. They'd now been gone more than the generous four months Brahe had estimated.

Brahe and his colleagues waited—week after week of steeling themselves to the persistent flies, keeping fires going to drive off mosquitoes, shooting rats. Aside from guarding the grazing animals and preparing meals, they had nothing to do but gaze out at the serene water hole and watch the birds. The lassitude of the Outback was sapping their will. They stopped fishing and shooting ducks. They simply ate meals of rice and tea and salt beef and pork and damper, a bread baked in the ashes of a campfire. And now William Patton, the blacksmith, was sick, his limbs swollen, his gums too sore to chew. Most of them felt these symptoms of scurvy, though not as badly. The sickness comes with the territory, unless you're willful enough to break the spell of this eerie, peaceful land and look after yourself.

Brahe couldn't. Day after day of heat and stillness and nothing to do . . . night after night of silent stars . . . the growing sense of human puniness in the vastness of eternity . . . all these produced a lassitude that has an almost crippling effect on those who venture into Australia's remoteness. They stare endlessly at the coals of a dying fire in the silent wildness, and simply give up thinking and planning.

Where was Burke's party? Had they died in the emptiness, or had Burke headed east to Queensland's coastal settlements? Brahe couldn't answer, and the need for an answer, a decision, became more and more compelling as the days passed. What was he to do? Remain and rot?

It never occurred to Burke, less than 50 miles away, that Brahe would do anything but stay. On the 20th they continued, Burke riding one camel, Wills and King switching off on the second. They camped that night with only one day's journey to go, so they divided up most of the last rations and downed them. At dawn on the 21st, they set forth.

Brahe had fixed on the 21st as the day to give up waiting and break camp. He buried a large share of the rations under the coolabah tree, then raked over the spot so the natives wouldn't see it. On the tree trunk the men carved: DIG / 3 FT. N.W. / APR. 21 1861.

They loaded the camels, strapped poor Patton on one, and painfully trudged southward from the Cooper. It was about 10:30 in the morning.

Less than 30 miles to the north, the gulf party was forcing itself to a final, desperate effort. On they went, passing landmarks that they remembered, feeling the closeness of their goal. The early night of April fell on them, the camels lurching behind the men. By moonlight they continued, sure now that they could see the tents of the depot.

At about 7:30, only nine hours after Brahe had left, they arrived at Cooper's Creek, Camp 65. There was no answer to their shouts, no joyous congratulations, no tender care, no triumph at all in the end.

And that *is* the true end of the Burke and Wills expedition. Of course they found the buried cache, and the food restored some strength. But it was not enough to repair weakness gone bone deep. The men headed for the settlements near Mount Hopeless, some 150 miles away, but had to give up and return to the Cooper. They were too weak. Ironically, it was the natives they had so scorned who now nursed them and taught them to make flour out of the seed of the nardoo fern. The little cakes tasted good, but they couldn't fend off starvation.

Near the end of June or the beginning of July, Wills died, then Burke. Wills kept his journal going to the end, even with a touch of humor: "My pulse are at forty-eight, and very weak, and my legs and arms are nearly skin and bone. I can only look out, like Mr. Micawber, 'for something to turn up. . . .' " And Burke, too, wrote a few words. Like a good officer, he tried to look first to the welfare of his men: "King has stayed with me till the last. He has left me, at my own request, unburied, and with my pistol in hand."

King was found alive by one of the rescue teams that started out after

Nothing now but the greatest good luck can save any of us.
JOURNAL OF WILLS

192

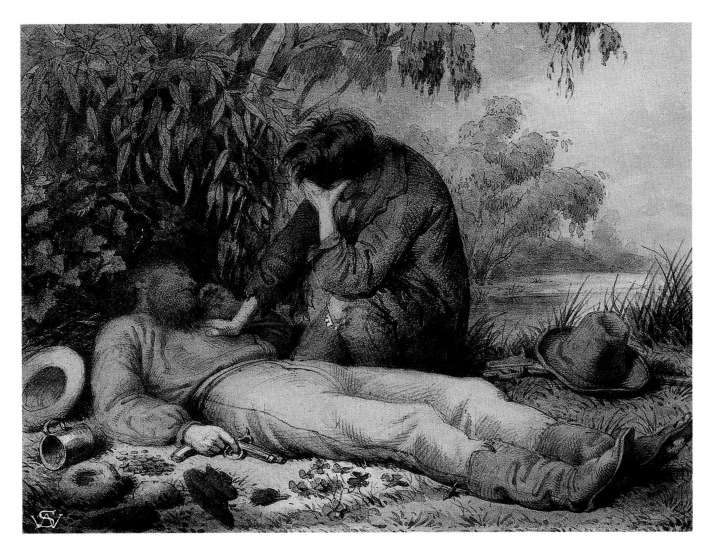

Death in the Outback—Burke with his pistol, mourned by King.

Brahe returned from Cooper's Creek (meeting Wright who, undone by lethargy and logistical problems, was just setting out). The blacks had nursed King and led the rescuers to him. He told of the triumphant attainment of the gulf, of the heartbreaking return to the deserted depot, and of the deaths of Burke and Wills. Brahe, who had been guiding the rescue team, heard King's story. His feelings can only be imagined. The Royal Commission that later looked into the affair chastised him.

In Melbourne, a monument was raised to Burke and Wills, along with a statue. The latter has been moved from its old place near the Parliament House and now stands by a gurgling fountain in a shopping center at City Square. But perhaps people still eye the statue as they munch a meat sandwich and sip a little good, brown beer. Perhaps they see that look in the sculptured eyes, that seeking. For what?

Perhaps for nine hours.

The journal of Wills was published in Melbourne in 1861. Alan Moorehead has written an absorbing narrative of the expedition, titled Cooper's Creek.

Fatal Africa

By Denis Hills

"He had long hair . . . interwoven with the bowels of oxen. . . . He had likewise a wreath of guts hung about his neck, and . . . about his middle." His body was wet with running butter. This Galla chief, mounted on a cow and decked out in all his finery to meet the ruler of Ethiopia, was one of the characters described by James Bruce, a wealthy Scottish laird, on his return to London from Ethiopia in 1774. Before Bruce's visit, Ethiopia and its ancient Coptic Christian Church had been a mystery to Europeans for 150 years—ever since the country had expelled its Portuguese Jesuit missionaries in a fit of nationalism.

But people scoffed at Bruce's descriptions of the handsome, cruel Ethiopians; at his tales of banquets at which raw beefsteaks were hacked from a living animal and chewed and swallowed on the spot, and guests of both sexes, gorged and drunk, gave themselves up to orgies of shameless debauchery. Then there were the massacres: Dismembered bodies, said Bruce, lay scattered about the streets of Gonder, and his own hunting dogs had brought home heads and arms.

His stories seemed too farfetched to be true and cast doubt on his claim to have discovered the source of the Nile—a goal sought since antiquity. Word went round that Bruce was an impostor. He withdrew in a huff to his estate in Scotland.

Bruce in fact had got his geography wrong. It was not, as he boasted, the source of the Nile that he had found but of its tributary, the Blue Nile. And he wasn't the first European to see it. Some Portuguese priests, whose accounts Bruce tried to discredit, had been there a century or more before him. But Bruce's observations about Ethiopia's terrain and customs proved essentially sound, being confirmed by other travelers after his death in 1794. He had lifted the veil from one corner of the African Continent and brought the question of the Nile's source dramatically to public attention.

"Travellers like poets are mostly an angry race," wrote explorer Richard Burton. He could have been thinking of Bruce and his anger over lack of recognition, or of many other European explorers of Africa, including himself. Most had a single-minded tenacity that brooked no rivalry. Africa, with its unknown interior, offered adventurers a new path to glory in an era of geographical curiosity awakened by Captain Cook's explorations of the Pacific.

In that new spirit of geographical inquiry, Sir Joseph Banks, the English botanist who had sailed with Cook, helped found the African Association in 1788 to fill in the "wide extended blank" of the African interior. Within this vast unmapped area lay the source of the Nile in central Africa and most of the Niger in West Africa. No European had explored the Niger or even identified its outlet, and reports from African and

A boatman pilots his dugout canoe through early morning fog on southern Africa's Okavango River, which Swedish naturalist Karell Johan Andersson explored in 1859. Many explorers took to rivers to avoid slogging across fiery sands or hacking through jungle, but cataracts, malarial swamps, and floating vegetation often blocked their way. Most Europeans who ventured inland in the 18th and 19th centuries lost their health, if not their lives, in the land one explorer dubbed Fatal Africa.

195

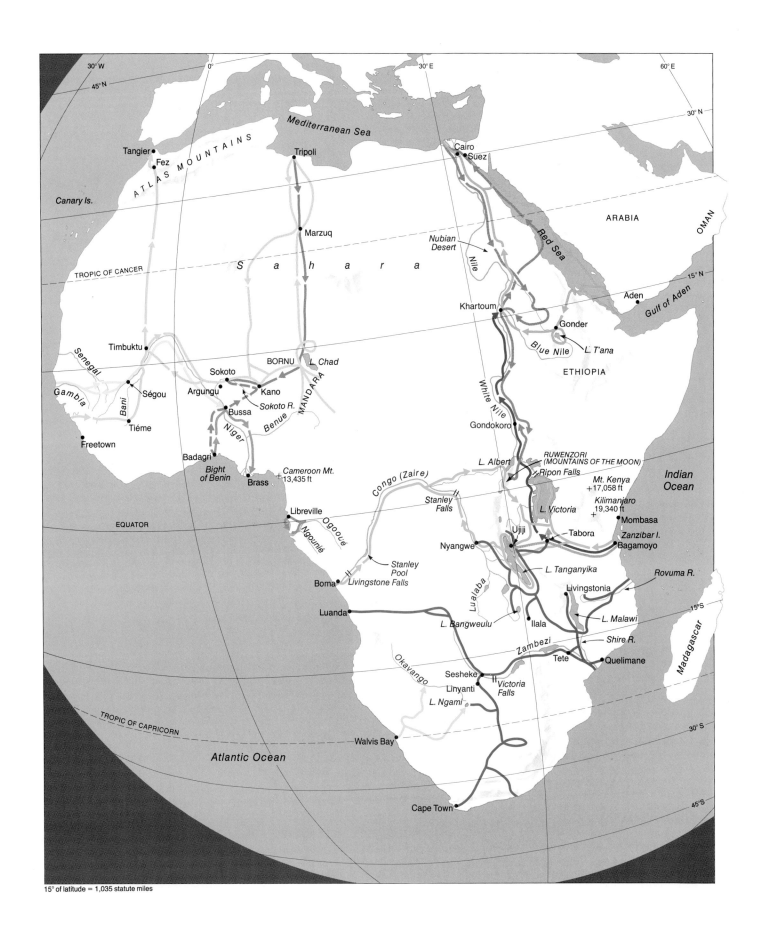

30° W

0°

30° E

60° E

45° N

30° N

15° N

EQUATOR

15° S

30° S

45° S

Mediterranean Sea

ATLAS MOUNTAINS

Tangier
Fez
Tripoli
Cairo
Suez

Canary Is.

ARABIA

OMAN

Marzuq

Nubian Desert

Nile

Red Sea

TROPIC OF CANCER

S   a   h   a   r   a

Aden

Gulf of Aden

Khartoum

Gonder
L. T'ana

Timbuktu

Blue Nile

ETHIOPIA

Senegal

Sokoto

BORNU

L. Chad

Gambia
Ségou
Argungu
Kano

Bani

Sokoto R.

Bussa

Tiéme

MANDARA

White Nile

Freetown

Niger

Benue

Gondokoro

Badagri

RUWENZORI
(MOUNTAINS OF THE MOON)

Bight of Benin

Brass

Cameroon Mt.
+13,435 ft

L. Albert

Ripon Falls

Mt. Kenya
+17,058 ft

Congo (Zaire)

Stanley Falls

Kilimanjaro
19,340 ft
+

Indian Ocean

Libreville

L. Victoria

Mombasa

EQUATOR

Ogooué

Ngounié

Ujiji
Tabora

Zanzibar I.
Bagamoyo

Nyangwe

Stanley Pool
Livingstone Falls

Rovuma R.

Boma

L. Tanganyika

Livingstonia

Lualaba

L. Malawi

Luanda

L. Bangweulu

Ilala

Shire R.

Okavango

Zambezi

Tete
Quelimane

Walvis Bay

Sesheke
Linyanti

Victoria Falls

Madagascar

L. Ngami

Atlantic Ocean

TROPIC OF CAPRICORN

Cape Town

15° of latitude = 1,035 statute miles

196

Adverse winds and currents delayed exploration of the African shoreline by European ships, but Portuguese, British, French, and Dutch traders had coastal toeholds by 1600. Deserts, disease, and hostile inhabitants kept them from mapping the interior for nearly 300 more years. Arabs led exploration in the north. Beginning in the 600s, Arab traders crisscrossed the Sahara, establishing Muslim settlements. By the 1800s Omani Arabs controlled much of the East African coast and the

slave trade on the island of Zanzibar.

A fanciful engraving (below) shows Scotsman James Bruce, one of the first European explorers to push inland, drinking a toast in 1770 from the source of the Blue Nile in Ethiopia. Bruce mistakenly claimed his find to be the chief source of the Nile. He brought back tales of brutal justice in Ethiopia, where the scavenging striped hyena (sketched by Bruce) roamed Gonder by night, feasting on the flesh of mutilated or executed criminals.

OVERLEAF: *Kebbawa fishermen surge into Nigeria's Sokoto River at Argungu, a town that German explorer Heinrich Barth described in the 1850s as a center of Kebbawa rebellion against the local sultan. The tribesmen perform an ancient ritual: Using nets with calabash floats, hundreds of men compete to catch the largest fish. Its size foretells how the gods will favor the Kebbawa in the coming year.*

Bruce 1768-1773
Park 1795-1806
Clapperton, Denham, and Oudney 1821-25
Clapperton and Lander 1825-27
Caillié 1827-28
R. and J. Lander 1830
Livingstone 1841-1873
Barth 1850-55
Andersson 1853-59
Burton and Speke 1857-59
Speke and Grant 1860-63
S. and F. Baker 1861-65
Stanley 1871-1889
Kingsley 1895

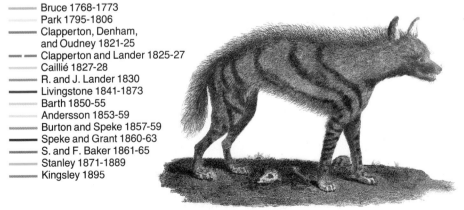

Arab travelers differed as to its direction of flow. In 1794 the African Association chose a young ship's surgeon, Mungo Park, as its geographical emissary to trace the Niger to its outlet and visit Timbuktu with its rumored hoards of gold.

The growing antislavery campaign in England had focused attention on West Africa. If slavery were abolished, perhaps the loss of profits could be made up by developing new markets for British commerce in the African interior. The coast had long been exploited for trade, mainly in slaves, but there had been no lasting white advance into the hinterland. Travel was hazardous, the inhabitants hostile, the climate lethal. The fever-ridden coast had earned the name "the white man's grave." (Africans today say that the mosquito was the black man's ally in keeping the white invaders out.) Slavers found it easier to wait off the coast for the black ivory to be brought to them by chiefs and slave dealers than to go hunting for it inland.

Mungo Park set off eastward from a town near the mouth of the Gambia in December 1795 with six Africans. As a white Christian bound for fanatically Muslim territories, poorly armed, and with few goods to barter for the favor of local chiefs, he was taking an enormous risk. But, avid for fame, Park was ready to gamble his life to achieve it. Throughout his journey he was insulted, threatened, and robbed. Moors hissed and spat in his face and his companions left him.

"A lonely captive, perishing of thirst," Scotsman Mungo Park drops to his knees and drinks with cows. Reduced to begging for sustenance during four months' captivity in a nomadic Muslim ruler's camps, Park often found himself too thirsty to sleep. On this night an old man yielded to his pleas but, fearing that Christian lips would taint the bucket, dumped the water in a trough.

Fired by youthful ambition, Park scouted the Niger River in West Africa in the 1790s and early 1800s, search-ing for its outlet. On his second Niger expedition, malaria and dysentery killed most of his European compan-ions, but Park struggled onward in a vessel patched together from the best parts of two rotting canoes.

At Bussa, by one account, tribes-men bombarded the explorers with rocks and poison arrows (opposite). The men returned fire until their ammunition failed. Then, all hope lost, they leapt to their deaths in the rushing waters of the Niger.

He was accused of being a spy and held captive for four months. Escap-ing, he struggled on to Ségou and at last caught his first glimpse of the "majestic Niger . . . as broad as the Thames at Westminster and flowing slowly to the eastward."

Park was by then starving and penniless. He was about to spend the night in a tree when a woman took pity on him, showed him to her hut, and cooked him a fish. Other women entertained him with an impromptu song—"Let us pity the white man; no mother has he," they sang.

A slave trader offered Park protec-tion during the 500-mile return jour-ney to the coast, which he reached in June 1797. In 1805 he was back again to search for the Niger's outlet, but this attempt failed too. Park and the few members of his party who survived the overland trip to the Ni-ger vanished. Their exact fate is un-known, but Africans said all the Eu-ropeans died in a fight on the river.

Mungo Park's account of his earlier Niger trip helped inspire a frail-looking young Frenchman named René Caillié. Caillié had dreamed of Africa since boyhood and was driven by a romantic ambition to visit the golden city of Timbuktu. Like Park, he resolved to reach his goal or perish in the attempt. In 1827, disguised as an Arab pilgrim, he joined a small caravan leaving the west coast. Experience had taught him to travel light, and one of his few, prized possessions was an umbrella.

At Tiéme he fell ill with scurvy: "The roof of my mouth became quite bare, part of the bones exfoliated and fell away, and my teeth seemed ready to drop out of their sockets. . . ." A village woman nursed him, forcing him to drink rice water. "At length, after six weeks of indescribable suffering . . . I began to feel better."

Caillié continued his journey by canoe down an upper tributary to the Niger—he traded his precious umbrella for a passage—and reached Timbuktu. But he was bitterly disappointed. "I had formed a totally different idea of the grandeur and wealth of Timbuctoo," he wrote. The fabled city was a dump of mean mud houses with a few stunted trees, roasting under a burning sun, and besieged by marauding bands of Tuareg horsemen. The grand myth died. Golden Timbuktu was nothing but a desert trading center whose main resource was salt.

To return home to France, Caillié traveled north to Tangier, crossing the Sahara with an Arab caravan, a journey no other European had completed. When he published the account of his travels, many readers disbelieved it. The British even accused him of finding and copying the journals of Maj. Alexander Gordon Laing, who was murdered on an earlier visit to Timbuktu. In 1838 Caillié died embittered at the age of 38.

No explorer had yet reached the lower part of the Niger, so the Colonial Office in London organized a fresh expedition, this time from the north. In 1822 two former navy men, Hugh Clapperton and Walter Oudney, and army major Dixon Denham left Tripoli for the kingdom of Bornu near Lake Chad. Clapperton and Oudney, who had planned the trip on their own, were furious when the Colonial Office sent Denham too, without even making clear who was the leader. Angry rivalry between Denham and Clapperton reached such a pitch that they parted ways. Denham turned east to explore the Lake Chad region. Oudney died while traveling west with Clapperton toward the Niger.

At Sokoto the sultan refused to let Clapperton continue to the Niger, only 150 miles away, and he retraced his steps to England in 1825. Later that year he tried again, taking along his servant Richard Lander, a young man of 20 who was to show heroic qualities of stamina and enterprise. They traveled north from the Bight of Benin. At Sokoto, Clapperton was reduced to a skeleton by dysen-

"Nothing but a mass of ill-looking houses, built of earth," wrote French explorer René Caillié in dismay. The first European to return from Timbuktu, in 1828, he exploded the myth of a glittering desert center of wealth and culture. Caillié's sketch of the city (left) with its mosques and crowded dwellings—an illustration in his 1830 book of travels—reveals an eye for detail. In modern Timbuktu (below), camels rest beside houses that might have come from Caillié's picture.

Timbuktu's inhabitants were devout Muslims. To travel in Muslim territory, Caillié posed as an Arab. Aware that Tuareg nomads had murdered Scotsman Alexander Gordon Laing near Timbuktu in 1826, he feared for his life if revealed as a Christian. The Frenchman hid notes and drawings when anyone approached and pretended to be studying loose pages of the Koran. He returned across the Sahara with an Arab caravan, limping into Tangier a sun-blackened skeleton.

tery. Lander, sick himself, nursed his master night and day, but in vain. Three days before he died, wrote Lander, Clapperton said "that he had heard with peculiar distinctness the tolling of an English funeral bell." He died in Lander's arms.

Determined to complete his dead master's task, Lander mounted a second expedition with his brother John in 1830. They reached the Niger, obtained canoes at Bussa, and traveled downstream through luxuriant scenery: "Magnificent festoons of creeping plants, always green, hung from the tops of the tallest trees, and dropping to the water's edge, formed immense natural grottoes," wrote John Lander. Surviving attacks by suspicious villagers, river

pirates, and "an incredible number of hippopotami," the brothers journeyed successfully to the river's outlet at Brass. The mouth of the Niger, sought by the British for over 30 years, had been discovered, an Admiralty spokesman said, "by a very humble but intelligent individual."

But still, the prime geographical mystery of the day remained the source of the Nile. German missionaries Johannes Rebmann and Johann Ludwig Krapf reported seeing snow on the peaks of two huge mountains near the Equator, Kilimanjaro and Kenya. Maybe melting snow drained into a great basin that gave birth to the Nile. Arab traders had spoken of a vast inland sea. Indian Army officers Richard Francis Burton and

A Wodaabe nomad, one of the Fulani people, herds cattle on a West African steppe south of the Sahara. Explorers Mungo Park, René Caillié, and Hugh Clapperton encountered militant Muslim subjects of the Fulani Empire, founded by jihad—holy war—in the 1790s. Muslim zealotry and nomad banditry barred exploration of West Africa to all but the most intrepid and resourceful infidels.

John Hanning Speke set out from Zanzibar to investigate these reports.

Burton certainly fitted his own epithet of the angry traveler, as did Speke. Jealousy would destroy their relationship. They were an ill-matched pair. Burton, an irascible intellectual with a gift for languages, had an almost perverse curiosity about native customs—in India his overzealous investigation of Hindu lovemaking and of homosexuality in the male brothels of Karachi had brought charges of ungentlemanly conduct and wrecked his army career. Speke had a passion for hunting and collecting specimens. He smarted under an imagined accusation of cowardice by Burton on a previous trip. Setting off in June 1857 with a well-equipped party of soldiers, porters, and baggage animals, Burton and Speke were soon plagued by sickness, desertions, and theft.

In February 1858 they came to Lake Tanganyika at Ujiji. Here, as today, egrets stepped delicately among the gentle wavelets and the fish eagle, poised on a bone white tree, uttered its witchlike scream. But Speke, temporarily blinded by ophthalmia, could not see the lake and Burton, weakened by malaria, had to be carried to its shore. After a brief canoe trip to the north end of the lake, they turned back for the coast, pausing to rest at Tabora. Here Burton remained, to question local sheikhs about the area, while Speke traveled north to check Arab reports of a great lake larger than

206

Lake Tanganyika. Within a few weeks he was back with astonishing news. He had seen an immense stretch of water, which he named Lake Victoria. He had no doubt that it was the true source of the Nile.

Burton ridiculed Speke's impulsive claim—"The fortunate discoverer's conviction was strong; his reasons were weak"—but the subject was dropped for the time being. Speke sailed ahead for England, promising to say nothing about the expedition until Burton got back. He broke his word, announcing his discovery while belittling Burton's part in the expedition, and soon returned to Africa with an old Indian Army friend, James Augustus Grant.

Grant was the ideal partner, loyal and compliant. Turning north from Tabora the two men traveled toward the court of Mutesa, king of Buganda, at the northwest corner of Lake Victoria. Grant was held up with an ulcerated leg, so Speke went on alone. He was impressed by the spacious reed huts of Mutesa's capital, by the neatly made cloaks of bark cloth and antelope skin the men wore, and by the people's courtesy. But the cruelty horrified him. Ears were cut off in punishment for negligible crimes, and for minor breaches of court etiquette young women were instantly executed.

The king regarded Speke, the first white man he had seen, as a rich prize and was unwilling to let him go. He fleeced him little by little of cloth, beads, guns, and ammunition until Grant arrived. Finally the king gave them permission to proceed. Grant marched north with the main party to Bunyoro. Speke turned east along the lake.

So Speke was alone with his bearers when on July 28, 1862, he stood at last at the waterfall where Lake Victoria poured into the Nile. He was entranced by "the roar of the waters, the thousands of passenger-fish, leaping at the falls . . . hippopotami and crocodiles lying sleepily on the water." He had managed to keep this ultimate triumph to himself.

Speke joined Grant near Bunyoro, where the ruler, Kamrasi, detained them for many weeks. Then they proceeded to Gondokoro. Here Speke's old sporting friend, Samuel Baker, met them with supplies. "The Nile is settled," Speke cabled London on his arrival in Cairo.

Back in England many people remained unconvinced by his claim, and a debate was arranged in September 1864 between Speke and Burton. As Burton awaited Speke on the platform, news came that he had shot himself accidentally the day before while out hunting. Burton broke down in his hotel and wept.

A fellow explorer at the debate would continue the search for the Nile's source: David Livingstone.

It was a humanitarian anger that first spurred Livingstone's forays into southern Africa after his arrival in 1841. He combined missionary and antislavery zeal with a practical interest in opening up routes for trade

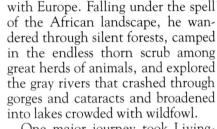

Fishing boats drift on Lake Victoria, chief source of the Nile, sought by explorers since Roman emperor Nero sent out an expedition in A.D. 60. In 1858 England's John Hanning Speke (below, right) became the first European to reach the lake, which he named for his queen. Speke went back to Tabora, where he had left his compatriot Richard Burton, and announced he had found the source of the Nile. Burton declared this conclusion hasty, and debate ripened into dispute in England.

Returning to Africa, Speke made his way to a waterfall he named Ripon Falls, where Lake Victoria emptied into a river he correctly identified as the White Nile. His companion on this successful expedition, Scotsman James Augustus Grant, portrayed Waganda musicians (left) playing the fife, the harplike nanga, and other instruments. Shells, beads, brass bells, and goat hair garnish the giant wooden kettledrum.

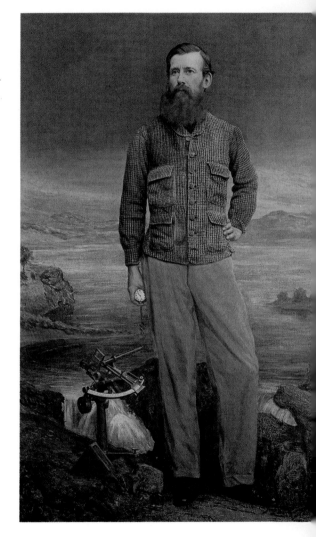

with Europe. Falling under the spell of the African landscape, he wandered through silent forests, camped in the endless thorn scrub among great herds of animals, and explored the gray rivers that crashed through gorges and cataracts and broadened into lakes crowded with wildfowl.

One major journey took Livingstone northwest from Linyanti across well over a thousand miles of almost unknown country to Luanda on the coast, which he reached in May 1854. After recuperating, he turned back the way he had come and proceeded east along the Zambezi River. Upon reaching Quelimane on the east coast, he became the first European to cross Africa. But his repeated attempts to establish a trade route on the Zambezi were thwarted by miles of rapids, and the Shire and Rovuma Rivers proved little better.

By now famous in England for his geographical exploits, Livingstone agreed to a proposal by the Royal Geographical Society to pursue the question of the Nile after Speke's death in 1864. Combining exploration with God's work, he could also check on the Arab slave trade. In 1866 he embarked on a lengthy search for the Nile's source, losing contact with the outside world. Everywhere he went, he found alarming evidence of the slave trade that supplied East Africa, Arabia, Persia, and India. Reduced to destitution by desertion and theft, he had to travel with Arab slave caravans himself, often marching with the victims.

Scottish missionary-explorer David Livingstone (right) reads the Bible to African villagers. He used it as a spiritual Baedeker to guide him, by example, through the tribulations that beset him as he explored southern Africa and challenged slavery, which he called the "great open sore of the world."

In 1853 he set out to "open up a path into the interior, or perish." While following the Zambezi east across the continent, Livingstone, mounted on an ox (below, right), glances back over his shoulder to see a wounded buffalo toss one of his bearers in the air. The man had stabbed the buffalo when it charged the line, and it turned on him. The bearer landed on his face but suffered no cuts or broken bones. "We shampooed him well," wrote Livingstone, "and then went on."

Artist Thomas Baines joined Livingstone's next venture in 1858 and painted "Poling up the Zambesi" (below, left). The boatmen found punting faster than rowing in shallow water.

In 1871 he witnessed a shocking incident. It started with a quarrel over the purchase of a fowl in the market of Nyangwe on the Lualaba and turned into a massacre. Livingstone was appalled as he watched Arabs shooting down helpless villagers, who tried to escape by canoe or by jumping into the river. He felt he was in hell. "I hear the loud wails . . . over those who are . . . slain," he wrote in his journal. "Oh, let Thy kingdom come!" He decided to halt his explorations and repair to Ujiji.

At this low point in his fortunes the miracle occurred. A column emerged out of the bush firing off salutes, with a white man striding forward and a servant carrying the American flag. It was Stanley. The American newspaperman had found the missing wanderer. Livingstone and Henry Morton Stanley greeted each other with a grotesque pretense of reserve. "Dr. Livingstone, I presume?" "Yes."

Newly equipped by Stanley, Livingstone set off on his last march. By now his search for the Nile had become an obsession. Sick, almost toothless, scarcely able to walk, he turned into a wandering guru seeking, if God willed, a lonely grave in the forest. In 1873 he finally collapsed in Ilala near Lake Bangweulu, where a servant found him dead one night, kneeling beside his bed.

Despite Livingstone's efforts, the slave trade was worse at his death than he had found it when he came

OVERLEAF: "The smoke that thunders" was the Makololo name for the Zambezi's Victoria Falls, whose billowing vapor Livingstone spied from five miles away in 1855. Perched at the brink, he watched the river "roll and wriggle" away from the 350-foot-deep chasm that slashes across its course.

211

214

Brash adventurer and revered missionary meet beneath the American flag: Tipping his pith helmet, Henry Morton Stanley inquires, "Dr. Livingstone, I presume?" The New York Herald had sent Stanley to find the famous explorer and interview him. Livingstone, sick and destitute, thought the journalist's arrival in 1871 at the Arab trading post of Ujiji was God's handiwork and persuaded Stanley to help him explore Lake Tanganyika. They became close friends. Trekking back to the coast, quick-tempered Stanley threatened to shoot a bearer (left) who stumbled midriver and nearly lost the letters and journal Livingstone was sending home.

In 1873 Livingstone's ruined body gave out. His African companions buried his heart and entrails under a tree, embalmed his corpse, and carried it to the coast—an eight-month journey. One of the Africans, former mission pupil Jacob Wainwright (below), sailed with Livingstone's coffin on the explorer's final voyage home to England.

to Africa. His report of the massacre at Nyangwe, however, so shocked the British government that they forced the sultan of Zanzibar to close his slave market.

During his brief friendship with Stanley, Livingstone had fired the imagination of the ambitious journalist. Angered by being considered an upstart in England and a fraud in America, Stanley was determined to prove his detractors wrong. He got two newspapers to sponsor an expedition to resolve the pattern of lakes and rivers in central Africa—to finish the work of his avowed hero.

He left Zanzibar late in 1874 with a huge caravan. Reaching Lake Victoria, he assembled his portable 40-foot boat, the Lady Alice, and sailed around the lake—establishing that it was a single lake and that Speke had been right about the Nile—and surveyed Lake Tanganyika.

He confirmed that the Lualaba flowed into the Congo (now the

Zaire), which he followed westward to the coast. It was an epic journey. Only 115 of his original party of 356 reached the sea. His men starved, drowned, and fell sick. The riverbanks resounded with war drums, and tribesmen attacked the party. Stanley retaliated by burning villages. He proved a harsh taskmaster, sometimes flogging offenders or putting them in leg chains. Under his relentless drive, men mutinied and deserted. His methods brought criticism, but they got results—a portent of the ruthless approach employed by the great powers in their scramble for Africa from the 1870s to the 1890s.

In contrast, Mary Kingsley's role in Africa was refreshingly humane. Any anger she felt was aimed at people who derided African religion. As an amateur English ethnologist striving to understand the Africans, she was ahead of her time.

After two earlier trips to West Africa, she sailed again for Freetown in 1895, dressed as always in severe Victorian clothes and a bonnet. She went on to spend about a year in the French Congo, Gabon, and Cameroon, journeying rough, often by canoe. Here she befriended the cannibal Fang tribe, whom she called "Fan," to avoid unfortunate associations. She learned to understand the reasons for witchcraft, or fetish, as it was called: Africans believed that misfortune and death were the work of malignant spirits whom it was necessary to propitiate by magic.

Once she fell into a 15-foot game trap, but her "good thick skirt" saved her from being "spiked to the bone and done for." Another time, in a village hut, she noticed a strong smell of "unmistakably organic origin" and found some bags full of human remains—a hand, "three big toes, four eyes, two ears, and other portions of the human frame." She learned that the Fan "like to keep a little something . . . as a memento."

On her return to England, she campaigned for colonial government that stressed justice, medical care, and anthropological study. She did not share the view commonly held by Europeans that the Africans were cruel or depraved children.

During Mary Kingsley's time, the exploration of Africa entered a second phase. Earlier explorers had only filled in the major geographical blanks—the river systems, the lakes, and the mountain ranges. Their accounts of the African people were often prejudiced by their own viewpoints and religious convictions. And they overestimated Africa's potential wealth and fertility.

From the 1890s to the 1920s, hundreds of colonial officials, army officers, and adventurous traders, whose names have mostly been forgotten, mapped Africa and did the donkeywork that made possible roads, railways, and cities. The traces of such men's devoted works remain in cairns or signposts on African hilltops. They paved the way for modern Africa and the independent black states that succeeded the colonies.

By James A. Cox

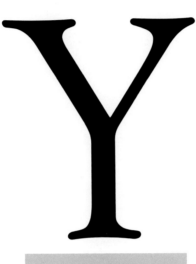

Tribal inspection: The Bunyoro people greet Sam and Florence Baker.

Y ou could make a movie about them—a real Saturday-afternoon-at-the-Bijou flick. The true-life experiences of Sam and Florence Baker as they search for the source of the White Nile! It's set in central Africa in the 1860s. The kind of tale that kept you riveted to your seat when you were a kid. And a great love story, too.

Sam Baker is positively larger than life. A British clubman. Widower in his late 30s with four daughters. Heir to a modest fortune. Solid, conservative, convinced of his own and Britain's superiority. Also strong and fearless, a sportsman who hunts stags on foot with only a knife because shooting them is too easy. *Also* a writer and artist, a skilled linguist, and a practical man who is at home in the wilderness, yet capricious enough to buy his second wife, a beautiful Hungarian refugee named Florence Finnian von Sass, in a Turkish slave market.

That's the scene to open with, the slave auction in 1859. Decadent Ottoman town on the lower Danube in what is now Bulgaria. Minarets reaching skyward, half-starved dogs scavenging in the streets below. Rough-voiced men—soldiers, Turkish traders, elegantly attired pashas—gather in a noisy crowd. Off to one side we spy a cluster of government officials and two visiting big-game hunters—a slim Indian maharaja and Sam Baker. The slaves—young white women and children—huddle together in terror. Now the auctioneer hauls forward a slender, teenage girl, her long golden hair swept back into a loose braid. Leering pashas begin the bid. Suddenly Sam charges through the crowd waving a fistful of Turkish liras and throws down the winning bid. The film title superimposes as he leads his purchase away.

The music stops abruptly, the scene begins to fade. We'll have a woman's voice—old but firm, with a lingering Balkan throatiness—say something like: "And that was how I met my Sam!"

We move to the formal English garden of a neo-Gothic stone manor

Sam fleeing the charge of a screaming bull elephant that he has wounded.

house where an old woman is tending roses. She is Lady Florence Baker, grande dame of the manor and alone since 1893, when Sam went to his reward. For our movie, she reveals the secret past that she only hinted at in real life. She explains briefly how she came to be sold as a slave: bloody uprisings in Hungary and the Balkans, her entire family slain, rescued by a faithful nurse, but finally left alone and defenseless. Florence ends by saying simply, "I owe everything to Sam."

She tells how Sam took her to the Black Sea, where he was involved in building a railroad. "But his heart was never in that," we'll have her say. "Africa—that's where he yearned to be, with the great explorers. Again and again he wrote to the Royal Geographical Society, hoping to join an expedition, but always he was turned down. So one day he decided to go up the Nile on his own. And I went with him." She laughs softly as the scene fades. Other people might worry about whether they were married then, but she would have followed Sam anywhere.

Now we see Sam and Florence in a kaleidoscope of scenes, all from Sam's journals: gliding up the Nile on a dahabeah, a small lateen-rigged houseboat; struggling across the Nubian Desert with 2 servants, 16 camels, and assorted baggage under a blazing sun; settling down beside a river in the Sudan, where Florence converts a round thatched hut into "the perfection of neatness," with a chintz- and muslin-covered dressing table and hunting knives on the wall; Sam hunting on horseback with the fearless Hamran Arabs who, armed only with swords, go after mighty elephants; Sam and Florence exploring and mapping the tributaries of the Nile that tumble out of Ethiopia, learning Arabic and as much of the central African languages as they can pick up.

After a year they decide they're ready for the big push. On to Khartoum, capital of the Egyptian Sudan, a frontier town built on the ivory and slave trades, and the jumping-off place for the interior.

Sam and Florence hate Khartoum. It is filthy, untamed, rotten to the core. Everyone, from Governor-General Moosa Pasha down, has a finger—or a fist—in the illegal slave trade. Sam presents his firman from the viceroy of Egypt, a permit that instructs local officials to give him every assistance. He is greeted with resentment, apathy, and antagonism. No one wants a meddling English gentleman poking about the slave-producing regions of the upper Nile. But Sam plows right ahead. He puts together an expedition of 3 boats, 40 boatmen, assorted horses, donkeys, and camels, an escort of 45 armed Arabs, and supplies for 4 months. Destination: Gondokoro, 1,000 miles south of Khartoum and the last stop before the vast unknown of darkest Africa.

The mail from England has brought a request from the Royal Geographical Society. Consul John Petherick was supposed to leave supplies at Gondokoro for the Speke-Grant expedition that is trying to pin down the source of the Nile. But no one has heard from Speke and Grant for a year, and Petherick is missing in the jungle and rumored dead. Will Sam take supplies to Gondokoro? Sam eagerly agrees. If he

A sudden storm on Lake Albert. The Bakers' canoe races for shore.

I at once named it the Albert N'yanza—N'yanza being the native name for "lake" or any sheet of water.
SAMUEL BAKER

finds the explorers before they reach the Nile's source, perhaps he will share in the glory. If they're dead, he may finish the search himself.

We follow Sam and Florence to Gondokoro. It turns out to be a string of riverside camps where traders keep slaves and ivory while awaiting the annual boats from Khartoum. The traders spend their time drinking, quarreling, killing each other, brutalizing the slaves, and terrorizing the local tribes. The place stinks of ordure and rotting food. Flies everywhere. Hordes of sleek rats. Clouds of mosquitoes, "the nightingales of the White Nile." Sam calls the place "a perfect hell."

Quickly Sam and Florence learn they are even less welcome here than they were in Khartoum, and for the same reason. The message rings loud and clear when a bullet shatters the skull of a boy in their boat. But they cannot leave without news of Speke and Grant. The threats escalate. When mutineers attack Sam, Florence rushes into the fray and fast-talks the ringleader into begging Sam's pardon. Their entourage begins to break up with desertions.

Finally one morning the rattle of gunfire from the south heralds the approach of a caravan. Sam's men race to his boat with news of two emaciated white men. *Speke and Grant!* Bursting with excitement, Sam ushers his bedraggled countrymen back to his dahabeah for refreshments. They are exhausted, their clothes in tatters, but they have much to tell, especially of Lake Victoria. The question of the Nile's source, Speke says confidently, is settled.

222

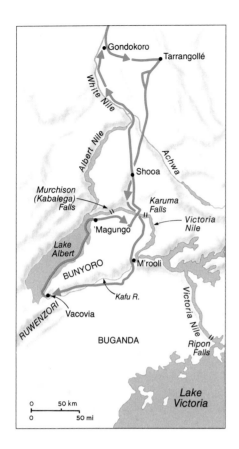

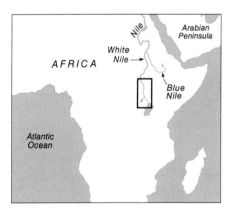

Sam cannot hide his disappointment. "Does not one leaf of the laurel remain for me?" he blurts. Speke tells him of rumors of another large lake to the west of Victoria that might also feed the river, and Grant draws up a rough map. To get there, they warn, glancing at Florence, will require hiking hundreds of miles, through the lands of implacably hostile tribes to the kingdom of Bunyoro, ruled by Kamrasi, "a sour, greedy African" who is likely to strip them of every possession. The grim warnings do nothing to dim Sam's enthusiasm. He can barely wait to get started. But their force has dwindled to only 17 men of doubtful loyalty, too small a party to travel on its own. They are forced to attach themselves to the caravan of a slave trader.

Now, by Sam's account, begins an almost unbelievable odyssey. The trading party takes its time. The rains come. Rivers are unfordable. Fever prostrates Sam and Florence for weeks on end. They run out of quinine. Their baggage animals die. Their food supplies dwindle, and they're reduced to eating grass. White ants and rats invade their hut. The war drums of the harassed tribes thump incessantly, spelling out a message of hatred for the slavers and all who associate with them. Even a friendly chief, Commoro of the Latooka, asks Sam: "Suppose you get to the great lake; what will you do with it? If you find that the large river does flow from it, what then? What's the good of it?"

In almost a year they move barely 150 miles closer to their goal. Shorthanded and ill, they cannot break away from the traders. At last, in January 1864 they reach the Victoria Nile and look across into Bunyoro. Kamrasi's tribesmen line the far bank. Sam puts on a tweed suit similar to that worn by Speke, and his interpreter calls out that Speke's brother has come to visit. The natives dance and sing in great excitement. But it is Florence who creates a sensation the next day when she undoes her hair and lets the golden tresses drop to her waist. The Bunyoro have never seen anything like it.

For all this brave show, Sam and Florence are so weak with fever by the time they reach Kamrasi's capital at M'rooli that Sam has to be carried into the king's presence. (Or at least Sam *thinks* he's the king. He's really the king's brother, M'Gambi, acting as stand-in, for security.) Sitting on a copper stool set on leopard skins, he counters every request for porters and a guide to the mysterious lake in the west with a demand for presents. The game goes on for days. Beads, shoes, a gun, necklaces, a sword, a cashmere shawl, a Persian carpet. Finally convinced he has picked his guests clean, M'Gambi says that Sam can go to the lake, but Florence must remain. He fancies her for a wife. It is not a mean-spirited demand: In exchange he will give Sam a pretty Bunyoro wife.

This is the last straw. Enraged, Sam hauls out his pistol and threatens to shoot him dead on the spot. Florence rises from her seat in wrath and screams at M'Gambi in Arabic. He doesn't understand the language, but he gets the meaning. He shrugs and tells them to go.

With porters and escort grudgingly supplied by M'Gambi, they set off. Food is scarce—their escort of Bunyoro warriors ranges ahead and

223

Women of Shooa dancing to celebrate the Bakers' return from Lake Albert.

strips villages along the way of everything edible. Fever and exhaustion dog every step. They have to cross the Kafu River, which is covered two feet deep with a matting of water grass and other plants. The porters run across, sinking only to their ankles. Sam starts after them. Florence can't make it. Sam looks back to see her doubling over, her face contorted and purple, sinking through the weeds. He races back and drags her to dry land, but she lies as if dead, her hands and teeth tightly clenched, her eyes wide and staring. Acute sunstroke!

They must keep moving. Sam trudges beside Florence's litter each day, keeps vigil at night. On the third morning she awakens, thrashing, raving deliriously with "brain fever." They reach a village—no food there. Sam dismisses the armed escort. He and his porters shoot some guinea fowl and find wild honey in the forest. Sam has been seven days with no sleep and little food. He reaches the end of his endurance. He covers Florence with a plaid and collapses, unconscious. His men fit a new handle on a pickax and look for a place to dig a grave. Fade out.

Fade in, many hours later. Sam wakes up. No longer is Florence thrashing about. She lies serenely, her face like marble. Sam is in agony, thinking she died while he slept. But then—a miracle! She opens her eyes for a moment and gives him a calm, clear look.

224

After two days the little caravan moves on. They are heading directly toward a high mountain range. Their hearts sink. There is no way they will be able to cross those towering peaks. But wait! Their guide tells them the mountains are on the *far* side of the lake; if they start early in the morning, they will reach the big water before midday!

Barely able to sleep, Sam rouses the expedition before dawn. They set out at a swinging pace, Florence and Sam riding oxen. The sun comes up on a beautiful day. They toil up a hill—and there, a quarter of a mile below them, stretches the lake, glittering like a sea of quicksilver, blue mountains rising from the far shore some 50 miles away. Sam had planned to lead his band in three lusty cheers. Instead he offers up a fervent prayer of thanks. Then he names the expanse Albert N'yanza—Lake Albert—for the late husband of Queen Victoria. At the shore he drinks deeply from this important secondary source of the Nile.

The scene shifts back to the manor garden in England, where the elderly Florence picks up the story. Explorers have two main problems, she explains. One is getting there. The other is getting back home. She and Sam did not have it easy (now another kaleidoscope of scenes): a stormy trip across the lake; their canoe almost capsized by a hippopotamus in crocodile-infested waters; an outbreak of plague; skirmishes with hostile villagers and Arabs; a trip in a dirty troop transport up the Red Sea. But at last, more than four years after they first set foot in Africa, they reach Suez. And for the first time Sam abandons Florence—for the hotel bar and a couple of tankards of ice-cold Allsopp's Pale Ale.

They land in England in October 1865, and almost right away they get married—a quiet ceremony—in St. James's Church in Piccadilly. While they were still in Africa Sam was awarded the Royal Geographical Society's gold medal. Knighthood soon follows, but there is a hitch: Sir Samuel Baker, discoverer of Lake Albert, is accepted at royal functions, but Lady Baker will never be received by Queen Victoria. *Nice women do not share intimacies with men until they marry them.*

We'll give Florence the last word, confident in her role as Sam's partner and adviser—his "prime minister," as he came to call her. A fine Hollywood speech: "I never thought I could forgive that woman. But then I realized something. What did a queen know of anything, locked away in a sterile court? How could she possibly know what it means to live in desperation, to face death day after day, and to love and be loved in spite of it all? There was nothing we could say to each other."

The scene dissolves to a green hilltop where Sam and Florence, holding hands, gaze proudly down at the lake they have discovered, their figures silhouetted against a blazing African sun. . . .

You'll find most of the details of our movie outline in Samuel Baker's book, The Albert N'yanza, *including quotations, except where we've indicated dialogue in the spirit of Hollywood. Richard Hall's* Lovers on the Nile *provides a gripping modern account. Sam's family loved and admired Florence. Descriptions of her come from a biography written by a great-grandson's wife and called by the name the Bunyoro gave Florence:* Morning Star.

Possessing a share of sangfroid *admirably adapted for African travel, Mrs. Baker was not a* screamer, *and never even whispered; in the moment of suspected danger, a touch of my sleeve was . . . a sufficient warning.*
SAMUEL BAKER

The Last Wildernesses

By Douglas H. Chadwick

"What a fabulous and extravagant country we're in!" marveled German naturalist Alexander von Humboldt when he arrived in South America in 1799. "Fantastic plants, electric eels, armadillos, monkeys, parrots. . . ." Such tropical wonders—here represented by macaws clustered near an Amazon River tributary—drew a new breed of explorer: the scientist in search of knowledge. Naturalists, geographers, and anthropologists now probed the world's intractable wilds in their quest to unravel nature's mysteries.

The sun has melted, red as macaw plumes, into the simmering mist. Now heat lightning blossoms from the Amazon twilight, flashing images of an earth-colored river flowing through walls of vegetation. And the swoosh of big bats chasing the lightning bugs blends with the jungle song: of a distant jaguar, whose eyes burn through the dark; of birds and frogs, Indians in the village, cicadas shrilling a wall of sound—of countless voices, most of them as yet uninterpreted.

In the 2.3-million-square-mile basin known as Amazonia, and in other tracts of wilderness surviving here and there on the globe, lie the major challenges for modern exploration: To find not just what is out there, but how it works. To understand the potentials of the last great wildernesses even as we transform them.

Scientific exploration came into its own in the 18th century, the Age of Reason as it was called. Earlier explorers sought glittering riches, slaves, souls, or imperial dominion. Now a new breed, the scientist-explorer, set out to learn about Earth's living resources—its flora, fauna, and indigenous cultures.

Charles-Marie de La Condamine, a friend of Voltaire's, descended the Amazon in 1743, after a visit to Ecuador. He was the first to map this largest of rivers using scientific instruments. The baggage he delivered to Europe was as promising as it was exotic: quinine-producing cinchona trees; the insecticide rotenone; platinum; and rubber, which he used to coat his quadrant. He also carried tales of a natural canal, the Casiquiare, linking Venezuela's Orinoco river system to that of the Amazon.

Determined to map this legendary stream—as well as to observe and study "the harmony in nature"—Alexander von Humboldt explored the Orinoco in 1800 with French botanist Aimé Bonpland. Humboldt touched barometer and thermometer to practically everything in his path. Meeting electric eels, he promptly started shocking himself with the long wriggling generators and dissecting them to learn about their anatomy. Humboldt's experiments would cause a sensation back home, where Alessandro Volta had just displayed the first electric battery.

Humboldt and Bonpland found the Casiquiare. It was real. The mystery there was how so many biting bugs could fit into the air at once. Day after ripe, green, windless day, the pair twitched, slapped, and mapped along the river, their big canoe awash with pressed plants and rock samples, its live cargo of seven parrots, a toucan, a motmot, and eight monkeys shrieking amidst the insect drone. At night, they built fires to smoke out the pests, while Humboldt recalled an Indian's words: "How comfortable must people be in the moon! . . . She looks so beautiful and so clear, that she must be free from mosquitoes."

Croaking like frogs, curl-crested tou-
cans swoop at British naturalist Henry
Bates (opposite) during his 1848-1859
study of the Amazon and its tributaries. In Bates's day, few uncharted
areas remained on maps of the world.
Into these came explorer-scientists to
study what—and who—lived there.

South America's sprawling forests
and volcanic peaks enticed Humboldt,
then Charles Darwin and Brazilian
explorer Cândido Rondon. The Villas
Boas brothers—Claudio, Orlando, and

Through Colombia, Ecuador, and
Peru, Humboldt's curiosity played
across the landscape like sun shafts
through clouds, illuminating tropical storm patterns, geomagnetic
fields, the way elevation affects plant
distribution, the strange behavior of
animals just before earthquakes, the
geology of volcanoes, and the cold
coastal current that now bears his
name. He marched up the Ecuador-
ian volcano Chimborazo, to an elevation of 19,286 feet by his calcula-
tions. He suffered altitude sickness.
He also figured out why, relating it
to a decrease in oxygen.

Another amateur naturalist with
boundless curiosity, Charles Darwin
took Humboldt's *Personal Narrative
of Travels* along on his 1831-36 journey on the *Beagle* around the world.
He also carried a just-published work
entitled *Principles of Geology*. Its author, Charles Lyell, argued that the
Earth was older than the 6,000 years
some biblical scholars had set, and
that its crust was continuously being
reshaped. Those were radical notions then, but the fossil seashells
Darwin collected at 12,000 feet in
the Andes would eventually make
him wonder: If the environment is so
changeable—evolving over time—
what of the organisms that dwell
within it? Tradition taught that species were immutable—fixed for all
time. After his return home, the
young man who had once entertained the notion of entering the
clergy found himself in a state of
creative flux that, years later, would

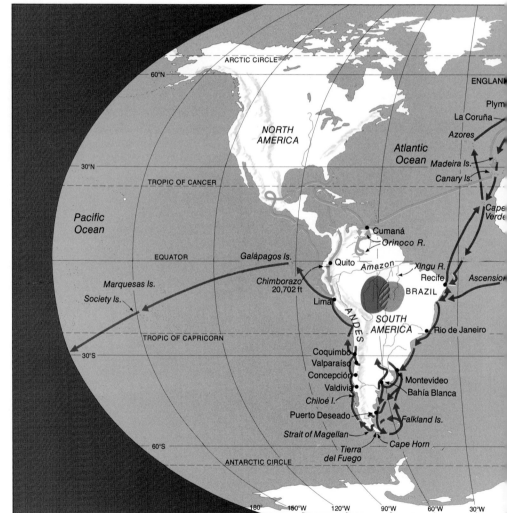

15° of latitude = 1,035 statute miles

Leonardo—followed, seeking isolated Indian tribes. Even today scientists from many nations probe this still largely unknown realm.

The deserts and mountains of central Asia also proved daunting; not until the late 1800s did scientists mount major expeditions to fathom their secrets. Swedish geographer Sven Hedin charted windswept deserts and Himalayan heights; American botanist Joseph Rock trekked central China in search of plants and anthropological knowledge; Roy Chapman Andrews, an American zoologist, searched the Gobi for fossils.

Italian naturalist Luigi D'Albertis and government officials of New Guinea challenged that island's tangled terrain, emerging with tales of cannibals, headhunters, birds of paradise—and with some of the last missing pieces of the mapmakers' global puzzle.

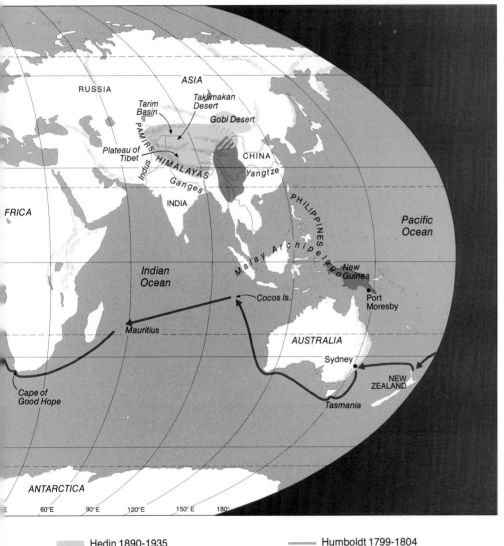

Hedin 1890-1935
Andrews 1922-1930
Rock 1922-1949
D'Albertis 1872-77
MacGregor 1888-1898
Champion 1926-1940
Hides 1935

Humboldt 1799-1804
Darwin and the *Beagle* 1831-36

Rondon 1907-1914
Villas Boas brothers 1943-1973

229

All bluff and no bite, an emerald tree snake no thicker than a finger shows its toothless gape in a forest in Amazonia. Most snakes in the Amazon basin pose little threat to humans—including a "wonderfully slender" six-foot serpent that dropped on Henry Bates and tangled him in its coils.

Serpentine tributaries writhe through a rain forest on their way to the Amazon. Using rivers as roads, scientists have explored the forests of Amazonia for more than two and a half centuries. The region may support 30 percent of Earth's species of plants and animals. Darwin's visit to Brazil in 1836 led him to describe the land as "one great wild, untidy, luxuriant hot-house which nature made for her menagerie."

culminate in the theory of evolution.

In the dreary factory town of Leicester, in the English Midlands, a hosier, Henry Bates, and a schoolteacher, Alfred Wallace, would read Darwin's *Voyage of the Beagle* and dream of orchid jungle light. In 1848, the two friends broke out for the Amazon, having arranged to sell specimens to wealthy collectors at threepence each.

Over the next 11 years, Bates amassed specimens of 14,712 species, 8,000 of them—mostly insects —previously unknown to science. From just one area in the state of Pará, Brazil, he netted 700 butterfly species, 310 more than inhabited Europe. Bates chased more than new creatures to classify. He also stalked relationships, focusing on how a single species of butterflies varies subtly from one habitat to the next, and how certain palatable varieties resemble noxious-tasting ones—an adaptation for fooling predators that we now term Batesian mimicry. "Nature writes, as on a tablet, the story of the modifications of species," he concluded and went on to publish eloquent proof.

Wallace, returning home earlier, had lost his hard-won collections during a fire at sea. He was quickly off again, though, this time to the steaming Malay Archipelago. Resting between malarial attacks and forays through lush tangles of life forms, he independently conceived the principle of natural selection at about the same time Darwin brought

forth his *Origin of Species* in 1859. Already systematic exploration of nature was offering glimpses of the unifying laws that shape existence— including, it would become apparent, our own.

More details of our past awaited discovery in central Asia, an expanse just as wide and uncharted as the Amazon. In 1893 the Swedish explorer Sven Hedin journeyed through southern Russia and on to the Taklimakan Desert, west of the

Names of more than a hundred plants crowd a slice in the flank of Chimborazo, a 20,702-foot volcano in Ecuador. Alexander von Humboldt devised this composite view of South American volcanoes to show how plant types change from tropical to temperate to arctic as altitude increases. He climbed mountains with a barometer to measure his altitude and ascended rivers with chronometer and sextant to fix his position. With thermometers he recorded air, ground, and water temperatures and with hygrometers, humidity; with compasses he took magnetic readings; with telescopes he studied meteor showers—and with a microscope he delighted the ladies of Cumaná, Venezuela, with visions of strange beasts that were their own head lice.

Gobi, to fill in what he called the "white spots" on maps. Some of the arid wilderness proved nearly as blank in reality; he soon ran out of bearings, then out of water. Two of his Muslim assistants drank camel urine. They died bloated with salt. Hedin crawled on for five nights, burrowing into the sand by day, until he found moonlight reflected in a muddy pool.

Once reoriented and reorganized, he pressed onward. From the dunes he sifted traces of forgotten, 2,000-year-old cities: Taklimakan and Karadong, flourishing when Buddhism spread northward from India. Later, along a spur of the old Silk Road, he located ruins of the Chinese city of Loulan. Within, preserved by the endless drought, bundles of some of the first paper invented proved to hold some of the first bureaucratic paperwork. Yet these writings whispered details of the daily commerce and administration, hopes and wor-

A Cacajao monkey sits for a sketch by Humboldt. Indians on the Casiquiare River sold him the small primate for a pet. It soon died of a stomach ailment —but not before Humboldt had studied its behavior.

Seated among instruments and specimens, Humboldt and his colleague, botanist Aimé Bonpland, are themselves captured on canvas by a 19th-century artist. Darwin praised Humboldt as "the greatest scientific traveler who ever lived."

ries, of a society old a millennium before Marco Polo passed that way.

White spots drew Hedin toward the Tibetan plateau. Ever since Alexander the Great first swept into India, geographers had assumed that the south-flowing Indus, Brahmaputra, and Sutlej Rivers originated in the Himalayas, the tallest mountains on Earth. Hedin proved that they flowed through that barrier and that their true sources lay in a more northern range, which he mapped and named the Transhimalayas.

Hedin kept crisscrossing white spots for more than 40 years. After a Mercury astronaut photographed Tibet from space in 1963, NASA used Hedin's surveys to help decide which wrinkles were which. Maybe the spacemen could imagine him somewhere among those map contours, watching stars blaze above his yak-dung fire, or fashioning ice skates from knife blades to carve sparkling free tracks across a frozen lake in the Tarim Basin.

Roy Chapman Andrews planned more elaborately for each of his five expeditions to the Gobi between 1922 and 1930. The zoologist from the American Museum of Natural History sought proof there for theories of mammalian evolution. Priding himself on overlooking no detail, he took care to select a team whose specialties would complement one another: surveyor, geologist, paleontologist, archaeologist, and others. He was among the earliest explorers to rely on 20th-century technology,

feeling that automobiles could cover ground ten times as efficiently as camel caravans.

Some overlooked details came calling anyway one cold night at an old Buddhist monument. For some reason, every poisonous snake in the area seemed bent on warming itself at camp. Vipers got into cots, shoes, a chauffeur's hat, gun cases; they lay in braids across the tent floor.

"Perils," Humboldt once said, "elevate the poetry of life." Here, then,

in the slithering dark is Andrews, stepping on a coil of rope and elevating straight for the ceiling while Walter Granger, patient analyzer of rock strata, stabs furiously at what turns out to be a pipe cleaner.

There were more reptiles along Flaming Cliffs, old ones: the first dinosaur eggs ever recognized, and to go with them, skeletons of embryonic dinosaurs. Until then, no one was certain whether the colossal reptiles laid eggs at all. Equally important

"A knot of enormous, clustered masses of snow-covered mountains, from which radiate the highest and mightiest ranges of the earth," wrote Sven Hedin of central Asia's Pamir mountains. Beneath this awesome backdrop amble a Kirghiz elder and his son. Hedin rode on camelback into these mountains in the 1890s to explore western China's Taklimakan Desert. Continuing on his way to Peking, he paused for a portrait with a Mongolian herdsman by a yurt of heavy felt.

was the discovery of small mammal remains in rock dating from the Age of Dinosaurs. The find continued the tradition of Darwin, tracing back our line toward its beginnings.

The Men of the Dragon Bones, as the local Mongol bandits called Andrews and his team, also unearthed bones of the largest known terrestrial mammal, *Baluchitherium*. And they found the largest known carnivorous mammal, hyenalike *Andrewsarchus*, as well as flint and fossil remnants of a people they named the Dune Dwellers. In one place, the crew found fragments of dinosaur eggshells worked into squares; the original discoverers of dinosaur eggs had been the Stone Age Dune Dwellers.

Elsewhere in the world Stone Age cultures still lived, many of them in New Guinea, an island long enough to reach from London to Istanbul. In 1876 a bearded, aria-singing Italian naturalist named Luigi Maria D'Albertis charged up the Fly River in a steam launch so loaded with crew, arms, and ammunition that its decks barely rose above water. For 45 days his men sweated and suffered from flies and monotony while D'Albertis collected natural specimens and cultural artifacts. To get the latter, he lobbed skyrockets into riverside villages, looting huts abandoned by the terrorized inhabitants. He even stole skeletons from their burial platforms. "Exclaim if you will, against my barbarity," he later wrote. "I am too delighted with my prize to heed reproof!" No one accused D'Albertis

of being a dull scientist. Or a very good one. But he did make one of the first significant penetrations of New Guinea's interior.

Fourteen years later, William MacGregor, the rugged administrator of British New Guinea, pushed 535 miles up the Fly River by steam launch. He was as keen to study natural history in the island's interior, with its spine of snowbound equatorial peaks, as he was to extend colonial authority. Blocked by rapids, his

235

A thrashing mule froths the Yalong River in central Asia, stuck in midstream on a cable of twisted cane greased with yak butter. Men of botanist Joseph Rock's expedition in the 1920s labor to haul their panicky pack animal toward the shore.

Wild terrain, cutthroat bandits, hostile tribes, petty wars, disease, and bad weather bedeviled Rock's expeditions for nearly three decades as he scoured China's central provinces for plants, seeds, and lore about native peoples.

At the Labrang Monastery in 1925, his camera caught all but the sonorous hoot as young Buddhist lamas unlimbered a chorus of six-foot-long trumpets which, like Europe's deep-voiced alpenhorns, could be easily heard from slope to mountainous slope.

expedition beat its way overland. Blocked by walls of bush, thunderstorms, and spear-tipped tribesmen, MacGregor had to call it quits just six miles short of the mountains.

On a later patrol, he topped the divide. Breaking out of the cloud forest on his way up one 13,210-foot summit, he found alpine meadows of daisies and buttercups. He found three new bird species there as well. Unfortunately, his assistant Joe Fiji ate two of them.

It wasn't until 1927-28 that the wider part of the island was traversed, from the Fly to the Sepik Rivers. On their second try, government officers Ivan Champion and Charles Karius bested an eerie central ridge of labyrinthine limestone so sharp that later visitors dubbed it "broken bottle country."

In 1935 a police patrol headed by Jack Hides explored the upper Strickland River in the southern highlands. After weeks of incessant

toil on short rations, Hides and his men crested a mountain wall.

"My mother!" blurted a sergeant, "What people are they?"

A huge, heavily populated valley dotted with cultivated fields of "mathematical exactness" lay before them. New Guinea had spawned legends aplenty but none as exotic as the truth. Hidden among those forbidding mountains were broad valleys of grass; terraced gardens silvered with the smoke from untold huts; battlegrounds and watchtowers. Explorers would find headhunters, pygmies, blond-haired people, eaters of their enemies, eaters of their own dead, people with jawbone belts, snake earrings, gourds on their penises, and feathers through their noses. You might say we had been speaking of mankind for centuries without fully knowing what we were talking about, for New Guinea supports perhaps the densest array of tribal cultures on the globe—some three million inhabitants, speaking more than 700 languages. About 40 percent dwell in the highlands.

Unlike Hides, who was attacked 9 times and who shot at least 32 natives while crossing the highlands, Champion usually avoided incidents. But then his idea of courage was different; he refused to raise his rifle even when bows were drawn taut against him.

The precedent had been set by a Brazilian explorer, Cândido Rondon, in his surveys of the Amazon's Mato Grosso hinterlands for the

An aerial view of New Guinea's upper Ramu River hints at the rumpled terrain—furrowed peaks, dark gorges, surging rivers, tangled forests, malarial swamps—that for centuries stymied explorers. But the sky opened pathways to inaccessible areas; in the 1920s floatplanes began bringing expeditions into the hinterlands, scouting routes from the air, and hauling supplies to remote camps.

A 1929 expedition (opposite, upper) mounted by the U. S. Department of Agriculture found itself mobbed by curious Papuans during a search for a disease-resistant strain of sugarcane. Using aerial photography, expedition members charted large parts of New Guinea that had never been explored by white men.

Arms in the air, explorer Jack Hides and a Tarifuroro tribesman discuss a safe route during the government official's 1935 trek, the last major expedition to probe the island's interior without radio or air support.

government, beginning in 1907. "Die if need be, but kill, never," was his motto. Part Indian himself, Rondon helped establish his country's first Indian protection agency.

His work continued under the Villas Boas brothers, Orlando, Claudio, and Leonardo. From the 1940s into the 1970s they probed the heart of the Amazon, seeking out remote, often unfriendly Indian tribes, some of whom had never seen a *civilizado*. It was delicate, dangerous work: leaving gifts, patient waiting, sudden flight when arrows whistled through the trees, more gifts—and at last the first wary encounter, the first touch, the first attempts at communication.

Humanitarianism is not the only reason for preserving tribal cultures. For much of the past decade, Darrell Posey, an American-born ethnobiologist, has lived among Kayapó Indians along a tributary of the Xingu River. He and a team of 20 specialists are conducting a study of Amazonia through native eyes.

Posey often works with Beptopup, a shaman. Beptopup claims to "speak" with certain animals, the spirits of dead people, and the world of energies beyond normal senses. You can make what you want of that; the practical point is that Beptopup carries volumes of unwritten information in his head. His specialty is the treatment of snakebites and scorpion stings. He knows how to graft wild medicinal plants onto fruit trees so as to have the remedies handy around garden plots. He knows how

239

to mulch with ant and termite nests to encourage plant growth; how to "transplant" colonies of *Azteca* ants, with their chemical secretions, to drive leaf-cutting ants from the gardens; and how to identify some 35 types of ants that can themselves be used for medicine.

Hike with him, and you might recognize *Colias* butterflies, bright flakes of color racing each other down jungle paths—just as Bates described them. You won't recognize the bugs sipping sweat off your forearms as minuscule bees. The shaman will. That pink one's hive has wax he can use to treat dizziness. The wax of the black one with gilt edges cures burns. And these leaves, crushed and rubbed on the body, will repel bees when you raid their hive.

"With ethnobiology, I think we're on a very exciting frontier," Posey says. "It's one thing to try to research and save plants and animals. But knowledge of how to use them is one of the Amazon's greatest resources." The project team has learned of uses the Kayapó have for over 600 plants that grow in this area. "The Kayapó have brought in many of these plants through trade and travel with other Indians from a region roughly the size of Western Europe, and they have domesticated dozens of wild varieties for their own needs."

In other words, what the civilizado sees as wilderness—for some a pristine paradise and for others a sprawling green hell to be conquered—the expert, the native, knows as a manageable neighborhood. His skills in working with living resources while increasing their diversity provides a rich source of conservation ideas.

As the scientist-explorers have shown us, the ultimate treasures were right there all along: in the soils and waters, the roots and leaves, the chorus of animals, and the manifold cultures of humanity. The hard scientific data need not diminish our sense of awe before creation. It doesn't for Beptopup. It didn't for Darwin. Watch his pen fly across the notebook as he makes one of his first excursions to the Brazilian interior: "Twiners entwining twiners—tresses like hair—beautiful lepidopters—silence—hosannah."

240

Charles Darwin

Edited by Margaret Sedeen

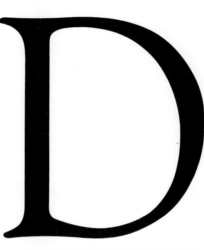

H.M.S. Beagle *at Sydney, Australia.*

At sea, February 1832

Dear sister Caroline,

We have crossed the Equator and are eight weeks out of Plymouth. Captain FitzRoy continues very kind to me in spite of my being underfoot in the crowded cabin we share. He is convinced that he can judge a man's character by his features, and tells me that when we first met he doubted whether anyone with my nose could possess sufficient energy and determination to voyage as naturalist aboard the *Beagle.* The Captain will be busy with coastline surveys for the Admiralty, and I will botanize and geologize to my heart's content at all our stops.

Our crew and passengers number above 70, including York, Fuegia, and Jemmy, the three natives of Tierra del Fuego whom Captain FitzRoy has educated in England. We are to bring them home. The *Beagle* is a splendid vessel, all fitted up with mahogany, brass armaments, 6 guns, and 24 chronometers! I find a ship a very comfortable house. Were it not for seasickness the whole world would be sailors.

I remember well the encouragement I received from Uncle Jos, that day when my mind was like a pendulum. Should I stay home, where all is familiar and my future as country parson a pretty sure thing? Or should I set out to explore a new world, to find I know not what? Well, I am here. My 23rd birthday has slipped by. My second life commences. Your affectionate brother, Charles Darwin

My dear Henslow,   *Rio de Janeiro, May 1832*

How are you all going on at Cambridge? But for your recommendation as my master in Natural History, I should not be aboard the *Beagle.* My first steps ashore, now some months ago, were in the Cape Verdes, where I feasted upon oranges and tasted a banana but did not like it. There I first saw the glory of tropical vegetation about which I have read

A *Bible reading on board the* Beagle.
The devout captain, Robert FitzRoy,
also led weekly Sunday services.

I think he was afterwards
well-satisfied that my nose
had spoken falsely.
DARWIN'S *AUTOBIOGRAPHY*

in Humboldt, and spent an unparalleled day hearing the notes of unknown birds and seeing new insects fluttering about still newer flowers.
I examined there a white band which runs for some miles along the face
of a sea cliff, about 45 feet above the water. Numerous seashells are embedded in this limestone band. It rests above ancient volcanic rocks and
below a gently sloping stream of basalt which covered the shelly bed
when it lay at the bottom of the sea. Geology is a pleasure like gam-
bling. When speculating on what rocks may be, I often mentally cry
out, "Three to one it is Tertiary!"

At Bahia I wandered in a Brazilian forest, delighted and bewildered
by the novelty of the parasitical plants, the glossy green of the foliage,
the flight of a gaudy butterfly. Already I am collecting and will send you
specimens to study. I am red-hot with spiders, they are so interesting. I
am overwhelmed by what I see, like a blind man suddenly given eyes.
Yours affectionately, Charles Darwin

My dear Henslow, *Tierra del Fuego, February 1833*
I have had my first sight of a real barbarian—of man in his lowest and
most savage state. This is a mountainous land, partly submerged in the
sea. A dusky mass of forest covers all the deep valleys. In the Strait of
Magellan the distant channels between mountains seem from their
gloom to lead beyond the confines of this world.

In December the *Beagle* got under weigh so that Captain FitzRoy

Charles Darwin in 1840, four years after the return of the Beagle.

could resettle York, Fuegia, and Jemmy. We had a smooth beginning, but Cape Horn demanded his tribute and sent us a wind directly in our teeth. Great black clouds rolled across the heavens, and violent squalls drove us into a cove. We pulled alongside a canoe with six Fuegians, the most abject creatures I anywhere beheld, with the rain trickling down their naked bodies. A woman suckling a child stared at our boat whilst the sleet fell and thawed on her bosom and on her baby.

We moored the *Beagle* and rowed in small boats with our Fuegians down a long channel where fires were lighted on every point. Men ran for miles along the shore and suddenly four or five came to the edge of a cliff. Their long hair streamed about their faces. They carried rugged staffs and waved their arms and sent forth hideous yells.

A few nights later we took up our quarters with Jemmy's people, the Tekeenica. They behaved quietly and joined the seamen to sing around a blazing fire. Although naked, they streamed with perspiration. We built large wooden wigwams and planted gardens for our Fuegians, but it was melancholy to leave them amongst their barbarous countrymen. Your obliged friend, Chas Darwin

My dear sister Catherine,   *Puerto Deseado, December 1833*

I am become quite a gaucho, drink my maté, smoke my cigar, then lie down and sleep as comfortably with the heavens for a canopy as in a feather bed. The danger from Indians is small as they are now collecting in the Cordillera for a battle against the Argentine army, which pursues a bloody war of extermination. After returning north to the pampas I traveled 600 miles, with guides, through a region until lately traveled only by Indians and never before by an Englishman. So fine an opportunity for geologizing was not to be lost.

In the pampas I found more fossil remains of the *Megatherium,* an extinct sloth the size of an elephant. It is the same that I found at Bahía Blanca in September along with several other remains, including a horse, a huge rodent-like animal, and a relative of the armadillo. These bones were embedded along with ancient shells similar to species even now living in the same bay. Here is evidence of Mr. Lyell's law that the longevity of mammal species is inferior to that of shelled invertebrates.

The gauchos are a singular race of countrymen. One's diet, traveling with them, is meat alone—puma, rhea, deer, armadillo (very good cooked in the shell), jaguar, especially beef. When we were at Montevideo, one gaucho showed great dexterity in forcing a restive horse to swim a flooded river. He stripped off his clothes and rode the horse into the water. Then he slipped off and hung onto the tail, splashing water in the horse's face each time it turned around. When the horse touched bottom on the other side, the gaucho pulled himself back on and grasped the bridle. A naked man on a naked horse is a fine spectacle; I had no idea how well the two animals suited each other.

We have had our Christmas here. The land deserves the name of desert but it supports many guanacos. I shot a good big one, so that we had fresh meat for all hands on Christmas Day. After dining we all went

245

Eruption of the Andean volcano Antuco—the center, Darwin speculated, of a shock wave that rocked Chile in 1835.

Tekeenica tribesman of Tierra del Fuego—as draped by the artist to accommodate Victorian sensibilities.

ashore for Olympic games of running, leaping, and wrestling. Old men with long beards and young men without any were playing like so many children. With affectionate love to my Father and to all of you.
Yours very sincerely, Charles Darwin

My dear Henslow,   *At sea, March 1835*

We are becalmed off Valparaíso, for which I am grateful as I am always sick when there is a sea. I have received a large bundle of letters from England. I hope you have gotten mine, as well as the collections I have sent. We have had a most interesting time progressing up the coast of Chile. Off Chiloé in January, at midnight on the 19th, the watch hailed me on deck when he saw on the horizon something like a large star. It increased in size and by three o'clock made a magnificent spectacle. The volcano of Osorno, 73 miles away was in action and cast a glare of red light on the water. We later heard that on this same night, 480 miles to the north, Aconcagua erupted, and Coseguina, 2,700 miles farther north, where there was also an earthquake. Whether this coincidence is accidental or shows some subterranean connection is hard to say, but the three vents do fall on the same great mountain chain.

In February at Valdivia I was at work ashore. Suddenly came on the great earthquake about which you have read in the newspapers. For two minutes the earth rocked. Standing upright made me giddy, as though I were skating on very thin ice. The earth, the very emblem of solidity, moved beneath our feet like a thin crust over a fluid.

In the town of Concepción people told us that during the fatal convulsion they threw themselves on the ground and gripped it to prevent being tossed over and over. Poultry flew about screaming. Horses stood with their legs spread, trembling. The earth cracked open and houses and the cathedral fell in blinding dust. This is one of the three most interesting spectacles I have beheld since leaving England—a Fuegian savage; tropical vegetation; and the ruins of Concepción. The land around the bay was raised two or three feet. It is a bitter thing to see such devastation, yet my compassion for the inhabitants was banished by my seeing a state of things produced in a moment which one is accustomed to attribute to a succession of ages.

Now I go to cross the Andes. Horsecloths, stirrups, pistols, and spurs are lying on all sides of me. So my dear Henslow, good night.
Your most obliged and affectionate friend, Charles Darwin

My dear Caroline,   *Coquimbo, Chile, May 1835*

It is worth coming from England once to enjoy these views. At 12,000 feet a transparency in the air and a confusion of distances and a stillness give the sensation of being in another world.

Our traveling from Valparaíso was delightfully independent. In the inhabited parts, we bought firewood, hired pasture for the animals, and bivouacked in a corner of the field with them. We cooked our suppers under a cloudless sky. My companions were my guide and an *arriero* with his ten mules and a *madrina,* an old, steady mare with a bell around

Movable feast: A gaff-wielding sailor prepares to overturn a giant land tortoise in the Galápagos Islands.

I have just got scent of some fossil bones . . . if gold or galloping will get them, they shall be mine.

DARWIN LETTER TO JOHN HENSLOW

her neck. Wherever she goes the mules, like good children, follow her.

The short breathing from the rarefied atmosphere is called *puna*. I experienced only a slight tightness across the head and chest. The inhabitants all recommend onions as a cure for the puna—for my part I found no remedy so good as my discovery of fossil shells on the highest ridges!

At about 7,000 feet in the Uspallata Range I found some snow white columns on a bare slope. They were petrified trees. I stood where a cluster of fine green trees once raised their lofty heads on the shores of the Atlantic, when that ocean—now driven back 700 miles—came to the foot of the Andes. I saw that they had sprung from a volcanic soil which had been raised above the level of the sea and then let down into the depths of the ocean, covered by sedimentary beds, then by submarine lava. I now beheld that ocean bed forming a chain of mountains.

Yet I miss you all so much that Snowdon to my mind looks higher and more beautiful than any peak in the Cordillera. I never cease marveling at all the marriages you have told me about. What a gang of little ones have come into the world since I left England. Give my love to all. Yours affectionately, Charles Darwin

My dear Henslow,   *Galápagos Islands, October 1835*

We anchored in several bays here for our surveying. The black sand is so hot that even in thick boots it is disagreeable to walk upon it; fields of lava in rugged waves are crossed by great fissures and stunted, sunburnt brushwood. One night I slept on shore. The next day was glowing hot, and the pits and craters—ancient chimneys for subterranean vapors—reminded me of the iron foundries of Staffordshire. Because many of the lava streams are still distinct, I believe that within a geologically recent period the unbroken ocean was here spread out. Both in space and time, therefore, I felt near that mystery of mysteries—the first appearance of new beings on this Earth.

Three species of Galápagos finches: Their varied beaks suggest adaptation to different environmental niches.

These islands appear paradises for the whole family of reptiles. There are large, clumsy lizards as black as the rocks. So many reddish ones lived on one island that we could not for some time find a spot free from their burrows on which to pitch our single tent. Of the giant tortoises, the inhabitants say that on one island their shells are thick in front and turned up like a Spanish saddle, whilst on another they are rounder, blacker, and taste better when cooked. The tortoises drink from springs high in the center of their island. It was comical to behold these huge creatures on their broad, well-beaten paths, one group eagerly traveling upwards with outstretched necks, another group returning, having drunk their fill. At the spring, the tortoise ignores onlookers, buries its head in the muddy water above its eyes, and greedily sucks in great mouthfuls. They travel by night and day. One, which I watched, walked at the rate of four miles a day—allowing it a little time to eat cactus on the road. I frequently got on their backs; then giving a few raps on the hinder part of their shells, they would rise up and walk away. Believe me, my dear Henslow, your most faithful, Charles Darwin

My dear Susan,   *At sea, September 1836*

I have lately received several letters from you and the other sisters. When I read in one that Professor Sedgewick says I shall be a leading man of science, I clambered over the mountains of Ascension with a bounding step and made the rocks resound under my hammer. Captain FitzRoy is readying his account of the voyage for publication. It warrants that all we have seen is evidence of the biblical tale of the Deluge.

For myself, I have been thinking about these five years wandering, and my imaginings haunt me. I must recount to you a strange dream I had last night. I sat in the clouds. Below me, in a primeval, tropical forest, were many animals: great fossil creatures covered with polygonal plates of armor; horses and cows and dogs; tortoises and lizards; mockingbirds, finches, hawks; apes, seamen, and Fuegian men and women. Then, my dear sister—surely you will think me mad—I saw in the forest an old gentleman with a long, white beard and a lantern in his hand. It was I! The old man turned the lantern's beam upon the wildest sight. The armored fossils began to change into armadillos, and a Fuegian man into Captain FitzRoy. All the people and animals began to melt together in a great lump, as though we all have one common ancestor.

Is this not ridiculous and fantastic, my dear Susan? Thanks to God, we are steering a direct course to England. God bless you all.
Your most affectionate brother, C. D.

While aboard the Beagle *Darwin kept a diary and wrote a stream of letters to family and friends, four of whom are addressed here. The diary and letters are the source material for these composite letters, where Darwin's own words are abridged, merged, and provided with transitions to make a coherent and completely faithful story. Only the dream event is made up, but it is not false: In words and images Darwin himself used later he "foresees" hints of the theory of evolution that came to him as a result of the* Beagle *voyage.*

The Call of the Ice

By Lynn Addison Yorke

Their shallow breathing made a rising, falling sea of fur. Huddled together, they lay untroubled, as if they knew—those 21 huskies—that their work was done. Thirty-five days of temperatures that dipped to minus 70°F, of hauling thousand-pound sledges over ice ridges 30 feet high. Now the plane's twin engines rumbled beneath them and they slept, going home.

Twenty-one others remained with six men and one woman on the ice of the Arctic Ocean. They were on their way to the North Pole in a 1986 reenactment of Robert E. Peary's 1908-09 trek. The removal of the dogs was one of the few concessions to modern sensibilities the explorers made; in another, two injured men were flown out, leaving the group finally at six. In an *exact* re-creation of Peary's expedition, the surplus dogs would have been killed and eaten as supply loads lightened; the injured men might have struggled on or turned back alone.

The expedition, led by Minnesotans Will Steger and Paul Schurke, had waited two days for the plane to come pick up the dogs. Flight was impossible while a four-day blizzard spent its fury nearly 800 miles south at their base camp in Resolute, Canada. The team had camped on ice that drifted west, drifted east, but somehow never toward the Pole. They had stayed behind waiting after the French doctor, Jean-Louis

Etienne, passed them on his way to the Pole—skiing alone with a 110-pound sledge harnessed to his chest and shoulders.

Now, on April 11, they could move on. Each day since their March 8 departure from the northern tip of Ellesmere Island meant the possibility of warming temperatures and breaking ice. Any day they might find themselves confronted with an impassable lead of open water that would force them to radio for planes to come and take them home.

Even if they reached the Pole, they would not be the first. But they would be the first *undisputed* dogsled expedition to reach the Pole without being resupplied. Team member Ann Bancroft would be the first woman to trek to either Pole. If Jean-Louis Etienne succeeded, he would be the first to walk alone to the North Pole.

"First" is a part of polar tradition. At the turn of the century, expedition followed expedition in a mad scramble to get "farthest north." An American explorer, Adolphus Greely, nearly died from starvation after being the first to reach 83° 24′ N in 1882, some 450 miles from the Pole but 4 miles closer than Englishman Sir Clements Markham had stood in 1875. Norwegian explorer Fridtjof Nansen sledged to 86° 14′ N in 1895. Six years later Umberto Cagni planted the Italian flag 28 miles closer at 86° 34′ N. But none of these men was as obsessed with being first as Robert E. Peary.

The near-freezing water of an open lead makes little impression on hardy huskies bred to battle the killing temperatures and fickle ice of the Arctic. No other mode of transport has served polar explorers so well: Inuit komatiks—wood sledges—drawn by Alaskan and Canadian dogs carried Robert Peary toward the North Pole and back in 1909. Roald Amundsen shipped the same tried-and-true technology south and conquered the South Pole in 1911.

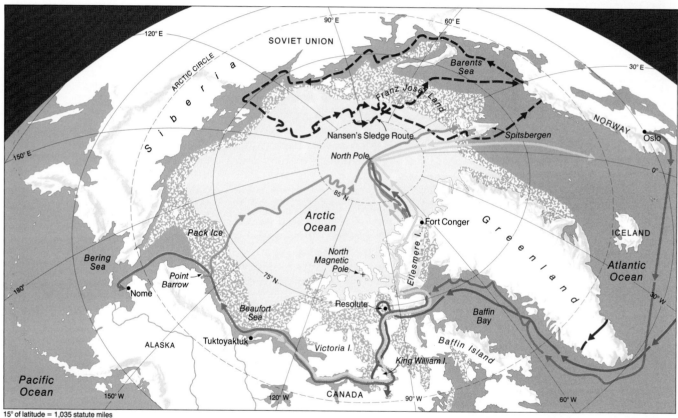

15° of latitude = 1,035 statute miles

▬▬▬	Franklin 1845-47
▬▬▬	Nansen 1888
▬ ▬ ▬	Nansen 1893-96
▬▬▬	Amundsen 1903-06
▬▬▬	Peary 1909
▬▬▬	Byrd 1926
▬▬▬	Plaisted 1963
▬▬▬	Herbert 1969
▬▬▬	Uemura 1978
▬▬▬	Fiennes 1979-1981
▬▬▬	Steger 1986

Whales first lured men to polar regions, but the dangers of the whale fishery (top) could not compare with the hazards that faced explorers who struck out over ice to reach the very ends of the Earth. The earliest Arctic expeditions attempted, like John Franklin, to navigate the icebound straits of the Northwest Passage. Later explorers headed for the Pole, sailing as far north as the seasonally fluctuating sea-ice limit allowed, then hauling sledges over the continually drifting, fracturing pack ice of the Arctic Ocean. The shortest route, chosen by Robert Peary, is from the tip of Ellesmere Island due north; many after Peary followed the same path by dogsled, by snowmobile, and on foot. Once the Pole was conquered, and outside support by airplane became available, explorers began to mastermind more challenging adventures like the long-range treks of Wally Herbert and Ranulph Fiennes.

252

As with the North Pole, the shortest route to the South Pole was favored by the first explorers. Ernest Shackleton, Robert Scott, and Roald Amundsen all approached the Pole by way of the Ross Sea. More recent explorers have traversed the entire continent. Edmund Hillary and Vivian Fuchs started out from opposite coasts and met at a chosen spot—a supply depot near 83° S. Still others, in the pursuit of science, have devoted their explorations to the seas surrounding Antarctica.

No ordinary ambition his; at 29, the young American naval officer planned a discovery as great as the one made by Columbus, "the man whose fame can be equalled only by him who shall one day stand with 360 degrees of longitude beneath his motionless foot, and for whom East and West shall have vanished; the discoverer of the North Pole."

Peary needed to be first because he needed to be famous. He wrote to his mother: "I *must* have fame and I cannot reconcile myself to years of commonplace drudgery and a name late in life when I see an opportunity to gain it now and sip the delicious draught. . . ."

Peary made four assaults on the Pole. During his second expedition, in 1899, he believed he was racing with Norwegian explorer Otto Sverdrup. In his effort to take the lead, Peary trudged through the darkness of midwinter in temperatures as low as minus 63°F.

When he arrived at Fort Conger on Ellesmere Island, his companion, Matthew Henson, had to peel the boots from Peary's frozen legs. As Henson ripped the rabbit-skin undershoes from Peary's bloodless feet, toes clung to the hide and snapped off at the first joint. "A few toes aren't much to give to achieve the Pole," said Peary. He lost them all.

In the end, he would lose more than toes in his pursuit of personal glory. Fifteen gold medals and three honorary doctorates could not wipe away the pain of bitter controversy

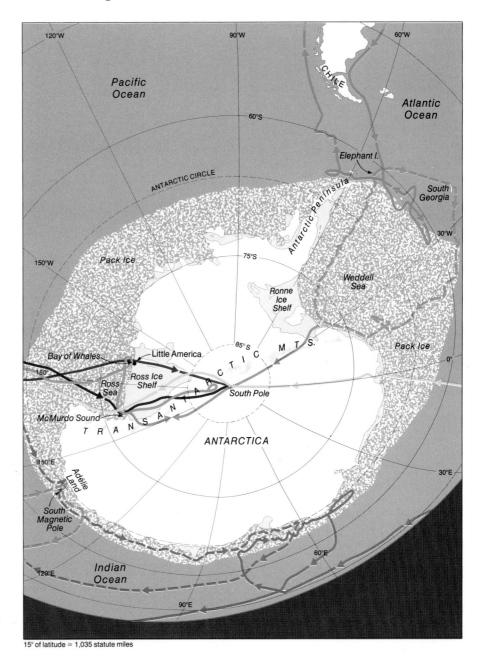

— D'Urville 1837-38
-- D'Urville 1840
— Shackleton 1908-09
-- Shackleton 1914-16
— Amundsen 1910-12
— Scott 1910-12
— Mawson 1929-1930
-- Mawson 1930-31
— Fuchs-Hillary 1957-58
— Fiennes 1979-1981

15° of latitude = 1,035 statute miles

Sea ice fractures under summer sun in Antarctica (right). Breakup here aids ships headed toward the continent. But once on land, explorers must negotiate glaciers laced with deep crevasses (below) before they reach more even terrain on the South Polar Plateau. In the Arctic, drifting floes mean treacherous going for explorers traversing the ice pack on their way to the North Pole; they dash across between March and May—after the minus 70°F days of winter but before summer breakup.

that followed the 1909 assertion of another American, Dr. Frederick Cook, that he had reached the North Pole a year before Peary. Neither claim could be verified and both men's records left room for doubt. Some said neither had reached the Pole. Peary's wife, Josephine, would write later that the congressional interrogation her husband underwent while his scientific observations were examined "did more toward the breaking down of his iron constitution than anything experienced in his explorations." Cook was eventually discredited and Peary vindicated by Congress, but Peary's bright star—his fame—was tarnished.

After 1909 it might have seemed that Peary had robbed the world of

one of its last great firsts. Not so. A string of successors contrived new ones. In 1926 Richard E. Byrd made the first flight over the North Pole, and in 1929 was first to fly over the South Pole. Ralph Plaisted reached the North Pole with a team of 12 men in 1968—the first to travel by snowmobile and the first arrival to be confirmed by airplane instruments. In 1978 Japanese Naomi Uemura was the first to journey solo to the North Pole by dogsled.

As polar firsts grew harder to conceive, they turned into "last great journeys." Even as Plaisted jounced to the Pole by Skidoo, British explorer Wally Herbert was traversing the Arctic Ocean by its longest axis—from Point Barrow, Alaska, to Spitsbergen, Norway, via the North Pole—in what he called "an epic trek . . . a journey that would complete the trilogy of the last three great pioneering geographical achievements" (the other two being the ascent of Mt. Everest by Edmund Hillary and Tenzing Norgay in 1953, and the Vivian Fuchs-Edmund Hillary Antarctic crossing in 1958).

Herbert, his three companions, and 34 huskies spent 16 months sledging over pack ice pressured by wind and current into a grinding, churning commotion of 30-foot ice walls and snow-filled valleys; knee-deep slush with all the characteristics of quicksand; young sea ice so thin and flexible that it bent like rubber nearly a foot from its normal plane as the sledges crossed it. They

260

"It is like a struggle between dwarfs and an ogre," wrote the Norwegian explorer Fridtjof Nansen (opposite) of efforts to break the stalwart Fram free from the Arctic Ocean's winter grip (left). But break free she did, north of Spitsbergen on June 13, 1896, after 35 months of drifting with the ice. The crew (below) guided the ship back to Norway, where they were reunited with Nansen and Hjalmar Johansen, who had left them to strike out for the Pole in March 1895. Nansen and Johansen made it to 86° 14' N—a new "farthest north," but still some 260 miles short of the Pole. They struggled by sledge and kayak back to Franz Josef Land, where a British expedition rescued them just as the Fram began to break loose from the pack.

drifted on floes that cracked apart beneath their tents, leaving men leaping desperately to save their lives. After reaching Spitsbergen Herbert declared, "We'd done it. That was the end . . . the end of a period of history."

Not quite. Ten years after Herbert's voyage, British explorer Ranulph Fiennes masterminded—and completed—an epic trek to end all epic treks. He would travel around the world via the Poles. He called his expedition "the last major polar challenge. The joining-up of the feats of the Antarctic, Arctic Ocean and Northwest Passage pioneers into a logical conclusion."

Such grandiose schemes might have been plots concocted to attract movie producers. In a way they were. Great expeditions are expensive. Herbert wrote that he expected his expedition to cost around £53,000, and literary contracts to yield £48,000. No wonder he took along only three rifles for four men. "Just supposing a polar bear comes along," he said. "If you have four rifles, no one's going to pick up a camera."

All the razzle-dazzle has its roots in more pragmatic human endeavor. During the late 1500s, when the Spaniards and Portuguese held a firm grip on trade routes to the rich Orient, other European navies headed north seeking an alternate passage from the Atlantic to the Pacific. Before long they realized that the plan was not only impractical, it was dan-

Polar bears stroll on Arctic ice (opposite) as they might have in 1897 beneath the hot-air balloon of Swedish explorer Salomon Andrée and his two companions, Knut Fraenkel and Nils Strindberg. Their plan was to fly the Eagle *across the Arctic Ocean from Spitsbergen to Siberia or Alaska. But not three days after lifting off, the balloon, leaking and ice coated, bounced through a debilitating fog to its final resting place on the sea ice. The explorers headed south by sledge and boat,* *but perished on an island east of Spitsbergen, where a ship passing 33 years later discovered their remains, diaries, and 17 rolls of film. The photographs (below), painstakingly developed by a Swedish technician, showed the downed balloon and a polar bear the explorers killed. One theory says the men died from trichinosis after eating undercooked bear meat.*

gerous. Men fled ships locked and crushed in the ice only to die of scurvy and starvation. Their efforts were not entirely in vain, though: A succession of explorers mapped hitherto unknown areas, and reports like John Davis's of "great store of Whales" began a whaling boom that lasted until the early 1900s, when bowhead whales neared extinction.

The whales provided Victorian ladies with flexible baleen for their corsets. But from thousands of women over hundreds of years, the Arctic exacted a heavy toll. No fewer than 129 sons and husbands waved a final good-bye when they left British soil to seek the Northwest Passage with John Franklin in 1845. Forty rescue missions took ten years to turn up the frozen remains of some 30 bodies on King William Island.

"The British love for their heroes to die," Wally Herbert once said. Indeed, it was Franklin whom the Royal Geographical Society recognized as the discoverer of the Northwest Passage, even though the men who searched for him mapped most of the territory in which the passage lies, and even though Roald Amundsen finally navigated the labyrinth of icy straits north of Canada's mainland. By then it was 1906, 60 years after Franklin disappeared. And Amundsen was Norwegian. The British needed a new hero—a man who would conquer the South Pole.

It was December 7, 1908—summer in Antarctica. On their stomachs, Ernest Shackleton and his

Triumphant at the North Pole: Matthew Henson, Robert Peary's black companion, poses flanked by four of some fifty able Inuit who helped push Peary in stages toward the Pole in 1908-09. Able indeed—it was the Inuit who taught Peary to travel by dogsled and to make the fur clothing he wore (left, lower). But triumphant? Perhaps not. Some question the ambitious explorer's sketchy records, and wonder why his famous diary entry (opposite) was written on a loose sheet of paper inserted among four blank pages. Graver doubts surrounded the claims of Frederick Cook (left, upper): Five days before Peary's 1909 announcement, Cook said he had reached the Pole in 1908. Cook was discredited by the Royal Geographical Society, and Peary was declared by Congress to be the discoverer of the Pole. But with irrefutable proof absent in both cases, some say neither man stood there—and that no one did until the first confirmed arrival, by Ralph Plaisted, in 1968.

three companions peered over the razor edge of a deep crevasse on Beardmore Glacier, seeing nothing but blackness, hearing nothing but silence; Socks had vanished down there. Socks was the last of the four Manchurian ponies that had left Cape Royds on McMurdo Sound on October 29, 1908, pulling sledges and heading for the South Pole.

One by one the ponies had fallen—sinking up to their bellies in deep snow, skittering helplessly over the ice, always in danger of tumbling into the deep cracks that form in the surfaces of glaciers inching over the earth. It was a miracle that Frank Wild had not plunged with Socks to certain death—the pony had crashed through the fragile snow bridge that hid the crevasse moments after the others had crossed it. Wild, leading the unsteady pony, had fallen too, barely grasping the opposite edge of the chasm with his outstretched hands.

Now Shackleton and Wild and the two others, Jameson Adams and Eric Marshall, would share the burden of the pony's thousand-pound sledge. The men were bruised from countless falls as they tripped and stumbled through fields of sastrugi—wavelike snow ridges sculptured by the wind. Their feet and shins were slashed by sharp ice. Shackleton's heels were cracked open from frostbite and his head ached continuously as they climbed from the Ross Ice Shelf up the Beardmore Glacier to an altitude of nearly 10,000 feet

in the Transantarctic Mountains.

In the even, dead white of sunlight diffused by clouds or mist, they could see no contours on the snow-covered ice. Snow blindness set in. It started with a runny nose, then they saw double, the blood vessels in their eyes swelled, and they felt a grittiness like sand under their lids. Their eyes streamed; their breath froze, then thawed in their beards, and condensed droplets trickled down inside their shirts to freeze again in sheets of ice on their chests.

On January 4, 1909, Shackleton wrote: "The end is in sight. We can only go for 3 more days at the most, for we are weakening rapidly." Five days later they turned around on the Polar Plateau, only 111 miles short of the Pole. The men barely made it back to the *Nimrod* in McMurdo Sound before she was forced in March to flee the encroaching ice of an Antarctic winter.

Shackleton would blame their failure partly on the loss of the pony. They had shot the other ponies, taking some of the meat and stashing the rest in depots for the return trip. If they could have eaten Socks, they might have made it farther south, maybe to the Pole.

Shackleton used ponies to haul sledges because he believed it was cruel to use dogs as pack animals. Even this was a concession to a British belief that nothing was so glorious as the triumph of human brute force over the power of nature. True achievement required true suffering.

An engraving of the north magnetic pole (below) by a member of James Clark Ross's party conveys a playfulness that matches the explorer's fanciful words about what might lie there: "an object as conspicuous and mysterious as the fabled mountain of Sindbad . . . or a magnet as large as Mont Blanc." In May 1831 he arrived at his goal—a featureless landscape near 72°N, 96°W.

Within the decade Ross turned south to circumnavigate Antarctica. In 1841 he entered the sea that would bear his name and encountered there the great tabular icebergs (opposite)—some more than 50 miles long—that calve from the Ross Ice Shelf.

OVERLEAF: Penguins like these might have greeted officers from the ship of French explorer Dumont d'Urville as they disembarked on Antarctica in 1840. D'Urville named the spot Adélie Land after his wife, Adèle. The penguins also inherited the name.

Real men walked, and pulled their sledges behind them.

No matter that experience proved otherwise—that huskies bred by the Inuit in the Arctic were surefooted and capable of pulling tremendous loads. Nansen and Vilhjalmur Stefansson, grandfathers of Arctic travel, knew that. Peary, and later explorers like Herbert and Steger, learned that. But back then, the British had to do it their way. That could be why Robert F. Scott, in 1911, lost the South Pole to Roald Amundsen, the Norwegian. And why Scott lost his life in the bargain.

To some extent, national chauvinism motivated most of them. Peary said in 1906: "To me the final and complete solution of the polar mystery, which has engaged the best thought and interest of some of the best men in the world, is the thing which should be done for the honor and credit of this country, the thing that I must do."

"What matters now," said Scott after Shackleton's failure in 1909, "is that the Pole should be attained by an Englishman."

Beneath the patriotic words, though, lay a drive so intensely personal that for some it approached compulsion beyond all reason.

Ambition. Says psychotherapist Evelyn Stefansson Nef, who traveled the Arctic with her explorer husband, Vilhjalmur Stefansson, before his death in 1962: "It's one of the characteristics that ties them together. The need to be famous."

She says Stefansson was different. "I am a scientist, not a tourist," he once replied when asked why he never cared to reach the North Pole. Stefansson, and others like him, eschewed the "firsts" and the "last great journeys." Dumont d'Urville, despite the orders of King Louis-Philippe in the late 1830s to penetrate as far south as possible in the Weddell Sea for the greater glory of France, cared far more about "the position of the magnetic pole, the knowledge of which is so important for the great problem respecting the laws of terrestrial magnetism."

Apsley Cherry-Garrard's only goal as a member of Scott's last expedition was to snatch a few emperor penguin eggs, incubated in the harsh winter darkness. "You will have your reward," he wrote in *The Worst Journey in the World*, "so long as all you want is a penguin's egg."

The scientists tend not to seek notoriety. But even they can display

On the deck of their corvette—a small ship ill suited to the crushing blows of Antarctic ice—Dumont d'Urville and his crew celebrated crossing the Antarctic Circle in 1840 (left). Their orders were to beat British explorer James Weddell's "farthest south"—74° 15'. But d'Urville was more interested in science than in flag-waving. His observations contributed to a 32-volume work containing watercolors of animals such as the leopard seal and the crab he named Lithodes antarctica *(above).*

A crew member bids adieu to the Endurance in the Weddell Sea. Ernest Shackleton wrote in his diary: "It was a one-sided battle. Millions of tons of ice pressed inexorably upon the gallant little ship which had dared the challenge of the Antarctic." Through the four-month winter night of 1915 the ship had remained locked in the ice; the men aboard had huddled by a coal fire (bottom) and fought World War I in their imaginations. They hoped to reach the continent; instead they fought their way to Elephant Island, where Shackleton and five others left 22 men to wait while they sailed 800 miles to South Georgia in a battered lifeboat. Four months later they returned on a Chilean steamer to rescue everyone.

A relic of Shackleton's 1908-09 march on the South Pole fared better than the Endurance. *The hut at Cape Royds in McMurdo Sound still stands (below). Shackleton wintered there with 14 men before his failed attempt to reach the Pole.*

curiously compulsive behavior at the ends of the Earth. They honor a tradition begun in 1912 by Australian explorer Douglas Mawson, who mapped over 1,800 miles of Antarctica's coast. They hack holes in Antarctic ice and skinny-dip in water that never gets much above freezing.

It helps to be compulsive. Filling a test tube with water from a frozen Antarctic lake involves hours with a gas-powered motor and a ten-inch-thick drill bit with enough extensions to reach 16 feet down. The setup has a torque so strong it drags the men who drive the drill in a slow circle on the ice. Wrote William J. Green of his scientific sojourn in Antarctica: "To be Ahab, to be monomaniacal in this polar quest, whatever its nature, is acceptable behavior. It is the norm."

It must be more than fame or national glory, more than adventure or science. It must be the wonder of a place as harsh as death. A place where in 1986 Steger and his five companions could arrive by dogsled at the North Pole; greet three planes carrying cameramen, reporters, and representatives from the National Geographic Society; and be forced to limit the festivities to a couple of hours so the planes, their engines left running because of the cold, would make it back to civilization on the fuel they could carry. A place where Etienne, arriving ten days later, had to pitch his tent and wait on the drifting ice pack for nearly four more, alone in his triumph, because

the weather would not permit flight.

And it must be the wind that blows the snow in gauze waves over the ice. It must be the blood red sunrise after six months of winter, the million shades of blue in a white landscape, the thunder of fracturing ice, the vapor trails that stretch out like veils behind the dogs.

It must be the place. Green wrote: "In the midst of a sentence that read, 'Water samples were collected with a 6.2 liter Kemmerer bottle attached to nylon line,' I wanted to say something about the afternoon shadows on the mountains or the murmuring of a distant stream or the way the wind was sapping my strength. I wanted to say something about the way water tastes on an antarctic lake after a ten-hour day. These things hovered like ghosts around the edges of scientific prose." They hover in the souls of explorers, adventurers, and scientists all, who answer the call of the ice.

When Richard E. Byrd piloted the Josephine Ford (opposite) over the North Pole in 1926, polar exploration entered a new age. Scientists could now fly to areas where even the most intrepid adventurers had never walked. In 1929 Byrd built an air base called Little America on the Ross Ice Shelf in Antarctica. He spent a winter there (opposite, below) and that summer became the first to fly over the South Pole. Today, scientists make regular visits to both Poles. Scientific bases surround the Arctic Ocean and drift stations float with the pack ice. In Antarctica, some 35 stations representing 18 nations coexist peacefully. During each Antarctic summer, expeditions such as the New Zealand geological survey (below) are dropped by plane into areas untouched by humans to continue exploring the mysteries of this frozen continent.

Roald Amundsen
Robert Falcon Scott

By Michael Parfit

Scott's expedition ship, Terra Nova, *seen from a cavern in an iceberg in McMurdo Sound.*

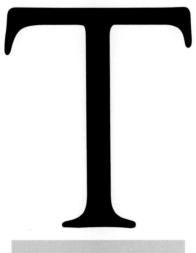

The canvas tent slapped and rattled under the lash of the Antarctic wind, and the three men inside listened without speaking. The wind was their mortal enemy—the wind that pressed through the cloth with its weight of cold, the wind that closed off their retreat, that pinned them to the ice of the Barrier and promised them that now, in the last days of March 1912, this tent would be their grave.

"The causes of the disaster," Robert Falcon Scott wrote slowly, "are not due to faulty organization but to misfortune in all risks which had to be undertaken." One of his feet was already frozen. He was failing of scurvy and cold. The last of the four men who had followed him to the end of the Earth—Birdie Bowers and Scott's old friend, Dr. Bill Wilson—were dying beside him. In the noisy little tent, the events of past years and months must have roared in Scott's ears like the drumming of the canvas: the daydreams of glory that drove him, the years of planning and preparation, and finally the endless toil of the great walk in the cold. Behind the noise, too, he must have heard whispers of the mistakes and defeats he acknowledged by writing those words of denial: the deaths of tractors, of ponies, of dogs, of Edgar Evans and Titus Oates; the triumph of Amundsen.

Amundsen! Amundsen, who left a flag to greet Scott at the Pole, the place that should have been virgin, who left a flag and a letter to be posted to the Norwegian king, as if Scott were a postman. Amundsen! Roald Engebreth Gravning Amundsen!

What did Scott know of this steady Norwegian who had beaten him so simply? He probably did not know his full name. He certainly knew his age: Amundsen was 39, four years younger than Scott. Amundsen was a civilian; Scott was a captain in the British Royal Navy. Amundsen had been to Antarctica in 1898 on the ship *Belgica,* and thus was among the first group of humans to spend a winter in the Antarctic

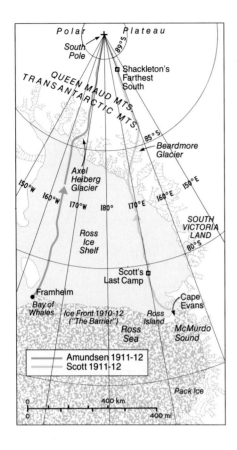

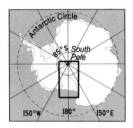

darkness; Scott had led an expedition south in 1901, and returned in 1904. Once, almost exactly two years ago—in March 1910—Scott had tried to meet Amundsen in Norway, but Amundsen, already planning his secret attack on the South Pole, had avoided him. The two men had never met. But in the tent, Amundsen was present—and triumphant.

If Scott let his mind wander back, he might have returned to Norway—his adversary's home. Scott had been there two years ago preparing for this journey. The motor-powered sledge he was depending on for travel on the Barrier ice had run beautifully. Scott had discovered how useful skis could be. He had thought himself a fortunate man.

He had also thought that Amundsen was going north. Amundsen had told the world that he was going to drift across the North Pole in the famous exploration ship *Fram.* The world believed him. Scott believed him. But when Amundsen's hopes of being first to the North Pole had been shattered by the claims of Peary and Cook, his mind had turned secretly but resolutely south.

Amundsen: that big black-and-white man, whom Scott had seen only in photographs, with his long steady face and his cursed equanimity. A man so unlike Scott—did he never have an emotion? Could he even imagine the swarms of doubt, the alternate despair and ecstasy, the agonies of self-evaluation that Scott endured? Amundsen: laconic, imperturbable. Always studying, considering methods: Inuit parkas, aerodynamic tents, the best use of dogs. Even when he was ill with scurvy on the *Belgica,* he made dispassionate notes to himself about how the illness softened and bewildered his own mind.

Were all those Norwegians so confoundingly cool? On his way south, at Melbourne, Scott had received a cable from Amundsen's brother: "Beg leave to inform you *Fram* proceeding Antarctic Amundsen." Suddenly Scott's ponderous expedition of motor sledges, ponies, and foot-slogging had become a race.

In the tent at the end of March, writing was bitter labor, but it was all Scott had left—of his strength, of his longing for glory. "I want to tell you that I was *not* too old for this job," Scott wrote as the snow hissed on the canvas. "It was the younger men that went under first. . . . After all we are setting a good example to our countrymen, if not by getting into a tight place, by facing it like men when we were there."

He wrote on, using his last energy on prose, gifted as few are with the chance to arrange and justify his life for others' eyes as his own filled with death. "I may not have proved a great explorer, but we have done the greatest march ever made and come very near to great success."

Confined by the flapping canvas, with his days full of the fury and cold of the storm, and his memory oppressed by nearly five months of steady plodding through snow and ice, he could have had only a glimpse of the full drama of the past two years. He could recall in detail the arrival of his ship, *Terra Nova,* at Ross Island in January 1911, and he knew Amundsen had disembarked at about the same time from *Fram* at the Bay of Whales, an indent in the enormous shelf of ice at the edge of the Ross Sea that both expeditions called the Barrier. Since the explo-

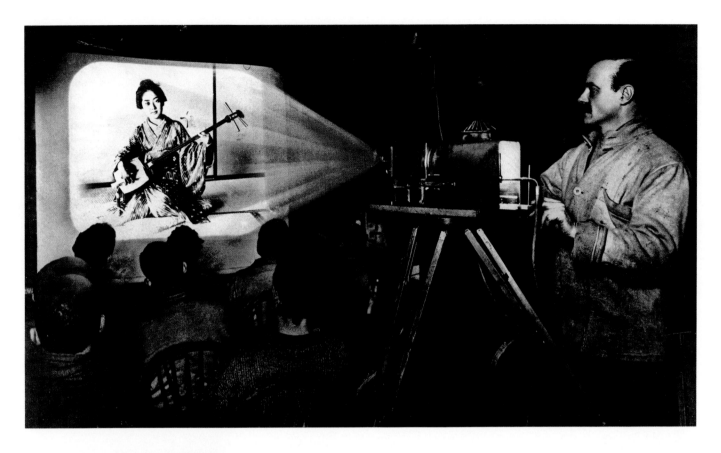

Work and play before the race: sewing at the Norwegian base, Framheim; movies for the British at Cape Evans.

ration season in Antarctica was so short, he knew that Amundsen too had spent the remaining months of daylight in 1911 planting depots of food up toward the Pole and testing his men and equipment.

For both teams the appearance of the sun in August signaled the start of the race to the Pole. Amundsen had begun fretting as soon as it was light. He was not, after all, immune to anxiety: "I always have the idea that I am the only one who is left behind," Amundsen wrote later. His haste drove him to an almost disastrous early start—September 8. Temperatures were in the minus 60s, so cold the heels of the men began to freeze. He had to retreat. He and the four others he had chosen to go south did not start off behind their dog teams again until October 19—but that was still 13 days before Scott harnessed his ponies and began.

"I don't know what to think of Amundsen's chances," Scott wrote in his diary just before he set off. "If he gets to the Pole, it must be before we do, as he is bound to travel fast with dogs and pretty certain to start early. On this account I decided at a very early date to act exactly as I should have done had he not existed. Any attempt to race must have wrecked my plan, besides which it doesn't appear the sort of thing one is out for." As if to persuade himself he wrote, "After all, it is the work that counts, not the applause that follows."

In the tent on the Barrier at the bitter end of March, the work was over, but Scott still must leave a record, as if he knew that the following spring expedition members searching from the base camp on Ross

279

> *The English have loudly and openly told the world that skis and dogs are unusable in these regions and that fur clothes are rubbish. We will see—we will see.*
>
> ROALD AMUNDSEN

A swig of whiskey for a chilled pony. Eventually, British ponies failed; Norwegian huskies fared better.

Island would find the tent and the bodies, the 35 pounds of geological samples they had hauled with them, scientific to the last; and the diaries under his shoulders. The wind and the noise of the slapping canvas went on and on, like torture. The three men spoke little in their pain and weariness, but Scott wrote. "Every detail of our food supplies, clothing and depots made on the interior ice sheet and over that long stretch of 700 miles to the Pole and back," he wrote in a statement he called message to public, "worked out to perfection."

In his delirium had he forgotten the disasters recorded in the diary he had written all those days? Could he forget the sight of those precious motor sledges broken down on the Barrier, the snow gathering around them like a shroud? Then the ponies had floundered and suffered so cruelly that they had to be shot far short of their goal, at the place called Shambles Camp. And there was the matter of dogs.

In the tent he yearned for the sound of dogs pulling sledges to his rescue—the dogs he had sent back to the base when he was more than 400 miles from the Pole. It was not just squeamishness at the "sordid necessity" of feeding dogmeat to dogs that had made him reject them; he was, after all, quite willing to shoot and eat his ponies. Nor was it just his expressed concern that dogs weren't reliable. He simply didn't want their help. In leaving the dogs behind he had chosen his daydreamed path to glory, the road, he had once written, on which men must struggle alone, and "the conquest is more nobly and splendidly won."

For Amundsen the only path that mattered was the one to the Pole. At about the same latitude at which Scott had sent the last dogs back to base, Amundsen had written: "It was a sheer marvel . . . that the dogs accomplished today. . . . 17 miles, with 5,000 foot climb. Come and say that dogs cannot be used here." In his last extremity, Scott must have had some idea how the dogs had pulled Amundsen away from him, so quickly and so far that on December 9, when Scott's team was killing ponies at Shambles Camp, 409 miles from the Pole, Amundsen had fewer than 115 miles to go. Even then, Amundsen was anxious. There, farther south than anyone had ever been, Amundsen and one of his men noticed a dog sniffing the southerly breeze and worried that Scott was ahead.

They needn't have been concerned. It had been warm on the high plateau for Amundsen—"Quite summer like:–0.4°F." But that same warm weather dumped wet snow on Scott, more than 200 miles behind, and raised the temperature at his lower altitude to above freezing; they joked about turning the tent into a boat. Melting snow soaked everything. "A hopeless feeling descends," Scott wrote in his diary, "What immense patience is needed for such occasions!"

But in the somber light of his canvas tomb, Scott found glory in the adversity he cursed. To him the greatness of the march was that the men did it all themselves, against odds that had been partly of their own making. When the machines were gone, and the ponies were gone, and the dogs were gone, Scott slipped into his harness and seemed, for once,

281

content. The terrible hardship of the climb to the plateau's 10,000-foot elevation was simple and difficult; it cleansed him of his doubt. He just put on the skis, leaned to the harness, and pulled. "I was very jubilant; all difficulties seemed to be vanishing. . . ." On Christmas Day, Birdie Bowers wrote, "Scott got fairly wound up and went on and on. . . ."

On the journey went, day blazing into day, with no ease of darkness, no cease of wind. But by Christmas Scott had already been beaten.

On January 16—two and a half months from the start—Bowers saw a hump of snow that looked man-made. He chose to think it was built by the wind. Then, Scott wrote: "half an hour later he detected a black speck ahead. Soon we knew that this could not be a natural snow feature. We marched on, found that it was a black flag tied to a sledge bearer; near by the remains of a camp; sledge tracks and ski tracks going and coming and the clear trace of dogs' paws—many dogs."

Amundsen had been there just a month before. The Pole was conquered. All Scott could do was look at the things Amundsen had left there in a tent, pick up the triumphant letter Amundsen had written to the king of Norway to make his own simple record in case he didn't get home. The presence of the letter, with a note asking Scott to forward it, at least showed Amundsen's respect for Scott's ability to get to the Pole and back, but that was no solace. On the night of the black flag, Scott wrote, "All the day dreams must go."

This moment, more than any others, must have haunted Scott in his final days, two months later, after the long and bitter trek homeward, after the rations proved inadequate, the fuel dwindled, and the cold and the scurvy wore the five men down; after Edgar Evans, ill and injured, fell in the snow and died; after Titus Oates, ruined by his frozen feet, volunteered for death, leaving behind the legend that Scott's diary gave him: "He said, 'I am just going outside and may be some time.' He went out into the blizzard and we have not seen him since." But Scott, when he stood at the Pole and wrote in his diary, "Great God! this is an awful place. . . ." would have been astonished to know how ambivalent Amundsen himself was as the victor.

"I had better be honest," Amundsen wrote later, "and admit straight out that I have never known any man to be placed in such a diametrically opposite position to the goal of his desires . . . the North Pole itself . . . had attracted me from childhood, and here I was at the South Pole. Can anything more topsy-turvy be imagined?"

Late in March, trapped on the Barrier in the impossible wind, 12 miles from the food cache known as One Ton Depot, Scott could not have known what was to come: That Amundsen would return to muted acclaim and that he himself would be honored beyond any of those daydreams. In a sense the journey gave each his goal. For Amundsen, who disappeared on a rescue flight in the far north in 1928, the journey itself was, as the historian Roland Huntford has written, his work of art. To the world he became the man who had made it look easy. But he had never sought fame; exploration itself was enough. Scott had written what was true of Amundsen: The applause was less important.

I wish to repeat now, what I said when I first heard of the presence of Amundsen, that this Expedition is going to lay its plans and carry on with its work just as if Amundsen did not exist.

ROBERT F. SCOTT

282

A victorious Amundsen (middle row, center), with ship and expedition crews, heading home.

But Britain, sliding into a war, needed once more to hear of honor and death, of valiant defeat, of the tragedy of one man, trapped by his flaws, still giving all. England would forgive Scott his failings—even honor them—if he died well. So at last, in the tent, perhaps he knew: He had come to play the Light Brigade for the Empire. All he had to do was write the noble words. Kathleen, his wife, would edit them for strength. That was the gift he left beside his body: "We are weak writing is difficult but for my own sake I do not regret this journey which has shown that Englishmen can endure hardships, help one another and meet death with as great a fortitude as ever in the past."

Bill Wilson and Birdie Bowers died in their sleep, folded in their sleeping bags. Robert Falcon Scott pulled his coat open to the cold and did it the hard way.

Our story on the feelings and imaginings of Scott and Amundsen is based largely on their diaries, Scott's Last Expedition *and* The South Pole.

Into the Deeps

By Philip Kopper

A sea fan and a group of redlings welcome a diver to the intricate ecosystem of a Red Sea reef. Plant and animal life abounds in the ocean's topmost layers, opened to explorers by the introduction of the Aqua-Lung in 1943. Farther down, by 5,000 feet, sunlight fades to darkness, and marine life dwindles to one-fiftieth of its surface numbers. This abyssal realm, where humans can venture only with submersibles, waits nearly untouched around a globe that is 70 percent underwater.

Two scuba divers tumble off a boat anchored in Cozumel's lee, shatter the shimmering surface of the Caribbean Sea, and sink to the reef 40 feet below. They fall weightlessly through crystal blue and glide like birds, then drift down through gardens bright with fish. As a barracuda pauses on patrol, one diver snaps its solemn portrait. A squadron of iridescent squid jets by. The divers follow a bank of ghostly rocks and thread a maze of coral.

It could be called the oldest frontier. Since first we looked beneath the waves, humans have been drawn to the undersea realm. In Mesopotamia, archaeologists have uncovered mother-of-pearl inlays that date to 4500 B.C. And early Greek writers lavished praise on sponge divers, considered braver than warriors.

Yet it is also the newest frontier. Not until Jacques-Yves Cousteau introduced the Aqua-Lung could scientists freely explore the ocean's upper layers as these Cozumel divers do now. To go deeper was even harder; the first men to reach the lowest seafloor did so just 14 months ahead of the first to reach orbit. Within the past two decades, discoveries from the deeps have revolutionized long-held notions about our planet.

Our progress into the ocean's depths is a history of inventions. Although skilled swimmers like Japan's *ama* divers and Polynesian spear fishermen commonly plunged a hundred feet for food, coral, or pearls, no free diver could stay down longer than one breath of air lasts.

People used tools to increase that air supply. Ancient Greek sponge divers would lower an inverted pot into the water and breathe the air trapped inside. In Renaissance Italy, humans hung in the water on suspended platforms fitted with glass bells. In 1620 a Dutch inventor took King James I of England for a ride under the Thames in one of the first self-propelled underwater craft. Oars fitted with greased leather gaskets powered it, and air came through a tube from bellows on the surface.

In 1837 the invention of the helmeted diving suit brought shallow seafloors closer. Salvage and construction workers used these clumsy suits, tethered to the surface by air hoses. But if they stayed below for too long, or went too deep, they faced another problem: pressure.

With every 33 feet of underwater depth, pressure increases by 14.7 pounds per square inch—the weight of the atmosphere at sea level. Even at swimming pool depths, water pressure starts to squeeze nitrogen into the blood and tissues as bubbles, which are reabsorbed if the pressure eases slowly. But a diver who ascends too fast suffers the bends: crippling agony in the joints and muscles and sometimes fatal embolisms.

Late in the 19th century physiologists learned to prevent the condition by carefully timed ascent. Dives were still limited by the time needed

to decompress. Scientists discovered other dysfunctions caused by the gases divers breathed: Pure oxygen, pressurized at depths below 25 feet, caused convulsions. Nitrogen caused narcosis, the mind-addling "rapture of the deep," which could transform even experienced divers into giggling clowns willing to share their air with fish. The solution: Match gas mixtures to different situations.

While helmets, diving suits, and new breathing mixtures helped open the upper ocean to exploration, the first serious study of the deep ocean began on the surface, under the guidance of Matthew Fontaine Maury. A U. S. Navy lieutenant with a flair for prose, Maury was in command at the Navy's Depot of Charts and Instruments when he launched history's first major deep-sea survey in 1849.

Maury dispatched two ingeniously equipped research ships, *Taney* and *Dolphin,* to sound the Atlantic systematically. Using weighted lines, his ships made new readings of the ocean depths. They also collected seafloor samples that Maury called "the feathers from old ocean's bed," from depths never reached before.

His chart of the Atlantic was the first bathymetric picture of an entire ocean, but it erroneously showed depths of more than seven miles, a distortion caused, perhaps, by the ship's drift, currents, and other factors. *Dolphin* also recorded a rising bottom in mid-Atlantic, a plateau that he dubbed Middle Ground. Little did he know its true extent.

In 1855 Maury wrote the earliest oceanography text, with a characteristically exuberant pen: "The wonders of the sea are as marvelous as the glories of the heavens; and they proclaim, in songs divine, that they too are the work of holy fingers." His images were devout, but his goal concrete: to bring "the physical geography of the sea regularly within the domains of science."

A British square-rigger named H.M.S. *Challenger* advanced that aim in 1872. Outfitted with two well-equipped laboratories, she embarked on a three-and-a-half-year exploration around the world. Her five scientists, the first interdisciplinary oceanographic team, sampled ocean water at many depths and found that it varied in salinity and temperature. *Challenger* sounded the Pacific floor near Earth's deepest point, the Mariana Trench. The expedition collected sessile and free-swimming organisms, identified 4,417 new plants and animals, and compiled enough data to fill 50 volumes. When *Challenger*'s leaders announced the discovery of a ridge running south from Maury's Middle Ground, speculation revived about a "lost Atlantis."

Answers would only come with new technology, which military interests supplied. As navies deployed better submarines, they also developed echoing devices that could find an unseen hull or chart the seafloor with new accuracy. In 1925 the German research ship *Meteor,* armed with early sonar, set out to make

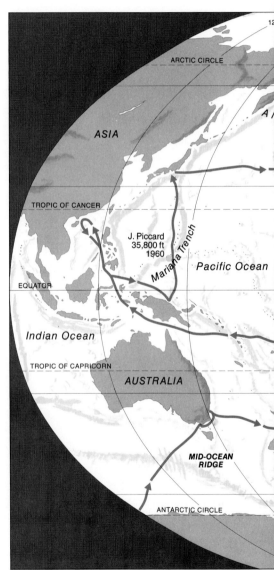

15° of latitude = 1,035 statute miles

286

Scientists peer through microscopes—one a long-barreled stereoscopic model—aboard H.M.S. Challenger. On her pioneering voyage of 79,292 miles, the British research vessel laid the foundation of modern oceanography, taking soundings around the globe with miles of hemp line. Dredges brought up samples for shipboard laboratories. Challenger returned with 13,000 kinds of plants and animals, proving the unexpected: Life could exist at great depths.

On a route crisscrossing the Atlantic (below), the German *Meteor* was first to record an entire ocean's currents. The succeeding decades brought more advances: William Beebe's bathysphere trips, Jacques-Yves Cousteau's Aqua-Lung, Auguste and Jacques Piccard's bathyscaph dives. Yet scientists have seen only a tiny fraction of Earth's 140 million square miles of ocean floor.

Not until the 1950s did geologists realize that a single feature, the Mid-Ocean Ridge, snaked through every ocean basin. While examining it with deep-towed cameras and an abyssal submarine off the Galápagos, startled investigators discovered unique colonies of sea life feeding around hot, mineral-rich springs far beyond the reach of sunlight. More vent systems were found at 21° North, and one rich in manganese on the Juan de Fuca Ridge. Project TAG (Trans-Atlantic Geotraverse) located the first vigorous vent system in the Atlantic.

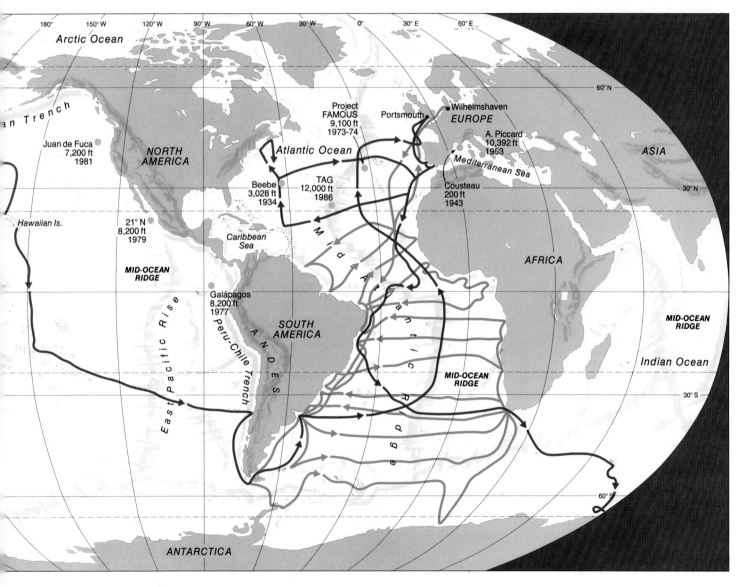

─── *Challenger* Expedition 1872-76
─── *Meteor* Expedition 1925-27
● Dive Site

In the three centuries since a crude diving bell took man 50 feet below, explorers have reached farther and farther into the deeps. Darkness and cold increase with depth, along with crushing pressure that tests the stoutest hulls. When Trieste hovered in the deepest known part of the sea, she had to withstand pressures of more than 960 atmospheres, or 960 times the weight of air at sea level. Scientists today often stay on the surface, operating their undersea vehicles by remote controls.

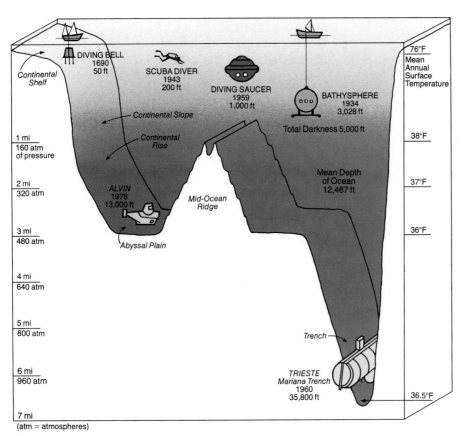

DIVING BELL
1690
50 ft

Continental Shelf

SCUBA DIVER
1943
200 ft

DIVING SAUCER
1959
1,000 ft

BATHYSPHERE
1934
3,028 ft

76°F
Mean Annual Surface Temperature

Continental Slope

Continental Rise

Total Darkness 5,000 ft

38°F

1 mi
160 atm of pressure

ALVIN
1978
13,000 ft

Mid-Ocean Ridge

Mean Depth of Ocean
12,467 ft

37°F

2 mi
320 atm

3 mi
480 atm

Abyssal Plain

36°F

4 mi
640 atm

5 mi
800 atm

Trench

6 mi
960 atm

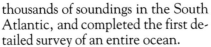

TRIESTE
Mariana Trench
1960
35,800 ft

36.5°F

7 mi

(atm = atmospheres)

thousands of soundings in the South Atlantic, and completed the first detailed survey of an entire ocean.

Meteor found no buried island of Atlantis but did show that the Mid-Atlantic Ridge curved around the Cape of Good Hope toward the Indian Ocean. Future research would establish the existence of a 46,000-mile mountain belt winding through every ocean: the Mid-Ocean Ridge, largest geologic feature on Earth. Geologists continued to wonder why

it was there, but for a closeup look they would have to wait.

Firsthand observation of the deeps was progressing slowly. In the 1930s naturalist William Beebe collaborated with engineer Otis Barton on the bathysphere (Greek for "deep ball"). Fitted with two observation ports, it dangled from a support ship's cable—a throwback to the suspended diving bells of old.

In 1934 Beebe and Barton rode it 3,028 feet down into the seas near

Helmeted in wicker to cushion a hard landing, Auguste Piccard (opposite, at right) pauses during preparations for a balloon ascent to the stratosphere in 1931. This Swiss physicist probed the upper atmosphere and then invented the bathyscaph called Trieste, a kind of underwater balloon, to explore the ocean depths with his son Jacques (in sagging knee socks). In 1953, father and son filled the huge metal bathyscaph with lighter-than-water gasoline off Naples, crawled into the vessel's

round cabin, and dived to 10,392 feet, deeper than anyone had gone before.

Less than a decade later, Jacques (below, far right) repairs the lurching Trieste. On this 1960 dive for the U. S. Navy, Jacques rode the submersible on an 8½-hour journey down into the 35,800-foot Mariana Trench. Trieste dumped 11 tons of steel shot at intervals to control her descent and ascent.

"Neither sun, nor moon, nor stars," wrote Auguste after one such dive, "nothing but opaque gloom."

Bermuda, observing new species as they went. Had Beebe's ball, tethered to its mother ship, approached the bottom, it might have been dashed against the seafloor as the tender bobbed on the surface.

Auguste Piccard, a Swiss physicist famed for his balloon designs, and his son Jacques overcame that problem with an untethered submersible. They called it a bathyscaph ("deep boat"), a thin-walled hollow float supporting a small, pressure-resistant cabin. It worked on the same principle as the high-altitude balloon Auguste Piccard took into the stratosphere in 1931. Employing the buoyancy principle, each vehicle rose and sank in the surrounding medium, whether air or water, by changing the mass within its suspending floats. Piccard's most ambitious bathyscaph, *Trieste*, had a float filled with lighter-than-water gasoline, which cold water compressed, causing the craft to descend. Free of fragile links

to a tender, the *Trieste* could land on the seafloor; she rose as his balloon had: by dumping ballast.

In January 1960 Jacques Piccard and U. S. Navy Lt. Don Walsh voyaged down 35,800 feet in *Trieste* to the floor of the Mariana Trench, a depth no one has reached since. From their vessel, squeezed by eight tons of pressure per square inch, Piccard and Walsh saw what many scientists had thought impossible at such depths—complex life. "A flat-

A polka-dot starfish in fluorescent camouflage spreads suction-cupped arms on coral 30 feet down in the Red Sea. Such sights reward sport divers, first ushered into the depths by Jacques-Yves Cousteau (below) and the Aqua-Lung. With underwater cameras, Cousteau brought millions of armchair aquanauts into his undersea world. In 1959 his "diving saucer" (right) lowered two divers to 1,000 feet, protected by a shell of pressure-resistant forged steel $^3/_4$ inch thick.

fish at the very nadir of the earth," Piccard wrote after seeing a fish briefly lit by *Trieste*'s lights. But this fish had eyes! Of what use were they in that blackness, he wondered? *Trieste* had no way to collect specimens, so the question remained.

About the same time that Auguste Piccard was working to free the bathysphere from its tether, Jacques-Yves Cousteau was freeing helmeted divers from theirs. In 1943 Cousteau developed the most liberating undersea invention of all, the portable Aqua-Lung. Why? Because, Cousteau said, "I needed it. All the things tested before were junk!"

For decades, divers had been trying breathing gadgets, all awkward, dangerous, or inefficient. One spewed air from bottles nonstop; others required the swimmer to squeeze a rubber bulb with his hand. Cousteau wanted "an automatic device that would release air to the diver without his thinking about it."

He explained it to Emile Gagnan, an engineer in wartime Paris who was making valves that allowed automobiles to run on cooking gas. Gagnan devised a regulator, a one-way valve the size of a man's wallet, connected to a mouthpiece. Each time a diver inhaled, it brought a supply of compressed air from a tank on his back, while another hose delivered exhaled air to exhaust ports. The valve supplied air at the right pressure at any depth. At last, divers could move with total freedom,

swim, and even turn somersaults.

Today, Cousteau says "devouring curiosity and obstinacy" drove him to find the right tools. In later years his team invented new devices, including battery-powered undersea scooters to extend the diver's range, and a "diving saucer" no bigger than a compact car for deeper work.

Cousteau considers himself an explorer more than a scientist. His films pay for further exploration and, he hopes, feed a love of the water world as deep as his: "I like to have guests at my table . . . and serve a meal of visions."

Equipped with what is now called scuba (self-contained underwater breathing apparatus), scientists began exploring Cousteau's world. Fishery experts discovered how conventional trawls damaged the fishes' habitat. Archaeologists found shipwrecks: undersea time capsules that preserved relics of ancient cultures. Diving surveys showed that pollution had alarmingly reduced natural flora and fauna in the upper Mediterranean. Biologists could at last observe marine organisms in their habitats, and put many myths to rest, such as the notion that sharks constantly cruised in order to breathe.

Perhaps the most surprising discovery about ocean life, however, was to come as scientists prepared to explore the Mid-Ocean Ridge. By the 1960s, magnetic readings of the ocean floor had helped gain general acceptance for the theory of plate tectonics: that all of the Earth's sur-

face rode on moving crustal plates. Where an ocean plate met a continental plate, the ocean floor slid beneath, forming trenches like the Mariana. Plates appeared to spread apart at the Mid-Ocean Ridge.

A firsthand look could confirm the theory, and new kinds of submersibles, smaller and less cumbersome than bathyscaphs, were now available. *Alvin*, an American minisub only 25 feet long, was easy to ship from place to place. Its robot arms could pick objects off the seafloor.

In 1974 *Alvin* investigated the Mid-Atlantic Ridge during Project FAMOUS (French-American Mid-Ocean Undersea Study). The trip down to the ridge took one and a half hours at a hundred feet a minute. There *Alvin*'s floodlights lit up treasures more precious than gold for explorer-geologist Robert D. Ballard: young pillow lava amid the mountainous terrain of the deep.

"We had to prove our contentions" that Earth was always being recreated, Ballard recalled. "When we first laid eyes on the obviously fresh lava, it was as if there lay the true birthplace of the Earth's crust."

The pillow-shaped rock had solidified when molten magma from the mantle, the layer below Earth's crust, came in contact with cold water. This recent volcanism meant crustal plates were indeed moving apart at the ridge. As new rock formed, it piled higher, building hills on the ocean floor. These were later pulled apart as the Earth's plates

wedged slowly away from each other, making room for newer lava to come billowing through.

Ballard dived again aboard *Alvin* in 1977 to the Galápagos Rift in the Pacific portion of the Mid-Ocean Ridge, where he and his colleagues suspected there were hydrothermal vents. They found the vents, which were fueling undreamed-of habitats.

Until then scientists had assumed that all food chains depended on sunlight, which could be converted

Oasis in a midnight desert (opposite): A fish and 18-inch tube worms flourish near a hydrothermal vent far under the Pacific's surface. Minisub divers using a temperature gauge found a "black smoker" (right, lower) of mineral-rich water at more than 662°F (350°C). Craft like Alvin (right) take explorers to the deeps to retrieve samples, study life, and even snap a self-portrait with a camera positioned by a flexible arm.

to food by plants through photosynthesis. They theorized that even creatures of the abyss relied on food filtering down from the sunlit layers above. (Perhaps Piccard's fish used its eyes to hunt small bioluminescent creatures that fed on this organic "snow.") Yet here in the pitch black was an ecosystem based not on photosynthesis but on chemosynthesis.

From their portholes *Alvin*'s passengers saw vents spouting milky blue water. Seawater that had seeped down toward the mantle was returning in superheated springs, rich in dissolved minerals like manganese and sulfur compounds. Bacteria absorbed the hydrogen sulfide and converted it into the organic products necessary for life, thus beginning the food chain for a surprising community of deep-sea animals: blind crabs, giant clams, and scarlet-plumed tube worms twelve feet tall.

Ballard plans each of his dives as an exploration—to a place never seen before. He caught the world's imagination in 1985 when, using a million-dollar camera sled named *Argo*, he found the *Titanic*, 12,500 feet deep, in an Atlantic canyon. In 1986 he took *Alvin* to visit and photograph the noble wreck.

Ballard points out that since 70 percent of what he calls Planet Ocean is submerged, "most of Earth has not been explored. We know less about the ocean's bottom than the moon's backside. Clearly the Lewis and Clark period of exploration in the deep sea is still underway."

William Beebe

By Thomas B. Allen

William Beebe wriggling into the sunlight after a three-hour dive; the inventor of the bathysphere, Otis Barton (in shorts), looks on.

Most afternoons, the Beebe boy disappeared. To watch the sunset and write about it, he said. An odd little boy. He began keeping a journal in 1889, when he was 12 years old. Already a naturalist, he wrote one of his earliest entries on an August day that year: "Today, I saw two Monarch Butterflies, *Danais archippus*, flying south."

And then there was the day he came running home, breathless and frightened. What had upset him so? Something about a kite, about the awful loneliness of a kite. No one in his little New Jersey town really knew him. He walked not in a world of childhood but in another world, a place full of mystery and discovery that he desperately tried to describe. He would rarely share his journal with anyone, or tell anyone about his fears. But, many years later, he wrote about the kite: "I remember pulling in a kite with all my might, trembling with terror, for I had sensed the ghastly isolation of that bit of paper aloft in sheer space, and the tug of the string appalled me with the thought of being myself drawn up and up, away from the solid earth."

When William Beebe wrote that, he was no longer a boy and he had already been like that kite. He had been drawn away from the solid Earth, not by going up and up but by going down and down . . . beneath the sea. There he found fame as a writer about the wonders of the undersea world, a new world he introduced to generations of readers. William Beebe, the man, had tethered himself to fame, but even as he soared into the glittery realm of the celebrity, he felt that he was losing touch with the world of the scientist, where people were expected to keep their feet on the ground. "Notorious," he jokingly called himself.

Beebe's underwater career began in 1925, when he donned a crude copper diving helmet and in the waters of the Galápagos discovered sea-

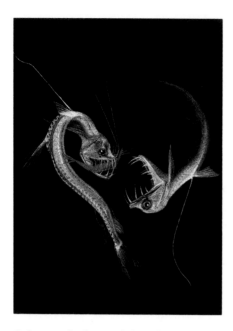

Saber-toothed Viperfish and shrimp at 1,700 feet, as rendered by an artist from Beebe's descriptions and notes.

scapes and creatures that rivaled in mystery and beauty what he had seen on land. He found a watery realm of towering ebony cliffs and jet black sand, scarlet crabs and a "great dusky octopus" that "slides out of its cave, perceives me, and, with a change of emotion, shifts its color to brick red and then to mottled red and gray."

He recorded sights never before seen, and he wrote about them with a sense of enchantment, not scientific detachment. And what enchanted readers often infuriated the scientists Beebe still considered his peers. Beebe did indeed have scientific credentials. He was head of the New York Zoological Society's Department of Tropical Research. He wrote for scientific journals. His four-volume monograph on pheasants of the world still stands as an important work. But a scientist did not write for the public or become the subject of a *New Yorker* cartoon. A scientist did not get divorced with messy publicity, as Beebe had, early in his career. A scientist did not go dancing in Manhattan jazz joints or employ comely young women as expedition members. A scientist did not become a celebrity, especially in an age that made celebrities of a flagpole sitter or a fan dancer.

On the printed page, he exuded humor, warmth, and a conspiratorial charm that invited readers to explore nature's wonders. Through 23 books and hundreds of articles, his army of faithful readers followed. But in person, Beebe could be aloof, sensitive to criticism, tough on assistants who did not work as hard as he did, and disdainful of some scientific peers. One day Beebe walked into a New York club where a friend was talking to Ivan T. Sanderson, a former British Museum scientist turned popular science writer. Since Beebe's own popular books about trekking through jungles had made him a celebrity, the friend, thinking that Beebe and Sanderson had something in common, said, "I don't believe you have met Ivan Sanderson, Will." Beebe looked coldly at Sanderson, the comfortable celebrity, and said, "No. And I never shall." Beebe turned and walked out of the room. A scientist should not associate with popularizers whom he considered reckless.

Beebe was a superb—and popular—interpreter of science. He had the instincts of a showman, though he denied that role as he grandly played it. What scientist would allow a radio announcer on a scientific expedition? Beebe did. In an era of hoopla and quests for frivolous firsts, scientists were not supposed to break records, but Beebe broke them. It was one way to get attention—and money—for other expeditions.

His vehicle was the bathysphere, the steel diving chamber that enabled Beebe to plunge to depths that humans had never seen. The bathysphere weighed 5,000 pounds and was more than four and a half feet in diameter. Its oxygen tanks provided about a six-hour air supply. Trays of soda lime absorbed carbon dioxide, while calcium chloride absorbed moisture. More than half a mile of $7/_8$-inch, nontwisting steel cable connected the bathysphere to a steam-driven winch on the deck of a tender. Tied to the cable at intervals were rubber-sheathed wires that sent electric power to the searchlights in the bathysphere and linked its telephone to one on the deck.

Beebe in the 20-pound copper diving helmet used on some of his earliest dives, off Bermuda.

Otis Barton had invented the bathysphere, financed its construction, and accompanied Beebe on every major dive. But Barton earned scant fame. Beebe in fact claimed that the inspiration for the bathysphere came from Teddy Roosevelt. And proof? "There remains," Beebe said, "only a smudged bit of paper with a cylinder drawn by myself and a sphere outlined by Colonel Roosevelt. . . ."

In a 1930 dive the bathysphere had taken Beebe down to 1,426 feet, a new record. At 600 feet, Beebe's disembodied voice crackled on the ship's telephone wire: "Only dead men have sunk below this." He wrote about the experience, in his now distinctive popular style, for the NATIONAL GEOGRAPHIC magazine: "Long strings of salpa drifted past, lovely as the finest lace, and schools of jellyfish throbbed on their directionless but energetic road through life."

Two years later, while preparing for a deeper dive, he sent the bathysphere down empty to 3,000 feet. When he hauled it up, it was almost full of water. As he and an assistant began to open the hatch, the water shot out under tremendous pressure. He concluded a dramatic account of the event with a dire note: If he had been in the bathysphere that day, "in the inky blackness we should have been crushed into shapeless tissues by nothing more substantial than air and water."

Thus adding death-defying daredevil to his showman role, in 1933 he asked the National Geographic Society to sponsor an expedition to explore the ocean deeps off the Bermuda island of Nonsuch, his usual diving site. He did not openly promise to break his own deep-diving record. But he accepted—along with a $10,000 grant—the Geographic's stipulation that the expedition would include "three descents in the bathysphere to approximately one-half mile depth. . . ."

Beebe readied the bathysphere, then on display at the Century of Progress Exposition in Chicago. On August 15, 1934, Beebe and Barton curled into the cold sphere and took up their stations at round quartz windows three inches thick.

The moment the bathysphere was hoisted to a boom and swung over the sea, Gloria Hollister, Beebe's beautiful young research associate, began speaking and listening on the deck-to-depths telephone. Beebe kept up his end of the conversation as he descended. They had agreed that five seconds of silence from the bathysphere signaled danger. So not all of the dialogue was scientific. "Gosh, it's cold," Beebe said. "Wear your red flannels next time," Hollister replied.

Beebe depended on Hollister to write down what he saw. And if he did not adequately describe what he saw, she would ask questions. "I willfully shut my eyes," Beebe wrote, "or turned them into the bathysphere to avoid whatever bewilderment might come while I was searching my memory for details of what had barely faded from my eye."

He now lived for these dives, when he knew no fear of the unknown sea or his unknown self, when, "forehead pressed close to the cold glass," he felt "a tremendous wave of emotion, a real appreciation of what was momentarily almost superhuman, cosmic . . . two conscious

Vanity Fair, 1933: "Professor William Beebe, gourmet and ichthyologist, secretly fries his new discovery, instead of pickling it for posterity."

human beings sat and peered into the abyssal darkness as we dangled in mid-water, isolated as a lost planet in outermost space."

"Surprises came at every few feet, and again the mass of life was totally unexpected, the total of creatures seen unbelievable. . . . At 2,100 feet two large fish . . . lighted up and then became one with the darkness about them. . . ." At 2,500 feet, he saw a "marine monster" about 20 feet long—"the supreme sight of the expedition."

Beebe ordered the dive ended with only a few turns of cable still left on the winch's drum. "Before we began to ascend, I had to stop making notes of my own, so numb were my fingers from the cold steel of the window sill. To change from my cushion to the metal floor was like shifting to a seat on a cake of ice," he wrote. The bathysphere had reached 3,028 feet—a record that stood for 15 years.

Beebe the showman liked the idea of breaking a record, but not Beebe the scientist. He later claimed that Gilbert Hovey Grosvenor, President of the National Geographic Society, had "demanded no condition of a new record, which is why I gave it to him." Beebe vowed that never again would he attempt record-breaking dives, "which really have no scientific value." He knew his dives for records had made him more vulnerable to the barbs of scientists. But wonder filled the man as it had filled the lonely child, and he had to rhapsodize about it:

"As fish after fish swam into my restricted line of vision—fish, which, heretofore, I had seen only dead and in my nets—as I saw their colors and . . . their activities and modes of swimming and clear evidence of their sociability or solitary habits, I felt that all the trouble and cost and risk were repaid many fold. . . . After these dives were past, when I came again to examine the deep-sea treasures in my nets, I would feel as an astronomer might who looks through his telescope after having rocketed to Mars and back. . . ."

On his dives Beebe marvelously, if unscientifically, described fish that he recognized, along with several he claimed as new species. His Pallid Sailfin was two feet long with "an unpleasant pale, olive drab" color, "the hue of water-soaked flesh," its body "bathed in a strange luminosity." His big-eyed Five-lined Constellation Fish glowed with strange yellow and purple lights. The six-foot-long Untouchable Bathysphere Fish, *Bathysphaera intacta,* had fangs in its large jaw and a "single line of strong lights, pale bluish," strung along its body.

Copeia, the journal of ichthyology and herpetology, scoffed at Beebe's fish stories. The reviewer especially mocked the Five-lined Constellation Fish: "I am forced to suggest that what the author saw might have been a phosphorescent coelenterate whose lights were beautified by halation in passing through a misty film breathed onto the quartz window by Mr. Beebe's eagerly appressed face."

No one ever reported seeing *Bathysphaera intacta* or the Five-lined Constellation Fish again. But not until 1986 did anyone hover off Bermuda as Beebe had, unobtrusive in his bathysphere. In a way, that zone of the sea remains Beebe's memorial. Perhaps someday others will see the wonders he saw, and science will accept his discoveries.

The New Yorker, *1934: "But Dr. Beebe? Where is he?"*

The half-mile dive climaxed Beebe's already long career, but for the rest of his life he would continue to look and wonder. In 1961 at the age of 84, on a walk at the New York Zoological Society's tropical field station in Trinidad, he saw six monarch butterflies going to roost together. Referring to his childhood journal entry of 71 years earlier, he now made a new observation about monarch butterflies: "The northern form is noted for its migrations, whereas the Trinidad insect is prone to roost in company but does not migrate."

William Beebe died in Trinidad the year after he saw those six butterflies. In a final gesture toward the curse of fame, he willed his journals to an associate and asked that no one write his biography too soon after his death. The man who had made a log of his life had closed the book.

This story is based on correspondence between William Beebe and the National Geographic Society and on the explorer's published works, particularly his book Half Mile Down. *More than 25 years after Beebe's death, his private journals remain in the hands of a friend, the contents undisclosed.*

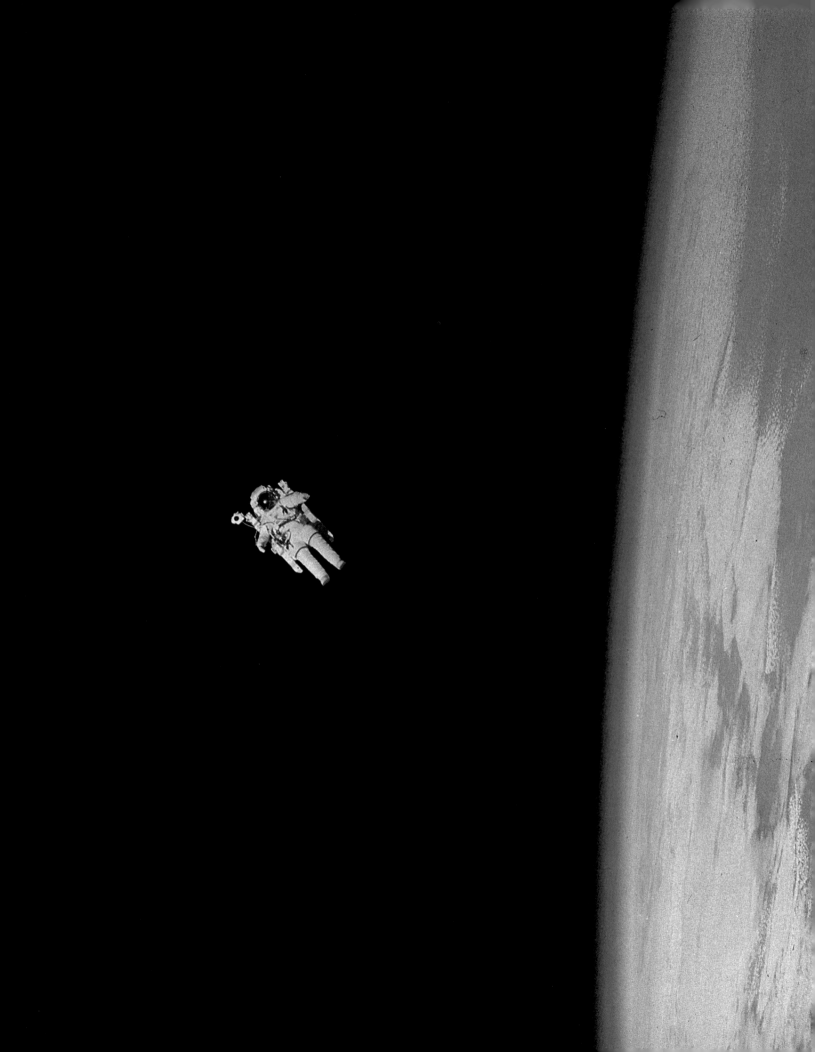

Out of the Cradle

By Jonathan B. Tourtellot

At ease in the void, Bruce McCandless becomes history's first human satellite in 1984, orbiting untethered near his space shuttle. The jet backpack gives astronauts maneuvering ability needed for such tasks as repairing satellites and building a space station. Soviet stations Salyut and Mir have become the first permanent footholds in a realm opened to humankind in 1961, when Russian Yuri Gagarin made a single orbit of Earth.

I t is 1986. The team is worried. It has taken years to prepare for this flyby of Uranus, and now a balky wheel on the Voyager 2 spacecraft is threatening to fail. Dr. Lonne Lane and his Photopolarimetry team, one of eleven Voyager science groups, wait in anxious expectation at the Jet Propulsion Laboratory in Pasadena. Except for TV monitors and computer printers, their fluorescent-lit workroom at JPL could pass for any modern office. But their thoughts are two billion miles away, at Uranus. Radio signals from Earth take $5^1/_2$ hours for a round trip, too long to test the repair command sent to Voyager. If it hasn't worked, the wheel will block part of the photopolarimeter sensor. Near one monitor a bottle of champagne waits, unopened.

It was 1957. President Dwight D. Eisenhower was playing lots of golf; Ford had introduced its new Edsel; "A White Sport Coat—and a Pink Carnation" was high on the charts. America was on top of the world.

October 4. Scientists from around the globe had gathered in Washington, D. C., to discuss the progress of the International Geophysical Year. Many were attending a Soviet Embassy reception when an American geophysicist left the room, returned, and tapped his glass for attention.

"I am informed by the New York Times," he announced as the guests fell silent, "that a satellite is in orbit at an elevation of 900 kilometers. I wish to congratulate our Soviet colleagues on their achievement."

Sputnik! From Western newspapers and airwaves a hubbub arose. How powerful was the rocket that could do this? That Sputnik signified the dawn of space exploration received little note; Americans had missiles on their minds. From backyards they could watch the spark of Soviet might sailing their evening skies, and its wake rocked the nation. DEMOCRATS CHARGE ADMINISTRATION WITH FAILURE TO EQUAL SOVIET, read a Times headline. A political cartoon portrayed a Sputnik hurtling past a soaring golf ball. An Eisenhower official hit back, belittling the "bauble in the sky."

Amid some embarrassingly fiery launch failures, the U. S., aided by German rocketry genius Wernher von Braun, managed to hoist Explorer 1 into orbit on January 31, 1958. Post-Sputnik American industry began tooling up for rocketry, post-Sputnik schools for science and math. Displeased with military control of the space effort, Eisenhower established the civilian National Aeronautics and Space Administration: NASA. The space race was on.

Why explore space? The answers lie as much in history as in the future. In 1957 the answer was national security. America went into space to counter Russia—as England sent Drake into the Pacific to counter Spain. And where satellites went, people would follow.

But no one knew whether space travel was even survivable. Would

303

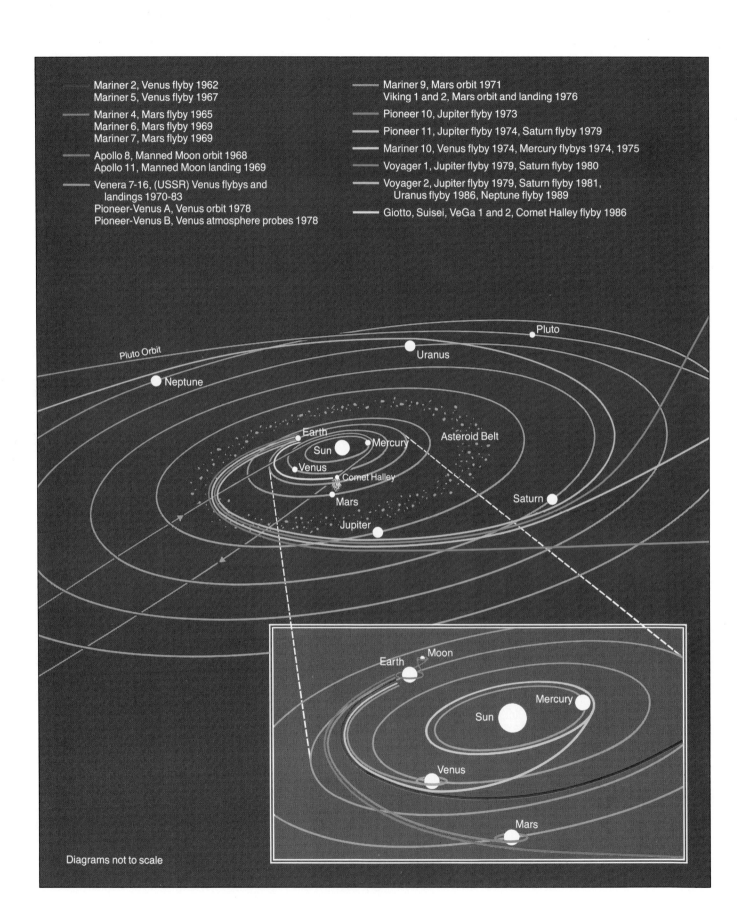

Mariner 2, Venus flyby 1962
Mariner 5, Venus flyby 1967

Mariner 4, Mars flyby 1965
Mariner 6, Mars flyby 1969
Mariner 7, Mars flyby 1969

Apollo 8, Manned Moon orbit 1968
Apollo 11, Manned Moon landing 1969

Venera 7-16, (USSR) Venus flybys and
    landings 1970-83
Pioneer-Venus A, Venus orbit 1978
Pioneer-Venus B, Venus atmosphere probes 1978

Mariner 9, Mars orbit 1971
Viking 1 and 2, Mars orbit and landing 1976

Pioneer 10, Jupiter flyby 1973

Pioneer 11, Jupiter flyby 1974, Saturn flyby 1979

Mariner 10, Venus flyby 1974, Mercury flybys 1974, 1975

Voyager 1, Jupiter flyby 1979, Saturn flyby 1980

Voyager 2, Jupiter flyby 1979, Saturn flyby 1981,
    Uranus flyby 1986, Neptune flyby 1989

Giotto, Suisei, VeGa 1 and 2, Comet Halley flyby 1986

Pluto Orbit

Pluto

Uranus

Neptune

Earth

Sun

Mercury

Asteroid Belt

Venus

Comet Halley

Mars

Jupiter

Saturn

Earth

Moon

Mercury

Sun

Venus

Mars

Diagrams not to scale

304

Robot spacecraft have spiraled out from Earth to explore the solar system since the early 1960s: U. S. Mariner and Soviet Venera probes to the inner planets; two U. S. Viking landers on Mars; and European, Japanese, and Russian probes to Comet Halley. Apollo 8 made the first manned trip out of Earth orbit in 1968. In the 1970s, the gas-giant planets of the outer solar system were so arrayed that each could act as a gravitational sling, speeding spacecraft from one world on to the next—four planets in all for Voyager 2.

A replica of Russia's trailblazing satellite, Sputnik 1, draws stares in Moscow. Satellites and space shuttles in low orbits circle the Earth every 90 minutes or so. Much farther out, communications and weather satellites can take 24 hours per orbit, and so seem to hang motionless over the Equator.

Sputnik 1
Launched 10/4/57

Mercury-Atlas 6 (John Glenn)
Launched 2/20/62

Space Shuttle
First launched 4/12/81

Communications Satellite
(geosynchronous orbit)

Military Satellite
(polar orbit)

g forces after lift-off crush the astronaut? Would cosmic rays fry him? Would weightlessness kill him? The Russians, aided by their own rocketry genius, Sergei Korolev, proved otherwise in April 1961. Yuri Gagarin, first man in space, made one full orbit and landed safely—and did it a month before the U. S. sent Alan Shepard on his short suborbital hop.

In May 1961, John F. Kennedy—launched into the presidency himself partly by Sputnik—spoke before Congress, calling on America to "commit itself to achieving the goal, before this decade is out, of landing a man on the Moon and returning him safely to the Earth." When, within a year, John Glenn made his three-orbit flight in a Mercury capsule, the goal began to look less improbable.

But Soviet firsts did not end with Sputnik or Gagarin. They kept coming: First probe to reach the Moon, 1959; first probe to see the back side of the Moon, a month later; first two spacecraft to meet in orbit, 1962; first woman in space—Valentina Tereshkova—1963; first multiple crew, 1964; first walk in space, 1965.

U. S. feats were less spectacular, but methodical. The Mercury program launched six lone astronauts. By 1965 pairs of astronauts in Gemini craft were practicing docking and space walks. A three-man Apollo would go to the Moon.

But in 1967 a fire inside Apollo 1 killed three astronauts during a launchpad test. Almost two years passed before a redesigned Apollo made its first manned flight in Earth orbit. Russia, too, lost momentum when a cosmonaut died on landing, only months after the Apollo fire.

And suddenly it all changed.

On December 21, 1968, a Saturn V, largest rocket ever built, thundered up from Cape Kennedy, Florida. To make up for lost time, NASA had decided to send Apollo 8 to circle the Moon ten times and return. By December 24, Frank Borman, James Lovell, and William Anders, the first men to leave Earth for another world, were in lunar orbit.

There they pointed their TV camera at the window and made a Christmas Eve broadcast. As the ancient, alien craters slid by beneath them and across the television screens of Earth, their thin radio-borne voices began to read: *In the beginning God created the heaven and the earth. . . .* And people listened to the words once spoken in a language of shepherds, 3,000 years earlier, and stared at their TV sets, some shaking their heads and saying "I don't believe it, I just don't believe it," but believing it.

The team has a new worry. Their photopolarimeter, which detects the way things reflect light, is to record a star's light as it passes through Uranus's rings. As Voyager's motion aligns the star behind the rings, the touchy wheel must work. If it does, Voyager will radio back data on the rings. Now comes news that rain may keep an antenna in Spain from picking up those faint signals.

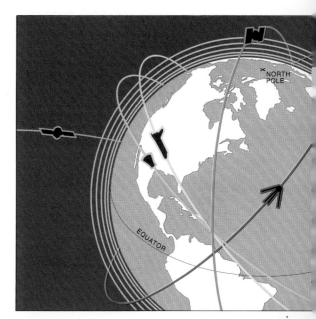

Thundering aloft in 1962, a Mercury-Atlas rocket blasts astronaut John Glenn into history as the first American to orbit the Earth. Project Mercury's six flights in the early 1960s launched the U. S. effort to reach the Moon. Astronauts rode atop liquid-fuel rockets invented in 1926, when space pioneer Robert Goddard sent his first crude prototype soaring 41 feet over a field in Auburn, Massachusetts.

It was July 21, 1969. Once again the thin radio-borne words reach Earth from the Moon, now from the lunar surface. "That's one small step for [a] man"—history has filled in the "a" Neil Armstrong's voice-activated mike may have lost—"one giant leap for mankind." Apollo 11 had won the never declared race to the Moon.

Fears of Russia forgotten, newspapers bannered the sheer triumph of exploration, a fantasy of the ages at last fulfilled. MEN WALK ON MOON roared the usually restrained *New York Times* in 72-point type, the largest in its history. A front-page poem by Archibald MacLeish honored the first footfall upon the "beaches" of the Moon. On inside pages the doubters still doubted, but now they questioned not America's lack of initiative, but its direction. Was this worth the cost? they asked.

Why explore the Moon? In 1969 it was for national prestige, just as when a young republic with 26 stars on its flag sent the Wilkes expedition off into the Pacific, for science, yes, but also for pride, to take a place among the questing nations of the world. Now that flag, with 50 stars, stood stiff on the windless Moon.

But there was something more this time: unexpected perspectives, brought by space travel itself. When Kennedy issued his challenge, no orbiting camera had yet revealed an Earth new to human eyes—fragile, dynamic, whole; Telstar had not yet linked televisions oceans apart; Apollo 8 had not filled those TV

A helicopter winches astronaut Alan Shepard from the sea just four minutes after his splashdown in the Atlantic. The smooth recovery capped his 302-mile suborbital flight in 1961, America's first manned space mission.

Requiring "more alterations than a bridal gown," pressurized flight suits (right) were tested against submersion, heat, and g forces. Astronauts wore vented long johns beneath to keep cool.

screens with its Christmas card of a living world rising over a lifeless one.

"O, a meaning!" wrote MacLeish: "over us on these silent beaches the bright earth, presence among us."

In every building on the campuslike grounds of JPL, even in the cafeteria, TV monitors display each new image coming from Voyager—the rings, a moon, the Uranian atmosphere—every picture new to history. The Imaging team's pictures attract throngs of reporters. The Photopolarimetry team can claim no such glamor; they hope only for strings of numbers. Yet such prosaic data are the brick and mortar of scientific exploration, building a foundation of knowledge for uses yet unknown.

It was 1976. Viking 1 landed on Mars. Cameras panned; sensors tasted the thin carbon dioxide atmosphere; and a tiny shovel extended itself to sample soil for a test, *the* test: Was there life on another planet?

Planetary exploration had begun only six months after John Glenn's three orbits. The U. S. Mariner 2, launched in 1962, made the first successful flyby of Venus, sending back hints of the ferocious heat trapped inside its thick atmosphere. Soviet Venera probes survived the 800°F climate long enough to radio back pictures of a rocky, baked surface.

More U. S. Mariner probes flew by Venus, and one went on to Mercury. Many others mapped Mars, in preparation for the Viking program.

Viking involved two orbiters, two

Making a rendezvous 185 miles high, Gemini 6 looks down on the Pacific and on Gemini 7, launched 11 days earlier. The two spacecraft sometimes flew only one foot apart. From 1964 to 1966, astronauts on ten manned Gemini missions honed skills such as rendezvous and docking—the kind of multiple-craft maneuvers needed to land men on the Moon and bring them home again.

June 1965: Edward White enjoys the first U. S. space walk—"extravehicular activity" in the poetry of NASA. A similar feat by Russian Alexei Leonov, three months earlier, persuaded NASA to let White leave his two-man Gemini 4 capsule, instead of simply standing in the hatchway. Tethered by a 25-foot lifeline, White cavorted outside for 20 minutes, propelling himself with a hand-held jet gun.

landers, and an army of 10,000 people. Deployed by program chief James Martin, a John-Wayne-like figure with a head for tactics, squadrons of technicians and subcontractors readied the invasion of Mars by remote control—the most complex exploration of another planet ever.

Why explore the planets? In 1976 it was for science, just as when an eager Alexander von Humboldt leaped off his ship and onto a Venezuelan beach—landfall on South America, his new planet—and plunged a thermometer into the sand.

Inside Viking 1, a pocket-size laboratory analyzed its shovelful of soil, and found ambiguous results, more typical of chemical reactions than biological ones. Partway around the martian globe, Viking 2 found the same. Life? Question unresolved.

And staying that way for a while. In the late 1970s something else took precedence: A rare alignment of the planets that would enable a probe to make a "grand tour" of the outer solar system—a once-in-180-year opportunity, not to be missed.

It almost was. The heroes of this exploration faced not stormy seas but the vexing halls of government. Months of argument and negotiation yielded funds, but only to explore Jupiter and Saturn—first by two simple Pioneer scouting probes, then by a pair of more complex Voyagers. So engineers performed their own heroics: They jury-rigged and reprogrammed and improvised so that Voyager 2 could continue on past

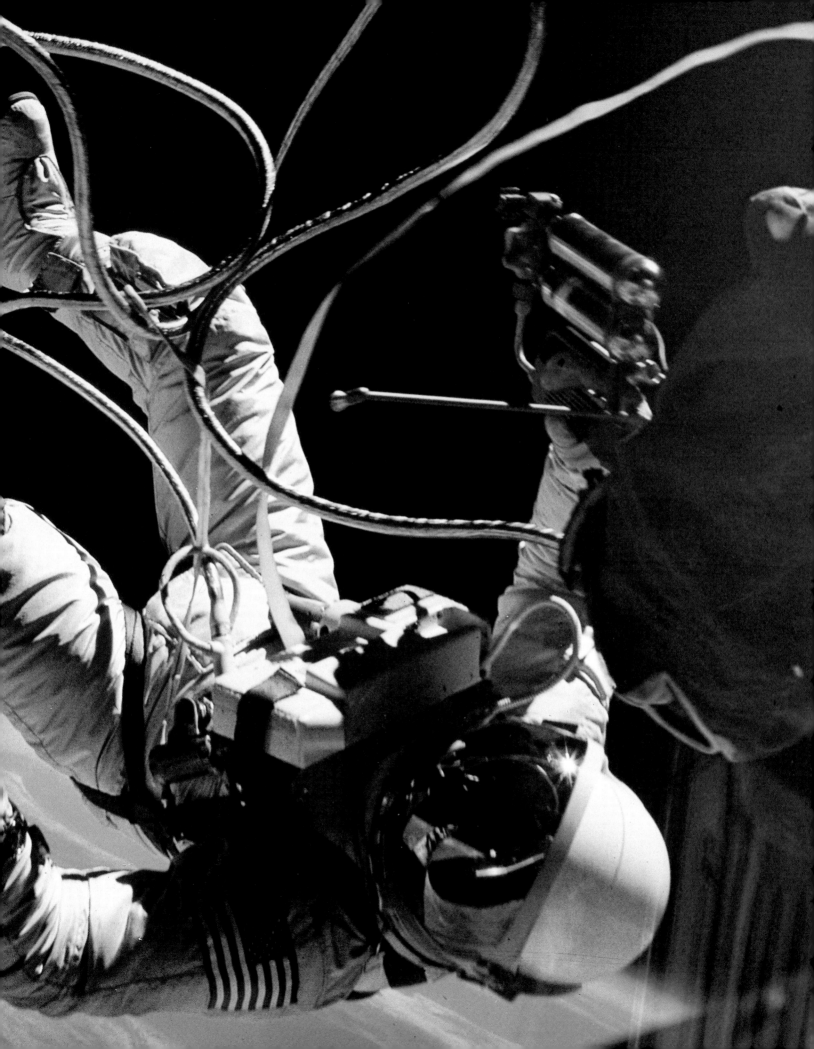

Saturn to Uranus and then Neptune.

The Voyagers were to make the most sweeping exploration in history. The probes were to reconnoiter ten new worlds—four giant planets and their six major moons—not to mention dozens of smaller satellites.

Somehow it worked. At Jupiter, Voyager discovered a ring girding the equator, centuries-old storms churning the atmosphere, volcanoes fountaining from the moon Io, and an iced-over ocean sheathing the moon Europa; at Saturn, it found rings—not the three that telescopes saw, but hundreds, shepherded by dark moonlets—and on the giant moon Titan an atmosphere like that of primordial Earth. From Saturn, Voyager 1, having inspected Titan rather than aiming for Uranus, sailed off toward interstellar space; Voyager 2 sped on to Uranus.

Voyager's discoveries inspired a trick question around NASA: Which planet have we learned the most about from space? Answer: Earth.

Much of that knowledge comes from low Earth orbit, of course—from manned laboratories, shuttle missions, and satellites. Satellites for oceanography, for geology, for climate, for radar-mapping, for agriculture, and satellites that guide explorers below. An orbiting navigation system helped Robert Ballard's team find the *Titanic*. Satellite radar has discovered Maya ruins and ancient riverbeds in the Sahara.

But the other planets teach us of Earth, too, placing it in the scheme of things. On Venus we see a runaway greenhouse effect, on Mars a runaway ice age. Io's surface is more volcanic; Titan's atmosphere more pristine. The ice of Comet Halley is older than life itself on Earth.

And not by chance, it seems. When European, Soviet, and Japanese probes looked at Halley, they found the same dark material Voyager was seeing a lot of in the moons and rings of the outer solar system: organic, carbonaceous matter—the stuff of life. Comets carried it inward to the sun-warmed Earth. Life born of comet dust! Some experts now ask if life might even exist in the carbon-rich outer worlds, too, far from the sun. If deep-ocean vent colonies that explorers found on Earth don't need sunlight, then how about a place like Europa, under the ice?

At JPL, Lane's team stares at the monitors. The rain has held off in Spain. Voyager's signals are now winging toward Earth at 186,000 miles per second. The 2-hour, 45-minute trip should be about to end. A timekeeper studies his watch. "The data should be on the ground—" he swings his arm down, "NOW!" As the screens fill with numbers, cheers fill the room.

It was 1986. Six months after the shuttle *Challenger* exploded, the Smithsonian's air and space museum was still the most popular museum in the world. In front of a Mars display a mother and her teenage daughter were reading about Mars' deep cold,

Apollo 17 astronaut Harrison Schmitt revels in a geologist's paradise as he investigates a 50-foot boulder in the Moon's Taurus-Littrow Valley. Like Apollo 15 and 16, this last U. S. lunar expedition, in 1972, brought a lunar rover (below, at right). Explorers covered 22.5 miles in it, studying terrain, collecting samples, and deploying scientific instruments.

The Victorian baby buggy (opposite) is actually Lunokhod 1, a robot vehicle landed by the Russians in 1970. Directed by earthbound controllers, it crawled for 6.5 miles, sampling rocks and soil and sending information home.

Lunar dust scooped up by Apollo explorers proved to be capable of making concrete stronger than terrestrial types—good news for future lunar-base builders. Apollo's rocks failed to verify any single pre-existing theory about how the Moon formed, and led to a new one: that a huge object hit the Earth over 4 billion years ago, ejecting debris that coalesced into the Moon.

OVERLEAF: High above Baja California in 1984, the space shuttle Challenger launches the first satellite ever built for recovery, LDEF-1. Challenger exploded after launch in January 1986, leaving it to other shuttles to retrieve the LDEF, a unit for testing how lengthy periods in space affect various materials. Shuttles may someday service a permanent space station made from substances that prove most durable.

Scene from the IMAX/OMNIMAX film, The Dream is Alive
Smithsonian Institution and Lockheed Corporation 1985

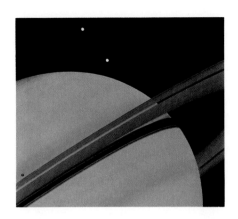

Close encounters of a clean kind: A technician at a McDonnell Douglas plant thrusts his arms into one of many pairs of inside-out rubber gauntlets on the sealed, germfree "glove box" in front of him. Parts of Viking 1 and 2 had to be assembled inside such sterile containers so that the spacecraft would not carry Earth microbes to Mars, where the contaminants might confuse the search for signs of life. Touching down on Mars' Plains of Utopia in 1976, the Viking 2 lander (below)

unfurls an array of cameras and sensors to gather data on weather, atmosphere, chemistry, and biology.

Computer-enhanced images of Saturn (left) from Voyager 1's 1980 flyby dazzled scientists with unexpected complexities in the planet's rings.

wisp-thin atmosphere, and apparent lifelessness.

"Not a very good place for a vacation," remarked the mother.

"Not yet," said the daughter.

Why explore space? In 1986, it was for all the reasons since Sputnik, but also for dreams. For the dreamers the roots of space exploration reach deep into time. Not since early humans left the Rift Valley in Africa has such an uninhabited vastness called. And just in time, say thinkers like Freeman Dyson, a physicist who argues that Earth, with no white spots left on its map, is "getting too homogenized. It's very hard for cultural minorities to survive. We're just too close together, whereas there's a lot of room out there."

Setbacks do not daunt visionaries. If a shuttle explodes, if discovery transforms the once-imagined jungles of Venus into an oven, or the canals of Mars to dust, the dreams live on. As Frémont went West with Manifest Destiny singing in his soul, or Livingstone to Africa with Christ singing in his, so the space dreamers seek the stars, singing of hope.

Their songs count, too. Inspired by the stories of Jules Verne, Konstantin Tsiolkovsky wrote, "Earth is the cradle of humanity, but humanity cannot remain in the cradle forever," and he wrote it in tsarist Russia in 1899. Tsiolkovsky was the first man to realize that rockets were the way into space. His research helped Korolev put Sputnik into orbit. And Korolev's rival, von Braun,

was inspired to seek the Moon by another visionary—H. G. Wells.

Between sips of champagne, team members laugh and chatter about what the data may hold. Relief and triumph under the fluorescents. Time will publish no pictures of their graphs, KCBS will air no film at 11. It doesn't matter. They have been to Uranus.

Each morning during the Uranus encounter, the science teams at JPL

gathered in private to discuss what new data Voyager had transmitted, what it meant, what to tell the eager press. "Instant science," the methodical scientists complained—but not too much. This was their hour.

They jammed into a conference room under TV monitors now revealing the moon Miranda. The Imaging team reported first: "One new satellite and one new ring, about half way between the Epsilon and Delta rings." Ultraviolet Spectroscopy

Ear to the sky, a Deep Space Network antenna in the Mojave desert picks up signals from Voyager 2 at Uranus, 2 billion miles away—a feat comparable to seeing a 20-watt light bulb from across the Atlantic. The signals carry encoded images such as this nightside view of the huge seventh planet. Voyager discovered that Uranus's smooth clouds may conceal a great ocean of searingly hot water.

threw graphs on a screen: atmospheric density as expected. Photopolarimetry—and Lonne Lane rose to report among first findings that the Gamma Ring was only 0.6 kilometers wide, "much, much smaller than ground data indicated." "Does that mean it's denser, since it's much narrower than people thought?" "Possibly." Another brick, mortar to come. Reporting moved on.

Today the two Pioneers and two Voyagers continue outward, heading for the stars. The relic craft are expected to survive for a billion years, long enough to circle the Milky Way galaxy four times. They are the first artifacts ever to leave our home star, bottled messages cast into the widest ocean of all. The dreamers made sure they carried diagrams, photographs, even an LP record of earthly sounds —all to greet any alien race, perhaps unborn, that finds them.

From here the story of exploration moves into science fiction's realm, where Yuri Gagarin was only a generation ago. Will people someday follow Voyager to the stars? They would measure their journeys, longer than any Captain Cook dreamed of, not in years and leagues, but in decades and light-years. Yet for every island Cook charted, the dreamers argue, there waits a galaxy; for every grain of sand he saw, a world.

Such starfarers would still share one thing with Cook—that same thrilling and frightening and hopeful question known to all explorers:

What's out there?

317

Neil Armstrong
Edwin Aldrin, Jr.
Michael Collins

By Michael Collins

A dream fulfilled by Apollo 11:
Neil Armstrong's photograph of his
foot on the Moon, July 20, 1969.

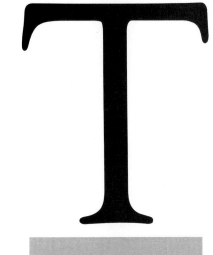

The big rocket engine used to wake my wife and me in the middle of the night. Its test stand was 17 miles away, across the dry lake bed at Edwards Air Force Base, California, but what's 17 miles to a Saturn V engine? Its deep roar rumbled right through our bedroom windows and rattled every teacup in our kitchen cabinet.

At that time, in the early sixties, I was just a test pilot and had no idea that before the end of the decade I'd be strapped atop a cluster of five of these monsters, ready to escape Earth's gravity and begin a three-day coast to the Moon.

A voyage of a quarter of a million miles begins with a thousand different steps. As with any complicated expedition, success depends on the details—all of them. In addition to the gigantic Saturn V, tall as a 35-story building, smaller but more densely packed machines had to be designed, tested, built, and filled with hundreds of items of complex equipment and a highly trained crew. This process took the better part of a decade, and at its height employed over 400,000 Americans.

Two of them would go with me: Edwin ("Buzz") Aldrin, our most learned pilot, and Neil Armstrong, the premier test pilot in the Apollo program, who would be first to step on the Moon. A good choice—Neil made decisions slowly and well, rolling them around in his mouth like fine wine and swallowing at the last minute.

By July 1969, six months before John F. Kennedy's deadline of "landing a man on the Moon," we were ready to give it a try. Personally I figured our chance of success was not much better than 50-50. Our trip would be complicated, and therefore fragile. I thought of it as a long daisy chain in which any severed link could result in failure, and perhaps death. Probably not my own, because I wasn't going all the way to the Moon's surface. As pilot of the command module, I would remain in lunar orbit while Neil and Buzz descended to the surface in the lunar

319

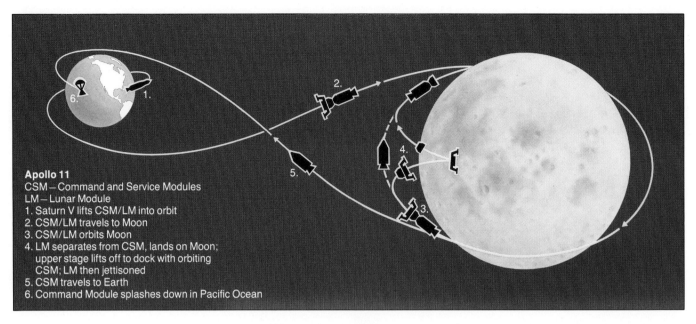

Apollo 11
CSM — Command and Service Modules
LM — Lunar Module
1. Saturn V lifts CSM/LM into orbit
2. CSM/LM travels to Moon
3. CSM/LM orbits Moon
4. LM separates from CSM, lands on Moon;
   upper stage lifts off to dock with orbiting
   CSM; LM then jettisoned
5. CSM travels to Earth
6. Command Module splashes down in Pacific Ocean

Not since Adam has a human known such solitude as Mike Collins is experiencing. . . .
NASA OFFICIAL

module. At our preflight press conference reporters kept asking whether I would feel terribly alone or frightened while orbiting the Moon by myself. I didn't know yet. I did have a secret fear, but not about that.

We had plenty enough to worry about. We were utterly dependent on the proper functioning of a frightening series of machines: the Saturn V, to reach Earth orbit and then escape velocity; the service module, for course corrections and braking into lunar orbit; the lunar module descent stage, to decelerate to a landing; the pressure suit and backpack, for extravehicular forays; the lunar module ascent stage, to blast off and rendezvous with the command module; the service module again, to escape the Moon and correct the trajectory to Earth; and parachutes, to bring our command module safely to splashdown.

Of all these links, the weakest, I thought, was Neil and Buzz's ascent and return to me in the command module. We had practiced this rendezvous over and over in the simulator, and it was a piece of cake as long as everything took place precisely on schedule, but it was terribly unforgiving of small deviations. Ideally, I would be in a circular orbit 69 miles over their heads when they lifted off. They would shoot for a lower, 52-mile orbit, calculated to give them a leisurely catch-up rate—but not too leisurely, because their oxygen was limited. A piece of cake. But suppose, for a host of possible reasons, Neil and Buzz were late taking off. Then we would have to try some new, untested orbit, in hopes of linking up before their oxygen ran out—the stuff of nightmares.

By launch day I am more than a little tense about rendezvous and a hundred other things, but eager to abandon the simulator and reenter the real world of spaceflight—nearly three years after my Earth-orbiting Gemini flight. I am everlastingly grateful that I have flown in space before. Still, Gemini 10 was a local affair. This Apollo 11, on the other hand, is serious business, with the ghost of John F. Kennedy riding with us in full view of a watchful world. Superimposed on the normal pres-

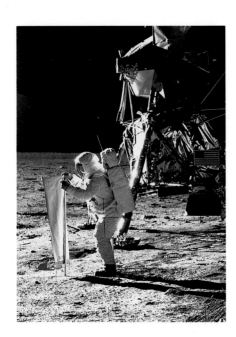

Edwin Aldrin, Jr., deploying foil for sampling solar-wind particles.

sure—the nagging worry of "What have I overlooked?"—is the imperative *not* to fail, to distill American expertise into eight flawless days, to drape that daisy chain around the Moon and return it to Earth.

A spaceflight begins when your helmet locks in place. From that moment on, no air will be breathed, only pure oxygen; no human voice heard, unless electronically piped in. The world can still be seen, but not smelled, or heard, or felt, or tasted. As Neil, Buzz, and I get out of a small van at the base of the launch tower, we can see it's a clear day, and we are told it's hot already, even at 6:45 a.m., a scorcher in the making. Usually this place is a beehive of activity, but now only a handful of us are left with our steaming tanks of liquid hydrogen and oxygen. A small elevator takes us 320 feet up to our command module, *Columbia.* I pause on the narrow walkway there to savor the view and consider the moment. If I cover my right eye I can see only the unsullied beach, the Florida of Ponce de León, and beyond it the ocean. If I cover my left I see the United States of America embodied in the most colossal pile of machinery ever assembled. I have to confess that the explorer in me pulls me toward the beach, but I have made my commitment to the machine. There will be time for beaches after the Moon, I hope.

At ignition the Saturn V gives us a little surprise. Instead of the hideous din one would expect, it is merely noisy inside. But the motion! As we leave the ground I feel our engines swiveling left and right, keeping us poised in delicate balance against crosswinds and sloshing fuel tanks. It is like a nervous novice driving a wide car down a narrow alley and jerking the wheel spasmodically back and forth. Still, the Saturn V is a gentle giant and pushes us back in our couches with an acceleration only slightly over four times that of gravity. Its first stage empties and separates at an altitude of 52 miles. Five more engines in the second stage take over. High above atmospheric disturbances now, our climb is smooth as glass. At 115 miles, the single third stage engine ignites and drives us down range, increasing our speed to the 17,500 miles per hour needed for orbit. The third stage is rough, buzzing and rattling, and I'm relieved when it shuts down. It is less than 12 minutes from launch.

Now we have an orbit and a half to make sure everything is operating properly before we reignite the third stage engine and commit ourselves to leaving the Earth's gravitational field. It all checks out, and Mission Control gives us their blessing in the esoteric patois of spaceflight: "Apollo 11, this is Houston. You are go for TLI"—translunar injection.

The burn is over in six minutes. We are 1,400 miles out now, climbing like a dingbat—six miles a second, far faster than a rifle bullet. Yet it is hard to tell that by looking out the window. We are entering a slow-motion domain where time and distance seem to mean more than speed. Distance from home especially. For the first time I know what "outward bound" means. We cannot watch the slowly shrinking Earth for long, because we must distribute the sun's heat by turning our craft broadside to it and rotating slowly, like a chicken on a barbecue spit.

Things are quiet on board *Columbia.* Neil and Buzz spend a lot of time studying their lunar module checklists, while I keep house. For three days between Earth and Moon we are in continual sunshine, but I notice that if I look downsun, and shield my eyes from all light, I can see stars. In this strange cislunar region we keep our watches and our circadian rhythm on Houston time. When sleeping, we use light nylon bags below our couches. It is pleasant to doze off with no pressure anywhere on the body—just floating and falling all the way to the Moon.

As we approach our destination we stop our barbecuing motion and swing around for our first closeup look at the Moon. The Moon I have known all my life, that flat, small yellow disk in the sky, has gone, replaced by the most awesome sphere I have ever seen. It is huge. It fills our windows, its belly bulging out toward us so that I feel I can almost reach out and touch it. The Sun, eclipsed behind it, sends light cascading around the lunar rim. Part of the Moon's face below us is in deep shadow, but another region basks in whitish light reflected from the Earth. This earthshine, as it's called, is considerably brighter than moonlight on Earth. The reddish yellow of the sun's corona, the blanched white of earthshine, and the pure black of the star-studded sky all combine to cast a bluish glow over the Moon. This cool, magnificent sphere hangs there ominously, a formidable presence without sound or motion, and issues us no invitation to invade its domain.

We brake into lunar orbit, from which we can examine the far side of the Moon, never visible from Earth. Unlike the front, it has no flat maria, or seas. It is all highlands, densely pocked by 4.6 billion years of meteoroid bombardment. Back over the near side it is just past dawn in the Sea of Tranquillity, and the sun's rays strike the landing site at such a shallow angle that craters cast long, jagged shadows. I don't see any place smooth enough to park a baby buggy, much less a lunar module.

Despite years of studying photographs of the Moon, I nevertheless find it a shock actually to be here and see the vivid contrast between Earth and Moon. One has to see the second world up close to truly appreciate the first. This withered, sun-seared peach pit out my window offers no competition to Earth's verdant valleys and misty waterfalls.

Neil and Buzz board their landing craft and undock. They have named it *Eagle,* but it doesn't look like one. The creature now suspended upside down outside my window is spindly and ungainly, with four legs jutting out above a body that has neither symmetry nor grace. Designed only for the vacuum of space, its shape ignores all streamlining rules, with antennas and other accessories stuck on at odd angles.

When *Eagle* begins its descent I am left alone with my thoughts in *Columbia.* Two hours per orbit, 48 minutes of which I am behind the Moon and unable to communicate with anyone. A census would count three billion plus two humans on one side of the Moon and one plus God only knows what on the other. Recalling reporters' questions about feeling lonely, though, I now know the answer is "absolutely

Lunar module returning to link up with author Collins in the command module.

not." I am accustomed to being alone in a flying machine and I like it—the more unusual the surroundings, the better. This is the ultimate solo flight. Far from fear, I feel satisfaction, confidence, almost exultation, as if I had a superhuman ability to cope with whatever might arise.

I am over the near side as the landing begins, so I can hear Buzz calling out altitude and velocity to Neil, whose eyes are glued to the window. "Forty feet" says Buzz. "Thirty seconds" says Houston—the fuel remaining. Better get it down, Neil. "Contact light!" calls out Buzz. "We copy you down, *Eagle*," says Houston, half statement and half question. Neil will later explain he was overflying a boulder field, trying to find the best place to land. Savoring the wine. Now he confirms, "Tranquillity Base here. The *Eagle* has landed." I am over the far side hours later when Neil speaks his historic first words on the Moon, but in radio range again as Buzz hops around like a kangaroo and Neil chats with President Nixon. They also gather a precious cargo of Moon rocks.

It is morning again and this, as far as I'm concerned, is the day of reckoning. As the moment of lift-off nears, I become more and more nervous. *Columbia* has no landing gear; I cannot rescue them from the surface. If they limp up into a lopsided orbit, I may not be able to catch them. For the past six months *that* has been my secret terror: to have to leave them here and return to Earth alone. If I must, I will, but. . . . It would almost be better not to have that option.

Buzz counts down, and now they are off! For the seven minutes of their powered ascent, I barely breathe. There is no backup for their engine; it must work. After much fiddling with my sextant, I finally see *Eagle,* first as a tiny blinking light in the darkness, and then as a golden bug in the light of sunrise, gliding through the crater fields below. Reassuringly they grow in my window, easing to a stop just 50 feet away.

As the Earth pops up over the horizon I snap a couple of pictures. I can't see Neil or Buzz, or the three billion on the small blue blob just behind them, but I know they are there—every human being in the entire universe, framed in my window. Now my rendezvous worries are over. I can throw away the book I have clipped to the front of my pressure suit, the book with 18 emergency variations on our rendezvous scheme. God knows we are still a long way from home. There are still fragile links in the quarter million miles of daisy chain ahead of us. I must dock with *Eagle,* and Neil and Buzz must transfer themselves and their two boxes of rocks back into *Columbia.* The service module engine behind me must ignite when I ask it, or we will become a permanent satellite of the Moon. A couple of days from now we must jettison the service module and slice into Earth's atmosphere at precisely the correct angle. Our parachutes must open. Yet despite all that, for the first time I feel we are going to carry it off. I can see it all out my window now, our beautiful home planet and my two compatriots, successfully returned to me. From now on it will be all downhill—for there they are!

Michael Collins continues to promote exploration, as a trustee of the National Geographic Society. His book Carrying the Fire *tells of Apollo 11's trip.*

Welcome home: Armstrong, Collins, and Aldrin waving to fans amid the blizzard of a ticker-tape parade, one of the largest in New York history.

"Aiming at the stars". . . is a problem to occupy generations, so that no matter how much progress one makes, there is always the thrill of just beginning.
ROBERT GODDARD, 1932

Explorers by the Ages

This list presents a selection of significant explorers, with their life dates, listed alphabetically for each of four major eras of exploration.

In the entries, you will find the regions in which they explored, their nationalities, what they did, and the years during which they did it. Explorer teams like Lewis and Clark are listed together.

Early Quests (3000 B.C.-A.D. 1000)

Alexander the Great (356-323 B.C.)
Asia: Greek; pushed into Egypt, Syria, Persia, and eastward to Indus River (334-323 B.C.).

Saint Brendan (ca A.D. 484-578)
Atlantic: Irish; sailed to Hebrides, Wales, and Brittany (A.D. 565-573). Legends say he reached North America.

Chang Ch'ien (?-114 B.C.)
Asia: Chinese; explored China's hinterlands and opened trade along Silk Road, primary means of East-West exchange for centuries.

Erik the Red (10th century A.D.)
Atlantic: Norwegian; explored Greenland (A.D. 982-85); established colony there (A.D. 986).

Leif Eriksson (ca A.D. 970-1020)
Atlantic: Norse; sailed from Greenland to Labrador, Newfoundland or Nova Scotia, and perhaps farther south (ca A.D. 1000).

Eudoxus (2nd century B.C.)
Asia: Greek; explored Arabian Sea and made two voyages to India; disappeared while attempting to circumnavigate Africa.

Hanno (5th century B.C.)
Africa: Carthaginian; explored from Carthage, colonizing down west African coast to Gambia, Sierra Leone, maybe Cameroon (ca 450 B.C.).

Pytheas (4th century B.C.)
Atlantic: Greek; sailed to Britain, Orkney Islands, and perhaps Iceland or Norway (325 B.C.).

Scylax (6th century B.C.)
Asia: Greek; followed Indus River to Indian Ocean, and home via Red Sea (ca 510 B.C.).

The World Discovered (1000-1600)

Diego de Almagro (1475-1538)
South America: Spanish; joined Pizarro in conquest of Peru (1532-35); explored Andes Mountains of northern Chile (1535-37).

Vasco Núñez de Balboa (1475-1519)
Central America: Spanish; explored Panama; first European to see Pacific Ocean (1513).

Álvar Núñez Cabeza de Vaca (ca 1490-1560)
Americas: Spanish; wandered Southwest in North America (1528-1536); explored southern Brazil and discovered Iguazú Falls (1541-44).

John Cabot (ca 1450-1499)
Canada: Italian sailing for British; searched for North American route to Asia, landed on Canada's east coast, claimed it for Britain (1497).

Pedro Álvares Cabral (1467-1520)
South America: Portuguese; en route to India, sailed down west coast of Africa, swung southwestward and discovered Brazil (1500-1501).

Jacques Cartier (1491-1557)
Canada: French; penetrated Gulf of St. Lawrence in search of Northwest Passage (1534-35).

Cheng Ho (15th century)
Asia, Africa: Chinese; sailed to Japan, India, and eastern Africa (1405-1433).

Christopher Columbus (1451-1506)
Americas: Italian sailing for Spanish; possibly landed at Samana Cay, Bahamas (1492-93); also discovered Dominica, Trinidad, and other Caribbean islands before return to Spain (1493-1500); then discovered Martinique, Honduras, and explored Panama's Caribbean coast (1502-04).

Francisco Vásquez de Coronado (ca 1510-1554)
Americas: Spanish; explored the Southwest; his patrol discovered Grand Canyon (1540-42).

Hernán Cortés (1485-1547)
Central America: Spanish; conquered Mexico (1518-1521); laid siege to Tenochtitlán (1521); explored southeast to Honduras (1524-26).

Vasco da Gama (1460-1524)
Asia, Africa: Portuguese; made first recorded voyage from Europe to India (1497-99).

John Davis (ca 1550-1605)
Arctic, Americas: English; searched for Northwest Passage on three voyages; sailed into Baffin Bay from Davis Strait (1585-87).

Hernando de Soto (ca 1496-1542)
North America: Spanish; explored Southeast; discovered Mississippi River (1539-1542).

Bartholomeu Dias (ca 1450-1500)
Asia: Portuguese; first European to make confirmed passage around Africa's Cape of Good Hope, opening sea route to India (1487-88).

Martin Frobisher (ca 1535-1594)
Arctic: English; searched for Northwest Passage and discovered Frobisher Bay (1576); returned there to search for gold (1577-78).

Ibn Battutah (ca 1304-1368)
Africa, Asia: Moroccan; ranged over 75,000 miles, as far as China and Sumatra, to visit and write about Muslim world (1325-1353).

Ferdinand Magellan (ca 1480-1521)
Pacific: Portuguese sailing for Spanish; led first expedition to sail around globe (1519-1521).

Francisco de Orellana (ca 1490-1546)
South America: Spanish; first European to explore Amazon River (1541-42).

Francisco Pizarro (ca 1475-1541)
South America: Spanish; with Balboa at discovery of Pacific (1513); conquered Incas (1532-35).

John of Plano Carpini (ca 1180-1252)
Asia: Italian; first European known to visit Mongol capital of Karakorum (1245-47).

Marco Polo (1254-1324)
Asia: Italian; with father and uncle, **Niccolò** and **Maffeo Polo,** opened overland route to China from Europe (1271-1295).

Juan Ponce de León (1460-1521)
North America: Spanish; discovered and explored Florida (1513).

Giovanni da Verrazano (ca 1485-1528)
North America: Italian; explored Atlantic coast from Cape Fear, probably to Cape Breton; discovered New York Bay and Narragansett Bay (1524).

Saint Francis Xavier (1506-1552)
Asia: Spanish; missionary who traveled to India and Japan to spread Christianity (1540-1552).

Yermak Timofeyevich (?-1585)
Asia: Russian; Cossack who crossed Urals, battled Tatars, and paved way for Russian conquest of Siberia (1581-85).

The World Explored (1600-1900)

Karell Johan Andersson (1827-1867)
Africa: Swedish; explored southwestern Africa and discovered Okavango River (1851-59).

Samuel W. Baker (1821-1893)
Africa: English; explored Nile tributaries in Ethiopia (1861-62); discovered Lake Albert (1864).

Heinrich Barth (1821-1865)
Africa: German; traveled through Sahara and West Africa, gathering detailed information about interior (1850-55).

Vitus Jonassen Bering (1681-1741)
North America: Danish; sailed through Bering Strait (1728); explored Alaskan coast and discovered Aleutian Islands (1741).

Louis-Antoine de Bougainville (1729-1811)
Pacific: French; circumnavigated globe; explored Tahiti, Samoa, New Hebrides, and other islands (1766-69).

James Bruce (1730-1794)
Africa: Scottish; explored Ethiopia; located source of Blue Nile (1768-1773).

Robert O'Hara Burke (1820-1861)
Australia: Irish-born, settled in Australia; with assistant **William John Wills,** led first expedition across continent, south to north (1860-61).

Richard Francis Burton (1821-1890)
Africa: British; with John Speke, explored Somali and Lake Tanganyika regions (1854).

René-Auguste Caillié (1799-1838)
Africa: French; disguised as Arab, he was first European to reach Timbuktu and return (1827-28).

Samuel de Champlain (ca 1567-1635)
North America: French; founded Quebec Colony (1608); discovered Lake Champlain (1609), Ottawa River (1613), and Great Lakes (1615).

Hugh Clapperton (1788-1827)
Africa: Scottish; with **Dixon Denham** and **Walter Oudney,** crossed Sahara from north; Denham explored Lake Chad region (1823); Oudney died; Clapperton reached Hausa region of Nigeria (1824), returned to Africa (1825-27) where he found and crossed Niger.

James Cook (1728-1779)
Pacific: English; explored most of world's largest ocean; disproved myth of a great Southern Continent; charted New Zealand, Bering Strait, and Canada's west coast; discovered Hawaiian Islands (1768-1779).

Charles R. Darwin (1809-1882)
South America, Australasia: English; naturalist on *Beagle*'s worldwide voyage (1831-36), which provided basis for his theory of evolution.

Benito de Goes (1562-1607)
Asia: Portuguese; Jesuit who went overland to China via Pamirs; confirmed that China and Cathay were same place (1602-07).

Charles Montagu Doughty (1843-1926)
Arabia: English; traveled undisguised through west and central Arabia and wrote about geography and culture (1876-78).

J.S.C. Dumont d'Urville (1790-1842)
Antarctic: French; first to Adélie Land (1840).

John Franklin (1786-1847)
Arctic: English; headed three Arctic expeditions (1818-1827). Perished with his men in Canada while seeking Northwest Passage.

Simon Fraser (1776-1862)
Canada: Canadian; explored westward from Rockies, through British Columbia to Pacific at Vancouver (1805-08).

John Charles Frémont (1813-1890)
North America: American; mapped Oregon Trail (1842); crossed Rockies to California (1845).

Henry Hudson (ca 1550-1611)
Arctic, North America: English; searched for Northwest Passage; discovered Hudson River and sailed upstream to Albany (1609); found Hudson Bay and died there after mutiny (1610-11).

Alexander von Humboldt (1769-1859)
Americas: German; naturalist who explored South America, Cuba, and Mexico; collected extensive scientific data (1799-1804).

Mary H. Kingsley (1862-1900)
Africa: English; explored Gabon, Congo, and Cameroon to study Fang and other tribes (1895).

Alexander Gordon Laing (1793-1826)
Africa: Scottish; first European to reach Timbuktu; killed as he left.

Richard Lemon Lander (1804-1834)
Africa: English; completed Clapperton's mission by finding mouth of Niger River (1830).

René-Robert Cavelier de La Salle (1643-1687)
North America: French; traveled through Mississippi Valley, claimed it for France (1682).

Meriwether Lewis (1774-1809)
North America: American; with **William Clark** led first crossing of continent to Pacific via Missouri and Columbia Rivers (1804-06).

David Livingstone (1813-1873)
Africa: Scottish; missionary and explorer of interior. Discovered Lake Ngami (1849), Zambezi River (1851), Victoria Falls (1855), and Lake Malawi (1859).

Alexander Mackenzie (1764-1820)
Canada: Scottish; charted Mackenzie River (1789); became first European to cross North America to Pacific, via Peace River (1793).

Jacques Marquette (1637-1675)
North America: French; missionary who, with **Louis Jolliet,** explored from Michigan down Mississippi River (1673).

Matthew Fontaine Maury (1806-1873)
Oceans: American; directed history's first major deep-sea survey, in Atlantic (1849).

Fridtjof Nansen (1861-1930)
Arctic: Norwegian; led first expedition across Greenland's ice cap (1888-89). Tried to drift across North Pole by ship, forced by ice to continue on foot, setting new latitude record (1895).

Mungo Park (1771-1806)
Africa: Scottish; probed West African interior (1795-96); explored Niger River to Bussa (1805-06).

Zebulon Montgomery Pike (1779-1813)
North America: American; mapped territory westward from St. Louis to Colorado (1806).

Nikolay Mikhaylovich Przhevalsky (1839-1888)
Asia: Russian; explored much of central Asia, bringing back extensive scientific data, such as route surveys, botanical collections (1870-1888).

Matteo Ricci (1552-1610)
Asia: Italian; Jesuit missionary who settled in China to spread Christianity and encourage

exchange of cultural and scientific information between East and West (1578-1610).

James Clark Ross (1800-1862)
Poles: Scottish; with his uncle, **John Ross,** located North Magnetic Pole (1831); commanded Antarctic expedition for geographical discovery (1840-43); searched Baffin Bay area for John Franklin (1848-49).

Jedediah Strong Smith (1799-1831)
North America: American; first to cross Great Basin into California (1826).

John Hanning Speke (1827-1864)
Africa: English; explored eastern Africa with Richard Burton; found primary source of White Nile at Lake Victoria (1857-59).

Henry Morton Stanley (1841-1904)
Africa: Welsh-born, settled in U.S.; commissioned by *New York Herald* to find David Livingstone in Africa (1871); circumnavigated Lake Victoria; discovered Lake Edward; descended Congo (Zaire) River (1874-77).

Abel Janszoon Tasman (1603-1659)
Pacific: Dutch; discovered Tasmania, New Zealand, and Fiji (1642-43); circumnavigated Australia without knowing it (1644).

Alfred R. Wallace (1823-1913)
South America: English; naturalist who made extensive collections in Amazonia with **Henry W. Bates** (1848-1852) and originated a theory of natural selection similar to Charles Darwin's (1858).

Samuel Wallis (1728-1795)
Pacific: English; discovered Tahiti during search for the mythical Southern Continent (1766-68).

Charles Wilkes (1798-1877)
Pacific: American; confirmed existence of Antarctica; charted Melanesian regions of Pacific (1838-1842).

Francis E. Younghusband (1863-1942)
Asia: British; crossed China from Peking to India (1886); probed Pamirs and Karakoram Range; led an army into forbidden city of Lhasa (1903-04).

To Worlds Beyond (1900-present)

Roald Amundsen (1872-1928)
Poles: Norwegian; first to sail through Northwest Passage (1903-06); first at South Pole (1911).

Roy Chapman Andrews (1884-1960)
Asia: American; led teams of specialists on five expeditions to Gobi Desert, where he uncovered dinosaur eggs and fossil evidence of Earth's largest land mammals (1922-1930).

Neil A. Armstrong (1930-   )
Space: American; first to walk on Moon (1969), after first lunar landing with **Edwin E. Aldrin, Jr.,** on Apollo 11 mission with **Michael Collins.**

Robert D. Ballard (1942-   )
Oceans: American; explored Mid-Atlantic Ridge (1973-74); found deep-sea life at hydrothermal vents in Pacific (1977); found *Titanic* (1985).

C. William Beebe (1877-1962)
Oceans: American; dived to record 3,028 feet in bathysphere (1934).

Frank Borman (1928-   )
Space: American; commander of Apollo 8, which first orbited Moon; accompanied by **James A. Lovell, Jr.,** and **William A. Anders** (1968).

Richard E. Byrd (1888-1957)
Poles: American; first to fly over North Pole (1926); first to fly over South Pole (1929); established American base in Antarctica (1929).

Jacques-Yves Cousteau (1910-   )
Oceans: French; developed Aqua-Lung with **Emile Gagnan** (1943); began worldwide ocean surveys on research ship *Calypso* (1950).

Alexandra David-Néel (1868-1969)
Asia: French; reached Lhasa by traveling in disguise as a poor Tibetan pilgrim (1923-24).

Ranulph Fiennes (1943-   )
World: British; led first Pole-to-Pole circumnavigation of globe (1979-1982).

Yuri Alekseyevich Gagarin (1934-1968)
Space: Russian; first man in space (1961).

John H. Glenn, Jr. (1921-   )
Space: American; first American to orbit Earth, in Mercury capsule *Friendship 7* (1962).

Sven Anders Hedin (1865-1952)
Asia: Swedish; explored and mapped central Asian highlands (1905-08).

Wally Herbert (1934-   )
Arctic: British; first to cross surface of Arctic Ocean via North Pole, by dogsled (1968-69).

Robert E. Peary (1856-1920)
Arctic: American; might have reached North Pole on fourth attempt (1909).

Auguste Piccard (1884-1962)
Oceans, skies: Swiss; designed balloon and made first manned ascent into stratosphere in it (1931); dived to record 10,392 feet in bathyscaph built

with son **Jacques** (1953). Jacques dived to ocean's deepest point, Mariana Trench, 35,800 feet (1960).

Ralph Plaisted (1927-   )
Arctic: American; first confirmed arrival at North Pole (1968).

Joseph F. Rock (1884-1962)
Asia: American; explored central China and unmapped borderlands of China's southwest (1922-1949).

Robert Falcon Scott (1868-1912)
Poles: English; reached South Pole one month after Amundsen (1912) and died on return trip.

Ernest H. Shackleton (1874-1922)
Antarctic: British; went farther south than anyone before him—111 miles from South Pole (1908-09).

Alan B. Shepard, Jr. (1923-   )
Space: American; first American in space (1961).

Vilhjalmur Stefansson (1879-1962)
Arctic: Canadian; explored Alaskan and Canadian Arctic (1913-18).

Claudio Villas Boas (ca 1916-   )
South America: Brazilian; explored southern Amazon basin with brothers **Orlando** and **Leonardo;** all studied Amazonian Indians and worked to preserve Indian cultures (1961).

About the Authors

Thomas B. Allen is a novelist, journalist, and former National Geographic book editor.

Elisabeth B. Booz lived in several Asian countries for 16 years. Her books include a novel set in India and the first comprehensive guidebook to Tibet.

Ian Cameron's name appears on many popular British books about adventure, including four published by the Royal Geographical Society.

Douglas H. Chadwick, writer and wildlife biologist, covers ecological topics on assignment from his home in Montana.

Michael Collins, pilot of the Apollo 11 command module, is an aerospace consultant and continues to write and speak about space.

James A. Cox, former National Geographic staffer, writes about many historical topics from his home in Nutley, New Jersey.

Ernest B. "Pat" Furgurson, a national columnist and chief of the Baltimore *Sun*'s Washington bureau, makes a specialty of seeking out-of-the-way datelines and offbeat Americana from Meddybemps, Maine, and West Frostproof, Florida, to Honolulu, Alaska.

Denis Hills, a British author and journalist who lived in Africa for many years, has written several books about the continent. In 1975 Ugandan president Idi Amin arrested him and sentenced him to death, sparking an international incident; the British Foreign Secretary successfully negotiated his release.

Philip Kopper, a Washington, D. C., author, journalist, and occasional scuba diver, writes about many topics, including seacoasts and history.

Loren McIntyre, writer, photographer, and seasoned expert on South America, has traveled most of the routes followed by the conquistadores.

Elizabeth L. Newhouse, National Geographic writer and book editor, grew up in Hernán Cortés's first New World conquest, Cuba.

Michael Parfit has lived for part of each season in Antarctica and written about it extensively.

Edwards Park, former National Geographic staffer, lived for years in Australia after World War II and returns there from time to time. He writes for *Smithsonian* and other publications, most often about matters historical.

Robert M. Poole, National Geographic writer and book editor, traced James Cook's routes through the Pacific from Tahiti to New Zealand, Australia, and Hawaii.

David F. Robinson, National Geographic writer and book editor, crews aboard the square-rigged *Maryland Dove* (pages 36-7), and has sailed the open ocean on the brigantine *Sheila Yeates*.

Margaret Sedeen, National Geographic writer and book editor, researches original documents to write her pieces about social history and scientific biography.

Jonathan B. Tourtellot, National Geographic writer and book editor, has followed space exploration issues for more than 25 years.

Lynn Addison Yorke, National Geographic writer and book editor, flew to 83° N for a brief rendezvous with the Steger International Polar Expedition on the frozen surface of the Arctic Ocean.

Acknowledgments

We gratefully acknowledge the individuals, groups, and institutions who gave us generous help in the preparation of this book: Richard P. Binzel, Planetary Science Institute, Tucson; Jim Brandenburg, Minneapolis; Geoffrey A. Briggs, NASA, Washington, D. C.; James A. Casada, Winthrop College, Rock Hill, SC; John Clune, Public Information Office, Australian Embassy; Michael Cooper, S. J., Sophia University, Tokyo; Bengt Danielsson, Papeete, Tahiti; J. Pieter deVries, Jet Propulsion Laboratory, Pasadena; W. Donald Duckworth, Bernice P. Bishop Museum, Honolulu; Liliana Gagliardi, Naples; James Gasperini, Steger International Polar Expedition, Stillwater, MN; Pericles B. Georges, Harvard University; Gordon D. Gibson, Escondido, CA; William H. Goetzmann, University of Texas; Carmen Gonzáles Sánchez, Madrid; Jocelyn Crane Griffin, Princeton, NJ; Gregory G. Guzman, Bradley University, Peoria; Sam Iftikhar, Library of Congress; Terry and Bezal Jesudason, High Arctic International, Resolute Bay, Canada; Robert McKerrow, Steger International Polar Expedition, Picton, New Zealand; Luis Marden, National Geographic Society; Earl J. Montoya, NASA, Washington, D. C.; Lee Motteler, Bernice P. Bishop Museum, Honolulu; Barbara Perry, National Library of Australia, Canberra; Capt. Geoffrey Pope of the *Sheila Yeates,* Excelsior, MN; Darrell A. Posey, Universidade Federal do Maranhão, São Luís, Brazil; Pierre Rouyer, Paris; Ahutiare Sanford, Office de Promotion et d'Animation Touristiques de Tahiti et ses Îles, Papeete, Tahiti; Denis Sinor, Indiana University; Yosihiko H. Sinoto, Bernice P. Bishop Museum, Honolulu; Capt. Eric Speth and the crew of the *Maryland Dove,* St. Mary's City, MD; Deborah Ward, Bernice P. Bishop Museum, Honolulu; Eric Widmer, Brown University; Diego R. Yuuki, S. J., Martyrs Museum, Nagasaki; and the National Geographic Society Library, Illustrations Library, Administrative Services, Translations Division, and Travel Office.

Illustration Credits

McIntyre. 82, Guillermo Aldana Espinoza. 85, GC. 86, Aspect Picture Library. 88-89, Aspect Picture Library. 90, Yva Momatiuk and John Eastcott, DRK Photo. 93, From the collection of Mr. and Mrs. Paul Mellon, Upperville, VA. 94-95, GC. 95(rt), LC. 95(rb), Public Archives Canada C-82974. 96-97, James Blair, NGP. 98, Culver Pictures. 99, U. S. Capitol Historical Society, NGP. 100, John de Visser. 101, BA. 102, Fred Mayer, Magnum. 103, BA. 104-105, Lowell Georgia. 105(r), Hudson's Bay Co. 106-107, Architect of the U. S. Capitol. 107(r), Tate Gallery, London. 108-109, Culver Pictures. 109(r), Hamlyn Publishing Group. 110, William Strode. 111(lt), GC. 111(rt,rb), SP Avery Collection, New York Public Library, Astor, Lenox and Tilden Foundations. 112, Historical Pictures Service, Chicago. 113, David Muench. 114(l), J. W. Powell. 114-115, Tom Bean. 116, Thomas Gilcrease Institute of American History and Art, Tulsa, OK. 119(lt,lb), Dick Durrance II. 120-121, 122, Montana Historical Society. 124-125, Amon Carter Museum, Fort Worth, TX. 126, Hiroji Kubota, Magnum. 128(l), Mansell Collection. 130-131, Gordon W. Gahan. 131(r), British Library. 132-133, Dean Conger, NGP. 133(r), Bibliothèque de l'Institut des Langues et Civilisations Orientales, SIM, Paris. 134-135, Christopher G. Knight. 135(r), Muséo Nacionale do Arte Antiqua, Lisbon, Tor Eigeland. 136, Mary Evans Picture Library. 137, Matthew Naythons, Liaison Agency. 138-139, Biblioteca Apostolica Vaticana, Ms. Barb. Or. 150. 139(t), Hiroji Kubota, Magnum. 140, Chester Beatty Library and Gallery of Oriental Art. 141(lt), Mary Evans Picture Library. 141(r), Fotomas Index London. 142-143, Roland and Sabrina Michaud. 144-145, Fotomas Index London. 145(r), Bibliothèque Nationale, Paris. 146, Roland and Sabrina Michaud, Rapho. 147, RGS. 148, BBC Hulton Picture Library. 149, Hiroji Kubota, Magnum. 150, 152, 154(rb), 154-155, AA. 156, GC. 157, AA. 158, 161, 162, 163, Archives Foundation Alexandra David-Néel, Digne, France. 164, Gordon W. Gahan. 167(r), NMM. 168-169, Nicholas DeVore III, Photographers Aspen. 170-171, Ardea London. 171(t), Musée de la Marine, Paris. 172-173, Gordon W. Gahan. 174, NMM. 175(b), Gordon W. Gahan. 175(t), Alexander Turnbull Library, Wellington, New Zealand. 176(lt), NMM. 176-177, Yale Collection of Western Americana, Beinecke Rare Book and Manuscript Library.

177(t), D. C. Blossom, NHPA. 178-179, John Ford, West Coast Whale Research Foundation. 180(l), President and Fellows of Harvard College, 1977, Peabody Museum, Harvard University, Hillel Burger. 180-181, 181(t), NMM. 182-183, Otis Imboden. 183(t), Bishop Museum. 184, Dixon Galleries, State Library of New South Wales, James A. Sugar. 185, Gordon W. Gahan. 186, National Library of Australia, Canberra. 189, 190-191, La Trobe Collection, State Library of Victoria. 193, Reproduced with the permission of the Victorian Parliamentary Library, Committee from William Strutt's *Victoria the Golden.* 194, Jim Brandenburg. 197(t), BBC Hulton Picture Library. 197(b), RGS. 198-199, Renato Berger. 200, 201, British Library. 202-203, Bibliothèque Centrale du Muséum National d'Histoire Naturelle, Jacques L'Hoir. 203(r), Douglas Waugh, Peter Arnold, Inc. 204-205, Carol Beckwith, from *Nomads of the Niger,* published by Harry N. Abrams, Inc., 1983. 206, 207, RGS. 208(t), Trustees of the National Library of Scotland. 208-209, Robert Caputo. 209(r), RGS. 210(l), David Livingstone Centre, Blantyre, Scotland. 210-211, Richard Hall. 211(t), AA. 212-213, Dieter Blum, Peter Arnold, Inc. 214, GC. 215(t), AA. 215(c), David Livingstone Centre, Blantyre, Scotland. 216-217, Hugo van Lawick. 218, AA. 220-221, 222, RGS. 224, Richard Hall. 226, Günter Ziesler. 229, British Library. 230, 231, Loren McIntyre. 232, Archiv für Kunst und Geschichte, Berlin. 233, Reproduced by permission of the Director of the Institute of Geography and Geoecology, Academy of Sciences of the GDR, Leipzig. 233(lt), Fotomas Index London. 234, Galen Rowell. 235, RGS. 236, National Geographic Society Collection. 237, Joseph F. Rock. 238-239, David Austen. 239(lt), R. K. Peck. 239(rb), LC. 240, Loren McIntyre. 240-241, Harald Schultz. 242, 244, NMM. 245, Down House, Royal College of Surgeons of England. 246, 247, LC. 248, BBC Hulton Picture Library. 249, LC. 250, Ivars Silis. 252(t), NMM. 254(l), Ranulph Fiennes. 254-255, Charles Swithinbank. 256-257, NMM. 258-259, George F. Mobley, NGP. 260(l),

AA. 260-261, Royal University Library, Oslo. 261(r), AA. 262, Martin Rogers. 263(t,b), Stiftelsen Gränna-Muséerna. 264(lt), LC. 246(bt), BA. 264-265, 265(lt), Cmdr. E. P. Stafford, USN, Ret., Adm. Robert E. Peary. 266, Dr. Uwe Kils. 267, NMM. 268-269, Colin Monteath, Hedgehog House, New Zealand. 270-271, 271(rt,rb), Bibliothèque Centrale du Muséum National d'Histoire Naturelle, Jacques L'Hoir. 272(t), Colin Monteath, Hedgehog House, New Zealand. 272(b), 273, RGS. 274(rt), LC. 274(l), Byrd Antarctic Expedition. 274-275, Shaun Norman, Twizgl, New Zealand. 276, 279(t), RGS. 279(b), Anne-Christina Jacobsen 1986, Photo by Roald Amundsen. 280(b), 280-281, AA. 281(lb), Anne-Christina Jacobsen 1986, Photo by Roald Amundsen, 1911. 283, Anne-Christina Jacobsen 1986, Photo by Roald Amundsen, 1912. 284, David Doubilet. 286(lt), Michael Holford. 288(r), Sygma. 289, Thomas J. Abercrombie, NGS. 290(t), 1985 Cousteau Society, a nonprofit environmental organization located at 930 W. 21st., Norfolk, VA. 290(b), Robert B. Goodman. 290-291, Jeff Rotman. 292, Emory Kristof, NGP. 293, Al Giddings. 294, National Science Foundation and Woods Hole Oceanographic Institution, Dr. John M. Edmond. 294(t), Emory Kristof, NGP. 295, National Science Foundation and Woods Hole Oceanographic Institution, Dr. John M. Edmond. 296, David Knudsen. 298, Ellie Bostelmann. 299, National Geographic Society Collection. 300, *Vanity Fair,* 1934 (renewed 1962) by Condé Nast Publications, Inc. 301, Drawing by Garrett Price; 1934, 1962 The New Yorker Magazine, Inc. 302, NASA. 305(b), John Bryson, *Life Magazine,* Time, Inc. 306, NASA photo courtesy James Long Associates. 307, Ralph Morse, *Life Magazine,* Time, Inc. 307(b), Dean Conger, NGP. 308-309, 309(r), 310(rt), 310-311, NASA. 312-313, Scene from the IMAX/OMNIMAX film, *The Dream is Alive,* Smithsonian Institution and Lockheed Corporation, 1985. 314, Scott Dine. 315(r), 315(lt), 316-317, 317(r), 318, 321, 323, 324-325, NASA.

Artist Michael Hampshire tinted the historical engravings and photographs in the 19th-century tradition of fine bookmaking. Colors were selected to match the style of each original and so, like the engravings themselves, do not necessarily depict the explorers' expeditions accurately.

Type composition by the Typographic section
of National Geographic Production Services,
Pre-Press Division. Color separations by
Chanticleer Co., Inc., New York, NY; Dai
Nippon Printing Company Ltd, Tokyo, Japan;
Graphic Color Plate Inc., Stamford, CT; The
Lanman Companies, Washington, D. C.;
Litho Studios Ltd, Dublin, Ireland. Printed
and Bound by Kingsport Press, Kingsport, TN.
Paper by Mead Paper Co., New York, NY.

Library of Congress CIP Data

Into the unknown.

    Includes index.
    1. Discoveries (in geography) I.
National Geographic Book Service. II.
National Geographic Society (U. S.)
G80.I58 1987   910'.9   87-5525
ISBN 0-87044-694-0 (alk. paper)
ISBN 0-87044-695-9 (deluxe: alk. paper)

You are invited to join the National
Geographic Society or to send gift
memberships to others. (Membership includes
a subscription to the NATIONAL GEOGRAPHIC
magazine.) For information call 800-638-4077
toll free, or write to the National Geographic
Society, Washington, D. C. 20036.